From the
Risale-i Nur Collection

EPITOMES OF LIGHT

(*MATHNAWI AL-NURIYA*)

THE ESSENTIALS OF
THE *RISALE-I NUR*

Said Nursi

Kaynak (Izmir) A.S. 1999

ISBN 975-7388-61-0

Published by
Kaynak (Izmir) A.S.
Sarnic Yolu No:5
(35410) Gaziemir-Izmir
Tel: 0-232-252 22 85
Fax: 0-232-251 38 96

Printed and bound in Turkey
by Caglayan A.S.

Contents

(As pointed out in the Introduction to the book by Fethullah Gülen, numerous topics, almost all of those discussed in the *Risale-i Nur* collection, are dealt with in *Epitomes of Light* (*Mathnawi al-Nuriya*) in a concise way. However, modern reader may not be able to reach a true understanding of the content of the book from the *Contents*. For this reason, at the end of each chapter, an index or brief summaries of the topics discussed in the chapter is given.)

BEDIUZZAMAN SAID NURSI
and THE *RISALE-I NUR*

In the many dimensions of his lifetime of achievement, as well as in his personality and character, Bediuzzaman was and, through his continuing influence, still is an important figure in the twentieth-century Muslim world. He represented in a most effective and profound way the intellectual, moral and spiritual strengths of Islam, evident in different degrees throughout its fourteen-century history. He lived for eighty-five years. He spent almost all of those years, overflowing with love and ardour for the cause of Islam, in a wise and measured activism based on sound reasoning and in the shade of the Qur'an and the Prophetic example.

Much has been said and written on the lofty ideal which Bediuzzaman pursued and his deep familiarity with the world and the age in which he lived, as well as the simplicity and austerity of his life, his human tenderness, loyalty to his friends, chastity, modesty and contentedness. Yet it is worth writing volumes on each of those dimensions of his legendary character and life.

Though strikingly simple in outward appearance, he was wholly original in many of his ideas and in his way of activity. He embraced all humanity, was deeply averse to unbelief, injustice and deviations, and never stopped struggling against all kinds of tyranny even at the cost of his life. He was as profound in belief and feelings as he was wise and rational in his ideas and approach to problems. In a manner that may seem to some paradoxical, to the same extent that he was an example of love, ardour and feeling, he was extraordinarily balanced in his thoughts and acts and in his treatment of matters. Also, he was very far-sighted in assessment and judgement of the conditions surrounding him, and in finding solutions to the problems he encountered.

Among his comtemporaries, those who knew him acknowledged, tacitly or explicitly, Bediuzzaman as the most serious and important thinker and writer of the twentieth-century Turkey or even of the Muslim world. Despite this and his indisputable leadership of a new Islamic revival in the intellectual, social and political conditions of time, he was never proud of himself and remained a humble servant of God Almighty and a most modest friend among human beings. 'Desire for fame is the same as show and ostentation and it is a 'poisonous honey' extinguishing the spiritual liveliness of the heart', is one of his golden sayings concerning humility.

Born in a small mountain village in an eastern province of Turkey, Bediuzzaman voiced the sighs and laments of the whole Muslim world, as well as its belief, hopes and aspirations. He said:

> I can bear my own sorrows, but the sorrows arising from the calamities visiting Islam and Muslims have crushed me. I feel each blow delivered at the Muslim world to be delivered first at my own heart. That is why I have been so shaken.

He also said:

> During my whole life-time of over eighty years, I have tasted nothing of the worldly pleasures. My life has passed on either battlefields or in prisons or other places of suffering. They have treated me as if I were a criminal; they have banished me from one town to another, and kept me under continual surveillance. There has been no persecution which I have not tasted and no oppression which I have not suffered. I care for neither Paradise nor fear Hell. If I see the faith of my nation secured, I will not care even burning in the flames of Hell. For while my body is burning, my heart will be as if in a rose garden.

Bediuzzaman lived in an age when materialism was at its peak and many crazed after communism, and the world was in great crisis. Shocked by the scientific and military victories of the West and under the influence of modern trends of thought, people all over the Muslim world were urged to break with their historical roots and many lost their faith. In that critical period when most Muslim intellectuals deviated from the Straight Path and lent their intellects to whatever would come from the West in the name of ideas, Bediuzzaman pointed people to the source of belief and inculcated in them a strong hope for an overall revival. He wrote to display the truth of the tenets of the Islamic faith and heroically resisted movements of deviation. In utmost reliance on God Almighty and unshakeable conviction in the truth of Islam, and with an infinite hope for a bright future awaiting the Muslim world, Bediuzzaman exerted a superhuman effort to defend Islam and bring up a new generation which would realize his hopes.

At a time when science and philosophy were used to mislead young generations into atheism, and nihilistic attitudes had a wide appeal, at a time when all this was done in the name of civilization, modernization and contemporary thinking and those who tried to resist them were subjected to the cruelest of persecutions, Bediuzzaman strove for the overall revival of a whole people, breathing into their minds and spirits whatever is taught in the institutions of both modern and traditional education and of spiritual training.

In the manner of an expert physician, Bediuzzaman diagnosed all the 'diseases' of Muslim communities, the diseases they had been suffering for centuries in all aspects of life, and offered the most effective remedies for them. Based on the Qur'an and the *Sunna* and the centuries-old Islamic tradition which originated therein, and travelling in mind through natural phenomena, which are each a sign of Divine existence and Unity, to fill his 'comb of the knowledge of God' with the 'nectar' he collected from them, Bediuzzaman concentrated first on proving the pillars of Islamic belief and then on the necessity of belief and worship, morality and good conduct, and finally on the social and economic issues which Muslims faced in this age.

The age in which Bediüzzaman lived and the remedies he offered for the centuries-old problems of the Muslim World

Bediuzzaman lived in both the dying years of the Ottoman State and the formative years of the Turkish Republic. He travelled from city to city, as far as the remotest corners of the country, and witnessed the ignorance, poverty and destitution and internal conflicts and seditions prevalent there and throughout the Muslim world. In 1911, he delivered a sermon in the Umayyad Mosque in Damascus. Approximately ten thousand people including one hundred high-ranking scholars packed the Mosque to listen to him. In this famous, historical sermon of his, he enumerated the disases which arrested Muslims in 'the Middle Ages', as follows:

The growth of despair among people, the loss of truthfulness in the social and political lives of Muslims; love of belligerency, ignorance of the bonds proper among believers; despotism in all fields of life, and egocentricity.

To cure these diseases, he offered hope, truthfulness and trustworthiness, mutual love, consultation, solidarity, and freedom in accordance with Islam, and emphasized the three points, which are as follows:

> History shows that Muslims increased in civilization and progressed in relation to the strength of their adherence to the truths of Islam; that is, to the degree that they acted in accordance with Islam, they drew force from its truths. History also shows that they fell into decline, disaster and defeat to the degree of their weakness in adherence to the truths of Islam. As for other religions, it is quite the reverse. That is to say, history shows that as they increased in civilization and progressed in relation to their weakness in adhering to their religions and bigotry, so were they also subject to decline and convulsions to the degree of their strength in adering to them.

> This is so because we Muslims, who are students of the Qur'an, follow proof; we do not abandon proof in favour of blind obedience and imitation of the clergy like some adherents of other religions. Therefore, in the future, when reason, sicence and knowledge prevail, the Qur'an will gain ascendancy, which relies on proof and calls reason to confirm its pronouncements.

> If we are to display through our actions the perfections of the moral qualities of Islam and the truths of belief, without doubt, the followers of other religions will enter Islam in whole communities. Some entire regions and states, even, on the earth will take refuge in Islam.

During the years when Bediuzzaman lived, as today, ignorance of God Almighty and the Prophet, upon him be peace and blessings, heedlessness of the religious commandments, indifference to the Islamic dynamics of prosperity in both worlds, and ignorance in modern sciences, were among the primary factors behind the wretched state of Muslims. He maintained that unless people were enlightened in both sciences and religious knowledge and knew how to think systematically, unless they were protected against misleading trends of thought and equipped with true knowledge to resist them, it was impossible for Muslims to recover from the maladies they suffered.

Ignorance was also one of the reasons for the poverty of Muslims. For as they lived unaware of the truth of their religion, they had also fallen far behind the West in science and technology. It was because of this that the vast plains remained uncultivated and the natural wealth of Muslim lands went into the treasuries of others.

Again, it was ignorance which was largely responsible for the inner conflicts and seditions in the Muslim world. Although the Qur'an strictly commands unity of Muslims, Muslim peoples were quarelling with each other, even while their lands were under foreign invasion and they were being subjected to all kinds of humiliation.

At the same time, the Muslim intellectuals, whom the masses expected to diagnose the problem honestly and offer remedies, were attracted by the violent storm of 'denial' blowing from the West. This storm had arisen in the previous century, blown up by human rooted in scienticism, rationalism and positivism. As a result of contradictions between the findings of sciences and corrupted Christianity and the attitude of the Church towards sciences and scientists, Europe had almost lost its belief and, consequently, Revelation was forced to yield to human reason. This storm of denial, unparalleled in history, shook to its roots the 'building' of Islam, which was old and had already decayed in many hearts and minds, in the individual as well as collective life of the Muslim community. What had to be done was, according to Bediuzzaman, while preserving this 'building' from further destructive influences from the storm of denial, to present the essentials of Islamic belief with all their branches, to all the faculties of modern man, including his power of reasoning. If Muslim community, which had plainly run aground on the oceans of the modern world, was ever to sail freely again, then, according to Bediuzzaman, the Muslims' present situation required an overall renewal in all the fields of Islam.

The reasons why the Muslims fell under the dominion of foreign powers

In explaining the reasons for the Ottoman collapse in the First World War and Western domination over the whole Muslim world, Bediuzzaman said:

The reasons why Destiny has allowed this calamity are our neglect in performing the commandments of Islam. The Almighty Creator wanted us to assign to daily prescribed prayers one out of the twenty-four hours of a day but we showed neglect. In return, by subjecting us to four years of training, troubles and continuous mobilization, He has forced us to a kind of prayer. He wanted us to force our carnal selves to fast one month a year but we pitied them. In return, He has made us fast for four years. He also wanted us to allocate one fortieth of the wealth He bestowed on us to the needy and poor but we refrained in stinginess. In return, He has taken from us the accumulated zakat of many years. Again, God Almighty wanted us to go on pilgrimage once in our whole lives in order that, besides other benefits of pilgrimage, we could come together as Muslims arriving from all parts of the world and exchange views on our common problems, but we did not do that. In return, He caused us to hasten from front to front for four years.

As for the reasons why unbelievers are triumphant over believers, we should consider the following four points:

The first point is that although every means of truth must be right, it cannot always be so in actual life, whereas it is not necessary for every means of falsehood to be false. Since falsehood may sometimes follow a true, right way, it can be triumphant over truth, which fails in following that way.

The second is that although a Muslim must be Muslim in all his attributes and actions, he cannot always be so in practical life. Likewise, it is not always the case with a transgressor or unbeliever that every attribute and action of his should originate in his unbelief or transgression. Therefore, by virtue of having Muslim attributes and acting in conformity with Islamic principles more than a Muslim who fails in practising Islam, an unbeliever may be victorious over a Muslim.

The third is that God has two kinds of laws: one is the Shari'a, known by everybody, which is the group comprising God's laws issuing from His Attribute of Speech and governing man's 'religious' life. The reward or punishment in following it or not usually pertains to the afterlife. The other group of Divine laws comprise those governing creation and life as a whole, which issue from His Attribute of Will and are generally (but wrongly) called the 'laws of nature'. The reward or punishmnet for them mostly pertains to this world. The Qur'an insistently draws attentions to 'natural' phenomena, which are the subject-matter of sciences, and urges their study. In the first five centuries of Islam, Muslims succeeded in uniting sciences with religion, the intellect with the heart, the material with the spiritual. However, in later centuries, the West took the initiative in sciences. This meant their obedience—although unconccious—to Divine laws of 'nature', which has resulted in their dominance over the Muslim world, which has failed to practise both the religious and scientific aspects of Islam. Power and force have some right in life, they have been created for some wise purpose. Equipped with force through sciences and technology, the West has got the upper hand over the Muslims.

The fourth point concerning the Muslims' defeat is that truth has been left without force or it has been diluted or lost its purity and authenticity in the hands of Muslims. Like causing the hawk to attack the sparrow and thereby urging the sparrow to develop its power of defence, God has allowed unbelief to triumphantly attack Islam so that Islam should be restored to its original purity and re-gain its force.

Belief, knowledge of God and worship in Bediüzzaman's way of thinking and struggle

Endowed with an extraordinary intelligence and learning capacity, Bediuzzaman had completed the normal course of madrasa (traditional religious school) education by the age of fourteen. Another striking characteristic he displayed from his early years was dissatisfaction with the existing education system. He had formulated his dissatisfaction with it into comprehensive proposals for its reform. At the heart of those proposals was the wedding of the traditional religious sciences with the modern ones and the founding of a university in important cities of Turkey, where his proposals could be put into practise. Although he had twice received funds for the construction of his university, and its foundations had been laid in 1913, it was never completed due to the consequences of the First World War and the vicissitudes of the time.

Contrary to the centuries-old practice of religious scholars, Bediuzzaman studied intently in the natural and social sciences, as well as in mathematics and philosophy. During the First World War he was held prisoner-of- war by the Russians for two years.

After his escape and return to Istanbul, he dedicated himself to expounding the pillars of the Islamic belief. The new, irreversible developments in Turkey which culminated in the establishment of a secular regime, and the rise of anti-Islamic trends and attitudes among intellectuals and the young as a result of deliberately positivist, even materialist, system of education, forced Bediuzzaman to concentrate primarily on the essentials of belief and worship and the main purposes pursued in the Qur'an, which he described as explaining and proving the Divine Existence and Unity, Prophethood, and the Resurrection and the necessity of worship and justice. He explains:

> Be certain of this, that the highest aim of creation and its most sublime result is belief in God. The most exalted rank of humanity is the knowledge of God. The most radiant happiness and sweetest bounty for jinn and mankind is the love of God contained within the knowledge of God; the purest joy for the human spirit and the purest delight for man's heart is the spiritual ecstasy contained within the love of God. Indeed, all true happiness, pure joy, sweet bounties and unclouded pleasure are undoubtedly contained within the knowledge and love of God.

> Belief is not restricted to a brief affirmation based on imitation. It has degrees and stages of expansion or development as from, say, the seed of a tree to the fully grown, fruit-bearing state of that tree, from the image of the sun in the mirror in your hand or in a drop of water to its images on the whole surface of the sea and to the sun itself. Belief contains so many truths pertaining to the one thousand and one Names of God and the realities contained in the universe, that the most perfect of all human sciences and knowledge and virtues is belief, and knowledge of God originating in belief based on argument and investigation. While belief based on imitation can easily be refuted in the face of doubts and questions raised by the modern way of thinking, belief based on argument and investigation has many degrees and grades of manifestation to the number of Divine Names. Those who have been able to attain the degree of certainty of belief coming from direct observation of the truths on which belief is based, can study the universe as a kind of Qur'an.

> In fact, The Qur'an, the universe and man are three kinds of manifestation of one truth. The Qur'an, having issued from the Divine Attrib-

ute of Speech, may be regarded as the universe written or composed, while the universe, having originated in the Divine Attributes of Power and Will, may be considered as the Qur'an created. So, from this point of view, the universe being the counterpart of the Qur'an and, in one respect, the collection of Divine laws of creation, the sciences which study the universe, can in no way be incompatible with Islam. Therefore, in the present time when sciences prevail, and in the future as well, which will be the age of knowledge, true belief should be based on argument and investigation, and on continual reflection on the 'signs' of God in the universe, on 'natural', social, historical and psychological phenomena. Belief is not something based on blind imitation. It should appeal to both the intellect or reason and the heart. It combines the acceptance and affirmation of the reason and the experience and submission of the heart.

There is another degree of belief, namely certainty coming from direct experience of its truths. This depends on regular worship and reflection. The one who has acquired this degree of belief can challenge the whole of the world. So, our first and foremost and most important duty should be to acquire this degree of belief and try in utmost sincerity and purely for the sake of God Almighty's good pleasure to communicate it to others. For, as is stated in a hadith, it is better for you than having all the world together with everything in it that one accepts belief by means of you.

In short, according to Bediüzzaman, belief consists in the acquisiton of the whole of Islam.

An outline of Bediüzzaman's life after 1925

When a revolt broke out in south-eastern Turkey in 1925, along with many others, Bediuzzaman was sent into internal exile and lived the remainder of his life until his death in 1960 under either strict surveillance or in prisons or under persecutions.

Bediuzzaman was first forced to live in Barla, a mountainous village in south-western Turkey. There he lived a wretched life isolated from almost everyone. However, he was able to find consolation, true consolation, in the Omnipresence of God Almighty and in utmost submission to Him.

The basic works of the *Risale-i Nur*, *The Words* and *The Letters*, were written in Barla under harsh conditions. Copies were made by hand and began to circulate throughout Turkey. This method of serving Islam caused reaction and hostility in the government. Accused of forming a secret society and working against the regime, a charge carrying the death penalty was laid against Bediuzzaman and one hundred and twenty of his students and, in 1935, tried in Eskisehir Criminal Court. Although during his whole life he had opposed revolt and all actions which would breach public peace and order, and had stressed that the rights of a single person could not be violated even for the sake of the whole society, he was accused of forming secret organizations to destroy the public order. When he was asked during the trial his opinion of the Republic, he replied: *My biography which you have in your hands proves that I was a religious republican before any of you came into the world.* He was held for eleven months in prison before acquittal.

Following his release, he was compelled to reside in Kastamonu. He stayed first on the top floor of the police station, then he was settled in a house immediately opposite it. His residence in Kastamonu continued for seven years, and a significant part of the *Risale-i Nur* was written there.

During this period, both he and his students [from Kastamonu and elsewhere] were under constant pressure from the authorities. This increased as time passed, culminating in widespread arrests and the Denizli trials and imprisonment in 1943-44. He was accused of forming a Sufi tariqa, and organizing a political society. Although the case would result in acquittal, Bediuzzaman was kept for nine months in solitary confinement under the most appalling conditions in a minute, dark, damp cell.

After release, Bediuzzaman was sent to reside in the town of Emirdag in the province of Afyon. In 1948 a new case was opened in Afyon Criminal Court, and although the Court sentenced him arbitrarily, the decision was quashed by the Appeal Court, and Bediuzzaman was acquitted together with his students. Following this, he stayed for brief periods in Emirdag, Isparta, Afyon, and Istanbul among other places. In 1952 he was tried once more, this time for his publication *A Guide for Youth*, and again acquitted. On his death in Urfa on 23rd March 1960, which may well have been the Night of Power in Ramadan, the coroner fixed his estate as a turban, a gown, and twenty lira. The real, invaluable estate which remained of this hero of Islam and humanity, who weighed only 40 kilos at his death, was the six-thousand-page *Risale-i Nur* Collection, which has been tried in different courts about two thousand times to this day, and his noble cause which was of dimensions that could not be contained in the coroner's records.

The Risale-i Nur

In order to comprehend the quality and main characteristic of the *Risale-i Nur*, the following experience of Dr Turner of Durham University, U.K. is worth quoting at length. Dr Turner writes:

"As someone born and raised in Britain, I am often asked what we as Muslims have to offer to the West. But before I answer, I should like to ask a question myself: Are we Muslims because we believe in God Almighty, or do we believe in God beacuse we are Muslims?

"The question occurred to me during a march through the streets of London, over a decade ago, to protest against the Russian occupation of Afghanistan. I'd made a formal conversion to Islam several years prior to this, and it wasn't my first demonstration. There were banners and placards and much shouting and chanting. Towards the end of the demonstration I was approached by a young man who introduced himself as someone interested in Islam. 'Excuse me,' he said, 'but what is the meaning of *La ilaha illa Allah?*'

"Without a moment's hesitation I answered, "There is no god but Allah."

'I'm not asking you to translate it,' he said, 'I'm asking you to tell me what it really means.' There was a long awkward silence as it dawned on me that I was unable to answer him.

"You are no doubt thinking, 'What kind of Muslim is it that does not know the real meaning of *La ilaha illa Allah?*' To this I would have to say: a typical one. That evening I pondered my ignorance; being in the majority didn't help, it simply made me more depressed.

"Islam simply made sense, in a way that nothing else ever had. It had rules of government, it had an economic system, it had regulations concerning every facet of day-to-day existence. It was egalitarian and addressed to all races, and it was clear and easy to understand. Oh, and it has a God, One God, in whom I had always vaguely believed. That was that. I said *La ilaha illa Allah* and I was part of the community. For the first time in my life I belonged.

"New converts are invariably enthusiastic to know as much as possible about their religion in the shortest possible time. In the few years that followed, my library grew rapidly. There was so much to learn, and so many books ready to teach. Books on the history of Islam, the economic system of Islam, the concept of government in Islam; countless manuals of Islamic jurisprudence, and, best of all, books on Islam and revolution, on how Muslims were to rise up and establish Islamic governments, Islamic republics. When I returned to Britain in early '79 from my trip to the Middle East to learn the meaning of *La ilaha illa Allah*, I was ready to introduce Islam to the West.

"It was to these books that I turned for an answer to the question "What is the meaning of *La ilaha illa Allah*?" Again I was disappointed. The books were about Islam, not about Allah. They covered every subject you could possibly imagine except for the one which really mattered. I put the question to the imam at the university mosque. He made an excuse and left. Then a brother who had overheard my impertinent question to the imam came over and said: 'I have a *tafsir* of *La ilaha illa Allah*. If you like we could read it together.' I imagined that it would be ten or twenty pages at the most. It turned out to have over 5000 pages, in several books. It was the *Risale-i Nur* by Bediuzzaman Said Nursi."[1]

Bediuzzaman had seen that modern unbelief originated from science and philosophy, not from ignorance as previously. Paradoxically, the Muslims' neglect of science and technology caused them to fall behind the West in economic and military fields. But the science and technology whic had provided the West with the power to achieve military and economic superiortiy in the world, had caused Western people to lose their faith and traditional moral and spiritual values and fall into a great pessimism, unhappiness and spiritual crisis. This was natural because although the Divine laws of 'na-

---

1. Quoted from Dr Turner's paper which he offered to the conference held about Bediüzzaman in Istanbul in 1993.

ture', which are the subject-matter of sciences, are the counterpart of the Divine Scripture or religion, they had been separated from each other in the West and, consequently, a secular morality and economic self-interest, had replaced religious and other traditional values. Bediuzzaman was of the opinion that nature is the collection of Divine signs and therefore science and religion cannot be conflicting disciplines. Rather, they are two (apparently) different expressions of the same truth. Minds should be enlightened with sciences, while hearts need to be illumined by religion.

In his heroic struggle to argue for the religious truths—Divine existence and Unity, the Resurrection, Prophethood, Divine origin of the Qur'an, the Unseen World and its inhabitants or immaterial dimensions of existence, the necessity of worship, morality, the ontological character of man, etc.—Bediuzzaman first tried to strengthen Islam with modern Western philosophy. Later, he saw that this way meant degrading Islam and that the essentials of Islam were too deep for the principles of human philosophy to reach. He then returned to the Qur'an almost exclusively. He writes:

> Thinkers accept the principles of human philosophy and the Western way of thinking and depend on them in their struggle against Europe. I too have filled my brain with the philosophical as well as the Islamic sciences. I thought the philosophical sciences were the means to spiritual progress and enlightenment, and was of the opinion that European way of thinking and philosophy could be used to reinforce and strenghten the truths of Islam. By grafting the shoots of philosophy, which we supposed deep-rooted, on the trunk of Islam, we imagined that could strenghten Islam. However, I have given up this way as it is very difficult and an improbable way to overcome the anti-Islamic trends, and since it means degrading Islam to some extent. The essentials of Islam are too deep for the principles of philosophy to reach.

In the struggle with the opponents of Islam, in resisting, even overcoming, modern (materialistic) trends of thought, the Qur'an sufficed:

> While there is a permanent miracle like the Qur'an, searching for further proof appears to my mind superfluous;

> While there is a proof of reality like the Qur'an, would silencing those who deny it weigh heavily on my heart?

Although wholly lacking in any positive rational arguments, unbelief and atheism coming from science and philosophy are more difficult to deal with and remove from hearts than unbelief coming from ignorance. It is unquestionably evident that creation of the universe and establishment of the relations among parts of it, requires an absolute, all-encompassing knowledge and will and power, and that 'being a design, not a designer, being something printed, not a printer, being a passive object, not an active agent, being a collection of Divine laws, not the law-giver', nature cannot be the creator of itself. Similarly, causes or the law of causality, being no more than things of nominal existence without any knowledge, will and power, cannot be creators of things either. If we ask those who attribute creation to causalty or causes what makes, for example, a flower, they will not be able to say water, earth and sunlight make it. They will not simply because they should first answer how earth or water or sunlight know what exactly to do, how they do that and what qualities they have that enable a flower to grow.

So, the *Risale-i Nur* removes the veil of 'sorcery' that materialist science has laid over creation. In the words of Dr Turner:

"The *Risale-i Nur* affirms that anyone who sincerely wishes to look upon the created world as it is, and not as he wishes or imagines to be, must inevitably come to the conclusion *La ilaha illa Allah*. For he will see order and harmony, beauty and equilibrium, justice and mercy, lordship, sustenance and munificence; and at the same time he will realize that those attributes are pointing not to the created beings themselves but to a Reality in which all of these attributes exist in perfection and absoluteness. He will see that the created world is thus a book of names, an index, which seek to tell about its Owner.

"The *Risale-i Nur* takes the interpretation of *La ilaha illa Allah* even further. The notion that it examines is that of causality, the cornerstone of materialism and the pillar upon which modern science has been constructed. Belief in causality gives rise to statements such as: It is natural; Nature created it; It happened by chance, and so on. With reasoned arguments, the *Risale-i Nur* explodes the myth of causality and demonstrates that those who adhere to this belief are looking at the cosmos not as it actually is, or how it appears to be, but how they would like to think it is.

"The *Risale-i Nur* demonstrates that all beings, on all levels, are interrelated, interconnected and interdependent, like concentric or intersecting circles. It shows that beings come into existence as though from nowhere, and, during their brief lives, each with its own particular purpose, goal and mission, act as mirrors in which various Divine Attributes, and countless configurations of Divine Names, are displayed.—Consider this: When you stand by a river, you see countless images of the sun reflecting in the floating bubbles on it. When those bubbles enter into a tunnel, the images are no longer seen. However, other bubbles coming to the point where you stand will also show the same reflections, and when they also go into the tunnel, the reflections will disappear. This evidently demonstrates that those images do not belong to the bubbles themselves: bubbles cannot own them. Rather, by reflecting its images, the bubbles show the sun's existence, and through their disapperance in the tunnel, they demonstrate their transience vis-à-vis the permanence of the sun.— It is just like this that through their coming into life, impotence and contingence, their total dependence on factors other than themselves, beings demonstrate beyond doubt that they owe their existence to the One Who necessarily exists, creates and has power over all things, and that through their transience and death, they show the permanence of that One.

"The materialists, however, see things differently—they do not see different things. They ask us to believe that this cosmos, whose innate order and harmony they do not deny, is ultimately the work of chance. Of chaos and disorder, of sheer accident. They then ask us to believe that this cosmos is sustained by the mechanistic interplay of causes—whatever they may be, and not even the materialists know for sure—causes which are themselves created, impotent, ignorant, transient and purposeless, but which somehow contrive, through laws which appeared out of nowhere, to produce the orderly works of art of symphonies of harmony and equilibrium that we see and hear around us.

"The *Risale-i Nur* destroys these myths and superstitions. Given that all things are interconnected, it reiterates, whatever it is that brings existence to the seed of a flower must also be responsible for the flower itself, as well as for the apparent causes of the flower's existence such as air, water, sunlight and earth; and given their interdependence, whatever brings into existence the flower must also be responsible for the tree; and given the fact that they are interrelated, whatever brings into existence the tree must also be responsible for the forest, and so on. Thus to be able to create a single atom, one must also be able to create the whole cosmos. That is surely a tall order for a cause which is blind, impotent, transient, dependent and devoid of knowledge of our purpose.

"The attribution of creative power to nature or natural laws is no more than a personal opinion reached not as the result of an objective, scientific investigation. Similarly, denial of the Creator of the cosmos, who has placed apparent causes there as veils to cover His hand of power, is not an act of reason but an act of will. In short, causality is a crude and cunning device with which man distributes the property of the Creator among the created in order that he might set himself up as absolute owner and ruler of all that he has, and all that he is.

"Inspired by the verse *La ilaha illa Allah*, the *Risale-i Nur* shows that the signs of God, these mirrors of His Names and Attributes, are revealed to us constantly in new and ever-changing forms and configurations, eliciting acknowledgement, acceptance, submission, love and worship. The *Risale-i Nur* shows that there is a distinct process involved in becoming Muslim in the true sense of the word: contemplation to knowledge, knowledge to affirmation, affirmation to belief or conviction, and from conviction to submission. And since each new moment, each new day, sees the revelation of fresh aspects of Divine truth, this process is a continuous one. The external practices of Islam, the formal acts of worship, also contribute to this process. Belief is therefore subject to increase or decrease, or strengthening or weakening, depending on the continuance of the process. Thus it is the reality of belief that deserves most of our attention; from there the realities of Islam will follow on inevitably.

"The *Risale-i Nur* also concentrates on the ontological character of man. Each of us is born in total ignorance; the desire to know ourselves and our world is an innate one. Thus "Who am I? Where did I come from? What is this place in which I find myself? What is my duty here? Who is responsible for bringing me into existence? What is that which life and death ask of us?"—these are questions

which each of us needs to answer and answers in his o
ther through direct observation or through blind accepta
answers suggested by others. And how one lives one's life, the c
terion by which one acts in this world, depends totally on the nature of those answers. According to the *Risale-i Nur*, all the answers
given to these questions, by which each of us determines his own
way of living and world-view, are given by either the Divine Revelation manifested in the form of Divine Religions or the ego of everyone. History records the conflicts between these two flows of human life or these two main branches of the tree of humanity,
namely religion and human ego. Rejecting to follow the Divine
Revelation, ego claims self-ownership in haughtiness, appropriating for itself whatever is given to it by the Creator, and attributing
to itself all the accomplishments God Almighty confers on it. This,
however, results in the abjection, wretchedness and unhapiness of
man. This branch of humanity has so far yielded the fruits of Pharaohs, Nimrods, Neros and other tyrants and those who, having
given in to their carnal desires, have themselves gone astray and
misled others. Opposite to this branch is the branch on which the
Prophets, saints, and other examples of virtuousness have grown.
This branch lies in one's being conscious of one's servanthood,
whose power lies in acknowledgement of one's inherent weakness
before God Almighty' absolute Power, and whose wealth lies in
admission of one's inherent poverty before His Riches. It also requires deep devotion and worship in absolute thankfulness, together with continous reflection on His signs in the universe, and a
never-ending enthusiasm in preaching His religion. The *Risale-i
Nur* is no less than a guided tour of the cosmos, as well as of man's
inner world, and the traveller is one who is seeking answers to the
questions above, and indeed finds them.'

Dr Turner continues:

"The secular, self-aborted society of the West is designed on all
levels to blind and stupefy. To mask the fact that the religion of the
self has failed to live up to its promises; that the secular trinity of
"unlimited progress, absolute freedom and unrestricted happiness"
is as meaningless as the Christian Trinity discarded centuries ago.
To cover up the fact that economic and scientific progress which
has secular humanism as its underlying ethos, has turned the West

into a spiritual wasteland and ravaged generation after generation. Yet there are those who are beginning to awake, to realize the illusion under which they have been living. It is to these that the disease of ego must be pointed out. One suffering from cancer cannot be cured by giving him a new coat. Yet it is not only modern Western man suffering from this diesase, it is common to almost all in the world. What is needed is a correct diagnosis, radical surgery and constant back-up treatment. The *Risale-i Nur* provides all of these.

"The *Risale-i Nur* envisages a revolution, a revolution of the mind, of the heart, of the soul and the spirit. It is designed to lead Muslims from belief by imitation to belief through investigation, study of nature and man's inner self and reflection on them, and worship, and through further intellectual enlightenment. It also aims to lead unbelievers from worship of the self to worship of God Almighty."

The *Risale-i Nur* is, according to Dr Turner, the only self-contained, comprehensive Islamic work that sees the cosmos as it actually is, presents the reality of belief as it truly is, interprets the Qur'an as the Prophet, upon him be peace and blessings, intended, diagnoses the real and very dangerous disesases that afflict modern man, and offers a cure. The *Risale-i Nur* also covers almost everything related to the essentials of belief, worship and morality, and it provides all the necessary criteria for understanding Islam and the Qur'an in the world we live in. A work such as the *Risale-i Nur*, which reflects the light of the Qur'an and illuminates the cosmos and man's inner world, cannot be ignored.

Mathnawi al-Nuriya

Fethullah Gülen

Mathnawi al-Nuriya is one of Bediüzzaman's works which he wrote before he started to write the main part of the *Risale-i Nur* collection. In this book, his golden thoughts revealed themselves each as a shoot, a drop, a bud. Each drop, each bud, each shoot later became like a bubbling stream, like a rose garden emanating perfume, like a forest murmuring with majesty. They stimulated and excited Muslim's feelings based on faith and meditation; while leading many unbelievers to make a new evaluation of their thoughts and ways.

Like all Islamic thinkers, according to Bediüzzaman, the greatest truth in the world is the truth of *iman* (faith) and *tawhid* (absolute Unity of the Divine Being). In his atmosphere of thought, existence —from atoms to the largest systems—is like a shuttle weaving the truth of Unity and like a needle and silk thread crocheting lace, embroidered everywhere with meanings belonging to Him. But everyone cannot grasp, understand and feel Unity to the same degree.

Belief in God's Unity has two degrees:

One is believing superficially that God has no partners and the universe can belong to none other than Him. It is possible that one who has this degree of belief may be susceptible to certain deviations and obscurities in his understanding.

The other degree is being firmly convinced that God is One and that everything belongs to Him exclusively, and that only He gives existence without any partners whatever and without needing any means to do so. The one with such degree of conviction sees His seal and observes His stamp on all things, and free from any doubts, feels himself always and everywhere in His Presence. Neither deviations nor doubts can find a way to dilute this degree of conviction.

One of the topics that Bediüzzaman persistently dwelt upon was that faith is like a prism that reveals the true dimensions of the nature of existence and man. According to him, by means of faith, the universe has become a readable book, an enjoyable exhibition, and man has become an index and proclamation.

Again according to Bediüzzaman, if all the facets of the truth of faith appear to be separate from one another, if they're sensed differently from different perspectives and felt differently, actually they're tightly connected and are the different faces of a whole:

> Know that belief in God, belief in the Prophet, belief in the Resurrection and affirmation of the existence of the universe require believing one another. That is, there is a perfect relation between these pillars of belief: believing one requires believing the others. Divinity requires Messengership; this world testifies to the other world.

During the "development" period of the *Risale-i Nur*, the Ninth Point of the Eleventh Ray is extremely original from the perspective of expressing the necessity among the essentials of faith.

One of Bediüzzaman's delightful observations is the truth that people, who have no depth in their spiritual and emotional lives, showing too much interest in mental and philosophical matters is both a sign of "disease" in heart, the centre of faith and emotions, and the virus that makes them ill.

> I have observed that the more one is preoccupied with philosophy, the more one increases in the spiritual disease of the heart, as I have also observed the more one increases in the spiritual disease of the heart, the more one is preoccupied with the ratinoal sciences. Spiritual diseases lead to preoccupation with rational sciences and preoccupation with rational sciences gives rise, in turn, to spiritual diseases.

The Thirtieth Word and Gleam of the *Resale-i Nur* collection put these balances forth in an interesting way.

Another original observation of Bediüzzaman is: Even though it is a responsibility to respect causes, attributing real influence to them would be obvious aberration and deviation; respecting them in addition to attributing the result to God is the true way.

> Know O friend! Attachment to material causes is the cause of humiliation and rejection. Do you not see that although the dog should be regarded as blessed by people due to its many good qualities, notably its proverbial loyalty, it has received the blow of being considered rit-

ually unclean. By contrast, other domestic animals such as the hen and the cow and even the cat, which do not have the feeling of gratitude and loyalty in return for the good done to them by human beings, enjoy being considered by people as blessed. This is because—provided it is not to backbite the dog and its heart be broken—on account of its disease of greed, the dog is attached to apparent causes to an extent which makes it blind to the true Bestower of Bounties. It supposes the means as truly effective [in the procurement of its food] and as the punishment for its blindness and indifference to the true Owner and Giver of Bounties, it suffers the stigma of ritual impurity.

As for the blessed animals, they do not recognize the means and causes or accord to them any real value or importance. For example, the cat implores you for food and when it gets what it desires, it behaves as if it did not know you or you did not know it. It does not feel gratitude to you. Instead, it thanks the true Giver of Bounties by mentioning: "O Compassionate One, O Compassionate One!"

The First Branch of the Twenty-fourth Word handles this truth from a different angle and presents a delightful observation with a unique sweetness to our feelings and thoughts.

One of the subjects that the Master—Bediüzzaman Said Nursi—carefully emphasizes is living in the orbit of the *Sunna*. As all of the *Ahl al-Sunna wal-Jama'a* scholars (those who follow the Prophetic example and the community of the Companions), he persistently reminds that the Prophet is an unerring, unerrable guide and the *Sunna* is the only road that takes us to happiness in this world and the next, and he calls us to unite in the *Sunna*.

A life journey that is not based on the *Sunna* is more like revolving around the edge of a whirlpool. Even if it appears to be like swimming and making progress, in reality it is nothing more than sliding towards a death hole.

Know O friend! I have observed in my journeying in the "layers of darkness", that the sayings and practices of the Prophet Muhammad, upon him be peace and blessings, and the principles of the Islamic law are like stars by which we can find our direction and radiate among innumerable dark and misguiding ways. By deviating from the way or Tradition of the Prophet [the *Sunna*], a man becomes a plaything of devils, an object of illusions and suspicions, a target of groundless

fears, and a mount of unbearable burdens, from which, when followed, the *Sunna* delivers him.

I have also observed that the principles of the *Sunna* are like ropes
hanging down from the heaven. Whoever holds fast to even a part of
them can be elevated. I have witnessed that who-ever opposes them
and relies on his own reason, even on public reason, is like him who
desires to obtain the means of travelling through the spheres of the
heavens in earthly vehicles and is ridiculed like Pharaoh, who said:
"O Haman! Build for me a tower to obtain the means [of travelling] in
the heavens!"

This subject is frequently mentioned in the *Risale-i Nur* collection; especially the Eleventh Gleam's Third Point is appropriated to
this subject and it is emphasized that the way of *Sunna* is the path
of God.

Bediüzzaman puts forth an original idea at the point of our relations with the world and our perspective on the world. He emphasizes that just as the world is not something to be disliked, to the
contrary it must be loved and he reminds us of three matters that
comprise the basic principles of this love.

The world has three facets.

The first facet of the world relates to the Names of God Almighty.

Its second facet is that it is the arable field of the Hereafter. These two
facets are beautiful.

As to the third facet of the world, it directly and exclusively relates to
the world itself and where man gratifies his bodily desires and seeks
to meet the needs of his transient worldly life.

In another approach related to this subject, these words greet us
a few pages later on:

What falls to one's part from the fruits and purposes of life is proportionate to the degree of one's part in ownership of one's life and disposal of it. The other purposes and fruits pertain to the Giver of Life, His
Majesty be exalted. Man is but the object of the manifestations of His
Names. God will display the colors and the radiations of His Mercy in
Paradise in the afterlife, which will consist of the fruits growing from
the seeds of this worldly life.

Man's relation with his life is like the relation between a steersman and the royal ship that he steers. What the steersman does is putting his fingers on the instruments necessary to move and steer the ship. What falls to his part from the uses and income of the ship is proportionate to his relation with the ship and the service he renders. It is no more than about one in thou-sands. This is the same relation with any living being and the ship of its existence and life. What falls to the part of a living being from the uses and purposes of its life is only one in thousands. Moreover, this one is not the part it has deserved by itself.

Another observation of Bediüzzaman: seeing and accepting man as greater than he is, is both an act of oppression and a step made towards idolatry. A person who takes this first step may not be able to turn back in some circumstances:

> *Know* O friend! Man unjustly attributes the fruits of the work of a group to a single person and assumes that that individual has produced those fruits. From this injustice a kind of secret association of partners with God arises. For assuming the result of the work of a community and the product of their free will to have originated from a single person means accepting that person has an extraordinary power which has reached the degree of creativity. The gods and goddesses of ancient Greeks and other pagan peoples were devised from such devilish assumptions.

Later he makes these observations on various subjects: Faith is a secret source of strength. Those who possess this source can possess worlds, and through dependence on God realized with faith, man can make everything a servant to himself:

> Whoever submits himself to the will of God and pursues His pleasure, everything serves him, and whoever, by contrast, disobeys God, everything turns against him. If one affirms that whatever exists belongs to Him exclusively, being a property of His, everything serves one.

The purport of the Qur'anic verse *Say, "if it weren't for your prayers, of what significance are you?"* is sufficient illumination and proof of this truth. Then just as a child who can't reach something asks for it from his father and mother, a servant should take refuge in his Lord with helplessness and need and ask for everything from Him. This matter is presented in more detail in the Fourth and Fifth Points of the Twenty-third Word.

Our Messenger is of the nature of the basis, essence and root of the universe. There is no point in the universe empty of the truth of his light. Just as the spirit and meaning in a seed are found in the body of a tree and shoot, he is a mirror to the First and the Last from the respect of his light comprising the essence of existence:

> If you see the universe as a great book, you will see the light of Muhammad, upon him be peace and blessings, as the ink of the pen with which that book has been written. If you see the universe in the form of a tree, you will see his light as originally its seed and consequently its fruit. If you see the universe as in the form of an animate being, you will see his light as its soul. If you see the universe in the form of a macro-human, you will see his light as his intellect. If you see the universe as a flower garden, you will see his light as its nightingale. If you see the universe as a lofty, richly-decorated castle with many rooms and apartments, which displays the splendor of the sovereignty of the Eternal Sovereign and the marvels of His Glory, as well as the beauties of the manifestations of His Grace and the wonderful designs of His Art, then you will see the light of the Prophet Muhammad, upon him be peace and blessings, as a spectator.

The Third Principle of the Thirty-first Word and the Second Part of the Addendum to the Tenth Word spread before the eye of our hearts a special depth and richness on this wonderful subject.

According to Bediüzzaman, the essential character of nature and man is both a deceiving idol and a secret prism showing the eternal Artist and eternal truth. For those who are spiritually prepared and who have grasped the perspective, both nature as a richly embroidered work of art and man as a crystal prism are each an unerring book, an eloquent speaker and a source of light illuminating the realm behind the visible world. Bediüzzaman puts this observation in the form of a victory song with his words:

> For thirty years I have struggled against two "rebels", one the ego within man, the other, nature in the outer world. I have seen the former as a shadowy mirror reflecting someone other than itself. Nevertheless, man views it as having an independent existence, showing itself, and therefore becoming, an unbending tyrant in rebellion against its Creator.
>
> As for nature, I have seen it as a work of Divine Art, a painting of the All-Merciful. However, as a result of viewing it heedlessly [of the

Creator], it has come to be regarded by materialists as if it were a deity, as self-originated and existing by itself, and made into an excuse for ingratitude which has resulted in unbelief.

Thanks be to God and praise be to Him, by the help of the One, Eternally Besought-of-All, and the enlightenment of the glorious Qur'an, my struggle has ended in the death of these two rebels, the smashing of these two idols.

Written during the period of *Nur's* evolvement, the First Aim of the Thirtieth Word approaches this subject with a unique breadth and richness, and again, the Twenty-third Gleam known as *The Treatise on Nature* destroys the idolization of nature in a language that people of every level can understand.

In Bediüzzaman's world of thought, sins are pictured as the reconnoitering hands of unbelief. In places where they are frequently seen, thought "sets sail" for immorality and faith is face to face with danger.

Surely there is the seed of unbelief in the essence of sins, especially if they are frequently committed. For a frequently committed sin makes the sinner indifferent to it and becomes an addiction whose only remedy lies in its abandonment. Then the sinner wishes for there to be no punishment for it and unconsciously tries to find an excuse to believe in the non-existence of eternal torment. This state of the sinner continues until he denies the eternal torment and the abode of punishment. Also, the shame arising from committing a sin not followed by remorse and asking forgiveness from God leads the sinner to deny that the sin he has committed is really a sin. It leads him to refute the existence of those—like the guarding angels—who oversee him and are aware of his sin. Because of the intensity of the shame he feels, the sinner wishes for there to be no reckoning in the other world. When he encounters even a false argument for its non-existence, he takes it as a strong proof and denies the final reckoning. Consequently, this ends in the darkening of the heart. May God save us from such a consequence! Amen.

In the First Point of the Second Gleam from *The Gleams*, one of the works written in the blossoming period of the Risale-i Nur, it is stated that sins are each a net on the road to unbelief. This approach of Bediüzzaman is also original.

Trying to delve deeper into the Qur'an was an unrelinquishable obsession of Bediüzzaman's. In a line extending from *Isharatu'l-I'jaz* (Signs of the Qur'an's Miraculousness) to the *Mathnawi*, from the *Mathnawi* to different *Words*, in particular the Twenty-fifth Word, he always breathed the Qur'an. With new and original interpretations, he frequently displayed its magical depths and excited thirsty hearts with his golden words, bringing Divine truths down to the comprehension level of the people.

In the Twenty-fifth Word the analysis attains a wonderful state of magic. The elaboration in that Word of the summary here in the *Mathnawi* is like the ocean to the drop and the forest to the seedling. In addition, it is not long after this brief reminder in the *Mathnawi* that a new delightful topic pertaining to the Qur'an whispers to us as if through a door slightly opened and then passes on.

> *Know*, O friend! While listening to the Qur'an, for each of its melodies, you can take on a new attitude and mood according to the degrees of guidance in consideration of the levels of its addressees, and try to assume the mood of the intermediaries ranging from Gabriel, who brought it to the Prophet, to the one from whom you hear it directly.
>
> While listening to it from the one reciting it where you are, you should try to hear it as if you were listening to it from the Prophet himself, upon him be peace and blessings, reciting it at the summit of Prophethood to the whole of mankind and other beings throughout the earth.
>
> Then, you should assume the manner of Gabriel while he recites it to the Prophet, upon him be peace and blessings, on the "highest horizon".
>
> Finally, if you can, you should try to hear it as if you were listening to it from behind seventy thousand veils from the Eternally Speaking One, Who speaks to the Prophet at "the distance of two bows' length".

Mathnawi al-Nuriya resembles an index of so many topics each of which could comprise a separate book to explain and which would later be elaborated in the *Risale-i Nur* each with a different tone and clarity.

Under the title of "Flower", in the notes that would later be discussed in the *Risale-i Nur*, numerous important truths are presented in a summary form.

The "Spark" is like a tiny seed-bed of piety and good works. There our worldly emotions are questioned... our thoughts are directed to Divine Unity once more... and the vastness of faith is shown.

The "Whiff" touches our hearts like a spectrum and points out before our eyes the depth and richness of the Qur'anic verses in a manner that surpasses poetry. It dwells on the purposes of the creation of human organs and, cleansing our eyes, it wipes away our habits that can be considered as a crust on our eye of discernment.

Under the title of the "Third Part of The Whiff", we are led around the "slopes" of Divine Destiny and Decree and the law of Sparing and then our hearts are told the secrets of the ways the Qur'anic verses conclude. Immediately after that we are offered a path to follow to the Turth, different from the paths of the past. The offer is made and our attention is turned towards essential human weakness and poverty. Two steps later under a different title, man's unique creationdifferent from all the other animate creaturesis pointed to and we are reminded of the fact that man is an index of the whole of existence. After that our attention is turned to prayer, a subject which is analyzed in several parts of the Risale-i Nur with its many dimensions; the meaning of God's answering prayers is explained and the desire of supplication in our hearts is excited. While travelling in the pure climate of the Mathnawi, we also encounter the difference between self-pride and man's proclaiming God's blessings upon him as a sign of gratitude to Him. Under the heading of Fourteenth Droplet the Qur'an's basic issues and essential purposes that can be considered as pivotal subjects in the *Risale-i Nur* are dwelt upon.

Under the title of "Radiance", we are led through the vastness of the Divine Existence whose "proper" name is *Allah* and our hearts are made to leap with the excitement of a unique knowledge of Him.

In another paragraph, the reader is introduced to grace and intercession that can be considered as active prayer. After pointing out the significance of soil as an element serving for the purpose of God's manifesting all His Names, attention is turned to humility which means being like soil upon which man prostrates himself before God. It is stressed that "a servant is closest to his Lord in prostration".

Under the heading "Point", in the name of the Divine Essence which Bediüzzaman frequently dealt with in the *Risale-i Nur*, in addition to the three important universal proofs, a fourth is dwelt upon. It is man's conscience, which is regarded as the union point of the world of the Unseen and the visible or material world.

The impossibility of evolution is emphasized and in clear language it is stated that mutation doesn't account for anything and there can be no passing or leaping from one species to another. With an absolute but sound thought and style of expression, he says "no" to evolution and settles the matter.

It is our earnest desire that these works be examined in depth within the body of an institute to be established related to the *Risale-i Nur*.

Rays from God's Unity as Bright as the Sun

In the name of God, the Merciful, the Compassionate.

God is the Creator of all things and He is guardian and watcher over everything. To Him belong the keys of the heavens and earth.[1]
Glory be to Him in Whose hand is the kingdom and inner dimensions of all things.[2]

There is nothing but with Us are the stores thereof.[3]

There is not a moving creature but He has grasp of it by the forelock.[4]

O you heedless one, who attribute all things and events in this world to the law of causality. The causes to which you ascribe creativity are only a veil over the operation of the Divine Power. The Dignity and Grandeur of God require such a veil. However, it is the Eternal Divine Power, absolutely independent of everything, which is ever active and creates. For the Divine Unity and Glory require that to be so.

Indeed, the Eternal Monarch has officers. However, they have no authority of their own to execute His orders independently so that they could be regarded as partners to His Sovereignty. They function only as media through which the acts and executions of His Lordship are watched and known. They function also as observers and witnesses. By doing so, they

---

1. *al-Zumar*, 39.62–3.
2. *Ya Sin*, 36.83.
3. *al-Hijr*, 15.21.
4. *Hud*, 11.56.

obey His laws and commands of creation and thereby perform their duty of worship required by their nature and disposition. In short, they exist because they must manifest the dignity of the Divine Power and majesty of the Divine Lordship and Sovereignty.

As for the human monarchs, they need officers and other means because of their incapability to execute their rule alone by themselves. There is neither a resemblance nor a relation between the Divine officers and human ones.

Since most of the heedless and ignorant do not discern the beauty and wisdom behind events, they make wrong complaints and impertinent objections. So, in order to divert such complaints from God to them, causes are placed as an intervening veil (between people and God's acts). However, causes cannot be a consideration in the view of one who is able to see the real beauty and wisdom in events.

There is a parable to clarify this point:

The Angel of Death complained to God that His servants would complain of him for his taking souls. God answered him: "I will put illnesses and misfortunes between you and them so that they will complain of them, not of you."

In sum: the Dignity and Grandeur of God require the apparent causes both to prevent improper complaints and so that those who reason superficially should not see the hand of Power as directly related to certain seemingly insignificant or vile things and affairs. The Unity and Glory of God require at the same time that, in both the creation and disposition of things, the apparent causes have no part.

A note

Belief in God's Unity has two degrees:

One is believing superficially that God has no partners and the universe can belong to none other than Him. It is possible that one who has this degree of belief may be susceptible to certain deviations and obscurities in his understanding.

The other degree is being firmly convinced that God is One and that everything belongs to Him exclusively, and that only He gives existence without any partners whatever and without needing any means to do so. The one with such degree of conviction sees His seal and observes His stamp on all things, and free from any doubts, feels himself always and everywhere in His Presence. Neither deviations nor doubts can find a way to dilute this degree of conviction.

In order that you may acquire such a degree of conviction in God's Unity, I will point out some rays of it which I have obtained from the Qur'an.

First ray

God Almighty has set a special seal on each of the things He has made which shows that He is the Creator of all things. He has set a special stamp on each of His creatures demonstrating that He is the Maker of all things. Also, on each of the "letters" that the Power "writes" there is an inimitable signature particular to the Eternal Monarch.

For example, among His innumerable seals, look at the one He has put on life. Consider how, through life, a single thing is made into many things, and many things into one thing. For example, water that we drink becomes, by God's leave, a means for the formation of innumerable animal organs and systems. Though a single entity, it becomes "many" by God's command. Conversely many varieties of foods become, by God's leave, a particular body or skin or a whole system or sub-system. Thus "many" things become, by God's command, a single entity. So, whoever has an intellect, consciousness and heart must conclude that making a single, simple entity from many things and using a single entity in making things of great diversity is a seal special to the Creator of all things.

Second ray

Among His innumerable stamps, look at only the one He has put on living things.

Being complex and inclusive in character, a living thing is like a miniature of the universe, a shining fruit of the tree of creation, a nucleus of the whole of creation, which the Creator has made a sample or a pattern of most species. It is as if that living thing is a drop filtered through wisdom from the whole of creation with absolutely exact measures, an all-inclusive point extracted from the whole of existence through knowledge with absolutely sensitive calculations. So, it is not possible for one who does not have the supreme disposition of the whole of creation, to create even the simplest of living things. Whoever has a sound intellect must conclude that the one who has made a honeybee an index of most things, and who has inserted in man's nature most parts of the book of creation must be the Creator. He has encoded in its tiny seed the future life of a fig tree. He has made the heart of man a small-scale copy of thousands of worlds and a window opening on them. He has recorded in man's memory his past life and everything related to it. The One Who has done all these and many other similar things cannot be but the Creator of all things, and His doing so is a stamp peculiar to the Lord of the Worlds.

Third ray

Look at the signature put on the acts of bringing to life and reviving. Out of innumerable possible examples, we shall mention only one:

From planets to drops of water and pieces of glass, in each transparent or apparently transparent thing there is a stamp—an image or reflection—particular to the sun.

So too, the Unique, Eternal Sun has set on each living thing a seal, a stamp, of reviving and bringing to life showing itself through the manifestations of all His Names on that thing. If all material causes—supposing they had power and will—came together to produce the like of that stamp, they would not be able to do so, even if they helped one another (*Qur'an*, 17.88).

Assume the images of the sun reflected in drops of water or

pieces of glass or in any transparent thing are not attributed to the sun itself. Then you would have to accept that there is a real, tiny sun in each drop facing the sun, and in each piece of glass reflecting the sun's light, and indeed that every transparent thing has become a sun.

Similarly, assume you do not attribute every living thing and life and every act of bringing to life, to the concentrated manifestation of all the Divine Names. Presume you do not accept that life is the focus of the manifestations of the Divine Names, which could be regarded as the rays of the Eternal Sun. Then you would have to admit that each living thing, even if it be a fly or a flower, has an infinite power of creation, an all-encompassing knowledge, and an absolute will. Also, you would have to attribute divinity to each atom, if you ascribe the existence of everything to itself. Likewise, you would have to attribute absolute divinity to each cause, if you ascribe the existence of everything to causes. This would also compel you to accept countless partners in Divinity which, necessarily, requires absolute independence and never accepts partnership.

Consider an atom or, particularly, a seed or fruit-stone and see how astonishing and well-arranged composition and relationships it has! It has relationships with all the parts of the living thing of which itself is a part. Rather, it has relationships also with all the members of its species and all other creatures. It has relationships and duties resembling those of a private with respect to all the military offices. If you cut off the connection of that atom or seed to the Absolute Power, then you would have to admit that it has eyes with which it sees all things and an all-comprehensive consciousness.

In summary, non-attribution to the sun of its images in drops of water requires the admission of the existence of many suns in the tiniest things. So, too, non-attribution of everything to the Absolutely Powerful One, in relation to Whose Power atoms and suns, particles and wholes, particulars and universals, the small and great, are all the same, necessitates the acceptance of countless divinities.

Fourth ray

For a book to be written by hand requires only a writer and a pen. Whereas, if you get it printed in a printing-machine, then there will have to be as many iron letters as the number of the letters and many people to make those letters and arrange them to print the book. The whole *sura Ya Sin* is written in very small letters inside the two letters *Ya* and *Sin*. If you chose to write a booklet in small, fine letters within a single word, then in order to print that single word you would need as many iron letters as the letters used in the booklet.

So too, if you affirm that the universe is a book written with the pen of a Single One, then you are following the easiest and most reasonable path. If, by contrast, you attribute the universe to nature or material causes, then this is, in fact, the most unreasonable and difficult of ways to follow. For, in this case, to "print" a single living thing would require as many instruments as printing most of the universe would demand. So, this ought to be an impossible supposition.

Suppose you attribute existence to nature or material causes again, for example, in the case of a flower or a fruit. There would have to be in each particle of earth, water and air as many "programs" and hidden factories [to produce it] as the number of all flowers and fruits in the world in all their diversity of color, taste and shape. Or each particle should possess as great power as to make all plants, and as much knowledge as to know all flowering and fruit-bearing plants and trees with all their parts and proportions. For any particle or atom of these three essential elements can be a means for the formation of all plants or most of them.

Suppose you have a pot filled with soil in which seeds of various plants have been buried. Then empty the pot and fill it with the soil taken especially from the surface of the earth. In both cases you will have almost the same result. This is not different from what you observe throughout the earth. Despite their variety in shape, color, taste and appearance, any earth could be the means for the growth of all flowery and fruit-bearing trees. Then each seed or fruit-stone, despite their simplicity and similarity to each other in formation, would have to have special machines or workshops to form the tree or plant in its entirety.

Fifth ray

Look! Any letter in a book points to itself to the extent of itself as a letter and in one respect only. However, it points to its writer in many respects.

Similarly, every "created" letter of the book of the universe points to itself only to the extent of being a letter. However, it points to its Maker in many respects both individually and in the words and sentences in which it is included, and manifests the titles of its Maker, describing them as if it were a long eulogy.

Sixth ray

Look! The Glorious Maker has put on each particular thing His special stamp and on each part of a whole, His peculiar seal. Likewise, He has put on each species and whole His special stamp. He has also put on all parts of the heavens and earth the stamp of His Unity by manifesting all His Names through out the parts of the universe. He has demonstrated His Unity and He has put on the whole universe the seal of His Oneness. By concentrating the manifestations of all His Names on the universe, He has displayed His Oneness.

Look at the stamp pointed out in the verse, *Look at the prints of God's Mercy, how He quickens the earth after its death. He verily is the Quickener of the dead in the same way, and He is powerful over all things*[5]. The quickening of the earth is really an astonishing "resurrection" or coming to life again. Hundreds of thousands of animal and vegetable species are raised to life. The members of many of those species are more numerous than the whole of the human population in the world. Nevertheless, to fulfil certain subtle purposes, most of those plants are not raised in their ex-

---

5. *al-Rum*, 30.50.

act former identities; rather, they are returned to life again in substantial and close resemblance to their previous forms. However they are revived, their being revived indicates the easiness of the Resurrection [which will take place at the end of time after the overall destruction of the universe].

Despite their being infinitely mixed with one another, the quickening of all those innumerable species without any confusion and with utmost exactitude in differentiating them, is a special stamp of the One of infinite Power and all-encompassing Knowledge.

The species are infinitely mixed and intermingled with one another and there is great similarity among them. On the page of the earth hundreds of thousands of "books" are written without any confusion and mistakes, with an infinite order and with absolute accuracy in distinguishing among them. This is, again, a special seal of the One in Whose hand are the kingdom and keys of all things. He is not prevented from doing one thing while doing another at the same time.

O man, you who consider the Resurrection as impossible and deny it! See, in the quickening of the earth, hundreds of thousands of examples of the Resurrection! Your considering the Resurrection impossible is like this:

A man saw one working miracles. He re-wrote innumerable lost books from memory, or composed new ones like the lost ones, all at once. The man is told that that author would write anew your book that he had composed in the twinkling of an eye and that had then been utterly dissolved in water. The man says: "Impossible! How can an obliterated book be written again in a moment?" He says that because he compares his own ignorant and impotent person to that miracle-working author who never forgets anything and who is able to do all things.

Assume a man says of one who lifts a mountain in order to demonstrate his strength that he cannot remove a rock blocking the way of the guests he has invited to the garden where he will offer them the most delicious foods and beverages. Would you not regard the man as foolish?

In this mighty disposition in spring there is an exalted, great and subtly embroidered seal belonging to the Lord, one showing itself in absolute accuracy and orderliness, abundance and extensiveness, with absolute speed and ease, and in perfectly distinguishing and separating utterly mixed things. This seal is particular to the One Whom doing something does not deter from doing another thing, from Whom nothing is hidden, and for Whom nothing is difficult.

In spring we observe on the face of the earth marvelous instances of an extraordinary art and activity based on purposefulness, insight, wisdom and munificence. They take place everywhere in the same way and in absolute exactness, orderliness and abundance. All this art and activity are but a seal of the One Who, despite being nowhere, is present everywhere through His Power and Knowledge, Whom nothing wearies and Who never needs help.

Seventh ray

Look! As the stamp of the One, Eternally Besought-of-All, is observed on the page of the earth, as well as in all parts of the heavens and earth, so too on the universe as a whole the stamp of Unity is clearly observed. The universe is like a magnificent palace, a well-ordered factory, and a well-planned city, among all of whose elements or parts there is a mutual collaboration and co-operation for great purposes. Even over long distances, the elements hasten to the aid of one another just on time without losing their ways. When you discern it, you will see how some of the parts give the others a hand to meet their needs. It is as if they respond to each other's requests for help and, in close co-operation and obedience to a single manager, they work in orderliness and serve living beings for specific purposes.

Look at this principle of mutual helping and cooperation. See how the sun and moon, day and night, and summer and winter, come to the aid of plants to urge them to help animals and convey to them their food that they take from the treasury of Mercy. Animals hasten to the aid of human beings. The honeybee and silkworm, for example, take honey and silk from the treasury of the All-Merciful One and carry them to man. Particles of earth, air and water come to the help of fruits and vegetation, each of which has a different taste and quality of nourishment. In turn, they go to the aid of the cells of the body in perfect orderliness and for great purposes.

This perfect, purposeful and well-arranged mutual helping is manifested by all those things, especially inanimate objects. It is an evident proof and a clear argument that they are servants of an All-Wise Sustainer, the workers of a Munificent Manager, working by His command and leave, and by His Power and Wisdom.

Eighth ray

Look! The food of living things is distributed among them just on time and according to the need of each. This well-arranged universal providence contained in an all-encompassing mercy implies love for and knowledge of those provided. The all-encompassing mercy combined with a perfect graciousness implies favoring and gratifying. The graciousness combined with a universal wisdom implies a certain purpose and consciousness. The universal wisdom is combined with a perfect arrangement, making all things dependent on one another. This dependence requires mutual helping and solidarity among all parts of existence. All this is a special stamp of the One Who is the Lord, Sustainer, Provider and Director of all things, and a seal particular to the One to Whose Command the sun, moon and stars are subjugated. He is the One Who has made all things good which He has created.[6] His command, when He wills a thing is only that He says unto it: Be! and it is.[7]

Ninth ray

As you see the stamp of Oneness on all individual things, and on the earth and the universe, you will also see it on the species

---

6. *al-Sajda*, 32.7.
7. *Ya Sin*, 36.82.

of beings and distributed throughout the world on the universal elements, namely air, water and earth.

Sowing seeds in an arable land indicates that the land is under the disposal of the owner of seeds, and the seeds belong to the one who disposes of the land. Their simplicity, uniformity and comprehensiveness imply an all-encompassing knowledge and wisdom. All those universal elements, where all things are "sown", and through their amazing distribution throughout the world for certain purposes, all creatures, these fruits of Mercy, miracles of Power, and words of Wisdom are all evidence. They bear witness to the fact that the comprehensive and comprehended, and the land and the seeds sown in it, are all at the disposal of a single Maker. Every species and element testify that each belongs to the One Who owns everything. Every flower or fruit or every animal or micro-organism is a seal proclaiming, or a stamp pronouncing, or a signature declaring, in the tongue of perfect harmony and orderliness and the purposes each serves: Whose property I am, this space is also His property. Whoever has created me, has also created it. Whoever uses me as a letter, has also "written" it, and Whoever has made me a stitch, has also woven it.

Again, the One Who disposes of the least of creatures and manages the life of the weakest of beings has the supreme disposition of all of the elements. Also, the One Who employs all of the elements manages the lives of all animals and plants and holds them in His hand of Lordship. This is a stamp of Unity that anyone whose eyes are not blind and heart is not sealed, must surely see.

Now, ask yourself and try whether you can claim absolute ownership and disposal of anything in the universe. Go and listen to what every individual being says — "whoever has the absolute ownership of the species I belong to, can claim the ownership of me, otherwise not." Then go to the species. You will hear every species saying, "whoever has the absolute ownership of the earth with its surface and interior, can claim the ownership of me, otherwise not." Afterwards, go to the earth and you will hear it saying, "whoever has the absolute ownership of the whole of the universe, can claim the ownership of me, otherwise not."

Tenth ray

After we have pointed out some stamps of Unity put on parts and individual beings and on the wholes, and on the universe, and put on life, living beings and bringing to life, now among the innumerable seals of Oneness on species and wholes, look at another one:

The difficulty or easiness in the creation of a tree and a fruit is the same, as both depend on the same law of growth and issue from the same center. The dependence on the same law of raising and upkeep diminishes difficulty and expenditure to the extent that there is no difference between the growth of a tree of numerous fruits by a single person and a single fruit by many people. The growth of a single fruit by many people would require as many tools as the growth of a tree bearing numerous fruits does. Similarly, the instruments, machines and factories needed to manufacture the equipment of a whole army would also be needed to equip a single soldier. The difference is only qualitative. Also, printing thousands of copies of a book in a printing-machine will not be much more expensive than printing a single copy. If you were to have those copies printed each in a different printing-machine, the amount you would have to pay would be thousands of times as great as that which you will pay for thousands of copies from the same machine.

In sum: when you do not attribute innumerably multiple things to a single source, then—besides having to attribute a single thing to innumerably multiple things—you will have as many difficulties as the number of those things. So, the extraordinary facility in coming into existence of so many species distributed all over the world comes from the Oneness of their Creator.

Eleventh ray

The essential similarities among the members of a species and the species of a class bear witness to the oneness of the stamp and the singleness of the "pen" and testify that all those similarities are the work of a single one. Also, the absolute facility [in their coming into existence in such abundance] and the littleness of the expenditure on them necessarily demonstrate that they are all the works of a Single Being. Or else, it would be impossibly difficult for them to come into existence. This observed facility and economy of means also makes impossible partnership with God Almighty in both His Essence and acts. Otherwise, as a result of the destruction of its order, the universe would go to ruin.

Twelfth ray

Look! Just as life is a proof of Divine Oneness and the necessity of His Existence, so too death is an evidence of His Permanence and Eternity.

The images of the sun reflected in the bubbles floating on a flowing river and in the waves of a sea, as well as in transparent things on the earth, bear witness to the sun. Those images disappear when the sun sets or the river enters a tunnel, and new ones appear the next day when the sun rises again or the river comes out of the tunnel. This testifies to the permanence of the sun's light and demonstrates that all those images are the work of a single sun. Through their existence they show the existence of the sun, and through their disappearance they demonstrate that there is only one sun which continually exists.

Similarly, through their existence, creatures testify to the necessary existence of the Necessarily Existent Being, and through their disappearance together with the causes of their existence and through their being followed by new ones, bear witness to His Permanence, Eternity and Oneness. For along with the alternation of days and nights and seasons and the flux of years and centuries, beautiful beings are renewed, fine creatures are replaced, with new ones, and they "set" while their likes "rise". All this evidently testifies to the existence of an Eternally Beautiful One Who continuously manifests Himself, and to His Per-

manence and Oneness. Also, the disappearance of causes together with their effects along with the succession of years and
centuries and their being followed by their likes, bear witness
for certainty that causes and their effects are created for subtle
purposes. It shows that they are therefore creatures powerless
in themselves, and that all of those fine beings coming in suc-
cessively are creatures of One All-Majestic and All-Gracious
and Beautiful, all of Whose Names are beautiful and holy. It testifies that they are His changing works, moving mirrors, and
successive stamps and seals.

Thirteenth ray

Look! From tiniest particles to planets and galaxies and from individual beings to suns and stars, everything, in the tongue of
its essential helplessness, points to the necessary existence of its
Creator. In the tongue of its functions and tasks which, despite
its helplessness, each is charged with in the general order of
creation, it indicates the Oneness of its Creator.

Everything testifies in two ways to the existence and Unity
of the Creator.

In every living being there are two signs of His Oneness and
absolute independence of creation.

Through the enlightenment of the Qur'an, I have seen that
each part of creation testifies to the Necessarily Existent Being,
One and Eternally Besought-of-All, in around fifty-five tongues,
which I once described briefly in one of my Arabic treatises
called *Qatra*—The Drop.

Fourteenth ray

Know that just as creatures bear witness to the All-Glorious
One's necessary existence and Oneness, so too they testify to
His Attributes of Majesty, Beauty and Perfection. They also bear
witness to the perfection of His Essence and that there is no de-
fect or deficiency in either His Being or essential "Qualities" or
Attributes or Names or acts.

Surely, the perfection of a work visibly and manifestly points to the perfection of the act. The perfection of the act evidently points to the perfection of the title. The perfection of the title necessarily points to the perfection of the attribute. The perfection of the attribute surely points to the essential capacity or indispensable quality of the being, and the perfection of the essential or indispensable quality points for certain to the perfection of the being himself.

Consider this: The perfection of the structure and decoration of a palace manifests the perfection of the work of the engineer who built it. The perfection of his work clearly shows the perfection of his title as an engineer. That is, you regard him as a skillful, expert and able engineer. The perfection of his title displays the perfection of the qualities he has an as engineer. That is, you recognize him by his knowledge, intelligence, ability and efficiency. The perfection of his qualities bears witness to these essential capacities. That is, he has superior capacities and distinguished potential he has fully realized. The perfection of his capacities reveals his perfection as an engineer.

Similarly, the perfection of the works we observe in the universe bears witness to the perfection of the activity behind them. The perfection of the activity evidently bears witness to the perfection of the titles of the one who does those works. The perfection of the titles necessarily testifies to the perfection of the qualities or attributes. For, as is known, names or titles issue from attributes. The perfection of the attributes reveals the perfection of the essential capacities that are the sources of the attributes. The perfection of the essential capacities testifies for certain to the perfection of the All-Glorious Being.

Actually, compared to His glorious Perfection and majestic Beauty, whatever perfection or beauty is in the universe, is only a dim or vague shadow.

INDEX OR BRIEF SUMMARIES OF THE TOPICS
DISCUSSED IN THE TREATISE

*Causes or causality to which some ascribe creativity are only a veil over the operation of the Divine Power. The Dignity and Grandeur of God require such a veil. (1)

*Belief in God's Unity has two degrees. (2)

*Life is an argument for God's Unity. Being complex and inclusive in character, a living thing is like a miniature of the universe, a shining fruit of the tree of creation, a nucleus of the whole of creation, which the Creator has made a sample or a pattern of most species. (4)

*If you affirm that the universe is a book written with the pen of a Single One, then you are following the easiest and most reasonable path. If, by contrast, you attribute the universe to nature or material causes, then this is, in fact, the most unreasonable and difficult of ways to follow. (6)

*Every "created" letter of the book of the universe points to itself only to the extent of being a letter. However, it points to its Maker in many respects both individually and in the words and sentences in which it is included, and manifests the titles of its Maker, describing them as if it were a long eulogy. (7)

*There are hundreds of thousands of examples of the Resurrection in the quickening of the earth in spring after winter. (8)

*The universe is like a magnificent palace, a well-ordered factory, and a well-planned city, among all of whose elements or parts there is a mutual collaboration and co-operation for great purposes. This manifestly points to the One Creator and Director. (9)

*The food of living things is distributed among them just on time and according to the need of each. This well-arranged universal providence contained in an all-encompassing mercy implies the Provider's love for and knowledge of those provided. (10)

*Every species and element testify that each belongs to the One Who owns everything. Every flower or fruit or every animal or micro-organism is a seal proclaiming, or a stamp pronouncing, or a signature declaring, in the tongue of perfect harmony and orderliness and the purposes each serves: Whose property I am, this space is also His property. Whoever has created me, has also created it. Whoever uses me as a letter, has also "written" it, and Whoever has made me a stitch, has also woven it. (11)

*When you do not attribute innumerably multiple things to a single source, then—besides having to attribute a single thing to innumerably multiple things—you will have as many difficulties as the number of those things. So, the extraordinary facility in coming into existence of so many species distributed all over the world comes from the Oneness of their Creator. (12)

*Through their existence, creatures testify to the necessary existence of the Necessarily Existent Being, and through their disappearance together with the causes of their existence and through their being followed by new ones, bear witness to His Permanence, Eternity and Oneness. (13)

*From tiniest particles to planets and galaxies and from individual beings to suns and stars, everything, in the tongue of its essential helplessness, points to the necessary existence of its Creator. In the tongue of its functions and tasks which, despite its helplessness, each is charged with in the general order of creation, it indicates the Oneness of its Creator. (14)

*The perfection of the works we observe in the universe bears witness to the perfection of the activity behind them. The perfection of the activity evidently bears witness to the perfection of the titles of the one who does those works. The perfection of the titles necessarily testifies to the perfection of the qualities or attributes. For, as is known, names or titles issue from attributes. The perfection of the attributes reveals the perfection of the essential capacities that are the sources of the attributes. The perfection of the essential capacities testifies for certain to the perfection of the All-Glorious Being. (15)

Droplets from the Ocean of Knowledge of the Prophet

A note

There are innumerable things that make our Lord known to us. The three greatest and most universal are:

The first is this universe, some signs of which [concerning the existence and Unity of our Lord] you have already heard.

The second is the Seal of the Prophets, upon him be peace and blessings. He is the greatest of our Lord's signs in the universe and the key to His hidden treasures.

The third is the holy Qur'an, which is the interpreter of the book of the universe and God's argument against creatures.

Surely, we should recognize the second sign, the Prophet Muhammad, upon him be peace and blessings, who is an articulate, indisputable "argument" [for our Lord], and then listen to what he says. From the ocean of knowledge of that sign, we shall mention a few droplets.

First droplet

Know that the Prophet Muhammad, upon him be peace and blessings, this indisputable, articulate argument for our Lord, has a universal personality. If you ask who he is and what kind of one he is:

He is such a one that due to the universality of his person, the surface of the earth is his mosque, with Makka being his place of worship and Madina, his pulpit. He is the leader of all believers, who, standing after him in rows, follow the orator of all mankind explaining to them the principles of happiness [in both worlds]. He is the chief of all the Prophets, clearing them of the calumnies their peoples spoke against them and affirming them and the essentials of their religions within his comprehensive religion. Muhammad, upon him be peace and blessings, is the master of all saints, guiding and educating them through the light of his Messengership and the "pivot" around whom there is the circle of recitation of God's Names formed of the Prophets, upon them be peace, the good, the truthful, and the righteous, who are all agreed on his Message. He is a luminous tree growing on the firm, healthy and lively roots of the previous Prophets and the heavenly principles they preached, and shooting out green, fresh branches and yielding the fine "fruit" of saints distinguished with knowledge of God. Whatever he claimed, it is confirmed by the whole of the Prophets based on their miracles, and the whole of saints based on their good or marvelous works. All the affirmations he made bear the seals of all perfected people. If you hear him declaring *There is no god but God* and therefore affirming Divine Unity, you will surely hear the same declaration from the past and future, from the illustrious, shining "suns" and stars of humanity reciting God's Names in His circle. Despite the differences in their approaches and temperaments, they agree with him on all his affirmations, as if saying in unison, "You declare the truth and speak the truth."

So, on the basis of a few mere illusions, how can one dare to raise an objection to a claim affirmed by innumerable witnesses whose miracles and marvelous good works display their pure characters and truthfulness?

Second droplet

Know that this illustrious person, who affirms Divine Unity and guides mankind to it, is himself confirmed by Prophethood and sainthood, which, for fourteen centuries, hundreds of millions of people have unanimously agreed that he enjoys. Also, in the previous heavenly Scriptures—the Torah, the Gospel, the

Psalms and others—there are verses predicting him and confirming his Prophethood. Again, he is confirmed by the marvels that, prior to his Prophethood, either he himself worked or took place connected with him. Besides, as is reported through reliable channels, his coming was predicted prior to his birth and Prophethood. In addition, he is affirmed by the hundreds of miracles he worked—such as his splitting of the moon, the abundant flow of water from his fingers, trees' moving in answer to his call, the coming of rain upon his prayer, satisfaction of many hungry people with very little food through his blessing, the speaking to him of rocks, trees and animals like the lizard, gazelle, camel and wolf—all of which were narrated by truthful traditionists and historians. He is also confirmed by the law contained in his religion that enables people to find happiness in both worlds.

You have already seen somewhere else the rays from the "sun" of the law contained in his religion diffusing happiness. If there is not a covering on your eyes and a seal on your heart, they will be enough for you.

Third droplet

Know that, besides numerous arguments for his Prophethood, the very person or character of the Prophet Muhammad, upon him be peace and blessings, proves his Prophethood. Like the sun [showing itself through its light, heat and other manifestations], all the praiseworthy virtues concentrated in his person and the merits and excellences he displayed in fulfilling his mission, confirm his Prophethood. His firm belief demonstrated by his austere life, his great fear of God and righteousness and his matchless servanthood to his Lord are further proofs. Muhammad's utmost submission to God to which his life testifies, the perfection of his earnestness, firmness and courage, and his utmost certainty in his movements testified to by his full confidence in his cause—all this confirms him in his cause. Also, just as green leaves, bright flowers and fresh, radiant fruits bear witness to the vigor of the tree, so his full adherence to his cause and following it in utmost certainty and strictness also confirm him in his claim.

Fourth droplet

Know that time and space have great influence on man's reasoning and thought. So, if you would like to, come and, freed from the influences of the present conditions of time and space, let us travel back through the stream of time as far as the Arabian Peninsula in the Age of Happiness. We should put on the clothes woven in that age and visit the "Axis of the Sphere of Divine Messengership" while he is at work.

Open your eyes and look carefully! What catches our eye first in that land is an extraordinary man excelling all others in beauty of appearance as well as in good conduct. He has with him a noble, miraculous book and speaks in an extraordinarily concise and wise way, giving an eternal address to the whole of creation including all of mankind and *jinn* and to all other creatures.

What strange things he speaks about! He speaks about a very important affair, a very awesome tiding. He removes the veil from the creation of the universe, and explains the reasons why it has been created. He also answers the three awesome questions that from the very beginning have occupied the mind of every conscious being and bewildered it: Who are you? Where do you come from? What is your purpose or final destination?

Fifth droplet

Look at that most illustrious being and see how he disseminates the truth with the light of which the night of mankind changes into daytime, and its winter into spring. Also, it is as if the universe changed form so that its vexed, distressful face became cheerful and smiling.

If we do not look at the universe in the light [of the truth] that man brought, then the universe seems as if full of sorrow, with its living creatures like strangers and enemies to one another and inanimate objects like frightening corpses. We see animals and human beings like orphans weeping at the pains of death and separation. The world in all its movements, and the changes and alterations it undergoes, and with all its decorations and adornments, seems like a plaything of chance, devoid of any meaning. Also, the helplessness of man becomes a continuous trouble for him and his poverty makes him unable to do anything. His reason or intellect continually upsets him with the sorrows of the past and anxieties of the future. As a result, man is reduced to being the lowest and most wretched of animals.

Now look at the universe with the light of the Prophet, upon him be peace and blessings, and observe it through the telescope of his religion. Look how the universe then appears! See how its appearance has suddenly changed! No longer a house of mourning, it has become a mosque where all beings praise and thank the Creator and reflect [on His works]. The creatures that formerly seemed like strangers and enemies to one another, have become friends and brothers. The inanimate objects, which you saw before as terrifying corpses, have all become like amiable living beings fulfilling certain important functions and, in the tongue of those functions or tasks, articulating their Creator's signs. The living beings whom you saw before like orphans weeping with pain and complaints, now appear as reciting the Creator's Names through their lives and thanking him for their discharge from their duties—that is, for their death. All the movements, changes and alterations taking place in the universe are no longer a meaningless plaything of chance. Rather they are messages from the rulership or mastership of the Creator, "pages" on which He writes His signs of creation and rules of the universe, and mirrors where His Names are reflected. In sum, the universe is a book of Divine Wisdom.

Now look at the past, that great tomb in darkness, and see how it has been illuminated with the suns of Prophets and stars of saints. Then look at the future, the darkest of nights, and see how it has been illuminated with the light of the Qur'an and appeared as gardens of Paradise.

Had it not been for that person, the universe with everything in it and man would have been reduced to something worthless and meaningless. Had it not been for that wonderful, superior person who makes known the universe and its Creator, this beautiful universe would not have existed. For we would have been unable to know what it means for us. How truthful He is Whose words are true and for Whom is the kingdom of all creation, in His declaration: *But for you, I would not have created the worlds.*

Sixth droplet

I have urged you to look and listen to what he says. He speaks about eternal happiness and brings good tidings of it. He unveils the infinite mercy and announces it to all people, calling them to it. He also heralds the beauties of the Divine rule and upbringing and reveals the secrets of the treasuries of the Divine Names.

Look at him from the viewpoint of his mission. You will see him as the proof and lamp of the truth, the sun of guidance and the means of happiness.

Then, look at him from the viewpoint of his person. You will see him as the epitome of the All-Merciful's love [of His creatures] and the embodiment of the Lord's mercy for them. He is also the honor of humanity and the most radiant and illustrious of the fruits of the tree of creation.

Now look at him and see how the light of his religion has reached the East and West with the speed of lightning and one fourth of mankind has wholeheartedly accepted the gift of his guidance.

Is it then at all possible for the carnal self and Satan to argue with reason and without sophistry against the affirmations of one like that man, especially against the foundation of all his affirmations, namely *There is no god but God?*

Seventh droplet

If you would like to know what it is that stimulates that being, it is a sacred power. Consider his accomplishments in that vast peninsula: do you not see in that vast, strange desert those savage peoples, fanatically adherent to their customs and unyielding in their tribalism and hostilities. They were so hard-hearted that they could bury their daughters alive in the soil without remorse or grief. How did that being remove from them in so short of time all such bad morals and equip them with high, laudable virtues? He made them teachers of humanity and masters of civilized peoples. Look again! He did all of that not, as most other rulers have sought to do it, by force of power and terror, but by conquering hearts and minds, and subjugating spirits and egos, becoming the beloved of hearts, the teacher of reasons, educator of selfhood and the ruler of spirits.

Eighth droplet

You know that removing a petty established bad habit like smoking from a small community requires a great effort and a powerful, determined ruler. However, that illustrious being removed many established bad habits from vast communities fanatically adherent to their customs and traditions and unyielding in character. He did so with a small force, little effort and over a very short time. Moreover, in place of their bad habits, he ingrained in them praiseworthy virtues and exalted merits. Look, for example, at 'Umar, may God be pleased with him, before and after his conversion to Islam. [You see him among the leading personages among his people in the time of pre-Islamic ignorance] with only a seed of virtue in his character, he became, following his conversion, like a "tall, excellent tree" [of most laudable merits]. Almost all of the accomplishments of that illustrious being, the Prophet, are extraordinary. Whoever blinds himself to that Age of Happiness, we call him to look into that peninsula in its present civilized state. He may test himself to see what he can achieve there. Let them take a hundred of their philosophers [psychologists and sociologists] and go to the Arabian Peninsula. I wonder whether they will be able to accomplish in a hundred years a hundredth of what that noble being accomplished in a single year.

Ninth droplet

You know, if you have some understanding of man's essential nature or character, that it is not easy for a sensible man, however infamous he is, to tell a lie that will embarrass him when it is found out. Even if it concerns an insignificant claim or matter and is told in the presence of a small group, still it is not easy. If he tells such a lie comfortably without blushing or feeling shame, this points to his being a lying trickster, and his opponents will publicize this trait of his. This being so, how can it be possible for one—especially if he is famed for his trustworthiness and truthfulness—who carries the greatest responsibility, to tell a lie concerning the most important and greatest mission before the whole of mankind until the Last Day? How could he lie before people who feel a strong antagonism towards him and are impatiently on the look-out for a lie to fall from his lips?

We see that noble being giving utterance to whatever he had to say without fear of his opponents and without any hesitation or anxiety, with absolute sincerity and enthusiasm, and in a way to vex and discomfit their reason, arguments and attitudes. Is it then possible for such a one to have lied and deceived people concerning his mission? No! [*Whatever he says*] *is but a revelation revealed.*[1]

Truth is absolutely free and independent of deception and has no need of it, and the eye able to see truth cannot be deceived. Therefore, the path of that noble being is true and therefore he is wholly free of deception of others, just as his truth-perceiving eyes were wholly free of being deceived by illusions.

Tenth droplet

Look and listen to what he says. He speaks about awesome events and warns people [about them]. He also speaks about matters that captivate hearts and inspire minds to reflect, and he brings mankind good tidings [of a happy future both in this world and the Hereafter].

---

1. *al-Najm*, 53.4.

You know that many people have so great a desire to know the reality of things and events as even to sacrifice their souls. If they told you that someone had come from the moon or Jupiter and was saying very interesting things about them and also foretelling everybody's future, would you not agree to sacrifice half of your belongings or even your life to find out what he had to tell? How surprising it is then, that while you would most probably agree to sacrifice half of your life or belongings only to satisfy your curiosity, you do not care what that noble being says. Yet the people of truth and expert knowledge including the Prophets, truthful and truth-seeking scholars and saints, have all confirmed him and are all agreed on whatever he said and whatever he predicted. He speaks about the acts of a Monarch in Whose kingdom the moon is no more than a fly flying around a moth. The moth itself flies around a lamp He has lit in one of the thousands of His mansions that He has prepared for His guests. He also speaks about a world full of wonders and marvels and about a revolution so unusual and extraordinary that if the earth exploded and its mountains flew like clouds, this would not be equal in strangeness to one thousandth of that revolution. If you would like to, hear about it from him:

> When the sun is folded up, and when the stars fall, losing their luster; and when the mountains are moved; and when camels ten-months pregnant are abandoned; and when the wild beasts are herded together; and when the seas are set boiling, and when souls are reunited, and when the girl-child that was buried alive is asked for what sin she was slain; and the records of men's deeds are laid upon; and when the heaven is torn away; and when the hell is set blazing; and when Paradise is brought near; then every soul will know what it has prepared.[2]

> When the sky is cleft asunder, and when the planets are dispersed, and when the oceans are poured forth, and when the graves are overturned, each soul will know what it has sent forward and what it has kept back.[3]

2. *al-Takwir*, 81.1-14.

3. *al-Infitar*, 82,1-5.

When the earth is shaken with its earthquake and the earth yields up its burdens, and man says: "What is the matter with it?" That day it will proclaim its tidings because your Lord inspired it. That day mankind will come forth in scattered groups to be shown their deeds. Whoever does good an atom's weight will see it then. And whoever does ill an atom's weight will see it then.[4]

The Clatterer! What is the Clatterer? Would that you knew what the Clatterer is! A day when men will become like scattered moths, and the mountains will become like carded wool. Then, as for him whose scales are heavy [with good deeds], he will be in a pleasing life. But as for him whose scales are light, the bottomless pit will be his home. What will convey to you what that is like! It is raging Fire.[5]

He gives tidings of a future, compared to which this world's future is like a drop from a mirage of water as compared to a limitless ocean. He brings good tidings of contentment compared to which worldly contentment is but a flash of lightning as compared to an ever-shining sun.

Beneath the veil of this universe of wonders there await us events wholly out of the ordinary, wholly beyond what we are used to. In order for us to be informed of those events there must surely be an extraordinary one who will witness them and then inform us about them. Indeed, we observe what that being does and how he lives and conclude that he witnesses them, and so either warns us [against them] or brings us good tidings [of the happy future awaiting us beyond them]. That being also informs us of the things pleasing to the Lord of the Worlds and the things He wants us to do, and of some awesome affairs we cannot escape, some strange realities which we are bound to face and without which happiness is impossible.

Woe to the heedless! Woe to the misguided! How amazing are the attitudes of some towards these realities! How can they blind themselves to truth and become deaf to these realities?

---

4. *al-Zilzal*, 99.1-8.
5. *al-Qari'a*, 101.1-11.

While souls should be sacrificed for his sake and everyone should renounce the world and whatever is in it to hasten to him, how can they not care about a being as wonderful as he?

Eleventh droplet

Know that that illustrious being whom we know by his most sublime character and the world recognizes by his matchless accomplishments, and who is an articulate, truthful argument for God's Oneness and a most true evidence of His Unity, is a decisive argument and definite evidence of eternal happiness. Through his call and guidance he is the means of gaining the eternal happiness, the creation of which he caused through his prayer and servanthood.

If you wish, look at him in the most comprehensive prayer that he leads before the inhabitants of the Arabian Peninsula, rather the inhabitants of the whole world. Look again: he is standing in that most comprehensive prayer in the Arabia of his century with all the virtuous descendants of Adam from the time of Adam to the end of time standing in rows behind him and following him. All down the centuries they follow him in worship and say "Amen" to his supplications. Be attentive to what he does and says in that worship. Look! He prays out of a deep, comprehensive and mighty need. The whole world, the heavens and all creatures accompany him in his prayer and say in the tongues of their behavior and dispositions: "Yes, O Lord, accept his prayer. We too ask what he asks of You; together with everything we have—our eyes, ears, tongues, hands, legs, heart, minds, etc.—as the manifestations of Your Names, we ask of You whatever He asks."

Now look at his manners and see how he supplicates in utmost consciousness of his poverty before his Lord and in a most ardent desire and deep sorrow! He stirs the universe to tears and it participates in his prayer. Then look for what he supplicates! He supplicates for the realization of such a purpose that if it is not realized, then the whole of mankind, indeed all creatures, will fall into the lowest of the low, with no value and meaning at all. However, by the realization of that purpose, all creatures will rise each to its rank of perfection according to its own capacity. Also, look how he supplicates with such deep yearning for help and such a pitiful request for mercy that the Divine Throne of Universal Rule and the heavens are moved to pity and love and say: "Amen, O God, Amen"! Again, look to Whom he applies for the realization of his purpose! He applies to the One All-Powerful, All-Hearing, All-Munificent, and All-Knowing, All-Seeing and All-Compassionate One Who hears the most secret petition which an animal makes in the most secret place for its most secret need, and manifestly answers it, satisfying that need. He also sees the least desire of the least living being for the least thing and manifestly enables it to realize its desire from a direction it had not reckoned. He gives freely and shows compassion in such a wise, orderly, regular way that no doubt remains that this kind of training, raising and sustenance can only be the work of One All-Hearing, All-Knowing, All-Seeing and All-Wise.

Twelfth droplet

How extraordinary! What does this being ask for, who stands on earth with all the Prophets, the most virtuous of mankind, behind him and, holding his hands towards the Supreme Throne of God, makes a supplication to which mankind and *jinn* say "Amen"? We know by his acts that he is the honor of humanity and pride of all beings and the unique one among creation at all times. He intercedes with God [for all beings] for the sake of all the Divine Names manifested in the "mirrors" of beings. Listen! He asks for eternal existence, meeting with God, Paradise and God's good pleasure. Eternal happiness is necessitated by (among other reasons) the Divine Mercy, Favoring, Wisdom and Justice, and God's Beautiful Names, almost all of which demand the existence of the other world. But even if it weren't so, a single prayer of that illustrious being would suffice for his Lord's building of Paradise for him and his followers, as He builds for us in every spring Paradise-like gardens ornamented with the miracles of His Art. Just as his mission of Messenger-ship caused the building of this world for trial and worship, so the prayer he makes as a requirement and dimension of his servanthood would cause the construction of the other world for reward and punishment.

The matchless beauty of the universe is so perfect that it prompted a man like Imam Ghazzali to say, "It is not possible for another creation more beautiful than the present one to come into existence." Is it then possible for that extraordinary order and harmony, that all-inclusive mercy and faultless artistry, and that matchless beauty to be combined and marred with detestable ugliness, terrifying injustice, and great confusion? The petition from the least creature for its least need is heard and answered most attentively. Would it not be a supreme ugliness and unequalled fault not to hear the loudest voice and a supplication made for the greatest need, and not to accept the best of requests made with a most beautiful desire and longing? God is absolutely free of such ugliness and fault. The faultless beauty observed throughout the universe does not admit such ugliness. It is impossible.

Thirteenth droplet

O fellow traveler! Does what you have so far seen not yet suffice you? If you desire to acquire complete knowledge of that illustrious person, even if we stay in this peninsula a hundred years, we will still not be able to comprehend fully even a single one of the dimensions of his mission and accomplishments. Let us return and, travelling back through centuries, see how each century "flourished" [with his Message] and to what extent it benefited from that Age of Happiness.

We see that in each century we passed through innumerable "flowers" opened in the "sun" of that Age of Happiness and that through the light of guidance that noble being diffused, each century yielded thousands of illustrious fruits such as Abu Hanifa,[6] Shaifi'i,[7] Abu Yazid al-Bistami,[8] Junayd al-Baghdadi,[9] Shaykh 'Abd al-Qadir al-Jilani,[10] Imam al-Ghazali,[11] Muhyi al-

Din ibn al-'Arabi,[12] Abu'l-Hasan al-Shadhili,[13] Shah Naqsh-band,[14] Imam Rabbani[15] and others. Postponing to another occasion the detail of our observations, let us call God's peace and blessings upon that illustrious, miracle-working being, namely our master Muhammad, upon him be peace and blessings:

> O God! Bestow peace and blessings on that illustrious being, on whom the wise Qur'an was sent down from the Supreme Throne of God by the All-Merciful, the All-Compassionate. He is our master Muhammad, upon whom be peace and blessings to the number of a thousand thousand and the good deeds of his Ummah. Peace be upon him whose Messengership was predicted in the Torah, the Gospels, the Psalms, and other Divine Scriptures. His Prophethood was prophesied by the miraculous events before his Prophethood and the foretellers among jinn and mankind and by saints of humankind; and by his gesture the moon split into two. He is our master and lord Muhammad, upon him be peace and blessings to the number of a thousand thousand and the breaths of his Ummah. Peace and blessings be upon him whose call trees answered, and at whose prayer rain came speedily, and whom the cloud shaded from

6. Abu Hanifa, Nu'man ibn Thabit (700-768): The founder of the Hanafi School of Law. He is one of the greatest Muslim faqihs—scholars of jurisprudence able to exercise *ijtihad*, that is, to deduce new laws from the Qur'an and *Sunnah* and was also well-versed in *kalam* (theology). He lived in Kufa and died in Baghdad. He trained many students.

7. Shafi'i (767-820). The founder of the Shafi'i School of Law. Born in Ghazza in Palestine and visited Mecca, Baghdad and Egypt to study Islamic sciences. Died in Egypt. Besides *fiqh* (Islamic jurisprudence), he was also well-versed in *hadith*, language and poetry. *Al-Umm* and *Ahkam al-Qur'an* are only two of his several works.

8. Abu Yazid al-Bistami (802-873). One of the most famous of Muslim spiritual masters and saints. He was born in Bistam, between Iraq and Khorasan, and died there.

9. Junayd al-Baghdadi (d.910). One of the most famous of early Sufis—Muslim spiritual masters. He was a disciple of Sirri al-Saqati and learned *fiqh* from Sufyan al-Thawri. He was widely respected to the point of being known as *sultan al-'arifin* (the prince of knowers of God).

10. 'Abd al-Qadir al-Jilani (1077-1166). One of the most celebrated Sufi masters in Islam. Born in Jilan but lived in Baghdad. He also studied *hadith* and *fiqh*. He was called the *qutb* (spiritual axis) of his age, and even the *ghawth al-a'zam* (the greatest succour). At his hand innumerable straying Muslims found the true way and numerous Christians and Jews became Muslims. *Kitab al-Ghunyah, Futuh al-Ghayb* and *al-Fath al-Rabbani* are only a few among his books.

heat. Hundreds of men were satisfied with a gallon of his food, and water flowed abundantly from his fingers. For him God made speak the lizard, the gazelle, the wolf, the camel, the mountain, the rock, and the tree. He ascended as far as the seventh heaven and the Supreme Throne of God and his eyes did not swerve. He is our master and intercessor Muhammad, upon him be peace and blessings to the number of a thousand thousand and the letters of the words of the Qur'an that have had forms by the All-Merciful's leave in the "mirrors" of air molecules during their recitation by every reciter from the first day of its revelation to the end of time. O God, for the sake of every blessing and peace called upon him, forgive us and have mercy on us. Amen! Amen! Amen!

The arguments for the Prophethood of Muhammad, upon him be peace and blessings, are uncountable, some few of which we mentioned in *The Nineteenth Word* and *The Nineteenth*

11. Imam al-Ghazali, Abu Hamid Muhammad (1058-1111). Theologian, jurist, sage, and one of those known as *Mujaddid* (revivers promised to come every century to restore Islam to its original purity and vitality). He was known in Europe as Algazel. An extraordinary figure, al-Ghazali was the architect of the later development of Islam. He left behind a vast collection of books, the most famous of which is *Ihya al-'Ulum al-Din* (Reviving the Islamic Sciences).

12. Muhiy al-Din ibn al-'Arabi (1165-1240). Born in Andalusia and died in Damascus. He was known as *shaykh al-akbar* (the greatest Sufi master). Because of his doctrine of the Transcendental Unity of Existence, which most people have mistaken for monism and pantheism, he has become the target of unending polemics. He wrote numerous books, among which *Fusus al-Hikam* and *al-Futuhat al-Makkiyah* are the best known.

13. al-Shadhili (1196-1258). The founder of the *Shadhiliyah*, one of the most important brotherhoods. Born in Ghumara, Tunisia, and buried in Humaithra, a village near the Red Sea, where he died while returning from the pilgrimage. He made Egypt the center of his activity and teaching.

14. Shah al-Naqshband (1316-1389). One of the most prominent spiritual masters in the history of Islam, and the founder of the Sufi order of *Naqshbandiyyah*. Born in Bukhara and studied in Samarqand. His order is still widespread in Turkey, the Caucasus and Central Asia. He died in Bukhara. Among his books are *Risalat al-Warida, al-Awrad al-Baha'iyya, Hayat-nama,* and *Tanbih al-Ghafilin.*

15. Imam Rabbani (1563-1624). Born in Sarhand, India. Known as the "reviver of the second millennium." Well-versed in Islamic sciences, he brought up many students and removed many elements of corruption from the Sufism of his time. He brought up Shah Alamgir or Awrangzeb (1618-1707), the ruler of Babur Muslim State in India, who had a committee of scholars to prepare the most comprehensive compendium of Islamic Law according to the Hanafi School.

Letter. The miracles he worked amount to one thousand. Moreover, the Qur'an, the aspects of whose miraculousness numbering around fifty we explained in *The Twenty-fifth Word*, also testifies to the Prophethood of Muhammad, upon him be peace and blessings. Again, with all the signs it contains, this universe bears witness to his Prophethood. Also, among the creatures distributed throughout the universe there are both innumerable signs of the Unity of the Divine Being and countless evidences of the Messengership of Muhammad, upon him be peace and blessings.

Among these signs and evidences, consider, for example, the fine artistry in creation. The perfection of the fine artistry in creation is a decisive evidence of Muhammad's Messengership, upon him be peace and blessings. For the beauty of these ornamented creatures manifests to the observer a fine artistry in their creation and a richly ornamented form and constitution. The fine artistry and ornamentation evidently point out that the Maker has a boundless will to make beautiful and ornamented. The will to make beautiful or ornamented clearly indicates that the Maker has an elevated love for His creation and a sacred desire to manifest the perfection of His Art. This love and desire decisively show that man—the most perfect and finest of creatures and most comprehensive of beings—is the comprehensive and excellent object and focus of this love and desire. Man's being the finest and most comprehensive of creatures means that he is the conscious fruit of the tree of creation. That is, he is like a conscious fruit that has grown on the tree of creation. His being like the fruit means that among the parts of creation, man is finer and more comprehensive than all the other parts. His being the finest and most comprehensive and conscious signifies that he has an all-encompassing view and universal consciousness. That is, he has a full view of the whole of the tree of creation and is fully aware of the Maker's purposes. He is the direct, special addressee of the Maker. His having an all-encompassing view and universal consciousness has been the reason of the Maker's choosing him as His direct, special addressee. There is one individual who focuses his all-encompassing view and universal consciousness exclusively on servanthood to the Maker and love of Him and on appreciation and exhibition of His Art. There is one who uses all his consciousness, attention and strength in thanksgiving to that Maker, Who demands thanksgiving in return for His bounties, and in calling all people to servanthood and thanksgiving to Him. Surely, this individual will be the first and foremost addressee of the Maker, the nearest to Him and most beloved by Him.

O mankind! Can you argue that this unique individual is not the Prophet Muhammad, upon him be peace and blessings? Is there in your history another one more worthy of this position than the Prophet Muhammad, upon him be peace and blessings? O one whose eyes are not blind and discernment is not dull! When you look at the human world in this universe, you will clearly see two spheres and scenes facing each other. The first sphere is that of the Divine Lordship infinitely magnificent and well-ordered. The first scene is that manifesting the infinitely perfect and splendid Art of the Maker. As for the second sphere, it is that of servanthood radiant with utmost submission, integrity and righteousness. The second scene is the scene of utmost contemplation and appreciation, and the firmest belief and fullest thanksgiving.

If you have discerned these two spheres and scenes, then look at the relationship between them. You will clearly see that the first sphere moves thoroughly in the name of the first one and works with all its strength for its sake. Again, you will surely observe with a little attention that, with all its content and meanings, the scene of contemplation, thanksgiving, appreciation and belief, is wholly turned to the scene of art and favoring.

When you have witnessed this reality with your own eyes, is it reasonable for you to deny the greatest relationship between the chief of the sphere of servanthood and the Owner of that of Lordship? By fully appreciating and exhibiting [the works of] His Art, that chief serves the purposes of the Maker most sincerely. Does your heart allow you to remain unconvinced of the fact that he has the greatest relationship and connection with the Maker, and that he speaks to the Maker directly and the Maker honors him with His Messengership? Indeed, he is evidently accepted and beloved by the Lord of the Whole Domain [of the heavens and the earth]; he is the most beloved by Him and the nearest to Him.

Is it reasonable for you, O man, that the Maker of these creatures ornamented with endless varieties of beauty, and the Giver of all these bounties, Who considers the delicacies of taste in the mouths of all creatures, is not attentive to that most perfect and beautiful creature? Muhammad, upon him be peace and blessings, turns to Him with perfect yearning, servanthood and love. He enraptures the heavens and earth with his loud songs of applause and appreciation of that Maker's Art. He throws the land and sea into ecstasies with his chants of gratitude for that Creator's favors and with the splendor of his glorification and magnification of the Grandeur of that Creator and Giver of Bounties.

Is it possible that such a Maker, Benevolent and Omnipotent, does not consider that appreciative and grateful one? Is it possible that He does not turn to him with affection? Is it possible that He does not speak to him? Is it possible that He does not love him? Is it possible that He does not draw him near to Him? Is it possible that He does not desire that his good conduct and refined manners be approved and imitated by all other people? Is it possible that He does not make him an example to be followed by others so that they may take his "color"? Is it possible that He does not send him as a Messenger to all human beings?

Is it possible that the Maker of these completely well-formed creatures, the delicacies of whose artistic design point to an infinite knowledge and boundless wisdom, is unaware and unconscious of that most perfect and most beautiful member of His creation?

Is it possible that He does not know and see him and not speak to him?

Is it possible that He does not make Himself known and loved through the ornaments of His creatures? Is it possible that He does not know and love the one who loves Him as much as He deserves and makes Him known as He must be known, who makes himself loved by Him through his faithfulness and worships Him most truly?

Fourteenth droplet

This contains "driblets" from the ocean of the greatest miracle [i.e. the Qur'an].

First driblet

Know that the arguments for the Prophethood of Muhammad, upon him be peace and blessings, are uncountable. Exacting scholars have written volumes to explain them. Despite my shortcomings, I humbly attempted to offer some "rays" from this "sun" in a Turkish treatise called *The Rays* and explain briefly some aspects of the Qur'an's miraculousness, numbering around fifty, in another treatise named *The Flashes*. I expounded its eloquence, which is only one of those aspects, in *Signs of Miraculousness*, an introduction to the interpretation of the holy Qur'an.

Second driblet

The Qur'an came from the Creator of the heavens and heavenly objects and this earth and earthly creatures. You must have understood from the foregoing explanations that the Qur'an, which makes our Lord, the Lord of the Worlds, known to us, deals with many issues in different degrees of priority.

If you ask what the Qur'an is, we have already described it elsewhere as follows:

> The Qur'an is the eternal translation of the universe and the everlasting translator of the "languages" expressive of the Divine Being's natural signs and the interpreter of the book of the universe. Also, it is the discloser of the secrets of the Divine Names' treasuries hidden on the "pages" of the heavens and earth, and the key to the truths which lie beneath the lines of events. Again, it is the tongue of the un-

seen world in the visible, material one; the treasury of the eternal Divine Speech and the eternal favors of the All-Merciful One. It is the foundation, plan and sun of the spiritual and intellectual world of Islam and the map of the world of the Hereafter. It is the expounder, the lucid interpreter, articulate proof, and clear translator of the Divine Essence, Attributes, Names and acts; the educator and trainer of the world of humanity and the water and light of Islam, which is the true and greatest humanity. It is the true wisdom of humankind and their true guide leading them to that which they were created for. As it is a book of law for human beings, it is also a book of wisdom for them. As it is a book of worship and servanthood to God, it is also a book of commands and invitation. As it is a book of invocation, it is also a book of contemplation. It is a single book, but a book containing many books for all the needs of mankind. It is also like a sacred library filled with books and treatises from which all the saints and eminently truthful ones, and all the purified and discerning scholars and gnostics of different temperaments and approach have derived their ways peculiar to each. It illuminates each of these ways and answers the needs of their followers who likewise have their different tastes and temperaments.

Third driblet

This is to explain the gleam of miraculousness in the repetitions or reiterations of the Qur'an. In this gleam there are six points:

First point

Know that since the Qur'an is a book of invocation, prayer and invitation, its reiteration is very good and in conformity with eloquence; indeed, it is a necessity. For invocation, prayer and invitation are enhanced and strengthened through repetition. Repetition of invocation brings spiritual enlightenment; reiteration of prayer brings satisfaction and peace; and invitation is strengthened through repetition.

Second point

Know that the Qur'an is a [Divine] address to, and a cure for [the "diseases" of] all classes of mankind. It addresses people from the most to the least intelligent, from the most God-fearing to the most sinful, and from the hard-working and those who show success in life or those who have renounced the world, to the miserable and abased and those engrossed in their work. For this reason, it is not always possible for everyone to recite the Qur'an from beginning to end, which is a cure for everybody at all times. So, in order to make it easy, the All-Wise and All-Compassionate One included most of the purposes of the Qur'an in most of its chapters, not only in the long ones, but also in the short ones. It encourages people, declaring, *In truth We have made the Qur'an easy for remembrance and warning. Is there any that will remember and take warning?*[16]

Third point

Bodily needs vary. Some of them like air are constantly needed. Others like water are needed on occasion of thirst or in response to heat. Some like food are needed everyday, others every month or every year or, those like medicine, on irregular occasions only. So too, man's spiritual needs vary. While some of the Qur'anic words and verses like *He* and *God* are constantly needed, among others there are those like *In the Name of God* that are usually needed, and those needed very frequently like *There is no god but God*.

So, the repetition of certain verses and words is because of the recurrence and intensity of the need for them. Again, in order to remind of the need for them and urge people to feel the need for certain "spiritual sustenance," certain verses and words are repeated in the Qur'an.

Fourth point

Know that the Qur'an has established this firm religion and laid down its foundations and the foundations of the Muslim world.

---

16. *al-Qamar*, 54.17.

It has also changed communities of mankind and united them in a shared culture and civilization. It hardly needs saying that for something to be established so firmly and extensively requires reinforcement and, therefore, repetition.

Also, in the Qur'an there are answers to the questions asked by many groups of diverse people, of different backgrounds and temperaments, and different levels of linguistic ability, understanding and thinking.

Fifth point

Know that the Qur'an mentions many important matters and calls hearts to believe in them, and speaks about subtle truths and invites reason or intellect to have certain knowledge of them. Obviously, in order to secure belief and understanding, reiteration in different styles and contexts is necessary.

Sixth point

The verses of the Qur'an have inward and outward meanings, inward and outward dimensions, and they serve an ultimate purpose for the betterment of mankind, inwardly and outwardly. For example, many legal injunctions and norms of conduct are intended to be derived from some verses, and the relative significance and applicability of injunctions and norms in different contexts require that the verses of the Qur'an should be accordingly reiterated in different ways and contexts. Similarly, in the inward dimensions of meaning, the intellect's effort to understand is challenged and rewarded by verses recurring in different contexts, enabling infinite variety and depth of nuances of meaning.

Fourth driblet

This is to explain the virtue of the Qur'an's not mentioning certain issues of relevance to science and referring to some others implicitly and succinctly. The explanation contains six points:

First point

If you ask why the Qur'an does not treat of the universe in the

manner of modern philosophy and science, I will tell you that
modern philosophy and science approach the universe in reference to itself and for its own sake. As for the Qur'an, which was
revealed in truth and guides to truth, it treats the universe not
in reference to itself, but in reference to its Creator and for the
sake of knowing and understanding Him.

Contrary to modern philosophy and science, the Qur'an does
not mention explicitly or mentions only succinctly and ambiguously the heavenly objects and the earth and their shape and
movements. If you ask why, I will tell you that the Qur'an's ambiguous or implicit reference is very significant and its succinct
mention of them is really beautiful.

For, first of all, the Qur'an mentions the universe by way of
digression or parenthetically in arguing for the Essence and Attributes of the Creator. An argument should be explicit and understandable to everybody in leading to the purpose. The purpose is to enable everybody to have sufficient knowledge of the
Essence of God and His Attributes and Names. If it had said as
scientists desire, "O people! Look at the sun in its motionlessness and the earth in its movements and see how their Creator
is powerful," the argument would have been more obscure and
secret than the purpose and remained incomprehensible for
most people in almost all epochs. Whereas the absolute majority
should be given precedence in guidance. Considering the level
of knowledge and understanding of the majority does not exclude scientists, philosophers and intellectuals, who form only a
small minority in any society. By contrast, giving precedence to
this minority would deprive the majority [from benefiting from
the guidance of the Qur'an].

Second, the rules of good speech in texts for guidance require that the minds of all those for whom the guidance is intended should not be confused by it. Rather, their views, feelings and level should be taken into consideration and they
should be addressed plainly and without going into detail, so
that they feel familiarity with the subject and can understand it
easily. [The guidance of the Qur'an is intended for the whole of

mankind in all epochs and its form of expression is universally accessible according to the degree of the individual attempting to benefit by it.]

Thirdly, as pointed out above, the Qur'an mentions the universe and what is happening in it not in relation to itself, but in relation to its Creator. What is of importance for the Qur'an is that the universe with everything and every occurrence in it should point to its Creator. As for science and modern philosophy, they deal with the universe for its own sake only. What is of importance for them is that whatever is and occurs in the universe should point to itself. There is as great a difference between the two as between the highest heaven and the earth.

Also, it has already been mentioned that the Qur'an is God's Word that lowered itself to the understanding of even the most common people. It considers the majority of people so that, freed from remaining restricted to the imitation of the élite, they could have direct access to firm knowledge of and belief in God. However, science speaks on behalf of scientists in a way to compel the commonalty to imitate and accept their views. It is because of this that where science goes into detail—although it is highly questionable to what extent it speaks the truth—the Qur'an speaks succinctly or ambiguously or keeps silent, according to how and to what extent all the people can benefit.

Fourthly, the Qur'an aims to guide all classes of mankind. Thus its rule of speech requires that the majority of people should not be misled in the facts accepted by them as unquestionably true by modes of argument which may be associated with sophistry and vying for superiority among human beings. It is also pointless, except when absolutely necessary, to change their views of such facts. It is rather better to keep silent or be succinct on matters that are of no use to them in respect of their essential duties to God or to each other.

For example, the Qur'an mentions the sun not on account of itself or its physical features but on account of the One Who has made it a light-giving lamp. It also mentions the function of the sun as the "pivot" of the universal system and the center of the order of creation. It is referred to as the shuttle of the weaving machine by which the works of the Eternal Designer are woven on the face of the earth and heavens with the threads of day and night and alternating seasons. The Qur'an does so in order that by showing us the magnificent system and arrangement in weaving and the extraordinary order and design of woven things, it could make known to us the perfection of their All-Wise Creator, their All-Knowing Maker. It is not of much importance from the viewpoint of the Qur'an's purposes whether the sun really moves or is motionless. Divine weaving of things is obviously splendid; therefore if the sun is really motionless as science asserts it is, this gives harm to neither the Qur'an's purposes nor its expression of them. [In any case, as scientists tells us, the motionlessness of the sun is relative only to the motion of the earth and other planets, not absolute.][17]

Second point

The Qur'an says, *[He] has made the sun a lamp*,[18] and, *The sun runs on unto a resting-place for it.*[19]

If you ask why when, according to science, it is the center of a huge system of which the earth is only a part and therefore is far from following the earth, the Qur'an refers to it as a lamp for the earth, my answer will be as follows:

By calling the sun a lamp, the Qur'an means that the universe is like a palace with the things in it as its furniture. It also

---

17. In recent decades, solar astronomers have been able to observe that (Bartusiac, M. (1994) 'Sounds of the Sun', *American Scientist*, January-February, pp.61-68) the sun is not in fact motionless. It quivers and shakes and continually rings like a well-hit gong. These vibrations of the sun reveal vital information about the sun's deep interior, its hidden layers, information which affects calculations of the age of the universe. Also, knowing exactly how the sun spins internally is important in testing Einstein's theory of general relativity. Like so many other significant findings in astronomy, this discovery about the sun was totally unexpected. Having discovered the quivering and ringing sun, some astronomers have commented that it is as if the sun were a symphony orchestra, with all the instruments being played simultaneously. All the vibrations combine at times to produce a net oscillation on the solar surface that is thousands of times stronger than any individual vibration. (Tr.)

18. *Nuh*, 71.16.

19. *Ya Sin*, 36.38.

contains other necessary equipment like food, which the All-Munificent and Compassionate One has prepared for its inhabitants who are in fact His guests and servants in it. The sun is the lamp of this palace at the command of the Owner of the palace. The description of the sun as a lamp suggests the mercy of the Creator in grandeur of His Lordship indicates His favoring in His comprehensive Mercy, and His generosity in the majesty of His Sovereignty. By demonstrating that the sun, which many have deified and worshipped during history, is only a lamp subjugated to God's command, it declares Divine Unity.

The expression "runs" implies the supreme, purposeful disposition and acts of God Almighty in the continuous alternation of day and night and succession of summer and winter. It thereby reminds of the vast power of the Maker in His being the Unique Lord of the universe.

When the sun and moon are mentioned together, minds automatically go to day and night, and summer and winter and therefrom to the events taking place during them. The expression "runs" implies all these meanings, and is not meant to define whether the sun really moves or not.

Look at the words and expressions of the Qur'an and see how, despite their apparent simplicity, they function as doors or keys to treasuries of subtle meanings. Then look at the words and expressions used by science and see that, despite their apparent glitter, they are of little use to you either spiritually or even intellectually or with respect to man's main purposes in life. They cause you to fall from the heaven of illumining unity to dark valleys of multiplicity. Listen to some part of what modern philosophy and science say concerning the sun:

"It is a huge mass of intense fire 1,300,000 times as big as the earth, and spins on its axis. The planets, including ours, were detached from it and, at different distances, fly around it attracted toward it through the general gravity. If, after some unpredictable event in the heavens (such as a collision with a passing comet), one of those planets leaves its orbit, it will result in the collapse of the solar system and the destruction of our world."

The probability of such an event fills people at times with terror.

Ask yourself whether such information is of any use to you in your normal, ordinary life. May God be glorified! How misguidance takes on the form of truth! The sun and its planets are but the creatures of the All-Wise Maker charged with certain tasks and subjugated to the Command and Power of the Creator. Despite its huge size, the sun is but a single shining drop on the face of the ocean of the heavens, on which a ray of the Divine Name the Light is manifested.

If scientists and philosophers had included in their issues a light from the Qur'an and said, "God uses these huge inanimate objects in important tasks for the order of the universe and they are in utmost obedience to Him," their knowledge would have had some meaning. But since they attribute [the creation of these celestial objects and their movements and the tasks they perform] to the objects themselves or to nature and material causes, they are included in the meaning of the Qur'anic verse, The man who serves other deities besides God is like the man who falls from the sky and the birds had snatched him, or the wind had blown him to a far-off place.[20]

Third point

Know that the Qur'an has four main purposes: Divine Unity, Messengership, the Resurrection, and justice together with worship. The other issues the Qur'an deals with are means for the realization of these purposes. It is a rule of good speech that going into detail in mentioning the means and ramifying the subject-matter with unnecessary additions or arguments causes a rupture from the main aim. For this reason, the Qur'an tends to omit certain points of explicitly scientific import or is ambiguous or succinct about them. The majority of people cannot be expected to understand the profound Divine truths without metaphors, comparisons and parables. Since most scientific and philosophical issues require a long time to be comprehended, the

---

20. *al-Hajj*, 22.31.

Qur'an refers to most such issues through metaphors, similes and parables and remains succinct on points which are to be understood with the passage of time [i.e. with progress in scientific inquiry].

Fourth point

Know O friend! Just as a clock ticks on continuously with the ceaseless working of the devices in it, so too the world, which can be regarded as a huge clockwork, is continuously active. The inclusion of time in this activity causes the occurrence of day and night like the second hand of the clock; years, like its minute hand; and centuries, like its hour hand. The inclusion of space in it causes the atmosphere to be, through the speed of changes it undergoes, like the second hand. The earth, through the changes observed on it in plants and animals and with respect to life and death, resembles the minute hand, and through the movements in it and the formation of mountains, the hour hand. The heavens, through the changes occurring in them and through the movements of their objects and the birth of new stars and death of old ones, are like the "day" hand.

The world is based on these seven basic elements—day, night, year, century, earth, atmosphere, and heavens—which, in fact, manifest the acts of the Divine Names and the inscriptions of the Pen of Divine Power and Destiny. Although the world based on these elements is moving, perishing, transient, journeying, and flowing like water, heedlessness and naturalism congeals it, making it a veil over the Hereafter. By urging people to excessive preoccupation with studies of nature and philosophy, the defective, vicious philosophy and corrupt civilization increases it in "density" and "opacity." As for the Qur'an, it makes the world like carded wool through its verses, and makes it transparent through its expressions. The Qur'an also melts the world through its rays, smashes its illusory eternity with its powerful warnings against death and eternal punishment, and removes heedlessness caused by naturalism with its thunder-like admonitions. With its essential character, the world convulsed in change recites the verse, *When the Qur'an is recited, give ear to it and pay heed, that you may obtain mercy.*[21]

It is for the reasons mentioned that the Qur'an remains brief where modern philosophy and science go into detail in description of things and their features. By contrast, where philosophy and science are brief or negligent in [description of] the functions of things as [servants of God] in utmost obedience to His commands of creation and life and pointing to their Creator's Names and acts, the Qur'an goes into detail.

In sum: the Qur'an explains the meanings of the book of the universe and what it refers to, while science describes only the material structure of the "letters" of this book together with their positions and reciprocal relationships. Science does not tell us that all things or creatures are meaningful words. If you would like to see the difference between the attitude of philosophy and science and the wisdom of the Qur'an, you may refer to the "Twelfth Word" in *The Words*. There this difference is explained from the perspective of the Qur'anic verse, *Whoever is given wisdom, has truly been given abundant good.*[22]

Fifth point

(You will find this point elaborated in *A Light from the Lights of the Verses of the Qur'an*, which is the last chapter of this book.)

Sixth point

Know O friend! As has already been stated in the *Fourth point* above, the Qur'an stresses the aspects of things pointing to the acts of the All-Mighty and how they manifest His Names, Exalted is He. The Qur'an also expounds how the Divine acts originate from the Divine Names and how, being the rays of the Divine Attributes, the Names encompass things.

In sum: the Qur'an deals with creatures with their aspects pointing to their Creator. As to science, it studies creatures with their aspects pointing to themselves and their causes. The pur-

---

21. *al-'Araf*, 7.204.
22. *al-Baqara*, 2.269.

pose of science is focused on either the scientific or technological benefit things provide. It is sheer ignorance, in thrall to materialism wedded to scientism, to accept science and philosophy as a criterion by which to judge the sacred Qur'anic expressions.

Fifth driblet

Know O friend! It is one of the virtues of the Qur'an, as affirmed by the sciences of semantics and rhetorical style, that it combines excellent fluency of style, a firm mutual support and coherence, harmony and assistance among its sentences and elements. It shows an extraordinary correspondence among its verses and their meanings. Although it was revealed piecemeal over twenty years on different occasions and sometimes in reply to specific questions, it displays such a miraculous harmony and consistency that it is as if it had been revealed on one occasion only or in reply to only one question. Also, it came to establish certain rules or explain certain commandments for different cases and fitted itself to the understanding of different peoples with different styles, tastes and approaches. But it has such a wonderful arrangement and smoothness of style that it is as if it had come for a single case and to satisfy a single taste and level of understanding. Furthermore, it has such a clarity of expression, beauty of diction, and purity of style that, although it takes into consideration every level of understanding and knowledge, everyone thinks that it directly addresses him. Again, although it came to guide all people of varying capacities each to his particular level of attainment in guidance with no deviations at all, it preserves the balance so perfectly that it is as if it had aimed at only one point of attainment in its guidance. So, whoever has a sound perception will certainly see in the Qur'an a viewpoint taking in the whole of the universe with its inward and outward dimensions as if it were viewing a single page, and see also that the Qur'an unveils all of its meanings and teaches them to whoever it desires.

Sixth driblet

This is to explain that the Qur'an cannot be compared to any other book or speech.

Know O friend! any speech derives its power, beauty and sublimity not only from the time, place and occasion which determine the way or manner of speaking and the subject matter, but also from three other things: the one who speaks, the one(s) spoken to, and the purpose. You consider the one who speaks, the one spoken to, what the speech is for, and under what circumstances it is made. Furthermore, if the speech contains a command or prohibition, the one who speaks should have certain authority and power and the greater authority and power the speaker has, the more forceful and exalted the speech is.

Consider the authority of the Divine Power in the command, for example, *O earth, swallow up your waters; O sky, withhold (your rain).*[23] He said to it [the sky] and to the earth: *Come both of you, willingly or unwillingly. They answered, We do come willingly.*[24] See how different it is from human power that does not have any authority over the sky and earth. The difference is like that between an order from a commander absolutely obeyed by a powerful obedient army and the order of an individual to whose person or command no one gives the least importance. See the difference between *When He wills a thing, He only says unto it: Be! and it is,*[25] and human words. Listen to *Have they not observed the sky above them, how We built it, and decked it out fair, and it has no cracks? And the earth—We stretched it forth, and cast on it firm mountains, and We brought forth in it all kinds of delightful plants. An enlightenment and reminder for every penitent servant. And We have sent down from the sky blessed water with which We have brought forth gardens and the harvest grain. And lofty date palms with ranged clusters: Provision for the servants; thereby giving new life to a dead land. Even so shall be the Resurrection.*[26] Listen to these Divine words and see the difference between the descriptions of the True Owner, Whose commands are absolutely influential, Who describes His acts in enumeration of His favors, and shallow, human descriptions unrelated with the Divine acts and favoring.

21. *Hud*, 11.44.
22. *Fussilat*, 41.11.
25. *Ya Sin*, 36.82.
26. *Qaf*, 50.6–11.

How vast the difference is between the "angels" of the words of the sun and moon's Creator diffusing the lights of guidance, and the mumbling noise of human beings "blowing on the knots" of their vain ambitions. How different are the words of the Qur'an which are the "mother-of-pearls" of guidance and the sources of the truths of belief and the essentials of Islam having issued from the Supreme Throne of the All-Merciful. They comprise the eternal address embedded in the Divine Knowledge, Power and Will. How different they are from the hollow human words of fancy and desire. The Qur'an is like a tree which has ramified, come to leaf, blossomed and yielded the fruit of the Islamic world with its spiritual values, principles, perfections, and purified scholars and saints. Many of the fruit-stones this illustrious tree has produced as principles of conduct have grown up into fruit-bearing trees. It has been declared about it: *Say: "If all men and jinn gathered together to produce the like of this Qur'an, they could not produce one like it, though they were helpers of one another."*[27]

The Qur'an is unique and beyond all compare with the beauty of its order and composition, the originality and uniqueness of its styles, the superiority, excellence and clarity of its explanations, the power and truth of its meanings, and the purity and fluency of its language. Its meaning is so comprehensive that the principles of all exacting jurists, the tastes of all gnostics, and the paths of all wayfarers to God and purified, perfected scholars have all originated in it. It has been able to remain original and fresh through the ages. Rather, with the passage of time, it has grown ever-fresher, satisfied all levels of knowledge and understanding in every age, and silenced those most distinguished in rhetoric and eloquence. Indeed it has made all humankind unable to produce even a single verse like it. So, the difference between it and human words is as great as that between the highest heaven and earth; indeed, no human words can be compared with it.

---

27. *al-Isra'*, 17.88.

O God! For the sake of the Qur'an and for the sake of him to whom the Qur'an was revealed, illumine our hearts with the light of the Qur'an. And make the Qur'an a cure for every illness of ours, and a companion for us both during this life and after death. Also, make it a confidant for us in the world, a friend in the grave, an intercessor on the Judgement Day. Make it a light on the Bridge, a veil and a cover from the Fire, a companion to Paradise, and a guide and leader to all good, through Your Grace, Mercy, Generosity, and Favoring, O Most Munificent of the Munificent, Most Merciful of the Merciful.

Bestow blessings and peace on him unto whom You sent the Qur'an and whom You sent as a mercy for all the worlds, and on his family and Companions, as will please You and himself and as will be approved, O Lord of the Worlds.

Revealer of the Qur'an! For the sake of the Qur'an, make this book say this prayer on my behalf when death has silenced me. Amen! A thousand times Amen!

INDEX OR BRIEF SUMMARIES OF THE TOPICS
DISCUSSED IN THE TREATISE

*There are innumerable things that make our Lord known to us. The three greatest and most universal are: The first is this universe. The second is the Seal of the Prophets, upon him be peace and blessings. The third is the holy Qur'an. (16)

*The Prophet Muhammad, upon him be peace and blessings, this indisputable, articulate argument for our Lord, has a universal personality.

*The Prophet Muhammad, upon him be peace and blessings, this indisputable, articulate argument for our Lord, has a universal personality. If you ask who he is and what kind of one he is:

He is such a one that due to the universality of his person, the surface of the earth is his mosque, with Makka being his place of worship and Madina, his pulpit. He is the leader of all believers, who, standing after him in rows, follow the orator of all mankind explaining to them the principles of happiness [in both worlds]. He is the chief of all the Prophets, clearing them of the calumnies their peoples spoke against them and affirming them and the essentials of their religions within his comprehensive religion. Muhammad, upon him be peace and blessings, is the master of all saints, guiding and educating them through the light of his Messengership and the "pivot" around whom there is the circle of recitation of God's Names formed of the Prophets, upon them be peace, the good, the truthful, and the righteous, who are all agreed on his Message. He is a luminous tree growing on the firm, healthy and lively roots of the previous Prophets and the heavenly principles they preached, and shooting out green, fresh branches and yielding the fine "fruit" of saints distinguished with knowledge of God. Whatever he claimed, it is confirmed by the whole of the Prophets based on their miracles, and the whole of saints based on their good or marvelous works. All the affirmations he made bear the seals of all perfected people. If you hear him declaring *There is no god but God* and therefore affirming Divine Unity, you will surely hear the same declaration from the past and future, from the il-lustrious, shining "suns" and stars of humanity reciting God's Names in His circle. Despite the differences in their approaches and temperaments, they agree with him on all his affirmations, as if saying in unison, "You declare the truth and speak the truth." (16–7)

*This illustrious person, who affirms Divine Unity and guides mankind to it, is himself confirmed by Prophethood and saint-hood, which, for fourteen centuries, hundreds of millions of people have unanimously agreed that he enjoys. Also, in the previous hea-venly Scriptures—the Torah, the Gospel, the Psalms and others—there are verses predicting him and confirming his Prophethood. Again, he is confirmed by the marvels that, prior to his Prophet-hood, either he himself worked or took place connected with him, and about one thousand miracles he worked during his Prophet-hood. (17–8)

*Besides numerous arguments for his Prophethood, the very person or character of the Prophet Muhammad, upon him be peace and blessings, proves his Prophethood. (18)

*He removes the veil from the creation of the universe, and ex-plains the reasons why it has been created. He also answers the three awesome questions that from the very beginning have occu-pied the mind of every conscious being and bewildered it: Who are you? Where do you come from? What is your purpose or final des-tination? (19)

*Had it not been for that person, the universe with everything in it and man would have been reduced to something worthless and meaningless. Had it not been for that person who makes known the universe and its Creator, this beautiful universe would not have existed. For we would have been unable to know what it means for us. (20-21)

*You will see him as the epitome of the All-Merciful's love [of His creatures] and the embodiment of the Lord's mercy for them. (21)

*The Prophet removed all bad morals from the hard-hearted people of 'Arabia and equipped them with such laudable virtues that he made them teachers of humanity and masters of civilized peoples. He did all of that not, as most other rulers have sought to do it, by force of power and terror, but by conquering hearts and minds, and subjugating spirits and egos, becoming the beloved of hearts, the teacher of reasons, educator of selfhood and the ruler of spirits. (22)

*That noble being gave utterance to whatever he had to say without fear of his opponents and without any hesitation or anxiety, with absolute sincerity and enthusiasm, and in a way to vex and discomfit their reason, arguments and attitudes. (23)

*He speaks about awesome events and warns people [about them]. He also speaks about matters that captivate hearts and inspire minds to reflect, and he brings mankind good tidings [of a happy future both in this world and the Hereafter]. (23–6)

*That illustrious being is a decisive argument and definite evidence of eternal happiness. Through his call and guidance he is the means of gaining the eternal happiness, the creation of which he caused through his prayer and servanthood. (26–7)

*He asks for eternal existence, meeting with God, Paradise and God's good pleasure. (27)

*In each century we passed through innumerable "flowers" opened in the "sun" of that Age of Happiness and that through the light of guidance that noble being diffused, each century yielded thousands of illustrious fruits in all fields of religious and "natural" sciences as well as in the inner dimension of religion, which we call Sufism. (28-30)

*The arguments for the Prophethood of Muhammad, upon him be peace and blessings, are uncountable, some few of which we mentioned in *The Nineteenth Word* and *The Nineteenth Letter*. The miracles he worked amount to one thousand. Moreover, the Qur'an, the aspects of whose miraculousness numbering around fifty we explained in *The Twenty-fifth Word*, also testifies to the Prophethood of Muhammad, upon him be peace and blessings. (31)

*The Qur'an, which makes our Lord, the Lord of the Worlds, known to us, deals with many issues in different degrees of priority. (34)

*Description of the Qur'an (34–5); the wisdom in repetitions in the Qur'an (35); whether the Qur'an mentions scientific facts, if it does, how? (37-44); the Qur'an's and science's approach to the universe (38-45); main purposes of the Qur'an (42); eloquence of the Qur'an (45)

*The Qur'an is unique and beyond all compare with the beauty of its order and composition, the originality and uniqueness of its styles, the superiority, excellence and clarity of its explanations, the power and truth of its meanings, and the purity and fluency of its language. Its meaning is so comprehensive that the principles of all exacting jurists, the tastes of all gnostics, and the paths of all wayfarers to God and purified, perfected scholars have all originated in it. It has been able to remain original and fresh through the ages. Rather, with the passage of time, it has grown ever-fresher, satisfied all levels of knowledge and understanding in every age, and silenced those most distinguished in rhetoric and eloquence. Indeed it has made all humankind unable to produce even a single verse like it. (47)

Particular Arguments for the Resurrection

In the Name of God, the All-Merciful, the All-Compassionate.

All praise be to God, to Whose necessary existence and Unity all the atoms and compounds of the universe testify with the tongue of their helplessness and poverty [before God]. Peace and blessings be upon His Prophet, the discoverer of the secrets of creation and the key to its signs [of God's existence and Unity], and upon his brothers of the Prophets and Messengers, and the angels nearest to God, and upon the righteous servants of God among the inhabitants of the heavens and earth.

Know, O friend, on whom naturalism and dogmatic adherence to causality have closed the door of thanksgiving [to the Creator] and opened the door of associating partners with Him. Surely, associating partners with God and unbelief in Him, together with ingratitude to Him, are based on innumerable impossibilities. Among those impossibilities, consider the following only:

If an unbeliever is awakened from the intoxication of ignorance and can think about his unbelief in the light of true scientific knowledge, he will be obliged to acknowledge that he has attributed to a single minute particle functions and missions unbearable for it. He will have to admit that he has accepted that each atom has millions of machines in it and such extraordinary skills as to produce all the subtleties of art contained in all creatures. For each particle of air, for example, can enter all plants, flowers, trees and fruits, and work therein. If you do not admit that it works in the name of One in Whose hand is the kingdom of all things, you will have to accept that it knows whatever it enters with all its formation, functions and features. Consider a single fruit: it is the miniature of the whole of the tree, and its stone is like the page where all the life-history of the tree has been inscribed. Rather, a fruit is connected with all the members of its species, even to the whole of the earth. Because of this, by virtue of the greatness of the art and meaning it contains, a fruit is as great as the earth in art. Therefore, the One Who brings a fruit into existence with all the art and meaning it has, can undoubtedly bring the earth into being and govern it.

Know O friend! Everything has two aspects: one its sensed physical aspect or form or body, which, like a garment, is "cut out" and shaped according to the measures determined by the functions and purposes assigned for it in life. The other is its immaterial aspect composed of the sum of the forms it has taken on during its growth in the course of time. This is like a circle formed by something with light attached to one end spinning around itself at speed. This immaterial aspect of something is, in one respect, its life-history determined by Destiny, which we call in everyday language "the fate or destiny of things." Whether with respect to its material aspect or its immaterial one, there are wise purposes for the existence and life of everything. The material aspect of something requires Power, while it is Destiny that determines its shape and growth. That is, Destiny draws outlines of something or makes its plan according to the purposes Wisdom has assigned for it, and Power builds it according to that plan.

O unbeliever! When you refer to true scientific knowledge and truth, your ingratitude and unbelief will compel you to admit that every minute particle and every "natural" cause has knowledge. They must have as much knowledge as to be able to cut out garments as many and different as the number of things, including, even, the forms they take on during their growth. Let alone minute particles, even man, the fruit of the tree of creation and, supposedly, the most powerful of causes and the most knowledgeable of them with a most comprehensive will-power, cannot cut out a single garment for a thorny tree properly fitted for it including all its members. However, its the All-Wise Maker Who clothes it in ever-new garments during the stages of its growth. He makes for it green, richly decorated and most fitting garments very swiftly and easily. *All glory be to Him Whose command, when He wills a thing, is only to say unto it, "Be!" and it is. Glory be to Him in Whose hand is the dominion of all things and unto Him you are returning.*[1]

Know O friend! Everything bears a stamp and seal particular to the One, Besought-of-All, and has signs testifying that He is the Maker and Owner of all things. Out of the innumerable stamps of His Oneness and seals of His being the Eternally Besought-of-All, look, if you will, at the stamp placed on the page of the earth in spring. The following successive paragraphs interrelated with one another will show you this stamp:

On the page of the earth we observe acts of ever-original and purposeful creation, which take place in infinite abundance together with beautiful artistry without faults or imperfections. They take place with absolute facility in perfect order and arrangement, with incredible speed combined without any loss in proportion or firmness or substantiality, in infinite extent of distribution of species together with the infinite beauty of each individual. These acts occur with the greatest economy or lowest cost imaginable while yet every individual is valuable beyond price, with the individuality of each perfectly distinguished out of absolute mixedness, with the highest correspondence and similarity between and among species in spite of vast distances in time and space. They are in balance with an absolute variety, with perfect individualization of characters and features in each creature though generated from similar or even the very same materials, structural principles and organization. Each of these articles is enough to manifest the stamp discussed, because the infinite abundance together with beautiful, ordered artistry is particular to Him Who has infinite power and Who is not distracted or prevented from doing one thing because He is doing some other. The absolute facility in perfect order and arrange-

---

1. *Ya Sin*, 36.82–3.

ment is particular to Him for Whom nothing is difficult and Who has infinite knowledge. The extraordinary speed at no cost to firmness and proportion is particular to Him to Whose Power and Command everything is submitted.

The vast extent of the distribution of species while maintaining the infinite beauty of each individual member is particular to Him Who is unconfined by space, but present near everything through His Power and Knowledge.

The wonderful economy and abundance while each individual is of immeasurable value is particular to Him Who is infinitely rich and disposes inexhaustible treasures.

The coherence of the members of various species despite the perfect distinction between individuals and without the least confusion and fault is particular to Him Who sees all things and is a witness over them. He is not hindered from doing one thing because of doing another and He hears the petition of all things at the same time without becoming confused.

The perfect correspondence and similarity in structure and form among species in spite of vast distances in time and space and in balance with an absolute variety —as if each member expects the order to be given to it by a single director—is particular to Him. Through His Knowledge, Power and Wisdom, He disposes the whole earth however He wills.

The perfect individualization of characters and features in each creature though generated from similar or even the very same materials, structural principles and organization is particular to Him Who has absolute will and freedom of choice. The perfect structure and beauty of each individual member of a species despite the vast abundance of the species is particular to One Whose Power is so absolute and inclusive that there is no difference for Him between atoms and galaxies.

Where each of the points above is enough to manifest the stamp of Divine Oneness, when considered together as a single act formed one within the other like concentric circles, you may guess how forcefully they display the same stamp of Divine Oneness. From this you can understand the meaning of the verse, *Assuredly, if you should ask them who created the heavens and the earth, they will surely say, "God".*[2] That is, when intellectually and logically awakened to this reality, an unbeliever cannot help but confess the Existence and Creative Power of God.

Know O friend! Belief in God, belief in the Prophet, belief in the Resurrection and affirmation of the existence of the universe require believing one another. That is, there is a perfect relation between these pillars of belief: believing one requires believing the others. Divinity requires Messengership; this world testifies to the other world.

It is impossible for a book like this one, the words and letters of which are interrelated with one another, to be without a writer. So too the existence of this book of the universe cannot be explained, except in a stupor of misguidance, without believing in the existence of the Eternal Designer. Also, a building containing many marvels of art, exquisite designs and wonderful decorations could not have come into being without an architect and builder. Neither can the existence of this world be affirmed without, unless one is drunk with misguidance, the confirmation of the existence of its Maker. Again, the images of the sun reflected in transparent things and the bubbles on rivers and seas cannot be explained except by attributing them to the sun. So it is also with all its smaller or bigger "suns"—heavenly objects—as many as transparent things and bubbles and drops of water in the world. The existence of this ever-changing and renewed universe cannot be explained, unless one has lost all reason, without confirming the necessary existence of its Creator and Builder, Who built this magnificent building. It is He Who planted this awesome tree, according to the principles of His Will and Wisdom, elaborated it according to the prescripts of His Destiny and Decree, and ordered it in accordance with the demands of His custom and manner of acting. He decorated it in accordance with the gifts of His Favoring and Mercy, and illuminated it through the manifestations of His Names and Attributes.

2. *al-Zumar*, 39.38.

Each living part of creation is like a miniature of the whole and therefore the God of that part is able to create the whole. The non-acceptance of the One Creator will make it necessary to accept as many divinities as the number of the atoms and compounds of the universe.

Then, just as it is inconceivable for the sun not to diffuse light, so too it is inconceivable for God not to manifest Himself by sending Messengers. An infinitely perfect beauty cannot fail to make itself known by means of a teaching Messenger. An infinitely beautiful art cannot fail to draw attention to itself by means of a herald who will describe it. It is inconceivable for the sovereignty of an all-encompassing Lordship not to proclaim, through one raised with the principles of happiness in both worlds, Its Oneness and Its being the Eternally Besought-of-All for all classes of beings. Nor can It fail to demand universal servanthood. An Infinite Beauty cannot fail to demand beautiful ones who will observe its subtleties and love It. Such a Beauty cannot fail to wish the existence of eyes to gaze upon It with appreciation, or fail to show Itself by means of a beloved servant, a Messenger, who will love It himself and make It loved by others. That is, that Messenger will be, through his servanthood, a mirror to reflect the Beautiful One and, through his Messengership, to have Him observed by others. A treasure replete with miracles and most precious jewels will certainly be exhibited by means of a goldsmith who will describe it with all its hidden subtleties.

Now, apart from our master Muhammad, upon him be peace and blessings, has anybody appeared in the world who contains in himself all the qualities mentioned above [to make the Lord of the Worlds known by all conscious beings]? Our master Muhammad, upon him be peace and blessings, is the most perfect, the noblest, and most virtuous of all. He is the king of the Messengers, of those who make the Divine Being known, who manifest His Beauties, and who convey His commandments. It is they who observe His miracles and have them observed by others, who worship Him and guide others to His worship, who love Him and have Him loved by others. Upon him and them and their families be the most meritorious of blessings and peace as long as the earth and heavens subsist.

***

Now consider the irrefutable arguments on which belief in the Resurrection and afterlife is based:

There cannot be a just ruler except that he rewards obedient subjects and punishes rebellious ones:

The more so if that ruler is infinitely munificent and disposes infinite treasures and has an awesome might which is the source of infinite honor and dignity.

The more so if that ruler has a boundless mercy requiring boundless graciousness, and majesty demanding the chastisement of those who slight it.

The more so if that ruler has an exalted wisdom requiring the preservation of his sovereignty by treating kindly those who take refuge in it, and an absolute justice demanding the maintenance of His glory by protecting the rights of his subjects.

The more so if that ruler has infinitely vast treasures and absolute generosity requiring a permanent abode of feasting and the permanent existence of those in need of his treasures.

The more so if he has secret perfections demanding to be manifested to those who fully appreciate them.

The more so if he has peerless beauties, incomparable subtleties of benevolence, all requiring to be observed by others in "mirrors," which requires the permanent existence of those who will gaze on them with yearning, wonder and appreciation. For permanent beauty and grace are not content with impermanent lovers.

The more so if that ruler has compassion and pity to the degree that he comes to the aid of all who are in need, answers all who petition him, and gratifies all the needs of his subjects down to the slightest need of the most insignificant among them. So, he will certainly gratify the need of the most favored with him among his subjects, especially if that need is the need of all and is very easy for the ruler to meet.

The more so if, despite the infinite splendor of his sovereignty, the subjects of that ruler are assembled in a small hospice filled and emptied every day, an ever-changing testing-ground. They stay only for a short time in that place prepared for the exhibition of samples of the marvels of the ruler's art and favor and which undergoes continuous transformations. Surely this implies that, behind this hospice, this testing-ground, this place of exhibition, are permanent palaces, everlasting abodes and open treasuries filled with the originals of the samples exhibited here.

The more so if that ruler is infinitely meticulous in the duties of his sovereignty so that he records and wants to have recorded the least of his subjects and the most insignificant of the deeds and services of each. If he orders that whatever happens in his kingdom be copied and preserved, this signifies that one day he will call his subjects, especially the leading ones among them, to account for what they are doing here in the world.

The more so if that ruler makes repeated promises and threats which are very easy for him to fulfil and of greatest significance for the subjects, and if breach of promise is infinitely contrary to the glory and dignity of his rule.

The more so if those who convey this information are unanimously agreed that the center of his mighty sovereignty is very distant from us and the mansions in this abode of trial are transient and bound to be changed for everlasting palaces. A magnificent, permanent sovereignty like that ruler's cannot be founded on perishing, changing and transitory things.

The more so if that ruler always demonstrates the samples of many of those permanent worlds in that transitory abode of trial. This means that all these gatherings and separations are not ends in themselves, rather they are rehearsals to be copied and preserved with their results. Proceedings in that vast place of gathering will be according to the consequences brought about by these rehearsals.

The more so if that ruler manifests in these decaying mansions, perishable grounds, transitory places of exhibition, the works and traces of his evident wisdom, visible bestowal of favor, lofty justice, and comprehensive mercy. Anyone with discernment must clearly conclude that it is impossible to find wisdom more perfect than his, favor more liberal than his, mercy more encompassing than his, and justice more glorious than his. In order that this wisdom, favoring, mercy and justice may manifest themselves, each with its essential or original truth, there must be in the center of his sovereignty permanent lofty abodes, everlasting elevated mansions, and inhabitants to reside in them eternally. Otherwise this would require the denial of this observed wisdom, discernible favor, noticed mercy, and this witnessed justice. It would also require the acceptance of the doer of all these acts, and owner of these instances of wisdom and munificence as a playful, capricious and unjust tyrant. This would require the change of truths to their opposites, which is inconceivable according to all men of sound judgement and reasoning except those who (like the sophists) are able to deny the existence of everything, themselves included.

As can be concluded from innumerable evidences, that ruler will transfer his subjects from these transitory mansions to the seat of his permanent sovereignty, and numberless signs show that this mutable ground will be changed for a perpetual one.

Also, it is in no way possible that this world should exist and the other one not, that the Creator should have created this universe but not the next one, whereas the sovereignty of His Lordship requires reward and punishment.

Moreover, as is understood from its instances, the Owner of this abode has a vast Munificence that demands a commensurate giving of favor and reward. He also has an immense Might and Dignity which require infinite sensitivity and zeal [to preserve that Dignity] and severe punishment. Whereas, this world does not suffice for the fulfillment of even a thousandth of what that Munificence and Dignity require.

And again, the Owner of this world has a Mercy encompass-

ing all things. The compassion of all mothers and the easy provision of plants and the weak and young among animals with
the food necessary for their survival and growth, are but a single radiation of this Mercy. This all-encompassing Mercy requires a commensurate bestowing of favor and benevolence.
Now, consider the ephemerality of those It favors and provides
for in the world that accounts for but a drop from the infinite
ocean of that Mercy. If that Mercy did not manifest itself fully in
another world, then favoring and beneficence stopped in this
world with no hope of restitution would change into a cause of
distress and suffering. Compassion [for things bound to eternal
extinction] is, in fact, a suffering, and love for them, a desperate
concern. Again, the intellect [which brings to mind the pains of
the past and pesters it with anxieties for the future] is, in a short
life, a means of torment, and passing pleasures, with no hope of
eternity, turn into pains.

Denial of the eternal life means denial of this Mercy, which is
in no way different from denial of the sun which every day we
clearly see filling the world with its light.

Also, as may be concluded from His free acts, the Owner of
this world has a Majesty and Glory, which require chastisement
of those who are not respectful to them and destruction of those
who disparage them. His eradication of rebellious peoples in
ancient times shows that He gives them respite but does not neglect them. His manner of acting also demonstrates that He attaches the greatest importance to His commands and prohibitions.

He makes Himself known to people and loved by them
through perfectly made, well-proportioned and beautiful things,
such as the lovely flowers in the world. He shows them His
Mercy through the attractive fruits therein. For those who do
not recognize Him by belief and make themselves loved by
Him through worship, and who do not respect Him through
thanksgiving, He has prepared an abode of punishment at the
seat of His eternal Lordship.

Particularly, as may be concluded from the purposes and
benefits He has attached to everything and the order and beau-

ty of art He displays in all creatures, the all-encompassing wisdom in His imperial acts requires the rewarding of those who are obedient and those who take refuge in Him. Also, He places everything just in its proper place, giving everything its due, answering every petition from everything whether for its life or provision or survival. From this it may be deduced that He dispenses an absolute, true Justice that requires preserving the glory of His Kingdom and Lordship and protecting the rights of His subjects in a supreme tribunal. Since this transient abode which is the realm of trial for conscious beings where they are allowed to act freely, is too small for His absolute Justice to manifest itself thoroughly, the All-Just, All-Wise One with absolute Beauty, Grace and Glory, must dispose an eternal Paradise and permanent Hell.

Again, the Owner of this world Who has free disposition of it has infinite Munificence and Generosity and treasuries of blessings and favor. Among the envelopes of these blessings and favor are those "suns" replete with lights and these trees full of fruits. This infinite Generosity and Wealth demand the existence of the eternal realm of feasting and the permanent existence of those with various needs. An infinite generosity requires infinite bestowal of favor that, in turn, demands the perpetual existence of those who will be favored and return with thanksgiving. Otherwise, returning that perpetual favoring would be restricted to the limited span of each individual lifetime.

Also, the One acting so wisely and generously has secret Perfections. All these miraculous works of His around us demonstrate that those Perfections must be manifested for those who will gaze upon them with appreciation. A perpetual perfection requires perpetual manifestation and the existence of those who will observe it with appreciation. A perfection loses its value in the view of an observer condemned to eternal extinction.

Again, the Maker of all these fine, ravishing, radiant and ornamented things has a peerless, transcendent Beauty; indeed each of His Names is perfectly beautiful because of the radiations of this Beauty. How could we grasp that Beauty? The earth (which is only one of His "solid" mirrors), with all its ever-changing scenes, displays to us every year, every season, even every moment, but shadows of a few radiations of that Beauty, and spring, only one of its flowers.

It is certain that a perfectly beautiful one must desire his beauty to be observed by both his own seeing of it and the seeing of others. He desires the existence of the "mirrors" to reflect radiations of his beauty and the lovers to show measures of its admired grace. Eternal grace and beauty require the eternity of their lovers and admirers, and are not content with ephemeral lovers. Since one feels enmity towards the thing one is unable to attain or comprehend, the love of an ephemeral lover for an eternal beauty turns into enmity. Therefore, just as this world evidently requires the existence of a Maker, so also the Maker doubtlessly demands the existence of an eternal realm.

Let us reflect further on the fact that the Owner of this world has such mercy and affection that He swiftly comes to the aid of those who ask Him for help and answers the petitions of those who pray to and take refuge in Him. We see that He gratifies the most insignificant need of the smallest of His creatures just on time and hears the softest voice of the most secret of His creatures and complies with its request.

When you consider how infants and the weak among living beings are cared and provided for, you will see the Divine Mercy and Affection as bright as the shining sun. Thus, this Mercy united with Generosity requires for a certainty that the greatest need of the greatest and most beloved of His servants should be met, especially if this need is the need of all conscious beings which they manifest either verbally or by actions. This is true especially if the gratification of that need is so important for all as to enable them to rise to the highest of the high and its refusal may cause them to fall to the lowest of the low. It is especially true if that need is presented through all of the Divine Names manifested in the universe in a way that these Names may intercede with the One called by them for its gratification. The gratification of that need is as easy for the One Who will meet it as to satisfy it in a twinkling of an eye. It is so especially if the most beloved servant supplicates to Him in a most humble and pitiable manner and in a way to make him loved through all acceptable acts of worship. All those who stand after him in acceptance of his leadership, among whom are the most virtuous fruits of the tree of creation, namely the Prophets, saints and the pure, exacting scholars, say "Amen" to his prayer and ask their Munificent Lord for Paradise, eternity, eternal happiness and approval. Then it is inconceivable for the all-encompassing Divine Mercy to do wrong and display ugliness in not accepting such a petition from such a beloved, accepted servant. Indeed, this beloved person who is the center or pivot of witnessing (the existence, Unity and acts of) the Eternal Witness and having others witness them, is a Messenger. Through his Messengership, he is the revealer of the mystery of creation, the herald of the Divine Unity amidst the whirl of multiplicity, and the cause of attaining the eternal happiness in Paradise. He is also a servant and, through his servanthood, the unveilor of the treasuries of Mercy, a mirror reflecting the beauty of the Divine Lordship, and the means of eternal happiness and the existence of Paradise. If, for the supposition's sake we imagined that there were no other reasons for the existence of Paradise, the request coming from such a beloved one would suffice for the generosity of the All-Generous, Who creates in every spring richly ornamented gardens resembling gardens of Paradise, to create Paradise. The creation of paradisiacal gardens on the earth is not easier for Him than the creation of Paradise. The one about whom was declared, "But for you, I would not have created the worlds," deserves to be addressed with "Had there not been anything else than your prayer, I would have created Paradise for your sake."

O God! Bestow blessings and peace on that beloved one, the lord of the two worlds, the pride of creation, the life of the two realms, the means of happiness in both worlds, who has the principles of a happy life in both worlds, the Messenger to both mankind and jinn, and on his family and Companions altogether, and on his brother Messengers and Prophets. Amen.

Think again and most particularly of how the Owner of this world, as may be concluded from His disposition of this world, His subjugation of suns, moons, trees, rivers, etc., enjoys a magnificent sovereignty in His awesome Lordship. However, this abode is subject to continuous transformations and bound to destruction. It therefore resembles only a hospice prepared for visitors, which is filled and emptied every day, or an arena of trial incessantly changing, or a place for the exhibition of models of the marvels of its Owner's art and samples of His bounties. The creatures assembled in this place are on a continuous journey and therefore allowed to stay therein only as long as they can get the answers to the questions they ask about what they see and hear, and at any time they may be called to leave that place. Therefore there must be behind this transient abode, this changing arena and place of exhibition, permanent castles, everlasting mansions and treasuries the doors of which are open and which are filled with the originals of those samples, where the eternal Sovereignty will manifest Itself with all Its magnificence.

Suppose anyone with the least consciousness comes across a splendid guesthouse that a benevolent ruler has built and richly decorated for travelers to stay only one night. He observes that most of the decorations are samples and visitors are allowed only to taste of the food offered, not to eat to full satisfaction. He also observes that whatever happens in that guesthouse and whatever visitors do or say is recorded with secret cameras and that the ruler changes the decorations every day with new ones for newcomers. Then he will certainly conclude that the owner of that guesthouse has limitless wealth and is infinitely generous. He will know that the guesthouse was built for a fixed period in order that a yearning may be aroused in his guests for the boundless and inexhaustible banquets that he has prepared for them in his permanent mansions.

Similarly, a truly human being will certainly understand that:

This world has not been created for its own sake, and it is

not an end in itself. Rather, it is a realm filled through births and emptied through deaths. Its inhabitants are guests only, whom the Munificent Lord invites to the realm of happiness. Its decorations are not for taking pleasure in endlessly, for after they give you a momentary pleasure they disappear and leave behind great pains. Your tasting of them only sharpens your appetite but you are not allowed satisfaction because of the shortness of either your existence or theirs. They are offered to you for reflection, thanksgiving, and yearning for their eternal originals. These decorations are only "pictures" or samples of the bounties that the All-Merciful has stored for believers in gardens of Paradise. Also, these transient things have not been created for eternal extinction. Rather, they have been assembled here to be copied with their forms and meanings and with the consequences of their existence. Everlasting scenes will be woven of them for the people of eternity. Or the One Who subjects them to incessant transformations will make from them whatever He wills in the eternal world.

Another proof for the fact that things are for eternal existence not for eternal extinction, or that their apparent decay or extinction means the end of their tasks in this world or their discharge from their worldly duties, is this:

For example, among the "words" of the Divine Power, consider a flower, which looks at us for a very short time and then goes away. You may think of it as a word uttered, which by God's permission, goes to thousands of ears, with its meanings understood by numerous intellects. Then, when the flower dies, it entrusts itself to the memories of those who have seen it, and its forms and meanings to its seeds. Thus the memory of each one who has seen it and each seed becomes like a record for the preservation of the decorations of its forms and a place for its permanence. You can compare with that flower other living beings that have a higher degree of life up to beings with eternal spirit.

Surely, man has not been left to "roam at will" and to do whatever he wishes. Rather, whatever he does and says is recorded and the consequences of his deeds are preserved for a final reckoning. The destruction in autumn of the beautiful things of spring means their discharge from their duties completed and making room for new things to come and do their duties. It is also a warning for the heedless and "intoxicated" that the Maker of this world is the All-Knowing and Eternal, Who drives and urges His servants to Him, and Who has prepared for them things that eyes have never seen, nor ears ever heard, nor hearts ever conceived of.

Reflect attentively on the reality that the Owner of this world is the All-Preserving; He misses nothing and whether it be the biggest or the smallest, He records and preserves everything in a manifest book. The balance, order, harmony and measure witnessed in the world are but a few lines of this book. Whoever completes his life and therefore his duties and goes away from the visible, material world, he goes with all his life recorded on preserved tablets and most of his deeds preserved in their results. The Creator keeps them in various "mirrors" from both the visible and unseen worlds. It is as if many things around man are charged with recording whatever he does and however he behaves towards the entities, living or non-living, with which he has some relation.

Look, if you will, at the memories of human beings, the fruits of trees, and the seeds of fruits and flowers, so that you may understand the comprehensiveness of the law of recording and preserving. The Owner of these creatures is infinitely careful about His activities of Sovereignty and has recorded whatever happens in His Kingdom. Everything is so perfectly ordered and measured in His Lordship that He records or has recorded even the most insignificant happening and the least service [rendered by His servants]. This recording and preservation point to, indeed clearly show, or rather, require a reckoning. Especially the comprehensive acts done by the noblest and most honorable of creatures, namely man, will certainly be judged. Man is the witness of all the acts of the Divine Lordship, the herald of the Divine Unity in the realm of multiplicity, and the observer of the glorifications of creatures. Because of this and innumerable other virtues, man has been honored with the Divine Trust—human self distinguished with free will, knowledge and speech and with the Divine religion—and God's vicegerency on the earth.

This honor and distinction must not be thought to exempt man from being called to account for what he does. *Does man think that he will be left to roam at will, that he will be left uncontrolled?*[3] No, indeed. He will be called to account for even the least of the things he does. He will be transferred to the Place of Supreme Gathering and eternal world. Destroying the world and raising the dead and assembling them for judgement in the Place of Gathering are as easy for the Divine Power as to create spring and autumn. All the past happenings, which are the miracles of His Power, testify for a certainty that He is able to do whatever He wills and promises to do in the future.

The Owner and Ruler of this world has particularly and repeatedly promised something the creation of which is extremely easy for Him and of infinite importance for His creatures, His servants. Breaking a promise is utterly contrary to the dignity and glory of His Power and the mercy of His Lordship. Since breaking a promise comes from, first, ignorance, and then, inability or impotence, it is inconceivable of the One with absolute Knowledge and Power. Building the other world through many revolutions and with all its Gardens is not more difficult for Him than creating spring with all its gardens and the transformations therein. His promise has been established and affirmed by the unanimous agreement of all the Prophets and the consensus of all the purified, exacting scholars. Hear the strength of His promise in this verse: *God—there is no god but He. He will surely gather you to the Resurrection Day, about which there is no doubt. Who is truer in tidings than God?*[4] Woe to man! How ungrateful he is! He does not confirm the word of Him Whose truthfulness all of these creatures, which are His true words,

---

3. *al-Qiyama*, 75.36.
4. *al-Nisa'*, 4.87.

definitely confirm and which, through its articulate signs, this universe affirms. The man who refuses is relying on illusions, nonsensical words of his carnal self and falsehoods of Satan. We seek refuge in God from being left without a true helper and from the evils of the carnal self and Satan.

We observe in this world the manifestations of a magnificent, eternal Lordship and the works of a permanent and splendid Sovereignty. Consider the grandeur of the Owner of this Lordship: how the ever-changing earth is under His command and submits to it like a tamed animal. He makes it die and brings it back to life, manages and directs it. The sun likewise, with all its satellites, is subjugated to His Power: He manages it and moves the system of which it is the center. However, this magnificent eternal Lordship, this comprehensive perpetual Sovereignty, which amazes intellects through its awesome acts, cannot be confined to those ever-changing momentary affairs related to this changeable, transient world. Among the pavilions of this Lordship, this world is but an arena of trial, a place of exhibition. It will be destroyed at an appointed time to be made into the foundation of everlasting palaces to which its inhabitants will be transferred. The Lord of this changeable, transient world disposes another, a perpetual world. There are those who, with enlightened intellects, illumined hearts and illuminating spirits, have been able to discover the inner reality of creation and things and acquired nearness to the All-Glorified God. They have informed us that God Almighty has prepared for the obedient and the rebellious an abode of reward and punishment, and to that end He makes strong promises and severe admonitions. He is absolutely free and glorified above breaking His promise and failing to fulfil it. In addition to the Prophets, saints and purified, exacting scholars who have given us that information, despite their differences in temperament and approaches, those who are experts in such matters are agreed on the truth of that information, which the universe also corroborates with its signs. Now, can there be any other news or information truer than this?

The Owner of this world displays many samples or models of the Place of Supreme Gathering in this narrow, transient arena of the earth every day, every year, every century, and every age. Ponder, if you will, the quickening of the earth in every "resurrection" of spring and see how hundreds of thousands of instances of resurrection take place with perfect order in so short a time as about six days. See how, while lying dead or almost dead on or under earth mixed with one another, innumerable plants and animals are revived with perfect distinction. How can anything tire the One who does this? Why should He be unable to create the heavens and earth in six days? Why should the resurrection of the dead not take place in a twinkling of an eye?

The One Who writes hundreds of thousands of books on a single page—the face of the earth—without any confusion and mistakes, can in no way be unable to re-write a book which He wrote before and destroyed. In order to understand the meaning of this comparison, reflect, if you will, on the verse, *Look at the imprints of God's Mercy, how He gives life to the earth after its death; surely He is the quickener of the dead, and He is powerful over everything.*[5] All such acts of His required by His being the All-Merciful and All-Powerful Lord of creation point out that all these happenings in the world—these gatherings and separations—are not ends in themselves. There is not an acceptable, reasonable relation between all these important "festivals" and ceremonies and their particular, impermanent consequences within a short, limited time. Therefore, all these festivals and ceremonies are only a representation to be copied and preserved with their consequences, so that the proceeding should take place according to them in the Place of Supreme Gathering and these fleeting things should yield perpetual forms, everlasting fruits and eternal meanings. So, this world is but an arable field to sow for harvesting on the Day of Resurrection and a store which will be emptied into Paradise and Hell.

Consider attentively how, in these transient mansions, these

5. *al-Rum*, 30.50.

fleeting places of exhibition, these ephemeral arenas, the Eternal Lord and Everlasting King visibly displays the works and traces of His manifest Wisdom, clear and flowering Favoring, lofty Justice, and all-comprehensive Mercy. He does so to the degree that anyone with eyes not blinded and heart unsealed must certainly conclude that there can be no wisdom more perfect than His, no favoring more gracious than His, no mercy more comprehensive than His, and no justice more glorified than His. All these works and traces may be the means for the manifestation of the truths of this Wisdom, Favoring, Mercy and Justice. If there were in His Kingdom no permanent lofty mansions with everlasting inhabitants in them, then it would require the denial of this observed Wisdom, this witnessed Favoring, this spectacular Mercy, and this evident Justice. It would also require the acceptance of the One Who does all these things originating in His Wisdom, Mercy, Munificence and Justice, as—God forbid such a thought! —a capricious trickster and a pitiless tyrant. Again, it would require the turning of truths into their opposites, which is impossible according to all men of sound reasoning except those who (like the sophists) are able to deny the existence of things and even of themselves.

***

O, friend, you who have accompanied me thus far in these reflections, do not suppose that the arguments for the Resurrection are limited to those we have so far mentioned. No! The wise Qur'an points to innumerable indications of it, and teaches that our Creator will transfer us from this ephemeral place of exhibition to the seat of His everlasting Lordship, and depicts numberless signs of the reality that He will change this fleeting, transitory realm for that perpetual one.

Nor suppose that the Divine Names requiring the Resurrection and next life are restricted to the All-Wise, the All-Munificent, the All-Compassionate, the All-Just and the All-Preserving. No! All of the Names manifested in the administration of the universe demand it.

In sum: the matter of the Resurrection is a matter agreed on by the All-Glorified One through His Grace, Beauty and Majesty and all other Names, and the Qur'an containing in itself all the books of the Prophets, upon them be peace, and by the saints and purified, exacting scholars, and by the Prophet Muhammad, upon him be peace and blessings, the most perfect of creation, and the bearer of the meaning of the consensus of the Messengers, Prophets, discoverers of hidden realities behind things and events, and truthful ones, who all have purified, exalted, and illuminating spirits, and by the universe with all the signs it contains.

All things in the universe, whether they be particular or universal, parts or wholes, have two aspects. One of them is related to their Creator and has numerous "tongues" all of which testify and point to the Divine Oneness. The other aspect is connected with the final purpose of the existence of each and the Hereafter, and also has lots of "tongues" pointing and bearing witness to the other world and the Last Day.

For example, just as through your existence as the best pattern of creation you point to the necessary Existence and Oneness of your Maker, so also, through your rapid decline despite your very comprehensive capacity, great talents and ungratified desires for a happy eternal life, you point to the Hereafter.

Divine Wisdom, the all-inclusive decoration and provision of Divine Favoring, the all-encompassing benevolence of His Mercy, His over-all Justice and comprehensive and meticulous Preservation establish the universal order. Just as these point to the All-Wise, All-Munificent, All-Compassionate, All-Just and All-Preserving Maker, so too they indicate or demonstrate the truth of the afterlife, the near and imminent coming of the Hour and the realization of the eternal happiness.

O God! Include us in the people of eternal happiness, resurrect and gather us among the group of the eternally happy, prosperous ones, and, through the intercession of Your chosen Prophet, admit us to Paradise in the company of the purified, virtuous ones.

Bestow blessings and peace on Your chosen Prophet and his family as befits Your Compassion and deserved by his being a holy, respectable one, and keep us and our religion in peace and security. Amen.

And all praise be to God, the Lord of the Worlds.

INDEX OR BRIEF SUMMARIES OF THE TOPICS
DISCUSSED IN THE TREATISE

*Naturalism and dogmatic adherence to causality have closed the door of thanksgiving [to the Creator] and opened the door of associating partners with Him. (49)

*Everything has two aspects: one its sensed physical aspect or form or body, which, like a garment, is "cut out" and shaped according to the measures determined by the functions and purposes assigned for it in life. The other is its immaterial aspect composed of the sum of the forms it has taken on during its growth in the course of time. (50)

*O unbeliever! When you refer to true scientific knowledge and truth, your ingratitude and unbelief will compel you to admit that every minute particle and every "natural" cause has as much knowledge as to be able to cut out garments as many and different as the number of things, including, even, the forms they take on during their growth. Let alone minute particles, even man, the fruit of the tree of creation and, supposedly, the most powerful of causes and the most knowledgeable of them with a most comprehensive will-power, cannot cut out a single garment for a thorny tree properly fitted for it including all its members. (50)

*The vast extent of the distribution of species while maintaining the infinite beauty of each individual member; the wonderful economy and abundance while each individual is of immeasurable value; the coherence of the members of various species despite the perfect distinction between individuals and without the least confusion and fault; the perfect correspondence and similarity in structure and form among species in spite of vast distances in time and space and in balance with an absolute variety; the perfect individualization of characters and features in each creature though generated from similar or even the very same materials, structural principles and organization ; the perfect structure and beauty of each individual member of a species despite the vast abundance of the species— all that is enough to manifest the existence and Oneness of an All-Knowing, All-Willing, All-Powerful and All-Wise Creator. (52)

*Just as it is inconceivable for the sun not to diffuse light, so too it is inconceivable for God not to manifest Himself by sending Messengers. (54)

*In addition to many other evidences, infinite justice, munificence, mercy, grace, generosity, dignity, majesty, recording and preservation, which are all indispensable to the Almighty, require the founding of a new, eternal world where every one will see the consequences of whatever he or she does in this world. (55-68)

*In sum: the matter of the Resurrection is a matter agreed on by the All-Glorified One through His Grace, Beauty and Majesty and all other Names, and the Qur'an containing in itself all the books of the Prophets, upon them be peace, and by the saints and purified, exacting scholars, and by the Prophet Muhammad, upon him be peace and blessings, the most perfect of creation, and the bearer of the meaning of the consensus of the Messengers, Prophets, discoverers of hidden realities behind things and events, and truthful ones, and by the universe with all the signs it contains.

All things in the universe, whether they be particular or universal, parts or wholes, have two aspects. One of them is related to their Creator and has numerous "tongues" all of which testify and point to the Divine Oneness. The other aspect is connected with the final purpose of the existence of each and the Hereafter, and also has lots of "tongues" pointing and bearing witness to the other world and the Last Day.

For example, just as through your existence as the best pattern of creation you point to the necessary Existence and Oneness of your Maker, so also, through your rapid decline despite your very comprehensive capacity, great talents and ungratified desires for a happy eternal life, you point to the Hereafter.

Divine Wisdom, the all-inclusive decoration and provision of Divine Favoring, the all-encompassing benevolence of His Mercy, His over-all Justice and comprehensive and meticulous Preservation establish the universal order. Just as these point to the All-Wise, All-Munificent, All-Compassionate, All-Just and All-Preserving Maker, so too they indicate or demonstrate the truth of the afterlife, the near and imminent coming of the Hour and the realization of the eternal happiness. (69)

Fourth treatise

A Drop from the Ocean of (the Proofs) of Divine Unity

In the Name of God, the Merciful, the Compassionate.
All praise be to God and blessings be upon His Prophet.

This treatise consists of an introduction, four chapters and a conclusion.

Introduction

Know O friend! During my whole life of forty years and study of thirty years, I have learned four words or phrases and four sentences, [each of which is a general ruling]. The phrases are: being, like a letter, a sign of the whole or pointing to others, being rather than itself; like a word, pointing to or representing itself; intention and viewpoint.[1]

That is, we should consider anything other than God not on account of itself but on account of God Almighty. To consider the universe on account of itself or material causes is wrong. Everything has two aspects: one pointing to the Creator, the other, creation. Any created being should be considered with respect to its first aspect, that is, with respect to its being a sign of the Almighty Creator. For example, any bounty or blessing should be associated with the Divine gift or Divine act of bestowing bounties and the means and causes should be made or seen as "mirrors" reflecting the disposals of Divine Power.

Similarly, intention and viewpoint change the nature of things and, as elixir turns earth into gold, good intention and correct viewpoint change evil acts into good ones. Also, intention makes

---

1. In Arabic, "letter" means a thing pointing to the meanings of others, not itself. As for "word", it is a thing pointing to itself in meaning. Considering something from the viewpoint of what a letter signifies or on account of the Creator means considering it as a "mirror" reflecting God's Names and Attributes manifested on it. (Tr.)

our everyday, ordinary acts into acts of worship and through viewpoint sciences become a means of acquiring knowledge about God. If the findings of sciences are considered on account of or from the viewpoint of material causes and means, they become a means of ignorance. If, by contrast, they are considered on account of God, then they give knowledge about God.

As for the four sentences I have learned during my lifetime, they are as follows:

The first: *I am neither the owner nor master of myself.* The one who owns me is the Owner of the whole creation, the One of Majesty and Munificence. I suppose myself as self-owner so that I may understand the Attributes of my Owner by comparison. Through my limitations [in power, attributes, capacities, etc.] I perceive the Infinite One. "When the sun rises and morning comes, stars set."

The second: *Death is inevitable.* This life and body cannot be a foundation on which this huge world will be founded. Made up of different things like flesh, blood and bones, which are bound to decompose at some time, life and body are not eternal. How, then, can a "palace" as large as the world be built with desires and fancies upon this loose foundation and rotting support?

The third: *My Lord is One.* All kinds of happiness for each one can be possible only through submission to One Lord. Or else everyone would need as many conflicting lords as the entities in the universe. For man, because of his comprehensive nature, needs almost all things and has connections with each. Whether consciously or unconsciously, he is impressed by all of them and suffers because of them. This is a hellish state for him. Whereas knowledge and recognition of One Lord before Whose Hand of power all those fancied or supposed lords are but a thin veil, is a paradisiacal state.

The fourth: *Human ego is a black dot, a point of comparison* [to know and recognize God] *intertwined with the "threads" of a conscious artistry.* It shows that its Owner is nearer to it than itself.

These sentences will be explained in the conclusion of the first chapter.

The first chapter

This is about [the profession of the creed]:

There is no god but God.

In the Name of God, the Merciful, the Compassionate

All praise be to the Lord of the Worlds, and peace and blessings be upon the master of the Messengers, and upon all his family and Companions.

Let all witnesses and all the witnessed witness that I bear witness that there is no god but God, Whose necessary existence and perfect Attributes, and also Whose Oneness, Unity, Singularity and being the Eternally Besought-of-All, are decisively established by the following arguments:

The first and foremost truthful witness whose truthfulness has been unanimously confirmed, and the articulate, verified proof is the lord of the Prophets and Messengers and the leader of all saints and God-fearing scholars. He holds the meaning of the confirmation of God's existence and Unity, and the consensus thereon of all the Prophets and Messengers and that of all the saints and scholars. He has manifest signs [to testify to his Prophethood] and numerous miracles unanimously confirmed and transmitted by the Companions and later generations and reliable authorities. He has lofty, laudable virtues and perfect, admirable morals. He is the center upon which the Divine Revelation is focused, and the traveler in the unseen worlds who has seen the spirits and conversed with angels. He is the guide of mankind and *jinn* and, through his person demonstrating that he is the favorite of the Creator of the universe, he is the embodiment of all the perfections shared by the whole of the creation. The law he has brought contains all the principles of happiness, such that it proves to be the order established by the Orderer of the universe. He is our master, who guides us to belief: Muhammad the son of Abdullah, the son of

be the best of blessings and the most perfect peace. At the head
of all witnesses, he informs us in this visible, material world of
what he witnesses in the world of the Unseen. As a bringer of
good tidings and a warner, with his fullest voice and all his
strength, with his perfect earnestness and utmost reliability and
with his infinite conviction and perfect faith, he announces to
all the generations to come through centuries in all parts of the
world, that *there is no god but God.*

Also, another witness of God's necessary existence and Oneness, and expounder of His Attributes of Majesty, Beauty, Grace
and Perfection, is the Wise Criterion, which is the Holy Qur'an.
It holds the meaning of the consensus of all the heavenly Scriptures that were sent to certain Prophets who came in different
times. It also holds the meaning of the unanimous agreement of
the books of all saints with different temperaments and all au-
thenticating monotheist scholars following different methods in
their studies. Those with sound power of reasoning and conscience and truly enlightened intellects have all affirmed the
commandments of the wise Qur'an, which is enlightening in all
its aspects.

The Qur'an is the Word of God and has proved to deserve
this name. As confirmed by those honored by the Divine Revelation and inspiration and the ability to unveil hidden truths, it
is pure Revelation and evidently pure guidance. It is also the
source of belief, which, obviously, contains all truths. Clearly, it
leads to happiness and continuously yields perfect fruits. It has
been accepted and adopted by angels and innumerable men
and *jinn.* All those with perfect power of reasoning and wisdom
and sound judgement and conscience have agreed that the
Qur'an is affirmed with rational proofs and confirmed with the
testimony of good character and disposition. Manifestly, it is an
eternal miracle, and the tongue of the Unseen, and it definitely
bears witness in the visible, material world to the fact that *there
is no god but God.*

Also, with all its chapters, sections, pages, lines, sentences
and letters, this great book (of the universe), with all its sys-

tems, organs, cells, atoms, attributes and states, this macro-human being, that is, this cosmos, testifies to God's necessary existence and Oneness, and His Attributes of Majesty, Beauty, Grace and Perfection. Through all its worlds and spheres, it says that *there is no god but God*, and through the main constituents of those worlds it says that *there is no creator but He*. Through the parts of those constituents it says that *there is no maker but He* and through the components of those parts it says that *there is no director but He*. Through the elements of those components it says that *there is no giver of certain form and disposition but He* and through the cells of those elements it says that *there is none but He with the necessary power of ordering and disposing them* Through the atoms or minutest particles of those cells it says that *there is no Creator but He*, and through the ocean of ether in which all atoms or particles are "sown" it says *there is no god but He*. In sum: with all the species inhabiting it, and with all its worlds, spheres, constituents, parts, components, atoms, and ether, the universe testifies in fifty-five languages to the necessary existence and Unity of the Eternal Designer.

Those fifty-five languages will be explained below. However, first we will make a brief mention of them:

Through the languages of its individual parts and well-ordered compounds and the poverty and neediness of the living creatures in it, the universe bears witness to the necessary existence and Oneness of its All-Powerful and Beginningless Creator. Through the well-ordered conditions or states it undergoes, the amazing and perfect forms it has, and its peculiar and ornamented designs, the universe points to His Attributes of Perfection. Through the lofty purposes it serves, the great benefits it produces, the extraordinary variation it displays and the well-arranged similarities it exhibits, the universe mentions and recites His All-Beautiful Names. Through the languages of the order and excellent measure observed in its wholes and parts, the good arrangement and regularity it manifests, and the firm and faultless artistry discerned in everything, the universe glorifies Him with praise. Through the mutual assistance among different inanimate objects, through the solidarity among dissimilar and varying things, through the languages of the universal wisdom and perfect favoring and comprehensive mercy and all-encompassing provision and all-permeating life, the universe interprets the verses of the wise Qur'an. Through the languages of beauty and making beautiful, the grace manifested everywhere, the true love, the attraction and being attracted, and the quality of nature as being the shadow of the Divine Truth, the universe contributes to the brightness of the light of Islam. Through the languages of acting for certain purposes, and making interchanges for certain benefits, and making transformations for certain instances of wisdom, all of which take place in it; and making alterations for certain aims, and ordering and arranging to perfections, the universe interprets the verses of the wise Qur'an. Through the languages of its being contingent and having a beginning; and its needs, poverty and destitution; and its helplessness, death, ignorance, and ephemerality, and being subject to ever-changing and final destruction to be built again, the universe declares God's power. Through the languages of the acts and forms of its worship, glorification, prayer, and seeking refuge [with Him]—in all such languages, and with all its individual parts and compounds, the universe strengthens submission to the Summit of Prophethood, and belief in the Necessarily-Existent Being, One and Single. In all such languages and under the command of the Eternal Word and presidency of the Master of All Creatures, primarily including the Messengers, the universe announces: *God, there is no god but He, the All-Living, the Self-Subsistent and Sustainer.*

Now give ear to the explanation of these languages:

1.   As a whole and with all its parts, the universe displays an evident order and an extraordinary solidarity among all its individual parts. This order and solidarity point to the necessary existence of Him in Whose Hand of power the universe is and bears witness in the tongue of this universal order to the fact that *God, there is no god but He.*

2.   In the universe everything is so exactly measured and

proportioned that it announces that *God, there is no god but He* Who has set this measure and made all things in admirable proportions and exactly commensurate with one another.

3.   The harmony and precise arrangement in the "house" of the universe, and the regularity of its working show that it is impossible for numerous different hands to interfere in it, and announces in the language of this harmony, arrangement and regularity that *God, there is no god but He.*

4.   The art and design exhibited in this "house" of the universe point to the fact that the One Who has designed and decorated the house is also its Owner, and testifies in the language of this art and design that *God, there is no god but He.*

5.   The perfection of the art which the Pen of Destiny displays in everything according to the capacity of each shows that the Pen is one and announces that *God, there is no god but He.*

6.   The mutual relationship between all things in the universe and faultless artistry displayed in each demonstrate that the one who has inscribed the page of the sky with stars and suns is He Who inscribes the pages of the honeybee and ant with their cells. In the language of all creatures in it the universe bears witness that *God, there is no god but He.*

7.   We observe in the universe that even the inanimate objects, no matter how distant they are from one another, come to the aid of one another for wise purposes. For example, [vaporizing waters come down onto the earth to "revive" it, and] corn and fruits become the sustenance of human cells. In the language of this mutual assistance the universe bears witness that *God, there is no god but He.*

8.   As between the sun and the planets, which are its "fruits", there is solidarity among different, distant objects in the universe. This solidarity shows that whatever is in the universe is under the command and disposition of only one being and in the language of this solidarity, the universe testifies that *God, there is no god but He.*

9.   The resemblance among certain things, among the stars

of the heavens, for example, is another language in which the universe proclaims that *God, there is no god but He.*

10. The proportion among certain other things, as, for example, among the flowers of the earth, demonstrates that whatever is in the universe belongs to the same Owner and is under the disposition of the same Power. In the language of this proportion, the universe testifies that *God, there is no god but He.*

11. Every living thing in the universe receives the manifestations of numerous Names. [For example, the Names the Creator, the Shaper, the All-Seeing, the All-Hearing, the Arranger, the Provider, the Sustainer, the All-Healing and many other Names manifest on the same being.] Like the seven colors in the light of the sun, these Names have each Its own beauty and imprints but they work to the same effect in each individual thing, including even cells. This shows that the One Who has these Names is the one and same being. That is, the All-Living Creator of something is also its Shaper, Provider and Sustainer, and the One Who provides something is the Creator of the sources of provision, and its Creator is He Who has dominion over every thing. This reality opens a window on the necessary existence and Unity of the One called by the Names mentioned, and in the language of every living thing the universe testifies that *God, there is no god but He.*

12. The connection among all things, the connection between, for example, the eyes of the honeybee and ant and the sun and the solar system, shows that both are the designs of a single Designer. In the language of this connection the universe bears witness that *God, there is no god but He.*

13. The indispensable relation among the parts of each thing and things themselves, down to that between the least and the largest, like that between the eyes of an ant or honeybee and the sun, demonstrates that everything is the work of a single Maker. In the language of this relation the universe testifies that *God, there is no god but He.*

14. The "brotherhood" between the gravitation among the minutest particles and atoms of an individual thing and the

general gravitation between stars and suns is indicative of the fact that both are the "inscriptions" of a single pen, the texture of a single weaver, the rays from a single "sun". This shows the necessity of Divine existence and Unity and in this language the universe bears witness that *God, there is no god but He*.

15.   All the minutest particles or atoms in compounds and then compounds within one another are placed each in its exact position. It is done according to such delicate calculations that, for example, any atom or particle in an eye is interrelated with the other atoms in the eye and all the systems and cells of the body. This necessarily demonstrates that the Creator of the eye with all its atoms and the body and the eye of the world—the sun— and their positioner is the Creator of all compounds in the universe. Thus, in the language of all the minutest particles and their positions and tasks, the universe bears witness that *God, there is no god but He*.

16.   The comprehensive disposition of the power of a species and the wide distribution of certain species like angels and fish indicate that the Creator of a single individual being is also the Creator of the species. The pen, which draws the lines of, say, Jack's face and thus identifies or individualizes him, has to be able to see all the faces together at the same time before it so that it could determine the distinguishing features of each. Otherwise individualization would be impossible and confusions would appear. This requires that the Creator of an individual should be the Creator of the family and species. The universe testifies in this language that *God, there is no god but He*.

17.   Those with defective view and reasoning may regard it as impossible for a single being to have created all things and therefore are misguided into denying the existence and Oneness of the Creator. Whereas the attribution of things to nature or to themselves or to material causes or to such "notions" as chance and necessity makes the existence of things infinitely improbable or impossible.

The creation of many things by a single one is much easier than the creation of a single thing by many "creators". The in-

terference of many "blind" hands in the production of a thing is
of no more use than increasing "blindness." If, for example, a
honeybee is not attributed to the power of a necessarily existent
being, then whatever is in the heavens and on the earth should
have participated in its existence. If the existence of a minute
particle or a single hair is attributed to other than a necessarily
existent being, to material causes, for example, it would be as
difficult as the existence of mountains. The organization and direction of a company by a single commander is much easier
than its direction by the soldiers themselves or many command-
ers. Also, everyone judges the shower of water sprinkled [on
the flowers in a garden] to be shooting from a sprinkler. All the
lines ending on the circumference of a circle originates from a
single center. Each of such results can easily be obtained with a
few acts of a single being.

Suppose, for example, the shower of water from a sprinkler
was attributed to the drops of water. Or suppose the existence
of a flower was attributed to the particles of earth, molecules of
water, rays of the sunlight and the constituent particles of the
flower itself, or to chance and the like. Then it would require
that each particle of these elements should have the attributes of
the Necessarily-Existent Being. It should have perfect artistry,
comprehensive consciousness, all-encompassing knowl-edge
and absolute will and power. Also, the attribution of creativity
to such causes besides God would mean the acceptance of innumerable partners with the Necessarily-Existent Being, Who
does not admit partnership at all. Again, the order and perfect
arrangement also require that each particle would both be dominant over others and be dominated by them at the same time.
In sum, the attribution of the existence of things to nature or
chance or material causes or to themselves would mean the admission of all such inconceivable requirements.

Suppose, by contrast, that everything is attributed to its true
Owner, Whose existence is absolutely necessary and Who is
One and Single. Then, like the drops of water each "containing"
and reflecting the sun and shining with its image, each minute

particle receives and reflects the rays of the manifestation of the infinite and eternal Power which includes the infinite and eternal Knowledge and Will. A minute particle that receives a single ray of this manifestation is more effective than the "sun" of material causes. The connection to that Power even through a minute particle produces much more effect than a mountain. For a transparent particle with the capacity of receiving and reflecting the manifestation of that Power possesses Its attributes and therefore acquires universality or functions like a universal thing. Furthermore, the Power is an essential Attribute of the Divine Being and therefore is infinite and has no opposites to admit division and dilution. Due to essential qualities in existence, namely transparency, reciprocity, balance and measurement, orderliness, abstraction and obedience,[2] the sun is as easy for that Power to create as the minutest particle or the smallest and the largest whole are the same in relation to a single ray of It. The operation of the Power can also be likened to light penetrating through a small hole and illuminating a large area.

Know that life, being and light are transparent and permeable and operate in the inner, immaterial dimension of existence. For this reason, it is always possible to discern the operation of the Power under the solid material causes. In order to have an image of the sun in a piece of glass, the sun's light needs only to penetrate through a small hole. A cluster of grapes grows at the end of a thin, slender stem. The illumination of a room requires the lighting of a candle or lamp. As in these examples, the Power operates behind such simple and delicate causes. If the Power is not discerned in such effects, then they must be attributed to the glass itself or the slender stem of the cluster or lighting a match.

Again, there are hearts or intellects which suffer from insurmountable difficulties or troubles issuing from the denial of a single Creator or associating partners with Him in creation of things. They can find peace only in attributing everything to the One Necessarily-Existent Being, through Whose Power all difficulties can be solved, Whose Will is the key to all problems and

---

2. These qualities are explained in the Second Aim of *The Twenty-ninth Word*. (Tr.)

mysteries, and through Whose remembrance hearts find peace and tranquility. There is no shelter or salvation except by taking refuge in Him and reliance on Him. The Almighty declares: *Flee to God*,[3] and *Assuredly in the remembrance of God do hearts find peace and tranquility*.[4] This undeniable truth opens a window on the light of Islam, and on obedience to Prophethood and the light of belief in the Necessarily-Existent Being of Oneness and Unity. In the language of all its parts, the universe testifies that *God, there is no god but He*.

18.   The apparent material causes, like bread and milk for satisfaction of hunger, are simple, limited in time and place and quantity, subject to disappearance or death, and changeable. They have no consciousness and will, and most of them are subject to "laws" which have only nominal, not material, existence and which are perceived only after the effects are brought about. When compared to their causes, the effects are extremely extraordinary and display splendid artistry. For example, the formation of cells and their relations with one another and the whole of the body are so complex and extraordinary that they require much more knowledge, much greater skills, much more comprehensive will and much vaster power than are disposed by the whole population of the world. Therefore, they can be explained with neither the food given nor the working of the unconscious and ignorant body.

Also, with what can the human memory be explained? It is like a copy of a person's life that the Hand of Power reproduces and gives to his hand so that he may remember all his deeds at the time of reckoning and be convinced that there is a permanent life behind the disturbances of this life. The All-Knowing One arranges things and events in it without any confusion despite their utmost intricacy and confusion. Again, human faculties like reflection, reasoning, thinking and speech and their operation can never be attributed to or explained by some systems and organs and their movements. [As is known, although creat-

---

3. *Qaf*, 50.3.
4. *al-Ra'd*, 13.28.

ed from and nourished of the same elements and formed of the same constituents, human beings are infinitely different in features, characters, desires, capacities, likes and dislikes, speech, etc.] Therefore, both these faculties or powers and the systems and organs can only be the work of One with an infinite Power, Knowledge and Will and the real agent in the universe can only be a Creator with a boundless Power. The material causes and means are only some excuses [to allow some space for human agency] and veils [before the operation of the Power]. Senses, faculties and qualities are some titles to the "pieces of glass" receiving and reflecting, according to their capacities, the manifestations of the Power, including the eternal and infinite Knowledge and Will. As for the things called laws, they are the names of the manifestations of the Knowledge, Command and Will on species. A law is but something issuing from the "realm" of Commands and Will. This truth opens another window on the necessary existence of the Divine Being, and in the language of all effects the universe testifies that *God, there is no god but He.*

19.   The wonderful works of a universal, perfect art and the utmost care shown in these works require a limitless power; not only these works but also each part of them demands this power.

This points to the fact that this universe has an All-Powerful Creator. There are no limits to the manifestations to His Power. Since It is infinite, It is absolutely independent of having partners and It does not need them at all. Partnership with something infinite is inconceivable, as it means limiting It. Divinity does not accept limitation and, since being limited means being contained in time and space and defective in the capacities and qualities which a divine being must necessarily have, any limited being cannot, obviously, be God. Also, absolute independence and freedom are essential to divinity. Besides, there is no room, no space and no need for partnership, and there are neither evidences nor signs for the existence of a partner. By contrast, through its parts and as a whole and in the language of all the events in it, the universe displays the stamp of Unity and shows that the agent ruling over it is One.

Consider that the most capable of creation, the most eminent of causes equipped with a free will, is man. The role of man in the acts he does out of free will, like eating and speaking, is one out of a hundred. While the most capable and honored of creation, one equipped with consciousness and free will, is limited to that degree in the acts in which he is most free, what part can inanimate objects have in the creation and operation of the universe? How can the handkerchief or envelope in which the gift of the king is wrapped, be a partner or helper of the king? This truth opens another window on the necessary existence and Unity of the Divine Being, and in the language of this truth, the universe bears witness that *God, there is no god but He.*

20. Although some of the Divine Names like the All-Knowing encompass all things, the Divine Names manifested in the universe coordinate in the creation, life and working of all its parts down to the minutest particles. Like the seven colors in the light of the sun, they work to the same effect. [For example, although the Names and Attributes manifested on a man, like Knowledge, Will and Power and the All-Seeing, the All-Hearing, the All-Shaping, the Provider, the Sustainer, etc. have their own manifestations and produce effects particular to themselves, the result they ultimately produce is an integral entity.] This evidently demonstrates that the Being called by these Names is one, and in the language of the co-ordination and solidarity among the Names manifested in it, the universe testifies that *God, there is no god but He.*

21. A universal wisdom is apparent in the whole of the universe, both as a whole and in parts. This wisdom, which includes a purpose, consciousness, will and preference, points to the necessary existence of an All-Wise One, as it is impossible for an act to be without a doer and a thing done or a part of it cannot be the doer.

22. The purposeful and gracious, all-encompassing favoring apparent throughout the universe necessarily testifies to the necessary existence of an All-Munificent Creator, as any favoring cannot be without a favorer.

23. The extensive mercy encompassing the whole of the universe, which contains wisdom, favoring, benevolence, munificence, kindness, gratifying, love and recognition, indicates the necessary existence of an All-Merciful, All-Compassionate One. This is so as any quality cannot be the one qualified by it and the earth and heavens can have been "clothed" by none other than that All-Merciful One.

24. The satisfaction of infinitely diverse needs of living creatures from the universal provision, which contains wisdom, favoring, mercy, protection, engagement [to provide them], intention, love and recognition, evidently points to the necessary existence of a Compassionate Provider.

25. The life and vigor widespread throughout the universe contain wisdom, favoring, mercy, provision, delicate artistry, elegant design, firmness, and care, and they are brought about by the manifestations of a purpose, consciousness, knowledge and will. This indicates the necessary existence of an All-Powerful, Self-Subsistent, All-Sustaining One, Who gives life and takes it. Life is a simple and unified or uniform phenomenon. Contrary to the principle of a rotten philosophy that only a single entity issues from something one and unified [suggesting that every different thing needs a different origin], something one and unified (like life) issues only from something one and unified or uniform. So, the creator of life is one and indivisible.

All these five truths, articles 21-25, which make a composition like the seven colors in the light of the sun or the concentric circles, clearly indicate that this universe has a Lord. They also indicate that He is the All-Powerful, the All-Knowing, the All-Wise, the All-Munificent, the All-Compassionate, the All-Merciful, the All-Providing, the All-Living, the Self-Subsistent and All-Sustaining, One qualified by the attributes of perfection. These five truths together open a window on the light of Islam together with submission to Prophethood and the light of belief that He is God, One and Necessarily Existent. In the language of the light composed of these truths, the universe bears witness that *God, there is no god but He.*

26. The grace observed throughout the universe making everything graceful indicates the necessary existence of the One to Whom grace is essential.

27. The innocent beauty on the cheeks of the universe signifies the necessary existence of the One with an absolute beauty.

28. The true love felt by the universe deeply in heart is a sign of the Truly-Beloved One.

29. The attraction and ecstasy felt by the universe demonstrate most profoundly the center of attraction towards which everything is attracted.

30. What we hear from all perfected people who describe their observations to us is that the whole of the creation is but a shadow of the light of the Single Being of Unity.

These five truths (26-30) necessarily point to the fact that the universe has a Lord, necessarily existent and qualified by the attributes of Majesty, Beauty and Perfection. In the language of these five truths, the universe testifies that *God, there is no god but He.*

31. Besides the species as a whole, we see each member of the species specifically disposed for certain benefits and purposes. This evidently points to the necessary existence of an All-Wise Disposer or Agent, as an act cannot be without its doer nor can the thing done or a part of it be the doer of itself.

32. Continuous changes are observed in the lives of plants and animals for certain benefits, which indicates the necessary existence of a Master Who directs them.

33. Again, continuous purposeful transformations are observed in the lives of plants and animals, either of each member of them or their species as a whole. This also points to the necessary existence of a Wise Master.

34. The alternation of day and night in the sphere of the earth for many purposes and benefits is another sign of the necessary existence of an Agent Who does whatever He wills.

35. An act of ordering cannot be without an orderer, and

the thing ordered and the order itself cannot be the doer of this act that requires consciousness. The order and arrangement made throughout the universe to make each thing attain its particular level of perfection, and to make the creation as a whole attain to its final point of perfection, testify to the necessary existence of an All-Powerful One, Self-Subsistent and Sustaining. Is it possible that a nightingale has clothed itself in its elegant, ornamented body? Is it conceivable that the earth itself has woven its so richly decorated dress?

Like the colors in the light of the sun or concentric circles, these five acts of disposing, changing, transforming, alternating, and ordering obviously show that this universe has a Master. They show He Who disposes it is wise, efficient, powerful, self-subsistent and sustaining, One Who does whatever He wills and is possessed of attributes of perfection. In the language of these acts, as if by five mouths, the universe announces that *God, there is no god but He.*

36.   The universe has a beginning; whether as a whole or in parts, it came into existence within time. While there were probabilities of infinite number as to how and of what properties it might be, it took its present form, which is one of perfect order, harmony and balance. This obviously demonstrates the necessary existence of One with free choice, One Who is All-Knowing, All-Wise and All-Powerful.

37.   Everything in the universe, whether big or small or a whole or a part, is in endless need with respect to sustenance and survival, and if it is a conscious living being, it has also spiritual and intellectual needs. Despite the inability of each to satisfy even the most insignificant of its needs, the needs of everything are gratified just on time and from whence it did not reckon. This necessarily points to the existence of a Lord Sustaining, Providing, Munificent, Merciful and Compassionate.

38.   Everything in the universe, big or small, a whole or a part, is in infinite destitution and unable to procure the necessities of its life. However, everything is provided in exact measures with whatever it needs to survive. This necessarily indi-

cates the existence of One Compassionate, Munificent, giving freely, All-Loving and All-Aware [of even the least needs of the least creature].

39. Despite their essential and extreme poverty, things like trees and earth, while appearing utterly dead and dried up in winter, display signs of vigor and power in spring. This indicates the necessary existence of One absolutely Powerful, in relation to Whose Power the minutest particles and the largest suns are equal.

40. Despite its essential poverty, as is displayed by the dried earth which becomes the source of provision for living creatures, the universe shows signs of absolute richness. This points to the necessary existence of One absolutely Rich. The sun and trees are only some "cells" of His treasures of mercy, and water and light are only two "streams" originating in His ocean of compassion.

41. Everything in the universe is essentially dead. The "lights" of life that all living creatures disseminate demonstrate the necessary existence of One All-Living and Self-Subsistent, One Who gives life and takes it.

42. Nothing in the universe has consciousness of its own.[5] Together with the powers of seeing and hearing, the encompassing consciousness which conscious living beings display shows the necessary existence of One All-Knowing and All-Aware (of everything).

43. The continuous, orderly changes and decay which everything, especially every living thing suffers, point to the necessary existence of One making changes but Himself Permanent and not changing.

44. We observe that those living, conscious beings who perform their duties of worship get the precisely weighed reward

5. Consider a human embryo, while a lump of flesh and bones, how it enters a stage of development in which it will acquire life and consciousness. It would be ridiculous to claim that it is the embryo itself or nature or certain biological laws with nominal existence only, which are all ignorant, unconscious and powerless, that equip the embryo with life and consciousness. (Tr.)

of worship and, attaining higher spiritual ranks, can get in some sort of touch with the inhabitants of invisible realms. The imprints of their worship are to be discerned in their lives, their manners and even on their faces. This indicates the necessary existence of One Who alone deserves worship.

45.   The glorification of the universe, whether in words or in acts, points to the necessary existence of One Whom *whatever is in the heavens and on earth glorifies.*[6] The testimony of "natural disposition" or actions is irrefutable. Therefore, how can the testimony of all beings through their dispositions, functions, lives and physical compositions to the necessary existence of Him Whom *whatever is in the heavens and on earth glorifies,* be refuted?

46.   The prayers and supplications that living creatures do [verbally or actually or in the language of neediness and helplessness] are answered or accepted and usually yield desired results.This indicates the necessary existence of One Who answers the supplication of the helpless when they supplicate to Him.

47.   The afflicted seek refuge consciously or unconsciously in their "unknown" Protector or their Creator. This testifies to the necessary existence of the Refuge of the Afflicted and Fearful, the Helper of those who seek help.

48.   Perfected people who penetrate the inner reality of existence and are based on their intuitions, spiritual experiences and observations, are all agreed that whatever exists contained in time and space is but a shadow of the lights of the "Eternal Sun" and testifies to Its necessary existence.

49.   [Despite their lifelessness, ignorance and unconsciousness,] inanimate objects, especially atoms and particles smaller than atoms serve very comprehensive, conscious and universal purposes. It is as obvious as if seen with the naked eye that the comprehensive movements or acts exhibited by them as the result of the manifestations of the Names on them originate from the rank of the Necessary Existence and Unity, not from the rank of contingency. This bears witness to the necessary exis-

---

6. *al-Hashr,* 59.24.

tence of a Holy One Who employs all things and is called by the Names manifested on them.

50.   [Those who refuse to admit the existence of a Divine Being as the sole Creator of all things, have all differed in explaining the origin of existence and life.] The Qur'an proclaims *Flee to God*[7] and *Assuredly in the remembrance of God do hearts find peace and tranquility*[8] and *Unto God all things are brought back.*[9] Only those who have acknowledged the truth of the such Divine proclamations have been able to find relief from the difficulties, bewilderment and insoluble problems arising from attributing existence to itself or to nature or to material causes. It is only by attributing existence to the Creator's Power that all difficulties and problems are easily solved, and that minds and hearts find peace. Truly, there is no creative agent other than God.

51.   In the universe everything is measured in exact proportions. [Also, most simply, as almost everyone has had some glimpses or clues of the future in dreams,] a universal Destiny, which pre-determined everything, prevails in the whole of the universe, [a fact which negates chance completely. Again, all seeds or fruit stones including the fully-grown state of plants or trees also point to that universal Destiny.] Because of the all-inclusive Destiny, every thing is perfectly ordered and serves pre-determined and evident purposes in accordance with which it has been given form and characteristics and endowed with necessary capacities. If you need an example, look at your body with all its lines and your hands with all their fingers. They tell you that they have been built and shaped according to the purposes they must serve and therefore signify the Destiny that has determined those purposes and their structure. According to the plan of the Destiny, the Power puts into "writing" the meanings established and kept by the Knowledge. The Destiny which has pre-planned all things and the Destiny which records the life-histories of all things indicate the necessary existence of

---

7. *al-Dhariyat,* 51.50.
8. *al-Ra'd,* 13.28.
9. *al-Fatir,* 35.4.

Him, the pen of Whose Destiny and Decree have drawn the outlines of all things.

52.   The comprehensive capacities with which man is endowed suggest that man is the fruit of the tree of creation and therefore the most perfect of creation. On account of one aspect of his nature, he is inclined or turned to non-existence, which is the dark face of the world. However, man's comprehensive capacity to offer worship implies that he has not been created to go into eternal non-existence. Rather, he must turn himself from darkness to light, from non-existence or eternal extinction to existence, from ephemerality to permanence, from the created to the Creator. Worship is like a chain connecting the beginning to the end in creation. The "natural" disposition of man thus bears witness to the necessary existence of Him Who has created the universe with whatever is in it to make himself known, Who has created men and jinn so that they should worship Him.

53.   In creation there are the stations of contingency, multiplication and being effected. [That is, whatever is created is contingent, its existence is not necessary and absolute; it is not unique or peerless, and it is something acted upon.] This certainly requires the position of necessity, oneness and agency. That is, there must be One Whose existence is absolutely necessary, Who is Himself unique, peerless and unitary, and Who is active.

54.   We observe in the universe that all things are in continuous movement each toward its particular point of perfection, and when they reach perfection, they stop moving and acquire stability and steadiness. Perfection requires stability and constancy. The existence of existence is by perfection and the perfection of perfection is by constancy. [That is, a thing exists truly only after attaining perfection and the true perfection of a thing lies in its continuing to be perfect.] So, the One Who is necessarily existent is absolutely perfect and all the perfections shared by contingent beings are but a shadow of the manifestations of the lights of His Perfection. This testifies that surely God is the Absolutely Perfect One both in His Divine Essence and His Attributes and acts.

55. The interior of something is much subtler and displays much greater artistry than its exterior. This points to the fact that its Maker is not distant from it. Also, the maintenance of the exact balance and proportions between it and other things indicates that its Maker is not contained in it. When we view a thing in respect of itself, its very being, we conclude that its Maker is All-Knowing and All-Wise. When we view it with respect to its relations with other things, we judge that its Maker is All-Hearing and All-Seeing, One Who sees all things from above and fashions them and regulates their relationships for certain purposes. This truth indicates the necessary existence of the Maker Who is not contained in the universe, nor distant or excluded from it.[10] He is the Most Inward of the inward, as He is the Most High of the high. He sees one thing at the same time as He sees all things.

The truths so far mentioned in articles 36-55 form a single, composite truth like the colors of a rainbow or concentric circles. They are radiant signs which point to the fact that surely this universe has an Owner, Ruler and Sustainer, Whose existence is absolutely necessary and Who is All-Knowing, All-Wise, All-Powerful, All-Merciful, All-Compassionate, All-Providing, All-Munificent, All-Wealthy, All-Living, Self-Subsistent, All-Aware, Ever-Lasting, Permanent, and deserving worship. He is One Who does whatever He wills, One Whom whatever is in the heavens and earth glorifies, Who answers the helpless when they supplicate to Him, Who is the refuge of those in fear, and the helper of those who ask Him for help. This universe is but a shadow of His lights and the manifestations of His Names and the imprints or works of His acts. He is the One in Whose remembrance hearts find peace and tranquility, unto Whom affairs are brought back, Who has created men and jinn only that they should worship Him, Who has ordered the universe through the laws of His Destiny and Decree. He is necessarily

10. By His Essence or Divine Being, He is not contained either in time or space. However, through the manifestations of His Names and Attributes, He is everywhere, nearer to everything than itself, as the sun places itself in the pupils of your eyes and penetrates your body through its light and heat.

existent and One, Unique, and He is absolutely perfect both in His Essence and His Attributes and acts. He is the All-Subtle, the All-Aware, the All-Hearing, the All-Seeing.

Through their lights they show the light of Islam, together with the necessity of submission to Prophethood which leads to believing that He is God, Whose existence is absolutely necessary, Who is One and Single. All these truths form a language in which the universe announces that *God, there is no god but He*.

Know that the pillar of belief that *God, there is no god but He*, establishes that there is no power and strength except with God.

Again, know that through all the proofs discussed, the belief that *God, there is no god but He*, requires believing that Muhammad is the Messenger of God. Believing in the Messengership of Muhammad, upon him be peace and blessings, necessarily includes the other five pillars of faith and, like a mirror, reflects the Attributes of God Almighty. For this reason, in the balance of faith, the belief that *Muhammad is the Messenger of God* weighs equally with the belief that *there is no god but God*. This is so because Prophethood has a universal, all-encompassing position by virtue of being the mirror reflecting the Attributes of God as the Ruler and Sustainer of the universe. The relation of sainthood to Prophethood is like the relation of God's being the Lord of the Worlds to His being the Lord of one single person, or like the relation of God's Supreme Throne to the heart of a believer. Or it is like the relation of the Ascension of the Prophet from the earth to the realms beyond all heavens to the "ascension" of a believer if he can realize it in his prostrations in prayer.

A note

Know that the point we have so far discussed is like a center around which we have drawn a circle through the arguments we have put forward. Each point on the circumference looks toward the center and between the points there is a solidarity that removes the weakness of some among them. The whole of the arguments produce a conviction which adds to the light of Islam and contributes to submission to Prophethood and then to faith. The arguments are sources from which this conviction originates, and as pointed out above, the weakness in some of them does not harm the strength of the conviction. Even if the solidarity among the arguments does not remove the weakness of some, it still maintains them as arguments notwithstanding that each may not be able to remain an independent argument as forceful as to prove the point discussed. Even if the weakness of some may cause them to lose their validity as arguments, this does not harm the completeness or integrity of the circle; it may only cause it to be smaller.

Supposing all the arguments were false, still this would not harm the truth of the point discussed and could not shake the firm belief in Prophethood and extinguish the light of faith. For there are innumerable other arguments supporting the truth of Islam, which is based on God's existence and Unity, and corroborating Prophethood and the Prophethood of Muhammad, upon him be peace and blessings.

It is a sign of a disease of the mind, or delusion by the evil-commanding self, to expect that each argument should be as forceful and convincing as all the arguments taken together. Such an expectation increases the disease or delusion and paves the way to denial and unbelief. May God save us from both! In order not to fall into such a delusion, if the argument through which we look at the point discussed seems to us so weak as to arouse doubts in us, we should refer to the arguments as a whole and consider them from the viewpoint of the result to be filtered from them.

Know that among the arguments are those like water and those like air and still others like light. For this reason, we should consider them with a comprehensive viewpoint and careful discernment so that they do not slip through our fingers.

Know that in order to have knowledge of its life, benefits and degree of strength, an elaborate, fruit-bearing tree is viewed in two ways: one is from its roots upwards, the other, from its fruits downwards. The first way is better and leads to correct conclusions, while the second is defective and leads to misconceptions [especially as a tree may not yield good fruits every year due to particular external factors].

In the same way, the tree of Islam is rooted in the heavens, while its branches are spread out throughout the world of multiplicity. In order to have knowledge of it, we can approach it from two viewpoints and there are two ways into its sphere:

The first viewpoint is that we view it from its roots. If we succeed in doing so properly, we will inevitably see that it originates in a massive pool whose source is perfectly pure: the Divine Revelation. The pool continuously increases (in "water") through the "signs" joining it from the outer world and the inner world of human beings. Its fruits derive their "nourishment" from this "pool." To prove the life of a single fruit, it is enough to establish the fruitfulness and vigor of the tree, as there is a basic connection between the roots and each fruit. However, the disappearance of a fruit does not establish the unproductivity of the tree. The source from which the tree derives vigor is a guarantee of the maintenance of its life. If the one who holds this viewpoint sees a dead fruit in the tree, he will attribute it to external factors. This viewpoint is the sound and correct one. May God provide us with it and hold us firmly to it.

The second viewpoint is the origin of misguidance and insurmountable difficulties. The one who holds this viewpoint views the tree from its fruits and with the intention of criticizing it. Since there is not the same connection among the fruits as that between the roots of the tree and each of its fruits, he has to examine and taste the fruits one by one in order to judge the tree. Also, he cannot see the coming of life to fruits from the roots of the tree. If he sees a dead fruit, he may conclude that the tree is lifeless. May God save us from holding such a viewpoint.

***

Conclusion

About four diseases

The first disease: *Despair*

Know that when you are fearful of the punishment of Hell and unable to perform your duty of servanthood to God, you desire the non-existence of that punishment and begin to look for an argument against it. When you see signs that seem to you capable of serving such an argument, devils get hold of you and recruit you in their legions. [If you are in such a state,] give a sincere and attentive ear to the following Qur'anic verse:

> Report [to them what I say]: "O My servants who have transgressed against their own selves! Do not despair of God's Mercy. Surely God forgives all sins; for He is the All-Forgiving, the Most Compassionate."[11]

The second disease: *Self-admiration (because of one's good deeds)*

Truly, o self, when in despair you are looking for a support against the punishment of Hell, you catch sight of your good deeds and deviate into self-admiration because of them. However, you have no right at all to appropriate them to yourself. Think over this!

O self! This body in which you dwell is not your own handiwork that you can claim ownership of it. Nor is it something that you found on the way so that you take possession of it. Again, it is neither the result of blind chance nor the product of lifeless causes that you can claim to own it. Rather, through its amazing design and the marvels of art it exhibits, this body of yours testifies that it is the handiwork of an All-Wise Maker, Who looks after it continually.

---

11. *al-Zumar*, 39.53.

Do you not see that your part in the operations of your body is hardly one in a million? Again, do you not see that although you are the noblest of causes, one having the most comprehensive will-power among creation, your part in your acts like eating and speaking which you do out of free will is but one in a hundred? Also, despite its apparent comprehensiveness, the area in which you are allowed to act freely is very narrow. You have faculties such as imagination that cannot be controlled by reason. How, then, can you consider them to be within the realm of your free will and be proud of them?

Furthermore, many things take place either against or in favor of you. Although you are unaware of many of them, they evidently serve many deliberate purposes. This means that the One Who causes them to take place is an All-Hearing, All-Seeing One of infinite consciousness. It is neither you nor deaf and blind causes which bring them about. So, you must give up claiming to own yourself and your good deeds. You should know that what falls to your share is only faults and defects. That is, by misusing your free will, you change the quality of the virtues pouring into the world as the result of incessant manifestations of the Divine Perfections. And your body, your dwelling place, is a loan entrusted to you gratis, and you are a guest in it. Your good deeds are therefore gifts to you, [which the Almighty enables you to do,] but your sins and evils are the products of your misuse of your will power. Therefore say: *His is the ownership (of all things in the universe) and to Him is all praise, and there is no power and strength except with Him.*

The third disease: *Vanity*

Because of the disease of vanity or conceit, you have a "distant view" of the preceding virtuous and illustrious great persons and belittle them. This causes you to be deprived of the blessing of their good deeds and virtues and prevents you from benefiting from them. You suffer illusions about them and hold an ill opinion of them. Therefore, view them closely and see how in forty days they accomplished what you could not accomplish in forty years.

The fourth disease: *Suspicion*

Because of your disease of suspicion of others, you think others suffer the same defects and vices that you have. This causes you to condemn everyone and blind yourself to the virtues of the illustrious ones among both the present and past generations, from whom you should benefit. Thus, you make daylight into night for yourself.

O God! Save us from despair, suspicion, self-admiration and conceit. Amen.

***

The Four Significant Truths

I witnessed in my intellectual and spiritual journey

In my (intellectual and spiritual) journey underground, I witnessed the following truths:

The first truth

Know O friend! Heedlessness or indifference to the True Owner (of creation), the All-Glorified and Majestic, causes one to claim absolute independence and ownership of one's self. Supposing himself to absolutely own his self, a person imagines a realm of dominion for himself and then, comparing other people and material causes to himself, he shares the rest of God's property or dominion among them. However, the Almighty has given him his (human) ego so that, taking it as a measure or means of comparison, he might comprehend the attributes of Divinity.[12] But he abuses his powers or faculties and attempts to oppose the Divine Commandments and contend against the Destiny and Decree of his Creator.

O you who are accompanying me in my journey! This truth has become manifest to me in all its dimensions as follows:

People can learn subtle truths, particularly abstract ones, through comparisons and infinite things can be perceived by imagining limits to them. So, man has been given the "ego," which is rooted in him through the "water" of heedlessness or indifference [to the True Owner of creation], only as a point of comparison. It allows him to perceive the Attributes of the Creator, Who has no partners at all, none to contend against Him either in His Sovereignty or Lordship or Divinity.

12. For example, starting from his being equipped with the limited powers of seeing, hearing and learning, he may conclude that his Creator must be the All-Seeing, the All-Hearing and the All-Knowing. Again, his poverty, helplessness and mortality may lead him to discover that the Creator is the Absolutely Wealthy, Powerful and Permanent. (Tr.)

The ego or selfhood is not the owner of either itself or its body. Nor is its body something found on the way, nor the result of chance, nor self-formed. Rather, it is an extremely complex, intricate and amazing Divine machine or factory in which the Pen of Divine Power continuously works in the hand of Destiny and Decree.

O selfhood! Give up this false claim. Submit the "property" to its owner and be a reliable trustee in fulfilling your responsibility towards it—the body entrusted to you. For when you attribute to yourself even the (ownership of) a single particle, then you are on the way to sharing out the property of God to your fellow beings and then to material causes. [Here lie the roots of many kinds of associating partners with God in the creation and rule of the universe.]

O selfhood! You are not the owner of yourself so that you can be the maker or creator of the body in which you dwell. Nor have material causes made it so that they claim to own it. How can you be a maker seeing that basically you are not different from a sheep. [It is clear that both of you have been made of the same elements and do not have the least part in your coming into existence.] How can a sheep claim that it is the maker of its body? And there is a close affinity between a sheep and a pomegranate. How can the dye of the pomegranate be the maker of its seeds? How can a fruit placed at the top of a tree be the creator of its tree? If a sheep is the maker of itself, if a pomegranate is the creator of its tree, then you can be the owner of yourself.

What is true is that any creature announces most loudly: "I am something an All-Knowing, All-Wise, All-Hearing and All-Seeing One has made in accordance with precise measures." All material causes are blind, deaf and lifeless. Their coming together and intermingling with one another increase them only in blindness and deafness; for the more of the blind and deaf there are, the more is their blindness and deafness. Consider that the preparation of a certain medicine requires proficiency in the sciences of medicine and pharmacology and knowing in what measures and amounts its ingredients should be mixed. Supposing there are the ingredients of a certain medicine each in a certain bottle placed on a roof. A wind blows and makes the bottles topple down, resulting in the substances in the bottles spilling and mixing with one another. Do you regard it possible that the required medicine could be formed by itself or by chance? Materialists and naturalists attribute creation either to itself or to causes or to nature. If you judge that the production of the required medicine is possible as in the example we have just given, you can claim that creation is either self-created or the product of chance and causes. Besides, the beginning of creation and the origin of things and life are other awesome questions to be answered. Anyway, the attribution of creation to other than an All-Knowing, All-Wise and All-Powerful Creator with an absolute Will is no more than sheer, arrogant folly.

The second truth

Know, o evil-commanding self! You have a world particular to yourself, which is very spacious and founded upon your aspirations, relationships and needs. The main pillar of that world is your life. However, this pillar is being nibbled by maggots— time, events and diseases incessantly corrode it. Therefore, your world is unsound and subject to decay. It may collapse at any time. And your body is not long-lasting; it is not composed of iron or rock, rather it is composed of flesh, bones and blood, ready to disintegrate at any time. Its decomposition means the destruction of your world on you. Look back at the past, it is a large grave containing the ruined worlds of the dead. The future is another similar grave waiting to be filled. Now you are between two large graves. Yesterday became the grave of my father and tomorrow will be that of mine, which means I am between two graves. Although the world we live in is one, it contains as many worlds as the number of the people living in it. One's death means the end of one's world or one's doom.

The third truth

I have seen this world with all its pleasures as a heavy burden.

No one except those with corrupted spirit is contented with it. Rather than suffering from dependence on almost the whole of the universe, being needy of all means and causes and appealing to numerous contending deaf and mute and blind masters, one should seek refuge in a single, All-Hearing and Seeing Master. If you place your trust in Him, He is sufficient for you.

The fourth truth

Know o ego! The scientific inventions woven around your head, the lines of conscious artistry connected to you, and the things put in your hands stretched out in neediness—all this demonstrates that your Creator, Maker and Helper hears the sighs of your destitution and your cries for help. Having mercy on you, He undertakes to gratify all your needs. Seeing that that Creator and Maker answers the calls for help of your tiniest cells, why should He—the All-Hearing, the All-Seeing—not answer your call and help you?

O spacious cell called ego or selfhood, which is built up of lesser cells! Say: "O God! O Lord! O my Creator! O my Fashioner! O my Owner! O my Master! O my Guardian! Yours is the dominion (of all things) and to You is all praise! I am a guest in this body, a property of Yours which You have entrusted to me."

O selfhood! Why do you claim to own a thing that you will never be able to own? Give up this false claim, which throws you into acute pains. Consider the emotions of pity and affection, which are among the exhilarating embellishments of the spirit: if they were left to your pretended ownership, they would harm the spirit as a torment for it.

For example, the misfortunes and calamities striking you or others would cause you to remain in continual pains and go so far as to blame the Destiny for them. However, when you see a soldier working directly under the king having lost his mount or whose residence has been burnt down by mistake, you do not feel much pity for him. If you consider that both the mount and residence belong to the king himself, you will see that their disappearance does not cause significant decrease in the king's property. Nor does it become a cause of much grief to the soldier—indeed, inasmuch as the soldier is poor, it is highly probable that out of pity the king compensates his losses with something better. In the same way, God is the All-Compassionate and always treats His servants out of utmost compassion. Therefore, compassion for creatures as creatures of God exhilarates the spirit. By contrast, the feeling of pity arising from the supposition that everything owns itself, continually suffocates and distresses the spirit.

One with a sound viewpoint based on belief in the Divine Unity sees every living being in his disposition of his body like a hired captain on a ship of the king who disposes his property as he wills. Such a viewpoint does not allow one to see an ant or a honeybee as contending with attacking causes. Rather, according to it, the ant and honeybee dispose one an earthly "vehicle", the other an "aircraft," the reins of which are in the hands of the Power of an All-Powerful One. Causes do not have much weight in the sight of either the ant or the honeybee, which depend on the True Owner (of all things).

By uttering *Surely we are God's and surely we are returning to Him*,[13] when struck by a misfortune, one means: All property is God's and I am under His command, journeying to Him. My relation with my body, which is His property, is like the relation of a soldier holding in his hand something belonging to the king. When robbers attack him to take what is in his hand, the soldier reacts: "Surely I am responsible for guarding this property entrusted to me. However, I am unable to guard it now. Like this property, I also belong to the king and am going to him." When one with such a viewpoint sees a fellow struck with misfortune or oneself suffers a misfortune, one is relieved of a continual distress. Otherwise, one is constantly weighed down with pains and distress.

---

13. *al-Baqara*, 2.156.

The second chapter

This is about [the phrase glorifying God]:

Subḥan Allah *(Glory be to God)*.

In the Name of God, the Merciful, the Compassionate.

Glory be to God, the Absolutely Powerful through the Power essential to His being as God, and the Absolutely Wealthy, and free and exempt from impotence and neediness.

Glory be to God, the Absolutely Perfect in His Being, Attributes and acts, and free and exempt from faults and defects. The perfections of His works point to the perfection of His acts, which, in turn, points to the perfection of His Names. The perfection of His Names indicates the perfection of His Attributes, which testifies to the perfection of His Essence, may His Majesty be exalted. All perfections and beauties in the universe are but a dim shadow in comparison with His Perfection and Beauty. All people of spiritual experience and discovery and those who unveil hidden truths in creation are unanimously agreed on the fact that the whole of the creation is a shadow of the lights of the Necessarily Existent Being.

Glory be to God, the One and Single, and free and exempt from having partners. He has no partners, either in His dominion, as the unity of the work points to the unity of its doer, or in His being the Lord and Sustainer, as is indicated by the unity of the Pen ["writing" on the "page" of time and space]. Nor does He have partners in His Divinity, as Divinity requires absolute independence and being unique and peerless.

Glory be to God, the All-Powerful and beginningless, and free and exempt from having helpers and ministers, as having helpers and ministers would mean putting limits on the infinite, perfect Power by means of finite contingencies.

Glory be to God, eternal and beginningless, and free and exempt from having likes and equals.

Glory be to God, the Necessarily Existent One, and free and exempt from necessities pertaining to contingencies.

Glory be to God, for Whom is the highest comparison in the heavens and earth,[14] and He is the All-Mighty, the All-Wise, and is free and exempt from the qualities that those having false beliefs attribute to Him or conceive of with respect to Him. He is also free and exempt from all defects. Faults and defects are particular to contingent mortals, so how could they be attributed to the Necessarily Existent Being?

Glory be to the Perpetual, Eternal One, free and exempt from all kinds of changing and alteration, as they are particular to contingent, created beings and contrary to His absolutely necessary existence and absolute Oneness.

Glory be to the Creator of all creation and space, free and exempt from division and being contained in space, as they are incompatible with the absolute independence essential to the Divine Being.

Glory be to the Eternal, Permanent One, free and exempt from having a beginning and end.

Glory be to the Necessarily Existent Being, free and exempt from whatever is not fitting for Him like incarnation and union.[15] What relation can earth or something of earth have with the Lord of all those who claim lordship? Being limited means being dominated and attribution of begetting to God means placing limits on Him. He is absolutely free and exempt from such false beliefs and conceptions, and far exalted above what wrongdoers and transgressors say.

Glory be to God, Whom all angels and all that is in the heavens and earth glorify through what the Pen of Destiny has inscribed on their foreheads.

---

14. Since God Almighty is absolutely infinite and therefore it is impossible to perceive His Essence, in order that we could have some knowledge and understanding of His Attributes, He usually speaks in parables and similitudes or comparisons. (Tr.)

15. Incarnation is the false belief that God takes a body in human form. Union is another false belief that by being united with God in spirit, a man becomes god but appears in human form. (Tr.)

The third chapter

This is about [the phrase in praise of God]:

aſ-ħamðu ſi-ſſaħ *(All praise be to God)*

In the Name of God, the Merciful, the Compassionate.

All praise be to God, Whom either verbally or in the languages of their lives and being all creatures and creations praise and exalt by manifesting His Attributes of Perfection. With all their kinds, supports, parts, and particles, and in the languages of their having a beginning and being contingent, in the languages of their neediness and destitution and the purposes they serve, all creatures praise His Majesty. In the languages of the artistry, orderliness, balance, firmness and perfections they display, and in the acts of worship and glorification they do, all creations recite His Attributes of Majesty. They affirm that surely He is God, Necessarily Existent, Beginningless, Perpetual, Eternal, One and Single, Peerless, Eternally Besought-of-All, and the All-Mighty, the All-Compelling, the Proud, the All-Overwhelming... They also praise Him with His Attributes of Beauty and Grace and say: He is our Creator, All-Merciful, All-Compassionate, All-Providing, All-Munificent, All-Generous, All-Loving, All-Diffusing (of blessings), All-Gracious, All-Subtle, All-Favoring, All-Beautiful... Again, they mention Him with His Attributes of Perfection and say: He is Our Creator and Owner, All-Living, Self-Subsistent, All-Sustaining, All-Knowing, All-Wise, All-Powerful, All-Willing, All-Hearing, All-Seeing, All-Speaking, All-Witnessing... Further, they recite His Beautiful Names manifested in the universe.

All praise be to God, Whom the universe with all that is in it praises, glorifies and exalts by manifesting His Attributes of Perfection. With all its chapters, sections, pages, lines, sentences and letters, and with the purposes it serves and the artistry and design it displays, this greatest book—the universe—is a whole in itself. All the things and beings in it are mirrors of different sorts reflecting the "lightning" of His Attributes of Majesty, the flashes of His Attributes of Grace and Beauty, the gleams of His Attributes of Perfection and the rays of His Beautiful Names.

All praise be to God for the existence He bestows on us— existence is pure good—and for the blessing of life by which existence is perfected, and for the blessing of faith, which is the essence of true life and by which life attains perfection.

All praise be to God for the light of faith, which removes darkness from around us and illuminates the outer world as well as our inner worlds. Faith is a source of light which consists in the six lights—the six pillars of belief—and from which originate the rays of the sun of knowledge of the Eternal Sovereign.

All praise be to God for belief in God, for through it the spirit is delivered from the darkness of all sorts of annihilation, from the feeling of utter desolation in the universe and from seeing all things in existence as singing dirges, and from innumerable other destructive sentiments.

All praise be to God for the light of faith, which shows us Refuge, Favoring, Munificence, Love, Pity, and Compassion. Faith unveils the eternal life for us and shows it to us with all its brilliance and brings us the good tidings of eternal happiness. It offers us a support and source of help, teaches us on Whom we should rely and from Whom we should ask help, and lifts the veil of lamentation from the face of the mercy enveloping the whole of creation. Faith also removes the pains of separation from lawful pleasures by comparing the two worlds and enables the continuation of favors and blessings by showing the everlasting tree of favors.

Also, the light of faith shows the true nature of all things and states supposed as controversial, strange, dead and fearful, and makes clear that they are all friendly, familiar, living and amicable.

Again, this light embraces all the worlds and the two realms, this one and the next, replete with the gifts of Mercy for all believers without one giving the other any trouble to benefit from them with all their senses, feelings and faculties. Therefore, every believer must say: "All praise be to God for whatever He has created," and approve of and be satisfied with no one in whose grasp of power the whole of creation is not, as the lord and master. Every believer must set his heart on no one other than Him as one deserving of worship and love and the object or goal of life.

All praise be to the Lord of the Worlds for His "mercy" for the worlds, which is our master Muhammad, upon him be peace and blessings. For through him and his Messengership did the lights of the conception of Divinity, which had been extinguished under the thick veil of corrupted philosophies and religions, rekindle and acquire stability and constancy. It is again through his Messengership that whatever is pleasing to the Lord of the Worlds became clear for mankind. Also, humanity has been guided through him to faith, which is the light of creation and existence.

All praise be to God for the blessing of Islam, which contains whatever is pleasing to the Lord of the Worlds. Islam has shown us what pleases Him and what our Lord, the Lord of the Worlds and the Lord of the heavens and earth, wills and approves.

All praise be to God for the light of faith which derives strength from *In the Name of God, the Merciful, the Compassionate*. The one who praises should turn his attention from the bounty to the act of giving bounties so that he may perceive that the Giver of bounties sees him and is nearer to him than himself and makes Himself known through giving bounties and loved through favoring. When a man becomes conscious of His seeking to make Himself known and loved, he feels compelled to be thankful to Him.

The fourth chapter

This is about the phrase exalting God:

Allahu akbar (*God is the Greatest*)

and it consists of two sections. The first section is very brief, while the second is in full detail.

The first section

In the Name of God, the Merciful, the Compassionate.

God is the Greatest, He is incomparably greater than all things, for He is the All-Powerful, Who is powerful over all things through an infinite power, in relation to which minute particles and stars, parts and wholes, individuals and species are easy to the same degree. Your creation and your raising from the dead are but as the creation and raising of a single soul.[16] Truly, a giant star, a whole and a species are not more difficult to create than a minute particle, a part and an individual .

God is the Greatest, for He is the All-Knowing, Who knows all things through a limitless knowledge, which is essential to God as the Divine Being. Nothing can escape Him, as He is present everywhere. The comprehensive wisdom, all-embracing favoring, all-encompassing consciousness, the decrees putting all things in exact order, fruitful ordinances and measurements, appointed hours, regular provision, mercy of universal diversity, firm and magnificent organization, and the exact care, which are witnessed throughout the universe, testify to the all-encom-passing Knowledge of the Almighty: *Should He Who creates not know?*[17]

God is the Greatest, for His Will includes all things. While it was infinitely probable for the universe with whatever is in it to

---

16. *Luqman*, 31.28.
17. *al-Mulk*, 67.14.

take a certain form, it was put in the present order in accordance with exact measures. Like a tree having leaves, blossoms and fruits, all well-ordered creatures were created of simple, inanimate elements. All this bears witness to the all-encompassing Will of the Almighty and demonstrates that whatever He wills is, and whatever He does not will is not, exalted be His Majesty.

God is the Greatest. If you ask why He is so and Who He is, the answer will be: He is the Eternal "Sun." This universe is but a shadow of His lights, manifestations of His Names and the imprints of His acts.

God is the Greatest; He is incomparably greater than all things. If you ask why He is so and Who He is, the answer will be: He is the Eternal Sovereign. All of these worlds are at His disposal in absolute dependence on the order and measure He has established, exalted be His Majesty.

God is the Greatest. If you ask why He is so and Who He is, the answer will be: He is the Eternal Ruler. He ordered the universe through the laws of His usual way of acting, the prescripts of His Destiny and Decree, the precepts of His Will and Wisdom, the requirements of His Favoring and Mercy, and the manifestations of His Names and Attributes. What we call laws (of nature) are but descriptions of the manifestations of His Knowledge, Command and Will on all species.

God is the Greatest. If you ask why He is so and Who He is, the answer will be: He is the Eternal Maker, Who has created and founded this macrocosm—the universe—and this microcosm—man. There is His stamp on the foreheads of both, nay, on each part of both.

God is the Greatest. If you ask why He is so and Who He is, the answer will be: He is the Eternal Designer. This universe consists in the lines of the "pen" of His Destiny and Decree, the designs of the "compasses" of His Wisdom, the fruits of the diffusion of His Mercy, the decorations of the "bright hand" of His Favoring, the flowers of the dispensations of His Munificence, and the rays of the manifestations of His Grace.

God is the Greatest. If you ask why He is so and Who He is, the answer will be: He is the Eternally Powerful. This universe consists in the miracles of His Power, which testify that surely He is powerful over all things. Nothing has been able, nor is able, to escape the dominion of His Power, in relation to which a minute particle and the sun are the same.

God is the Greatest. If you ask why He is so and Who He is, the answer will be: He is the Creator, the Originator, and the Fashioner, for Whom are the Beautiful Names. All those heavenly objects are shining proofs of His Divinity and Grandeur and radiating witnesses of His Lordship and Splendor, exalted be His Majesty.

God is the Greatest. If you ask why He is so and Who He is, the answer will be: He is the Creator of all things. He is the Provider of all living beings, the Giver of bounties to all in need of bounty, the Merciful in both worlds—our master Muhammad, upon him be peace and blessings, and Paradise are works of His comprehensive Mercy. He is the Lord and Sustainer of all things, One rearing, training and maintaining all things.

God is the Greatest. If you ask Who He is, the answer will be: He is the Fashioner of all things, One Who has ordered this world and disposes all things.

God is the Greatest, and high exalted above being comprehended by intellects and absolutely free and exempt from incompetence and defects.

God is the Greatest. He is incomparably greater than all things. That is, He is the Greatest, the Most High, the Most Beautiful, the Best because of Himself, and the Most Grand, the Most Majestic by Himself.

A note

These blessed phrases—*Subhan Allah, al-hamdu li-llah, Allahu akbar*—are repeatedly recited after the daily prayers in order to establish their meanings, which support one another, in minds and hearts and confirm them.

For example, you throw a stone into the center of a large pool and as greater and greater circles are formed one after the other, you say, greater... greater... greater... Like this, following the five daily prayers, we repeatedly recite *Subhan Allah, al-hamdu li-llah, Allahu akbar*, to establish and confirm their meanings and obtain the fruits expected of their recitation.

***

Question

What is the meaning of comparing God with creatures by saying *God is the Greatest*, and of what value contingencies are that we say *the One of Necessary Existence is greater than them*? Are there creators or all-compassionate beings other than the Almighty that we describe Him as *the Best of Creators* and *the All-Compassionate of the Compassionate*?

Answer

There is none greater and more exalted than Him, and there can be none better and more beautiful apart from Him, nor can there be, besides Him, any more grand and more majestic. He is essentially greater than whatever minds may conceive of. He should be greater than all that is in your minds and hearts and more important than all your desires and aims. Again, He is too great for the veil of creation to conceal.

As for the phrase, *the Best of Creators*, it means: He is essentially better than the creators conceived in minds as the result of the reflection in them of the attribute of creativity. This is like saying the sun is more radiant than suns, implying that the sun itself is more radiant than its images in mirrors or mirror-like things. Also, He is better than whatever minds may conceive of as a creator. Again, consciously or unconsciously, we may sometimes attribute creativity to material causes or creatures themselves, so *God is the Best of Creators* means that He is the best as creator without being veiled by causes and therefore we must always turn to Him, without considering apparent material causes. Then, such comparisons relate to us and the things we are related to; in essence they do not relate to the Almighty. For example, when we say to a private concerning his particular duty, the king is better and grander, we mean: the part of the king in your duty is greater than those of your immediate superiors.

God is too great for minds to comprehend and for incompetence and defects to touch. He is absolutely perfect in His Essence, Attributes and acts, exalted be His Majesty.

The second section

The ranks of
God is the Greatest

The first rank

In the Name of God, the Merciful, the Compassionate.

Say: "All praise be to God, Who has never taken to Himself a son, and Who has no partner in sovereignty. Nor (needs) He any guardian due to weakness and humiliation, and magnify Him with all magnificence".[18] We believe and we are at Your command. God is the Greatest, greater than all things in power and knowledge. For He is the Fashioner, Who has made man by His Power like the universe and inscribed the universe with the "pen" of His Destiny as He has inscribed man with the same "pen." Like the microcosm—man—this macrocosm—the universe—is something made by His Power, "inscribed" by His Destiny. He has made it a "mosque," while making man the worshipper in it. He has founded the former as an abode, while making the latter as a servant inhabiting it. His art in the former has been manifested as a book, while His coloring of the latter has flourished as speech. His Power in the former displays His Majesty, while His Mercy in the latter arranges His provision. His Majesty in the former bears witness that He is One, while His provision in the latter announces that He is Single. His stamp in the former both on it as a whole and in its parts shows itself in apparent calm-

---

18. *al-Kahf*, 18.111.

ness in never-ending motion, while His seal in the latter is on both the whole of the body and its parts down to its each cell and particle.

Look at His works, all of which are firmly well ordered. There is an absolute order despite absolute abundance, an absolute measure and balance despite absolute speed, and an absolute firmness despite the absolute facility. There is an absolute beauty of art despite absolute heterogeneity, an absolute harmony and correlation despite absolute distance, an absolute distinction despite absolute compositeness, and absolute worth and value despite infinite economy. This obvious quality of existence bears witness for a verifying, sensible one and compels a foolish denying one to admit, that existence belongs to the One Absolutely Powerful, Who is also absolutely All-Knowing.

There is absolute ease in explaining existence by attributing it to One Divine Being, whereas there are insurmountable barriers in the way of attributing it to various origins. If it is attributed to the One Divine Being, the whole of the universe will be as easy to create as a honeybee, and a honeybee, as a fruit. If, by contrast, it is ascribed to multiple origins, the creation of a honeybee will be as difficult as that of the universe as a whole, and the creation of a fruit, as that of all trees in the universe. For with a single movement a single being can produce an effect and deal with a whole. If that effect or treatment is to be expected of multiple beings, it will only be obtained, if it can be at all, with extreme difficulties and after many controversies. You can judge which is much easier or much more difficult: the management of an army by a single commander or the soldiers themselves, the construction of a building by a builder or by the stones themselves, the revolution of many planets around a single sun or vice versa....

When existence is attributed to One Divine Being, the connection between existence and that Being becomes like a boundless power and causes do not have to be of the same power. Also, the effect produced becomes great proportionally to the Being it is attributed to. Otherwise, each cause has to be as infinitely powerful as to originate existence and the effect produced becomes of its own size only.

Also, when all things are attributed to One Divine Being, they do not have to be created from absolute non-existence. Rather, creation means giving external, material existence to things that already exist in knowledge. It is like developing a form reflected in a mirror or putting in words the meaning in mind or by rubbing a substance, making visible a letter written in colorless ink. However, when things are ascribed to themselves or their causes, then they would have to be created from absolute non-existence. This is impossibly difficult, if indeed it is not inconceivable. The facility in the former way makes the existence of things as easy as if it is absolutely necessary for them to be howsoever, and the difficulty in the latter is of the degree of inconceivability. For the existence of a living being requires that the particles to form it spread out in earth, water and air should come together and therefore each has to have a universal knowledge and absolute will. Anything with such knowledge and will would be absolutely independent of and indifferent to admitting any partners. There is not in the universe even the weakest sign of the existence of such things and partners. Again, the creation of the heavens and earth observably requires a perfect, infinite power, which must be independent of having partners. Otherwise, it would require that this power should be limited by a finite power. This is inconceivable because a power that is infinite does not need partners at all, nor is it by any means obliged to admit them. Again, in the universe there are no signs of the existence of partners with that Power.

As this Power does not have any partners, It has also no assistants and ministers at all. Material causes are but a thin veil before the operation of the Eternal Power and do not have any creative affect in the existence of things. The noblest of causes, one equipped with will-power, is man. Yet it is doubtful whether he has even a hundredth part in his acts like eating, speaking and thinking, which he does by his free will. Now man, the noblest of causes and one equipped with a free will, is short of disposing himself, how then can animals, plants and inanimate objects [and the lifeless, blind and deaf laws that only have nominal existence] be partners with the Creator of the heavens and earth in the creation and disposing of things? Obviously, the "envelope" in which the King puts His gifts or the "handkerchief" in which He enwraps His offerings or the "private soldier" by means of whom He sends you His bounties, cannot be partners with Him in His Kingdom. Nature and causes, which are like "soldiers" by means of whom the Absolute Sovereign sends us His bounties or envelopes or chests in which He stores His offerings to us or handkerchiefs in which He wraps His gifts for us, cannot be either partners with Him or means of creative effect in the execution of His commands.

The second rank

God is the greatest, greater than all things in power and knowledge. For He is the Creator, the All-Knowing, the Maker, the All-Wise, the All-Merciful, the All-Compassionate, and all earthly creatures and heavenly objects are manifestly the miracles of the Power of an All-Knowing Creator. All these multi-coloured and decorated plants, and adorned animals of innumerable kinds, distributed throughout the garden of earth, are the wonders of the Art of an All-Wise Maker. Also, all these smiling flowers and bedecked fruits in the parts of this garden are the gifts of the Mercy of an All-Merciful, All-Compassionate One. All of those creatures or objects attest and announce that surely the Creator of these, the Fashioner of those, the Giver of gifts, is powerful over all things, and knows everything, and encompasses all things in mercy and knowledge. In relation to His Power minute particles and stars, and the few and abundant, and the little and great, and the finite and infinite, are all equal. Again, all past events, ordinary or extraordinary, are the miracles of the Art of an All-Wise Maker, which bear witness that that Maker is powerful over all contingencies of the future, that is, He is able to do whatever He wills in the future, whether ordinary or extraordinary, for He is the All-Knowing Creator, the All-Wise and Mighty.

Glory be to Him Who has made the garden of earth an exhibition of the works of His Art, the assembling ground of the products of His Creativity, a place where His Power and Wisdom are manifested, a garden where His Mercy blossoms, the field to be sown for Paradise, and a place where creatures come and depart in a continuous flux according to fixed measures.

Ornamented animals, bedecked birds, fruit-bearing trees, flowering plants—these are all the miracles of His Knowledge, the marvels of His Art, the gifts of His Generosity, the proofs of His Favouring.

The smiling of flowers promising fruits, the singing of birds at the invigorating time of dawn, the splashing drops of rain on the cheeks of flowers, the compassion of mothers for infants—these are all the instances of an All-Loving One making Himself known and an All-Merciful One making Himself loved, and the imprints of the Compassion of an All-Pitying One and the Pitying of a Most Kind One, for jinn and mankind and spirit beings and angels and animals. The seeds and fruits and grains and flowers are all the miracles of Wisdom, the marvels of Art, the gifts of Mercy, the proofs of [Divine] Oneness, and the witnesses of His Bountifulness in the Hereafter. They are truthful witnesses that surely their Creator is powerful over all things and knows everything. And He encompasses all things in mercy, knowledge, creativity, sustaining, making and fashioning. In relation to His Attributes of creating, arranging and maintaining, and of making and fashioning, the sun is like a seed, and the star like a flower, and the earth like a grain. Seeds and fruits are mirrors of [Divine] Unity in the realm of multiplicity, and the signs of Destiny, and the indications of Power. The source of the multiplicity—the universe with whatever is in it—is the realm of Unity. The multiplicity testifies to the oneness of the Creator in originating and fashioning, and ends in Unity pointing out the Wisdom of the Maker in creating and sustaining and maintaining. Wisdom manifests that—as the universal view encompasses and considers all particulars—the Creator of all things considers the particular. For if the particular is, for example, a fruit, obviously it is the purpose for the creation of the tree. Man is the fruit of the universe and the most manifest purpose of the Creator [in creating the universe]. The heart is like a seed or the nucleus [of man] and the brightest mirror of the Maker of creation. It may be concluded from this that man in this universe is the pivot on which the wheel of creation turns, and for the sake of which the universe continuously undergoes destructions, changes, transformations and renewals.

God is the greatest: O Great One! O God, You are One Whose Grandeur, Greatness and Majesty intellects cannot grasp.

All things announce in unison: *there is no god but He*, and continually seek: *O Truth,* and eternally say: *O Living One!*

The third rank

God is the Greatest, greater than all things in power and knowledge. For He is the All-Powerful, the All-Determining, the All-Knowing, the All-Wise, the All-Fashioning, the All-Munificent, the All-Subtle and Favouring, the All-Decorating, the All-Loving, the One Making Himself Known, the All-Merciful, the All-Compassionate, the All-Pitying, the All-Beautiful, the One with Absolute Beauty and Perfection, the Eternal Designer. The truths of the worlds as a whole or in parts, and the truths of creation as a whole or in parts and in existence and maintenance—they all consist in the lines drawn by the "pen" of His Decree and Destiny according to a definite ordering, determining, knowledge and wisdom, and in the designs made by the "compasses" of His Knowledge and Wisdom according to a definite art and fashion. They also consist in the decorations made by the "bright hand" of His Art, Fashioning, Decorating, and Illustrating with favouring and munificence, and in the flowers of His Favouring, Munificence, Making Known and Loving with mercy and bountifulness, and in the fruits of the overflowing of the spring of His Mercy, Bountifulness, Pitying and Affection with grace and perfection. Again, they consist in the radiations of an everlasting Beauty and perpetual Perfection, as is attested by the fact that the mirrors [reflecting those truths—that is, all creatures] are mortal and the reflections are subject to disappearance, while the manifestations of the Beauty are permanent through the passage of seasons, centuries and ages, and conferring bounties continues through days and years despite the mortality of the creatures living on those bounties.

The mortality of mirrors and the decay of creatures despite the perpetual manifestation [of Divine Names, Attributes and acts] in utmost abundance, is a most clear sign and most convincing argument that the manifest Beauty and flowering Perfection do not belong to those on which they are manifested, and a most eloquent explanation and most evident proof of the abstract Beauty and ever-renewed Benevolence, and of the Necessarily Existent and the All-Loving, Permanent One.

A perfect work evidently points to a perfect act. A perfect act necessarily indicates a perfect name and a perfect agent. A perfect name doubtlessly betokens a perfect attribute. A perfect attribute convincingly shows a perfect function or essential capacity. A perfect function or essential capacity certainly demonstrates the perfection of the Being through what is befitting for that Being, Who is the Most Evident Truth.

The fourth rank

His Majesty be exalted: God is the greatest. For He is the All-Just and the source of justice, and the All-Judging, the All-Ruling and and the All-Wise. He has founded the tree of this universe in six days by the principles of His Will and Wisdom, ramified it by the prescripts of His Decree and Destiny, arranged it by the rules of His way of acting, decorated it by the precepts of His Favouring and Mercy, and illuminated it through the manifestations of His Names and Attributes, as is attested by the orderliness and balance in His creation, the decorations of His creatures, and the similarity, proportionateness, mutual assistance and answering among them, and by the firm, conscious artistry in all things which Destiny has determined for each according to its capacity.

The comprehensive wisdom in the ordering of creation, the perfect favouring in its decoration, the all-encompassing mercy in gratifying the needs of creation, the all-inclusive provision in its raising, the amazing life conferred on it to make it the object of its Originator's essential manifestations, the beauties granted to it for certain purposes; the permanence of the manifestations of His Grace on it despite the decay of its individual members; the true love ingrained in its heart for its sole Object of Worship; the attraction it feels towards its Creator; the unanimous agreement of its perfect, conscious members on the Unity of its Originator; the purposeful disposal in its parts; the wise sustaining of its plants and the munificent breeding, nursing and taming of its animals; the perfect order in the changing of its pillars; the extensive goals in its order as a whole; the perfect artistry it has despite its coming into existence as if all at once; the infinitely wise and purposeful individualization in it despite the endless potentialities before it; the gratification of each creature's needs just on time from whence it does not reckon, despite the infinite multiplicity and diversity of creation and the creature's inability to meet even the least of its demands; the absolute strength lying in its weakness; the absolute power lying in its helplessness; the life manifested on its inanimate matter; the comprehensive consciousness lying in its ignorance; the perfect order and arrangement in the changes it undergoes requiring the existence of an Immutable One to change it; the concord —like that of concentric circles —in its glorifications; the acceptance of the prayers it does in the languages of capacity, essential neediness and utter constraint; the supplications it does and the discoveries of certain invisible truths it achieves and radiations it is favoured with in its worship; the measure and balance in its acts of worship, the peace and tranquility it attains through remembrance of its Originator, its worship being the line uniting its beginning and end and the cause of the emergence of its perfections and the realization of the purposes of its Maker in its creation—all such qualities of creation and many others unmentioned are witnesses that it is under the management of a single All-Wise One and sustained and raised by a single, All-Munificent Lord, One Besought-of-All, and it serves a single Master and is at the disposal of a single Ruler. Also, the origin of creation is a single Power, the stamps of Whose Oneness appear on each of Its "missives", on each of Its "pages", and as abundantly as the number of those missives and pages.

Every flower and fruit, and every plant and tree, and every animal and rock, indeed, every particle of sand and stone in every valley and hill, and in every desert and plain—all this is a manifest seal demonstrating that the One Who has placed it is the "Inscriber" of this space all meaningfully and the "Inscriber" of land and sea with whatever is in them. He is also the Designer of the sun and moon on the meaningful page of the heavens: the Majesty of that Designer be exalted, He is God the Greatest.

Whence the world sings in unison, *There is no god but He.*

The fifth rank

God is the greatest. For He is the Creator, All-Powerful, Fashioner, All-Seeing. All those celestial bodies, those pearl-like stars, are radiations of the proofs of His Divinity and Grandeur, and the rays of the witnesses of His Lordship and Might. They all attest and proclaim the splendor of the Kingdom of His Lordship and proclaim the vastness of His Rule and Wisdom and the magnificence and greatness of His Power.

Give ear to the verse, Do they not look at the heavens above them, how We have built it and decorated it?[19], and then look at the face of the sky and see the serene silence, the purposeful motion, and the magnificent glittering smile, together with the orderliness in its creation and its well-proportioned art. Its "lamp" shines for the changing of seasons, its "lantern" radiates for the illumination of the world and its stars glitter for the decoration of the worlds. All this announces to the people of good sense and judgement the boundless Sovereignty in the organization and maintaining of the universe.

---

19. *al-Qaf*, 50.6.

That All-Powerful Creator knows all things and has a Will so comprehensive that whatever He wills is, and whatever He wills not is not. He is powerful over all things by an absolute, all-encompassing Power essential to His Divine Being. As it is inconceivable for the sun to exist without light and heat, so it is also inconceivable for the God and Creator of the heavens to be without an all-encompassing Knowledge and an absolute Power. He knows all things by an all-encompassing Knowledge essential to His Divine Being. Nothing can escape it, by virtue of its relation with all things, and its penetrative capability and comprehensiveness.

Whatever is observed in the whole of creation—orderliness, balance, and harmony, and all-inclusive wisdom, perfect favouring, well-established measures, well-arranged dispensation, fruitful decrees, appointed hours, regular provision, pleasing care [given to all things], and perfect, distinguishing measurement, order and firmness, and the absolute facility thereof—testifies to the all-encompassing Knowledge of the Knower of the Unseen, and of all things. The verse, *Does the One Who creates not know? He is the All-Subtle, the All-Aware*[20], points out that the existence of something requires knowing it. If the beauty of art in a man's work points to his consciousness to the extent of the brightness of a little star on a pitch-dark night, the creation of man is indicative of the Knowledge of his Creator to the extent of the splendour of the sun at noon.

As He knows all things, He has also a Will encompassing all things. Nothing takes place without His Will.

The Power produces the effect, the Knowledge distinguishes and the Will apportions and individualizes and thus things come into existence. There are as many witnesses of the Will of the Almighty as characteristics, attributes and states of things.

The creation and fashioning of things each with distinguishing character and attributes purposefully chosen for it out of innumerable alternatives and potentialities and forming each most

---

20. *al-Mulk*, 67.14.

delicately and with most sensitive measures in an infinitely diverse flux, and the creation of diverse, well-formed living beings from simple, inanimate elements—the creation of man, for example, with his senses and all other systems and organs of his body from a sperm, a bird with the systems of its body from an egg, a tree with all its parts from a seed or fruit-stone—bear witness that every thing is given its individual character and attributes by the Will and Choice of the Almighty, glory be to Him.

The correspondence between the members of a species in structure and basic systems of their bodies necessarily points out that their Maker is One and Single. However, each having a distinct character and distinguishing features demonstrate that that One and Single Maker does whatever He wills and judges however He wishes, His Majesty be exalted.

As the All-Knowing and All-Willing Creator has an all-encompassing Knowledge and all-inclusive Will, He has also a perfect Power issuing from and essential to His Divine Being. It is impossible that there is an opposite of that Power to interfere with It, for in that case it requires the agreement or combination of two opposites, which is, by universal assent, inconceivable. There can also be no grades in that Power: in relation to It minute particles and stars, the few and many, the little and great, the part and whole, the particular and universal, a man and the world, a seed and tree, are the same due to Its being immaterial, the transparency of the immaterial dimension of existence with which It deals, the interrelation among things, the exact balance in creation, the perfect order of existence, and the utmost obedience of existence to It.[21] The absolute order and harmony in creation and the absolute measuredness and the absolute distinctness observed in it, despite the speed and facility of creation and the infinite multiplicitiy, individualization and diversity of the created, also testify to this fact. Again, by virtue of the Oneness and Singleness of the One Who has that Power and the necessity of His existence and His not being of the same identity and quality or nature as the created; owing to His being unre-

---

21. These qualities are explained in the Second Aim of the *Twenty-ninth Word*. (Tr.)

stricted and indivisible and uncontained by space; since there can be nothing to impede Him, rather, whatever seems as an impediment serves as a means of facility although He has no need for anything like the nervous system in man to conduct and execute His commands; and due to the fact that a minute particle or an individual or a part or the few or the small or a man or a seed is not less in the art it contains than a star or a species or a whole or the many or the great or the world or a tree, it is as easy for that Power to create a star or a species or a whole or the many or the great or the world or a tree as to create a minute particle or an individual or a part or the few or the small or a man or a seed. Whoever has created the latter has also created the former. The One Who creates a seed, which is in fact a small-scale copy of its tree into which the Creator has included the tree by the principles of His Knowledge, must undoubtedly be the Creator of the tree. It is not difficult for the Power Which brings into existence the particulars to create the universals.

As the copy of the "Qur'an of wisdom" inscribed in an atom with the particles of ether is not less in beauty and art than the copy of the "Qur'an of grandeur" written on the pages of the heavens in the ink of stars and suns, so also the creation of a honeybee and an ant does not require less skill and artistry than the creation of a date palm, and the art a rose contains is not less than the art in a pearl-like star. Again, while the utmost and perfect facility in creation of things causes the misguided to confuse creation with self-formation, which in fact requires the acceptance of such impossibilites and superstitions as are detestable to sound reasoning and judgements, it leads the people of truth to admit with utmost certainty that planets and minute particles are the same in relation to the Power of the Creator of the universe, His Majesty be exalted, His Name be extolled, and there is no God but He.

The sixth rank

His Majesty be exalted, and His Name be Extolled—God is the Greatest, greater than all things in power and knowledge. For He is the All-Just, the All-Wise, the All-Powerful, the All-

Knowing, the One, the Single, the Eternal Sovereign: all these worlds are at the disposal of His "hands" of order and balance, arranging and measuring, Justice and Wisdom, and Knowledge and Power, and manifest His Oneness and Singleness. For there is nothing excluded from His order and balance and His arrangement and measuring. The order and balance and the arrangement and measuring are two "chapters" of the Manifest Record and the Manifest Book, which are the titles to the Knowledge and Command of the All-Knowing and All-Wise, and the Power and Will of the All-Mighty and All-Compassionate.[22] The order and balance in this Book, together with that Record, clearly testify for whoever has the power of understanding in his head and eyes in his face, that there is nothing in time and space excluded from the disposal of the All-Merciful, the ordering of the All-Pitying, the decorating of the All-Gracious and the measuring of the All-Ruling.

In sum: the manifestations of the Divine Names the First and the Last in creation refer to the beginning and end, the origin and issue, the past and future, the command and knowledge, and point to the Manifest Record. The manifestations of the Names the Outward and the Inward on things connected with God's Attribute of Creation, point to the Manifest Book.

The universe is like a huge tree, and each world in it is also like a tree. The creation of the universe and its ramification into worlds and species of creation may be likened to a tree. A tree has an origin, which is a seed from which the tree grows. It has also issue which continues its duties after its death, which is the seed in its fruit. As the beginning and end are the results of the manifestations of the Names the First and the Last, through its composition and the purposes it serves, the original seed is an index or encoded commands for the formation of the tree, and therefore is the object of the manifestation of the Name the First. The seeds in the tree's fruits are the objects of the manifestation of the Name, the Last.

---

22. The Manifest Record and Manifest Book are explained in detail in the *Thirtieth Word*. Therefore, we have mentioned them here briefly.

The seeds or stones in fruits are like miniature chests in which the index and the encoded commands for the formation of new trees exactly resembling the original one are included or inscribed by the Pen of Destiny. The exterior of the tree is the object of the manifestation of the Name the Outward and, through the perfect, well-ordered structure and decoration it has and purposes it serves, is like a well-woven and well-fitting, richly decorated and bejewelled dress cut out with perfect wisdom and favouring according to the tree's size. The inside of the tree is the object of the manifestation of the Name the Inward. Through the perfect, amazing organization it displays and the conduct of the food for the life of the tree into all of its parts with perfect order, the inside of the tree is like an extraordinary machine or factory working in perfect order and balance. The origin of the tree resembling extraordinarily encoded commands and its end like an extraordinary index, point to the Manifest Record. And its exterior like an artistically woven dress and its inside resembling an extremely well-ordered machine, point to the Manifest Book, just as the memory in man indicates the Supreme Guarded Tablet, the original seeds and fruits in all trees also indicate the Manifest Record, and the exteriors and insides of them symbolize the Manifest Book. You can compare with that particular tree the "tree" of the earth with its past and future, and the "tree" of the universe with its beginning and future, and the "tree" of man with his ancestors and descendants. The Majesty of their Creator be exalted, and there is no god but He... O God! You are the One Whose Greatness and Grandeur minds are unable to describe and Whose Splendor minds cannot grasp.

The seventh rank

His Majesty be exalted—God is the Greatest, greater than all things in power and knowledge. For He is the Creator, the Opener, the All-Acting, the All-Knowing, the Giver of Gifts, the Distributor of Blessings,[23] the Eternal "Sun". With all its kinds

---

23. By viewing through these Names the Divine acts and imprints behind creatures, it is possible to move to the One called by these Names.

and the creatures they contain, all the worlds comprising the universe are the shadows of His lights, the works of His acts, the colors of the embroiders of the manifestations of His Names, the lines of the "pen" of His Destiny and Decree, the mirrors of the manifestations of His attributes Beauty, Majesty, and Perfection, as is attested by the Eternal Witness—the Almighty Himself—with all His Books, Pages or Scrolls, and signs of creation and verses of the Qur'an, and by the earth with the absolute riches and wealth manifested on it despite its essential destitution and neediness, and by the Prophets, saints and purified, exacting scholars having enlightened intellects and illumined hearts with all their investigations, spiritual discoveries and supplications and the blessings with which they are favoured. With utmost certainty, conviction, and affirmation, and accepting the testimony of the signs of creation and verses of the Qur'an and the testament of the heavenly Books and Pages, which contain the testimony of the Necessarily Existent One, all of these witnesses—the earth, the heavenly bodies and the most illustrious members of humanity—are all agreed on the fact that all these creatures are the works of His Power, the inscriptions of His Destiny, the mirrors of His Names, and the images of His lights. His Majesty be exalted, and there is no god but He.

Conclusion

Different experienced issues

Know, O friend!

As long as I am alive, I say as Mawlana Jalal al-Din al-Rumi, may God sanctify him, said:

I am a servant of the Qur'an as long as I am alive; I am the soil of the way of Muhammad, the Chosen One.

For I see the Qur'an as the source of all intellectual and spiritual radiation and whatever of truths is in my books is among the radiations of the Qur'an. For this reason I cannot agree that any of my books lacks references to the miraculousness of the Qur'an. From as many as forty aspects of the Qur'an's miraculousness that I mentioned in the "Gleams" affixed to *The Words*, I will include here only one as a means of blessing for this book. It is as follows:

Ponder these questions concerning a speech made or a word uttered:

Who said it? To whom was it said? Why was it said? About what was it said?

A word derives its strength and beauty from the one who speaks it, the one to whom it is spoken, the purpose of its utterance and the occasion on which it is spoken. Some literary men have erred by accepting the occasion as the only source of the beauty of a word. The wording or the words chosen to express a meaning are not the body of a speech; they are its dress. The apparent or superficial meaning of a speech is not its "spirit", but its body. A speech derives its life from the intention and feelings of the speaker, and therefore its spirit is the meaning intended by the speaker. If the speech made or the words uttered contain an order or prohibition, then surely they have authority proportionate to the degree of the power of the speaker, which adds to the strength and sublimity of the words.

Then, see how great the difference is between an unauthoritative order issuing from whimsies of one [who has not enough power enough to put his orders into effect] and a forceful and powerful command issuing from a determined authority! How different is the order, *O earth, swallow up your water, and O heaven, withdraw (your rain)*![24] [which issued from the sole Sovereign of the universe] from such orders which you suppose to issue from human beings to lifeless elements as—O earth, be still and come to a rest; O heaven, split asunder; O world, destroy yourself utterly and be built again for the Resurrection! Also, consider the difference between the command "March"! issuing from a commander absolutely obeyed to a mighty obedient army, which attack the enemies of God and defeat them, and that which issues from one whose person and whose orders are alike given no importance. How different is the account of acts by their true owner, an absolutely authoritative commander, a maker who makes whatever he wishes, and a generous bestower of gifts, such as "I have done and I do such and such... I have made the earth a bed for you and the heavens a ceiling". How different is this account from that which a human being makes superficially concerning the deeds and things with which he has no direct relation. See the difference between the stars themselves and their images in pieces of glass which have no real existence. Again, how different are the "angels" of the words of the Speech of the Creator of the sun and moon from the noises of human beings resembling the hum of wasps! How different are the words of the Qur'an, which are the "mothers of the pearls" of guidance and truths of belief and, of the principles diffusing from the Supreme Throne of God, and which constitute the Eternal Speech containing knowledge, power and will——how different they are from hollow human words coming from whims and fancies! Lastly, how different is the tree which has ramified and then come to leaf and blossomed and yielded

---

24. *Hud*, 11.44.

fruit from a substance obtained from some of the fruits of that tree by changing their form and removing from them the nucleus of life and mixing them with another element!

Surely, the Qur'an is like a tree each seed of which has grown into principles of conduct, into fruit-bearing trees, and from which the world of Islam has formed with all its aspects. Minds have derived from it ideas and the exalted truths originating from it have become incontestable principles and branches of knowledge. If one appears and takes one of those truths and, making changes in it and removing from it its nucleus of life, decorates it according to one's own corrupted fancies and makes one's taste a criterion to judge the verses of the Qur'an— if one does so, you may judge whether it is justifiable at all to compare the forms given to precious stones, to pearls, for example, according to childish desires and those stones themselves.

I have personally experienced and observed that to experience the beauty of the Qur'an requires a sound, purified heart. A heart tainted with [spiritual diseases] can feel only what his diseases have soiled and muddied. The styles of the Qur'an and the heart are two corresponding mirrors reflecting each other.

A subtle point

Belief establishes brotherhood and affinity among all things and therefore there is not found in the heart of a believer a strong greed, nor enmity and hatred, nor the feeling of desolation. A believer sees even his strongest enemy as a human brother to him. As to unbelief, it is the cause of separation and alienness, not affinity, among all things, and therefore an unbeliever is severe in greed, enmity and self-preference and self-reliance. It is for this reason that unbelievers can be usually successful in worldly life. They see the reward of their virtues mostly in the world, whereas the believers suffer there the consequences of some of their shortcomings and sins. That is why the Prophet, upon him be peace and blessings, declared: *The world is the prison of the believer but the paradise of the unbeliever.*[25]

---

25. *Muslim*, Zuhd, No. 2959; *Tirmidhi*, Zuhd, No. 2324; *Ibn Maja*, Zuhd, No. 4113.

Know that if the elixir of belief enters a heart, a man becomes like a jewel worthy of eternity and Paradise, but unbelief reduces him to something like a valueless, perishable stone devoid of most sublime feelings and virtues. Belief unveils the sound, pleasant kernel or essence within the perishable covering and shows as a radiant diamond what is supposed as perishable foam. While unbelief shows the covering as the kernel and clings to it firmly. Through unbelief, man is reduced from the degree of being like a diamond to the degree of a piece of glass or a piece of ice or foam. This is what I have observed concerning belief and unbelief.

A point

I have observed that the more one is preoccupied with philosophy, the more one increases in the spiritual disease of the heart, as I have also observed the more one increases in the spiritual disease of the heart, the more one is preoccupied with the rational sciences. Spiritual diseases lead to preoccupation with rational sciences and preoccupation with rational sciences gives rise, in turn, to spiritual diseases.

It is, again, my observation that the world has two aspects:

Its first aspect is that outwardly it is partly and temporarily attractive whereas inwardly it is eternally horrible.

Its second aspect is that outwardly it is partly horrible while inwardly eternally beautiful.

The Qur'an draws attention to the second aspect of the world, which relates to the Hereafter. As for its first aspect, it is connected with eternal annihilation as contrary to the eternal afterlife.

I have also observed that existence based on human ego ends in non-existence whereas self-annihilation or annihilation in ego or selfhood results in existence and leads to the Necessarily Existent Being. If you desire existence and find it, try to realize annihilation in selfhood.

A subtle point

Know O friend! Surely, intention is one of the four words

which I mentioned in the *Introduction* as the attainment of my
forty years of age.

Intention is a mysterious elixir changing ordinary acts and
customs into acts of worship. It is a penetrating and pervading
spirit through which inanimate states and deeds acquire life
and become "living" acts of worship. It is also through a peculiar quality of intention that evils change into virtues or good
deeds.

Intention is itself a "spirit" or soul which causes ordinary
deeds and customs to become "living" acts of worship, and the
soul of intention is sincerity or acting solely for the sake of God
Almighty. There is no salvation except by sincerity of action in
the way of God. Sincerity multiplies actions in worth and
through sincerity or solely acting for God's sake one can buy
Paradise with a little action in a short life.

It is again through the purity of intention that one becomes
continuously thankful to God, for the worldly bounties and
pleasures have two aspects.

Pertaining to their first aspect which concerns the purity of
intention, a man confesses that the bounties he consumes are
conferred on him by the "hand" of Mercy and Favouring, and
thus he passes from bounties to the Divine act of giving bounties and the pleasure he gets therein increases.

The second aspect of bounties is that a man pursues pleasures only to gratify his bodily desires. He does not recollect the
Divine act of giving bounties and concentrates on the bounty
and pleasure themselves. He looks upon bounties as something
falling to his lot for nothing and does not consider in what way
he takes hold of them.

With respect to the first aspect, when the pleasure disappears, its spirit lasts. That is, by thinking, "the mercy of the Giver of Bounties does not forget me", a man feels unbreakable
connection with the Giver of Bounties. However, concerning
the second aspect, the disappearance of the pleasure does not
allow its spirit to last, rather, when the pleasure dies away, its

"smoke" remains. The "smoke" of the pleasure is the sins [arising from unthankfulness and the unlawful ways in obtaining bounties and consuming them].

When viewed with the light of belief, lawful pleasures in the world and bounties in the Hereafter form a virtuous circle in which they follow one another. Neither the disappearance of pleasures nor separation from bounties gives pains, for the pleasures of belief and thankfulness are permanent. However, without belief, pleasures change into pains for the decay of pleasures, even thinking of their decay is itself a pain. Since in the way of unbelief each pleasure is an end in itself, its disappearance leaves behind it pains in the heart.

A point

Know O friend! Attachment to material causes is the cause of humiliation and rejection. Do you not see that although the dog should be regarded as blessed by people due to its many good qualities, notably its proverbial loyalty, it has received the blow of being considered ritually unclean. By contrast, other domestic animals such as the hen and the cow and even the cat, which do not have the feeling of gratitude and loyalty in return for the good done to them by human beings, enjoy being considered by people as blessed. This is because—provided it is not to backbite the dog and its heart be broken—on account of its disease of greed, the dog is attached to apparent causes to an extent which makes it blind to the true Bestower of Bounties. It supposes the means as truly effective [in the procurement of its food] and as the punishment for its blindness and indifference to the true Owner and Giver of Bounties, it suffers the stigma of ritual impurity.

As for the blessed animals, they do not recognize the means and causes or accord to them any real value or importance. For example, the cat implores you for food and when it gets what it desires, it behaves as if it did not know you or you did not know it. It does not feel gratitude to you. Instead, it thanks the true Giver of Bounties by mentioning: "O Compassionate One,

O Compassionate One!" By disposition, it recognizes its Creator and worships Him consciously or unconsciously.

A subtle point

If all things are not attributed to the Almighty, then it requires the admission of an infinite number of deities, all of whom are essentially opposite to one another but identical at the same time for a given moment. Because of the interrelation among all things of the universe and the essential quality of divinity, their number increases in proportion to the number of the particles and compounds of creation.

For example, the power of the deity who creates a honeybee or a single grape should be able to exert its rule and influence on all the elements of the universe, as a honeybee or a grape is a miniature of the whole of the creation. Furthermore, in existence there is no room for a divine being other than a Single Necessarily Existent One. If things are attributed to themselves, then this requires that each minute particle—the smallest unit of an element—should be a deity. Do you not see that the stones in the dome of the Ayasofya (Hagia Sophia) should be each like its architect, if we do not attribute it to an architect? The testimony of the universe to its Single Creator is more manifest, more radiant, clearer, and more expressive than its testimony to its own existence. Even if the existence of the universe is denied, it is impossible to deny the existence of the One, Who is powerful over all things.

A point

How strange it is that heedlessness and misguidance conclude the law of causality from the concourse or concurrence of causes and the series of creation in the production of a result and attribute creativity to that law. However, this requires the acceptance of an endless series of impossibilities, in addition to the fact that there has never been identified a sign in the universe for the existence of a partner with the Creator. Rather, the structure of every thing and the art in it unveil an infinite power which must belong to an All-Powerful, Necessarily Existent

One. How great a loss man suffers and how ignorant he is! How strange it is that associating partners with the All-Powerful Creator can find room in him, in his mind!

A subtle point

The letter *nun* [meaning we] in *na'budu* [we worship] has a universal meaning. While reciting *na'budu* [we worship], a believer who prays in a congregation consciously of performing a prayer in a congregation and aware of its meaning and significance, regards the face of the earth as a mosque where the whole community of believers are standing in line to pray God Almighty and sees himself as a member of this huge community. By virtue of the concensus of all the Prophets and saints on *There is no god but God* and because all individuals in the cogregation utter the same recitation, the believer can easily conceive time as a circle of reciters under the leadership of the Leader of the Prophets. With the Prophets sitting on the right side of the circle—representing the past—and the saints on the left—representing the future—the whole circle is mentioning God and reciting His Names so loudly that whoever gives ear can hear this recitation. One with a keener sight and hearing can hear all creatures reciting God's Names and sees himself in this universal circle of recitation.

A point

Know O friend! Loving all else besides God has two aspects. The first aspect is that one loves God and because of His love he loves those that God loves. Love of God does not diminish this love, rather it increases it.

The second aspect is that one loves the means [to attain love of God] and makes this love a step to reach love of God. This aspect of the love of all else besides God has many kinds. If one encounters a strong, attractive means, it hinders one from further advance, and even if one is able to attain love of God, it will be defective.

A subtle point

Know, O friend! As is declared in the verse, *There is not a mov-*

ing creature in the earth but its provision falls upon God,[26] God has undertaken the provision of all creatures. However, provision falls into two categories: that which is absolutely necessary for life and that which is superfluous. It is the absolutely necessary provision which God has undertaken. As to the superfluous provision, it is that which, although unnecessary, is made necessary through misuse of will and bad habits and customs. This kind of provision is not included in that which God has declared He has undertaken in the verse mentioned. Whoever reflects on eggplants, which are the "fish" of the land, and the fish, which are the "eggplants" of the sea—whoever reflects on how the Creative Power makes them all fleshy and how their provision comes to them abundantly from whence they do not reckon—surely understands that it is stupidity to feel groundless anxieties about provision and blame the All-Providing One.

A point

Know, O friend! In the misfortunes happening to innocent children and animals there are reasons people usually fail to notice. For example, the Divine laws of nature and life are the principles of the Divine Will which are not applied only to intellectual beings so that the creatures that do not have reason are not obliged to obey them. Those laws also appeal to the heart and feelings and senses. A child may be considered as mature in the senses or feelings of the heart, indeed the feelings of your child may be more perfect than your reason and more alert. It may happen that your reason does not prevent you from oppressing an orphan but the compassion of your child who watches you doing it drives him to tears.

That being so, if a child does not heed his feeling of compassion or pity and kills a honeybee to indulge an impulse, he may have his head broken as a deserved punishment.

For example, a female leopard has great affection towards its young and owns the feeling of protection towards its mate. However, when these two of its feelings do not prevent it from

---

26. *Hud,* 11.6.

cutting a young gazelle to pieces, it may be the target of the bullet of a hunter. Is this not its desert, just as its lawful food is the carcasses of other animals? [Like human beings,] animals also do not own themselves; they cannot behave however they wish. The true Owner of the universe, the One of Majesty and Favouring, is the Owner and sole Ruler of the whole of the creation including all of the kingdoms of living beings, and disposes in His realm of dominion however He wills. He is the One Who does whatever He wishes. *He is not to be questioned concerning what He does but they are to be questioned.*[27]

---

27. *al-Anbiya'*, 21.23.

Addendum

In the Name of God, the Merciful, the Compassionate.

All praise to God, the Lord of the Worlds.

Blessings and peace be upon our master Muhammad and all of his family and Companions.

Symbol

Know, O friend! It is commendable [for a believer] to perform the daily prayers each at the beginning of its time and imagine the Ka'ba before him. The one who prays imagines the believers standing in prayer around the Ka'ba in lines as concentric circles, the first line being the nearest to the Ka'ba and the last encircling the Muslim world, and feels a strong yearning to join them wholeheartedly. After joining, the consensus of this huge community and the unity of its members become a decisive proof and evidence for the truth of all meanings and causes contained in the prayer.

For example, when the one who prays says *All praise be to God*, it is as if all the believers praying in the mosque of the earth say in answer, "I agree. You say the truth!" Whatever doubt and suspicion Satan whispers, they all disappear from his heart. Each of his senses and faculties derives belief and a pleasure particular to itself and questions such as *Why*? and *How*? cannot form an obstacle to him. The huge congregation of the pious, God-fearing believers is formed at the beginning of the prayer's time, and because of the uniformity of the prayer in acts and recitations, the differences of times of prayers in different regions of the world do not prevent the imagination of the praying believer.

Wherever the praying believer is, he turns to the Ka'ba. While imagining the Ka'ba before him and the community of the believers standing in circling lines around the Ka'ba, the praying believer should not busy himself intentionally with this imagination, rather, a simple imagination is enough. How do you know that Destiny which neglects nothing does not record every act and recitation of those orderly, blessed lines on the pages of the world of symbols or immaterial forms, in which all things are preserved eternally?

Symbol

Know O friend! I have observed in my journeying in the "layers of darkness", that the sayings and practices of the Prophet Muhammad, upon him be peace and blessings, and the principles of the Islamic law are like stars by which we can find our direction and radiate among innumerable dark and misguiding ways. By deviating from the way or Tradition of the Prophet [the *Sunna*], a man becomes a plaything of devils, an object of illusions and suspicions, a target of groundless fears, and a mount of unbearable burdens, from which, when followed, the *Sunna* delivers him.

I have also observed that the principles of the *Sunna* are like ropes hanging down from the heaven. Whoever holds fast to even a part of them can be elevated. I have witnessed that whoever opposes them and relies on his own reason, even on public reason, is like him who desires to obtain the means of travelling through the spheres of the heavens in earthly vehicles and is ridiculed like Pharaoh, who said: "O Haman! Build for me a tower to obtain the means [of travelling] in the heavens!"[28]

Symbol

Know O friend! In the soul there is an important, obscure knot which causes an opposite to give birth to its opposite, and by which the soul regards what is against it as in its favor.

For example, the sun passes its "hand" to you and either caresses you or slaps you. Whereas you cannot pass your hand to it and exert no influence on it. It is nearer to you than yourself despite its great distance from you. If you think that because of

28. *al-Mu'min*, 40.36.

your distance from it the sun cannot exert any influence on you and because of its nearness to you you can have an affect on it, this will be sheer ignorance on your part. It is in this way that, if the carnal self views its Creator with the eye of conceit and whimsy and, despite His being nearer to it than itself, sees Him as distant from it, this will be the cause of its misguidance.

Again, when the carnal self encounters a great reward, it sighs, saying, "If only I had done the same! Alas! If only I had behaved that way"! However, when it comes across a terrible punishment, it consoles itself by ignoring or denying it.

O stupid dark dot, stupid carnal self! The acts of the Almighty are, first of all, concerned with Him, not with you and your narrow mind. And the wheel of creation does not revolve according to your fancies. Also, He did not make you a witness to His creation of the universe. Surely, Imam Rabbani told the truth: "The gifts of the Sovereign can be borne only by those qualified for them."

Symbol

Know, O friend! Surely, the One Who has decorated your head beautifully and embellished it with the power of sight, sees you better than yourself. The Maker Who has embellished your head with the "gems" of eyes and the "mothers-of-pearl" of ears, and suspended the tongue of "coral" in the cavity of your mouth to converse with—surely He sees and hears you better than yourself, is nearer to you than yourself, and more compassionate for you than yourself.

Symbol

Know, O friend! The prayers of especially those in great difficulty and under severe strain and constraint produce great results. They cause the mightiest and greatest thing to be subjected to the weakest and smallest one. For example, the fury of a roaring sea may subside in answer to the prayer of a broken-hearted infant on a piece of wood floating on it. This means the One Who answers prayers has absolute authority over all things and He is the Lord of all creation.

Symbol

Know, O friend! It is one of the important diseases of a misguided human selfhood that it seeks the splendor of a whole in each of its parts and the glory of a king in a private. When it does not find it, it rejects the whole or the king. For example, it seeks to see all the manifestations of the sun in its image in a bubble, and when it cannot see them, it refuses to accept that the image belongs to the sun.

O selfhood! The oneness of the sun does not require that its manifestations should also be one. Also, something which points to something else does not require to contain that something else. Again, something which describes something else with certain qualifications does not require to have the same qualifications. A minute transparent object points to the sun and displays some of its qualities. Similarly, a beehive exhibits the Attributes of the All-Wise Maker.

Symbol

Know, O friend! Walking along the way of unbelief is like walking on ice or under earth and essentially repulsive, and therefore very difficult for him who inclines to this way knowingly to walk along it. However, one with a careless, imitative view cannot discern this difficulty. As for the way of belief, going along it is like travelling in water or air or light, and essentially attractive, and therefore very easy for him who is inclined to follow it.

For example, if you would like to benefit from the sun from all the six sides of you, you will either expose the whole of your body to the sun by turning round and lying or have the sun come down from that great distance and turn around you. The first alternative is an example of the easiness of following the way of believing in the Oneness of God, while the other is an example of the difficulty of going along the way of unbelief.

Question

Despite its difficulty to that degree, why do numerous people accept unbelief and reject belief despite its being so easy?

Answer

Almost no one accepts unbelief consciously. Rather, unbelief sticks to a man because of the apparent attractiveness of his bodily desires and dirties him. Whereas one accepts belief knowingly and consciously and belief is established in one's heart.

Symbol

Know, O friend! It makes no difference that a word uttered is heard by an individual or millions of people. In relation to the Eternal Power, there is no difference between an individual and a species.

Symbol

Know, O friend! The Qur'an is infinitely comprehensive in meaning and encompasses all levels of understanding, and it considers the feelings of all whom it addresses, especially lowering itself to the level of the commonalty, which constitute the absolute majority of people and therefore are the first to be addressed by the Qur'an. Although this is one of the reasons of the perfection of the Qur'an, diseased carnal selves are misguided because of it. This is because such selves seek the most exalted styles and the most balanced ways of expressions in the simplest manner of descriptions required for the topics discussed and the levels of addressees, and make the styles, which should naturally consider the feelings and levels of the addressees, a criterion and "observatory" to see and judge the Speaker—the Almighty. This is why they go far astray.

Symbol

How can one be pleased with the third facet of the world and take delight in it? The world has three facets.

The first facet of the world relates to the Names of God Almighty.

Its second facet is that it is the arable field of the Hereafter. These two facets are beautiful.

As to the third facet of the world, it directly and exclusively relates to the world itself and where man gratifies his bodily desires and seeks to meet the needs of his transient worldly life.

I am forced to wear a flesh that is essentially lifeless. Today is my coffin, between yesterday and tomorrow, which are the graves of my father and "his son". I am pressed between two dead bodies and graves. But be aware that, with respect to its facet as the arable field of the Hereafter, the world and viewing it with the light of belief give spiritual pleasures of Paradise.

Symbol

Know O friend! Your body is like a publicly owned rifle or horse entrusted to a soldier to use. Just as the soldier is responsible for the care of the rifle or horse, so too you are charged with the preservation of the trust in your hand—your body.

Know O friend! The reason why I have said so is that I saw my carnal self proud of having virtues. I told it: "You own nothing." It answered: "Then, I do not care for what I do not own of the body." I said: "You should not fall behind a fly [in caring for your body]. If you would like to, look at that fly how it cleans its wings with its legs and wipes its eyes with its hands!" Glory be to Him Who has inspired the fly to do that and made it an instructor to me, thus silencing my self through it.

Symbol

Know, O friend! It is one of the causes of error and deviation that one confuses the decrees and acts of the Divine Name the Inward with those of the Outward and expects from the Former what one should expect from the Latter. One also confuses the necessities of the Divine Power with those of the Divine Wisdom, and seeks to see in the Former what one should seek to see in the Latter. Again, to confuse the requirements of the realm where the law of causality has part of its own in God's acts with those of belief in the absolute Unity of God, and the acts and ways of the manifestation of the Divine Power with the manifestations of Divine Existence or those of other Divine Attributes and seek to find the rules and laws of the Former in the

Latter—this is another cause of error and deviation. For example, your coming into existence and growth in this world is gradual but in the mirrors of the intermediate realms between this material realm and purely spiritual realms—as in dreams, for example—it is all at once. This is so because the Divine Attributes vary in manifesting themselves, and creation and manifestation are different from each other.

Symbol

Know, O friend! Surely, Islam is a universal mercy, to such an extent that it is thanks to Islam that even unbelievers find some happiness in their worldly lives and the pleasures they take in life do not change into endless pains. This is so because Islam has changed the absolute unbelief and denial causing painful despair and severe pains into doubt and hesitation. Influenced by the clear announcements of the Qur'an, an unbeliever may come to regard the eternal life as probable and is relieved from the suffocating pains [arising from the thought of eternal extinction] and since he is not convinced of the coming of that life, he feels free from the obligations required by it. Like an ostrich—a bird resembling a camel—which, when told to fly, replies, "I'm a camel, not a bird"; but when told to bear a burden like a camel, answers, "I'm a bird, not a camel". Deluded by Satan, [paradoxically, with false hopes of salvation in the Hereafter on the one hand and with denial of the eternal life to be free from fulfilling the religious obligations on the other], unbelievers and transgressors [of the Divine rules of conduct] find a superficial happiness in the worldly life, in contrast to atheists and sincere believers.

Symbol

Know, O friend! In order to maintain the dominion it claims in its own realm, the human selfhood or ego does not wish to admit or conceive of something proceeding from itself less valuable than that created by the Power of the Creator. So long as the human selfhood does not regard itself as the least of creatures or nothing in essence, it is not possible for one to be absolutely saved from denying the Attributes of the Creator or inwardly associating partners with God.

Symbol

Know, O friend! Because of its indolence in doing its duties, the human selfhood wishes there would be none to oversee it and seeks to remain hidden. It considers the non-existence of the Owner of all things over and over again and seeks absolute freedom. First it desires, then it considers and thereafter it conceives. After that, it begins to believe in the non-existence of an Owner and Ruler above itself. Finally, it deserts its faith or becomes an apostate. However, if it knew what great, consuming sufferings and unbearable pains are under the freedom and ease it aspires to and the irresponsibility it seeks, it would not show the least of such inclinations, rather, it would flee them, keep away from them, or repent of them or die.

Symbol

Things differ according to the difference of their points of support. For example, a private connected with and supported by a great, powerful sovereign can do what a king is unable to do. [Owing to his point of support,] this private is "seven degrees" greater than one who is normally greater than him in "seventy degrees". It is because of this reality that a mosquito appointed by the Eternal Power can defeat a most powerful ruler of the world who is the most obstinate in unbelief.[29] By the leave of God Almighty, the Splitter of Grains and Seeds, a fruit stone contains whatever a huge "palm tree" needs. Factories built in an area the size of nine villages cannot manufacture what that tree needs.

Know O friend! The difference between the way established by the Qur'an (and that I have followed in *The Drop*) and that of philosophers is this: I dig the ground wherever I am and water comes out. Philosophers attempt to open canals through the

---

29. Referring to the historical fact that a mosquito entering through one of his nostrils caused the death of Nimrod, the tyrant who had cast the Prophet Abraham, upon him be peace, into flames (Tr.)

universe and lay down pipes to provide water. They go as far as beyond the Divine Throne. Since they attach much importance to material causes, in order to protect the pipes they should have millions of guards along the long way against the attacks and destructions of whispering, deluding satans. However, what the Qur'an has taught me is like the Staff of Moses: wherever I strike with it, even if I am on a rock, the water of life gushes forth. I do not feel compelled to make a long journey beyond the world and protect very long pipes from breaking or destruction. The saying, *In each thing there is a sign demonstrating that He is One*, clarifies this point.

Symbol

Alas! What a pity! Human selfhood or the carnal self [which is the source of all defects and lusts] is essentially blind. So long as it continues to exist [in man as the source of defects and lusts, without being disciplined], even if as something as small as the wing of a gnat, it remains a veil to blind itself to the sun of truth. Actually, because it concentrates on its own existence [and, with the tendency to appropriate for itself whatever is given to it by the Creator, does not want to recognize a supreme dominant power over itself], when it sees a defect in one of the stones of a big castle built of stones of decisive proofs [of that Power's existence], it denies the existence of the castle. You can judge from this the extent of the ignorance of the selfhood arising from its attachment to its own existence.

Symbol

Know, O ego! You have already known that what belongs to you of yourself is one out of thousands, if indeed it really belongs to you! So, put on that small, weak part, which is your free will, as much load as you can bear. Do not load your consciousness, so weak as a hair, with "huge rocks". Do not put anything upon what does not belong to you, except by the leave of its Owner.

When you act heedlessly on your own behalf, do not overstep your limits. The field of your movement is as narrow as a hair.

When you act on behalf of the Lord of all dominion, you can load yourself with whatever you see provided it is according to His orders and Will, not according to your own will. You should learn His permission and Will from His Law—the *Shari'a*.

Symbol

O one who seeks fame and reputation! Hear this from me: Fame is identical with show and ostentation and kills the heart. No one seeks it except to be a slave to human beings. If it happens to you, say: *Surely we belong to God and surely we are on the way of return to Him.*[30]

---

30. *al-Baqara*, 2.156.

INDEX OR BRIEF SUMMARIES OF THE TOPICS DISCUSSED IN THE TREATISE

*We should consider anything other than God not on account of itself but on account of God Almighty. To consider the universe on account of itself or material causes is wrong. Everything has two aspects: one pointing to the Creator, the other, creation. (71)

*Intention and viewpoint change the nature of things and, as elixir turns earth into gold, good intention and correct viewpoint change evil acts into good ones. (71)

*The four sentences I have learned during my lifetime are:

I am neither the owner nor master of myself.

Death is inevitable.

My Lord is One.

Human ego is a black dot, a point of comparison [to know and recognize God] intertwined with the "threads" of a conscious artistry. It shows that its Owner is nearer to it than itself. (72)

*First of all, the Prophet Muhammad, upon him be peace and blessings, and the Qur'an are the most articulate proofs of Divine existence and Oneness.

•All the Prophets, upon them be peace, saints, purified, truth-seeking scholars and hundreds of millions of believers, and all of the heavenly books are evident proofs of Divine existence and Oneness.

•Angels and jinn and other kinds of spirit beings, the existence of whom all the Prophets, saints and exacting, purified scholars are agreed constitute another decisive proof for God's existence and Unity;

•Islam and other heavenly religions with all the truths they contain show the existence and Unity of God.

•The exact, very precise order;

•everything being in exact measures and proportions;

•the harmony, precise arrangement and design in the "house" of the universe;

•the perfection of the art which the Pen of Destiny displays in everything according to the capacity of each;

•the mutual relationship between all things and faultless artistry displayed in each thing;

•everything being hastened to the aid of everything else, for example, for the existence of a single pomegranate the sun, air, earth and such "laws" as germination and growth being sent to the aid of the seed of the pomegranate;

•solidarity among different, distant objects;

•utmost resemblance within utmost variety; absolute orderliness despite absolute facility, being absolutely valuable despite absolute abundance, absolute distinguishment within absolute mingledness;

•the connection among all things, the connection between, for example, the eyes of the honeybee and ant and the sun and the solar system;

•the interrelatedness among all objects and parts of an object;

•everything being in need of everything else;

•the indispensable relation among the parts of each thing and things themselves;

•all the minutest particles or atoms in compounds and then compounds within one another being placed each in its exact position;

•the absolute facility in attributing all things to a single Creator while it is absolutely difficult that they are brought into existence either by themselves or by causes or nature or matter;

•utmost inconceivability that blind, deaf, lifeless and ignorant causes or matter could have created the universe which, with all its parts, require the existence of one with absolute knowledge, power, and will;

•the extensive mercy encompassing the whole of the universe, which contains wisdom, favoring, benevolence, munificence, kindness, gratifying, love and recognition, which are all observed throughout the universe;

•also the grace, beauty, love and attraction witnessed in the whole of creation, which show the existence of an all-gracious, all-beautiful and all-loving one;

• absolute wisdom and purposeviness observed in the life and existence of each thing;

• life, consciousness and will-power and numerous kinds of feelings innate in conscious beings;

• comprehensive capacities enjoyed by men and other living beings;

• continuous movement observed in the universe as a whole and in each being toward a point of perfection;

—all this and other facts and evidences prove the existence and Oneness of a Creator. (73-95)

*Despair, self-admiration because of one's good deeds, vanity and suspicion as four diseases of heart. (96–8)

*The four significant truths that Said Nursi witnessed in his spiritual and intellectual journeying. (99-103)

*Reflections on Glory be to God. (104–5)

*Reflections on All praise be to God. (106–8)

*Reflections an God is the Greatest. (109-113)

*The ranks of God is the Greatest. (113–127)

*The Qur'an from the viewpoint of the questions concerning a speech made or a word uttered: Who said it? To whom was it said? Why was it said? About what was it said?

A word derives its strength and beauty from the one who speaks it, the one to whom it is spoken, the purpose of its utterance and the occasion on which it is spoken. (128–30)

*Belief establishes brotherhood and affinity among all things and therefore there is not found in the heart of a believer a strong greed, nor enmity and hatred, nor the feeling of desolation. As to unbelief, it is the cause of separation and alienness, not affinity, among all things, and therefore an unbeliever is severe in greed, enmity and self-preference and self-reliance. It is for this reason that unbelievers can be usually successful in worldly life. They see the reward of their virtues mostly in the world, whereas the believers suffer there the consequences of some of their shortcomings and sins. (130–31)

*The more one is preoccupied with philosophy, the more one

*It is one of the important diseases of a misguided human self-hood that it seeks the splendor of a whole in each of its parts and the glory of a king in a private. (141)

*Walking along the way of unbelief is like walking on ice or under earth and essentially repulsive, and therefore very difficult for him who inclines to this way knowingly to walk along it. (141)

*It makes no difference that a word uttered is heard by an individual or millions of people. In relation to the Eternal Power, there is no difference between an individual and a species. (142)

*The Qur'an is infinitely comprehensive in meaning and encompasses all levels of understanding, and it considers the feelings of all whom it addresses. (142)

*The world has three facets. The first facet of the world relates to the Names of God Almighty. Its second facet is that it is the arable field of the Hereafter. These two facets are beautiful. As to the third facet of the world, it directly and exclusively relates to the world itself and where man gratifies his bodily desires and seeks to meet the needs of his transient worldly life. (143)

*It is one of the causes of error and deviation that one confuses the decrees and acts of the Divine Name the Inward with those of the Outward and expects from the Former what one should expect from the Latter. (143)

*Islam is a universal mercy, to such an extent that it is thanks to Islam that even unbelievers find some happiness in their worldly lives and the pleasures they take in life do not change into endless pains. (144)

*In order to maintain the dominion it claims in its own realm, the human selfhood or ego does not wish to admit or conceive of something proceeding from itself less valuable than that created by the Power of the Creator. (144)

*Because of its indolence in doing its duties, the human self-hood wishes there would be none to oversee it and seeks to remain hidden. (145)

*Things differ according to the difference of their points of support. For example, a private connected with and supported by a great, powerful sovereign can do what a king is unable to do. (145)

A Bubble from the Ocean of the Wise Qur'an

My Lord is Munificent: He buys His property from you;
He preserves it on your behalf and gives, in return, a great price.

In the Name of God, the Merciful, the Compassionate.

All praise be to the Lord of the Worlds, and peace and blessings be
on our master Muhammad and all of his family and Companions.

Know, O believer, who performs the prescribed prayers and recites God's Names! When you say, for example, "I bear witness
that there is no god but God" or "Muhammad is the Messenger
of God" or "All praise be to God," you have made a claim, announced a cause and conviction, and declared a conclusion. At
the moment you have done this, hundreds of millions testify to
your truthfulness in your cause and you feel as if millions of
millions of believers who lived before you and uttered the same
pronouncements confirm you. Also, whatever testifies to the
truth of Islam, whatever confirms its essentials or judgements,
and all the proofs and witnesses by which portions of the castle
of Islam are supported—all this affirms you in your cause and
strengthens your conviction and conclusion. Again, your pronouncements receive innumerable blessings and gifts, and
countless rewards pour down in return for them. They are surrounded by an attractive halo of meaning and an enlivening, in-
spiring spirit formed of the radiations of the spiritual ecstasies
of the community of believers and the light showers emitted by
the hearts of those believing in the Unity of God who absorb the
water of life from the fountains of these blessed words.

Know, O friend! It is an established rule that the one who affirms something is preferred to him who negates it. This is so because negation is self-restricted whereas affirmation is not to be limited to a single source or means. If a thousand people negate something, this negation will not be stronger than that of a single one. But if a thousand people affirm something, the affirmation of one of them will be as strong as that of all of them. Assume a man sees the moon through a window, and another one through another, and a third one through a third, and so on. Since each has seen the moon through his own window and all of them confirm one another, the affirmation by one of the existence of the moon will be as strong as that of the number of all those who have declared that they have seen the moon. By contrast, assume a man has not seen the moon because he does not have a window to look through, another one, because of the weakness of his sight, and a third one, because he has not looked, and so on. Then the strength of the negation of each will be restricted to itself. Their denial of the existence of the appearance of the moon does not at all mean that the moon does not exist in itself. The denial of each does not support that of the other because of the variation of reasons, despite the multiplicity of those who deny. Thus, the denial of each is restricted to the one who denies.

If you have understood this subtle point, know that even if the whole world of misguidance and unbelief were agreed upon the denial of an issue of belief, their denial would be like the denial of a single person. It has no value other than being a defective argument restricted to a single one. As for the agreement of the guided on the matters of belief, since all of them confirm all and each, each of them has as many witnesses as the number of all.

Know, O friend! The parts or stones of a strong building support one another and each derives strength from the whole, and the weakness of each separately is removed because of each supporting the other. It is as if the whole building helps each of its parts. Likewise, knowing the properties of each of the branches and fruits of a tree depends on knowing the whole of the tree, while each provides knowledge for the whole. It is as if each of them is a window to look through at each, and serves as a standard to know it. It is in this way that each of the radiations of belief and Islam, and their subject-matters, is supported by the whole and can be more clear and understandable in parallel with the number of the whole. The more belief and Islam are ramified, the more we are convinced and sure of the truth of each of their parts. Despite this fact, the carnal self and Satan tend towards the opposite way: they take the weakness of a part as a pretext to see the whole as weak.

Know, O friend! Each part of the universe serves as a unit of comparison to see the possibility of the existence of all of its other parts. Conversely, the parts of the universe serve as units of comparison to see the possibility of the existence of each of its parts.

Know, O friend! The least part of a very great whole needs [for its being] whatever the whole needs [for its being]. Whatever a tree needs, a fruit needs it also. So, the Creator of the fruit, rather, of the least of its individual cells, is surely the Creator of the tree, and (by the same token), of the whole of the earth and the whole tree of creation.

Know, O friend! (This is an) issue the two halves of which are infinitely distant from each other and each, like a seed, has flourished and grown into an elaborate tree. [After the evidence of its growth] no one should retain any doubt of the uniqueness and authenticity of that issue. It is possible to have some doubt of the nature of seeds as long as they remain as seeds under earth. But after each has grown into a tree and yielded fruit, if you still have doubt of its kind while its fruits witness to what kind it is, and if you confound it with some other seed, its fruits will contradict you.

For example, it will not be easy for you to assume a seed that has become an apple tree as the seed of bitter gourd, unless you fancy it to be so or all of its fruits change into gourds, which is impossible.

Prophethood is like a seed from which the tree of Islam has grown with all its flowers and fruits. The Qur'an is a sun which has yielded the fruits of the planets of the eleven pillars of Islam.[1] [Is it possible to still have doubt of the authenticity and soundness of that seed after we have seen all its invaluable fruits?]

Know, O friend! An egg hatches and a peacock chick or other fine young bird comes out. Then this chick or young bird grows into a big, beautiful peacock or other beautiful bird flying in the sky. Or a tree grows from a seed and stretches its branches high into the sky and yields fruit. If one seeks to find in the eggshell what he has heard of the beauties and qualities of the peacock or the bird, he has surely deceived himself. Or if he desires to find in the husk of its seed under earth what he has heard of the grandeur and flowers and fruits of the tree, he has surely made a fool of himself.

Similarly, if one views our Prophet, upon him be peace and blessings, superficially, in the light of what history books narrate of the beginning of his life, one will not be able to perceive him and appreciate his worth and recognize fully his character. However, the religion of Islam and the world civilization of Islam have flourished from him. One should consider the narrations of history and biography books as a thin cover which, like the moon that split in two by a gesture of the Prophet's finger, would be torn apart to show him as the seed and founder of this civilization. One should regard what one sees of the merely human dimension of his being as the shell of a seed from which the blessed tree of Prophet Muhammad has grown. It is a tree that has been watered by Divine blessings and has flourished continually through time by the help of Divine favoring. Whatever one hears of his merely human qualities and states, and of the beginning of his life, one should never get stuck there. Rather, one should immediately direct one's attention to the degree of greatness he had attained at the final point of his greatness, being something that is impossible for one to perceive.

---

1. That is, the six pillars of belief and five pillars of Islam (Tr.).

Also, someone who is studying his character with a doubting or idle curiosity cannot distinguish between being a subject and being an object, a source and a mirror. He cannot differentiate between being like a letter, which has no meaning in itself and therefore draws attention to other than itself, and being like a word which, having a meaning in itself, attracts attention to itself. He cannot distinguish between what is essential to or inherent in the Divine Being and what is disseminated or manifested by Him. The Prophet, upon him be peace and blessings, is purely a created servant of God Almighty, one much more advanced than anybody else in worshipping and servanthood to Him. We must view him as one who is the object of Divine manifestations. Whatever he has of perfections is from the Almighty.

As we have repeatedly mentioned, nothing, whether big or small, can be, of itself, the real source or origin of anything. But, the tiniest particle can, like a mirror [reflecting what is manifested in it of God's manifestations], contain even the stars of the heavens. However, one heedless of the reality of things views each thing in respect of itself, and not in respect of the origin of what is manifested in it, and is so misled into conceiving of the Divine art as nature.

Know, O friend! Surely prayer or supplication contains the meanings of belief in One God and worship. The one who prays secretly and silently, should be convinced that the One to Whom he prays hears and knows his desires and needs and is able to supply them. This requires holding the conviction that the One to Whom he prays knows all things and is powerful over all things.

Know, O friend! By way of manifestation, the sun—the lamp of the world—can enter the eye of a gnat and illuminate it. But the flame produced by lighting a match cannot enter that eye by itself. If it entered it, the eye would be blind. In the same way, a minute particle can be an object of the manifestations of the Names of the Eternal "Sun", whereas it is impossible for it to contain something truly effective and operative in creation, even if that something is smaller than the minutest of particles.

Know, O friend! O selfhood, obstinate, conceited and proud! Look at how weak, impotent, destitute and abject you are! A microbe that can be seen only by magnifying it hundreds of times can confront you and utterly defeat you.

Know, O friend! It shows to what degree man is weak and impotent when left to his devices and before the Creator's Power and Grandeur, that when he sets out to traverse his memory, which is said to occupy a space in the brain the size of a mustard grain, he finds this tiny grain stretch before him like a vast desert impossible to cross. While man cannot finish travelling across his memory, the size of a mustard grain, how can he travel through the whole [of his mind]? If, with respect to the mind, the memory becomes like a boundless desert, the mind will be like an unfathomable ocean. Glory be to Him Who has made the grain [of memory] like a world for the mind and the world like a grain for it!

Know O friend! Man unjustly attributes the fruits of the work of a group to a single person and assumes that that individual has produced those fruits. From this injustice a kind of secret association of partners with God arises. For assuming the result of the work of a community and the product of their free will to have originated from a single person means accepting that person has an extraordinary power which has reached the degree of creativity. The gods and goddesses of ancient Greeks and other pagan peoples were devised from such devilish assumptions.

Know, O friend! Man is surrounded by concentric circles. One of those circles is formed of his clothes and body. Another circle, of his native town, and another, of the earth, and still another, of the material, visible world, and so on. However, except the smallest one, he has no part in or influence on any of these circles. He is unable to do anything substantial with respect to the other circles; rather, they have an effect on him. He can only benefit from them both materially and spiritually. If he ventures to interfere with them, he only diminishes his benefit from them because of his defective nature.

Know, O friend! The one who recites God's Names benefits from them through many of his faculties. Through some of those faculties he benefits from the recitation consciously and through others, unconsciously. Therefore, the recitation made unconsciously cannot be said to give no benefit.

Know, O friend! God Almighty has created man of a very strange composition. He is a uniform being composed of a great multitude of parts. He is both simple and complex at the same time. He is a single individual but composed of organs, limbs, systems, senses, feelings and faculties, each of which has its own pains and pleasures, together with others related to and coming from the whole of the body. There is a swift, mutual helping and support among them. By virtue of such genuine creation of his, if he assumes the way of servanthood to God, man will be rewarded, especially in the Hereafter, with all kinds of pleasures and blessings and all degrees and varieties of perfections. If, by contrast, he follows the misleading way of egoism, he will be the target of all sorts of pains and sufferings and all forms of torments. Toothache is different from earache. The pleasures of the eyes are different from the pleasures of the tongue. Also, the pleasures and pains originating in touch, imagination, the reason and the heart, are all different from one another.

Know, O friend! The benefits of the non-definition of the time of death are a clear proof of its being definite in the knowledge of the Originator. Had it been made definite [for man], supposing it to be dependent on a "natural" law, man would have thought that it is undefined within the Divine Knowledge. Since it is not defined for man, man is left no right to suppose it is also undefined [in the Divine Knowledge].

Know, O friend! The regular recitation of certain Divine Names is among the marks or signs of Islam. The signs of Islam are too exalted for the "hand" of ostentation and hypocrisy to reach.

Know, O friend! The repetition of the formula proclaiming the Divine Unity—*There is no god but God*—is for the purpose of isolating the heart from sorts of [inner] relations with [whatever separates man from God] and false objects of worship. For the one who recites this formula has many faculties and senses, each of which should be convinced of the Divine Unity and absolutely isolated from polytheistic attitudes particular to itself.

Know, O friend! It makes no difference whether you send as a gift the reward of the recitation of, say, the Opening Chapter of the Qur'an—*sura al-Fatiha*—to one man or to thousands or millions of people, as there is no difference between one man and thousands in hearing a word uttered. For immaterial things multiply or spread very rapidly, without one copy thereof hindering any other, like a light being reflected in one or in millions of mirrors.

Know, O friend! Calling blessings and peace upon the Prophet, upon him be peace and blessings, is like answering the invitation of the Giver of Bounties Who spreads His blessings freely and has laid the table of His bounties on him whom He honored with Ascension. When the one who calls blessings and peace upon the Prophet, upon him be peace and blessings, mentions the Prophet with a (good) attribute, he should concentrate and reflect on the one he praises so that he may grow in zeal to call peace and blessings on him over and over again.

Know, O religious scholar! Do not grieve about people's indifference to your knowledge and the inadequacy of the wage they pay you. For the worldly payment or reward comes in proportion to need, not to the degree of personal merit. The reward of personal merit will be given in the Hereafter. It is not permissible for you to sell it—your personal merit—at a small price, for the delusive provisions of this world.

Know, O writer and public speaker who addresses people in the language of the media! You should be humble [before people] and feel free to announce your defects, repenting. However, you have no right to feel self-pride and publicize what is against the marks or signs of Islam. Who has allowed you, who has deputed you, and from where have you taken the right, to spread groundless doubts about the religion of Islam, to disseminate misguidance among the nation and the Muslim community? Do you think that the whole of the nation is misguided like you? No one is permitted to see or show others as deviated. From where have you taken the permission to condemn with suspicion the whole of the Muslim community as deviated from the symbols of Islam? Surely, to publish in the media what the majority of believers do not accept is calling to deviation, and the one who publishes such matter is a caller to deviation.

Know, O friend! Since unbelief is the opposite of belief, the unbelievers are hostile to the believers. It is for this reason that love of the unbelievers, with whom it is impossible to establish friendship, is of no use at all. The wise Qur'an has condemned the unbelievers and their unbelieving ancestors to eternal punishment in Hell. O people of the Qur'an! Do not expect them to love and help you! Say: *God is sufficient for us. What a good guardian He is and what a good helper*!

Know, O friend! The difference between the civilization of unbelievers and that of (true) believers is this:

The former is barbarism which disguises itself as civilization. Outwardly it is glittering but inwardly hideous. It is apparently pleasing but in reality frightening. As for the civilization of believers, its inside is more exalted than its outside. In meaning it is more perfect than in appearance. It is composed of friendliness, love and mutual helping. This is so because, on account of his belief in and affirmation of the Divine Unity, a believer sees brotherhood among all things in the universe and friendship and loving among all it parts, particularly among human beings, and particularly among the believers. He also sees brotherhood in origin and union in the end. [That is, all things issue from a single origin and, after ramification like the branches of a tree, come together in the end.] As for the unbeliever, on account of his unbelief, he sees all things as hostile and alien to and separated from one another. He sees hostility even among brothers since, in his view, brotherhood is only a point of meeting between two lines of disunity or separation, one line extending back into eternity in the past and the other forwards into eternity in the future. It is only through national zeal or racial passion that the feeling of brotherhood among unbelievers may be strong for a short, limited period, but the love an unbeliever seems to feel for his brother is in fact for himself. The acceptable humanitarian aspects of the civilization of the unbelievers and the spiritual virtues to be seen in it are either borrowings from the civilization of Islam or leftovers from the heavenly religions or are owed to the guidance of the Qur'an [being in the world].

If you wish, imagine yourself among a group in the presence of a Muslim spiritual leader in any village whose conversation emits rays of the Islamic civilization. In his presence you will find lords sitting with the poor and angels mixed with human beings. Then, go to a European capital and join a meeting of the barons or lords. You will find there "scorpions" clothed in human dress and "demons" in the form of human beings.

Know, O friend, who desires *ijtihad*—the evolution through reasoning of new religious precedents in the Islamic law—that the door to *ijtihad* is open. However, it is not permissible to go in through that door in the following circumstances:

One: At a time when winter gales are blowing and when it is proper for even small holes to be closed up, how can doors be opened? In the same way, at a time when unacceptable acts are done freely, innovations opposed to the spirit of religion come in floods and destructive thoughts attack from all sides, it is not reasonable, nor permissible, to cause the destruction of the "wall" by making breaches in it.

Two: The essentials of Islam cannot be made subject to *ijtihad*. They are like nourishment or sustenance for Muslims and are neglected, ever rejected, today. For this reason, we must strive with all our strength to revive them and apply them in our practical life. Then, if need arises, *ijtihad* may be applied in secondary, theoretical matters, which have, in fact, been made by earlier scholars spacious enough to encompass the answers to the needs of all times.

Three: Every epoch or period has goods in great demand in

its market. The goods in demand in the market of today are politics and securing [the necessities of] the worldly life. However, in the time of the centuries following that of the Prophet, upon him be peace and blessings, what was in demand was inferring from His *Word*—the Qur'an—the things pleasing to the Creator of the universe and securing eternal happiness. Since minds, hearts and spirits were all concentrated at that time on knowing the things pleasing to the Lord of the heavens and earth, whoever had potential or capacity learned, consciously or unconsciously, from the circumstances, and the happenings and conversations, prevailing at that time. It was as if everything served to teach and prepare those with enough capacity for *ijtihad*, so that the fuel of their minds ignited even if they were not lit with the "match" of special study. When they turned to *ijtihad*, this meant light upon light for them. But today minds and hearts are in great confusion. [Because of the disorienting complexity of modern life] people cannot concentrate on one subject and modern trends of thought and politics dominate minds. For this reason, for an individual with the same degree of intelligence as Sufyan ibn Uyayna[2] to attain the competence to do *ijtihad* requires tenfold the time that Sufyan did. For when Sufyan, at the age of puberty, started to study for *ijtihad*, his capacity was like a match ready to ignite. But the capacity of his modern counterpart is distant from *ijtihad* to the extent of being deeply grounded [and bounded] in modern, non-religious sciences and hardened by them to the degree of his preoccupation with them.

Four: If one who desires to do *ijtihad*, to expand the sphere of the Islamic secondary matters, aims to attain to the higher degrees of piety and follow the essentials of Islam more strictly, this desire causes perfection. However, if one who neglects to follow the pillars of Islam and prefers the worldly life over the

---

2. Sufyan ibn Uyayna was one of the greatest scholars of Islamic history. Born in 726, he died in 814. He was well-versed in *Hadith* and *Fiqh*. He met more than eighty scholars belonging to the generation following the Companions. He narrated Hadith from Zuhri, Ibn Munkadir, Ibn al-Zinad, A'mash and others. Imam al-Shafi'i, Shu'ba, Ibn Ishaq, Ibn Jurayh and Yahya ibn Kathir and some others narrated from him. He was a very pious and God-fearing scholar.

Hereafter, then his desire to do *ijtihad* is an inclination to destruction insofar as it is, in reality, a seeking of ways to be freed from religious responsibilities.

Five: The benefit from a religious obligation is the cause of preferring to fulfil it; that benefit is not the cause of its being legislated in the first place. However, the modern view tends to make the benefit to be expected from it the cause of something being legislated. The modern view also considers worldly happiness first. But the view of the *Shari'a* considers, first of all, the eternal happiness and then takes the worldly life into consideration proportionally to its being the means of acquiring the eternal happiness. Furthermore, many of the modern "needs" to which people have become habituated have only become "necessities of life" because of people's abuse of their will and unlawful tendencies. Therefore, their "necessity" cannot be put forward, except as an unlawful pretext, as the reason for new dispensations and means of making unlawful things lawful. This is the same principle whereby, for a drunken man—one who has drunk of his free will—the plea of drunkenness cannot be admitted in excuse for criminal conduct. So, any *ijtihad* to be done with that view and in such modern considerations will be "earthly", not "heavenly". And any addition or amendment in the laws of the Creator of the heavens and earth and ruling His servants without His authority is to be rejected.

Know, O one who is enveloped by heedlessness and the darkness of naturalism, and consequently has become "blind" and "deaf", a "worshipper" of material causes in the darkness of imagining nature as the origin of existence! I will only explain to you one of the fifty-five "languages" spoken by each of the minute particles and compounds of the universe to witness the necessary existence of the Almighty and His Unity in His Divinity and Lordship. It concerns that anguish of mind and spirit that follows from the misguidance of attributing things to themselves or to material causes. From this anguish spirits and minds seek refuge with the Necessarily Existent Being, One and Single, with Whose Power it is possible to explain all difficulties, and with Whose Will all ambiguities can be clarified, and in Whose remembrance all hearts find peace and tranquility.

If you wish to understand it clearly, consider this: Creation is to be attributed to either creatures themselves and causes or the One, Necessarily Existent Being. Because of defective reasoning, it may be supposed difficult to attribute all things to the Necessarily Existent Being. Then, because of the absolute inadequacy of any cause to give existence to any creature, attributing their existence to self-creation or material causes is not something to be supposed, but really and certainly is impossible. What is supposed in the first alternative is certain in the second. Furthermore, while there is only one supposed difficulty in attributing creation to a Single, Necessarily Existent Being, the obvious difficulty and impossibility in attributing it to creatures themselves or causes are as many as the number of the parts of the universe. For example, if a honeybee is not attributed to a Single, Necessarily Existent Being, because of its interrelation with all parts of the world, all the heavens and earth would have to take part in its coming into existence. Also, the origination of multiple things from a single source is by far easier than a single thing's origination from numerous sources that are in contradiction with one another and deaf and blind and whose coming together increases them only in deafness and blindness.

As has been mentioned, if the supposed difficulty in attributing things to a Single Being is only as great as a minute particle, then, it will become as big as mountains when creatures are attributed to themselves or to causes. For with a single movement a single being can produce a result and give a form or order to multiple things. However, it will not be easy for multiple things to produce the same result even with many movements, and they will be able to give the same form or order only after exerting great effort and suffering much difficulty. For example, a single commander can command numerous soldiers very easily, which is impossibly difficult for the soldiers themselves. Innumerable drops come from a single water jet.

The one supposed difficulty in the former case becomes innumerable impossibilities in the second. Some of these impossibilities are as follows:

Since the perfect artistry and design observed in things requires an all-encompassing knowledge, an absolute sight, a perfect power and an all-inclusive will, each of the particles forming them should have the attributes of the Necessarily Existent Being.

If things are not attributed to a Single, Necessarily Existent Being, then it would be necessary to attribute divinity to each thing and thereby associate partners with the Divine Being in His Divinity and Necessary Existence, which should be absolutely free from having partners.

If we do not attribute a dome to a builder, then the faultless construction of the dome, impossible to occur by chance, would require that each of the stones forming it should be as knowledgeable and skillful as an engineer. Like those stones, if things are not attributed to a Single Being, the particles or atoms forming a thing should be both consciously dominant over and dominated by each other and the thing itself.

Since the absolute balance, solidarity, mutual helping and correlation observed in the universe require a comprehensive consciousness and absolute power of seeing, each of the particles forming things and causes should have this degree of consciousness and knowledge and power of seeing. If things are attributed to themselves, they themselves or even each of the particles forming them should have these attributes, and if they are attributed to causes, then causes should have them.

Many other such impossibilities and false conceptions like the ones mentioned will arise in the non-acceptance of a Single, Necessarily Existent Being as the originator of all things.

Whereas, when things are attributed to their true Lord, Who necessarily exists and is One, particles and compounds become like the drops of rain bearing images of the sun by way of reflection. They are objects coming into existence by the rays of the manifestations of the Divine Power, absolute, luminous, comprehensive, eternal and infinite, based on, rather, including, the eternal, infinite Knowledge and Will. It is the Power to Which the miracles of creatures testify and Whose single ray is more radiant and penetrating than the sun, as the lights of the sun can be hindered, refracted, divided and scattered in the world of multiplicity—the (material) world where things exist separately and in abundance. The least portion of that Power is greater than the largest of material causes, as a partial manifestation of something luminous possesses the properties of the whole even in the world of multiplicity—like the sun being "contained" even in the smallest piece of glass.

The difference between attributing things to themselves or causes and to the One, Necessarily Existent Being is like the difference between the image of the sun reflected in a drop of water and claiming that image as the sun itself. How inconceivable a claim that is! By contrast, there is no difficulty in the eternal Divine Power penetrating even the least thing. In relation to It, particles and stars, parts and wholes, individuals and species, the few and the many, the small and big, you and the universe, the seed and the tree, are each and all the same. For that Power is essential and intrinsic to the Divine Being Himself, eternal and infinite, and therefore it is inconceivable that It has an opposite. It has also no degrees and, in respect of It, any limitation or impotence is inconceivable. Since It has no degrees, the least and the greatest are the same in relation to It.

In order to understand this point more clearly through comparisons from the sphere of contingencies and multiplicity, consider the following—God's is the highest comparison, that is, concerning God the highest and most sublime similitudes should be coined:

Because of *transparency*, in receiving the manifestations of the sun in the form of images, pieces of glass, oceans and planets are the same. Because of *facing each other*, in reflecting the light of a lamp standing at a central point, the least of the mirrors on the smallest circle (around that center) and all of the mirrors on the largest circle are the same. Because of *being imma-*

terial, in benefiting from it—as from a source of light, for example—great numbers of things are not hindrances to one another. For example, in hearing a word uttered, one and thousands are the same—it can be heard by thousands of people at the same time without one hindering the other. [There is a very precise *balance* or *measurement* in the universe. In order to understand the preciseness of this measurement,] consider a balance so large and so sensitive that things as small as walnuts or as big as mountains can be weighed with the same exactness. Suppose we were to weigh a pair of things, whether as big and heavy as two suns or as small and light as two walnuts, if a walnut is put on either of the scales, the scales would be worlds apart from each other on account of the sensitivity of the balance. Because of exact *orderliness* and *interconnection* among things, it will not be more difficult for a child to start or steer a huge vessel than starting or steering his toy ship. Because of *obedience*, with the command of "March," a commander can move a huge army as easily as a single private. Since the reality of existence is incorporeal and what gives a species its nature is not its physical composition, the smallest member of a species is of the same nature as its biggest member, as well as all the members of it. Thus, because of such essential properties of things or basic characteristics of existence, in relation to the Divine Power, the few and the many and the big and small are the same.

The inner dimension of existence [which is its essential dimension, while the outward visible, material forms are transient and accidental] is transparent. The face of all things in existence is turned toward the Divine Power, which is incorporeal and of pure light. There is an infinitely precise balance in existence and all things are infinitely well ordered and interconnected with one another. All of the particles forming things are "enthusiastically" obedient to the Divine laws and orders of creation that may be summed up in the word *Be*! And the Necessarily Existent Being is absolutely free from corporeality and detached from corporeal things. Because of these properties belonging to things and the Divine Power, it is equally easy for the Divine

Power to bring back to life a single fly and the earth after their death, to create a honeybee and the heavens and earth, to originate a minute particle and the sun. Actually, this ease is visible and tangible enough not to need proof; (for example, the apparently dry dead wood of vines or palm trees produces clusters of grapes or dates]. The Divine Power, Whose nature is unknown to us, but Whose miraculous acts are not unknown to us, is such that if Its acts are attributed to causes or themselves, innumerable difficulties will certainly arise. Whereas the Divine Power penetrates the inner, transparent dimensions of things or their archetypes—which constitute the essence of their existence in Divine Knowledge—even through such small openings as the eye of a needle and manifests on them by Its creativity.

In sum, what we all see concerning the creation of the Power of things demonstrates:

One: that means and apparent causes are to serve as veils to preserve the dignity of the Power [in the eyes of people] in Its dealing with the corporeal aspects of things. [For people, because of their inability to see the true wisdom of the Power in creating things and events construed as misfortunes, may blame the Divine Being. Thus, in order to save them from such a perilous impudence, God acts behind causes in the visible, material world.]

Two: that in dealing with things like life, existence and light, which are transparent in both their outer and inner aspects, veils—means and causes—are not put between them and the Divine Power.

Three: that the Divine Power does not have the least difficulty in dealing with things. Nothing is difficult for that Power, Which makes a huge fig tree from its seed, tiny as a particle of dust, and hangs a cluster of grapes from a stem, thin as a thread. Actually, the existence of the Owner of that eternal Power is more manifest than the existence of the universe. Each creature testifies to its own existence in a few ways, whereas it bears witness to the existence of its Maker in many observable and intelligible and rational ways. Whatever creature it is, if all heavenly and earthly causes came together and supported one another, they would not be able to produce a like of it. In the art they contain and the skill they require to be made, neither is the seed of a fig tree less than the tree itself nor is a man less than the whole earth. So, the Power Who originates the seed and man has no difficulty at all in creating the tree and the earth.

O you who go astray by supposing it impossible to attribute things to the One Necessarily Existent Being! You have seen that the difficulty and impossibility lie in attributing existence to itself or to causes. The anguishes of mind and spirit arising from the deviation of attributing things to themselves or to causes cease only in fleeing and submission to the One Necessarily Existent Being, by Whose Power alone the existence of all things can be explained. It is by referring to His Will that all ambiguities can be clarified, and through His remembrance and dependence on His Name that hearts and minds can find peace and tranquility.

Know, O friend! The area where man's mind and heart move is too spacious to be encompassed. Although he sometimes travels within a minute particle, floats in a drop, and imprisons himself in a dot, he actually puts the whole of the world before his eyes and includes in his intellect the whole of creation, aspiring to see the Necessarily Existent Being. Sometimes he becomes smaller than a minute particle but sometimes he is greater than the heavens. While at times he enters a drop, at other times he includes the whole of existence with all its species and parts.

Know, O friend! For the gifts God has ordained for man to attain to or make use of, there are conditions some of which are established by God and some pertain to man himself. For example, light, air, food and speech are God's gifts, benefiting from which depends on having sound and healthy eyes, nose, mouth and ears etc. All such senses and organs have been created by God Almighty; our part in having them is only doing what we should do to keep them sound and healthy. You should never suppose that they are things found on the way by chance so that you can own and dispose of them however you wish. They come to you by the Will of the One Who bestows them on you, and you keep them working by your own will and use them according to the wish of the One Who grants them.

Know, O friend! Things are not more ordered and sound in their beginning than in their end. Nor are their outward appearances and forms more beautiful in art and more exalted in wisdom than their insides. Never suppose that things are left to the hand of chance to play with in their end and inner aspects. Do you not see that the flower and the fruit growing from it display more wisdom than the seed and the shoot growing from it? The Maker, His Majesty be exalted, is He Who is the First, the Last, the Outward and the Inward, and Who knows all things.

Know, O friend! The miraculousness of the Qur'an saves the Qur'an from corruption. It is impossibly difficult for the words of anyone, whether that one be an interpreter of the Qur'an or a writer or a translator or a corrupter or any other, to be confused with the verses of the Qur'an. It is not possible for that one to put on the Qur'an's "dress", as happened with the other revealed books which were confused and mixed with the words of others and finally corrupted.

Know, O friend! There is repetition of the verse, *Which of the blessings of your Lord do you deny?* in *sura al-Rahman* at the end of the revealed verses pointing to diverse "natural" phenomena—each being a sign of Divine Existence and Oneness. It indicates that the disobedience of mankind and jinn [to God's commands] and their rebelliousness and ingratitude mostly arise from their blindness to the Divine act of bestowing bounties, and heedlessness to the One Who bestows, and therefore their attribution of bounties to causes and chance. Consequently, they become deniers of God's blessings. It is therefore necessary for a believer to recite at the beginning of using or consuming each bounty, *In the Name of God, the Merciful, the Compassionate.* This means that it is from God and he takes it in His Name and for His sake, not for the sake of means and causes, and therefore to Him belongs all praise and gratitude.

Know, O friend, who is exposed to the whisperings of Satan and involuntary thoughts and suggestions arising from the heart and carnal self, and before whom some obscene scenes and imaginations appear when he sets about considering and reflecting on Divine truths! Dark, disgusting clouds of obscenity and malice pass before your eyes, with the imagination of which you tremble when you look at the "Sun" of truths. It is as if your hands became fouled with the filth of your imagination when you stretch them for the glorification of God and your eyes soiled with the excretion of your carnal self when you fix them on God's praise and extolling. Then, this filth and excretion were reflected on things sacred in your view, making you suffer because of them and drawing your attention to them more closely. Do not suffer from them and do not abandon yourself to pondering them in order to be saved from this state. They give no harm unless you suppose them as harmful and concentrate on them. Look at the sun and its light, and the sky and its stars, and a garden and its flowers, through the holes of a garment stained with various bits of dirt. Do you not see that it is impossible that what you see can become smeared with those bits of dirt. The suggestions and thoughts occurring to you unintentionally are like certain insects and bees. If you attempt to struggle with them in order to be protected against them, they will crowd and pester you more. If you cease to struggle with them, they will leave you.

Know, O friend, who, preoccupied with philosophy and preferring reason to Revelation, comments on Revelation, and thereby rather corrupts it as he cannot comprehend it with his defective reason and because of his vainglory and engrossment in philosophy. Once I thought as you think now. But later I saw a high, brilliant castle whose floors are connected to the ceiling of the heavens, from whose windows are hung different ropes. Some of these ropes are close to the earth. Whoever is able to overcome his carnal self to hold fast to any of them can rise to the highest stations. Then, I have seen some people who, lost in their vainglory and in heedlessness to those ropes, attempt to rise on things like stones which they pile up under their feet. After rising a little, they fall. What do they have to do with rising? I have seen others who, relying on their refractory, haughty egos, drive nails into the walls of the castle and try to clamber up by them. However, they also fall and have their necks broken. And so on. I have observed that whatever a man has of abilities and intellectual faculties is given to him to use them according to his capacity and to use in order to rise to the ropes, not to the stations. Your reason is a rope by which you are fettered, while you can rise by Revelation. Whoever relies on God, God is sufficient for him.

Know, O friend, who wonders about the triumph of the sinful wrongdoers over the pious and about the supremacy of the wicked over the righteous in the worldly life! In a vision I saw a castle. There were pavilions in it one within another. Their inhabitants varied in beauty, exaltedness, glory and luster. The one who was sitting in the center resembled the king. Below him down to the portal were rooms whose residents varied in rank and distinction. The one who stood by the door was a servant and before the door lay a fawning dog. Then I saw another castle with a glittering front. In wonder, I looked into it and saw there the king was playing with the dog in front of the portal. The women dressed immodestly were making jokes with the children and while the important tasks were left undone, the duties or functions of the dog, children and servants of the lowest degree seemed to have acquired prominence. The residents were busy with shameful things. However glittering, fortified and magnificent the castle was in appearance, in reality it was dark and in a wretched state.[3] You may take the castles as representing men. For I have seen an individual man like a castle. I have even seen my carnal self as a castle. The inhabitants of cas-

---

3. Of the castles, the first stands for a believer who, although in appearance dull and not glittering, is in reality happy and brilliant, and whose faculties like the heart and intellect and senses and organs perform their functions according to the will of the Creator. The second castle represents a modern unbeliever who, glittering and happy in appearance, is unhappy and uses his faculties, senses and organs only for the temporary pleasures of the world. (Tr.)

tles are of infinitely different degrees or ranks [in knowledge and/or morality or having human values.] I have observed that what modern civilized people call progress is falling and degeneration. What they call acquiring and holding power is vulgarization and loss of value. What they call being awake, revival and enlightenment is deepening in sleep of heedlessness. And what they call politeness is show and hypocrisy; cleverness, Satanic intriguing, and humanity being metamorphosed into beasts. However, as a result of his God-given radiating faculties being together with his dark soul, some graceful and attractive scenes may appear in this fallen, rebellious man. But as for the pious believer obeying God Almighty, his carnal self represents the sorrowful-looking dog in front of the door. He uses his God-given faculties not to gratify his lowly desires and fancies but to guide the misguided and help them to get back to what they were created for. If God Almighty loves a servant of His, He does not make him love the beauties of the world; rather, He makes him, through certain misfortunes, despise them.

Alas! What a pity that this corrupt civilization has developed certain attractive devices and charming toys by which the inhabitants of the castle of man are fascinated, like moths attracted by lights, which become burning fire for them.

Know, O wretched, sinful Said! Why is this self-conceit, heedlessness and indifference [to God's blessings]? Don't you see that you have a free will no stronger than a hair and power no greater than a minute particle? Don't you see that you have a life no more enduring than a flash of light, consciousness no brighter than a dim, decaying ray of light, time no longer than a passing moment, and space the size of a grave? However, your impotence is endless, your needs are infinite, your poverty is boundless, and your ambitions are limitless. Should one so needy and impotent rely on what is in his hand and depend on his self or should he rely on God, the All-Merciful and the All-Compassionate? Among the wrappings of His Mercy and chests of bounties there are those light-filled and light-diffusing suns and fruit-bearing trees, and among the streams rising from the source of His blessings and the floods of His Mercy are water and light.

Know, O friend, who regards the conclusion as too great for the evidence declared to lead to! Every individual element among the truths of belief for which there is an evidence is corroborated, supported and strengthened by every other that indicates the truth of Islam and each part of Islam. It is as if the innumerable evidences, witnesses, and signs of the truth of Islam and the truths of belief corroborate the truth of each and set the seal of approval on it. For, as was mentioned at the beginning of this treatise, while (because of the incompatibility of reasons) the negation or rejection of one thousand people is no stronger than the negation of only one, the more of those who confirm, the more strong their argument.

Know, O friend! Intensity of love causes denial of the thing loved. This is also true for the intensity of fear, the excess of greatness [the excessive greatness of one causes one to be denied], and comprehensiveness of reason. Intensity of love for that which may not be attained can lead the thing loved to be denied. So also, the intensity of fear may cause one to deny that which one fears. Likewise, the greatness that is beyond the grasp of reason may, being beyond its grasp, be denied by that reason.

Know, O friend! I am as fully convinced as if I had directly observed that the seed of unbelief potentially bears Hell, in the way that a mustard plant is compacted in its seed. Likewise, belief potentially bears the seed of Paradise, in the way that the palm-tree is compacted in its fruit stone. It is not strange that a seed or a stone grows into a plant or a tree, the plant of mustard or the palm in our example. Similarly, it should not be considered as impossible or odd that the essence of misguidance is embodied as a tormenting hell and the lights of guidance are embodied as a sweet paradise.

Know, O friend! If a seed or fruit-stone is pierced in the heart, it cannot grow to become 'proud' of itself. Similarly, when the hard grain of the human ego is pierced with the rays and burning "flames" of regular recitation of the Divine Name, it cannot grow and become strengthened to be proud of itself in heedlessness like Pharao by relying on the accomplishments of its species (humankind) and contentiously rebelling against the All-Compelling and Overwhelming Lord of the heavens and earth. The saints belonging to the order of *Naqshbandiya* have been able to open up the grain of the heart and find a short way to ignite the rocky mountain of ego, smashing the head of the conceited self with the "drill" of the silent recitation of God's Names. While through the loud recitation of those Names the idol of (philosophical) naturalism is destroyed or broken into pieces.

Know, O friend! As in other spheres of multiplicity—the corporeal spheres where things exist separately and in abundance —in the most remote, largest and delicate of them, the imprints of wisdom, care and making firm and perfect are clearly observed. If you want an example, look at the remotest ends of the skin enveloping the human body. See how on the page of its forehead and on its face and in its palms the Pen of the Divine Power has inscribed lines and designs pointing to the meanings in the spirit of man. The invisible, immaterial copy of the history of his whole life is hung around his neck which points to his destiny included in his creation. This inscription [which indicates man's destiny] does not leave an opening through which blind chance and other "blind" or "squint-eyed" agents [like causality] can penetrate.

Know, O friend, who is fond of this worldly life. You think that the purpose of life and of whatever the Eternal Power has entrusted to the essence of man and living beings—such as wonderful systems and extraordinary faculties—is only to maintain this fleeting life, to secure its continuance! No, it cannot be! If the purpose of life consists in its continuance, then the most manifest, clearest and radiant proofs of wisdom, favoring and orderliness and the absolute lack of futility, which are observed throughout the universe and witnessed by the overall order of the universe, would become, [since everything perishes,] the

most astonishing instances of futility, wastefulness, purposelessness and chaos. What falls to one's part from the fruits and
purposes of life is proportionate to the degree of one's part in
ownership of one's life and disposal of it. The other purposes
and fruits pertain to the Giver of Life, His Majesty be exalted.
Man is but the object of the manifestations of His Names. God
will display the colors and the radiations of His Mercy in Paradise in the afterlife, which will consist of the fruits growing from
the seeds of this worldly life.

Man's relation with his life is like the relation between a
steersman and the royal ship that he steers. What the steersman
does is putting his fingers on the instruments necessary to move
and steer the ship. What falls to his part from the uses and income of the ship is proportionate to his relation with the ship
and the service he renders. It is no more than about one in thousands. This is the same relation with any living being and the
ship of its existence and life. What falls to the part of a living being from the uses and purposes of its life is only one in thousands. Moreover, this one is not the part it has deserved by itself.

Know, O my heart! The pleasures of the world and its beauties without knowledge of our Creator, our Owner, our Lord,
even if they are at the degree of those of Paradise, are no more
than a hell. This is my experience and observation. With His
knowledge, a blessing like compassion becomes so pleasing and
sweet that it may make man indifferent to whatever is in the
world, even to Paradise.

Know, O my heart! Whatever happens in the world has two
aspects: one pertaining to the world, the carnal self and man's
worldly desires and fancies; the other pertaining to the Hereafter. With respect to the worldly aspect, the greatest, the most
important and the most established of affairs is of the degree of
the smallest, the most insignificant and the most fleeting in itself. So, it is not worth worrying and grieving about and attaching importance to it.

Know, O my heart! Have you seen any more stupid and more

ignorant than one who sees the image of the sun in a transient tiny object or its manifestation on a flower as color, and then demands that that image or color should be all that may be demanded from the light and heat-diffusing lamp on the ceiling of the world, which enjoys the central position in the solar system and makes the planets revolve around it? Furthermore, when what he sees in the tiny object or the flower disappears, because of his restricted and defective view, he denies the existence of the sun at midday, even if all things, dew-drops, rain-drops, all drops and bubbles of water anywhere, testify to it in broad daylight.

Then, that ignorant one confuses a shadow existence formed through manifestation or reflection according to the capacity of the thing determined by Destiny, with the main, substantial existence. For example, he sees the image of the sun in a transparent object and says, "Is the sun so little? Where is its amazing heat and other properties?" And so on.

Within such objections, there is a mistaken wish to take hold of a brand of the sun's fire or touch it with the hands or exert some sort of influence upon the sun. The one objecting does not understand that his being "near" to the sun does not mean or necessitate that the sun should be influenced by his acts. Further, he sees that the smallest things are made surprisingly firm, with astonishing care and very pleasing art, and for significant purposes; then, making a false, misleading analogy, he supposes that their Maker must have exerted superfluous effort in making them. He says, "What value does, for example, this gnat have that the Wise Maker has expended such great labor upon it?"

O you who think like a sophist! God's is the highest comparison and for Him the highest of examples and similitudes should be coined, and God is the Creator of all things and the Guardian over all things—you should keep in mind the following four points so that that matter may remain clear in your thinking:

The first point: On account of what it bears [from His Attributes], everything from minute particles to massive suns indicates the Almighty in the perfection of His Lordship. Whatever that thing has [of good] is from Him; it [i.e. that good] is not to be ascribed to it as its own [good].

The second point: In everything there are doors opened on the Almighty's Light. If some shortsighted, narrow-minded person sees one of those doors as closed, it does not follow that all the other doors are to be supposed to be also closed. Rather, one open door should be taken as an indication meaning that all of the doors are in fact open.

The third point: Destiny, which is a reflection of God's all-encompassing Knowledge, has determined for each thing a particular, fitting character out of the radiations of the absolutely luminous Names of God.

The fourth point: *His command, when He wills a thing, is but to say to it "Be!" and it is.*[4] *Your creation and your resurrection are but like [the creation and resurrection of] a single soul.*[5] If things are attributed to themselves or to possible causes, then it will require that all people of sound reasoning should accept all kinds of impossibilities, inconceivabilities, issuing from this foolish judgement, [as really possible].

Know, O friend! The Qur'an of miraculous expression explains many truths through parables and comparisons, as the abstract Divine truths take on or are presented in limited, concrete forms in this [material] sphere of contingencies. A contingent being considers the concrete forms in the sphere of contingencies and contemplates in the light of them the acts issuing from the sphere of Absolute Necessity, that is, the sphere of Divinity.

Know, O friend! The heart has the same meaning for you as the Divine Throne[6] has for the universe. Your heart in you is the "outer dimension" of your being. You are the "inner dimen-

---

4. *Ya Sin*, 36.82.

5. *Luqman*, 31.28.

6. The truth and real identity of the Divine Throne is unknown. With respect to its relationship with the creation or symbolically, it may be seen as an immaterial center by means of which God's commands are conveyed or conducted throughout the universe. For example, water is regarded as the Throne of Mercy, that is, the conductor of God's Mercy, and earth, as the conductor of life (Tr.).

sion" of your being in your heart. In the sphere of the Divine Name the Outward, the Divine Throne encompasses all things. In the sphere of the Divine Name the Inward, It is like the heart of creation. In the sphere of the Name the First, It is pointed to by *His Throne was upon the water*.[7] In the Divine Name the Last, it is symbolized by *The ceiling of Paradise is God's Throne*.[8] The Divine Throne has the qualities of being the first, the last, the outward and the inward issuing from the verse, *He is the First, the Last, the Outward, and the Inward*.[9]

Know, O friend! Helplessness gives rise to entreating and need causes praying.

O Lord, O Creator, O Owner! I entreat You, I pray to You, because I am needy. I take shelter in You through my prayer, because I am in destitution. My helplessness is my means of imploring You and asking You for help. My weakness is my treasure. My ambitions and pains are my capital. Your Beloved—the Prophet, upon him be peace and blessings—and Your Mercy are my intercessors. Pardon me, forgive my sins and have mercy on me, O God, O Merciful, O Compassionate!

---

7. A saying of the Prophet related by Ibn Maja and Ibn 'Asakir. *Jami' al-Saghir*, No. 3116.

8. *Hud*, 11.7.

9. *al-Hadid*, 57.3.

A supplication

O Lord! I looked around in all six directions, searching for a cure for my pains. Alas, I could find no cure for them.

I looked to past time on my right to find solace, but yesterday appeared to me in the form of my father's grave.

Then, I looked to the future on the left. I could find no cure. Rather, tomorrow appeared to me in the form of my grave.

I looked at the present day, and I saw it like a coffin, carrying my desperately struggling corpse.

I raised my head and saw that my corpse was looking down at me from the top.

I lowered my head and saw that the dust of my bones underfoot had mixed with the dust of my first creation.

Turning away from that direction too, I looked behind and saw a temporary world with no foundation revolving in valleys of nothingness and darkness of non-existence.

Since I saw no good from that direction either, I cast my eye ahaed of me. I saw that the door of my grave stood open at the end of my way, behind which the highway leading to eternity caught my eyes from afar.

What I have is but a insignificant free will. It lacks power, its range is short.

It can neither penetrate the past nor discern the future.

The arena where the will-power is active is brief present time and the passing present instant.

Despite all my destitution and helplessness, the "pen" of Your Power has incribed in my nature infinite desires and ambitions extending to eternity.

The sphere of need is as extensive as the eye reaches. In fact, wherever the imagination goes, the sphere of need extends that far.

Whereas the extent of my power is as narrow as my arm reaches.

My wants and needs are of infinite quantity.

Whereas my capital is as little and insignificant as an atom.

So, what does that insignificant will-power signify in the face of these needs as extensive as to encompass the universe?

However, O Lord, I give up my free will in Your way, and abandon my ego.

So that Your absolute Mercy may help and support me.

One who finds the boundless sea of Mercy, does not rely on his own free will which is no more than a "drop" from "mirage".

O Lord, this passing life is but a sleep; this life too flies like the wind.

O my wretched soul, fond of living and desirous of a long life, awaken and come to your senses!

Your Creator is He in Whose hand is all life and existence.

His is the whole of existence and it is He Who gives life and existence.

So, sacrifice your self in His way so that it will gain permanence.

For a negation negated is an affirmation.

Thus, if our non-being is negated (in favour of Being), our being finds true existence.

O God, O All-Generous and Munificent! Grant to me a life and place from Your Presence.

And make me of limitless value in Your sight, for surely You are the All-Preserver, the All-Protector.

An address to the Parliament[10]

In the Name of God, the Merciful, the Compassionate.

Surely, the prayer is made obligatory on the believers. at fixed hours.

O members of parliament! You will be resurrected for a mighty day!

O soldiers of Islam! O supreme advisory council of the nation!

I request you to listen to some words of advice from this humble one on a matter [of the highest importance]. The advice is offered in ten sections.

First: The extraordinary Divine blessing contained in this victory requires thanksgiving so that it may last. If a blessing is not returned with thanksgiving, it disappears. Now that you have saved the Qur'an from the attacks of the enemy by God's help, in order that its blessings may constantly come to you, you must obey its clearest, most decisive injunctions such as the prescribed prayer.

Second: You have given joy to the Muslim world and won its love and favorable inclination. Nevertheless, this love and inclination can only endure by your fulfilling the commandments of Islam, which demonstrate that this country is a Muslim one. For Muslims love you because of your being Muslims.

Third: You have commanded the soldiers of Islam who have either been martyred or survived, and who may be regarded as having attained the rank of sainthood. So, you are expected to perform the commandments of the Qur'an so that you may be in the company of those illustrious persons in the other world. Otherwise, though you hold a position of authority in this world, you will have to beg an ordinary soldier for light in the other.

---

10. This address was made to the Turkish Parliament on January 19th, 1923.

For all that it contains of fame and honor, this base world is not something so worthwhile as to suffice you and be an end for you.

Fourth: Muslim peoples, even if they themselves do not do the prescribed prayers and even if they commit some great sins, still desire that those leading them should be pious. What the people in southeastern Turkey first ask about their officials is whether they do the prescribed prayers. If the officials do the prayers, the people place their trust in them. Otherwise they condemn them, even if they are eminent officials. Once the tribes of Bayt al-Shabab rebelled against their government. When I asked them the reason for their rebellion, they answered: "Our governor does not do the prescribed prayers and he drinks alcohol. How shall we obey an irreligious one such as he?" Those who gave that answer did not themselves perform the prescribed prayer. Moreover, they were robbers.

Fifth: Most of the Prophets appeared in the East, while most of the philosophers have emerged in the West. This is a sign of Destiny that the main impulse for the progress of the East is religion and the "heart", not reason and philosophy. You have awakened the East, now direct it in a course appropriate for its disposition and temperament. Otherwise your efforts will either go in vain or be of temporary use and superficial.

Sixth: The Western powers which are enemies of you and of Islam have made, and are still making, much use of your neglect in religion and indifference to it. I can even say that certain others who likewise exploit your neglect in religion do you and Islam as much harm as your enemies. For the sake of the well-being of Islam and the security and prosperity of the nation, you should renounce this neglect and resume your religious duties. Do you not see that, despite their extraordinary resolution and steadfastness and causing some degree of awakening among the Muslims, the followers of the Union and Progress Party were despised and hated by the people because they showed some degree of indifference and carelessness in practicing the religion? If the Muslims living in other countries showed them

respect, they did so because they did not witness their neglect
in practicing the religion.

Seventh: The world of unbelief has been in continuous on-
slaught against the Muslim world for centuries with all its power. With all its technological facilities, its civilization, philosophy, sciences and missionary organizations, it has established
superiority over the Muslim world in material and military
fields. However, it has not been able to triumph over it in religion. All the deviant religious groups within the state have long
been despised and remained negligible factions. Islam has preserved its firmness and fortitude through the adherence [of the
many] to the way of the Prophet and preserved our internal cohesion and unity. This being the case, now an irreligious movement originating from the corrupt elements of the European
civilization cannot be allowed to arise and grow through heedlessness. Revolutionary, important accomplishments in the Muslim world are possible only by obedience to the pillars of Islam,
otherwise not. Even if some achievements have been witnessed,
they have not been lasting.

Eighth: At a time when the corrupt European civilization
which has caused indifference to religion is on the verge of decline while a new Qur'anic civilization is about to appear, it is
not possible to achieve what is good by indifference to Islam.
As to realizing negative, destructive trends, the world of Islam,
after having suffered so much damage, does not need them.

Ninth: Those who appreciate the services you have rendered
and the victory you have won in this War of Independence and
who love you from the bottom of their hearts are the believing
majority of this country, particularly the common people who
are strong Muslims. They sincerely love you, support you and
appreciate your sacrifices, and feel indebted to you. They present
you a vast, very great power that has been awakened. So, for
the benefit of Islam, it is necessary for you to build a connection
with them and rely on them by performing the commandments
of the Qur'an. Otherwise, since it runs against the well-being of
Islam and Muslims to prefer over the Muslim masses a fortu-

nate, deviant minority who wholeheartedly imitate the West, the Muslim world will turn away from you and seek help from others.

Tenth: Only an insanely bold one who is tired of living ventures to follow a way which is ninety per cent certain to lead to perdition. There is ninety-nine per cent of salvation in the prescribed prayers, which are an indispensable obligation of Islam taking only one out of the twenty-four hours of the day to perform. There can come at most one per cent of worldly harm from heedlessness and indolence in doing the prayers. Whereas there is ninety-nine per cent of harm in not carrying out the obligations of Islam. Therefore I wonder what excuse can be shown for neglecting or not-performing the Islamic obligations, which is certain to bring man harm with respect to both this world and the next. How does religious and national zeal allow it?

People imitate this group of Muslim soldiers, the members of the parliament, in their acts. As for their defects and shortcomings, the people either imitate these also or criticize their leaders because of them. Whichever they do, it will cause harm. This means that the rights due from God to them contain also the rights due from people to them. There are those who follow the suggestions of their carnal selves and the whims and fancies whispered by Satan. They do not listen to a clear message on which the whole Muslim community has been agreed for centuries. They do not heed the countless proofs for its truth and its being beneficial and the warnings made against neglect of it. These people cannot be expected to realize good, significant accomplishments.

This mighty revolution should be based on sound foundations. By virtue of the power it enjoys, the collective person of this honored parliament has assumed the meaning and function of the Sultanate. It should not fail to assume the function of Caliphate by fulfilling and making the people fulfil those principles of Islam which show whether a country is a Muslim one or not. This parliament should not fail to satisfy the religious need of this people who, while needing four things for life, feel needy of religion at least five times a day. They have not been degenerated by the seductive pleasures of modern civilization, and have not forgotten their spiritual needs. They will accept as the Caliph the one whom you have named as Caliph, and give him wholehearted support to act as the Caliph. Any support and the power it provides that do not originate in and depend on the parliament, will cause internal discord and rifts, which is contrary to the Qur'anic commandment, *Hold fast, all together, to the rope of God.*[11]

This is the time to be a united community and establish collective consciousness. The collective personality originating in the community is firm and more able to enforce the commandments of the Shari'a. A single person who assumes the burdens of Caliphate can fulfil the requirements of Caliphate only by depending on the collective person [represented in the parliament for the people]. If this collective person is upright, the services it is able to provide will be much better and more extensive than those of a single individual. But if it is corrupt, then the corruption it will cause will also be greater and more extensive.

Whatever a single individual does, whether it be good or bad, is generally limited [in its effects]. Whereas, the good or bad which a community does is boundless. By causing evils and corruption within the country, do not destroy and make fruitless the good and merits you have obtained by fighting against the external enemy. You know well that your external enemies and adversaries wish to destroy the main pillars of Islam. Therefore, you are obliged to restore and preserve these pillars. Otherwise you will be unconsciously abetting the conscious will of the enemy. Neglect and apathy in practicing the main commandments of Islam demonstrate the weakness of the nation, and that weakness does not stop the nation's enemies from attacking; rather, it encourages them.

God is sufficient for us and how good a Protector He is. What a good Lord and what a good Helper!

11, *Al 'Imran*, 3.103.

Addendum

In the Name of God, the Merciful, the Compassionate.

Praise be to God Who is infinitely exalted above having a like both in His Essence and Attributes. He is the Creator, such that that macro-cosmos is His creation, and this micro-cosmos, that is, man, is His invention. That is His construction and this is His building. That is His work of art, and this is His painting. That is His design and this is His adornment. That is His mercy and this is His bounty. That is His power and this is His wisdom. That is His grandeur and this is His Lordship. That is His creature and this is His fashioning. That is His kingdom and this is His slave. That is His place of worship and this is His worshipping servant. On the sides of both, nay, on each part of both is a stamp showing that whatever there is is His property.

O God, O One sustaining the earth and heavens! Be witness and let those bearing Your Throne and Your angels be witnesses—together with the witnessing of all Your Prophets, Your saints, Your signs, Your verses (in the Books You sent), and the whole of Your creation—that You are God, there is no god but You, One, and having no partners. Forgive us, we turn to You in repentance and we bear witness that surely Muhammad is Your servant and Messenger whom You sent as a mercy for all the worlds.

O God! Bestow Your blessings on him as befits the reverence he deserves and Your mercy of which he is worthy, and on all his family and Companions.

Know, O friend! Your body and the things necessary for it's maintenance that God has bestowed on you, have not been given into your possession so that you may dispose of them however you wish. Rather, you have the right of disposal in whatever has been given to you only in accordance with the consent of

Him Who has given them to you, just as a guest cannot waste or dispose of anything belonging to the host without the approval of the latter.

Know, O friend who regards the Resurrection as impossible and improbable! Do you not see innumerable instances of resurrection and assembling and destruction happening on small scales in front of your eyes? While observing numerous instances of death and revival every year displayed by even every fruit-bearing or flowering tree, how can you regard as improbable the final great destruction of the world and its re-construction? If you desire conviction to come from direct observation, take your intellect with you and stand under, for example, an apricot or mulberry tree at the end of spring and summer. See how their sweet and lively fruits are re-created and re-presented. Those fresh, pleasant and enjoyable fruits smiling at your face are almost identical with those that died in the previous year. If, like human beings, they had spirits, they would be the exactly identical fruits that died in the previous year. Then reflect on the fact that despite itself being dried wood and the complexity and narrowness of its capillary tubes through which the food reaches the flowers and fruits, the head of the tree suddenly becomes a dazzling "world." It describes for a careful observer the meaning of *When the graves are overturned [to bring forth their contents].*"[12] It is true that nothing is difficult for the Power that produces from the dried tree those sweet, pleasant things— flowers, leaves and fruits. It is true, and we believe!

Know, O friend! Each *sura* of the Qur'an contains in epitome the whole contents of the Qur'an and the purposes the other *suras* pursue as well as the important stories they contain. This is so that those who are able to recite only a single short *sura* of the Qur'an, not the whole of it, due to either being unlettered or some sort of incapacity or shortcoming, may not be deprived of the reward coming from reciting the whole of it. It is by virtue of this gleam of miraculousness that for the one who recites it, a single *sura* substitutes for the whole of the Qur'an.

12, *al-Infitar,* 82.4.

Know, O friend! It is not necessary for a single one disposing multiple things to personally be among them and in direct, physical contact with them. This is so especially if that one is not of the same nature as the things he disposes and especially, again, if that one is, contrary to the things, not a contingent, corporeal entity. In order to enforce his command on his troops, a commander does not always have to personally be among them, rather, his command is usually enforced through his orders and decrees. If the duty of commanding were to be left to the troops themselves, then each of them would have to act the role of both commander and commanded and therefore would have to have the ability to command. The All-Glorious One, despite His infinite grandeur and being infinitely high above being among us or in physical contact with us, disposes us as He wishes. Like the sun, the All-Glorious One is nearer to us than ourselves and we are distant from Him, may His Majesty be exalted.

Know, O friend! Like a tree ending in its fruit, by virtue of a part including the properties of the whole [and the unity of the origin or Originator], multiple things result in unity. A single whole thing becomes like the whole of its species and a part the whole of the thing of which it is a part. For example, since each particle of the sun's light diffused throughout the space contains an image of the sun, the vibrating particles of the light become as if each a tiny sun because of its uninterrupted connection with the sun. For God the highest comparison or similitude should be coined—the Names of the Eternal Light of Lights are manifested in a similar way: each manifestation is seen both on each individual and on the whole of its species.

Know, O one who is satisfied with the world and content with it! Your like is the like of him who rolls down from the top of a very high castle, and the castle rolls down in a flood which falls from a very steep mountain. And the mountain collapses into the depths of the earth with unending quakes.

The castle of life collapses and the "plane" of the life-span flies with lightning speed. You will soon be buried in the pit of the grave wrapped in your white shroud. The stream of time turns its wheels with horrifying speed, and the "ship" of the earth floats like the floating of clouds. If one who travels on a train going at very high speed stretches his hand out to the thorny flowers alongside the railways, and the thorns tear his hands, then he should not blame anyone other than himself. Do not covet the pleasures of the world, nor stretch your hands out to them, for if the pains coming from the feeling of separation at the time you have reached them tear the heart, you may guess what will happen at the time of final separation.

O evil-commanding self! You may worship whomever you wish and claim whatever you wish. As for me, I worship no one else other than Him Who has created me and subjected to me the sun, the moon, and the earth with the many things on it. I ask help of no one else other than Him Who conducts me on the "plain" of life moving through the "space" of Destiny and has subjected to me the "space-ship" among the planets. I ask help of no one but Him Who makes me mount the "train" of time travelling with the speed of lightning through the time tunnel under the mountain of life toward the gate of the grave along the way to eternity. Sitting on it by His leave, I recall Him in the compartment of this day connected to both yesterday and tomorrow. I call and ask help of only Him Who is able to stop the wheel of Destiny, which apparently moves the ship of the earth, and bring the movement of time to a rest by re-uniting the sun and moon. I ask help of only Him Who is able, by transforming the earth into another earth, to steady this changing world rolling down from the summits of existence into the depths of the valleys of decay and non-existence. For I have ambitions and aims connected with all things. My ambitions are related to the passing of time and the movement of the arth. I also feel a deep connection with the joys and sorrows of all beings, particularly of humanity, and most particularly of the righteous ones among the inhabitants of the heavens and earth. So, I worship none other than Him Who is aware of even the most secret thoughts occurring to my heart and satisfies the least of the ambitions and inclinations of my heart. He is also able, by destroying the world and changing it into the Hereafter, to realize the desire of my intellect and imagination, namely, to establish the eternal happiness for mankind. His hand reaches both the tiniest particle and the largest sun at the same instant and nothing, however small it is, can be too small to be hidden from Him, nor can it be, however big, too big for His Power to encompass. For He is such that if you know Him, your pains change into pleasures and, without Him, sciences result in sheer fantasies and conjectures, and philosophies in fallacies.

Without His light, instances of existence change into instances of non-existence, lights into layers of darkness, living creatures into dead things, pleasures into pains and sins, beloved ones, indeed all things, into enemies. Without Him, permanence becomes a disaster, perfection goes to nothing, life is wasted and becomes a torment, intellect becomes a means of suffering and misery, and ambitions become pains.

Whoever submits himself to the will of God and pursues His pleasure, everything serves him, and whoever, by contrast, disobeys God, everything turns against him. If one affirms that whatever exists belongs to Him exclusively, being a property of His, everything serves one. He has created you surrounded by circles of needs one round the other and equipped you with the devices with which you can satisfy only those in the smallest circle if you rely on your will and power. Some of your other needs are related to so large a circle that it stretches from the eternity in the past to the eternity in the future and between the center of the earth and the Throne of God. In order to satisfy these needs, He has equipped you with prayer or supplication. It is decreed in the Revelation, *Say: "My Lord will not be concerned for you, were it not for your supplication."*[13] An infant calls his parents to obtain what his hands cannot reach, and a servant prays to his Lord for what he is unable [to obtain or overcome].

Know, O friend! The perfection of art in everything and its firm structure come from the unity [of origin]. But for the unity

---

13. *al-Furqan*, 25.77.

of origin that does not admit division and disintegration and cannot be prevented from manifestation, there would be disharmony and disorder in existence. For example, the sun, one and single, exists in whatever it touches with its light, from a transparent minute particle to the face of an ocean, and its reflection or manifestation in one thing does not prevent it from being manifested in another. This is so for the sun, a contingent, contained, inanimate physical object, and a "drop" shining by the manifestation of a ray of the Divine Name the Light. You may guess how it can be for the Ever-Existing Sun, the Eternal Sovereign, the Necessarily Existent and Permanently Self-Subsistent, the One and Single, the Ever-Living, the All-Powerful, the Eternally Besought-of-All, may His Majesty be exalted. *For God the highest comparison or similitude should be coined*—the unity of the encompassing light points to the oneness, and the existence of the sun with all its properties in every part and particle through the manifestation of its light implies unity. Ponder this!

Know, O friend! Among the most truthful witnesses of Divine Oneness are:

the unity or miraculously harmonious organization in everything which extends from the particles of the cells of your eyes to the whole of the universe,

the perfectly firm structure everything has according to its capacity determined by the Divine Decree and Destiny,

and the absolute facility in the invention and building of all things. This absolute facility also points to the fact that the existence of the Creator is not of the same kind as the existence of the created. The existence of the Creator is infinitely more deeply rooted and established than the created.

Know, O friend! The earth gives you, sells you, its produce and the goods in its hand extremely cheaply. If all that it gives you were its own or the produce of material causes, you would not be able to buy a single pomegranate in return for what you spend to obtain all that you receive from the earth through the hands of its trees and fields. For you see that the Maker has shown the utmost care in [creating] everything down to grains, making it infinitely firm and furnishing it most elaborately. He has also included in it what He includes with perfect conscious- ness and wisest skill, equipping it with the subtleties of color, nourishment and fragrance to attract the attention of customers. He has no difficulty at all in creating it and no need to have physical contact with it. Had it not been the creature of Him for Whom a grain and a garden, an individual and a whole species, a minute particle and the sun, are, evidently and doubtlessly, the same in relation with His Power, it would not be of its present perfect quality. Since it has been created so firmly and artistically and in such abundance, then those grapes or those grains of pomegranate, for example, cannot have been created only to satisfy the temporary pleasures and particular desires of some animate beings. Were that true, it would require that their Creator should be—God forbid such a thought!—without con- science, will, knowledge, choice and perfections. However, the perfect, conscious, wise and purposeful art in everything utterly contradicts such a hypothesis.

The Necessarily Existent Being is All-Powerful, All-Willing, All-Knowing, All-Wise and has the absolute dominion of every- thing. *When He wills a thing, His command is only to say to it "Be!" and it is.*[14] *Your creation and your resurrection is but like [that of] a single soul.*[15] And in each creature He has instances of wisdom and purposes connected with the manifestations of His Names and the meaning of His acts as God Almighty, not connected only with the benefits it gives to consumers of it. It is impossible that this universal banquet is prepared by a blind power and that all those fruits, those products, coming in floods, are a play- thing of chance and coincidences. The particular form, color, smell and taste assigned to each for certain purposes and the services each is consciously made to render reject decisively the intervention of blind chance and coincidences. On the contrary, there is abundance and cheapness, and the facility in their com-

---

14. *Ya Sin*, 36.82.
15. *Luqman*, 31.28.

ing into being both individually and in species, and their firm
structure and, despite their infinite variety, their formation out
of only a few substances—all these testify to the absolute generosity of the absolutely Generous, Wise and Powerful One, may
His Majesty be exalted. His gifts encompass and His favoring
include all.

Glory be to Him Who has combined infinite, absolute generosity with infinite wisdom and economy. Glory be to Him Who
has put the unrestricted, absolute free-giving within the limits
of a perfect order, a sensitive balance or measure and an absolute justice. This order, balance and justice are to such extent
that an elephant is compelled to protect itself against a fly biting
it on a point on its huge body, and that haughty, too-conceited
man is obliged to fight against the little "spear" of a mosquito.
—*O mankind! A parable is set forth, so listen to it: Surely, those
whom you invoke, apart from God, will never create a fly even if they
combine together for the purpose. And if the fly take something from
them, they cannot rescue it from it. Hence, weak are both the seeker
and the sought.*[15] — And the fury of a sea and the rage of storms
subside, and the severity of coldness diminishes, through a silent supplication of a broken-hearted child and the child is carried to safety. —*Is not He [best] Who answers the oppressed one
when he supplicates Him and takes away [his] ills?*[16]— The One
Who hears the beatings of the heart and is aware of whatever
occurs to it answers him and directs the movements of the sun
and moon—may His sovereignty be exalted.

Know, O friend who ascribes everything to the law of causality! The creation of a cause and making it the cause of an effect,
furnishing it with the equipment necessary for the effect to come
into being, is not easier and a more perfect and wonderful act
than the creation of the effect with the command of "Be!" issuing
from Him in relation to Whom particles and suns are the same.

Know, O my heart! The sufferings, decaying and deaths that

14. *Ya Sin*, 36.82.
15. *Luqman*, 31.28.

you see filling the world consist in fact in the further and further recurrences of the things and events all alike. In each separation and decay, instead of the pain of decline and disappearance, a believer finds the pleasure of renewal. Believe and find security and satisfaction; submit yourself to Him and find peace and happiness!

Know, O friend! Racism is a combination of heedlessness, ignorance, misguidance, ostentation and wrongdoing, which support and give strength to one another. Racists make a fetish of their race. —We seek refuge with God from such deviations! — As for the zeal for Islam, it is a bright light coming from belief.

Know, O friend engaged in disputes with heretics and agnostics and imitators of the Western atheists! You are in a great danger. For if you are not a perfectly purified one fully convinced of the truths of belief and Islam, you may gradually and unconsciously be drawn to the side of your opponents. You cannot trust in your evil-commanding self in a dispute today called objective reasoning. For in the mind of a just disputant who ponders the ideas of his opponent and temporarily supposes them as true to find answers to them, a seed of criticizing and faultfinding germinates and the disputant himself begins to behave like a deputy for his opponent. Taking advantage of this, Satan seats himself in his mind and tries to grow that seed.

However, if you have a pure intention [in disputing], when you feel that you have begun to behave like a deputy for your opponent, you immediately turn to struggle against your greatest enemy within you and insistently ask forgiveness from God in utter humility.

Know, O friend! Suppose a wonderful palace is being built and decorated for a mighty king. Whoever witnesses and sees the instruments used and the workers employed without knowing for what purposes the palace is being built, will certainly conclude that the workers are working not on behalf of themselves but on behalf of the one who employs them for certain lofty purposes. In the same way, look at the animate and inanimate beings employed in the universe for numerous noble and subtle aims and purposes many of which even the elect of scholars are unable to perceive. Ponder the exquisiteness that flowers display in order to make themselves loved by those who look at them. You will certainly be convinced that like other beings, animals, for example, the flowers are charged by the Generous, All-Wise One with serving His guests on the earth and making Him loved by them.

Do flowers have feeling and animals consciousness that they could perceive the purposes for the designs and decorations and the graces of generosity they are made to display? So, they are to make the Generous Lord known and loved by His conscious servants, His guests. May His Majesty be exalted and His gifts encompass and His favoring include all.

Know, O ill-meaning, evil-commanding self! You demand to see what is necessary for all the grades of existence in a single grade, and what is needed by all the senses in a single sense. You also seek to experience the whole of the pleasures you can experience with all of your feelings, faculties and senses with each of them separately. You seek to see the rays of all the Divine Beautiful Names in each Name, and the splendor of the Creator in each creature, and to find the real, manifested meaning of everything in its reflection in the mind. Whereas, in order not to be exposed to evil suggestions and thoughts about the Creator, you should seek to find in each thing what it deserves and can encompass.

Know, O friend! When you have a high opinion of yourself, consider those greater than you. When you see those, like insects, that are smaller than you, consider the cells of your body and concentrate on only one among them. You will see that even a fly and those greater than that are greater than you. However, this should not cause you to despise the wisdom, mercy, favoring and the perfectness of art in you. When you see the innumerable bounties of the same kind conferred on you, consider the extent of your neediness and weakness and the purposes for those bounties so that you should not despise them.

Does it lessen your need for the eye that all animals have eyes? Or does it reduce the inclusiveness of a particular bounty and of the purpose for it? No, rather, it intensifies the need for it and increases its inclusiveness.

Know, O friend! There are innumerable purposes for the life of every living creature. Only one among them is concerned with the living creature itself, while the others concerned with the Life-Giving One are in proportion to the extent of His limitless Ownership. No one one among the creation, however great it may be, has the right to boast to those less than it. Although there is not the least uselessness and purposelessness in creation, yet, by considering everything with respect to their own interests and wishes, some arrogant, selfish ones may regard those things they see as irrelevant to their own uses as futile and purposeless. The universal table spread on the earth is a gift to mankind due to his responsibility to render the earth prosperous in the name of God, provided he fulfils this responsibility. That table does not belong to him, nor is it spread for his use only.

Know, O friend! If one whispers to you: "You are but an animal among those countless others. The ant is your brother and the bee, your sister. How can you have a relation with the One *Who rolls up the heavens like a scroll rolled up for books? The whole earth is His handful on the Day of Resurrection, and the heavens will be rolled up in His right hand,*" say to him:

"My admission of my impotence, poverty and insignificance before Him, together with my recognition and conviction of Him, becomes a mirror to show me His Power, Wealth and Dignity. It is because of this that I have progressed from the rank of being an animal to the rank of humanity. The perfection of His Grandeur and comprehensiveness of His Power require that He should hear my call and see my needs, and that His sustaining the earth and heavens should not prevent Him from sustaining me and directing my affairs."

God's concerning Himself with insignificant-seeming things and events does not contradict His Grandeur. Rather, if He did not concern Himself with them, this would be a lack on the part of the Grandeur of His Lordship. Do you not see that every bubble, every drop of water and every piece of glass, however small it is, contains the image of the sun? If it could speak, it would say, "The sun belongs to me, it is in me or it accompanies me." Neither those drops and pieces nor the planets, nor the faces of seas, hinder one another from having a relation with the sun, nor does the greatness of the sun prevent those relations. Rather, as in this example, the more we know the Almighty and the more we are aware of our poverty and insignificance before Him, the nearer we are to Him. How good is the position of one who does not forget his poverty and impotence before Him to Whose Wealth, Power, Dignity and Grandeur there are no limits.

Glory be to Him Who has included limitless kindness in limitless grandeur, and boundless tenderness in boundless majesty, Who has combined infinite nearness with infinite distance, Who has established brotherhood between minute particles and suns, and Who manifests His Power by combining opposites.

Look how His majestic sustaining and directing the earth and heavens does not prevent Him from His affectionate sustaining of insects. See how His sustaining and administering does not hinder Him from the creation of the smallest of bees and birds and giving life to the least of fish in the depths of seas. See how the violence of the gales of the earth and the fury of seas do not distract Him from His perfect kindness and goodness to the most hidden, weak, helpless and minute animate creature in the most hidden place in the darkness of sea in the darkest night.

Mercy appears smilingly amidst the fury of the sea and behind its stern, frowning face. For while it cries with a roaring tone, "O All-Mighty God, All-Majestic, Greatest! Glory be to You, how grand You are," that little creature responds to its roaring, calling silently, "O All-Subtle and Gracious God, All-Munificent, All-Providing, Most Compassionate! How gracious Your favoring is!" In these two types of calling God by His Names and glorification of Him are a gentle, gracious splendor and a splendid grace and gentleness as well as an exalted type of worshipping the One, Single and Eternally Besought-of-All, may His Majesty be exalted and His favoring encompass all.

Know, O friend! After acquiring the necessary knowledge about faith, it is incumbent upon you to do good and righteous deeds. For, following faith, the Wise Qur'an declares: *Those who do good, righteous deeds.*

This short life-span suffices only for doing what is most important and necessary. As for the sciences and technology, they are necessary insofar as they help the satisfaction of essential needs, the progress of mankind both intellectually and spiritually and their prosperity in both worlds. If they cause dissipation and sedition, they are harmful.

O God, O Most Compassionate of the Compassionate! Have mercy on Muhammad's umma, and illumine their hearts with the light of faith and the Qur'an, and brighten the proof of the Qur'an, and exalt Islam! Amen.

* * *

INDEX OR BRIEF SUMMARIES OF THE TOPICS DISCUSSED IN THE TREATISE

*O believer, who performs the prescribed prayers and recites God's Names! When you say, for example, "I bear witness that there is no god but God" or "Muhammad is the Messenger of God" or "All praise be to God," you have made a claim, announced a cause and conviction, and declared a conclusion. At the moment you have done this, hundreds of millions testify to your truthfulness in your cause and you feel as if millions of millions of believers who lived before you and uttered the same pronouncements confirm you. (148)

*Each of the radiations of belief and Islam, and their subject-matters, is supported by the whole and can be more clear and understandable in parallel with the number of the whole. The more belief and Islam are ramified, the more we are convinced and sure of the truth of each of their parts. (150)

*The least part of a very great whole needs [for its being] whatever the whole needs [for its being]. (150)

*Prophethood is like a seed from which the tree of Islam has grown with all its flowers and fruits. The Qur'an is a sun which has yielded the fruits of the planets of the eleven pillars of Islam. (151)

*If one views our Prophet, upon him be peace and blessings, superficially, in the light of what history books narrate of the beginning of his life, one will not be able to perceive him and appreciate his worth and recognize fully his character. However, the religion of Islam and the world civilization of Islam have flourished from him. One should regard what one sees of the merely human dimension of his being as the shell of a seed from which the blessed tree of Prophet Muhammad has grown. (151)

*By way of manifestation, the sun can enter the eye of a gnat and illuminate it. But the flame produced by lighting a match cannot enter that eye by itself. If it entered it, the eye would be blind. In the same way, a minute particle can be an object of the manifestations of the Names of the Eternal "Sun", whereas it is impossible for it to contain something truly effective and operative in creation, even if that something is smaller than the minutest of particles. (152)

*Man unjustly attributes the fruits of the work of a group to a single person and assumes that that individual has produced those fruits. From this injustice a kind of secret association of partners with God arises. (153)

* Man is surrounded by concentric circles. (153)

*By virtue of the genuine creation of his, if man assumes the way of servanthood to God, he will be rewarded, especially in the Hereafter, with all kinds of pleasures and blessings and all degrees and varieties of perfections. If, by contrast, he follows the misleading way of egoism, he will be the target of all sorts of pains and sufferings and all forms of torments. (154)

*The benefits of the non-definition of the time of death are a clear proof of its being definite in the knowledge of the Originator. (154)

*Calling blessings and peace upon the Prophet, upon him be peace and blessings, is like answering the invitation of the Giver of Bounties Who spreads His blessings freely and has laid the table of His bounties on him whom He honored with Ascension. (155)

*The difference between the civilization of unbelievers and that of (true) believers: (156)

*The door to *ijtihad* is open. However, it is not permissible to go in through that door in the following circumstances: (157–9)

*Only one of the fifty-five "languages" spoken by each of the minute particles and compounds of the universe to witness the necessary existence of the Almighty and His Unity in His Divinity and Lordship. (159–65)

*The area where man's mind and heart move is too spacious to be encompassed. (165)

*For the gifts God has ordained for man to attain to or make use of, there are conditions some of which are established by God and some pertain to man himself. (165)

*The miraculousness of the Qur'an saves the Qur'an from corruption. (166)

*The disobedience of mankind and jinn [to God's commands] and their rebelliousness and ingratitude mostly arise from their blindness to the Divine act of bestowing bounties, and heedlessness to the One Who bestows. (166)

*Whisperings of Satan and involuntary thoughts and suggestions arising from the heart and carnal self. (167)

*About philosopehrs' critics of Islam and the triumph of the sinful wrongdoers over the pious and the supremacy of the wicked over the righteous in the worldly life. (167–9)

*Intensity of love causes denial of the thing loved. (170)

*The seed of unbelief potentially bears Hell, in the way that a mustard plant is compacted in its seed. (170)

*Man's relation with his life is like the relation between a steersman and the royal ship that he steers. (172)

*What value does, for example, the gnat have that the Wise Maker has expended such great labor upon it? (173–4)

*The Qur'an explains many truths through parables and comparisons, as the abstract Divine truths take on or are presented in limited, concrete forms in this [material] sphere of contingencies. (174)

*The heart has the same meaning for you as the Divine Throne. (174)

*A supplication. (176–7)

*An address to the Turkish Parliament just after the Turkish Independence War. (178–82)

*Your body and the things necessary for it's maintenance that God has bestowed on you, have not been given into your possession so that you may dispose of them however you wish. (183)

*Each *sura* of the Qur'an contains in epitome the whole contents of the Qur'an and the purposes the other *sura*s pursue as well as the important stories they contain. (184)

*Whoever submits himself to the will of God and pursues His pleasure, everything serves him, and whoever, by contrast, disobeys God, everything turns against him. (187)

A Grain Contained by a Fruit in the Garden of the Qur'an

The grain says:

I am a branch of a tree laden with the fruits of Divine Unity,
Or a dew drop from the sea full of the pearls of praise unto Him.

In the Name of God, the Merciful, the Compassionate.

Praise be to God for the religion of Islam and perfection of faith. May God's blessings and peace be upon Muhammad, who is the center of the circle of Islam and the source of the lights of faith, and on all his family and Companions so long as days and nights continue and the sun and moon move in their courses.

Know, O friend! If you see the universe as a great book, you will see the light of Muhammad, upon him be peace and blessings, as the ink of the pen with which that book has been written. If you see the universe in the form of a tree, you will see his light as originally its seed and consequently its fruit. If you see the universe as in the form of an animate being, you will see his light as its soul. If you see the universe in the form of a macrohuman, you will see his light as his intellect. If you see the universe as a flower garden, you will see his light as its nightingale. If you see the universe as a lofty, richly-decorated castle with many rooms and apartments, which displays the splendor of the sovereignty of the Eternal Sovereign and the marvels of His Glory, as well as the beauties of the manifestations of His Grace and the wonderful designs of His Art, then you will see the light of the Prophet Muhammad, upon him be peace and blessings, as a spectator. He first views them on His behalf and then announces: "O people! Come and look on these pleasant sights!

Hasten to receive your share in them—love, amazement, refreshment, appreciation, enlightenment, reflection and many other lofty things." He shows all these to them; he observes them and has them observed by people. As he is himself amazed at them, he also causes people to be amazed at them. He loves their Owner and makes Him loved by people. As he himself is illumined through them, he also has others illumined. He benefits from them and makes others also benefit.

Know, O friend! Man is the fruit of the tree of creation. A fruit is the most perfect of the parts of a tree and the farthest from the roots. It is also the most comprehensive of them which has the properties of the whole tree.

Among human beings there must be one from whom the All-Powerful One, may His Majesty be exalted, grew this tree of creation. Then, the Creator made that one the fruit of the tree. Afterwards, the All-Merciful One made that illustrious fruit the seed of the tree of Islam, and the lamp of its world, and the sun of its system.

Without doubt, what is necessary for a tree is also necessary for its seed. Compared to the huge size of the tree, the tiny size of the seed, like the seed of a fig, does not exclude it from this rule.

There is a grain also within man. If man had been a fruit, this grain would have been its seed. Beware, this grain is the heart.

I have seen that, because of the variety of his needs, man has relations with all species of creation, nay, with all its individual parts, and due to the intensity of his neediness and poverty, he has connections with all the lights of the Divine Beautiful Names. It is as if man has as many needs as the parts of creation; he has world-filling adversities and hostilities. He is not to be satisfied with any but the one who is able to make him independent of, and protect him against, everything.

I have also seen that like a map or an index or a sample, man has a capacity to include or represent the whole of creation. He has a seed that does not accept but the One, Single. It is not contented with anything else save what is eternal and perpetual. This seed is the grain of the heart, which is to be watered by Islam and receive light from belief. If in the soil of servanthood and purity of intention it is watered by Islam and awakened to life by belief, it grows into such an illustrious spiritual tree that it becomes the spirit of its corporeal body. If it is not watered, it remains a dried seed having to burn in fire until it acquires the quality of light.

In the seed there are very subtle, delicate things like nerves, each of which, in case where the seed germinates properly, fulfils an important duty. Also, the grain of the heart has inactive servants which, when activated and developed with the life of the heart, travel through the gardens of the universe like birds. Consequently, the grain of the heart expands to the degree that man says: "Praise be to God for all His creatures, for all of them are bounties conferred on me." (The grain of the heart expands to the degree that), for example, imagination, the weakest and feeblest of the servants of the heart, is burdened with a strange duty. Through it, man, confined in a narrow place, enters an exhilarating garden and, while performing the prescribed prayer in the remotest corner of the east or west, puts his head under the Black Stone at the Ka'ba and entrusts to it his testifying (to God's being his Lord).

As is known, grain is threshed in the threshing-ground and preserved. Like this, the Plain of Resurrection is the ground awaiting man, the fruit of creation, [to separate the grain from the chaff].

Know, O friend! Within this world everyone has a particular world completely identical with the outer world, except that in the center of this particular world lies the man himself who has it, not the sun. The keys to this world are in the hands of the man and connected with his senses and faculties. This world takes its color after its center—the man to whom it belongs—

and again it depends on the man himself whether his world is a prosperous, beautiful or ugly one, an illumined or dark one. Just as the views that a garden reflected in a mirror will have, and the changes it will display, depend on the mirror, so the particular world of everyone depends on the one who has it in all its views and characteristics. So, do not think that your small size of body may be an excuse for the insignificance of your sins. A negligibly little darkness or hardness in your heart may cause all the stars of your particular world to be extinguished.

Know, O friend! For thirty years I have struggled against two "rebels", one the ego within man, the other, nature in the outer world. I have seen the former as a shadowy mirror reflecting someone other than itself. Nevertheless, man views it as having an independent existence, showing itself, and therefore becoming, an unbending tyrant in rebellion against its Creator.

As for nature, I have seen it as a work of Divine Art, a painting of the All-Merciful. However, as a result of viewing it heedlessly [of the Creator], it has come to be regarded by materialists as if it were a deity, as self-originated and existing by itself, and made into an excuse for ingratitude which has resulted in unbelief.

Thanks be to God and praise be to Him, by the help of the One, Eternally Besought-of-All, and the enlightenment of the glorious Qur'an, my struggle has ended in the death of these two rebels, the smashing of these two idols. As is discussed in *The Point, The Drop, The Particle, The Breath, The Grain,* and *The Bubble,* behind the veil of nature has appeared a work of Divine Art, a collection of the Divine laws of creation and operation of the universe. And ego has broken into pieces, and behind it has emerged the One like Whom there is nothing, may His Majesty be exalted.

Know, O ego! There are nine things the nature and consequences of which you live unaware:

One of them is your body. It is like a fruit that is fresh, pleasant and enjoyable in summer, but dried and rotten in winter.

The other is your animal quality. Look at the animals and see how speedily decay and death come to them.

The third is your human quality. It vacillates between extinction and purification and between decay and permanence. Preserve that part of it which is inclined to remain forever through constant remembrance of the Permanent One.

The fourth is the life-span assigned to you. It is short and limited and lasts until the hour appointed for it, which is neither antedated nor postponed. Therefore do not grieve for it, nor be anxious about it, nor burden it with worldly ambitions impossible to achieve within it.

The fifth is your material existence. It is at the hand of the True Owner of all things. He cares for it much more than you. If you interfere with it unnecessarily without His permission, you will give it harm. Do you not see how avarice brings despair and disappointment and how insistence on sleeping causes one to lose one's sleep and become restless?

The sixth is the misfortunes befalling you. They are not really bitter, for they disappear quickly. They give pleasure by disappearance and being followed by fortunes. Besides, they cause you to turn from what is fleeting to what is permanent through the Permanent One.

The seventh is that you are a guest here, wherever you are in the world. A guest does not set his heart upon what does not concern him and what does not follow him throughout his journeying. As you will depart from here soon, you will also depart from this town: you will either go out of it or be buried in it. As you will leave it anyway, you will also leave this transient world or be expelled from it. So abandon it, renounce it, with honor and dignity, before you are expelled in humiliation.

The eighth is that you should sacrifice your material existence for the One Who has given it. For He buys it for a very high price. Make haste to sell it, rather, to sacrifice it. For, first of all, it goes away for nothing. Second, it belongs to Him and will be returned to Him. Thirdly, if you rely on it, you will fall into non-existence. For your existence is in fact a door opened onto Him. If you open that door by renouncing it, you will find the permanent existence. And fourthly, if you hold fast to your existence, only a part the size of a point remains of it in your hand, and you will be enveloped by a thick darkness of non-existence. But if you blow off that part, the lights of existence will surround you from all sides.

The ninth concerns worldly pleasures or enjoyments. Whatever Destiny apportioned to you, it will come to you. Therefore, do not be worried about it. A sensible one does not set his heart upon fleeting things. However your own particular world will end, you had better renounce worldly pleasures. If it will end in happiness, one can attain happiness by renouncing pleasures; if it will end in misery, how can one waiting to be hanged get pleasure from the decoration of the gallows? Even one who, because of unbelief, supposes himself to be going into absolute non-existence—I seek refuge with God from such a supposition!—had better renounce worldly pleasures. For the recurrent disappearance of these pleasures makes an unbeliever constantly feel the pains of the absolute non-existence he supposes to follow death, and those pains are much more acute than the pleasures he will get in the enjoyments of life.

Know, O friend! Your likeness when stricken with the misfortunes thrown by Destiny is that of the sheep at which the shepherd throws stones to make them turn back when they enter the public pasture. The sheep struck by the stones of the shepherd turn back as if saying: "We are under the command of the shepherd. He knows us better than ourselves, so we must return."

O my soul! You are not more astray than the sheep. When stricken with misfortunes, say, "We belong to God and we are bound to return to Him."

Know, O friend! Out of innumerable evidences that the heart has not been created to be occupied primarily with worldly affairs, heed the following:

When the heart is attached to something, it is attached to it very strongly. It sets itself upon it too zealously, and seeking in it permanence and eternity, is lost in it completely. When it stretches out its hand to grasp something of it, it stretches it out to take a share as big as a huge rock but the share it can grasp out of the world is no bigger than a hair or it is left empty-handed.

The heart is the mirror to reflect the Eternally Besought-of-All. It does not admit an idol carved out of stone. That stone breaks it. A lover mostly suffers at the hand of his beloved. This is because the beloved unconsciously rejects what in fact does not belong to him or her, as the lover is not worthy to reside in the heart of the beloved.

Know, O friend! The Qur'an was sent and with it was sent a heavenly table on which is found whatever human beings differing in their intellectual appetites need. The foods are found on this Divine table in certain order or arrangement. First comes the food to be offered to the commonalty that form the great majority of mankind. For example, the share of the commonalty in *The heavens and earth were at first one piece, then We parted them*[1] is: There was no relationship between the heavens and earth. The heavens were clean and without clouds, unable to send rain, while the earth was dried and barren. Then, by the Will and permission of the Almighty a relationship, a contact, was established between them and, consequently, while the heavens gave birth to rain, the earth began to bring forth its produce. The part of the verse just following the sentences above, and *We have made every living thing from water*, alludes to that meaning.

The meaning those of higher level of understanding will infer from the Qur'anic expressions mentioned above is: The sun and planets were separated from the matter created from the light of the chief of all creation, upon him be peace and blessings, and susceptible of taking any shape like dough. This is indicated by the hadith, *What God created first is my light*.[2]

---

1. *al-Anbiya'*, 21.30.
2. Ajluni, *Kashf al-Khafa'*, 1.205.

Another example: *Were we then worn out by the first creation? Yet they are in doubt about a new creation.*[3]

The commonalty understand from this verse that those who cannot admit the Resurrection do affirm their creation, which they ought to recognize as much more astonishing. They regard the Resurrection as improbable, although it will be easier. Beyond or above this level of understanding lies a bright evidence for the perfect easiness of the Resurrection: O deniers of the Resurrection! You are revived, resurrected, many times in your life, nay, in each year of your life, nay, on each day. Like changing clothes in the morning and evening, you put on your bodies and then take them off every day.

Know O friend! How foolish the human ego or selfhood is: it sees in itself the imprints, traces and signs of an absolutely Free, All-Wise Lord's making, sustaining, and administering, and discerns that this is also true of all other individual beings and species and kinds as a universal, all-encompassing rule. It must therefore be convinced of this as an undeniable reality confirmed by the whole of the creation. Yet the foolish ego unfortunately deceives itself by supposing such overall manifestation of the Divine Beautiful Names, which are also manifested on it, throughout the universe, as a sign of (Divine) neglect of it and a veil under which it can hide from the watching and inspection [of the Lord]. The universality and intensity of these manifestations lead the unfortunate selfhood to suppose that there is none to watch it. Even Satan is ashamed of a sophistry such as this.

Know, O distressed, restless soul! Like the rising of the sun in the morning and its setting in the evening, whatever will happen to you throughout your life, in whatever conditions you will be, has all been pre-determined by the Pen of Destiny and inscribed on your forehead. If you wish, you may strike your head against the "anvil" of Destiny but only to see your distress and depression increase. Be convinced that the one who is unable to penetrate the regions, the depths, of the heavens and the

---

3. *Qaf*, 50.15.

earth, must willingly consent to the Lordship of the One Who has created everything and decreed its destiny.

Know, O friend! If the maker of a thing were within it, he would be of the same nature as it, and there would have to be as many makers as the things made. Otherwise not. For example, look at this book. It is written with a single pen but printed by using as many different letters as the letters of the alphabet. [Or a single man types it by pressing many keys on a typewriter.] The designs or embroideries in a work of art are not made by the work itself, nor are the fruits of a tree made by the tree itself, nor the letters of a piece of writing produced by that piece itself. Otherwise the order would be destroyed and everything would go to chaos. But we see that there is a perfect order and stability in the creation. This is so because everything is inscribed by the Pen of the Divine Power on the lines of Destiny.

Know, O friend! How strange it is that the intellect which comprehends the universe and goes so far beyond it out of the sphere of the created, is sometimes drowned in a drop. It disappears in an atom, is lost in a hair, and restricts existence to what it is lost in, wishing to include all that it comprehends in the point which has swallowed it.

Know, O friend! If the right of possession and disposal of this material domain belonged to you, the fears and anxieties of maintaining it would make it very distressing for you to benefit from it. Whereas the All-Munificent Bestower of Bounties undertakes to provide for you whatever you need. What falls to you is only to eat from the table of His favors and thank Him. Thanking Him is a reason for the increase of His favors upon you, for it means seeing the act of favoring or giving bounties in bounties. Seeing the act of favoring removes the grief arising from the disappearance of bounties. For the disappearance of a bounty is not its eternal disappearance so that it gives sorrow. But like the fruits of a tree consumed this year being succeeded by new ones next year, it means departing in order to make room for the coming of a new one, and so it gives you the delight of taking ever-renewed pleasures. Their latest call, *All praise be to God, the Lord of the Worlds,*[4] indicates that praising itself is a pleasure. It is true. Praising is to see the tree of [Divine] favoring in the favor of fruits. It removes the pains arising from the thought of their disappearance and becomes the pleasure itself.

Know, O friend! The information provided by materialistic sciences and philosophy about the outer world cannot always be free from doubtfulness and errors. However, the information based on one's sound conscience is mostly free from giving doubts and troubles. Therefore, look from your inner world, your conscience, toward the outer world. Do not do otherwise and so avoid error.

Know, O friend! As this corrupt civilization has made the world so small as a town, people know and hear from one another through media, and help one another in sinful acts and in what does not interest and is of no benefit for them. This leads them to wrong and thickens the veil of heedlessness [over faith and the religious life]. This veil can be torn apart only with a mighty effort and struggle. This civilization has also made in the soul of man innumerable openings on the world, which it is possible for no one save him for whom God has special mercy to close.

Know, O friend! A minute transparent particle contains the image of the sun, even though it cannot hold two particles of its own size and nature. The drops of rain [and the bubbles on the face of an ocean] shine with the images of the sun held by them. Similarly, all the constituent particles and compounds of the universe have the capacity of receiving the manifestations of the luminous, absolute and eternal Divine Power, accompanied by the eternal, infinite Divine Knowledge and Will. It is impossible for a constituent particle of a cell in your eye to be the origin of the power, consciousness and will it requires to fulfil its functions in all your veins, arteries and nervous system and in your powers of seeing, hearing, thinking and describing, etc.

---

4. *Yunus*, 10.10.

This perfect, astounding art, this full decorated and orderly design, and this profound, subtle wisdom can be explained in two ways. Either each of the constituent particles and compounds of the universe is the origin of the perfect, absolute, and all-encompassing attributes [such as power, will, knowledge and consciousness], or each is an object receiving and reflecting the radiations of the Eternal "Sun" having all such attributes.

In the first alternative, there are as many impossibilities as the number of the particles and compounds of the universe. The approval of this alternative means that a bee is as powerful as to bear the mountains of Ararat and Subhan[5] on its wings and that rivers like the Nile and Euphrates can flow from the eyes of a gnat. Whereas, being unable to bear whatever is beyond its power, every particle testifies that there is no creator, sustainer, upbringer and administrator, no owner, no self-subsistent, no deity, save God. And all the particles and compounds of the universe announce in different tongues and bear witness in different ways:

Our expressions differ but You are always the One of the same beauty;

So whatever exists points to that All-Beautiful "Face."

Every letter of the book of the universe points to its own existence only in one way and to the measure of being a letter, while it indicates its Writer and Artist in numerous ways. It sings a long poem of praise in the tongue of the Names manifested on it.

Reflect upon the lines of the [book of the] universe,

For they are letters to you from the Highest Realm.

Know, O friend! The "mirrors" in which Divine manifestations are reflected are of great variety: pieces of glass, water, air, the world of symbols or immaterial forms, the spirit, the intellect, the imagination, time, and many other things which we do not know. The reflections of solid, material things in mirrors are

5. Ararat and Subhan are two mountains in eastern Turkey. (Tr.)

dead and regarded as separated or disconnected from themselves. They do not have the essential characteristics of their
originals and therefore are not identical with them. This is indicated by the fact that when their pictures are taken, they are
seen only with their outer, physical forms. But the reflections of
luminous things are not separated from their originals. They are
connected to them and bear their characteristics or attributes.
[Although not exactly identical with their originals,] they are
not things other than them either. If the Creator, may His Majesty be exalted, had made the heat of the sun its soul, its light, its
consciousness, and the colors in its light, its senses, the sun
would have spoken to you through the "heart" of the mirror in
your hand. It would be like talking to you through your telephone or the "mirror"of your heart. For, according to its capacity, the image of the sun in the mirror in your hand would have
had the heat of life and the light of consciousness and the colors
of senses. It is because of this fact that the Prophet, upon him be
peace and blessings, luminous in identity, becomes aware of all
the blessings called upon himself at the same moment. This is a
key to many mysterious truths.

Know, O friend! *Glory be to God* and *praise be to God* describe
the Almighty with His Attributes of Majesty and Grace. *Glory be
to God* implies the contingent nature of the servant and his distance from God, the Necessarily Existent One, the High and
Grand. *Praise be to God* implies God's nearness to the servant
and His creatures with His Mercy and Grace. Consider: The sun
is near to you, it makes its heat and light reach you and has certain disposal of you by the leave of its Creator. Thus it functions
as a mirror for the manifestation of the Divine Name the Light
and a receptacle of His bounties of heat and light. Whereas you
are very far from it and can do nothing with respect to it. While
it has affect on you, you can exert no influence on it. Similarly
to this—*to God applies the highest similitude*—God, may His Majesty be exalted, is near to us so that we praise Him, and we are
distant from Him so that we glorify Him. Praise Him for you
see that He is near with His Mercy. Glorify Him for you see that

you are distant from Him. Do not confuse His nearness to you with your distance from Him lest you become bewildered on the straight path. Provided you do not make any confusion, you can consider His nearness from the viewpoint of your distance and your distance from the viewpoint of His nearness, and you can combine these two considerations and say: *Glory be to God with His praise!*

Know, O friend, who strives for the world! You must renounce the world for the following four reasons:

First, it goes swiftly and decays. The pains arising from decay and separation remove the pleasure of attainment of or union with something subject to decay.

Second, what is left of its pleasures are only pains and grief.

Thirdly, what is awaiting you and what you are travelling toward directly without turning away from it—the grave, which is the door to the other world—does not accept from you the ornaments of the world as a gift, for they will change into errors and sins there.

Fourthly, [in order to understand the difference between this world and the Hereafter, reflect on] the difference between staying among enemies and vermin for an hour and staying in a place for years where all of your most beloved friends and elders are. The Lord of earthly and spiritual dominion calls you to give up that one hour of pleasure so that you may have perfect comfort and satisfaction in the company of your beloved ones in those years. Therefore, answer the call of God before you are sent to Him fettered.

All glory be to God, how great are His mercy and favor toward man that He buys from man at a very high price the property which He has entrusted to him and preserves it permanently for him. If man claims ownership of it and does not sell it to God, he is exposed to great calamities and misfortunes, as he undertakes to preserve and carry it with a very slight, insufficient power. If he attempts to carry it on his back, it will weigh on his back too heavily to carry. It will disappear from him swiftly and go all for nothing, leaving to him only the sins it has caused.

Know, O friend! It is as if the following couplet were said about me:

My eyes were in sleep during the night of my youth;

They woke up only when it was the morning of old age.

I have come to see that what I regarded as the greatest wakefulness in my youth was in fact the deepest of sleepiness. So, what the modernists describe as enlightenment and wakefulness must resemble that wakefulness of mine in my youth. They are like him who has a dream in which he wakes up from a sleep and relates his dream to some others. Whereas, by dreaming he has proceeded from a less heavy sleep to a more heavy one. How can a sleeping one, resembling a dead one, wake up the awake? How can a sleeping one make himself heard from behind the thick veils of sleep?

O sleeping ones regarding themselves as awake! Do not approach modern civilized ones by making concessions to them, and trying to resemble them in religion. Do not think that by doing so you can build a bridge or fill up the valley between them and us. No! The distance between the believers and unbelievers is too great to remove, and the valley between is too deep to fill up. It is probable that you either join them or greatly deviate from the right path.

Know, O friend! Surely there is the seed of unbelief in the essence of sins, especially if they are frequently committed. For a frequently committed sin makes the sinner indifferent to it and becomes an addiction whose only remedy lies in its abandonment. Then the sinner wishes for there to be no punishment for it and unconsciously tries to find an excuse to believe in the non-existence of eternal torment. This state of the sinner continues until he denies the eternal torment and the abode of punishment. Also, the shame arising from committing a sin not followed by remorse and asking forgiveness from God leads the sinner to deny that the sin he has committed is really a sin. It leads him to refute the existence of those—like the guarding angels—who oversee him and are aware of his sin. Because of the intensity of the shame he feels, the sinner wishes for there to be no reckoning in the other world. When he encounters even a false argument for its non-existence, he takes it as a strong proof and denies the final reckoning. Consequently, this ends in the darkening of the heart. May God save us from such a consequence! Amen.

Know, O friend! The radiations of the miraculousness of the Qur'an amount to about forty kinds. The following are only some among its many aspects of eloquence:

It has a pure, genuine fluency and is absolutely free from all defects in wording and meaning. There is a firm solidarity and proportionateness among its sentences and paragraphs, which corroborate one another. Although revealed in parts over twenty odd years on different occasions, there is, as the sciences of rhetorical style and semantics testify, so firm a cohesion and accord among its verses and purposes that it is as if it had been revealed at once and on one occasion. Although many parts of it came as answers to different questions, it contains no contradiction in meaning, and there is such an agreement and harmony among its parts that it is as if it had come to answer one question only. It also came to explain and judge happenings different in character, but it has such an order that it is as if it had come to judge only one happening. It is God Who speaks in it in styles suited for all levels of understanding. It came down, first of all, to the Prophet, upon him be peace and blessings, in his different moods, but it has such a smoothness and correspondence among its parts that it is as if it had come down to him while he was always in the same mood. Although it addresses all peoples at all times, it speaks so smoothly, fluently, orderly and clearly that it is as if it were addressing only one level of understanding. (It speaks in such a way that) every class of its addressees thinks that it directly and primarily addresses them. It came down to guide everyone and enable them to attain to their varying degrees of guidance but it is so balanced, orderly and straightforward that it is as if it pursued a single purpose. Whereas the goals and purposes it pursues can be summed up in these four or five: the Divine Unity, Prophethood, the Resurrection and justice and worship or devotion to God in creed and practical life. Since it primarily concentrates on the Divine Unity, it is perfectly coherent, harmonious, consistent and orderly.

Whoever has eyes will see that the Qur'an has an eye seeing all the creation like a clear page. It makes reiterations to establish its purposes in minds and hearts and repeatedly narrates the stories of certain Prophets to reinforce the warnings and lessons it intends to give. However, its reiterations never fatigue, nor spoil the taste for it. Where it makes repetitions, it fixes its purposes deeply in minds and hearts. Like musk giving more scent as it is worn away, the more the Qur'an reiterates a subject, the more it perfumes and the more "breaths of the All-Merciful" are diffused from it. The more you read it, if you are a man of good taste with a sound heart, the more delight you will take in it. This is because it nourishes the heart and gives cure and strength to the spirit. The nourishment essential to the body like air, water and bread does not fatigue when taken repeatedly; rather, the body needs them all the time. A man needs air at every instant, water, a few times a day, and food, at least once a day. He also needs light. Since he needs these basic substances of nourishment all the time, rather than boring him, taking them repeatedly gives him ever-renewed pleasure. Similarly, with respect to his intellectual and spiritual life, man needs whatever is in the Qur'an. He needs some of its elements like *He... God*, at every instant, and the spirit refreshes itself through them; and some like *In the Name of God*, at every hour, and still some others, every day, each according to the degree of need for it. So, the Qur'an makes repetitions in accordance with the degree of the need the life of the heart feels.

For example, since *He... God* or *In the Name of God* is like fresh air to be taken to refresh the body and oxygenate the blood, it must be repeated all the time. Again, the Qur'an repeatedly mentions a particular event each time from a different perspective and thus points to certain universal principles. For instance, the phrases and sentences used in relating the story of the Prophet Moses, upon him be peace, are more beneficial to mankind than the staff of Moses and their benefits are not restricted to a certain time and people.

In sum: the wise Qur'an is a book of recitation of Divine Names, a book of reflection, a book of legislation, a book of knowledge, a book of truths, and a book of law. It is a cure for what is in human breasts, and a pure guidance and mercy for the believers.

Know, O friend! Man is of such a strange nature that at the time of heedlessness he confuses the functions of his physical senses and organs and his intellectual and spiritual faculties. He is like an insane one who, because of the neighborhood between his eyes and hands, stretches his hand to grasp whatever he sees with his eyes. A man unaware of the difference between what is Divine and what is human, who is unable to accomplish the least matter concerning himself, attempts in his vanity to interfere with God's disposal of the universe. There is little difference among human beings in physical form and structure. But again, it is peculiar of man's nature that there is, contrary to animals, as great variety and difference among them in character, disposition and spirit as that between an atom and the sun and the sun of suns. Even if there is a great difference between, for example, a fish and bird in bodily form and structure, there is not so much difference between them in being animals. Whereas it is as if man stands at the top central point of the "cone of existence" and everything, whether it be an atom or the sun or the sun of suns, is at the same distance from him. This is so because his faculties or powers—his lusts, anger, intellect, etc.— are not restricted. He is reduced through egotism and vanity to the lowest of the low. By contrast, by abandoning egotism and vanity and through worship and servanthood and by the grace of God, he can be elevated to the highest of the high, to the degree of being "the sun of suns" like the Prophet Muhammad, upon him be peace and blessings.

Know, O friend! What is essential to things is that the Eternal One does not allow them to go into absolute non-existence. Even the things swiftly decaying or disappearing like the words uttered and the conceptions formed momentarily in the mind are preserved in certain places. However, they may take on different forms according to the places where they are preserved. It is as if things are charged with preserving a thing whether in its exact form and nature or with one aspect only. Although science has discovered this reality, it has not been able to comprehend it perfectly yet. It errs by attributing the chemical processes such as combination, composition and dissolution to things themselves and thus by ascribing eternity to matter. Whereas matter cannot be eternal and God Almighty dissolves, compounds and composes things and He creates and makes them die. He acts however He wishes and ordains and judges however He wills.

Know, O wretched Said! The grave is a door; inside it is mercy and happiness, whereas outside it lie suffering and wretchedness. Almost all of your beloved ones, your friends, dwell on the other side of this door. Is it not time yet for you to feel desire to join them and their world? You should be purified [of your sins]; otherwise they will be disgusted at you.

If, for example, you were told that Imam Rabbani Ahmad al-Faruqi, may God bless him, was living in India at the present, surely you would leave your homeland and risk all the troubles of journeying to visit him. Whereas there are thousands of stars called Ahmad round the "sun" mentioned as Ahmad in the Bible, as Ahyad in the Torah and Muhammad in the Qur'an. And there are millions called Muhammad. All of those are now inside the door of the grave, enveloped by the Mercy of God. Therefore you must always bear in mind the following principles:

If you are a good servant wholly submitted to God, then everything is subjugated to you. If, by contrast, you are not submitted to God, everything is an adversary to you.

Everything was preordained. Therefore be satisfied with what comes to you so that you may be at rest. Otherwise you are exposed to suffering after suffering.

Your life and body belong to God but have been entrusted to you. However, He wishes to buy them from you to preserve for you permanently. If they are left with you, they will go for nothing.

You need Him in every respect and under any circumstances.

You are surrounded from all of your four sides and being driven to the grave awaiting you.

The heart does not derive pure pleasure from what is not lasting. You are decaying, so are your world and the world of all other people.

The universe will be stripped of its present cloth and dressed in another garment. It is as if the universe was a huge clock the seconds, minutes and hours of which follow one another so that it should come to its appointed hour. So do not attach importance to the works and traces left of you in this fleeting world and which will be of no benefit to you in the Hereafter.

Do not view His disposition of creation with mercy and favoring from the perspective of your smallness and being distant from Him and of His Grandeur and Might. [That is, seeing creation as too distant from Him and too insignificant for Him to treat it with favor and mercy, do not think why He should condescend Himself to favor you and provide you.] However, such kind of relation of Him with creation requires you to glorify Him, as He deserves.

Nor view His Attributes of Majesty from the perspective of His nearness to creation and enveloping it with His Knowledge and Mercy and of your being His creature included in His favoring and munificence. For, then, suspicions and misconceptions [about His Might and Grandeur] will attack you.

Glory be to Him Who is absolutely free and exempt from being comprehended by minds and intellects, and praise be to Him Whose Mercy encompasses all things. There is no deity save He, One, and He has no partners. His is the dominion of all things and His all praise; He gives life and causes to die. In His hand is all good, and He is powerful over all things.

Know, O friend! When a man having a "living heart" turns his attention to the universe, he sees mighty, comprehensive affairs beyond his understanding and at which he is astonished. To find a cure for his pains of astonishment, like a thirsty one hurrying to sweet water, he cannot help but utter *Glory be to God!*

He sees the subtleties of Divine Favoring and experiences the pleasures that compel him to express his delight. He desires the increase of the pleasures by discerning the act of favoring in the bounties he consumes and the Giver of Bounties in the act of favoring. Then like one who has found out a buried treasure, he is relieved by uttering *All praise be to God!*

When he sees very strange and remarkable creatures that he is left unable to describe, the desire he feels to find the truth about them occupies his mind and he finds relief only in uttering *God is the Greatest!* That is, their Creator is incomparably and immeasurably great and it does not give Him the least difficulty to create and govern them. He is like one who, on seeing the moon rotating around itself, is greatly astounded or one who, on witnessing a mountain coming forth out of earth during an earthquake, is frightened. He is saved from the "burden" of astonishment and fright by putting it on the "ship" of the All-Powerful, the All-Strong, the All-Firm, may His Majesty be exalted.

Know, O friend! With your sins and evils you cannot attach to God any harm but you harm only yourself. For example, in reality, God has no partners at all. By conceiving of a partner with Him, you cannot have any effect on His perfect, absolute sovereignty and rule over the universe. Your associating partners with Him only harms your own world and causes your home to be destroyed over your head.

Know, O friend! Whoever relies on God, God is sufficient for Him. So, say: *God is sufficient for me, what an excellent guardian He is!*

First of all, He is absolutely perfect: absolute perfection is loved for its own sake and souls are sacrificed for it.

Second, since He is loved for His own sake, He is the true beloved, and love requires sacrifice.

Thirdly, He is the Necessarily Existent One. In His nearness originate lights of existence, while being absent from Him brings about darkness of extinction or non-existence, and gives the human soul incurable pains because of the extinction of its aspirations.

Fourthly, He is the refuge of the human soul suffocated within the narrow confines of material existence, suffering from the filth, the deceiving ornaments of the world, and crushed under the burden of the pains arising from the soul's affection toward the creation.

Fifthly, He is the Permanent, by Whom is permanence and without Whom is decay and extinction, which cause only grief and sorrow. Without Him, pains are accumulated on the human soul, whereas lights pour from everywhere over one who finds Him and trusts in Him.

Sixthly, He is the sole Owner of all existence. He wants to bear for you the burdens of life and bodily existence that He has entrusted to you, as you are unable to carry them and are bound to be left in painful torments if you suppose yourself to own them. If you desire their permanence and the continuance of His favoring, do not be grieved at His taking them from you. The bubbles of water containing images of the sun do not grieve at their passing away. For the renewal of the reflections of the sun, they joyfully sacrifice their apparent forms. Also, neither fruits are grieved at their separation from the tree, nor seeds, over the disintegration of the fruit in earth. You know that its disintegration means the growth of a new tree that will yield numerous fruits.

You are also a fruit, an embodiment, of His favoring.

Seventhly, He is the All-Wealthy and Giver of Wealth. In His hand are the keys to all things. If you become a sincere servant of Him and then look at the universe, you will see the sovereignty and magnificence of your Master and get relief. You will then come to view the universe as if it were your property that you own without any trouble and for the disappearance of which you will feel no grief. A sincere servant of the King who is annihilated in His love, becomes proud of whatever belongs to Him.

Eighthly, He is the Lord of all the Messengers and Prophets, and saints and the God-fearing pious, all of whom are happy in His mercy. If you have a sound, uncorrupted heart, your knowledge of their happiness must give you happiness and pleasure.

Know, O friend! If you have a sound intellect, it is not fitting for you to either rejoice at or grieve over or be angry or complain about what you obtain or lose from among worldly things. For the world is decaying, so is your world, and especially so too are you. You are not [created] to stay here permanently, nor are you made from iron or wood so that you could stay longer. You are from ever-renewed flesh and blood and delicate limbs and you are vulnerable to the least of things. One part or component of you breaks, the other freezes, and still the other dissolves through the disintegration of its atoms. Look, the dawn of old age has broken on your head and it has covered half of it like a white shroud. The diseases visiting you, nay, intending to inhabit you, are the forerunners of death. They destroy the pleasures [of life]. Whereas there is an eternal life before you. Your comfort and happiness in that life depend on the efforts you make here. However, your avarice is of a degree as if you would remain in the world forever. Awake before the throes of death awaken you.

Know, O friend! When you turn to the Almighty supposing that He is One known and recognized, He will become unknown and unrecognized. For your supposition of His being known and recognized is based on a commonplace, imitative knowledge about Him. Such knowledge has, in most cases, nothing to do with truth. The meaning it conveys to your mind is far from explaining the absolute Divine Attributes.

If, however, you turn to the Almighty accepting Him as One existent but unknown, then the rays of true knowledge of Him will be revealed to you and the all-encompassing, absolute Divine Attributes manifested in the universe will appear in the light of this knowledge.

Know, O friend! It suffices for you as a limitless source of pride that you have a Master, an Owner, powerful over all things. He is such a Powerful One that on Doomsday the heavens will be rolled in His "right hand" and the earth will be His handful. He brings up, trains and sustains you with a caring and compassion much more perfect than your parents'. As for you, you are like a drop in the sea, and the sea is like a point in the known part of the universe and this part, like a minute particle among His huge creatures. He is the Light of Lights, and the Knower of all secrets. If an earthly, human king is not busied with the details of the affairs of his kingdom, it is not because he is too great but because he is not able enough to be so. By contrast, because of the grandeur of the Eternal Sovereign, He inscribes the signs of His Divinity on the page of the sky with the pen of His making in the ink of pearl-like stars. At the same time, He inscribes the signs of His Lordship on the page of the pupil of the eye with the same pen in the ink of atoms.

Glory be to Him for Whose Divinity and Grandeur all those heavenly objects, those pearl-like planets, are bright proofs, and for Whose Lordship all those smiling, luminous stars are rays of witnesses.

Know, O friend! Like the light containing the seven colors, the Divine Beautiful Names contain and imply one another. They also testify to one another and give effect to one another. They are reflected in one another. They may be recited as if they are both analogies and the conclusions reached through them at the same time or both the arguments and the conclusions reached through them. Any of the Greatest Names contains all of the other Names in the greatest degree. It may be possible for some to reach the light of the Greatest Name through some other Name or Names and what the Greatest Name is differs according to one who tries to find it out and reach it. God best knows the truth.

A supplication

O God! It is incumbent upon me not to care either if I lose both lives—this one and the next—or if the whole of the universe becomes mine, as you are my Lord, my Creator and my God. I am one created and made by You. Despite my extreme rebelliousness and limitless remoteness from other connections of grace, I have a connection to You, which is my being Your creature. I supplicate in the tongue of this connection:

O my Creator, O my Lord, O my Provider, O my Owner, O my Fashioner, O my God!

For the sake of Your Beautiful Names and Your Greatest Name, and for the sake of Your wise Criterion—the Qur'an—your Noble Beloved—the Prophet Muhammad, upon him be peace and blessings—Your eternal Speech, and Your Greatest Throne, and for the sake of thousands of thousands, *Say: He is God, the One,* have mercy on me, O God, O All-Merciful, O All-Pitying, O All-Bounteous, O Supreme Ruler! Forgive me, O All-Forgiving, O All-Covering [of sins], O All-Relenting, O Free-Giving! Pardon me, O All-Loving, O All-Clement, O All-Pardoning, O All-Excusing! Favor me with Your kindness and gentleness, O All-Kind, O All-Aware, O All-Hearing, O All-Seeing! Overlook my faults, O All-Forbearing, O All-Knowing, O All-Munificent, O All-Compassionate! Guide us to the Straight Path, O Lord, O Eternally Besought-of-All, O All-Guiding! Always favor me with Your grace and generosity, O Originator, O All-Permanent, O All-Just, O He! Enliven my heart and [illuminate] my grave with the light of belief and the Qur'an, O Light, O Truth, O All-Living, O Self-Subsistent and All-Subsisting, O Master of All Domains, O One Having Majesty and Benevolence, O First, O Last, O Outward, O Inward, O All-Strong, O All-Powerful, O my Master, O Forgiving, O Most Merciful of the Merciful! For the sake of Your Greatest Name in the Qur'an and the Prophet Muhammad, upon him be peace and blessings, who is the greatest embodiment of the meaning You have given to the creation, I ask you to open through these Beautiful Names windows through which the lights of Your Greatest Name may come into my heart while in this world and to my spirit while in my grave. Let this page be the ceiling of my grave and these Names, the windows through which the rays of the sun of truth pour into my spirit.

O God! I desire that I should have an everlasting tongue with which I always call You until the Last Day. Accept these lines as a perpetual substitute for my mortal tongue.

O God! Bestow peace and blessings on our master Muhammad in a way by which You will save us from all misfortunes and calamities and meet all our needs and purify us of all our evils and forgive us all our sins and faults.

O God! O One Who answers all prayers! Accept from me at each moment during my life and after my life thousands by thousands and by thousands of calling blessing and peace on our master Muhammad and on His family, Companions, helpers and followers. Increase these callings of blessings to the number of my breaths I take in and out during my life, and forgive me and have mercy on me for the sake of each calling of blessing and for the sake of Your Mercy, O Most Merciful of the Merciful! Amen.

Addendum

O friend! I believe myself to be somehow compelled to try and unveil something very important through my confused works. I wish I knew whether I had been able to discover it or if it is yet to appear or if I am a means to make it easy for a discoverer to come to reach it.

There is no power and strength save with God. God is sufficient for us, what a good guardian He is! O God! Do not take us out of the world but as martyrs and believers!

In the Name of God, the Merciful, the Compassionate.

All praise be to God for the blessing of faith and Islam, to the number of the drops of rain, and the waves of seas, and the fruits of trees, and the "embroideries" of flowers, and the songs of birds, and the rays of lights, and thanks to Him for each of His bounties in all circumstances, to the number of all His bounties at all times.

Peace and blessings be upon the lord of pure saints and the good of human beings—the chosen Prophet, Muhammad—and on his purified family and Companions, each like a luminous, guiding star, as long as nights and days continue.

Know, O friend! There are conditions special to each of the stations a traveler calls on. One journeying on the path to God should likewise put on an attitude special to each of the stations, ranks and veils that come on the way and which he is to pass by or through, and each of the states he is to experience during his journeying. Whoever confuses these [with one another] makes mistakes. He would be like the one who hears the neighing of a horse coming from a stable at the village he happens to be visiting. Then he goes to a town and, on hearing the singing of a nightingale in the house where he is received as a guest, he confuses the neighing of the horse with the singing of the nightingale or expects the nightingale to neigh like a horse.

Know, O friend! One of the reasons why you see the worldly life as beautiful is the preceding illustrious, great persons shining as stars of guidance in the "mirror" of the world. This is so because the future is the mirror of the past and the past has already been mixed into the intermediate realm between this world and the next, leaving its form in the mirror of the future and in history and the memories of people. In loving the worldly life because of your love of those persons you resemble one who comes across on the road a huge mirror where he sees the images of his friends and beloved ones who have already emigrated to "the east", who appear in the mirror to have gone to the west. Terrified of the east, he turns back and hastens toward "the west." If the veil of unawareness and heedlessness is lifted up from your face, you will see yourself hastening in a vast desert toward a mirage and torment, not toward a source of sweet water.

Know, O friend! One of the aspects of the greatness of the Qur'an and most truthful evidences of its truth is as follows:

It contains whatever is necessary for all degrees of confirmation of Divine Unity and its varieties—Unity in Essence, Unity in Attributes, Unity in Names and Unity in Acts—and observes the balance among all exalted Divine truths. Again, it comprehends whatever is required by the Divine Beautiful Names and preserves the proportion among them, and also encompasses the essential qualities of Lordship and Divinity with perfect balance. This quality of the Qur'an is not to be found in the products of any human mind whether he be among the saints penetrating the inner dimension of existence or among illuminist philosophers (*Ishraqiyyun*) having insight into the inner side of things and events or among the perfect, purified scholars seeing into the unseen world. They cannot comprehend the absolute truth with their limited views. They only observe an aspect of it and, in their attempts to grasp it, they handle it in some extreme, unjust ways. This destroys the balance and removes the proportionateness.

Their like is the like of divers who probe at the bottom of a sea a treasure of all kinds of precious stones. Some of them happen to find a long diamond and conclude that the treasure consists of only that kind of diamond. When they hear that some of their friends have found other stones, they think that those stones are the gems to be set in that diamond. Some others encounter a round ruby, and still others, a square amber. Each group supposes that the treasure consists of what they have found and what the others have found are its parts or the parts to be added to them. Obviously, this would destroy the balance and proportionateness and lead the groups to make false or unacceptable comments on the findings of each other and even to deny them. Whoever examines according to the criteria established by the *Sunna* the works of illuminist philosophers and spiritual masters based on their particular findings and observations will not hesitate to confirm me in this judgement.

Then look at the wise Qur'an. You see that it is also a diver. But it has an open eye which sees the whole of the treasure with whatever it comprises, and describes it exactly as it is, without going to extremes and neglecting anything, nor destroying the balance and proportion among the parts of the treasure. For example:

It contains whatever is necessary to describe the Grandeur of God Almighty, such as:

The whole earth is His handful on Doomsday, and the heavens will be rolled up in His right hand.[6]

On that day We shall roll up the heavens like rolling up a scroll for books.[7]

He fashions you in the wombs as He pleases.[8]

There is no moving creature but He has grasped it by the forelock.[9]

He has created the heavens and the earth.[10]

6. al-Zumar, 39.67.
7. al-Anbiya', 21.104.
8. Al 'Imran, 3.6.
9. Hud, 11.56.
10. al-An'am, 6.73.

He creates you and whatever you do.[11]

He revives the earth.[12]

Your Lord has inspired the bee.[13]

The sun, the moon, and the stars are all subjugated to His command. [14]

Have they not seen the birds above them flying in lines with their wings spread out and alighting [with their wings] closed? None save the All-Merciful One sustains them. He is Seer of all things.[15]

He inscribes the page of the heavens with stars and suns like inscribing the wing of a bee with its cells and particles.

His Seat embraces the heavens and the earth. [16]

He is with you wherever you may be.[17]

He is the First, the Last, the Outward and the Inward, and He knows all things.[18]

What is observed in different deviant sects is that they have all deviated because of their leaders who have "set out" into the inner dimension of existence and turned back halfway in reliance on their findings. They have obtained something and lost many things.

Know, O friend! Describing the heaven with the world in *We decorated the heaven of the world*[19] and mentioning the world as the opposite of the Hereafter, point to the fact that the remaining six heavens are related to the worlds of the Hereafter from the intermediate world of the grave to Paradise. The heaven that we see with its stars is the heaven of the world. However, God knows best.

---

11. *al-Saffat*, 38.96.
12. *al-Rum*, 30.50.
13. *al-Nahl*, 16.68.
14. *al-'Araf*, 7.54.
15. *al-Mulk*, 67.19.
16. *al-Baqara*, 2.255.
17. *al-Hadid*, 57.4.
18. *al-Hadid*, 57.3.
19. *Fussilat*, 41.12.

Know, O friend! You were brought into existence out of non-existence. Then, your Originator favored you by elevating you from the lowest level of existence to the level of being a Muslim human being. Whatever you received and whatever happened between your first movement at the beginning of your existence and your present state is a favor of God on you. From each of these favors there is a fruit attached to you and a color put on you. You are like a necklace or a cluster or a spike on which the "beads" or "grains" of favor have been strung. You are as if an index of the Almighty's favors. Existence requires a cause, while non-existence does not. You will be asked how you have attained so many favors during the course of obtaining a full, perfect existence from the level of being a particle to death, how you have deserved them, and whether you have thanked [God] for them. No one with a bit of intellect asks a stone why it has not become a tree or a tree why it has not become a human being.

O Said, wretched, arrogant creature! You are a point in the middle of the series of creatures. You have been distinguished with favors to the number of the creatures below you as far as non-existence. You are responsible for giving thanks for each of them. As for the favors conferred on those above you, they are not for you. You are not to be questioned concerning any of the favors which it is impossible for you to attain, just as a particle has no right to sigh, saying: "Alas! Why did I not become a sun?" or a bee to complain to its Creator: "I wished you had created me as a fruit-bearing date-palm!"

Know, O ego! It is a cause of your perishing and it leads you to perdition and deviation, and it humiliates you, that you do not give everything its due and put on it the burden it has the capacity to bear. You go to extremes and burden a single soldier with all the requirements of an army. You want to see the sun itself with all its grandeur and planets in the image of it in the eye of a drop or on the face of a flower. In truth, a drop or a flower describes the sun to you [each according to its capacity to reflect the sun], but they do not have the qualities of the sun.

Know, O friend! The ownership and dominion of all things

belongs to Him. He also owns your body, which He has entrusted to you. There is no benefit in worrying about it and no good in what is not permanent. Avoid breaching your undertakings. You are destined to die, and the death resulting in life is better than this life resulting in death.

Know, O friend! While the image of something reflected in a mirror is not identical with that thing itself, it is not other than that, either. Paradoxically, the image is both identical with the thing and other than it at the same time. On account of the image being the form of the "meaning" reflected in the mirror, it is identical with the thing and what is true of the thing is also true of the image. Whereas, on account of the image consisting only in the form of the thing reflected in the mirror, it is other than the thing. In that way, while it is not identical with the thing itself, it is not something other than the thing either. Similarly, what is reflected in the mirror of the mind, since it is the form of the meaning, it is something known, whereas, since it is the description of the thing reflected, it is knowledge.

Know, O friend! Many worlds are situated in existence without one preventing the other. If on a pitch-dark night you enter a room illuminated with an electric lamp and the walls of which are looking glasses,

first, you will see in the walls numerous illuminated places and the town itself reflected and illuminated;

second, you can make any changes and alterations in those reflected places;

third, you will see the lamp is nearest to the remotest of the reflected lamps, for it is the original of all the reflected lamps;

fourth, a part of this existence, the size of a grain, can contain a whole world of the reflected existence.

All these four qualities are also true of many other things, even of the Necessary Existence and the world of contingencies, which are the shadows of the lights of the One Whose existence is absolutely necessary. Although the existence of the world of contingencies is illusionary by itself, it has stability by the command of the Almighty and is visible, sensed, by the creation of the Necessarily Existent One.

Know, O friend! It is inconceivable that this domain of existence should not have One Who has brought it into existence and owns it. It is also inconceivable that that Owner should not make Himself known to man who is able to perceive the beauties of this domain testifying to the perfection of the Owner. Man, who has been made a ruler in this cradle of his—the earth— leveled and prepared for his dwelling, has disposal of both his cradle and its ceiling of the heaven. In addition, despite his weakness and smallness, as testified by his strange and wonderful disposition, man is the noblest of creatures. Also, among the causes [that God has made a veil before His acts and free disposing], man is the most comprehensive and influential in choice and free decision. So, the Owner sends him who will make the Owner known to the inhabitants of His domain unaware of Him and inform them of what is pleasing to Him and demand it from them.

Know, O friend! All of man's feelings and faculties including even those of supposition and imagination are compelled to be finally agreed on truth and take refuge in it. It is impossible for falsehood to have room in them. They affirm that it is impossible for the universe to be different from how the Qur'an describes it.

Know, O friend! There is no collision and repulsion between the worlds of light, heat, air, electricity and gravitation and also those of ether and ideas or immaterial forms and the intermediate world of the grave. They exist together with you where you are without one preventing and being mixed with the other. Similarly, although much more spacious or larger than this narrow world, many of the worlds of the Unseen can exist together. Also, air does not prevent us from journeying, nor water, from going [on or through it], as glass does not stop light from passing through it and a solid object does not hinder the penetration of X-rays and the light of the intellect and the spirit of an angel. Iron cannot form an obstacle before the permeation of heat and the conduction of electricity. Nothing can stop the penetration of the power of gravitation and the movement of the spirit and the light of the intellect. Likewise, this solid, material world does not stop or prevent spirit beings from circulating, the jinn from moving around, Satan from infiltrating and penetrating, and angels from journeying.

Know, O friend! The light and what is of light are like the eye and the lamp and the sun. It is equal to them [to encompass with their manifestations] whether it be an individual thing or a species as a whole or a partial thing or a whole or a single thing or by thousands. Look at the sun and see how at the same time and with the same facility the planets or oceans or bubbles or drops or dewdrops or raindrops or tiniest particles of glass contain and reflect its images!

For God should the highest similitude be set forth—the disposition of the book of the universe by the Eternal Sun, the Light of Lights, is similar. He writes all its chapters, sections, paragraphs, lines, sentences, words and letters at the same time with the same absolute facility, with no difficulty at all. He declares, *Your creation and resurrection are like those of a single soul.*[20] We believe and confirm.

Know O friend! One who reflects upon the tiniest component particles of things and their travel as far as the farthest point they should go to and be settled at for many purposes and results, becomes convinced that there is One Who orders them: "Stop and be settled!" It is like the casting-mould ordering the melting gold in the tongue of iron: "Do not flow! Be fixed and stable within the borders of the mould made for some particular purpose!"

What commands the tiniest component particles of things is the Encompassing Knowledge that manifests Itself as Destiny— the power destining, determining and ordaining. Destiny becomes a fixed measure or amount and the measure becomes a mould.

---

20. *Luqman*, 30.28.

Know, O friend! Just as the verses of the Qur'an interpret one another, so the parts of the book of the universe also interpret one another. Also, just as the corporeal world truly needs the sun from which the lights of the favorings of the Almighty diffuse upon it, so too the spiritual world needs the sun of Prophethood for the diffusion of the lights of the Almighty's compassion upon it. The Prophethood of Ahmad—Muhammad—upon him be peace and blessings, is as manifest, clear, and certain as the sun at noon [on a clear summer-day]. Does daytime need any evidence?

Know, O friend! The purposes for the existence of a living thing do not concern only the life, benefit and perfection of that thing itself. While they concern the thing itself in one respect only, they relate to the Giver of Life in innumerable respects. The realization of the purpose for the thing itself needs a long time but the purposes relating to the Giver of Life are realized in an instant. By being a mirror reflecting the manifestations of His Most Beautiful Names, a living thing fulfils in an instant its function of praising its Creator with all His Attributes of Perfection, Grace and Majesty.

Know, O friend! Each individual human being is like a species of other beings. Because:

A human being has a past and a future: [since all his cells are renewed every six months] his two individual forms depart from him every year but only after depositing in him their pains, sins, ambitions, etc. It is as if he is an all-inclusive individual. Also, his intellectual capacity and comprehensive thoughts, feelings and emotions make him like a species. Again, he is individually as well as as a species, responsible for improving the world in accordance with the commands of God [which we call vice-gerency] and being the pivot around which his particular world, as well as the whole of the world, rotates. His conscious concern with all other parts of creation and disposal of many species of plants, animals and elements—all this also makes him like a species. It is as if each individual human being is a species in himself. Furthermore, the prayer of a believer for the whole of the inhabitants of the heavens and the earth points to the fact that an individual human being becomes like a world or its center through belief. Consider whatever takes place in a species of animals and plants every year in the name of death and revival and renewal. Look at the imprints and traces of God's Mercy manifested every year in the fruits renewed or recruited with almost their identicals, and at the resurrection of many species of insects and vermin with perfect facility. The same thing happens in every individual human being. Through all these "verses" of creation the book of the universe indicates the overall destruction of the world on mankind and their resurrection, a fact which the Qur'an points to with its verses of Revelation. I have mentioned rational arguments for the Resurrection in "The Tenth and Twenty-ninth Words" in the book of *The Words*.[21]

Know, O friend! While listening to the Qur'an, for each of its melodies, you can take on a new attitude and mood according to the degrees of guidance in consideration of the levels of its addressees, and try to assume the mood of the intermediaries ranging from Gabriel, who brought it to the Prophet, to the one from whom you hear it directly.

While listening to it from the one reciting it where you are, you should try to hear it as if you were listening to it from the Prophet himself, upon him be peace and blessings, reciting it at the summit of Prophethood to the whole of mankind and other beings throughout the earth.

Then, you should assume the manner of Gabriel while he recites it to the Prophet, upon him be peace and blessings, on the "highest horizon".

Finally, if you can, you should try to hear it as if you were listening to it from behind seventy thousand veils from the Eternally Speaking One, Who speaks to the Prophet at "the distance of two bows' length".[22]

---

21. *The Words* has been published in two volumes. (*Kaynak Koll. Şti.* 871 Sok. No. 4, Konak-İzmir-Turkey.) (Tr.)

22. "The distance of two bows' length" is mentioned in the Qur'an (53.9) to express the nearness to God the Prophet Muhammad achieved during his Ascension. It is purely metaphorical. (Tr.)

Know, O friend! What falls to your part from consciousness and knowledge is proportional to your share in your existence. This is because there is no waste in existence and the cause is proportionate to its effect, and the power to the result. When compared to the part in your existence belonging to Him Who has created you, your share is only as much as a hair compared to a thick rope or as a fiber compared to clothes. As for your consciousness and knowledge of yourself compared to your Creator's knowledge and sight of you, they are like the light of a firefly in the bright sun shining at midday. You are in the darkness of heedlessness and the night of nature or naturalism shows your light as if it was a piercing star.

Know, O friend! Between God's acts there is a proportion and between His works, a similarity. His Names are reflected on one another, His Attributes are intermixed and His essential qualities, commingled, with one another. However, each of these has a particular attitude and way of manifestation and operation, with the others dependent on and subordinate to it. In the sphere of the manifestation and operation of one, the rule and consequence are not to be attributed to others, nor should the imprints and works of others be sought from that one.

Therefore, out of His works, when you look at inanimate objects, consider, first of all, His Power and Grandeur. Then, the manifestations of other Names will appear to you as subordinate to these.

When you look at animals, consider, first of all, the Names manifested on them most. For each thing there is a measure with Him. All things has He created and established for it a measure.

Know, O friend! *There is no force and strength save with God* has a relation or concern with each of the stages a man undergoes during the course of his coming into existence, from the stage of being a component of elements in nature to that of being a believing human being. In connection with each of these stages and [for the satisfaction of] each of his senses and faculties, man has different needs and expectations, and suffers different pains:

There is no force to bring forth from non-existence *and no strength* to give existence, save with God.

There is no force to save from decay *and no strength* to give permanence, save with God.

There is no force to cause harm *and no strength* to give benefit, save with God.

There is no force to save from misfortunes and *no strength* to meet needs, save with God.

There is no force to enable one to resist against sins *and no strength* to enable one to be sustained in worship of and obedience to God, save with God.

There is no force to save from pains and torments *and no strength* to bestow bounties, save with God.

There is no force to save from evils *and no strength* to earn grace and do good, save with God.

There is no force to enable one to endure pains *and no strength* to enable one to attain one's ambitions, save with God.

There is no force to remove the veil of darkness *and no strength* to send illuminating lights, save with God, the High, the Grand.

Know, O friend! Whoever trusts in God and relies upon Him, He is sufficient for him [to protect against evils and attain all good.]

God is sufficient for us and what a good Guardian He is. For He is our owner and the owner of all things. Therefore, if we submit ourselves to Him, it will be as if everything is in our possession.

God is sufficient for us and what a good Guardian He is. For He is the Absolutely Perfect One and perfection is loved by Him and it is worth being sacrificed for the sake of that perfection.

God is sufficient for us and what a good Guardian He is. For He is the All-Majestic and the All-Beautiful One having absolute perfection. Beauty is loved by Him and for the sake of the zeal and ecstasy produced by the renewals that the manifestations of His Beauty bring about, we die smiling and are revived rejoicing.

God is sufficient for us and what a good Guardian He is. For He is the Necessarily Existent One, Who gives existence to all things. Our knowledge of the absolute necessity of His existence makes the whole of existence subservient to us and bestows on us eternal existence. Our ignorance or denial of His necessary existence leaves us enveloped by the worldwide darkness of non-existence.

God is sufficient for us and what a good Guardian He is. For He is everlasting and eternal, uncontained by time and space. *All things are perishing except His "Face".*[23]

God is sufficient for us and what a good Guardian He is. For the world is transient and life is ephemeral.

God is sufficient for us and what a good Guardian He is. For without Him all pleasures of the world change into pains, whereas through turning to Him and connection with His Mercy, one is saved from the pains of being mortal and fleeting pleasures gain permanence.

God is sufficient for us and what a good Guardian He is. For one receives the lights of existence through Him, while without Him one falls into the darkness of non-existence.

God is sufficient for us and what a good Guardian He is. For if we recognize Him and refer to Him our needs and complaints, He will suffice for all our needs. If, by contrast, we turn to causes and refer to them our needs and complaints—although causes are blind and deaf, unable to see and hear us—we are confused and lost in our ways. We are like one who, although he needs to and should refer his complaints directly to the king who is able to answer them instantly, applies to the whole population of the country one by one to help him.

Know, O friend! Among the subtleties of the miraculousness of the Qur'an and the evidences that it is an all-encompassing mercy for the whole of creation, are the following:

Just as out of this world each person has a particular world of himself, so also out of the Qur'an each person has a Qur'an addressing his temperament and educating him and curing his [spiritual] diseases and answering his intellectual quests.

---

23. al-Qasas, 28.88.

Among the Qur'an's merits of guidance are the following:

There is a perfect coherence, consistency, and connection among its verses, which enables each person to pick out verses from different chapters for his guidance and the cure of his spiritual diseases. This is what scholars and spiritual guides belonging to different schools do. Although the Qur'an was revealed in parts on different occasions, you see its verses arranged like the beads of a necklace in perfect harmony and coherence with one another. Neither its division into verses and chapters causes disaccord and disunity and distraction from its main purposes nor transition to other verses or groups of verses causes any disruption. Most of its verses are subtly interlinked with one another so that they can be mentioned together or gathered together to form, for example, a compilation of supplications.

The verses of *sura al-Ikhlas* corroborate one another: they are both arguments for one another and conclusions to be reached from those arguments.[24] Similarly, because of the interrelation among its verses and the comprehensiveness of their meaning, there are thousands of thousands of Qur'ans within the single Qur'an, and a book is formed around each of its truths.

O God, the Revealer of the Qur'an, for the sake of the Qur'an, make the Qur'an an intimate friend for me in my life and following my death, and a light in my heart and in my grave.

There is no god but God. Muhammad is His Messenger.

---

24. *Sura al-Ikhlas* is: Say: *"He is God, (He is) One. God is the Eternally Besought-of-All. He begets not, nor was He begotten. There is none comparable to Him"*. (112.1-4) For its verses corroborating one another and being both arguments for one another and conclusions to be reached from those arguments, see, *The Words 2*, Kaynak (İzmir), Turkey, 1997, p.10. (Tr.)

Second Addendum

In the Name of God, the Merciful, the Compassionate.

All praise be to God, the Merciful, among the greatest fruits of the sacred tree of Whose Mercy are our master Muhammad, upon him be peace and blessings, and Paradise, both hanging down to both worlds—this and the next one. He is the All-Powerful One: all these ever-renewed, spectacular creatures and the heavenly objects are witnesses of His Lordship. These multi-colored plants and diverse kinds of animals in the garden of the earth are the marvels of His Art and evidences of His Divinity. These lustrous flowers and, with all their leaves, blossoms and fruits, these fruit-bearing trees are the miracles of His Power and proofs of His Mercy. All testify that He is powerful over all things.

Past events are miracles of His Power pointing to the fact that He is able to make their likes in the future. There is nothing that either happened in the past or can happen in the future, beyond the decree of His Power. In relation to Him, the tiniest particles and the largest suns are the same. He is the Evident Truth, One, Single. In their various tongues, the particles and components of the universe point to His absolute Beauty, pronouncing:

Though we differ in expressing, You have the same Beauty;
Whatever exists [in the universe] points to that Beauty.

With all its chapters, sections, paragraphs, sentences, words and letters, the book of the universe reads the signs of His absolute necessary existence and Unity, and its lines announce to the intelligent:

Ponder the lines of the universe
For they are messages to you from the highest abode.

Peace and blessings be upon our master Muhammad and on all his family and Companions.

Know, O rebellious Said! Do not fix your eyes on what is not for you; rather, look at yourself. What kind of one are you? Of what value are you? What do you rely on? You are an embodiment of impotence and neediness; whatever you have is conferred on you by God. And you are in a sleep that you regard as wakefulness.

Impotence is your body in which neediness is its spirit inciting it to move. With all that you have, you are an embodiment of God's favoring. Your life consists in sleep. Alas! I have drowned in a drop that has become an ocean swallowing me. I am lost in a moment that has become like eternity for me. I suppose this flash of life as a shining sun that will never set.

O wretched Said! You have a capital of about only sixty dollars. You have already spent forty-five dollars of it to satisfy your needs in the caravanserai of the world. You have forgotten and neglected your house and your property has become a debt for you to pay and a fire. As for the remaining fifteen dollars, it is doubtful whether you will be able to spend all of it or only some of it or whether you will be able to spend any of it. Whatever amount you will be able to spend of it, spend it on your permanent house. Let one third of it, at least, be a light for you. How ignorant you are! What a great loss you are in! You have spent on this passing life all of the amount you have been given out of your capital and the amount left in your hand for your eternal abode is the least of the little. You are a heedless traveler: you departed from your family home and hometown and you are about to step out of this transient world.

Know, O friend! Dreadful is the word that comes out of the mouths of some when they say, "things are formed by themselves" or "causes have brought it about" or "nature requires it [to be so]". All of these three statements are false and contain many impossibilities. You exist: according to the first statement, you are your own creature. According to the second one, [material] causes have brought you about. Or according to the last one, some unconscious, deaf and blind laws or forces [which they attribute to nature] or lifeless things forming what they call nature have required your coming into existence. Whereas truth requires that you are a creature of God the Almighty.

As for the first statement, *things cannot be formed by themselves* because:

Each of the particles or atoms forming your body should have an eye to see the whole of your body, nay, the whole of the creation, and also consciousness [to be aware of all the requirements of life and existence]. This is what your perfect composition, the perfection of art in you, require, and because all particles of existence are in vital and substantial relations with one another and with the whole of the creation.

Also, for even a simple book to be printed in a printing house there must be as many iron letters or keys as the number of the letters and symbols used in writing it. So, for you to be made by yourself, there must be in you as many moulds as the atoms of you in conscious relation and communication with one another.

Again, you have a uniform composition, all parts of which are in close interrelation with one another. Therefore, like the stones forming an arch or a dome, all your atoms or building blocks of your body should both be dominant over and dominated by one another. They should also be, like the manifestations of the Names and Attributes of the One Who rolls up the heavens like a scroll rolled up for books, both opposite and complementary to one another.

Causes cannot bring about anything by themselves because:

Consider that the bottles in a pharmacy containing the ingredients of certain medicine topple over and certain amounts of the substances in them pour out and mix together on the ground in exact measures to form the desired medicine. If that is possible then your formation by chance, by random causes, may also be possible.

Also, if innumerable deaf, blind and unconscious causes were to come together, they would only increase in deafness and blindness. It is inconceivable that a thing in perfect order issues from them. Whereas man is a most perfect work of art [intelligent, conscious and equipped with endless and extremely complex feelings, senses and faculties, and feeling numberless needs]. So, your creation by deaf, blind and unconscious causes is infinitely impossible.

Thirdly, assume it is possible that numberless causes come together in a most orderly fashion and in exact measures to create, say, a single cell in your eye. Then it is not more difficult than this that the basic parts or elements of the universe including huge heavenly objects, assemble themselves in your palm or even in each of your cells. For if one works in a house, this means the house contains him. All the parts of the universe such as air, water, earth, the sun, plants and animals etc. are related with man. So, if it is causes that make man, then, the universe, with all its parts, should be able to operate within each part of your body and be contained by a cell of yours. This is a most inconceivable sophistry.

Nature cannot be a creator because:

Nature is something supposed to exist, a name given by the heedless and misguided. However, in its true meaning, it is a Divine art, a painting by the All-Merciful.

As for what they call "natural forces," they are the manifestations of the Power of the All-Merciful, the All-Knowing, the All-Aware, the All-Willing. What they call "chance" is only a supposition issuing from misguidance put forward by those unaware of or denying the Single Maker. In many of my treatises such as T*he Point*, *The Drop* and its Addendum, and in *The Breath*, *The Particle* and in *The Grain* and its Addendum, I have argued that this wonderful art [which constitutes the essence of what they call nature] can not be other than the work of the Power of the All-Aware, the All-Seeing, having all the attributes of His Perfection.

How can it be possible that something restricted, solid, inanimate, and of which it is equally possible that it should exist or not exist, and therefore needs one who prefers its existence and brings it into being, can have woven the garment of the universe? How can it be possible that a gnat can have had a part in weaving these best designed and adorned garments all those worlds are dressed in? So, the only explanation for your existence as well as the existence of all the creation is that you and all other things are creatures of an Eternal Maker, the witnesses to Whose being the Creator are as many as the number of creatures. Among these witnesses, with all its particles and compounds, the visible, corporeal universe testifies to Him in fifty-five tongues, which were explained in *The Drop*.

Among those witnesses are the Qur'an and all other books revealed to different Prophets and written by saints and those who believe in the existence and Unity of God, together with whatever is and takes place in the universe.

Among them are the lord of creation and all other Prophets, saints and angels—the Prophet Muhammad, upon him be peace and blessings.

Among them are mankind and jinn with all their "natural" needs.

Among them is: *God testifies that surely there is no god but He*.[25] Also, listen to what is to follow:

Know, O friend! The falsehood of attributing creation to things themselves or nature or causes can be explained through the example of a fruit-bearing tree. If you attribute a fruit-bearing tree to God, the One and Single, you have attributed it to its seed and the laws of germination, creation and growth which issue from the Necessarily Existent Being, the One and Single, and on which that seed depends. It is dependent on the laws issuing from a Single Creator, because of the facility coming from the Oneness of Him Who governs its germination, growth and life. It is equally easy for that Single Creator to grow that seed into a tree, whether it be a large coconut palm bearing countless fruits or a very small one with only a few fruits.

Whereas, if you attribute a tree to itself or causes or nature, then each of its fruits, flowers, leaves, branches and twigs would

---

25. Al-i 'Imran, 3.18.

need whatever the whole of that tree does. For each of its parts is an epitome of a whole and whatever a whole needs, each of its parts also needs it. Now you may consider these two alternatives in explaining the origin and existence of things: the difference between them is the difference between what is absolutely necessary and what is inconceivable. The facility coming from the former is to the degree that it makes the existence of things necessary, while the difficulty issuing from the latter makes the existence of things inconceivable.

In short: if you attribute the existence of things to whatever is other than God Almighty, if you attribute their existence to things themselves, then you will have to accept that every cell of your body is of the quality to encompass the whole universe. If you attribute it to material causes, to builders other than God, then you will have to affirm that every cell is like a room where all the causes operating in the universe are included. For all cells are the same with one another and display the same structure. This uniformity of cells leads you to the unity in diversity, to the interrelatedness in the whole of the universe, and therefore to the unity of the Maker. Something unified, displaying uniformity, something composed all of whose parts are in basic relationship with one another, cannot have been created by more than one Creator. How can a cell in which even two wings of a gnat cannot be included contain the many material, bodily causes needed for it to function?

Something of external, material existence is more established, stable and fixed than something of only ideal, immaterial, existence. A tiny particle of the former can contain a mountain belonging to the latter. [For example, the reflected form of a mountain can be included in a small mirror.] [Whereas, whatever exists in the universe is contingent, it was equally possible for it to come into existence or not, and its coming into existence was the result of a preference by One having the absolute authority of preference. That One has an absolutely necessary existence, without which it would have been impossible for anything to exist. Therefore,] that necessary existence is more established, stable and fixed than all material existence. It is the Real Existence. It cannot be contained by contingent existence. Contingent things—whatever exists other than The Necessarily Existent One—are reflected in the mirror of the Eternal, all-encompassing Knowledge, their real existence consists in their existence in that Knowledge [as meaning]. They come into the material existence through the manifestation of the lights of the Necessary Existence. Therefore they show the existence of the Necessarily Existent One. Their material existence in the corporeal world, which is the result of their transference from the all-en-compassing sphere of Knowledge, can never be of the same essence and quality and of the same existential degree as the Real Existence.

Know, O friend! One who ponders creation will see that solid, material and corporeal things are acted on and affected by immaterial things or the things of light. For example, look at the light of the sun and that mountain. The former comes from the sky and operates on the earth freely, while the latter, despite its huge size, cannot do anything, nor can it have any effect on its environment. The subtler and more of light something is, the more effective and active, while the more material and solid, the more susceptible to being acted on and affected. We can conclude from this that the Creator of causes and effects is He Who is the Light of Lights: *Nothing is like Him, He is the All-Hearing, the All-Seeing.*[26] *Vision comprehends Him not, but He comprehends all vision. He is the All-Subtle, the All-Aware.*[27]

Know, O friend! Reflection [on creation, on the signs of God in the universe] is like light; it removes or melts the frozen heedlessness to and unawareness of [God]. Being careful and attentive is like fire, it burns the "dried rubbish" of doubts and suspicions [about Him]. However, when you reflect on yourself, your inner world, the world of your feelings, emotions, faculties and your conscience, reflect as deeply and in as much detail as possible, as the Divine Name the Inward wants you to do so. For the perfection of an art shows itself in details and ramifications.

---

26. *al-Shura'*, 42.11.
27. *al-An'am*, 6.103.

When you reflect on the outer world, reflect on it briefly and superficially, without going into detail. It is enough for you to understand the foundations upon which that world is based. This is what the Name the Outward requires. For the splendor of art becomes more evident and more dazzling when looked on and examined as a whole, and the outer world is very spacious. If you dive in it, since it has no shores, you may be drowned.

If you go deep in your inner world but make a brief and fast journey in the outer world, you can approach unity. Individual parts acquire wholeness, compounds become composites and composites become unified. And from this issues the light of conviction of unity.

When you do it otherwise, that is, when you make a brief and superficial examination of your inner world while going into detail in your traveling in the outer world, then the diversity of things throws you into confusion and causes doubts in you. Your egotism is strengthened and heedlessness becomes ingrained in you. Then, you are inclined to naturalism. This is the way leading from the diversity of things to misguidance. O God, do not include us among the misguided! Amen.

Know, O friend! It is narrated that when a man moves [with greed], his providence stops. When he stops [showing greed], his providence moves. This is to explain a profound truth. Look at trees: they stand motionless in their places and their providence comes to them. Whereas since animals move with greed, their providence stops motionless on the stems of plants. With all its diverse colors and smells, a plant invites to itself hungry animals and rouses them to move towards it.

Know, O friend! How ignorant is the heedless man, how misguided he is and how harmful he is to himself! He abandons a great good for fear of the harm he may suffer from it in the world at a probability of one out of ten. Whereas, while there are thousands of proofs for its truth, he abandons true guidance for a slight doubt and thereby falls into misguidance. Man is a being as cautious as to abandon a thing the probability of whose giving him harm in the world is one out of ten. How is it that he does not refrain from a thing that it is ninety-nine percent certain will give him the greatest harm in the Hereafter?

Know, O friend! The soul of man has endless needs and suffers from endless pains, and it has an appetite for endless pleasures and nourishes endless ambitions. Even compassion may cause endless pains for a misguided soul [because of its unbelief in God and its distrust in His Destiny and true Compassion]. So you cannot say, " What is my worth and what value do I have that God will destroy this world to re-build it and judge me therein?"

O misguided, doubtful one! Do not be deceived in this world! The pleasure you will take in it is dependent on a misleading argument. A misguided one, who is doubtful about the existence of the afterlife and terrified of being mortal and the thought of eternal extinction, may seek relief in the probability that there is eternal happiness in the other world. However, when he feels obliged to do religious duties, then he seeks relief in the probability that there is not another world where people will be called to account for what they did in this world. He thus seeks to escape both kinds of pains. But it is not long before the problem is solved and the truth is unveiled. As the first alternative throws him all at once into accumulated pains, rather than lessening them, so the second alternative causes him to encounter the torments of Hell.

He also consoles himself for a limited time by thinking: The coming calamity [death and the punishment to follow] will embrace most of the people. So, since I will be like everyone else, I don't care. However, when its time comes before long, his pains increase proportionally to the number of the afflicted. In addition to his own, he also feels the pains of his relatives and friends. Since man feels innate relations with his fellow men, the generality of the misfortune causes his pains only to increase.

O doubting, heedless one! Do not think that what you taste in heedlessness and doubts as real pleasure, rather there are severe pains accumulated in it. They will attack you all at once and appear as the torments of Hell. If you desire these pains should become renewed pleasures for you and that fire should change into light, give up conceit and bow and prostrate yourself before God in humility five times a day. Be so humble before God that the "table" of the Divine Criterion—the Qur'an—should descend with the light and gifts of belief. Also, persist in reflection on the verses of the Qur'an and the "natural" phenomena and in practising your duties of worship regularly. Thus the veil of doubt and heedlessness may burn away and the sweet taste of being saved from the bitterness of misguidance may emerge and the pleasure of supplicating to God Almighty arise.

Know, O friend! Servanthood to God Almighty requires submission. A man cannot test God [whether He will fulfil His promise]. The Lord has the right to test His servant, not the servant his Lord.

Know, O friend! The spheres of the Divine Names the Inward and the Outward are both within and face each other. Those who limit themselves to the latter, seeking Him only in nature, cannot escape associating partners with God by attributing to causes and nature creativity and creative effect. While those seeking to reach Him only in the light of the former cannot escape false beliefs of attributing to God division and union [with certain human beings]. For the images of the sun in transparent things carry the attributes of the sun and therefore may lead one unable to distinguish between the sun and its images to suppose each of the images as the sun itself. Similarly, one who seeks to reach God only in the light of the Divine Name the Inward may confuse the manifestations of God in himself, in his heart and other inner senses and faculties, with God Himself. This may lead him to see himself as the incarnation of God. The likes of those who limit themselves to the Name the Outward and those restricted to the Name the Inward, are like those who, respectively, follow only the superficial interpretation of the Qur'an and reject the *Sunna* and those following only an esoteric interpretation of Islam. Whereas Islam is the middle, straight way.

O Revealer of the Qur'an! For the sake of the Qur'an, guide us to the middle, straight way! Amen. Amen. Amen.

INDEX OR BRIEF SUMMARIES OF THE TOPICS DISCUSSED IN THE TREATISE

*Man is the fruit of the tree of creation. A fruit is the most perfect of the parts of a tree and the farthest from the roots. It is also the most comprehensive of them which has the properties of the whole tree. (197)

*Within this world everyone has a particular world. In the center of this particular world lies the man himself who has it, not the sun. The keys to this world are in the hands of the man and connected with his senses and faculties. (198)

*For thirty years I have struggled against two "rebels", one the ego within man, the other, nature in the outer world. (199)

*O ego! There are nine things the nature and consequences of which you live unaware: (199-201)

*Your likeness when stricken with the misfortunes thrown by Destiny is that of the sheep at which the shepherd throws stones to make them turn back when they enter the public pasture. (201)

*Heart has not been created to be occupied primarily with worldly affairs. (201–2)

*The Qur'an was sent and with it was sent a heavenly table on which is found whatever human beings differing in their intellectual appetites need. (202)

*O restless soul! Like the rising of the sun in the morning and its setting in the evening, whatever will happen to you throughout your life, in whatever conditions you will be, has all been predetermined by Destiny and inscribed on your forehead. (203)

*If the right of possession and disposal of this material domain belonged to you, the fears and anxieties of maintaining it would make it very distressing for you to benefit from it. (204)

*A minute transparent particle contains the image of the sun, even though it cannot hold two particles of its own size and nature. The drops of rain [and the bubbles on the face of an ocean] shine with the images of the sun held by them. Similarly, all the constituent particles and compounds of the universe have the capacity of receiving the manifestations of the luminous, absolute Divine Power, accompanied by the Divine Knowledge and Will. (205–6)

*Glory be to God implies the contingent nature of the servant and his distance from God. Praise be to God implies God's nearness to the servant and His creatures with His Mercy and Grace. (207)

*All glory be to God, how great are His mercy and favor toward man that He buys from man at a high price the property which He has entrusted to him and preserves it permanently for him. (208)

*Surely there is the seed of unbelief in the essence of sins, especially if they are frequently committed. (209)

*The radiations of the miraculousness of the Qur'an amount to about forty kinds. A few among its many aspects of eloquence are: (210–12)

*What is essential to things is that the Eternal One does not allow them to go into absolute non-existence. (213)

*The grave is a door; inside it is mercy and happiness, whereas outside it lie suffering and wretchedness. (213)

*O friend! With your sins and evils you cannot attach to God any harm but you harm only yourself. (215)

*Whoever relies on God, God is sufficient for Him. (215*7, 232*3)

*If you have a sound intellect, it is not fitting for you to either rejoice at or grieve over or be angry or complain about what you obtain or lose from among worldly things.(217)

*When you turn to the Almighty supposing that He is One known and recognized, He will become unknown and unrecognized. If you turn to Him accepting that He is One, existent but unknown, then the rays of true knowledge of Him will be revealed to you and the all-encompassing Divine Attributes manifested in the universe will appear in the light of this knowledge. (217–8)

*It suffices for you as a limitless source of pride that you have a Master, an Owner, powerful over all things. (328)

*Like the light containing the seven colors, the Divine Beautiful Names contain and imply one another. (218)

*A supplication. (219–20)

*There are conditions special to each of the stations a traveler calls on during his spiritual journeying (221).

*Among the subtleties of the miraculousness of the Qur'an and the evidences that it is an all-encompassing mercy for the whole of creation, are: (233–4)

*Do not fix your eyes on what is not for you; rather, look at yourself. What kind of one are you? Of what value are you? What do you rely on? You are an embodiment of impotence and neediness; whatever you have is conferred on you by God. And you are in a sleep that you regard as wakefulness. (236)

*Dreadful is the word that comes out of the mouths of some when they say, "things are formed by themselves" or "causes have brought it about" or "nature requires it [to be so]". (236–9)

*The falsehood of attributing creation to things themselves or nature or causes can be explained through the example of a fruit-bearing tree.(239–40)

*Reflection [on creation, on the signs of God in the universe] is like light; it removes or melts the frozen heedlessness to and unawareness of [God]. However, when you reflect on yourself, your inner world, the world of your feelings, emotions, faculties and your conscience, reflect as deeply and in as much detail as possible, as the Divine Name the Inward wants you to do so. When you reflect on the outer world, reflect on it briefly and superficially, without going into detail. (241–2)

*When a man moves [with greed], his providence stops. When he stops [showing greed], his providence moves. (242)

*Man abandons a great good for fear of the harm he may suffer from it in the world at a probability of one out of ten. Whereas, while there are thousands of proofs for its truth, he abandons true guidance for a slight doubt and thereby falls into misguidance. (242)

*The spheres of the Divine Names the Inward and the Outward are both within and face each other. Those who limit themselves to the latter, seeking Him only in nature, cannot escape associating partners with God by attributing to causes and nature creativity and creative effect. While those seeking to reach Him only in the light of the former cannot escape false beliefs of attributing to God division and union [with certain human beings]. (244)

A Flower from the Garden of the Wise Qur'an

Every living creature in the world is like a regular soldier who works on behalf of the king and in his name. Whoever supposes himself as his lord is subject to perishing.

The absolute order and balance observed in the universe are two titles of the two principles of the All-Merciful and two chapters from the manifest book and the book of the universe.

The Qur'an is the expounder or translator of these two books, the index of the two chapters and the concise summary of the two principles.

In the Name of God, the Merciful, the Compassionate.

All praise be to God, the All-Wise Ruler, Who has ordered and organized this universe with the laws of His way of acting, given it a certain shape and form with the principles of His Decree and Destiny. He has built it with the rules of His Will and Wisdom, decorated it with the standards of His Favoring and Mercy, and illuminated it with the manifestations of His Names and Attributes. He is the All-Powerful, Self-Subsistent and Ever-Lasting, such that this universe, with all its outer and inner features and properties, and with all its contents, decorations, and beauties, consists in but the lines of the Pen of His Decree and Destiny. It is but the designs of the compasses of His Knowledge and Wisdom and the decorations of the "Bright Hand" of His Art and Favoring. The universe consists of the flowers of the gardens of His Kindness and Munificence, the fruits of His gushing Mercy and Benevolence, and the gleams of the manifestations of His Absolute Beauty and Perfection. May His Glory be exalted! Praise be to Him to the number of all of the particles in the whole of the universe multiplied by themselves.

O One Who has manifested all those wonderful creatures through the lightning-like manifestation of His Names!

O One in relation with Whose Power the minutest particles and planets are the same (in creation and direction)!

O One Who has inscribed all those adorned worlds according to the measures of the Manifest Book—the source of the order and balance!

Before every pause and start by which all the particles and compounds of the universe start moving, we offer You the testimony of faith: We testify that there is no god but You—You are One with no partners at all. We also testify that Muhammad is Your servant and Messenger, whom You sent as a mercy for all the worlds.

O God! Bestow peace and blessings on him, his family and his Companions, to the number of the letters of the words of the Qur'an. It takes on forms by Your leave in the mirrors of the molecules of air during their recitation by every reciter from the first day of its revelation to the Day of the Resurrection!

Know, O wretched Said! Whatever reaches you in the name of livelihood reaches you either as a result of some other's choice or without the intervention of any free choice. What comes to you without the intervention of any choice or will, comes in the Name of God and for His sake. Receive it and eat it uttering the Name of God, offering all your thanks to Him exclusively. As for what comes to you as a result of a choice, do not receive and eat that on which God's Name is not invoked. Do not eat that which is given to you without remembering or considering its real Owner and directing your attention to Him—as alluded to in the verse: *Eat not of that on which God's Name is not mentioned.*[1] However, if they give it to you howsoever and you have to receive it, invoke God's Name on it and consider the One Who has bestowed it on him (who gives it to you) and on you. Consider the act of bestowing in what is bestowed and the real Be-

1. *al-An'am*, 6.121.

stower in the act of bestowing. Such a consideration means thanksgiving. Then, if you would like to, you can thank him who has been a means of that thing reaching you, as it has come to you through him. But beware, O my heart! Beware that first of all you must consider the real Bestower!

In short: You must mention God's Name twice on what comes to you by means of someone other and once on the other—that which comes to you by means of no one. Beware, O my soul! Beware, lest you take the means for a real cause. Seeing that any bounty comes to you as a result of someone's action, your defective view supposes that action to be the real cause for that bounty's coming to you. No! Beware that, seeing the absence of bounty as the result of the absence of some thing, act or person, you do not ascribe the existence of the bounty to the existence of that one or thing or act. While, according to God's way of acting or practice, the absence of even one of the conditions or parts or causes necessary for the existence of something results in the absence of that thing, its existence depends on the existence of all those conditions or parts or causes. So, is it right that if one whose duty is to turn on and off the main valve of the irrigation canals of a garden where many plants are produced, claims that he is the real maker and owner of all those plants? This is a criterion to understand the degrees of unawareness and forgetfulness of the real Maker, Owner and Director and of associating partners with Him unknowingly.

Beware, O my heart! Beware that you do not ascribe any work or product resulting from the corporate effort of a whole community to yourself or anyone other who represents that community, or to its leader or guide. Such an ascription is a grave wrongdoing that will lead him to whom the work is ascribed to a false and awful self-conceit, arrogance and egotism. It opens the door to a kind of associating partners with God unknowingly. The means is taken for the doer and therefore becomes the one sought and appealed to and the"doorman" appears in the form of the"king."

Beware, again beware, that when you see that a certain effu-

sion of spiritual radiance and ecstasy reaches you through someone, you must not suppose him as the source or mine of that radiance. What he does is only a reflecting [like a mirror] of what
is manifested in him. However, your devotion to him causes you
to imagine that what flows to your heart from the Director of
Hearts is first received by your spiritual guide and then reflected to you consciously. You resemble one who fixes one's gaze
on a piece of glass and, after certain period of concentration, begins to travel in the world of symbols or immaterial forms, and
witnesses some marvels and thinks that they really appear or
are manifested in the mirror. No!

Know, O one who seeks help from [material or natural] causes! You are having recourse to a wrong source and making a
wrong appeal, like one who supposes gaining weight because
of an illness to be a sign of good health.

Imagine you see a wonderful building, a palace, made of different, marvelous jewels some of which can, at the time of construction, be found only in China, some others in Morocco, and
some others in the Yemen, and still some others in Siberia, and so
on. Will you not testify that only one who dominates the whole
of the world and has anything he wants brought from any part
of the world just at the time of need, can build that palace?

It is in this way that each living thing is like a building, and
each animal is like a Divine palace. Especially man is the most
beautiful and wonderful of those palaces, [the jewels—particles
or atoms—of which are gathered together from many worlds—
the world of spirits, the world of symbols, the Supreme Preserved Tablet, and from the worlds of air, water, earth, light
and fire]. The range of man's needs stretches into eternity, and
his desires encompass the heavens and the earth. He has connections with whatever is included in the spheres of the world
and the Hereafter. So, O man! It does not befit you, nor do you
have the right, to regard yourself as one who must pray to and
worship one other than Him Who dominates the earth and
heavens and holds the reins of the world and the Hereafter.

Know, O my heart! The most stupid person is he who does not recognize the sun while he sees its image in a mirror, and loves only the mirror and tries to preserve it passionately with the aim of holding on to the sun permanently. However, if he were to understand that the sun does not perish with the perishing of the mirror, nor does it disappear with the breaking of it, he would direct all his love to the sun itself. For what he sees in the mirror does not depend on the mirror for its permanence, rather, the permanence of the mirror depends on it, whereas it subsists by itself. The permanence of the "liveliness" of the mirror and its shining [with the sun in it] are possible through the permanence of the manifestations of the sun and the mirror's facing the sun. Thus, your heart is like that mirror, and the love of permanence implanted in your nature is to be directed not to itself but to what is manifested in it. So, say, "O Permanent One, You are the Permanent" and turn to Him so that you too become permanent. Then let mortality do with us whatever it wishes, and we do not mind whatever befalls us.

Know, O man! It is one of the strange characteristics the All-Wise Creator has implanted in your nature that the world cannot contain you so that, as if in a suffocating dungeon, you frequently utter a sound of disgust. Yet so little a thing as a mustard seed or a cell or a memory or a minute of time absorbs you so much so that you are lost in it and passionately attracted to it. The Creator has given you such faculties that some of them are not satisfied even if they swallow up the whole of the world. Some others feel bored with even so small a thing as the minutest particle and cannot put up with even a hair in the wrong place. You know that the eye cannot bear even a hair, it harms the eye or prevents its proper working.

So, be alert and be careful in your acts. Be afraid lest you are ruined and ruin the most subtle of your faculties because of a morsel or a word or a glance or a beckoning or a kiss. For everything has an aspect with respect to non-existence such that it can ruin and swallow you. Look at the mirror in your hand and see how the sky is contained in it with all its stars. See how the

Truth inscribes in your memory, which is no bigger than the size
of a mustard seed, most of your acts or deeds and even most of
your life! Glory be to Him, the All-Powerful, the Self-Subsistent!

Know O friend! Your own private world is a grave-like, narrow place. But since its "walls" are made of "glass", you see it
as spacious to the extent of your sight. With respect to the material dimension of the worldly life, the past has gone out, while
the future does not exist. However, being the two mirror-like
walls of your world facing each other, they come together at the
point of your present time and make it difficult for you to distinguish between the real and the reflected [in them]. The "line"
of your present extends into [your past and future] and becomes an area. When you are made to move by misfortunes,
you strike your head against the walls, suffering disappoint-
ments in your imagination and losing sleep. You see your world
narrower than a grave and a bridge, and your life moves faster
than a river and even lightning.

Know, O one who wants to see the witnesses of the manifestations of the Divine Name the All-Recording and Preserving.
This Name is referred to in the verses: *Whoever does an atom's
weight of good shall see it, and whoever does an atom's weight of evil
shall see it.*[2] *Not an atom's weight in the earth and in the heaven es-
capes your Lord, nor is there anything smaller or greater, but it is in a
manifest book.*[3] Know, O one who wants to see them in the sheets
of the book of the universe inscribed according to the standards
of the Manifest Book![4] Take a handful of the seeds of various

---

2. *al-Zilzal*, 99.7-8.

3. *Yunus*, 10.61.

4. The "Manifest Record" and the "Manifest Book" are metioned in several places in
the Qur'an. The Manifest Record is an expression for one aspect of Divine Knowledge
and Commands in which every thing has an essential, archetypal existence. It is an index and programme of the tree of creation as a whole, a book of Divine Destiny or a
register of Divine laws that are operative in the creation and life of the universe with
whatever is in it. As for the Manifest Book, it is an expression for Divine Power and
Will. Everything is given existence according to the law of that Will and the principles
of that Power. Through the dictation of the "Manifest Record", that is through the decree and instruction of Divine Destiny, Divine Power employs particles in creating beings or manifesting them on the "page" of time. For further information for the Manifest Book, see, *The Words 2*, Kaynak Koll. Şti, İzmir, 1997, pp. 244–46. (Tr.)

flowers and trees. Although they belong to different species and are of different characteristics, they are so like one another in form and shape that you are nearly unable to distinguish one from the other. Then bury them together in darkness—the darkness of simple, lifeless-seeming soil. Afterwards supply them with water—water that has no measure and standards to know and distinguish them. To whatever direction you sprinkle it, it goes there. Look at them at the time of the yearly resurrection when the whole of nature comes to life again through the trumpet-blow of thunder in spring.

See how those mingled seeds resembling one another have obeyed the orders of creation given by the All-Wise Creator (and grown each into a different flower or tree) in a way to manifest the perfection of His Wisdom, Knowledge, Will, Purpose, Discernment and Consciousness. Do you not see how all those similar things were distinguished so that this fig tree spreads over your head?—How excellent its Lord! Do you not see that those flowers have been adorned for you and smile at you, making them loved by you? Do you not see that those fruits sharpening your appetite invite you to themselves and sacrifice themselves to you? This handful (of seeds) has changed by the leave of its Creator into a Paradise-like garden full of various flowers and trees. Look whether you can see in it any error or defect? *Then look again! Can you see any rift?*[5] Rather, the All-Preserving One has given each of them exactly and completely what was passed on to it from the property of its parent. The One Who does this is He Who alone is able to destroy the universe and re-build it on the Last Day. The One Who does this also does that. The act of perfect recording and preserving observed here even in trifling, perishable things is an undeniable evidence for the recording and preservation of important things whose effects extend into eternity. Recorded are the deeds and works of those honored with ruling the earth according to Divine laws, and the acts and speeches of those who assumed the Supreme Trust, and the good deeds and evils of the servants of

---

5. *al-Mulk*, 67.3.

the One, the Single. *Does man think that he will be left to his own devices, uncontrolled, without purpose?*[6] Rather, he is bound to journey to eternity and be called to give account of whatever he does and says here in the world.

[There are so many examples of or analogies for the Divine act of recording and preserving that] this one which you have woven is not a handful of wheat out of a heap, nor is it a handful of water out of an ocean. It is rather a single grain of sand out of a vast desert or a drop of water out of the rain of the heavens. Glory be to Him, the All-Preserving, the All-Controlling, the All-Witnessing, the All-Reckoning.

Know, O heedless Said! It does not befit you to set your heart on what will not accompany you after the annihilation of this world, what will abandon you together with its destruction. Such being the truth, how can you set your heart on what will leave you after the end of your century? Why set your heart on what will not accompany you during your journeying to the intermediate world of the grave? How can you count on what will abandon you eternally in one or two years, debiting your account with its sins, and on what forsakes you against your desire just at the moment of your being delighted to have obtained it.

If you are sensible, do not be anxious and care about what will not accompany you in your journeying to eternity—what perishes under the tumults and convulsions of the world, the continuously changing conditions of the intermediate world of the grave and the revolutions of the Hereafter. Do you not see that there is something in you that is not pleased with anything but eternity and the Eternal only and does not turn to any but Him only. It does not lower itself before any but Him. That thing is the king of your faculties. Obey that king of yours which is obedient to the command of its All-Wise Creator, may His Glory be exalted.

Know! I saw myself in a dream telling people: O people! It is one of the principles of the Qur'an that you must not consider

---

6. *al-Qiyama*, 75.36.

anything other than Him, the Glorious One, as greater than you in such a way that you adopt an attitude of worship before it. Nor must you consider yourself as greater than anything in such a manner that you claim absolute dominion over it. Anything whatever other than Him is equal to any other—in its distance from being the Object of Worship and in respect of its being a created thing.

Know, O heedless Said! You look around you and since you see the world around you as stable and perpetual, you have the illusion that you too are stable and perpetual and therefore are frightened only of the final destruction of the world as though you would live until that destruction. This is not truth. You and your own world are decaying every moment. With this illusion, you are like one in whose hand there is a mirror in which a mansion or a town or a garden is reflected. The least movement of the mirror and making a slight change in it cause a tumult in that mansion or town or garden with which he is so content. Their apparent, actual-seeming permanence is of no benefit to you. For what falls to your share of them is what the mirror reflects according to its capacity. Consider your mirror and how it is possible for it, as well as for what is reflected in it, to perish at any moment. So, do not burden it with what it is unable to bear.

Know that it is a usual practice of the All-Wise Creator that He returns (to life again) what is of great value over epochs and seasons recurring periodically together with renewals in most things. When you look at the types of resurrection occurring every day, every year and every century, you see this established, regular law. Sciences are agreed that man is the most perfect fruit of the tree of creation having the greatest importance and value. Each individual human being is like a species of other living beings. So every human being will be resurrected on the Judgement Day with his exact identity, body, title and form.

Know, O ignorant, arrogant soul! Every station or position has a shadow, rather, many different shadows. How can a shadow be equal to the original? Does it befit him who sees the throne of the king in water or in his dream and is seated on it, that he

supposes himself as the king or as equal to the king? Or he sees
stars in his pool and supposes himself to be in the sky like one
who is journeying among stars or above them. One who relies
on his intellect and knowledge in his journeying in the inner dimension of existence is in perilous arrogance. This is so because,
although his is only one of the shadows of the original station,
he is proud of his knowledge that he attributes to himself solely, he sees himself as comparable with the real owner of that
station. Thus he makes a very great error because of conceit and
begins to say in ingratitude: "What I have has been given to me
because of my knowledge." However, it is but a means of testing him.

Know O friend! The phrases or sentences usually coming at
the end of the Qur'anic verses have connections, not only with
those verses themselves, but also with the whole of the subject-
matter discussed, the whole of the *sura* and, indeed, the whole
of the Qur'an itself. They connect the verses with one another,
causing one to recollect and consider them. Do not judge what
is stated by those phrases by the meanings of the verses where
they are, nor seek their grandeur only where they are mentioned. For example, *Thus We detail the signs and revelations;*[7] and
We make recurring explanations in this Qur'an;[8] and *We coined for
mankind in the Qur'an all kinds of similitudes;*[9] and *Surely, God is
All-Dignified, All-Wise;*[10] and *Surely, God is All-Knowing, All-
Powerful;*[11] and *that You may reflect;*[12] and *that You may deserve
God's protection,*[13] and other similar verses have eyes looking at
most of the Qur'anic verses, most of God's signs of creation,
and general conditions and affairs of human life and characteristics of humanity.

Those concluding phrases or sentences with which the vers-

---

7. *al-'Araf*, 7.174.
8. *al-Isra'*, 17.41.
9. *al-Rum*, 30.58.
10. *al-Tawba*, 9.58.
11. *al-Nahl*, 16.70.
12. *al-Dhariyat*, 51.49.
13. *al-Baqara*, 2.183.

es are sealed and confirmed, in addition to other excellencies of eloquence they have, draw the attention of the addressee from the mingled and detailed particular affairs to universal and inclusive laws and truths. And they direct his attention toward higher aims and purposes.

Know, O my heart! Satan deceives you by offering to your attention what is in infinite abundance and thereby diminishing the value of the bounties conferred on you. In order to save yourself from this deception, consider how needy and, with respect to meeting your needs, how impotent you are, and reflect upon the purposive wisdom in the bounties you are given and the purposeful act of giving bounties. Also, you should meditate on the boundless manifestations of the Divine Power, Knowledge and Will, and on the purposes for your existence and its consequences with respect to the One Who has given you existence, the One Who owns the All-Beautiful Names.

The whisperer (of evils)—Satan—also deceives you by making use of your egotism and formidable conceit. He calls to your attention small creatures and vermin. He says, "What is the use of creating such short-lived things?" Implying that the purpose of life lies in life itself and it derives its value from perpetuity, this argument suggests to you that the creation of those short-lived creatures is meaningless. It thereby reduces in your view the value of mercy, favoring and the perfect artistry in what you observe, causing you to forget, even deny, the Maker. Respond to this deception of Satan by showing him the heaven with its stars and the earth with all its animate creatures. Compared with you, their huge size will awaken you. When you look at what is smaller than you, look, O greatest cell, at the cells of your body. See how marvelous they are and how wonderfully they fulfil their tasks, and again see what vital tasks the white and red blood corpuscles in your moving blood perform so long as you remain in this abode. You may also look at the subtle faculties springing from your heart.

Know, O Europe! There are two Europes. One is that which, having benefited from the religion of Jesus and Islamic civiliza-

tion, has invented and made things which will make mankind
comfortable in this life. The other is that which, based on natu-
ralistic and materialistic philosophy, opposes the heavenly religions, whose evils surpass the good of the former one, and
which has become the cause of the wretchedness and suffering
of the majority of mankind. Here I am addressing this second
Europe:

You have taken in your right hand the dark, deviating philosophy and in your left hand the corrupt, harmful civilization,
and claim that the happiness of mankind lie in them. I wish
these hands of yours were broken and those offerings the cause
of your death!

O you that spread unbelief and ingratitude! Is it possible for
one with a corrupt conscience and suffering from mental and
spiritual illnesses to be happy only with rich clothes and worldly belongings? Do you not see how, for a person disappointed
or disillusioned by seeing even one of his expectations unreal-
ized, the sweet turns sour, pleasure changes into pain and the
world becomes narrow? How can one exposed to your evils
and stricken in the depths of his heart and spirit with the misguidance you cause, and thereby frustrated in all his aspirations
and distressed, find happiness with what you offer him? Is it
possible to describe one whose body is in a deceiving, fleeting
paradisiacal state while his spirit and heart are in hellish torments, as happy?

Listen, O intriguing and corrupting spirit, to what will be
told you below! I will tell you only one of your thousands of
perils and troubles that you have brought upon mankind. In order to make it more understandable, I will coin a parable:

There are two roads before us. First we take that one and see
at every step a helpless man attacked by a band of thugs who
rob him of his things and belongings and destroy his hut. They
also inflict on him such blows that even heaven weeps for him.
Wherever we look, we see the same scene where the shouts of
oppressors and the cries and lamentations of the oppressed are
heard. Since a man feels pain because of the pains of others,

man's conscience cannot bear so much injustice and lamentation. So, the one who witnesses them, because of hopelessness and inability to do anything to stop them, abandons all his human feelings and, with a heart no longer concerned about the destruction of all other men so long as he himself is safe, surrenders to the utmost degree of savagery.

O Europe! Through your squint-eyed genius, you have brought upon mankind this hellish state as a gift and then, seeing that that is an incurable illness, you have offered people charming amusements and fancies as a cure to anaesthetize them. However, that cure of yours will be the cause of your death.

Then, we follow the other road and see at every station, in every place and in every town, soldiers doing some duties. Now and then some officials come and discharge them from their duties, taking their weapons and other belongings lent them by the government and giving them their documents of discharge. The soldiers are pleased with their discharge and returning to the king who dispatched them, although outwardly they look sad because of being discharged. If the officials of the king encounter a recruit who does not know them, that recruit tells them: "I am a soldier of the king and in his service. My final destination is with him. If you came here by his leave and consent, you are welcome. Otherwise keep yourself away from me, for even if you are thousands of people, I would fight with you not for myself but for the preservation of the trust of my lord and protection of his royal dignity and honor." Thus along our way and during our journey, we witness ever new troops concentrated or mobilized with joy and praises of the king—called births—while many others are discharged with contentment and glorifications of the king—called deaths. The wise Qur'an has offered mankind a gift. If they are respectful to it and make it a guide in their travel, they follow it and enter this second road. Then no fear shall come upon them, neither shall they grieve.[14]

---

14. *Yunus*, 10.62.

O Europe! You assume that all living creatures from the smallest of fish to the greatest of angels are lords over themselves and work only in their own name and for their own pleasure. That their only aim in life is to try to survive. Do you not see that there is a universal mutual helping among them, as established by their Creator? Plants come to the help of animals, and animals to the help of human beings. However, you see this as conflict and contention and have concluded that life consists in conflict. Glory be to God! How can it be a conflict and contention that the particles or atoms of all kinds of food are made to hasten to the help of the nourishment of the cells of the body? It is by the order of a Munificent Lord that there is such mutual assistance, which proves that no living creature is the lord of itself. This is so also because:

Among living agents in the world man is the most honorable, endowed with free choice with a wider field of activity. Despite this, his part even in the everyday acts he does out of free will such as eating, speaking and thinking, is so little as almost one out of hundred. If the most honorable of creatures endowed with free will with the widest field of activity has so little part in owning and lording over himself, you can compare to what degree other animate and lifeless things can claim lordship over themselves.

What, O Europe, what makes you fall into such an error is your squint-eyed genius which has led you to forget your Lord —the Creator of everything. Therefore, founded upon an illusion about nature, you attribute all things and acts in the universe to (material) causes and share what really belongs to God among false "claimants" to divinity. This compels man and all other living beings to struggle with innumerable aversions and hostilities to satisfy their endless needs through an atom's weight of power, a hair's capacity of will, a single gleam's light of consciousness, and a tiny sparkle of life. Whatever they have (in the name of power, will, consciousness and life) is not enough for the satisfaction of even a single one of their needs. When a misfortune visits them, they seek help from deaf and blind causes;

however, *the appeals of unbelievers are of no use.*[15] Your dark and darkening genius has changed the day of mankind into night illuminated only with false, illusory lights. In the view of the students of that squint-eyed genius of yours, every living being is like the wretched ones we saw along the other way attacked by darkness from all sides. They see the world as an abode of lamentations and all the voices in it as wailings over death and groans of orphans.

The students completely educated by your genius become each a "Pharaoh", a tyrant, but a tyrant who adores even the meanest of things and is attached to every beneficial means as if his lord. He is apparently refractory but lowers himself in utmost humiliation for the sake of pleasures and kisses even the feet of the devil for the sake of the meanest benefit. He is seemingly very powerful but due to being devoid of a point of support (in his inner world), he is infinitely weak.

All the efforts of your student are for the satisfaction of the desires of his stomach and private parts or for the benefit of his tribe but not in the name of his tribe but in the name of his own interests or satisfying his greed and conceit. He loves only his own self and can sacrifice every thing for it.

As for the sincere student of the Qur'an, he is a "servant" but he does not lower himself even before the greatest of the created and the greatest of interests even if it be Paradise. He is "mild and gentle" but he demeans himself before none except his Creator and by His leave. He is "poor" but the richest of all through what his Munificent Lord has stored in him. He is "weak" but relies on the strength of his Master Whose power is infinite. The sincere student of the Qur'an, let alone seeking this fleeting world, does not seek even to enter Paradise as his aim, nor is he pleased with it. [His aim is to obtain the good pleasure of his Lord.]

Consider then the degree of difference between the objectives of those two students.

---

15. *al-Ra'd*, 13.14.,

Also, the student of the Qur'an sees even the most immense of things such as the Supreme Throne of God and the sun but as creatures helpless in themselves, dutiful and subjugated. He finds in his spirit a very strong relation to all the pious from amongst the inhabitants of the heavens and the earth and prays for them from the bottom of his heart, as a man prays for his family.

Consider the difference between the qualities those students have: while one flees from even his brother for his own interest, the other regards all the servants of God as brothers. The Qur'an gives its students as prayer beads all the particles of the universe to glorify God. In place of the rosaries with ninety-nine beads in their hands, it gives them all the chains of the atoms of the universe to say their beads and mention their Lord to the number of all those chains or even more than that. Look at the saintly students of that Divine Revelation such as 'Abd al-Qadir al-Jilani, or al-Rufa'i[16] or al-Shadhali and see how they took in their hands all the chains of atoms, drops of rain, breaths of creatures and the like and glorified, mentioned and praised God to the number of them. They even regarded as little what they did and stretched their hands to what is infinite and referred to the knowledge of the Knower of the Unseen. Look at that man. Although defeated even by a microbe and driven to distress and despair by the least grief and anxiety, see to what exalted ranks he rises and to what extent his faculties are developed by the enlightening guidance of the Qur'an. He regards the world with whatever is in it as insufficient to say his beads and belittles Paradise as the aim of his praises and glorification. Despite this, he does not see himself as greater and more virtuous than the least of God's creatures.

The Qur'an guides man and says to him: "O man! What you hold in your hand is a trust and belongs to the Owner (of all

---

16. Ahmad ibn 'Ali ibn Yahya al-Rufa'i (1120-1184) is one of the most renowned and celebrated Sufi saints of the history of Islam. He founded the Sufi order of Rufa'iya. He was born in Wasit in Iraq and studied there. Then he dwelt it Umm-u 'Ubayda, a village between Wasit and Basra in Iraq and died there. (Tr.)

things) Who has power over all things and knows everything. He pities you and is munificent. He buys from you His property that He entrusted to you, to preserve on your behalf so that it should not go out of your hands. In return He gives you a very great price. Like a soldier, you have responsibilities and are charged with certain duties, so act in His Name and for His sake. He provides you with whatever you need and protects you against whatever you are incapable of overcoming."

The purpose for your life is that you must reflect the manifestations of His Names and Essential Qualities. When a misfortune visits you, say, "We are God's and in His service. If you have come, O misfortune, by His leave and consent, you are welcome. We are returning unto Him and very desirous of vision of Him. He will set us free from the duties and difficulties of life whenever He wishes. If, O misfortune, this will happen by your hand, it is OK. Whereas, if you have come by His will and order to test the degree of my truthfulness to His trust but without His consent to my submitting myself to you, then, so long as I am able to, I will never submit His trust—the life He has given me—to any other than one worthy of trust."

This is the reality concerning the two ways we have seen. Nevertheless, people vary in guidance and misguidance, and heedlessness has different degrees. The degree of heedlessness that has caught the civilized has made them insensible to those acute pains. However, through the increase in scientific sensitivity and the warning of death, this veil of heedlessness may yet be torn up.

O young of the world, especially the young of Muslim lands! After you have suffered all those misfortunes at the hands of this second Europe, will you still continue to follow them in their debaucheries and ideas and join their lines unconsciously? Will joining them be in contradiction with your claim of patriotism, as it means despising devotion to national values and ridiculing the nation? May God guide us and you to the Straight Path!

Know, O one shaken by the abundance of unbelievers and their agreement of denial of some truths of faith!

First of all, value is not judged by quantity. If a man cannot remain human, he turns into a devilish animal. As he advances in animal greed and appetites like deniers of religions, he increases in bestiality. In the same way, you see that in the world there are too many animals in return for human beings, although human beings are created as vicegerents of God on the earth.

Secondly, denial is a negation and a thousand people who negate are not preferred to two people who affirm.

If you ask what an unbeliever, an atheist, is, the answer is this. Unbelievers do not believe in any religion and they are a vicious species among God's animals created for the improvement of material life in this world and the Fire (in the other). They may serve for a measure of comparison in understanding the degrees of the Almighty's blessings upon His believing servants.

As to their agreement on denial of the Truth, their agreement has no weight. For denial, even if in the form of affirmation, is negation, repudiation, rejection, ignorance and acceptance of non-existence. For example, assume all the people of Istanbul rejected the sight of the crescent (at the beginning of Ramadan), while two people affirmed that they had seen it. Due to the affirmers' support of each other, two affirmations are preferred to the negation of all the other people, no matter how many they are. Affirmation relates to the reality or fact itself, whereas negation depends on him who negates. For example, suppose there is a thick cloud on the face of the sky and except a few, we cannot see the sun when we raise our heads. Will it be acceptable that you say, "Those who cannot see the sun are more than those who have seen it, therefore we should decide according to the majority"? Of course, no! For those who cannot see the sun will say, "I cannot see the sun," not "There is not a sun on the face of the sky." It is in the same way that since those who negate or deny the truths or essentials of faith will offer similar excuses, their denials do not corroborate one another. They are unlike those agreed on confirming a reality who, as in the case of those who help and support one another in, for example, lifting a huge rock, get support and strength from one another. The agreement of deniers is like coming together to go through a narrow hole and therefore is of no use and has no weight and value.

Know, O one who urges Muslims strongly to strive for the worldly life and invites them only to material progress! Beware that some of the ropes connecting them to religion are thin. So take care that they are not broken and their social life is not harmed greatly. For unlike an unbeliever, an apostate goes completely bad and causes corruption. Again, unlike the followers of another divinely revealed religion living among Muslims, one who commits major sins openly and without feeling any shame is treated like a traitor and his testimony is not accepted in a court, as his conscience is guilty and corrupt. So think over and over again and take heed! However, do not be deceived by the abundance of such transgressors, for a transgressor is not pleased with transgression. Without seeking transgression, he has found himself in it. There are almost no transgressors who do not desire to be pious and devout Muslims and to see their superiors as pious and righteous. Do you think that Muslims never love the world and need awakening and that they forget their share in the world? It is not so, rather, greed has intensified and it is the cause of loss for a believer. Also, the factors inviting to the world are many, such as carnal self, needs, passions, desires, Satan, bad friends like you, the sweetness of immediate profit and the like, while those inviting to the Hereafter are few. Patriotic feelings and efforts should add to the few. Do you also think that our poverty comes from our ascetic tendencies? No! Do you not see that the Magians and Buddhists and others subjected to the assaults and domination of Europeans are poorer than us? Are you so blind as not to see that whatever there is in the hands of Muslims is more than they need to be able to make ends meet and live well enough, but it is usurped and swindled from them by Westerners through different tricks? If you expect that following their civilization will enable you to realize a better rule and security in the country, you are taking the wrong road. For controlling and governing a hundred transgressors with bad morals and weak, shaken belief is more difficult than thousands of pious believers. So, Muslims do not need to be urged to strive for the world greedily; what they need is a good organization of labor and arrangement of their working hours, and a profitable co-operation and internal security, which is possible only through fear of God and piety.

Know O friend! Out of His perfect Mercy, the Truth, Glory be to Him, has included a part of the reward of service in the act of serving itself, and the reward of action in the action itself. It is because of this that creatures, including even lifeless ones, obey God's commands of creation and operation of the universe with perfect zeal and pleasure and by obeying those commands, they reflect the manifestations of the Names of the Light of Lights. A minute seed buried in the darkness of earth, for example, turns to the sun with its pure heart and, by making its heart the throne of the sun, smiles at your face. Suppose minute particles and compounds have consciousness, like the seed mentioned developing from being a very simple object to the rank of utmost flourishing and illumination. They take pleasure from receiving and reflecting the manifestations of the Names of the One of absolute Majesty, Beauty and Perfection and thereby realizing a great development through obeying the Creator's commands.

Look at your senses and organs and the services they are made to render for your survival or the survival of the human species. See how they take pleasure in giving service so much so that stopping service becomes a torment for them.

Then look at the animals and see how they take pleasure in fulfilling their duties! Do you not see, for example, that cock: how it prefers hens to itself and calls them to eat the food it happens to find? It is understood from its manner that it does so with zeal, pleasure and pride. Also, the hen leading its chicks does the same. Like mothers of other animals, it leaves them when they have grown enough to direct themselves. This shows that it does that, not for its own sake, nor for its own perfection, but for the sake of Him Who employs it and gives it out of His Mercy pleasure in fulfilling its task.

Again, look at plants and trees and see how they obey the commands of their Creator in a manner displaying zeal and delight. For their adornment and giving out scent display their zeal, and their sacrifice of themselves for their sprouts and fruits shows that their pleasure lies in obeying those commands. It is as if they ask the purest of sustenance from the door of Mercy and feed their fruits with it by the leave of their Lord. Do you not see how a fig tree supplies figs with pure milk that it takes from the treasury of Mercy, while itself is fed on mud. And a pomegranate tree offers its fruits pure sherbet that its Lord gives it, while itself drinks water. And so on.

Again, look at the seeds under the earth and see how, like a prisoner in a very narrow dungeon who earnestly desires to go out to a garden, they are zealous to grow and put shoots out into the air. This Divine law prevalent throughout the universe shows that an inactive thing gets more tired than an active, ever-renewed one. For while the former complains about the slowness of time and its life, the latter is full of thanks. Comfort lies in fighting with troubles and breasting difficulties, while trouble lies in sitting idly.

Again, when you look at lifeless things, you see what is in them potentially moves to become actual in a manner which appears as if they felt pleasure in that movement. Do you not see how a drop of water opens its heart enthusiastically by the command of its Originator? Despite its weakness and tenderness, when it hears the command "O water! Turn into ice and expand by the leave of your Lord", through the intensity of the zeal it "feels," it cracks the hard iron.

From the movement of minutest particles to the revolution of the sun, all the movements and efforts in the universe depend on the law of Destiny and are determined and controlled by Divine Power. They manifest themselves by the Divine command of creation containing Knowledge and Will and even Power. Each particle or atom and each compound, each living creature is like a soldier who has relations with all of the military spheres and duties accordingly. For example, a particle in one of the cells of your eye has relations with your eye, the nerves in your face and the veins of your body, and functions with respect to its relations. In the tongue of its essential impotence to bear what it is unable to and the duties it is charged with in the order of the universe and maintenance of the balance among the Divine laws of nature, every thing testifies to the necessary existence of the All-Powerful One. For the order and balance are two important, subtle "chapters" of the visible book of the universe. How could, for example, a particle or a bee read that book in the hands of the One Who will roll up the heavens as rolling up a scroll. Also, although itself an individual, through its relations with compounds one within or over the other and the duties it fulfils accordingly and through its position with respect to all parts of those compounds, each and every thing bears witness to the Unity of the Necessarily-Existent-Being, the Truth, the Glorified. Again, the All-Wise Creator determined for everything principles out of the two chapters—order and balance—of the visible book of the universe particular to it and according to its needs. When it acts according to those principles, it acts, even though unconsciously, in compliance with the laws of that book.

For example, when a gnat comes to the world, it immediately comes out of its home and attacks the face of man, striking it with its staff and taking out the water of life for itself. Who is it that has taught it this art of fighting? I acknowledge that if I were in its place, I could not have learned it except after a long period of instruction and many trials. You can compare with the gnat, bee and spider, able to receive Divine inspiration, and all other animals and plants, into the "hands" of each of whom the absolutely Generous One, Glory be to Him, has given a "guidebook" written in the ink of pleasure and need. All glory be to Him! See how He has included the secrets in the lines of the two chapters of the visible book of the universe into the "guidebook" inserted in the head of, for example, the bee. The key of which is the pleasure particular to the bee charged with certain tasks.

From all that you have heard so far, you can conclude through faith a significant message out of many included in *My Mercy embraces all things.*[17] You can see another in *There is nothing that does not glorify Him with praise but you do not understand their praising;*[18] and another in *When He wills a thing, His command is only saying to it 'Be'! and it is. Glory be to Him in Whose Hand the dominion of all things is, and unto Him you are returning.*[19]

Know, O one who calls Muslims to the world. You are wrong. Do you think, O heedless one, that the essential purpose for man's life is restricted to material progress, scientific and technological development, earning a livelihood and the like concerning the worldly life. Whereas the Lord and Ruler of the creation Whose command is only saying "Be!" says a word confirmed by existence, creation, realities and the feelings and faculties included in human nature: *I have not created jinn and mankind except to worship Me,*[20] and *There is not a moving creature that bears its own provision, but God provides for it and you.*[21] Do you think that the One Who has made you and continues to make you anew all the time by renewing your body, is in need of what you make in His Kingdom and of your assistance in His disposals? Do you not see that even the most sophisticated thing man makes cannot be equal in art and creation to a date palm or a bee or an eye or a tongue?

Know, O heedless one! It is absolutely inconceivable that the One Who has created you does not know what is happening to you while you move through social conditions and worldly circumstances. Whatever your beliefs and thoughts are or even if you are an atheist and materialist, you cannot but accept that there is a creative act, an art and a disposal in a sperm or an egg or a grain or a seed. Is it rational for you that whoever or whatever disposes in the seed—it is a wise, conscious disposal which

17. *al-'Araf*, 7.156.
18. *al-Isra'*, 17.44.
19. *Ya Sin*, 36.82–3.
20. *adh-Dhariyat*, 51.56.
21. *al-Ankabut*, 29.60.

considers the relations of the seed with the world of its species and with him who is going to benefit from it—is unaware of the world of trees with all its conditions and relations with other worlds? That the One Who splits the seed and makes it grow into first a young plant and then into an elaborate tree, does not see and observe him who sows it and why he sows it and what he obtains from it, and its relations with the world of animals, its environment and what is happening in that environment? Is it rational for you to imagine that the One Who forms and shapes the egg in a way to hatch and equips it with the tools belonging to the world of birds, does not see the conditions of the world of birds and the worlds of the species with which the world of birds have near relations? Is it conceivable for you that the One Who created of a drop of seed a clot suspended, then of the clot a tissue, then of the tissue bones, then garmented the bones in flesh, and thereafter produced it as another creation with life; Who gave that creature a form displaying artistry which manifestly belongs to one with boundless knowledge, sight and wisdom, and equipped it with the tools which the man, created out of a drop of seed, uses in his relations with most of the other species and worlds—do you suppose that that One, the Creator, does not see the world of mankind with all its conditions and whatever happens around humankind? That He does not know the periods man goes through and the worlds in which man moves with his body, feelings, spirit, intellect, imagination and all the other faculties he is endowed with to observe the worlds and discern the truths?

O heedless one! Do you think that you are free and exempt from the intervention of the One Who stretches pomegranates to your hand by means of wooden branches and by means of fibre-like stems melons and water-melons, grown and prepared for you? Because of heedlessness, you assume that the Maker of a melon is unaware of its eater. Because of blindness, you fancy that the Maker of a pomegranate is so blind as not to be aware of what He does for those who eat it and are astonished at the artistry it displays proclaiming "Glory be to Him Who has formed and shaped me, how beautifully He has formed me!'; for those who reflect on its beauty proclaiming *So blessed be God, the Best of Creators!*[22]; and for those who think over its firm, perfect structure proclaiming loudly, *Should He not know, Who creates? He is the All-Subtle, the All-Aware.*[23] Or do you think, O arrogant, that the One Who sends us those fruits to satisfy our needs does not see and know us? Or He does not observe us Who has scattered before us and throughout our world domesticated and other species of animals for our benefit?

Know, O one who relies on his self, causes and the world! You resemble a firefly which relies on its light and changes daylight with night. Or your like is the like of a private who assumes that his king embraces with his favouring and kindness all people down to the most ordinary soldiers with no rank and even animals but then sits and says to himself: "What value do I have that he may show me special consideration out of the innumerable people to whom he shows kindness? However, my heart feels the need for an affectionate, beloved one who will protect and support me. So I had better find another protector and supporter." Thereafter he sets out to find another protector without considering the martial laws and, tried and found a rebel, is sentenced to imprisonment. They tell him: "Do you not know, O wretched one, that the treasury of the king is sufficient to meet all your needs and the needs of all other soldiers. Whereas what is in your hand and in the hands of those to whom you appeal does not suffice to meet even the least of your needs, for you are enveloped by innumerable enemies and endless ambitions. The law of the king does not exclude you, rather it includes everyone whoever he may be. Even if you alone were in the military service, again you would have the same treatment as if the king were specially concerned with you by means of his law and saw you with the eyes of his law. Furthermore, if the king is a saintly one able to be present in many places at the same time, he will not be unaware of your needs even for a moment. You see

---

22. *al-Mu'minun*, 23.14.
23. *al-Mulk*, 67.14.

that the needs of each being is met particularly to itself, which shows that in the overall favouring there is an eye with which you particularly are seen. This is so because the king concerns himself with each being while being interested in the needs of the general public. It is like the sun illuminating every single object and being seen in every transparent object while giving light to the whole of the world, or it is like the perfect, universal order prevailing in each thing amidst the apparent confusion arising from things being all mingled with one another."

In short: Your Creator and Owner is more compassionate, munificent and affectionate to you than any other friend or beloved and He knows you with all your secrets. He is also able to meet all your demands including the greatest and most secret ones. So leave all but Him and put your trust in Him.

Know O friend! The book of the universe which is the book of Power is inscribed according to the measures of the Manifest Book which is the book of knowledge—the latter being like a lined paper placed under the former to be written in exact measures. This is attested by the fact that the universal order and balance are two "chapters" of these two books and a line of connection between them. They are also two titles of the two Grasps of the All-Merciful: there is not a wet or dry thing which is not included in these two chapters of the Manifest Book. Since there is nothing in existence or creation excluded from these two chapters, everything is included in that book.

As for the Qur'an, which is the book issuing from the Divine Attribute of Speech, it is the translator of the books of the seen and Unseen, the books of Power and Knowledge. It is the index of the two chapters just mentioned and the concise expression of the two Grasps referred to.

It is one of the principles of these three books issuing from the three Divine Attributes of Knowledge, Power and Speech, that every living creature, indeed each and every thing, is like a regular soldier or a servant charged with special duties. It works for the sake and in the name of the King Who owns it, not for the sake of itself and its own ownership. It works not for the sake of its own pleasure but for the sake of the pleasure lying in fulfilling its duties. Whoever assumes that he owns himself, whoever claims self-ownership, is subject to perishing, to being torn into pieces.

Know O friend! The heavens are made without any rift that you can see. Their Maker is so mighty, dignified, glorified and great that it is not difficult at all for Him to create every particular thing in its exact place, nor can anything escape His kingdom. The individual members of a species are found all mingled with one another, which shows that the Creator of a species such as fish and flies, is the Creator of all species. His is the kingdom and His is praise; His is creation and His is the command and also His is the judgement; there is no god but He...

Know O friend! The Prophet, upon him be peace and blessings, and his Prophethood are the best of and the epitome of the perfection and good shared by the whole humankind. His way and religion are the most perfect expression of absolute happiness and pure beauty. We see in his creation a superior perfection, an articulate truth, distinguished good and a radiant beauty, and right and truth are to be found on the side of the Prophet, and misguidance, illusions and extinctions on the opposing one. If you desire, out of thousands times thousands of the beauties and virtues that the Prophet brought, look at only this: the hearts and tongues of all those who believe in the Unity of God are united on many occasions such as the five daily and Friday congregational prayers and the congregational prayer performed on the days of religious festivals. For on such occasions every individual person responds to the illustrious and majestic address of the Eternal Object of Worship with the sounds of the hearts of all the believers and their supplications and recitations. Such a vast agreement and encompassing solidarity are witnessed that it is as if the whole of the earth were speaking and praying with all its parts and fulfilling with all its regions the order "Perform the prayer correctly!" which issued in all its awe from above the seven heavens. By executing this order and participating in the huge congregation of praying believers, that weak, helpless man becomes—despite his being a small one like a minute particle amidst those worlds—a servant loved by the Creator of the earth and heavens and honoured with ruling on the earth in His Name; he also becomes the head of all animate beings in the world and the final purpose for the creation of the universe. Do you not see that if, as in the world of the Unseen, those exalting God in this world numbering hundreds of millions uttered "God is the Greatest" all at the same moment during and after the congregational prayer of religious festive days, it would be equal to the exaltation—if it exalted as man does—of the whole of the earth. It would be as if the earth shook with a great shaking on the festive day, exalting God with all its spheres and stakes—mountains—uttering "God is the Greatest" with its mouth of Makka with the sincerity of its heart of *qibla*—the Ka'ba. The words coming out of its caves—the mouths of believers scattered throughout it, rather, throughout the intermediate world and the heavens—rose in waves. May the Glory of Him Who has created it—the earth—and made it like a cradle and a place of prostration for His servants, be exalted, and may He be glorified.

Know, O one who would like to see and reach the light of knowledge of the Truth, glory be to Him, through the windows of arguments and evidences and through the mirrors of His signs and witnesses! Do not meddle with what happens around you by raising your finger of objection, nor approach what occurs to you with suspicion, and extend your hands to seize the light appearing to you. Stand abstracted from the conditions of heedlessness, expose yourself to their coming to you and turn to them wholeheartedly. It is my personal experience that the witnesses and evidences of knowledge of God are of three categories:

Some of them are like water, you can feel and see them but you cannot hold them with your hands. So free yourself from random thoughts and be absorbed in them with all your being. Do not touch them with your fingers of criticism or with an inquisitive manner, for they flow away and are not pleased with being touched by the fingers.

The second category of them is like air, you can feel them but you cannot see and seize them. So expose your face, mouth and spirit to those breezes of Mercy. Do not, instead of breathing them in by your spirit, respond to them with your hands stretched out to seize them, nor with criticism and suspicion. Otherwise they disappear. It is not the hands where these witnesses and evidences reside.

The third category of them is like light, you can see them but you cannot touch and receive them. Turn to them with the eyes of your insight and expose your heart to them. Light can be seized and hunted only with light [the light of heart and insight]. So do not extend your hand to it ambitiously, nor measure it with material tools of measurement. Otherwise it hides itself, though not extinguished. It is not pleased with material or physical confinements and restrictions and solid owners.

Know, O friend, and look at the degree of the Qur'an's mercy and affection for the common people and see how it respects and considers the simplicity of their understanding. It reiterates the clear signs inscribed on the foreheads of the heavens and earth and makes them read in capital letters perfectly easy to see and read, such as the creation of the heavens and earth, sending down rain from the heaven, reviving the earth (in each spring) and the like. The common people can barely discern the writings written in small, delicate letters. Also consider the purity and eloquence of the Qur'anic expressions, how it reads to man what the Power has written on the sheets of the universe. It is as if the Qur'an is the recitation of the universe and its order and harmony and the pronouncement of its Composer and His acts. If you like, listen with a wakeful heart to the *suras* such as the Tiding and verses like *Say: "O God! The Lord of Sovereignty..."*[24]

Know that although they should be kept secret, I write the supplications of my heart to my Lord because I expect of the Al-

---

24. *Al 'Imran*, 3.26.

mighty's Mercy that He accepts the speech of my book in place of me after death has silenced my tongue. This is a part of the supplications of my heart:

O Merciful Lord, O Munificent God!

My life and youth have passed in misuses of my will-power; what is left of their fruits is only painful and humiliating sins, devastating and deviating pains and troubles and annoying, paralyzing anxieties. With this heavy burden, diseased heart, and ashamed face, like my ancestors, beloved ones, relatives and equals-in-age, I am approaching with utmost speed and out of my free will to the door of the grave, the house of loneliness on the way to eternity after separation from this transient, fleeting abode, the abode which is subject to waning, and unpitying and deceiving for those who, like me, follow their carnal, evil-commanding selves.

O Compassionate, Munificent Lord!

The appointed hour is at hand and I see that I have put on my shroud, got into my coffin, bid farewell to my friends and headed for my grave. I am crying at the door of your Mercy: Help! Help, O All-Affectionate, All-Bounteous One! Save me from the shame of rebellion!

Ah! I am in my shroud, standing beside my grave and, raising my head toward the door of Your Mercy, crying: Help! Help, O All-Merciful, All-Affectionate One! Deliver me from the heavy burden of rebellion!

Ah! I am in my shroud, lying in my grave. Those who saw me off have left me. I am expecting Your forgiveness: seeing that there is no shelter and refuge except in You, crying: Help! Help against the narrowness of this place, the loneliness my rebellions have caused and the ugliness of my face because of sins! O All-Merciful, All-Affectionate, All-Bounteous, All-Requiter (of good and evil), save me from the company of sins and rebellion.

O God! Your Mercy is my refuge and my means to reach You. I make complaint of my anguish and sorrow unto You.

O Munificent Creator! O Compassionate Lord! O Master! O Guardian!

Your impotent, heedless, ignorant, diseased, abject, sinful, old, wretched and fugitive creature, Your work of art, and Your servant, has returned to Your door after forty years taking shelter in Your Mercy, acknowledging his sins and errors, addicted to illusions and ailments, and supplicating to You in utmost humility. If You admit him, forgive and pity him, that is what is expected of You, as You are the Most Compassionate of the Compassionate. Otherwise, which other door is there to be sought save Yours? While You are the Lord to be sought and the Truth to be worshipped, and there is no god save You alone with no partners at all.

In conclusion:

I bear witness that there is no god but God and I also bear witness that Muhammad is the Messenger of God.

Addendum

In the Name of God, the Merciful, the Compassionate.

All praise be to God for His favouring us by sending down the Qur'an and for His mercy manifested by sending to us the master of creation, Muhammad, upon him and his family be peace and blessings.

Know O friend! The All-Wise Creator, may His Glory be exalted, has made vegetable and animal kingdoms—particularly the species of small size among them—one of the broadest arenas for the disposals of His Power and the manifestations of His Attributes in the greatest abundance, and one of the fields where there are most of the "mirrors" reflecting His Names. This is so because of certain wise, lofty purposes, some of which are as follows:

Vegetables or plants serve as seeds for the earth, and animals are fruits of the world. A seed or fruit-stone is the miniature content of a tree, and the fruit the miniature index of it. Whatever is manifested in a tree is also manifested in both the seed and fruit. The purpose for existence and life is to receive and reflect the manifestations of the Names of the All-Majestic and Beautiful One of absolute Perfection. Divine Favouring manifests itself through the ramification or elaboration and reproduction of plants and animals especially with all their most delicate parts and individual members, and this is what is most suitable to the eternal Wisdom.

It is narrated that the Prophet Moses, upon him be peace, complained to God about the abundance of gnats attacking him and asked: "What is the wisdom in creating them so abundantly?" God revealed to him in answer: "The gnat asks: 'Why have you created that man of such a huge size? He is unaware and heedless of You. If you had made up his head of gnats, You would have had tens of thousands of those glorifying You with praise and mentioning You and displaying the manifestations of Your Names and the embroideries of Your art through their tongues and disposition.'" True! While the invisible Qur'an inscribed in the ink of stars on the sheets of the spheres of the heavens reads to eyes the signs of the grandeur and splendour of creation, the Qur'an inscribed in the ink of sub-atomic particles on the atoms in your eye reads the signs of Knowledge and Wisdom.

When you hear from the former, "Glory be to Him! How splendid His essential qualities are!", you hear from the latter, "Glory be to Him! How delicate His Wisdom, how subtle His art!" Although both of the Qur'ans are of the same value and significance, since it is of no use to observers and watchers to multiply the big one, the multiplication of the small is certainly of great importance for those numberless angels, jinn, and men and others who study it and reflect on it. When it is multiplied, it will not remain the same, single book but will be of different, endless variations of different uses and with different meanings, and thereby increase in beauty and purity of expression. Furthermore, when many of the chapters of the small Qur'an and its copies are inserted in some of the letters of the big one, the small Qur'an excels the big one to the degree of its smallness.

Another wise purpose for the creation of animals and plants in great numbers is that the most perfect of Divine manifestations is that God manifests Himself with all His Names focused on a single being. And art becomes the most perfect when the greatest thing is inserted in the smallest with all its embroideries. The seed and fruit with respect to the tree, the plant and animal with respect to the earth, man and the Prophet with respect to the universe, and the heart and innermost sense or faculty of man with respect to man—these are essential, compact samples receiving and reflecting all of the Names manifested on the originals growing from them. A fruit, for example, being as a part of the tree and the tree representing the whole, points to Unity—the manifestation of Divine Names on all fruits and trees. However, being a sample of the tree (containing whatever is in the tree) and the tree representing the total growing from it and resulting in it, it indicates Divine Oneness—the manifestation of Divine Names as focused on the fruit.[25]

For example—and God's is the highest comparison—the sun's light illuminating the world in daytime is an example for the manifestation of Unity, while the sun's image being reflected in each transparent object, in a drop of water, in a pool, in an ocean and in planets is an example or analogy for the manifestation of Oneness. When you see the sun in your mirror as having taken on the colour and attributes of the mirror and then see it in other mirrors, you will understand and witness what Oneness or Unity means. It is the same and only sun which is manifested in all the mirrors, which announce:

> We speak in different tongues but
> Your beauty is one and the same.

Whatever is in existence points to that Beauty. It is understood from this that the All-Wise Creator with glorified wisdom and delicate art, turns with His most subtle Power, most complete Favouring, most perfect Mercy and most sensitive Wisdom, from the whole of creation to the earth, and therefrom to living beings, and therefrom to man, and therefrom to man's heart, and from humankind to what is the heart of humankind and creation and its seed from which the universe was created,

---

25. The manifestation of Oneness and that of Unity and part and whole and sample or particular and total are important points requiring explanation: For example, an arm or a leg or a head is a part of man's body, the body being the whole. But man is a sample or particular representing humankind and therefore a sample while humankind stand for the total. Whatever is in the whole is not to be found in the part: whatever is in man is not to be found in his arm or egg or head. But whatever is in the total is found in the sample or particular. The Divine Names manifested on the whole, on a man, are not to be sought on a part, but the Names manifested on the total, on humankind, are also manifested on the sample, on the individual man. The manifestation of the Divine Names on the total or the whole—which is called *tajalli-i wahidiya*—is translated here as manifestation of Unity, while the manifestation of Divine Names which are manifested on the total as focused on the part or individual—called *tajalli-i ahadiya*—is translated as manifestation of Oneness. (Tr.)

and also its illustrious fruit which is the final purpose for the creation of the universe and the embodiment of the love of the Creator and His Mercy. That exalted, noblest, pure, unblemished heart is Muhammad, our master and the master of the whole of creation, upon him be peace and blessings to the number of the fruits of the tree of creation.

Know, O one who fancies that some creatures exist in nature over-abundantly and in vain! The perfection of order and balance in creation refutes such a fancy, for the order is a design interwoven by the raison d'êtres of all the parts, particulars or individuals and details in creation. It is impossible for one to observe the purposes of all details of a palace, nor does he neglect the main purpose expected of building it. Since the main purpose is considered while building it with all its details, the secondary purposes expected of the details are thus observed. If you would like to verify this, hear with a vigilant heart and keen sense of hearing:

There are subtle purposes behind everything related with the All-Living, Self-Subsistent Owner in proportion to His Ownership and disposal and the extent of the manifestation of His Names on that thing. The purposes related to the thing itself are also in proportion to its life and existence.

Everything has been appointed an aim in life, which is studied by intelligent beings. If a man cannot discern it here, others can discern it, and there are many ways of benefiting from each thing. *God has uncountable hosts. None knows the hosts of your Lord but He.*[26] There is nothing in existence but on it is focused the attentive gaze of innumerable beings. Among them are angels glorifying and exalting God with all their kinds and varieties, and jinn observing creation in amazement and reflecting on it with all their classes and groups, and spirit beings extolling God and pronouncing His Unity with all their classes and tribes for whom the solidity of things does not form an obstacle to see what is in them and whom observation of a thing does not prevent from

---

26. *al-Muddaththir*, 74.31.

observing others. Above all, the Maker of all things looks on the works of His art. Also, many awake, enlightened believers and many animals moved by their perceptions look on God's works of art.

Question

The signs in the book of the universe point to the existence of those other than men who gaze on and study them in amazement and reflection and then set out to glorify God. Which line in that book indicates this?

Answer

The order on the line of balance in the page of wisdom indicates it. When you enter a theatre building where a play is being performed, you see many kinds of marvels amazing those who see them, many sorts of melodies pleasing to those who hear them, and many types of charms in which minds and imaginations take pleasure. There are also many other things which give pleasure to the innumerable faculties, feelings and senses of man. Then you look at the spectators' hall and see only, except a few, paralyzed, deaf and blind children. You will certainly conclude that behind the veils hanging in front of the walls there are various intelligent beings with different tastes and temperaments who have come for an innocent amusement and are pleased with and desirous of seeing every novelty in the play. They see you and the play from where you cannot see them.

If you understand the meaning of this comparison, look at those creatures together with the world they are in. You will see "carpets" spread, "couches" raised, "raiments" worn, and "sheets" unrolled. There are also flowers and fresh fruits inviting living, needy beings to themselves with their colors, tastes and smells, and appealing to intelligent beings and men of understanding with their designs, decorations and art. Again, there are plants rising straight upon their stalks to fulfil their duty of creation, and animals standing on their legs to do their duty of worship. Most of those creatures are not conscious of the astonishing, pure beauties and excellent faculties lodged in their creation.

Those faculties and beauties are not for those unconscious, mute creatures that bear them. They are for others who have the powers of seeing and hearing. Despite all this attractive majesty, charming adornment, kinds of favoring, things and events arousing the curiosity to know and feelings of love for the One behind them, and despite all undertakings, intentions and decisions, self-ornamentations, smiles, beckonings and flirtations, and many other similar attractions and charms that almost start to talk and tell their meanings, from amongst intelligent, living beings of understanding, we can apparently see in the world only those two kinds of beings of weight—men and jinn—most of whom heedlessness has made like deaf and blind children with paralyzed minds in the darkness of materialism and naturalism. This obviously shows and it is evidently reasonable that, apart from men and jinn, the universe is full of beings with spirit who reflect on existence and glorify God, as it is declared in the Qur'an: The seven heavens and the earth, and whoever is in them, glorify Him; there is nothing that does glorify Him with praise but you do not understand their glorification.[27]

Know O friend! The vaster the disposal of Divine Power in particulars is and the more in number those similar to them are, the greater the favouring on an individual. Do not say: "I am a drop in an ocean to be forgotten because of the vastness of the ocean." No! Rather, as the ocean testifies, in proportion to the expanse of your environment, you are under the protection of the firm order prevailing with all its strength in all the things like you. For the smaller, the more concealed from eyes and the more strictly surrounded a thing is, the greater care it is given and the less neglected and more protected it is against the interference of others and the tricks of coincidences. It becomes more favored as a created thing.

Do you not see that the centre is more guarded against the assault of others; the seed is under greater protection against the tricks of coincidences and harassment of storms, and it is given a greater care?

---

27. *al-Isra'*, 17.44.

O man! You are the seed of the earth and the earth is the egg of the universe. It is because of this that the Qur'an mentions many times the creation of the heavens and earth together and means by this the creation of all things.

Know and see that the perfection of favoring is through the perfection of wisdom, and the perfection of wisdom is through the perfection of order, and the perfection of order is through the perfection of balance or measures as, for example, in the art of the five senses of man. For the Creator has created man's five senses in such a composition and equipped them with such instruments that man senses nature with them and recognizes with them the features and qualities of all fruits, flowers, sounds, smells and the like. It is for such reasons that the sense of taste has so many delicate, well-ordered pieces of equipment that they are to the number of the varieties of fruits and all kinds of food and drink. Also, the sense of hearing has the capacity of receiving and distinguishing among innumerable varieties of sounds. You can compare with these the other external senses and the inner ones more in number and richer in equipment. This comprehensive nature of his has made man what he is, one able to receive and reflect endless kinds of manifestations of his Creator's Names, may His Qualities be glorified, and taste endlessly varieties of His bounties.

Your like, O man, is a telephone exchange. As in the telephone exchange there is a central key to make the connections within a city, you have a central sense to taste all the varieties of God's bounties and special keys attached to your head and faculties to experience the pleasure of your being able to receive and reflect the numberless kinds of His manifestations. Use those keys as will please your Originator by behaving in accordance with the balance of His *Shari'a*.

It is because of the differences in the degrees of the capacity to use those keys that there will be infinite degrees between two persons in experiencing the pleasures of Paradise although they are in the same place. Although the good tiding a man will be together with the one whom he loves[28] brings the highest and lowest together in the same place, (experiencing the pleasures of Paradise will be of infinitely different degrees according to how and to what extent people use the senses, feelings and faculties settled in their nature).

Know O friend! The apparent confusion and commingled state of things is not because they are playthings of chance, rather they are the most delicate embroideries of the general design of the book of the universe. However, that kind of design cannot be discerned easily with a superficial, untrained look directed into the reflections of things in the mirror of illusions.

Do you not see that commingled seeds of different plants scattered at random display a perfect order when they grow? The Pen of Destiny puts them in that amazing order.

Know O friend! It is a decisive proof for the fact that Muhammad is the seal of Prophets that he extended the bounds of religion in all respects to the point that no one can conceive of an order more comprehensive and more perfect. For example, concerning Divine Unity and Lordship, he says: *In His hand is the dominion of all things;*[29] *He grasps everything by the forelock;*[30] *The heavens are rolled up in His right hand;*[31] *He it is Who forms you in the wombs as He wills;*[32] *He is the First and the Last, the Outward and the Inward; and He has perfect knowledge of all things;*[33] *You will not unless God wills;*[34] *We are nearer to him than his jugular vein.*[35]

Also, the religion Muhammad, upon him be peace and blessings, brought decrees that the farthest points into which matter is divided and in which the limits of material things end, in which atoms and even sub-atomic parts come together with the biggest fruits of creation such as suns and planets, are all equal

28. *Bukhari*, Adab, 96; *Muslim*, No. 2640.
29. *Ya Sin*, 36.83.
30. *Hud*, 11.56.
31. *al-Zumar*, 39.67.
32. *Al-i 'Imran*, 3.6.
33. *al-Hadid*, 57.6.
34. *al-Insan*, 76.30.
35. *Qaf*, 50.16.

and stand shoulder-to-shoulder in obeying the commands of their Creator, Who is free from being of the same qualities as them and exempt from being in need of what they need. With respect to the issues of the Resurrection and Divine Unity, that religion has also reached a point which it is evidently impossible to surpass. So it is in every other respect: it is not possible at all to make new additions to any of its matters to complete and perfect it. So it has deserved to be eternal, to continue until the Last Day.

Know O friend! Moved by the touching appearance of the environment, I cried and the tears I shed are as follows:

I am mortal, but I do not want the mortal.

I am impotent, so I do not desire the impotent.

I surrendered my spirit to the All-Merciful One, so I desire none else.

I want only One Who will remain my friend forever.

I am but an insignificant particle, but I desire an everlasting sun.

I am nothing in essence, but I wish for the whole of creation.

***

Do not invite me to the world, I came, and found it evil and mortal.

Heedlessness was a veil; I saw the light of Truth concealed.

All things, the whole of creation, I saw were mortal and full of harm.

Existence, indeed I put it on. Alas! It was non-existence; I suffered much.

As to life, I experienced it; I saw it was torment within torment.

Intellect became pure retribution; I saw permanence to be tribulation.

Life was like a wind, it passed in whims; I saw perfection to be pure loss.

Deeds were only for show; I saw ambitions to be pure pain.

Union was in fact separation; I saw the cure to be the ailment.

These lights became darkness; I saw these friends to be orphans.

These voices were announcements of death; I saw the living to be dead.

Knowledge changed into whims; I saw in science thousands of ailments.

Pleasures became unmixed pain; I saw existence to be compounded non-existence.

I have found the True Beloved; Ah! I suffered much pain because of separation.

I have finally found God:

(You will never be able to find Him save only by renouncing worldly things.)

With this light I have found Paradise in the world;

The dead have started to be revived.

I have seen that voices are glorifications of God and recitations of His Names.

Things have become familiar.

Pleasures lie in suffering and pains.

Life has become a mirror reflecting the lights of the Truth.

Permanence, I have seen, lies in self-annihilation.

All particles recite God's Names.

Everything bears witness to the Truth.

> In everything there is a sign
> Pointing to the fact that He is One.

Know O one who fancies that pleasures and happiness of the world lie in heedlessness and not coming under the restrictions of religion: I once tested my carnal self and saw myself on a bridge lying between the peaks of two mountains, under which was a very deep valley. There was darkness everywhere. I looked right into the past and saw only frightening levels of darkness. I looked left into the future and again saw only terrifying darkness. Then I looked down and saw a deep, bottomless precipice. I looked up and saw dark, deaf and mute clouds sending down only sorrow, grief, despair and harm. Afterwards I looked ahead and saw amidst darkness demons of the most malicious kind, scorpions, lions, and wolves with teeth ready to tear. When, finally, I looked back, I saw neither help nor helper.

While in a state of hopelessness, and tired of being tested in the world, Divine guidance came to my help and I saw the moon of Islam rise over creatures and the sun of the Qur'an illuminate all sides. I also saw the bridge (of life) as a road extending between the bounties of the Glorified One and Paradise of the All-Merciful. To my right extended the gardens of the past full of the flowers of the righteous and the illustrious fruits of Prophets and saints, under which flowed rivers of time carrying those to eternity. To my left were also gardens where the flowers of ambitions and expectations opened by the Mercy of the All-Affectionate, All-Bounteous. Above me hovered the clouds of mercy sending down on us the water of life profusely in the middle of which the sun was smiling with the lights of guidance and eternal happiness. In the fields extending in front of me there were my brothers, friends and tame animals, which the darkness of misguidance had showed me as wild, harmful beasts.

To understand this vision, read the verse: *God is the protecting friend of those who believe. He brings them out of the levels of darkness into the light. As to the unbelievers, their protecting friends are those leading unbelief and rebellion. They bring them out of the light into the levels of darkness.*[36]

O Light of Lights! For the sake of Your Name the Light, bring us from the levels of darkness into the light! Amen.

Know O insane, wretched Said! Your like is the like of a silly child sitting on the seashore and weeping uninterruptedly over

---

36. *al-Baqara*, 2.257.

the disappearance of the bubbles reflecting the sun. As each bubble disappears, he weeps thinking that the smiling image of the sun reflected in it will die out eternally. He weeps as he sees the bubbles becoming turbid and unpleasant with the mixture of solid things. He does not raise his head until he understands that all the images reflected in bubbles are manifestations of the lights of the sun renewed on the surface of the sea and on the cheeks of waves and in the eyes of drops. The sun does not disappear with the disappearance of the mirrors where it is reflected and therefore the disappearance of its images in some bubbles is not a painful decay or a distressing separation. With its radiant face and beauties and the perfection of its majesty, the sun is perpetual alongside the continuous renewal of its manifestations in the multiplicity of the mirrors (where it is reflected). As for the mirrors and others objects receiving the sun's manifestations, they fulfil their tasks merrily and cheerfully and when they complete their tasks, they hide smilingly.

It is in the same way that, sitting on the shore of the ocean of life, you weep in grief over the setting of beings of perfection, beauty and grace, and the decay of the fruits of the Divine blessing when their time is due. In heedlessness, you suppose that the beauties belong to the beautiful things themselves and the fruits to the trees. The storms of chance blow and snatch them away and, according to your assumption, they disappear in the darkness of eternal non-existence. Do you not think that the One Who has illuminated the things you love with the light of beauty is He Who has illuminated all the flowers in the garden of the universe and stirs the hearts of loving nightingales toward them.

How much more will you weep, O wretched one, over the disappearance of the fruits in your hand? Consider the continuity of the bounties of the Splitter of the Grain and Stones by maintaining the tree of those fruits. Even if that tree stops yielding fruit, then consider the extent of the sphere of His favouring throughout the world where innumerable trees of the same kind are found. If there is shortage of fruit this year, then consider the extent of His favouring renewed with the renewals of seasons and years. Then consider the extent of the sphere of His favouring continuing in the world of symbols or immaterial forms and in the intermediate world with the likes of what you see in this visible world. Then consider the extent of the vastest, eternal sphere of His in the Hereafter where you will find the likes of what you have made friends with in the garden of the world. And so on.

Do not think about the bounties heedlessly of the act of bestowing bounties. Otherwise you will have to seek consolation in weeping. In bounties see the act of bestowing and its continuance and in the act of bestowing see the Bestower together with the comprehensiveness of His pouring out His bounties freely and the perfection of His Mercy. Smile with gratitude to Him and become relieved by His graciousness.

Whenever your eyes water and your heart wails over the separation of decaying beautiful things, consider the multiplicity and vastness of the spheres one within the other containing all that you love. The pleasure of their renewal in their likes will cause you to forget the pains of separation. All those spheres infinitely different in size from your ring to the zone of constellations, and infinitely different in life-span from a moment and minute to the life of the world and eternity, are all mirrors for the reflections of, or means for, the manifestations of the shadows of the lights of the Beauty of the All-Majestic, Munificent One, Eternal, Perpetual, Self-Subsistent, Permanent, and exalted above having a beginning and end and exempt from changes and mutations. Never think that what is reflected in the mirror is owned by the mirror so that you will weep over it because of the breaking or death of the mirror. Detach your attention from the world with respect to its maintenance and turn to the mirror of your heart so that you may see the Sun of Beauty and come to know that whatever you see and love in the world is a sign of Him. Among the signs of His Grace and Beauty is that He has decorated the heavens with lamps and the earth with flowers. And among the signs of His Beauty is that He has created man in the best pattern and of fairest stature and written the book of the universe in the most marvellous letters. Also, among the signs of His excellence is that He made shining and brilliant the spirits of the Prophets and illuminated the inner senses of saints and decorated the hearts of gnostics, with the lights of His Beauty, may His Glory be exalted.

Know O haughty ego! You are in absolute impotence and absolute poverty, and confined within so many limitations and restrictions that you are like a minute particle lost among the heaps of things or like an ant crushed under the burden of events as heavy as mountains or a bee blown here and there by tempests. So, as you yourself see, there cannot be any comparison between you and Him to Whose Power and Wealth there is no limit and to the manifestations of Whose Names and Attributes there are no restrictions. The whole of creation is in the grasp of His Power and the heavens are rolled up in His right hand; even a minutest particle cannot move without His leave, and there is no partner with Him in His Sovereignty and Divinity, and no one can contend with Him in His absolute dominion and Lordship. There is no god but He.

If your duty in the world were to enter into partnership with your Creator in His Lordship, glory be to Him, there would be comparable relationship between you and Him. But you see that there is not, nor can ever be, such a relationship! How can a "gnat" weave those richly decorated garments cut out and fashioned for those worlds just according to the size of each? The duty expected of you is being a worshipping servant, in which the perfection of your potentials lies. Servanthood is based on and flourishes by humility and acknowledgement of one's being nothing before God. It begins with this acknowledgement and ends in being a beloved of God, yielding the fruit of being beloved by God. Servanthood is the opposite of Lordship and Sovereignty and the comparison between them is that there is no comparison. You are loved by God and deserve His mercy to the extent of your awareness of your being distant from Lordship and Sovereignty.

Like a black page showing the letters written on it in light, servanthood reflects and shows Lordship by contrast. The more black the page is, the more clearly and radiantly it shows Lordship. The more conscious of their nothingness before God beings are, the more radiantly and apparently they reflect the manifestations of the existence of the Necessarily Existent Being, may His Glory be exalted and there is no god but He.

Know, O one who fancies that there is exaggeration in some of the Prophetic sayings concerning the virtues of religious deeds. There are narrations that, for example, whoever does certain virtuous deeds, he is given as much reward as that of mankind and jinn. Some have interpreted such sayings as meaning to encourage people to do them, while some others are of the opinion that they were uttered to express how meritorious they are. However, it is possible to gain the reward promised in such narrations requiring interpretation but it depends on certain conditions. It is enough to establish their truth that, some, not all, who do such deeds, may gain the promised reward not at any time they do them but in certain circumstances.

Such sayings were uttered to convey the idea that there is a potential reward in such deeds, although it cannot be gained by everyone. That reward cannot be gained whenever those deeds are done, as it requires utmost sincerity and their being acceptable by God to gain it. Also, any reward comes from the overflowing Grace and Munificence of God, and the servant will feel infinite need for reward in the everlasting abode. So, the view of the servant cannot comprehend what is given by Him to Whose overflowing kindness to such infinitely needy servants there is no limit.

When you consider God's kindness from the viewpoint of God Himself, it denotes infinity and therefore is beyond the knowledge of the servant. For example, it is narrated that whoever recites such and such supplication, he is given as much reward as that of Moses and Aaron, upon them be peace. The reward to be given for reading such and such verse does not increase in your limited view in this limited world. However, when approached with respect to God's infinite kindness, the reward promised in the narration depends on sincerity or purity of intention and its being acceptable by God. Also, the comparison in the narration is made to express quantity, not quality. A drop containing the image of the sun can say to the sea: "Your face is not vaster than my eye to receive the light of the sun and the colors it contains."

The reward promised in the Prophetic sayings in question relates to the world of unconditioned existence. A minute particle of that world can contain a world from this material realm, as the smallest piece of glass can contain the heavens with all their stars. Again, it sometimes occurs that one can easily open a treasury of Mercy with a good word in a blessed, auspicious state. People (look at everything through their own mirrors and) tend to judge the absolute and universal by their partial, individual criteria. However, the knowledge is with the Knower of the Unseen and the Converter of hearts, may His Glory be exalted.

INDEX OR BRIEF SUMMARIES OF THE TOPICS DISCUSSED IN THE TREATISE

*Whatever reaches you in the name of livelihood reaches you either as a result of some other's choice or without the intervention of any free choice. What comes to you without the intervention of any choice or will, comes in the Name of God and for His sake. Receive it and eat it uttering the Name of God, offering all your thanks to Him exclusively. (246)

*The range of man's needs stretches into eternity, and his desires encompass the heavens and the earth. He has connections with whatever is included in the spheres of the world and the Hereafter. So, O man! It does not befit you, nor do you have the right, to regard yourself as one who must pray to and worship one other than Him Who dominates the earth and heavens and holds the reins of the world and the Hereafter. (248)

*O my heart! The most stupid person is he who does not recognize the sun while he sees its image in a mirror, and loves only the mirror and tries to preserve it passionately with the aim of holding on to the sun permanently. (249)

*O man! It is one of the strange characteristics the All-Wise Creator has implanted in your nature that the world cannot contain you so that, as if in a suffocating dungeon, you frequently utter a sound of disgust. Yet so little a thing as a mustard seed or a cell or a memory or a minute of time absorbs you so much so that you are lost in it and passionately attracted to it. The Creator has given you such faculties that some of them are not satisfied even if they swallow up the whole of the world. Some others feel bored with even so small a thing as the minutest particle and cannot put up with even a hair in the wrong place. You know that the eye cannot bear even a hair, it harms the eye or prevents its proper working.

So, be alert and be careful in your acts. Be afraid lest you are ruined and ruin the most subtle of your faculties because of a morsel or a word or a glance or a beckoning or a kiss. (249)

*O one shaken by the abundance of unbelievers and their agreement of denial of some truths of faith! (262)

*O one who urges Muslims strongly to strive for the worldly life and invites them only to material progress, who calls them (263, 267)

*Out of His perfect Mercy, the Truth, Glory be to Him, has included a part of the reward of service in the act of serving itself, and the reward of action in the action itself. (264–7

*O one who relies on his self, causes and the world! You resemble a firefly which relies on its light and changes daylight with night (269)

*The book of the universe which is the book of Power is inscribed according to the measures of the Manifest Book which is the book of knowledge—the latter being like a lined paper placed under the former to be written in exact measures. As for the Qur'an, which is the book issuing from the Divine Attribute of Speech, it is the translator of the books of the seen and Unseen, the books of Power and Knowledge. (270)

*The Prophet, upon him be peace and blessings, and his Prophethood are the best of and the epitome of the perfection and good shared by the whole humankind. (271)

* The witnesses and evidences of knowledge of God are of three categories: (272–3)

*The All-Wise Creator has made vegetable and animal kingdoms one of the broadest arenas for the disposals of His Power and the manifestations of His Attributes in the greatest abundance, and one of the fields where there are most of the "mirrors" reflecting His Names. This is so because of certain wise, lofty purposes, some of which are: (276–9)

*O one who fancies that some creatures exist in nature overabundantly and in vain! (279)

*The vaster the disposal of Divine Power in particulars is and the more in number those similar to them are, the greater the favouring on an individual. (281)

*The perfection of favoring is through the perfection of wisdom, and the perfection of wisdom is through the perfection of order, and the perfection of order is through the perfection of balance or measures as, for example, in the art of the five senses of man. (282)

*It is a decisive proof for the fact that Muhammad is the seal of Prophets that he extended the bounds of religion in all respects to the point that no one can conceive of an order more comprehensive and more perfect. (283–4)

*The world of the misguided and the world of the rightly guided. (284–5)

*O one who fancies that pleasures and happiness of the world lie in heedlessness and not coming under the restrictions of religion: (285)

*O haughty ego! You are in absolute impotence and absolute poverty, and confined within so many limitations and restrictions that you are like a minute particle lost among the heaps of things or like an ant crushed under the burden of events as heavy as mountains or a bee blown here and there by tempests. (289)

*O one who fancies that there is exaggeration in some of the Prophetic sayings concerning the virtues of religious deeds. (290–91)

Eighth treatise

A Spark from the Rays of the Qur'an's Guidance

O One for Whom is the dominion (of all existence) and praise! Bestow peace and blessings on the lord of mankind whom You addressed as *O Prophet (who has all the qualities of Prophethood in the most perfect degree)*![1]

He responded, "Here I am, at your service." His response is echoed even through the hills of the angels of the highest heavens. You ordered him, "Give good tidings and warn!" He made the call, *O mankind! Worship your Lord!*[2] His call has echoed through the periods of time and all sections of space, and himself has become *a bringer of good tiding and a warner.*[3] He sees and bears witness to the truth of what he sees, making calls to all the generations of mankind across centuries and regions. He called at the top of his voice and has been heard by all times and places. For the world has been filled with the call of the Qur'an and he has brought under his rule a considerable part of the world, which he has attracted to himself and the Qur'an. He attracted with his perfect earnestness—as attested by his life and conduct —and his utmost trustworthiness and confidence in his Message — as attested by the simplicity of his life and his abstention from the pleasures of the world. He also attracted with his infinite conviction and peace of mind and heart—as attested by the strength of his principles and teaching—and with the perfection of his belief—as testified by the fact that he was the most advanced in servanthood to God and most careful in avoiding sins.

---

1. *al-Anfal*, 8.64.
2. *al-Baqara*, 2.21.
3. *al-Baqara*, 2.119.

Know, O ignorant soul! The doors opened toward God are to the number of the parts of the (book of the) universe and its pages, and to the number of its compounds one over or under the other. What great ignorance it is to fancy that all of those doors are closed when one of them is closed to you! With this fancy, you are like one who, when he cannot see a cavalryman in some one town, concludes that there is not a king in that country. He ignores all the king's rules and instructions, although the country is full of the soldiers of the king and his officials and government offices.

Know O friend! It is a proof for the fact that the inward of existence is more perfect and excellent and more vigorous in life and more decorated and subtle and better than its outer that what the outer displays in the name of life, consciousness and perfection, is only a sign of the life, consciousness and perfection of the inward. It is impossible that the outward could display life and consciousness while the inward is lifeless. Your stomach is much more orderly than your house, your skin more excellently woven than your garment, and your memory better designed than your book. You can compare with these particular examples the material and immaterial worlds and the visible and invisible worlds and this world and the next. Ah, woe for the carnal selves! The carnal, evil-commanding self looking with the eye of fancy and desires, sees the outward as animated and lovely and spread over the lifeless, dark and dreadful inward.

Know O friend! Your face has features distinguishing you from all other people past and to come, although the faces of all people are the same in their main parts and structure. It is as if unity has manifested itself within multiplicity on your face. It evidently shows the Oneness of the Maker that all people and most of animals have the same basic parts of structure, while the infinite differences distinguishing individuals from one another necessarily indicates that the Maker is infinitely independent and Wise and has absolute free choice. This reality becomes more significant when people are considered all individually. It is infinitely inconceivable that that wise distinguishing, fruitful differentiation and beneficial distinction are not by the purpose-ful choice of an All-independent and the will of an absolutely Willing and the knowledge of an All-knowing One.

All glory be to Him Who includes and inscribes endless fea-tures on the page of your face. Although they cannot be com-prehended by reason and beheld with a superficial look, they are discerned with the power of insight and can be perceived in detail by a careful look. It is impossible that such purposely-arranged and beneficial differences among men and the corre-spondent similarity among the members of the species such as wheat and grapes and also bees, ants and fish, are the work of blind chance and coincidence. No, no! They are the art of an All-Hearing, All-Seeing, All-Knowing and All-Wise One. The broad-est, the most distant, the most insignificant-seeming and the most elaborate section of multiplicity is closed to chance and preserved against its interference, and not neglected and left to its own devices. It is the arena for the operations of an all-wise purpose and intention, an all-knowing free choice and an all-hearing and seeing will. So O chance, there is no room for you in the domain of God. With your brother of naturalism and fa-ther of associating partners with God, go to the hell of non-existence and eternal annihilation. The verse *Among His signs is the creation of the heavens and earth and the variety of your tongues and colors*[4] points to the first and last levels of the manifestation of Divine Wisdom.

Know O friend! It is one of the whisperings of Satan that he says, "If, for example, a cow is a creature and design of the All-Knowing, Eternal Power, why is it so poor an animal? If it is the Pen of the Destiny of an All-Knowing One of absolute Will which works under its skin and within its body, why is the out-er side of its skin—the apparent part of its body—so docile, ig-norant, helpless and miserable?"

Answer: O human devil who teaches the Satan of jinn! First of all, if the art of the Eternal Power did not give everything

---

4. *al-Rum*, 30.22.

what is suitable for it with the necessary amount, the ear of your donkey would be more intelligent and skilful than you and your teachers. For example, the inside of your fingers would excel you in consciousness and willing. Also, there would be in your fingers greater consciousness and will-power than your present consciousness and will power. Everything has been given a certain capacity, together with a potential to expand and develop.

Secondly, Divine Destiny appoints for everything a certain measure and a receptacle or mould according to that measure. This determines the capacity of that thing which it has received from the absolute source of everything. What is emitted from inside to outside is according to the will-power and its capacity and in proportion to the need and its degree, and to the extent of the ability and according to the measure fixed by the Divine Names manifested on that thing. A cow is not an exception to this rule; it is not the inside of another creature that determines its outside. One who expects to see in its image in a bubble all the qualities of the sun such as illuminating the world, attracting the planets toward itself and being the center of the solar system, must be insane. The sun's image in a bubble points to the sun but does not bear all the qualities the sun has.

Know O friend! You are a conscious work of art made with wisdom, one indicating the Attributes of the Maker. You are a living one reflecting the Wisdom embroidering creation, the Knowledge with an absolute power of choice, and the Power seeing what you deserve. You are the fruit of a Mercy hearing the calls of your neediness. You are an embodiment of an act of the All-Willing willing what your potential wills and of the favoring of an All-Knowing knowing your demands. You are also a form of shaping, measuring Destiny aware of what is fitted for your construction. How is it possible for you to be excluded from the general rule of creation with your partial will and consciousness, and then compare the whole to the part? How can you be heedless of your Lord and Owner Who owns and exerts lordship over everything? And how can you fancy that despite the knowledge encompassing the whole of creation, there is not one watching you, One All-Hearing, All-Seeing, All-Knowing, All-Answering (the calls and prayers), All-Helping, Who hears your wailing, sees your destitution and knows your crimes?

O wretched soul! Why do you fancy that you are excluded from the sphere of Divine laws and wrong all other beings without attaching to them any importance or feel constrained to bow before them or see yourself as responsible for the management of them? This is a burden that is impossible for you to bear. So, you must leave such sort of associating partners with God, which means diversion from the primordial nature He has given to creation, and enter the sphere of God's dominion. By doing so, you can find peace of mind and heart and become a respected brother of all other beings. Otherwise you are like one who is charged with steering one of the wheels of the vessel full of the goods belonging to the king. Instead of putting his load on the ship and steering the wheel lightly, he carries his load on his back. If he has a bit of intellect, he must say, "I travel on this vessel, so I must place my load near the goods of the king, my lord and administrator."

In addition, O wretched soul, in order to be at rest and find peace, you should also place the Islamic rules and principles on the vessel of the mind of the Muslim world.

Know O friend! The One Who has created you must also have created the universe with whatever is in it, for whatever is in you also exists in it. It is necessary that your Creator must be the Creator of all things, for the Creator of a melon is not other than the Creator of its seed, which is its miniature sample taken from it and contained in it.

Know O friend! You are a restricted being, having a restricted body, a restricted lifetime and a restricted power. So, you must not spend this short, transient life of yours on transient things so that it goes to waste. Instead, you must spend it for the sake of what is permanent so that it may gain permanence. You can make use of your life here at the most for a hundred years, as if eating a hundred dried dates. Without the tree that yields them, they give, though less than the difficulties they cause, some benefit only during your life, for they are of no use to you after your death. If you aim at the afterlife (and bury those dates in the soil of the afterlife,) giving them the water of Shari'a, you can obtain a hundred marvelous date palms. One who sells a hundred excellent date palms for a hundred dried dates deserves only to be wood for the Fire.

Know O friend! It is the source of illusions, doubts and even misguidance that the carnal self supposes itself as excluded from the sphere of the manifestations of Destiny and Divine Attributes. Then, because of that supposed exclusion, the carnal self supposes itself as independent of Divine rule. Afterwards, whatever it comes across in existence which is in fact dependent on Divine Destiny and ruled by one or more than one Divine Name, it also excludes it from the kingdom of God and disposal of His Power. Through forced analogies and interpretations which will make it the teacher of devils, the carnal self reflects some of its states coming from associating partners with God, to that innocent thing.

The carnal, evil-commanding self resembles an ostrich: it thinks what is against it as in its favor. Or it is like sophists; it says to one of the two opponets who argue with each other, "The arguments of your opponent reject you." Then it turns to the other and says, "The arguments of that one invalidate yours. You are both wrong."

Know O friend! The carnal self supposes the other world as an expansion of this one and seeks to continue its heedlessness. With the thought of the afterlife—although it is not convinced of its coming—it seeks to be relieved from the terror of the annihilation of the world and the pains of decline. Taking refuge in heedlessness or doubts (about the afterlife), it seeks to be saved from the troubles of working for the afterlife. It looks upon the deceased generations as living but concealed from us and does not take a lesson from death. Under the illusion of implanting its worldly expectations in the soil of the afterlife (that is, using the afterlife as an excuse for clinging to its worldly expectations) it thinks, "These expectations of mine have two aspects.

One is related to the world, which has no permanence and goes like dust scattered. The other aspect relates to afterlife which is built on the same foundations as the world and its expansion." For example, knowledge has two aspects, one illumined, the other dark. The devilish carnal self shows you the illumined side and offers you the dark one under its guise. That is, by trying to convince you that knowledge will give fruit in the Hereafter, it calls you to use it for worldly benefits. In short, the carnal self is like an ostrich or a devilish sophist.

Know O friend! I am absolutely convinced that if God is not accepted as the Creator of all things, then He is not the creator of anything. For the whole of creation forms a complete entity (like an organism) all parts of which are interlinked and related to one another. It does not accept division. Whatever we acknowledge with respect to something necessitates the acceptance of it with respect to everything. Also, the Creator is either one or endless in number. For if there were not a true Creator, (for the same reasons as requiring His being the Creator of the whole universe), there would have to be true creators in infinite number. (It is absolutely inconceivable for there to be many beings with the same infinite attributes and it is infinitely impossible that there should be more than one infinite being.) This would necessitate the acceptance of many strange inconceivabilities and the non-existence of unity in absolute terms and, finally, the acceptance of the impossibility of the existence of a Creator.

It is impossible for a being giving light to be himself without light, a being giving existence to be himself non-existent and a being making the existence of something necessary to be himself unnecessary in existence. Similarly it is inconceivable to the same degree for a being bestowing knowledge to be himself without knowledge, a being granting consciousness to be himself without consciousness, a being endowing will-power to be himself without will-power, and a being giving perfection to be himself imperfect. Is it possible that one who shapes the eye and gives the power of seeing is himself without sight? It is absolutely necessary that all sorts of perfection shared by the created should be from the Perfection of the Maker. When a microscopic organism that knows only gnats from among birds, sees an eagle, since what a gnat has is not found in an eagle, it concludes that the eagle is not a bird.

Know O friend! What a human soul desires most is permanence and perpetuity. If it does not deceive itself with an illusive permanence, it cannot take pleasure in anything in life. O soul demanding permanence! Continue to mention the Permanent One so that you may gain permanence, and be like a mirror reflecting His Light so that you may not be extinguished. Also, in order to be purified, be a mother of His pearl. To be eternally alive, be a body for the breeze of His remembrance. In order not to fall into the bottomless pit of non-existence, hold fast to a beam of the rays of one of His Names. If a fruit is heedless of what sustains and maintains it and is attracted to a foreign light smiling at its face, it is disconnected from its stem and falls headlong.

O soul! Hold fast to Him Who sustains and maintains you, for nine hundred and ninety-nine parts of your being are in His charge, the remaining one only being entrusted to yourself. Place also that remaining one on the vessel carrying His property and find peace. Know that if you are unable to create and maintain yourself, and if your hands are too short to bring you any good, then all other people and more distant causes or agents are more unable to have a hand in your creation and maintenance. Look whether you can make your tongue that is a tree of words, a pool of tastes and an exchange of communication. If you cannot do it, and you will never be able to do it, then do not ascribe partners to God, for *ascribing partners to God is a tremendous wrong.*[5]

Know O friend! The world is a Divine shop or store in which there are all kinds of cloth, food and drink, some of which are thick and solid, some thin, some short-lived, some perpetual, some as kernel, some as fluid and some as gaseous. Some of them are woven from nothing, are created, while some others

---

5. *Luqman,* 31.13.

are fashioned through the manifestations (of the relevant Divine Name or Names). (Most) philosophers have gone astray by seeing the existence of all as self-necessitated and confusing creation with fashioning.

Know O friend! When associating partners with God in a veiled form arising from human egotism is solidified and condensed, it turns into associating material causes as partners with God. (First of all, it sees itself as the originator and the real cause of its successes or attributes its successes to itself rather than to God). If it is to continue, it changes into attributing to God nothing with respect to its life, and if it is still to continue, it changes—may God save us from falling into such a state— into atheism.

Know O friend! To seek light within darkness—by remaining under the influence of the carnal self and making that state into one's nature—is a severe pain and a disrespect to light and defilement of it. You must, instead, go out of darkness and then look toward light away from it, not from within it.

Know O friend! Man has been created to open and unveil (the treasuries of Divine Names and Attributes), be a luminous sign (guiding to God), receive and reflect (Divine manifestations), be a light-giving moon reflecting the Eternal Power, and be a mirror for the manifestations of the Eternal Beauty. He has gained greater refinement and purity and become more polished by undertaking the Trust from bearing of which the heavens, the earth and mountains shrank. It is one of the requirements of undertaking this Trust that man should be a unit of comparison to understand the all-encompassing Attributes of God. His ego— which becomes a dark point through heedlessness and associating partners with God—should be a switch to turn on the lights of those Attributes. (Contrary to those essential functions of man), why and how do most people become veils and barriers? While man is charged with opening, how and why does he close? While he must illuminate, why and how does he darken? While he must believe in the Oneness of God, why and how does he associate partners with Him? He must view God through the observatory specially created for looking to Him and acknowledge His property and kingdom as belonging to Him exclusively. Instead, viewing the creation through the observatory of his own ego, man shares the property of God among creatures. So, man is a wrongdoer and ignorant.

Know, O soul! If you please your Creator through abstaining from sins and obeying His commands and through righteous deeds, this also suffices to please the created. If the created are pleased with you on behalf of the Almighty, it is of use to you, but if they are pleased on behalf of themselves, it is useless. For they are impotent like you. If you choose the first alternative, please your Lord; if you are to choose the second one, you have associated partners with God in vain. Do you not see that if one, who goes to the capital to have a job of his done, pleases the king, his job will be easily done and he will gain the love of the subjects? If, by contrast, he expects his job to be done by those under the rule of the king, he will encounter many difficulties, nay, he will have to please all of them and procure their agreement on the fulfillment of his need. What is more, if he has been able to procure the agreement of all those under the king's rule, again he will need the permission of the king, which depends on pleasing him.

Know O friend! The Necessarily-Existent Being does not resemble the contingent—all of the beings other than God for whom it is equally possible whether they exist or not and therefore whose existence absolutely depends on the Necessarily-Existent-Being—in His Essence and qualities. So He does not resemble them in His acts either. For example, in relation with Him, there is no difference between the near and the distant, the few and the many, the small and the big, the individual and the species, and the part and the whole. Also, unlike the contingent, He has no difficulty at all in His acts, nor does it take Him any time to do them, nor does He busy Himself with anything specially. It is for this reason that the intellect is bewildered to understand the nature of the Almighty's acts and goes so far as to deny the One Who does them.

The teeth and claws of a lion point to the fact that what is expected of a lion is to tear, and the delight of a melon shows that it is for eating. So too the potential of man indicates that his essential duty is to worship God. The loftiness of his spiritual dimension and his longing for permanence and eternity point out that man was first created (in spirit) in a world more subtle and refined than this one and then sent here to obtain the necessary equipment to return to where he came from. His being the fruit of the tree of creation indicates that among human beings there is one who is the seed of humanity from which the Maker has grown the tree of creation. That seed can only be the one upon whose being the most virtuous and greatest of the creation all perfected men, nay, half of mankind—as the creation has been painted in his spiritual color—have agreed. He is the master of all creation, upon him be peace and blessings.

The Second Part of the Spark

In the Name of God, the Merciful, the Compassionate.

Know O friend! God has put the heavens and earth in order and wraps night and day around the head of the earth, which is our cradle, like a lined turban. How is it conceivable that He has committed the disposal of some sections of the creation to the charge of some poor, contingent beings? Is it possible for other than the Lord of the Throne to dispose what is under that Supreme Throne? No! For the Power is not short of having control and authority over all things and leaves no room for the intervention of others. Besides, the honor and dignity of His absolute authority and independence and His will to be known and loved do not allow others—however and whatever or whoever they are—to be a veil (between Him and His creation). Nor do they allow others to be a nominal means to attract the attraction of God's servants to themselves. Disposals of the whole and the part and the species and the individual take place all at the same time and one within and supporting the other. Therefore it is impossible to share them even between two agents. For the One Who has ordered the creation sustains, brings up and directs man at the same time as He governs and conducts our cradle—the earth. At the same time when He conducts the affairs of species, He also makes the cells of man's body and creates particles—the smallest parts of things—with the same Power controlling all sections of the creation. Rather, by putting in order He controls and manages, by controlling and managing He sustains, trains and brings up, and by sustaining, training and upbringing He disposes and creates. It is not possible for the sun to illuminate the whole of the face of an ocean without illuminating all at the same time the cheeks of bubbles, the eyes of drops and the pupils of the rain drops falling unto it. So also it is not possible for other than the Power Which wraps night and day around the earth to interfere with any of the particles of the cells belonging to the smallest organ of any inhabitant of the earth. The One Who has made, fashioned and ordered the mind of a fly and the eye of a microbe will not let your actions go without being recorded. He records them in a manifest book and will call you to give account of them.

Know O friend! The absolute disposal, all-encompassing power and all-seeing wisdom observed in every creature down to a particle—together with all they relate to and what takes place around them—are a clear evidence and a manifest sign of the fact that the Maker of all things is One without any partner at all. There is not any division, nor separation, nor distribution, in His Power. If a contingent being were the Maker, there would be division, separation and sharing in his disposals and executing his power and will. So, it is absolutely necessary that the Maker is One, His existence is Necessary. There is no limit to and no division in His Power Which operates according to the measures of His Destiny and "inscribes" on Its lines.

Know O friend! Small animals like the gnat, spider and flea are more intelligent, more sophisticated in structure and subtler in art than big ones such as the elephant, water buffalo and camel. Despite this, their life is shorter and, in appearance, they benefit from the world less than the others. This clearly shows that the Maker has no difficulty at all in creating things, and that He does not specially busy Himself in any of them. He only says, "Be!" and they are. Nothing can compel Him to do anything; He does whatever He wishes and acts however He wills. There is no god but He.

Know O friend! The image of the sun in a bubble is both a part (of the bubble) and an individual, tiny sun bearing the attributes of the sun. As it bears the attributes of the sun, it has the identity of the sun; but it is not of the same nature with the sun. In short, it is neither the sun itself nor something other than the sun. The shares of all other things in the sun, that is, the sun's giving light and heat and color to the whole of the world, does not decrease anything in the share of the bubble. It makes no difference for it whether all other things exist or not. The bubble can say, "The sun belongs to me exclusively and is contained in me, and it exists for me."

Know O friend! What recedes from the vastest sphere of the Name the Outward and sees itself as almost nothing before it, comes near and restricts itself to the relative or real sphere of the Name the Inward. In either case, *God surrounds them all*[6] through His Names, through His Knowledge, Will, Power and other Attributes of His. With his partial, limited mind lost in what it deals with, man views the Grandeur of the Almighty and His administration of the planets around the sun, and deems it unlikely that He concerns Himself with the creation of, for example, a fly. He compares the absolutely Necessary One with the poor and contingent—a comparison provoked by Satan. Such a comparison means despising small creatures, which is a great injustice, for there is not a thing that does not glorify its Creator. Nothing lowers itself to accept as its Lord any except the One for Whom this world is but one of His houses, the sun but one of His lanterns and the stars but a few of His lamps, as if there were nothing living in the world save He. A big thing has no right to see itself greater than a small one and feel pride, for like right being right without any difference between its great and little, the existence of a little thing is of the same value as a big one.

Know O friend! When viewed carefully, from the sun of suns to the fruits of trees, everything is chosen and distinguished among what is endless. Whatever is related to what is infinite, none but only the One, to the manifestations of Whose Attributes there is no limit, disposes it.

Know O friend! All-encompassing provision does not exclude

---

6. *al-Buruj*, 85.20.

the provision of each being particularly. For the bounties of God are not like rain or the water of a river from which everyone can benefit without considering particular needs of individuals so that individuals do not need to feel particular gratitude for them. The needs of individuals are not like pots and pans they have made for themselves to fill with Divine bounties they assume as pouring like rain. Rather, the real Giver of Bounties, may His Glory be exalted, Who takes each individual into consideration with all his peculiarities, makes a particular pot for everyone and then fills it with the food of His bounties. So, as thanksgiving is incumbent on everyone for the general favoring, so also it is incumbent on each individual for the bounties coming to him particularly.

Know O friend! Most human beings do not give their due to the observed book of the universe and the glorious book of the Qur'an recited and heard. For the philosophers among them attribute to the Necessary Being no more than a little part, a thin covering and a compound of nominal value, and then they share the rest among causes, rather, among certain impossibilities and mere notions. *God assail them! How they are perverted!*[7] Whereas one who believes in His Unity says, "Whatever is in existence belongs to Him, has come from Him, is returning to Him and subsists by Him."

As for how they wrong the Qur'an, the learned among human beings, deceived by succession of ideas and findings over time, ascribe to the Lord of the Supreme Throne from that magnificent palace—the Qur'an—from among its firm foundations, well-established principles, golden building blocks and flowery trees, no more than only some parts of the wording and a part of the meaning, and then share the rest of those "heavenly stars" among the inhabitants of the earth.

Woe to the intellect which is deceived by the supposition or imagination that man reaches the heavens and makes some disposals in some of the planets! Its like is like him who apportions

---

7. *al-Tawba*, 9.30.

only a few bubbles for the one who fills the ocean or who ascribes the overflowing of the ocean to a few bubbles. Whereas a truth-loving believer says, "Whatever is in the Qur'an from the first of its foundations to the last embroideries of its design, to the last letters of its text, is from God and belongs to Him." The Qur'an is interwoven in the styles which consider thousands of different levels of understanding and the temperaments of its addressees. Also, having come to us through seventy thousand veils, the Qur'an penetrates the depths of hearts and spirits, spreading its blessings through all levels of human societies. Every era understands and knows it; every age acknowledges its perfection and accepts it; every epoch makes friends with it and accepts it as its teacher, and every period needs it and respects it to the degree that it supposes it as revealed to it particularly. It is not a superficial, shallow book. It is a bottomless ocean, a shining sun and a profound guidance.

Know O friend! Look at the water and air, how gentle and permeating they are in creation! Glory be to Him Who provides and feeds both a microbe and an elephant! Look at the Chef of Power, how He makes food which both passes through the throat of a bee and fills the mouth of an elephant, which is not too big for the mouth of a microbe, nor so small that the mouth of a rhinoceros disdains it. Also, a word uttered is both received by the ear of an atom and fills the ear of the sun. That word is so multiplied that as a cave is filled with it and echoes it back to you, yet it is not too big for the cells in the ear of a gnat.

Know O friend! At the times of daily prayers, you can imagine the Muslim world as a mosque, with Mekka being the *mihrab*—the place where the leader of prayer stands—and Ka'ba the central point of that *mihrab*. In this mosque generations perform prayer. The mosque is continuously filled with and emptied of the generations coming one after the other.

Know, O Said! If you find happiness and maintain your dignity, you should leave today with honor and dignity what will leave you tomorrow, throwing you into humiliation and miseries. If you abandon the world, you will save yourself from its evils and inherit its good. If, by contrast, it abandons you, then you will be devoid of its good and reap its evils.

Know O friend! The modern corrupt civilization has opened a door to such an enormous, disgusting show and hypocrisy that, in the name of fame and reputation, they make show and behave hypocritically toward not only individuals but the whole nation. The mass media make them known to people and as modern concepts of history and history books written recently acclaim them, they also urge others to do so. The lives of individuals are sacrificed for racial considerations under the guise of nationalism.

Know O friend! On coming together to make a sound unity, a community of women can acquire firm manliness, while a weak unity of men becomes woman-like. The Qur'anic phrases *women say*[8] [the verb in whose original Arabic comes in the masculine form while according to Arabic grammar it should have come in the feminine], and *the (male) Arabs of the desert say*[9] [the verb in whose original Arabic comes in the feminine form], point to this fact. The community of the weak is strong, while the community of the powerful is weak.

Know O friend! By rejecting devils and overcoming them, the doors of Paradise are opened.

Know O friend! Divine Unity is one of the clearest proofs of Muhammad's Prophethood. For it is our master Muhammad, upon him be peace and blessings, who raised the flag of Divine Unity above the heads of all beings and planted it at the peak of the universe. He also proclaimed Divine Unity to all beings with all the degrees of its manifestation and expounded in detail what the previous Prophets had left in an outlined and generalized form.

---

8. *Yusuf*, 12, 30.
9. *al-Hujurat*, 48.14.

The Third Part of the Spark

In the Name of God, the Merciful, the Compassionate.

Know O friend! Those decorations, perfections and beautiful spectacles and the majesty of Divine Lordship and the splendor of Divinity observed in the universe require an observer to observe them in amazement. Reflecting on them, he must move therefrom to the Majesty of their Maker and Owner and to His Power and Perfection. Despite his ignorance and tendency to injustices, man has so comprehensive a capacity that it can be said that he is a sample of the whole of creation and he has been entrusted with a trust by which he can perceive the "hidden treasury" and open it. His powers or faculties have not been restricted in creation so that he may have a universal consciousness to understand the splendor of the kingdom of the eternal Sovereign and the magnificent beauty of His Divinity. Just as a beauty demands the beholding of a lover (to see it), so also the Lordship of the Eternal Designer requires the existence of man who will watch It in appreciation, amazement and reflection. That Lordship also necessitates the permanence of that reflecting, bewildered observer so that he can accompany what he is bewildered at along the way to eternity.

The One Who has adorned the faces of flowers, has surely created insects and birds in love with them, and as He adorned the cheeks of the beautiful, He has also created lovers longing for them. He has made the face of the world so ornate and attractive and its eyes shining with those smiling lamps. He has embroidered the world with so many kinds of excellent beauties, making each embroidery so faultless and exceptional that it arouses the feelings of love for its Maker and curiosity to know

Him. Such a Creator would certainly not leave it devoid of those lovers amazed, reflecting, fascinated, those aware of the value each beauty has. With his comprehensive nature, the perfect, universal man has become the raison d'être of the creation of the universe. Its happiness and real pleasure lie in his forsaking everything, including even his existence, for the sake of God, for His Glory is exalted, His existence is absolutely necessary, He is the absolutely Perfect One and He is One of absolute Majesty, Grace and Beauty. May whatever I have, indeed the whole of my existence and whatever exists, be sacrificed for Him.

Know O friend! Just as the correspondence and similarities among things point to the Oneness and Unity of the Maker, so too, the orderly and purposeful dissimilarities and distinctions among them indicate that the Maker is All-Wise and has absolute Will, doing whatever He wishes. For example, the similarity among the limbs and organs of people, particularly the symmetry between the organs a man has in pairs, are decisive proofs for the Oneness of the Creator. And the essential dissimilarity among people, each being a different individual having distinguishing marks, is a clear sign that the Creator has absolute Will and Wisdom.

Know O friend! Man is the most unjust among beings. Consider how great are his injustices! Due to his intense love of himself, he does not give things any value except in proportion to how much use they have for him. He also considers their fruits only relatively with their benefit for him. He supposes that the aim of life is life itself. Whereas in every creature there are instances of wisdom relating to the Creator that are difficult for intellects to understand. Why should it not be that those short-lived animate beings and those living organisms swiftly going to decline are not the samples, examples, foundations and seeds for their wonderful likes in the intermediate worlds between this and the next and between the material and the spiritual and in the realm of the inner dimension of existence? Why should they not be the manifestations or reflections and fruits in this world of the disposals of Divine Power in the world of the Unseen.

Know O friend! As the eye restricts itself to what it sees or what exists before itself, so too the carnal, evil-commanding self denies the existence of what it does not see, even if that is the most evident of the evident.

Know O friend! Through the perfection of His Power, God has subjugated all the particles and compounds of the universe to His laws and commands of creation. As He says to a gnat "Be so!" and it becomes so, He also says with the same facility to all animals "Be of such and such features and forms and with such length of life!" and they easily are how they are ordered to be.

Know O friend! The Power Which has taken those heavenly objects in Its hand and arranged them as you have set the gems on the frame of your mirror, is never unable to do anything, nor does It allow anything to interfere in the sphere of Its disposals.

Know O friend! There is no doubt that a drop of water is of the same nature with an ocean because both are water, and with a river because both form from clouds. Also, the image of the sun in a drop of water is almost of the same identity with the sun itself and a minnow is of the same species with a basking shark because both are fish. Again, a grain of wheat is not different from a heap of wheat. It is in this way that the Divine Name manifested on the tiniest cell comes together on the thing on which It is manifested with the Name manifested on the whole of creation. For example, the Name the All-Knowing manifests Itself on that cell together with the Name the Creator manifested for the creation of that cell. It manifests Itself on that bee together with the Name the Fashioner, on that fruit together with the Name the Builder, and on that illness together with the Name the Healer. It is inconceivable for a Name with the broadest sphere of manifestation not to be manifested on the smallest thing.

Know O friend! Inertia, motionlessness and inactivity and remaining unchanging in the same conditions mean a kind of death or non-existence for a contingent thing whose life and survival depend on activity and changing. Non-existence is a pain by itself and evil. Activity is a great pleasure by itself and renewal by changing brings great good. Although there may be some pains and sorrows in changing and renewal, those pains and sorrows are good in many respects. Being the light of existence, life is refined through sorrows and purified through pains. Life is measured according to how it receives and reflects the manifestations and qualities of the Giver of Life, may His Glory be exalted. For in a life there are many aspects related to the Giver of Life, while there is only one for the living thing itself.

A bubble adorned with the reflection of the sun has no right to oppose the sun and demand anything from it. When man, who is like a bubble in the ocean of existence, believes, he becomes through belief like a transparent, shining object as if a glittering star, whose lamps are lighted from the rays of the Eternal Sun.

Know O friend! A single builder builds a huge palace and furnishes it with whatever is necessary. Then he builds and furnishes another, smaller palace by using whatever he has used in the former. Now is it at all possible that the builder's main aim is not to build the second, small palace and that the purposes for its construction are not related to the builder? O man! You are that small palace, and the earth is a palace, and so is the universe.

Know O friend! God, may His Glory be exalted, makes Himself known to us through His creatures and the works of His art and loved through His Mercy, bounties and provisions. For certain purposes such as those mentioned, He manifests almost all His Names. Whoever—by God's enabling him to do so—understands perfectly why each Name manifests Itself and then explains it to others perfectly by His leave, may His Qualities be exalted, he deserves to be addressed as, "But for you, I would not have created the worlds." He is such a firm, trustworthy bond between the earth and the heavens that the earth is connected to God's Supreme Throne by the rope woven in his heart. As a human being, he is the most honorable of creation;

as the sample of humankind, he is the most perfect of living beings, and as an individual, he is the master, the lord, of the species honored with God's vicegerency on the earth. He is the master of the Messengers, the leader of the pious, the beloved of the Lord of the Worlds—Muhammad, upon him and his family and Companions be peace and blessings until eternity.

Conclusion

Whatever is suffered for God is good; how sweet it is even if apparently bitter! For it makes you taste the pleasure of supplicating and praying to Him.

Ibn Sam'un[10] says, "Every speech unconcerned with Him is idle talk."

Know that I am journeying to the Hereafter. I have so many sins that not only my life but also many other lives do not suffice to ask forgiveness for them. Therefore I depute my book to supplicate to God for the forgiveness of my sins forever after me as follows:

Alas! How pitiful, how regrettable, how deplorable it is that I have wasted my life, health and youth in sins and rebellion and for the sake of harmful, transient desires and fancies! What is left to my old age and ill health is sins and pains. With this heavy burden, dark face and diseased heart, I am approaching the door of the grave for an eternal separation from the transient world. How humiliated I will be when my Lord orders: Drive all hypocrites to the Fire!

O God! There is no shelter and refuge save the door of Your Compassion.

O God! Your rebellious servant has come
acknowledging his sins, and he prays to You.
If You forgive him, this is what You love to do;
if You repel him, who else will have mercy on him?[11]

---

10. Abu'l-Husayn Muhammad ibn Ahmad ibn Isma'il or Sam'un. A Muslim ascetic from Baghdad, renowned for his wisdom and wise sayings; he lived between 913 and 997. (tr.)

11. Attributed to Ibrahim ibn Adham. (tr.)

O God! I regret my sins and repent of them;
and I am ashamed of my evil words and deeds.
Pour blessings into my heart from the world of holiness
so that fancies may be removed from my heart.

I ask You to open the door of Mercy with the call of Mawla-na:

O God! Repeatedly I call O God, O God!
And utter things for God on Your way.

O God! Guide me to the way leading to You;
I am astray, looking for the right way.

O God! I am not worthy of the highest floor of Paradise,
Nor do I have strength to bear Hellfire.
Enable me to feel repentant of my sins
and ask forgiveness for them, and forgive me.
For You are the Forgiver of sins, however great they are.

* * *

INDEX OR BRIEF SUMMARIES OF THE TOPICS
DISCUSSED IN THE TREATISE

ing making the existence of something necessary to be himself unnecessary in existence. (298)

*What a human soul desires most is permanence and perpetuity. (299)

*When associating partners with God in a veiled form arising from human egotism is solidified and condensed, it turns into associating material causes as partners with God. (300)

*Man has been created to open and unveil (the treasuries of Divine Names and Attributes), be a luminous sign (guiding to God), receive and reflect (Divine manifestations), be a light-giving moon reflecting the Eternal Power, and be a mirror for the manifestations of the Eternal Beauty. (300)

*If you please your Creator through abstaining from sins and obeying His commands and through righteous deeds, this also suffices to please the created. (301)

*The Necessarily-Existent Being does not resemble the contingent in His Essence and qualities. So He does not resemble them in His acts either. (301)

*The teeth and claws of a lion point to the fact that what is expected of a lion is to tear, and the delight of a melon shows that it is for eating. So too the potential of man indicates that his essential duty is to worship God. (302)

*Small animals like the gnat, spider and flea are more intelligent, more sophisticated in structure and subtler in art than big ones such as the elephant, water buffalo and camel. (304)

*All-encompassing provision does not exclude the provision of each being particularly. (305*6)

*Most human beings do not give their due to the observed book of the universe and the glorious book of the Qur'an recited and heard. (306)

*At the times of daily prayers, you can imagine the Muslim world as a mosque, with Mekka being the *mihrab*—the place where the leader of prayer stands—and Ka'ba the central point of that *mihrab*. In this mosque generations perform prayer. The mosque is continuously filled with and emptied of the generations coming one after the other. (307)

*If you find happiness and maintain your dignity, you should leave today with honor and dignity what will leave you tomorrow, throwing you into humiliation and miseries. (307)

*The modern corrupt civilization has opened a door to such an enormous, disgusting show and hypocrisy that, in the name of fame and reputation, they make show and behave hypocritically toward not only individuals but the whole nation. (308)

*On coming together to make a sound unity, a community of women can acquire firm manliness, while a weak unity of men becomes woman-like. (308)

*Divine Unity is one of the clearest proofs of Muhammad's Prophethood. (308)

*Those decorations, perfections and beautiful spectacles and the majesty of Divine Lordship and the splendor of Divinity observed in the universe require an observer to observe them in amazement. (309)

*Just as the correspondence and similarities among things point to the Oneness and Unity of the Maker, so too, the orderly and purposeful dissimilarities and distinctions among them indicate that the Maker is All-Wise and has absolute Will, doing whatever He wishes. (310)

*Man is the most unjust among beings. (310)

*Through the perfection of His Power, God has subjugated all the particles and compounds of the universe to His laws and commands of creation. (311)

*Inertia, motionlessness and inactivity and remaining unchanging in the same conditions mean a kind of death or non-existence for a contingent thing whose life and survival depend on activity and changing. (311)

*God, may His Glory be exalted, makes Himself known to us through His creatures and the works of His art and loved through His Mercy, bounties and provisions. (312)

*Whatever is suffered for God is good; how sweet it is even if apparently bitter! For it makes you taste the pleasure of supplicating and praying to Him. (314)

*O God! Your rebellious servant has come
acknowledging his sins, and he prays to You.
If You forgive him, this is what You love to do;
if You repel him, who else will have mercy on him? (314)

*O God! I am not worthy of the highest floor of Paradise,
Nor do I have strength to bear Hellfire.
Enable me to feel repentant of my sins
and ask forgiveness for them, and forgive me.
For You are the Forgiver of sins, however great they are. (315)

A Whiff from Breezes of the Qur'an's Guidance

In the Name of God, the Merciful, the Compassionate.

Praise be to God, the Lord of the Worlds, for His mercy to the worlds through the Messengership of Muhammad, the master of the Messengers, upon him, his family and Companions be peace and blessings.

Know O friend! With all its species and sections in both the worlds of the Unseen and this visible world, the whole of creation testifies that *There is no god but He*, which is also required and displayed by the co-operation and solidarity among those species and sections.

The pillars of creation and structures from the solar system to others (smaller or larger), testify that *There is no lord[1] but He*, which is also required and displayed by the similarity and correspondence among those pillars and structures.

All the organs and limbs of all beings living on the earth testify that *There is no owner and master but He*, which is also required and displayed by those organs and limbs having almost the same formation and functions.

All the parts of all plants and animals testify that *There is no director and organizer but He*, which is also required and displayed by the mutual helping among those parts.

All the sub-divisions of the parts of plants and animals testi-

---

1. The Divine Name *al-Rabb*, usually translated into English as Lord, denotes God as One Who raises, brings up, sustains, educates, trains and administers all things. (Tr.)

fy that *There is no trainer but He.* It is also required and displayed by the fact that the correspondence among individual members of species—in that they have almost the same organs and structures—shows the same Pen and indicates that the Trainer is one. The diversity among countenances bears witness that the Inscriber is absolutely free, doing whatever He wills.

All the cells forming the parts and organs testify that *There is no disposer but He,* and there cannot be any disposal save by His commands of creation and operation. For if the Disposer were not one and single, there would have to be disposers of infinite number, who are both equal to one another in qualities and opposite, both independent and dependent, both unrestricted and restricted, and so on.

All the atoms forming the cells testify that *There is no orderer but He,* as is also required and displayed by the similarities and correspondence among the structures, working and functions of atoms.

And with all its particles, the main substance of creation—ether—testifies that *There is no god but He,* as is also required and displayed by the simplicity, calm and immobility of ether and the speed it shows in fulfilling the orders of the Creator.

Know O friend! No one has the right to complain about and object to the Maker of the universe. To satisfy the complainant may result in violation or sacrifice of thousands of instances of wisdom having parts in the general order of creation which rejects the satisfaction of the fancy of that complainant. If truth had followed their caprices, the heavens and the earth and whoever is in them would surely have been corrupted.[2]

O complaining one! How dare you raise objections and make your caprices the standard for the order of the universe and your corrupt taste as the measure of the degrees of Divine bounties? How do you know that what you see as a misfortune is not a blessing? Are you authorized to change the direction of the turning of the wheels of creation in order to satisfy your tri-

---

2. *al-Mu'minun*, 23.71.

fling fancies that do not have as much weight as the wing of a gnat? You can only make your complaints to Him, not about Him, for what falls to your lot from Him is only a "grain" out of heaps of corn, and one who is owned cannot be the owner. Know your place and do not overstep the limits of your authority.

Know O friend! Who operates in a cell of the body is surely operating in the whole of the body, for he must operate in a cell according to its relation with the body. The operation in a cell is under the command of the Creator of all things.

Know O friend! How can it befit the Wisdom and Attribute of Preserving of the One Who preserves the eggs of vermin and fish and the seeds of plants for wise, merciful purposes, that He neglects to record and preserve your deeds? Those deeds are the seeds of the trees that will yield their fruit in the Hereafter, especially considering that you are a bearer of His trust and His vicegerent on earth. Every living being cherishes the strong desire and inclination to preserve its life. This and the tendency in creation to reconcile the opposites for the continuation of life point out that worldly existence will result in eternal permanence through the manifestation of the Names, the All-Living, the All-Preserving and the All-Permanent. They also allude to a fact determined by Divine Destiny that each perishable, transitory thing has a vital, permanent point or aspect.

Know O friend! The One Who preserves the seed of a fig tree through the changes it undergoes until itself ends in the fig, and protects it with perfect care from rotting in earth through the seasons with whatever it has to grow into a fig tree—that All-Preserving and Protecting One Who also protects all other plants and animals, will not neglect at all the deeds of man, who is His vicegerent on the earth.

Know O friend! The material existence of the meaning—letters and words—may change and be effaced but the meaning continues to exist. A covering may be rent apart but the essence or kernel remains. Clothes are worn out but the body survives and the body ruins but the spirit survives. The body gets old but ego remains young; multiplicity and the multiple are divided and decay but unity and the unitary remain permanent; matter dissolves but light endures. Despite its putting on different "bodies", undergoing many changes and experiencing lots of different conditions, the "meaning" endures from the beginning of its life to its end and maintains its unity, that is, remains without changing. This shows that it will pass over the "ditch" of death and, freed from its hooks and stripped of its body, continue its journeying to eternity safe and sound. The strong tendency of material things—essentially subject to decay—to remain and survive clearly points out that simple things such as the meaning, light and spirit—essentially inclined to permanence—will remain eternally.

Know O friend! The grandeur of God's Divinity and Its dignity and absolute independence require that whether big or small, all things should be under His disposal. Your physically small size and some of your seemingly unimportant states do not necessitate your being excluded from it. Your distance from Him does not mean His being distant from you, the insignificance of some of your attributes the insignificance of your existence, and your being foul in character, mind and life-style your being foul with respect to the universal wisdom in your existence. So, the greatness of the Creator does not require that small things should be excluded from His disposal, as greatness necessitates being encompassing in disposing and independent in creating.

Know O friend! As material, solid things get larger, they lose their sensitivity to delicate, subtle things. Whereas, as light expands and spreads, it pervades more and penetrates more deeply into hidden and subtle things. Also, as light becomes more refined, like X-rays, it becomes more and more penetrating. If this is so with respect to the dimensions of contingent existence, you can consider how it is with respect to the Light of the Lights, Necessarily Existent and Single, Knower of all secrets and the hidden and the Disposer of night and day. His greatness necessitates being all-encompassing, penetrating and pervasive.

Know and see how the Qur'an considers and regards the level of understanding of the common people who constitute the absolute majority. In a matter possible to describe in different ways and degrees, it chooses the way most comprehensible by them. Otherwise, the argument would have been more abstruse than the conclusion.

The Qur'an mentions the natural phenomena to deduce the Attributes of the Creator, may His Glory be exalted! What is more comprehensible by the common people, is also more suitable for guidance. For example:

The Qur'an says, *And of His signs is the creation of the heavens and the earth and the difference of your tongues and colors.*[3] Behind the difference of colors lies God's determination of individuals with the distinguishing marks and countenances of each, as was mentioned in *The Spark*, the previous treatise.

The Qur'an also says, *There are signs in the creation of the heavens and the earth and the alternation of night and day.*[4] Under the "sheet" of night and day is revealed the rotation of the earth on its axis and revolution around the sun.

Again, the Qur'an says, *(We have made) the mountains as pegs.*[5] In this verse, the earth is likened to a ship (sailing in the ocean of space) or a tent fastened and made steady with pegs. Those pegs—mountains—also serve for the subsidence of the wrath of the earth, *which would nearly burst with rage*[6] because of the convulsions within it. Through mountains, the earth also respires. But for the mountains, the earth would cleave apart; it is by virtue of its mountains that it only quakes and then settles down. It is also seen that mountains are reservoirs of water and filters of air. They also serve for the protection of soil from the invasion of seas. So, in a figurative meaning, mountains are pegs, that is, pillars, of life.

You can compare other similar verses with the examples just given.

3. *al-Rum*, 30.22.
4. *Al 'Imran*, 3.190.
5. *al-Naba'*, 78.7.
6. *al-Mulk*, 67.8.

The Qur'an considers the common people first of all. For the same reason, Islamic law recognizes the sighting of the crescent (to determine the beginning and end of the holy month of Ramadan, the month of fasting, and the beginning of *Dhu'l-Hijja*, the month of *Hajj*), rather than astronomical calculation. It is again for this reason that in the Qur'an there are reiterations to establish and repetitions to confirm.

Know O friend! The Qur'anic verses are far richer in meaning than the imaginations in poetry and they are exalted above being in verse. The One Who speaks in the verses describes His essential Qualities and acts but most of poetry talks about others. The Qur'an that describes the ordinary is mostly extraordinary, whereas the poetry talking about the extraordinary is mostly ordinary.

Know O friend! The mirrors reflecting and the "pages" (of creation) bearing witness to God's Unity are infinite in number and multifarious; and they are one within the other, originating from the same center. Seeing one of them requires seeing the others; unveiling one of them makes possible to enter into all of them. It is not the other way, that is, not being able to see one never requires their all being veiled or non-existent. Despite this, the carnal, evil-commanding self, instructed by Satan, denies what is essentially true and confirms what is essentially false.

Know O friend! It is impossible that the writer of a word in a book can be other than the writer of a letter in it. It is impossible that the writer of a line be other than the writer of the page where it is, and the writer of the page other than the writer of the book itself. So also it is not possible that the Creator of an ant can be other than the Creator of all animal species and the Creator of all animal species other than the Lord of the worlds.

It is one of the signs of the absolute, all-encompassing Lordship that a word or even a book is inscribed in a big letter. A sea is one of those big letters in the universe, trees are lines of the book of the universe and the earth is like a point in the whole of the universe. The Creator inscribes, creates, the word of fish in the letter of the sea, some earthly moving creatures in the lines of trees and animals in the point of the earth. An ant in any place or corner of the earth may be supposed to be neglected, although it is not. As the whole of the *sura Ya Sin* can be inscribed within its initial letters of *Ya* and *Sin*, creatures are inscribed in their eggs or seeds.

Know O friend! There is resemblance among stars and suns. This shows that their Lord cannot be of their kind, nor can He be one among them. The Lord of one among them is necessarily the Lord of all of them and the Lord of all things.

O man! If only you were just and fair-minded in respect of what you suffer from creatures such as fleas and gnats! While those fine, innocent creatures bear with a perfect submission your biting of all fruits and most of animals, is it fairness not to bear the retaliation of the slightest degree you suffer at the hands of some pestering creatures?

Know O friend! An individual human being is a community formed of responsible organs and limbs. For each of the external and inner senses is a particular form of worship, as it may be rebellious or sinful through a kind of misguidance. The prostration of the head before anything and anyone other than God is misguidance. So too, the prostration of the imaginations of poets in excessive amazement and adoration before beauties other than that of God and not for the sake of God, is another kind of misguidance which leads the imagination to transgress (the limits established by God). Compare with the imagination other senses and faculties.

Know O friend! It is one of the widest causes of misguidance that man supposes as known what he has familiarity with because of its being common and usual. Whereas in most cases such sort of familiarity may cause compound ignorance. Nevertheless, because of that kind of familiarity, man does not need to reflect on what is usual and common, although those he sees as common are miracles of Divine Power. He only pays attention to what he sees as extraordinary because of rarity. He is like one who, without considering the whole of the sea with all its animals and flora, sees only the waves caused by wind and the sea's shining with the images of the sun. Then he mentions them as the proofs of the grandeur of the Owner of the sea and its Maker, may His Glory be exalted.

Know O friend. Most of the knowledge of people about the earth and what they see as evident are based on a superficial familiarity, which is a veil spread on compound ignorance. They do not have any real foundations. For this reason, the Qur'an draws the attention of man to the usual and ordinary. With its piercing expressions it draws aside the veil of superficial familiarity, shows man how the things seen as usual and ordinary under the veil of familiarity are in fact extraordinary.

Know O friend! The relationship and conversation between two things do not require their being equal or similar to each other. A drop of rain and a blossom have some sort of relationship and transaction with the sun. O man! Never suppose that your smallness veils you from the favoring of the Creator of all things.

Know O friend! The expansion of time for some saints should not be regarded as unlikely and denied. For example, Imam Sha'rani[7] (as is recorded at the end of *al-Yawaqit wa'l-Jawahir* ("Rubies and Other Kinds of Gems"), studied *al-Futuhat al-Makkiya* ("Makkan Discoveries"—a compendium of four great volumes by Muhy al-Din ibn al-'Arabi) two and a half times in a day. There are examples that can make it comprehensible. Do you not see that in a dream lasting a few seconds it is as if you lived a year? If you were to read the Qur'an in place of what happens to you within that period, you would read it from beginning to end a few times. This expansion of time in dreams in ordinary experience is what certain saints who can unveil the

---

7. Imam Sha'rani, 'Abd al-Wahhab ibn Ahmad ibn 'Ali al-Hanafi (1493-1564) was one of the Sufi scholars. He was born and lived in Egypt. He has several books among which *al-Mizan al-Kubra'* ("The Greatest Balance") and *al-Anwar al-Qudsiya fi Ma'rifat A'dab al-'Ubudiya* ("Sacred Lights in Knowing the Manners of Servanthood") are the most famous. (Tr.)

things hidden to other people experience in great dimensions while awake. They approach the sphere of the spirit uncontained by time.

Motion is like the body of time or time is like the color of motion: whatever takes place in one also takes place in the other. So, why should it not be possible for a saint whose spirit dominates his bodily existence to move with the speed of the spirit or imagination?

Know O friend! Some people are unable to comprehend the consequences of Divine Unity; their corrupt imaginations cannot bear them. They attempt to reject the authentic, decisive proofs to establish the Divine Unity and, arguing that it is impossible for such a proof to give such a tremendous result, try to damage their authenticity. They do not know that what supports and leads to the consequence is belief, the proof being only a window through which to look at it, or like a brush to sweep away the (dust of) illusions on it. Besides, there is not only one proof for the Divine Unity, rather, there are as many as the specks of dust of deserts, the drops of rain and the waves of oceans.

Know O friend! The One Who prepares melons and apples for you to eat knows better than you what you need to eat and is aware of what your conscience takes pleasure in. Is it possible for the branches and stems of plants and trees to know that? Such means or causes of Divine bounties are only the channels of Mercy and canals of bounties.

The Second Part of the Whiff

In the Name of God, the Merciful, the Compassionate.

Glory be to God! How thin is the veil between the manifest and inner, invisible dimensions of existence, while how great is the distance between them! How short, yet, how long is the way between the world and the Hereafter! How fine, yet, how thick, is the veil between knowledge and ignorance! How transparent, yet, how dense, is the space between belief and unbelief! How short is the distance between servanthood to God and rebellion, despite their being as far apart as are Paradise and Hell! How short is life, while how great ambitions are!

Likewise, between yesterday and today there is a thin veil that cannot hinder the spirit from passing and penetrate into yesterday and the past beyond that. Whereas, with respect to the body, this distance is so great as to require a year to travel. Also, the veils between the outer and inner dimensions of existence and between the world and the Hereafter are thin and transparent for the men of heart and spirit, while they are extremely thick for those obeying their carnal selves and bodily desires.

Similarly, between your night and day there is a fine interval, which is your "eyelid". When you open the eye of your self, your night disappears and your day shines. If, on the other hand, you forget what you are, you fall into a permanent night. Also, whoever looks at the universe for the sake of the Almighty, whatever he witnesses becomes a (source of) knowledge for him; if he looks with a view of heedlessness and from the perspective of material or natural causes, whatever he regards as knowledge becomes sheer ignorance.

Again, between the illimunation of *Aya Sofya* (Hagia Sophia) and its being in thick darkness at night there is a time as short as switching off the lights. The flash of lightning and its disappearance take place almost at the same instant. The darkening of the sky with dark clouds and its clearing through the removal of dark clouds from the face of the sun by a breeze of mercy happen just one after the other in a short time. One who looks and sees with the light of faith and belief in Divine Unity, sees the universe filled with light and in friendship, mutual love and affection, and all things and beings in it as amiable, living brothers. Whereas one who looks with unbelief, sees all things and beings as dreadful corpses, strangers hostile to one another. He also sees the universe in veils of darkness one above the other and himself in a deep sea covered by waves riding upon waves, above which are clouds; when he puts forth his hand, he can hardly see it.

Also, the veil between the two faces of a mirror is thinner than a leaf but there is as great a difference between them as the distance between east and west. With a movement of a finger, the mirror either smiles at you or your face is completely dark. In the same way, the deeds of man have two aspects or "faces". The deeds done with the intention to please God provide you with a transparent face in the depth of which numberless manifestations are reflected. The lack of such intention or the deeds not done for the sake of God show the dark, opaque face which bears nothing in the name of truth.

While the dark face has no depth and can contain nothing, with the exception of occupying space the size of itself, the transparent face, because of its relation to the immaterial world of ideas or symbols can, by virtue of its transparency, contain numberless huge things. In the same way, life has two faces, the first of which relates to the world and is dark, narrow and transient, while the other relating to the Truth is transparent, broad and permanent. The heedless carnal self, under the influence of a devilish sophistry, wears the dark face but demands what is possible in the transparent face like seeking eternity.

Know O friend! The key of creation is in the hands of man, in his ego. Although the doors of creation seem to be open, they are actually closed. The Truth, glory be to Him, has entrusted man with a key with which all the doors of creation are opened and the treasury of the Creator is unveiled. The key entrusted to you is ego, which is itself an enigma. When you solve that enigma by knowing its nature, creation is opened to you.

God Almighty, may His Glory be exalted, has given man ego so that it should serve as a unit of comparison to understand the attributes of Divine Lordship.

When man knows what ego is, he comes to see it as fine and weak like a conscious hair in the rope of man's existence, like a thin stripe in the cloth of man's nature, like an *alif*—the first Arabic letter—in the book of the individual. It has also two faces, one turned to good, a passive recipient of God's bounties and blessings, not the agent, the other turned to evils and non-existence and being itself agent. It has an illusory nature, imagined lordship and sovereignty, and existence as weak as not to bear anything by itself. It is to function like a thermometer or other like instrument with which things and properties are measured. It is a measure with which to know the absolute, all-encompassing Attributes of the Necessarily-Existent Being.

Man should be well aware of this and, becoming a referent of *He has indeed prospered who purifies it*,[8] fulfil what is due to the Trust he has been charged with.

If you reflect on ego as a unit of comparison to comprehend the Creator's Attributes and Names, it becomes an eye for you to see whatever exists in the universe. The information you get from the universe finds in ego what will confirm it and make it into real knowledge. Then its claim of lordship or sovereignty and self-ownership comes to an end, and it perceives that its existence is only an illusory one. Whereas if you consider ego as having an independent existence of itself and thereby breach the Trust, you will be among those referred to in *And indeed he*

---

8. *al-Shams*, 91.9.

has ruined it who stunts and spoils it.[9] For it is ego which the heavens, the earth and mountains shrank from bearing since, with that aspect of it, ego is the source of associating partners with God, all evils and kinds of misguidance. If ego hides itself from you, it grows thick and swells until it swallows you and, with all your existence, you become an ego. Then it grows stronger with tribal and then racial fanaticism until it has become a devil contending against the commandment of its Maker. Then it likens other people and things and natural causes with itself, attributing to each self-ownership and sovereignty, and thus falls into a tremendous kind of associating partners with God. While in this state, if you move your eyes throughout the creation, everything is closed in your face just when it seems to have opened to you, for your eyes return to your self and you see everything as colored by ego. The color of ego is associating partners with God or denial of Him. Even if all the horizons were clearly filled with the most manifest signs (of the existence and Unity of the Creator), what remains in ego would be a dark point covering all those signs.

An important matter

Ego has two faces, one represented by Prophethood, the other by human philosophy.

The first face is the origin of pure servanthood to God. With this face, ego points to God, not itself, and has an illusory, dependent existence. Although it appears to be self-owning, in fact it is owned and disposed by another—God. It has a supposed, not an established, reality. Its duty is to be a measure, a unit of comparison, to understand the Attributes of the Creator. This is the reality of ego, as it was seen by the Prophets, who submitted the whole of existence to God. They affirmed and demonstrated that God has no partners at all, either in His Sovereignty or in His Lordship or Divinity. In His hand are the keys of all things and He has absolute power over all things. From this transparent face of ego, the All-Compassionate has grown a

9. *al-Shams*, 91.10.

blessed tree of servanthood whose blessed branches spreading through the garden of the universe hang with clusters of fruits of Messengers, Prophets, saints, and truth-seeking, pure scholars glittering in darkness like stars.

As to philosophy, it considers ego as having an independent, self-owned existence showing to itself. Philosophers have supposed that ego has an established reality and that its duty is to be perfected through self-love. In this supposition many kinds of associating partners with God have originated and on the head of ego has grown the accursed tree of misguidance. The branch of the power of lust of this tree, which appreciates unjust might or force and physical beauty enamoured of show, has given to mankind idols deified (by their admirers) while themselves bow (before their admirers) in an attitude of adoration. The branch of the power of wrath has saddled mankind with Pharaohs and Nimrods. The branch of the power of reason has produced atheists and materialists. Philosophers attribute to God only a part of His kingdom and attribute the rest to other than the Almighty.

Although ego is essentially like air or vapor, because of the philosophers' ill-omened view, it grows denser, becoming like fluid and then, because of superficial familiarity, like a solid thing. Afterwards, because of heedlessness it gets frozen and, thereafter, because of rebellion, gets stronger and swells until it swallows its owner. It becomes broader with tribal or racial attitudes and then, because of ascribing to other people and natural causes self-existence and ownership and even creativity, as it ascribes the same to itself, ego starts to contend against the commandment of its Creator. Some philosophers have felt compelled to believe that natural causes have real effect in creation and control of things, and attribute creativity to nature and chance. That is why they deny the Resurrection and accept that spirits or, as is the case with materialists, matter have no beginning. May God assail them! How perverse they are! Because of conceit, they have become playthings of devils, who have thrown them into the pits of misguidance.

Ego in the normo-cosmos—man—is the counterpart of nature in the macro-cosmos: both have been attributed partnership with God and therefore deified. *Whoever denies false deities and believes in God, has laid hold of the most firm handle that is impossible to break. God is All-Hearing, All-Knowing.*[10]

Know O friend! Good deeds acquire vitality through sincere intention and are corrupted through show, ostentation and hypocrisy. Whereas the feelings for and (natural) tendencies toward good ingrained in conscience lose their purity through conscious intentions. As intention is the life of deeds, it is also the death of natural states. For example, intention to be humble spoils humility and intention to be great provokes contempt. Also, intention to have relief causes the disappearance of relief and intention to be sad decreases sadness, and so on.

Know O friend! The law of growth operates in a tree. The seed of a tree, from which it grows, is the essence of that tree. As is known, the seed is contained by the fruit and, unless somehow impeded, it grows by eternal Favoring into the tree and again is placed in the fruit growing on that tree. The fruit is the most valuable, most esteemed, most pleasant, most important and most illustrious part of the tree, being the aim of its existence. The universe is a tree, the basic elements like earth, water, air and fire being its branches, plants its leaves, animals its flowers and mankind its fruits.

The most radiant of those fruits and the most illustrious, greatest, most beautiful, most noble, most comprehensive and most beneficial of them is the Prophet Muhammad, upon him be peace and blessings, the master of the Messengers, the leader of the pious, and the beloved of the Lord of the Worlds. He made the Ascension and his eyes did not swerve. The moon split for him and the lizard, the gazelle, the wolf, the camel, the mountain, the rock, the pole, the tree, and the clod of earth spoke to him. From his fingers water flowed out like the Spring of *Kawthar*. He is the most virtuous of mankind, one carrying all

---

10. *al-Baqara*, 2.256.

truths of faith in his person, by whom all manifestations of Divine Favoring reach creatures, and on whom all mysteries of God being the All-Merciful are concentrated. He is the commander of the "cavalry" of the Prophets and the pious ones faithful to their allegiance and promises, and the most virtuous of all creatures. He is the bearer of the standard of the greatest glory through belief in and submission to Divine Unity and the owner of the most esteemed and dignified rope through Islam. He is the witness of eternal mysteries and observer of the lights and the translator of the tongues of those preceding him. He is the source of knowledge, forbearance and wisdom. He attained the highest rank of servanthood and was distinguished with the highest morality of the purest ranks: the greatest friend of God and His most noble beloved, upon him be the most meritorious of blessings and peace so long as the heavens and earth remain.

Take my hand, O master of the Messengers,
You are the desired and sought, O manifest light of God's Munificence;
I have no leader, no refuge, other than you.
My proof is, "There is no god but God and Muhammad is God's Messenger."

O God! I wish I had thousands of tongues to ask You for forgiveness until the Day of Judgement. O God! Substitute this treatise of mine for those tongues asking for forgiveness and calling blessings upon the Prophet on behalf of me so long as pens exist and continue to write.

O God! Sins have made me dumb and the abundance of my rebellions brings shame on me. The greatness of my heedlessness causes me to lower my voice. I knock on the door of Your Mercy and cry at the door of Your Forgiveness in the tongue of my master and support, Shaykh 'Abd al-Qadir al-Jilani, may God bless him, and with his appeal, acceptable and familiar to the door-keeper:

O One Whose Mercy embraces all things! O One in Whose hand is the dominion of all things! O One to Whom nothing can give harm, nor can it give benefit; Whom nothing can overcome and from Whom nothing can be hidden; Whom nothing tires, nor helps, nor doing something can prevent from doing another thing; and Whom nothing resembles, nor baffles! Forgive me for whatever (displeasing to You) I do so that you may not call me to account for anything (sinful) I did.

O One Who holds everything by the forelock and in Whose hand are the keys of all things! O One Who is the First, before all things, the Last, after all things, the Outward, above all things, and the Inward, inmost of all things, One overwhelming all things! Forgive me for all things. You are powerful over all things. O One knowing all things, encompassing all things, seeing all things, beholding all things, overseeing all things, penetrating all things, well aware of all things! Forgive me for all my sins and errors so that You may not call me to account for anything. You are powerful over all things.

O God! I take refuge in the might of Your Majesty and the majesty of Your Might, and in the power of Your Sovereignty ant the sovereignty of Your Power, from disconnection of my relation to You and lethal fancies. O the Neighbor of those who seek Your neighborhood! Guard me from satanic lusts, clean me of human dirt and purify me through sincere love of Your Prophet Muhammad, upon him be peace and blessings, from the rust of heedlessness and fancies of ignorance, so that I may be freed of my selfhood, my ego, and only what is for You, with You, to You and from You may remain; and that I may be overwhelmed by God's favor in the ocean of God's kindness, being among those made victorious by God's Sword, favored with God's gifts, and kept away by God's protection from any engagement interrupting from God.

O Light of Lights! O Knower of secrets! O Director of night and day! O Sovereign! O Mighty! O Overwhelming! O Compassionate! O Loving! O Forgiving! O Knower of the Unseen! O Turner of hearts and eyes! O Veiler of defects (of His servants)! O Forgiver of sins! Forgive me for my sins and have mercy on him who is in insurmountable difficulties, to whom all doors are closed, for whom it is difficult to follow the path of the righteous, and whose days are spent in the places of heedlessness, rebellion and sins. O One Who answers when He is called! O One swift at reckoning! O Munificent! O Bestower! Have mercy on him who has severe ills difficult to be cured, who have little, weak means while stricken with grave misfortunes! You are His refuge and his hope.

O God! I complain to You about my difficulties and afflictions. O God! My document is my needs, and whatever I have in the name of means is only my lack of means and my helplessness. O God! A single drop from the ocean of Your Grace makes me rich and a single droplet from the flood of Your Forgiveness suffices me.

O Loving! O Loving! O Loving! O Owner of the Supreme Throne! O Starter and Returner! O One doing whatever He wills! I ask You, for the sake of the light of Your "Face" which fills all the columns of Your Throne, and Your Power with which You are powerful over all Your creatures, and Your Mercy which embraces all things. There is no god but You, O Helper. I ask You to help me and forgive all my sins and the blunders of my tongue throughout all my life, for the sake of Your Mercy, O Most Merciful of the merciful! Amen. Amen. Amen.

O one who recites this cry of asking forgiveness! Recite it first on your behalf and then on my behalf for the sake of God. For I lie in my grave unable to do anything and to say nothing. I can speak only with your tongue through this book of mine, so speak on my behalf only for the sake of God.

The Third Part of the Whiff

In the Name of God, the Merciful, the Compassionate.

I ask God for help to continue on my way.

Glory be to Him Who makes the heavens speak with His praise and glorification with the words of the planets and other stars.

O One Who makes the earth speak with His praise and glorification with the words of trees and plants. Who makes trees and plants speak with the words of flowers and fruits. Who makes flowers and fruits speak with the words of seeds and stones. Who makes the seeds and stones speak with the words of spikes and grains.

Glory be to You Whom light glorifies with praise in all its radiations, and air with its winds, and water with its rivers, and earth with its rocks, and plants with their flowers, and trees with their fruits, and atmosphere with its birds, and clouds with their rain, and the sky with its moons.

Blessings and peace be upon our master Muhammad, who is the lamp of the Prophets, the moon of purified scholars, the star of saints, the sun of mankind and jinn, and the light of the east and west, and upon his family, the stars of guidance, and Companions, the lamps illuminating darkness.

Know O one who has great difficulty in understanding the meaning of *We have made them missiles for devils*.[11] In order to reach the sky of this verse, we need a ladder with seven steps.

First step: The heavens have inhabitants of their own called angels. Since, despite its insignificant size compared with the heavens, the earth is full of living, conscious beings, the heav-

---

11. *al-Mulk*, 67.5.

ens having constellations, those decorated castles, must also be full of conscious beings particular to themselves.

The universe is richly adorned with all those beauties, designs, and embroideries requiring the existence of beings to reflect on them with appreciation and amazement. For beauty is only displayed for its lover, as food is given to the hungry. Mankind and jinn, with respect to either their numbers or their lack of enough capacity, are far from fulfilling this function— the function of observing and reflecting on the beauties of existence—with all its majesty, which requires the existence of many kinds of numberless angels and other spirit beings.

Second step: There is a close relationship and there are transactions between the earth and heavens. For example, light, heat and other similar blessings come from the heavens. This shows and requires that there is a way for mankind to ascend the heavens, as is realized by the Prophets, saints and spirit being10s stripped of their bodily weight.

Third step: The order, peace and tranquillity of the heavens point out that their inhabitants must not resemble the inhabitants of the earth where confusion, convulsions, conflicts and testing prevail due to opposites like the good and evils existing mingled with each other. Whereas the inhabitants of the heavens are obedient, doing what they are ordered.

Fourth step: The Master of the Day of Reckoning and the Lord of the Worlds has Names with different rulings and requiring different manifestations. For example, the Name Which required the sending of angels to fight against unbelievers in the lines of the Prophet's Companions, also requires the struggle between angels and devils, between the good of the heavens and the evils of the earth. Do you not see how a king behaves? When his might and majesty require the rewarding or punishment before witnesses of those who deserve either, and honouring of some of his servants or officials, instead of doing that through his special telephone, he orders one of his ministers to gather people in a great place to exhibit the splendour of his rule, and to organize a magnificent parade.

Fifth step: It is beyond question that the evil ones among spirit beings imitate the good among them in attempting to ascend the heavens. The inhabitants of the heavens confront them and repel them because of their evils. The wisdom of the Sovereignty of Divine Lordship requires that this heavenly contest should have a sign in this visible, material world so that man, one of whose main duties is to watch and observe, can be informed of it. The best way of bringing this struggle before the sight of man is to shoot stars or meteors from the high towers of constellations. Unlike all other cosmic events having many instances of wisdom, there is no wisdom proper to that event of shooting stars other than their being a sign of the heavenly struggle between angels and devils—an instance of wisdom known and witnessed by all truth-seeking people.

Sixth step: The wise, miraculous Qur'an seeks to guide man to truth and hold them back from rebellion with lofty styles and exalted analogies or comparisons. For example, consider the warning in *O company of men and jinn, if you are able to penetrate the spheres of the heavens and the earth, then penetrate (them)! You will not penetrate them except with an authority*.[12] The verse proclaims the helplessness of mankind and jinn before the vastness and immensity of the kingdom of Divine Lordship, as if to say: "O man, helpless, poor, and tiny! How dare you rebel against a King Whom obey all suns, moons, stars and angels, who throw at devils missiles as large as mountains or even larger? How dare you rebel in the kingdom of a King among Whose soldiery there are those who are able to shoot in the face of enemies stars the size of your earth as easily as you throw walnuts or hazelnuts?"

Seventh step: Like angels and fish, from their biggest to the smallest, stars have many kinds. Whatever shines in the heavens is called a star. As there are among them those glittering like jewels and adorning the heavens as fruits adorn a garden and fish a sea, there are also others with which devils are shot to death as a sign of the existence of guards on the alert, obedi-

---

12. *al-Rahman*, 55.33.

ent and refraining from mingling with the rebellious, or a symbol of the law of struggle or contest prevailing in the vastest sphere of existence. For God is the perfect, most conclusive argument and the greatest wisdom.

Know O friend! There are many Qur'anic verses explicitly stating that things are recorded before and during their physical existence such as *Nothing of wet or dry but (it is recorded) in a manifest book.*[13] This is confirmed by the systems and compositions in the book of the universe and its "verses", especially those of universal order, harmony, balance, fashioning, adornment and distinguishing.

Among the evidences showing that all things are recorded before their coming into existence are seeds, measures and forms. For seeds are tiny cases into which the contents of what Divine Destiny measured, determined and appointed have been entrusted. Divine Power builds according to the precise measures of Destiny and employs particles in that building. The measures are the exact moulds (pre-)existing in Divine Knowledge. Despite their being blind, deaf and unconscious, particles move for the growth of things in exact measures: without ever overstepping the limits determined for them, as if having very acute sight and hearing, they go and settle just where they must for great results like fruits. You can compare with this many other evidences of the recording of things before they come into existence. As for the evidences for the recording during the existence of things, all fruits, which are like the rolls of sheets where the "deeds" of trees have been recorded, bring before the sight of witnesses what their origins have experienced as they were buried in earth and burst forth in spring. Also, man's memory, the size of a mustard-seed, is like a document which the Hand of Divine Power has copied out of the notebook of his deeds with the Pen of Destiny to give him at the time of the Final Reckoning so that he himself may see what he did while in the world. Memory also shows that behind this hustle and bustle, behind this turmoil and decay, there are mirrors of permanence

---

13. *al-An'am*, 6.59.

where the All-Powerful One records the pictures and identities of all decaying things, and there are also boards or tablets on which the All-Preserving, the All-Knowing One writes the meaning and realities of transient things.

Know O friend! As a clock is not stable, with its parts vibrating and moving, the world, which is like a huge clock, is also shaking and moving. With the inclusion of time in its movement, night and day occur as if a hand pointing to seconds, and a year being like another hand pointing to minutes and a century pointing to hours. With the inclusion of space, atmosphere occurs, undergoing very swift changes and alterations, like the second hand of the clock, and the earth the surface of which displays continuous changes of plants and animals through the cycle of death and life, like the minute hand of the clock. The inside of the earth also exhibits, like the hour hand, great changes and convulsions with the bursting out of hills and mountains from within it. Like the hand pointing to days, the heavens become the vastest scene of changes with the movement of its bodies, the appearance of comets and meteors and the birth and death of stars.

The world or worldly life is based on these seven pillars—day and night, year and century, the earth, atmosphere, and the heavens. Despite its describing the Divine Names by being a scene where they are manifested and the Pen of Power and Destiny continuously works, it is in a continuous flow like a river and is also fleeting, transient and perishable. Nevertheless, it is seen as permanent and perpetual with the eye of heedlessness and as stable with the eye fixed on "nature" and the view of naturalism, being a veil over the Hereafter.

Viewing the world or worldly life on behalf of itself and concentrating on its physical side with the modern, defective, materialistic-scientific attitude, modern, corrupt philosophy makes that veil thicker and presents it as a lot more stable and perpetual. However, the Qur'an "cards" the world with its verses and makes it like carded wool. It makes it transparent with its statements and melts its with its light and heat. The Qur'an also smashes its illusory permanence with its announcements (of death, the dreadful end of previous rebellious peoples and frightening events of afterlife) and disperses with its "thunderbolts" the heedlessness that gives rise to and breeds naturalism. The reality of the ever-shaking world recites in the tongue of its actual state the verse: *When the Qur'an is recited, give ear to it and pay heed, haply so you will find and be treated with mercy.*[14]

Know O friend! One of the factors distinguishing man from animals is that man has relations with both the past and the future and he has such comprehensive perception as to comprehend both his inner and the outer worlds. He can also find out the apparent causes of events and knows what is necessary for obtaining a result in his life. However, his greatest and most prominent duty for the fulfilment of which he is equipped with very important faculties is to glorify and praise God. Indeed, man glorifies his Maker with the tongues of both the past, the present and the future and the tongues of his inner world and the outer world. That is, he praises his Lord and glorifies Him for the blessings and bounties bestowed on him in the past and present and which will be bestowed in the future and also for the blessings he finds himself endowed with in his inner world and the outer world. As he also witnesses the glorifications of other creatures, he extols the Maker of things by discerning the Names manifested for the creation of things and the purposes for their lives.

Glory be to God praised and glorified in both amazement and appreciation, in both awe and love, Whose Holiness and exemption from all defects are proclaimed, and Whose Grandeur is beyond perception.

Know O friend! God destines and decrees, executes His decrees and spares (that is, He forgives and withdraws the execution of His decrees). His decree yields to His sparing, as hard rock and earth yield to very thin, fibre-like roots and the resistance of iron breaks in the face of frozen water. For it sometimes

---

14. *al-A'raf*, 7.204.

occurs that the law of Destiny is prevented from enactment by
His Decree. Also, it is often witnessed that a universal law which
is the destiny of a species or group is not enacted for a special
member of that species. (For example, a helpless, little baby is
found surviving a great calamity which has caused many
deaths and great destruction.) This is to point to the fact that the
All-Glorified One is absolutely free in His acts, He does whatever He wills and decrees however He wishes. What He gives
cannot be prevented and His decrees cannot be resisted.

The relation of sparing with the execution of decrees is like
the relation of the decree to Destiny. That is, sparing means
making exceptional to or excluded from the law of decree and
decree is sometimes excluded from the law of Destiny. One
who is well aware of such acts of God cannot help but say: "O
God! My good deeds are from Your sparing and I know that
Your decree will eventually come. But for Your sparing, I will
be among those who perish." Because of its aptitude for evils,
the evil-commanding self deserves to perish.

Know O friend! The reason for many Qur'anic verses ending
with Divine Names is that the wise Qur'an brings Divine works
before the sight of the reader with its miraculous expressions
and then concludes with the Divine Names Which are the origins of those works, as in the verse: *He it is Who originates creation, then causes it to return again, and it is easier for Him. His is the
highest comparison in the heavens and the earth. He is the All-
Mighty, the All-Wise.*[15]

The Qur'an also unfolds the weavings of His art before the
eyes of mankind and then wraps them in Divine Names. Again,
it expounds Divine acts and then summarizes with the Divine
Names. Again, it mentions creatures and shows through them
the order, balance and favoring and then offers the Divine
Names as if the creatures mentioned were the "words" of those
Names which are the meanings included in them or the water
of life reviving them or the seeds from which they grow or their

---

15. *al-Rum*, 30.27.

concise summaries containing the information given in them. Again, it mentions particular, material, changeable things of certain qualities and then summarizes them with the Divine Names with universal manifestations.

Again, it displays things growing freely and found in many places and then places on them the stamp of unity, drawing the attention toward the common points shared by them. Again, it manifests the great, comprehensive effects or results together with their apparent causes in order to show the great distance between what is seen as causes and their results, and that causes cannot be the real origin of results, as there is a great distance between the horizon and the sky, although they seem as if adjacent to or even touching each other. For even the most tremendous of causes are unable to produce the least of effects. The Qur'an fills in the great gap between causes and effects with the relevant Divine Names.

Again, it mentions the evil deeds of creatures and threatens them and then consoles them by mentioning the Names containing mercy. It also mentions certain particular purposes and then establishes them with the Names which contain universal laws ensuring those purposes.

Know O friend! Like love, helplessness is also a way leading to God, a way even more direct and safer than the way of love. Those who have been initiated in the ways seeking to reach God by silent recitation prefer to purify their ten faculties (such as the heart, spirit and other innermost ones, each "beneath" and more hidden than the other), and the others who seek to reach God by loud recitation choose to purify their selves with seven kinds or levels (such as carnal, evil-commanding self, the self resisted but still unsubmissive and accusing itself of its evils, the self obedient and at rest, and the self well-pleasing and pleased with God's decrees about it, etc.). As for the way of helplessness (which is based on acknowledgement of one's helplessness before God), it is a more direct, safer and levelled way with four steps.

The first step is that which is indicated by the verse: *Do not hold yourselves (to be) purified.*[16]

The second step is that indicated by the verse: *Be not as those who forgot God, so that He caused them to forget themselves.*[17]

The third step is what is pointed to by the verse: *Whatever of good befalls you is from God, and whatever ill befalls you is from yourself.*[18]

The fourth step is what is pointed to by the verse: Everything is perishable save His "Face".[19]

The first step

Man loves himself on account of himself; restricting all his love to himself. He praises himself as though worthy of being worshipped, defends himself strongly and holds himself to be free from all defects, without seeing in himself any fault. Like one who has taken his desires as his god, he exploits the faculties entrusted to him to praise and glorify God, the True Worshipped One, for the glorification of his own self. A man can purify himself in this stage only by not holding himself to be purified.

The second step

Man holds back at the time of bearing hardships and rendering services, but considers he should be the first to receive the reward at the time of collecting fruits. A man can purify himself in this stage by behaving otherwise, by forgetting himself at the time of receiving the reward.

The third step

At this step, man should find in himself only defects, insufficiency, helplessness and poverty, be convinced that all the beauties he has are blessings from His Creator requiring His praise, not self-glorification. His purification in this stage is possible by

---

16. *al-Najm*, 53.32.
17. *al-Hashr*, 59.19.
18. *al-Nisa'*, 4.79.
19. *al-Qasas*, 28.88.

knowing his perfection to lie in confession of his imperfection, his power in perception of his helplessness, and his wealth in acceptance of his essential poverty and inadequacy.

The fourth step

Man must perceive that with respect to his own self, he is essentially non-existent, contingent, ephemeral and mortal, but only on account of being a mirror reflecting the Names of his Maker, he is existent, experiencing and experienced. He can purify himself in this stage by perceiving that his non-existence lies in regarding himself as self-existent and his existence in confession of his essential non-existence. Also, he must continually repeat and be convinced that to the Almighty is due all existence and also to Him is due all praise.

Those who follow the way of the Unity of Existence (*Wahdat al-Wujud*) regard the universe as actually non-existent. And those who follow the way of the Unity of the Witnessed (*Wahdat al-Shuhud*) confine all existence within the prison of absolute oblivion. Whereas, what I have inferred from the way of the Qur'an requires neither the denial nor the ignoring of the actual existence of the universe, and employs all things in the duty of showing the Divine Names as mirrors reflecting them. It considers all existence on behalf of the Almighty, not on behalf of itself.

In man's being, there are different spheres of existence one within the other and levels of creation one over the other. For man is both a plant and an animal and a human being and a believer. (That is, his being has vegetable, animal and human dimensions and, if he is a believer, a believing one.)

The process of purification begins in the fourth level—the level of belief—and continues downward to the vegetable one where the severest resistance is shown. This treatment continues day and night uninterruptedly. During the treatment, man may make errors by confusing the levels and he says: "Whatever is on the earth has been created for me." He errs by thinking that humanity is restricted to being vegetable or animal; he also

errs by considering the purposes for the lives of things restricted to their benefits to himself and seeing them as only valuable
as they are beneficial to himself, and therefore he does not exchange a fragrant flower for Venus.

Know O friend! Worship is the result and price of the bounties already accorded to man. It is not the means of future, expected reward.

O man! You have already received your wages, for He has
created you in the fairest form and as a pattern of all existence
and made Himself known to you by bestowing belief on you.

Again, by giving you a stomach, He has given you innumerable substances of food, and also granted you life by virtue of
which this visible, material world has become for you a table
full of bounties. By giving you human selfhood, He has made
the visible and invisible worlds as if a table filled to the brim
with bounties. Furthermore, by bestowing belief on you, in addition to the tables mentioned, He has granted you other kinds
of tables stored in the treasuries of His Names. Also, by granting you His love, He has opened for you and bestowed on you
other sorts of indescribable bounties and blessings. Since you
have already received bounties and blessings such as those
mentioned, it is incumbent on you to serve Him. What He gives
you after your services is purely extra out of His Grace.

Know O friend! The infinite abundance of the members of
species, especially those of little creatures, without the least defect in their structure and with perfect orderliness, points to,
even explicitly shows, that there are no limits to the manifestations of the Maker and that He is absolutely different from all of
them and all things are the same in relation to His Power and
Necessary Existence. This abundance and creation are the result
of His Necessary Existence and are evidences for it. The abundance in species pertains to His Majesty, while the firm and de-
fect-free creation of members pertain to His Grace.

Know O friend! Making something is as easy for a man as the
extent of his knowledge of it and it is difficult for him to the ex-

tent of his ignorance of it. This is especially true when the small things with many little, delicate parts are concerned. The more informed of them he is, the easier they are for him. The absolute facility and swiftness observed in the creation of things and their creation in absolute abundance and without the least defect decisively demonstrate that their Maker has infinite knowledge. The verse *Our command (or doing something) is but one (word) (and it is fulfilled) in the twinkling of an eye*[20] points to that facility.

Know O friend! One who produces a work of art delicately embroidered and covers it with "garments"—like the derma and epidermis—extremely delicately woven of the same substance of the work of art, hewing cavities in it to set different instruments working all in close relation with one another—it is without doubt that that work of art, with its inside and outside, is the work of a single being and belongs to him exclusively.

Similarly, the One Who creates innumerable species of beings of almost infinite variety most delicately embroidered of almost the same simple things and clothes them in garments woven from elements according to the size and structure of each, One Who includes those creatures, especially animals that are the miniatures of the worlds, in the abdomens of those worlds built one within the other to house the creatures that are their fruits or seeds—that One is but One and Besought-of-All, manifesting Himself with all His Names on each of those creatures separately and on the worlds as a whole.

Know O friend! As a king has different titles to designate his authority in the departments of his government and the offices of his state and among his subjects, and to denote his duties of kingship as if he was present in person and superintending in all those departments and offices, so—and God's is the highest comparison—the One with the All-Beautiful Names manifests Himself in the departments of His Sovereignty with His Names with one Name being dominant in a department and the others subordinate. He executes His Lordship in each level of His rule by

---

20. *al-Qamar*, 54.50.

manifesting one of His Names particular to that level as if that Name was particular only to that level. In the levels of His Lordship, the All-Glorified One has essential disposals corresponding to one another; in the spheres of His Divinity, He has Names reflecting one another; in the mirrors of His Splendour, He has different representations; in the operations of His Power, He has varied titles; in the manifestations of His Attributes, He has flowering ways of disclosing Himself; in His modes of acting, He has corresponding disposals; in His division of creatures into species, He has manifestations of His Lordship specified for each creature surrounded by the manifestations on the species as a whole. Prophet Muhammad, the translator of the Eternal Tongue —the Qur'an—upon him be peace and blessings, points to this reality in his supplication named *al-Jawshan al-Kabir* ("The Great Armour"). This supplication has ninety-nine sections like cases of jewels each of which contains twelve gems of Divine Unity. When the Almighty is called by one of them, the Name or Attribute mentioned is specified for Him exclusively. For example, when we call "O Perpetual!", we mean "O One save Whom there is no perpetual in existence!" As is narrated from the Prophet, upon him be peace and blessingsthe All-Glorified One has as many as seventy thousand veils of light.[21] For an Existence penetrating all levels, Whose essential disposals correspond to one another, Whose Names reflect one another, Whose representations and titles are one within the other, Whose ways of closing Itself resemble one another, Whose ways of making Itself known support one another, the manifestations of Whose Lordship corroborate one another, and the manifestations of Whose Names concentrated on a thing are encompassed by their manifestations on a group of things as a whole—it is certainly necessary and inevitable for one who knows that Existence, glory be to It, by one of those Names or Attributes or ways of manifestations mentioned that one cannot but know It by the others also.

Surely We have created man in the fairest creation.[22]

---

21. Tabarani, *al-Mu'jam al-Kabir*, 2.580.
22. *al-Tin*, 95.4.

Know O friend! It is a peculiarity of the comprehensiveness of man's primordial nature that the All-Wise Creator has included in that small object innumerable meters to measure what is endlessly stored in His Mercy, and equipped him with countless faculties to understand what is contained in infinite number in the treasuries of His All-Beautiful Names.

Look at your ten senses and see how by means of them you become aware of the worlds of the things seen, heard, tasted, etc. with all their varieties. Also, He has given man highly restricted attributes or powers of will, knowledge, and hearing etc. to understand His encompassing Attributes and essential, all-embracing Qualities. He has also knit his ego as many fibres (referring to man's feelings, desires, faculties and senses) as the worlds with all their varieties through which to know its nature. Again, He has clothed his essential nature in as many garments as the veils of Lordship so that he may rend them apart and realize intellectual and spiritual progress. Again, he has endowed him with a faculty of perception so amazing that it travels without stopping in memory, the size mustard-seed, as if it were an infinitely vast world and cannot reach its frontiers. More than that, that vast world sometimes becomes so narrow for that faculty that the faculty encompasses it but is itself, together with all the spheres through which it travels and the books in has studied, is encompassed by that mustard-seed, the memory. Glory be to Him Who makes it so small despite its infinite vastness.

It is because of this amazing nature of man that there are extremely great differences among men. Among them is one who is lost in a particle and another in whom the world is lost. Also, one opens with one of the keys granted to him a vast one among the worlds of multiplicity and is lost there having strayed. He cannot reach Unity and belief in Divine Unity except with great difficulties. Men also greatly vary in following a way in their spiritual journeying. Some advance very easily and attain peace and unity, while others are overcome by fancies and heedlessness and, completely lost in multiplicity (of things), forgets unity.

Those regarding themselves as civilized who suppose corruption and regression to be progress, compound ignorance to be certified knowledge, the deepest phase of sleep to be fully awake, are among that second group who have fallen to the lowest of the low.

Know O friend! The manifestation of Divine Oneness (*Wahidiya*)—the manifestation of a Name on a whole—shows that the Divine Name manifested encompasses all things. While the manifestation of Divine Unity (*Ahadiya*)—the manifestation of many Names on a particular thing—points out that a living creature indicates all the Names relating to creation.

Know O friend! Groups, wholes and species are the objects of the manifestation of Divine Majesty and the absolute abundance in species is due to that manifestation, while most of the "mirrors" where the Grace is manifested are individual parts of the members of those groups and species. The beauty of individuals, the radiance of "mirrors", firmness in structure and orderliness are due to that manifestation.

Again, Majesty arises from the manifestation of Divine Oneness and Grace comes from the manifestation of Divine Unity. However, it also occurs that Grace arises from Majesty and Majesty arises from Grace. How beautiful is Majesty in the eye of Grace and how beautiful is Grace in the eye of Majesty!

Know O friend! While "bejewelled" creatures are seen with the power of sight, the disability of the power of insight to see the Creator is because of either the blindness of the insight or its insufficiency to perceive the importance of the matter or its being devoid of necessary guidance. Denial of the Creator would otherwise be much more ridiculous than denial of the power of sight.

Know O friend! The seeds sown in a field make that field protected by him who has sown it and prevent the field from the intervention and disposal of others. The seeds thus function as a sort of invisible wall built around the field. In the same way, every species among species of plants and animals is like a field sown and found in many parts of the earth. It denies other than him who has "sown" it disposal and intervention in itself. All of them together and with their individual members constitute so strong a wall that they never allow others to dispose of and interfere with them.

Know O friend! Some who would like to see and display the matchless beauty and splendour of their Paradise-like gardens, (according to the principle that things are better known through their opposites), put some shapeless rocks, crooked statutes and other similar things in them at random and dig some caves here and there in them. The order or harmony of those gardens seem to lie in their being disordered. However, one who discerns those gardens carefully concludes that it is the apparent disorder which shows them as beautiful and orderly.

Similarly, among well-proportioned creatures and things (in the garden of the earth), there are deserts, hills and rocks of different sizes and shapes scattered in a way that one with a superficial view may suppose that the Hand of Disposal has made them playthings. However, they are the elements added by the All-Wise Maker, the All-Knowing Creator, purposefully in order to contribute to the general order and harmony of existence. Look at the trees having thorns and the plants equipped with thorns to defend themselves against plant-eating animals. You see in them an amazing orderliness and a delicate beauty. It is one of the signs which display that the All-Wise Maker has a special purpose for that apparent lack of orderliness, that those things seemingly outside the general order of their species, are each of a different size and shape. Difference shows purpose and rejects chance. (The facial differences among men are a clear evidence for this.)

Know O friend! It is by virtue of the comprehensive nature of man and one of the factors distinguishing him from animals that he can comprehend the salutations living beings offer to the Bestower of Life. That is, as he perceives the speech of his inner self, he also perceives with the ear of belief all the words living beings, even inanimate ones, utter to glorify their Creator. While, like a deaf man who can speak inwardly or to his self only, each of those beings can perceive the speech of its own inner self, man is one capable of both speaking and perceiving all the sounds produced by all creatures all at the same time as signs of the Divine Beautiful Names. The value of every other being is restricted to itself, whereas a believing man is as valuable as the total of all beings. Though an individual, he is like a species, even all species. God knows the truth.

Know O friend! Although the truth of something consists in or is restricted to its outward aspect, there is a great distance between them. For example, the belief of an ordinary one in the Unity of God is that he attributes things to none other than the Almighty. This is a simple denial of attributability of all things to any being other than God. Whereas the belief of those who have attained the truth of what Divine Unity really means is that whatever they see and experience, they attribute it to the All-Glorified One. They see on everything His stamp and notice His seal. Such an acknowledgement gives peace to the mind and heart and prevents heedlessness.

Know O friend! The wisdom in God's giving respite to the unbelievers who only aim to live the worldly life is that, albeit unconsciously, they serve to manifest various blessings of God by their labour and artifices, and make arrangements, albeit without knowing, to display the beauties and excellencies of the works of Divine Art, offering them to the views of people. Unbelievers do that unknowingly as a clock tells you the time without knowing what it does.

Know O friend! It is possible for one receiving God's help to proceed from the outward to truth without passing through the intermediate realm of spiritual orders. I have seen in the Qur'an that way leading direct to truth without initiating into a spiritual order and another way leading to attainment of desired (religious) sciences without studying instrumental sciences (such as logic, mathematics, methodology, etc.)

It is what is expected from all-embracing Divine Mercy that

It grants the children of the present time—a time flowing too fast—a short, yet safe, way.

Know O friend! As the existence of a thing and its life is a decisive proof for the necessary existence of its Creator and His Attributes, and a radiant sign that the Creator is One, to Whom all things belong, and that He holds all (material or natural) causes in His "hand", so its decay and death to be replaced with its likes is a manifest evidence for the permanence of the Originator, Returner, Heir to all, and Reviver, and also shows that He has no partners, that is, nothing else has a part in creation, and that He also dominates the inner selves of things, preventing them from controlling their inner selves.

Know O friend! Life says, *There is no god but He, One*, and denies causes having any part in it. While death says, *There is no god but He, having no partners at all*, and denies the inner selves of things having any part in it.

Know O friend! One of the duties of human life is that it should witness the salutations of living beings to the Bestower of Life. It should also witness the worship of all things and announce it as if it was the representative of all of them and their tongue proclaiming their deeds to their Master.

Know O friend! The Qur'an and the one to whom the Qur'an was sent down both inform us of awesome matters and establish tremendous truths. They also lay down immense foundations. For example, they prove and establish the Oneness of the One:

He will roll up the heavens as rolling up scrolls for books; [23]

The earth altogether shall be His handful on Doomsday, and the heavens shall be rolled up in His right hand; [24]

In relation to Him, the matter of the Hour is as a twinkling of the eye, or nearer; [25]

---

23. *al-Anbiya'*, 21.104.
24. *al-Zumar*, 39.67.
25. *al-Nahl*, 16.77.

The seven heavens and the earth and whoever is in them glorify Him.[26]

He has created the heavens and the earth in six days;[27]

He revives the earth after its death;[28] and He resurrects during that revival hundreds of thousands of species of plants and animals, and "inscribes" them on the sheet of the earth all mingled with one another but distinguishing them from one another without the least confusion. The resurrection of all men on the Day of Judgement is not more difficult than that yearly resurrection, for only the number of the flies brought to life in a single summer is many times more the whole number of men to live on the earth from their appearance on the earth until the Last Day. The Qur'an and the one to whom the Qur'an was sent down also say:

God is the Creator of all things and He is Guardian over all things. His is the keys of the heavens and the earth;[29]

He creates you and what you do;[30]

He has prepared a painful torment;[31] and

Whoever does an atom's weight of evil, shall see it.[32]

Concerning the most evident and important matters, the Qur'an and the one on whom the Qur'an was sent down do not view the universe as modern science, philosophy and other human beings do. They instruct you in an art or provide you with a skill with which to know your Maker, Who holds all creatures in His hand and disposes them howsoever He wills, and they show you the inner dimension of existence together with its other dimensions and parts and what they mean for their Creator. They instruct you in a book with all its meaning and connotations. As for the modern scientific approach and philosophy,

---

26. *al-Isra'*, 17.44.
27. *al-A'raf*, 7.54.
28. *al-Rum*, 30.19.
29. *al-Zumar*, 39.62–3.
30. *al-Saffat*, 37. 96.
31. *al-Ahzab*, 33.8.
32. *al-Zilzal*, 99.8.

they describe the creatures completely beyond the reach of their disposal in the true, absolute sense of the word and only the outer aspects of what they can see and not the inner dimensions and meanings, of which they are unaware of. Like a mind occupied with involuntary evil thoughts or whisperings of Satan, they occupy your mind with superficial issues of no use and worth in essence and, without knowing anything of the meaning they bear, instruct you in their outward forms and the parts thereof. They instruct you in a bejewelled book ornate with the explanations of the forms and structures of its letters and their positions with respect to one another.

Since this is the truth, do not judge the truths of the Qur'an and the one on whom it was sent down by the standards of sciences and philosophy, nor weigh them by their balances. The mountains deeply fixed in earth are not weighed on the balances of jewels. The "earthly"—profane—principles of sciences and philosophy are not to be applied to the appraisal and confirmation of the truths of the Qur'an and/or of the one on whom it was sent down. Do not pay any attention to the critics of some small details of those truths who are misguided by fancies issuing from sciences and philosophy.

Know, O one long suffering for some particular misfortunes! Do not divide your "forces" of patience to confront both past and present misfortunes. Dispatch them only against the present ones. For the painful days of the past have joined your "forces" with the spiritual blessings that remain of them and the rewards they gained for you for your next life. Nor do you use up your forces of patience to confront the misfortunes likely to come to you in the future. For the future has not come yet and what it will bring depends on Divine Will. Dispatch all your forces of patience for today, even for this hour. Furthermore, reinforce your forces by smiling at the misfortunes and loving them to make them join your forces and by receiving help from reliance on your Owner, the All-Munificent, the All-Compassionate, the All-Wise. When you do that, your weakest patience will suffice for the greatest of misfortunes.

Know O friend! The Traditions that some persons of defective understanding dismiss as being exaggerated in fact contain some valuable truths. For example, the Prophet, upon him be peace and blessings, is recorded to have said: *If the world had as much weight in the view of God as the wing of a gnat, an unbeliever could not drink a sip of water from it.*[33] The Tradition means that what is manifested in the mirror of your fleeting life from the external face of the world is of no more weight than the wing of a gnat from the eternal world, as a single grain of corn which has the potential to gain permanence by growing into a plant is preferable to so much straw as would fill a vast threshing field but which has only the potential to blow away. Everyone has a world particular to him out of this world. If he views his world as having its meaning in pointing to its true Owner rather than to itself, and as the tillage of the Hereafter and the area where the Divine Beautiful Names are manifested, then it gains a very great value. Otherwise, with respect to its fleeting aspect, it does not have as much value as a single grain. You can compare to this the Traditions concerning the merit of certain particular recitations.

Know O friend! One of the demonstrations that life is based upon mutual assistance, and not upon conflict as some misguided and misguiding philosophers and scientists assert, is that dense earth and hard rocks do not show resistance against the penetration of delicate roots of plants. Rocks crack their hardened hearts by the touching of the silk-like fingers of the daughters of plants, and earth opens its hard breast for the penetration of the veins of plants. The parts of the (body of) the universe co-operate with its sun and moon for the benefit of animals; plants hasten to the aid of animals as food; the elements of sustenance compete to be sustenance for fruits; fruits are adorned to attract the attention of those needing provision; particles (of earth, air and water) co-operate to be food for the cells of the body, and so on. All this is a decisive proof that the general principle in life is mutual assistance. Conflict is only a particular, exceptional principle, notably among some wild animals.

---

33. Related by Tirmidhi, who judged it as authentic, in *al-Jami' al-Saghir*, No. 5168.

Know O friend! The absolute, observable facility in things coming into existence is one of the most evident proofs of the Unity of God. For every thing, especially every living thing, requires for its existence what is necessary for the existence of the whole.[34] If there were more than one Creator—God forbid such a thought and belief—the existence of a single thing would be as difficult as the existence of the whole of the universe.[35]

Know, O carnal, evil-commanding self! You deserve condemnation even for the most noble-seeming of your demands. For although you deeply desire the things pertaining to the Hereafter, you desire them not for the sake of the Hereafter but with the hope of being relieved from the gloom of transience and finding consolation for the pains of mortality. Woe to you for your despicable attitude! How can a king serve a mortal, despicable creature? You build an inn on the columns made of jewels you have taken from the royal castle for one night's dwelling of some animals. (That is, you use the precious faculties given to you to employ for the Hereafter for the satisfaction of your carnal, fleeting desires.) You will cause the castle to collapse on you. You eat up the fruits of the everlasting Paradise in the illusory paradise of the world.

Know, O soul enamoured of itself and relying on its physical existence! You became content with a drop from a mirage of the

----

34. For example, the existence of a single entity, say, a cherry requires the existence and co-operation of the sun, air, earth, water and the elements of its tree. Despite this, the absolute facility in a cherry coming into existence evidently shows that the sun, air, water, earth and its tree are all in the absolutely independent disposal of a single Creator. (Tr.)

35. For, since the creation and disposal of all things require infinite knowledge and power, the existence of more than one creator having infinite knowledge and power is inconceivable because there cannot be two infinites at the same time. Second, it is again inconceivable that a different creator is responsible for the creation and disposal of a certain part of existence and that the creators co-operate among themselves. For as this would cause disagreements among the creators because independence is an essential quality of divinity, and therefore existence would go into utter disorder, the unity and inter-relatedness in existence again require that all the creators supposed must be as knowledgeable and powerful as to know and dispose all existence, which makes the existence of more than one creator of the same qualities absolutely unnecessary. Therefore, association of partners with God, in whatever way or name it is done is utter nonsense, absurdity and ignorance. (Tr.)

ocean of the water of life and a weak radiance at night from the sun of a clear day. The relation of your physical existence with the manifestations of your Creator's Existence is like the relation of the existence of a single soul with all the creatures multiplied by the particles forming those creatures. Your existence points to itself in that respect only, while pointing to the Existence of its Creator in endless respects, as does every creature. With respect to yours, His existence is as manifest as the extent of the greatness of the universe with respect to you. As for your love of your selfhood, it is because your selfhood is the source of your carnal pleasures, the centre of your existence and the mine of your interests and because it is nearer to you than anything else. However, you confuse a dim, fleeting shadow with the very origin of all existence. If you love your selfhood for a transient pleasure, then you have to love Him Who is able to give you infinite eternal pleasures and creates all of that whose happiness makes you happy. If your selfhood is the centre of your existence, then your Lord is the One Who has given you that existence and maintains it together with all those with whose existence yours is related.

If your existence is the mine of your interests, then your Provider is Him in Whose hand is all good. He is the Permanent, Benevolent One and with Him are all your benefits and the benefits of those beneficial to you. If your selfhood is nearer to you (than anything else), then Your Creator is nearer to you than it. His hand reaches what the hand of your selfhood cannot reach and what is beyond the reach of its consciousness. So, you should unite all your love divided among creatures and, adding to it your love of your selfhood, direct it to the Almighty, True Beloved One.

Know O friend! What veils you from God and keeps you in heedlessness is that you restrict your view to things and parts separately and see them attributable to chance and causes. Whereas one who raises his head and can look at the whole and universal with a comprehensive view must find it impossible to attribute even the least thing to the greatest of causes. For example, you can ascribe your food to some causes, but when you see the wilderness of the earth and its utter destitution in winter and then its being adorned and filled with the varieties of food which Divine Power has cooked in the pans of trees and cauldrons of fields and orchards, you will be convinced that it is impossible that the one who provides you could be other than the One Who provides all living things by reviving the earth after its death.

For example, again, you can ascribe the illumination of your house and your (intellectual and spiritual) enlightenment to some apparent causes and say *What has been given to me is because of certain knowledge that I have.*[36] However, when you see that your light comes from the light of daytime and your enlightenment essentially depends on the Source of all lights, you will acquire the conviction that no one other than Him Who alternates day and night by moving the solar system and Who misguides whomever He wills of the shameless sinful souls and guides whomever He wills of the righteous souls by sending down Scriptures for the consideration of the free-willed, is able to illuminate your body and enlighten your mind and heart.

Know, O man! There are awesome issues before you which compel every conscious being to pay attention to them. One of those issues is death, your separation from all that you love and the world together with whatever is in it. Another is your journeying to eternity through awful circumstances. Another issue is your utmost impotence added to your endless poverty in your journeying not restricted to this limited span of your life.

How is it that you can behave as if oblivious of and blind to those issues in the manner of an ostrich which buries its head in the sand so as not to see the hunter? How much longer will you be absorbed in transient, perishable drops—trivialities—and pay no attention to fearful oceans?

Know O friend! Thanks to God, He makes it possible to solve the greatest ontological problems by means of a single rule of

---

36. *al-Qasas*, 28.78.

linguistics. It is the meaning related to the letter and the meaning related to the name.[37] So, this universe is a book and the creatures in it are the words it comprises. Those words should be viewed not on behalf of themselves but on behalf of their Inscriber. That is, they are messages of the Lord manifesting His All-Beautiful Names. The first view, that is, considering creatures on behalf of themselves, is the cause of compound ignorance, obstinate ingratitude and falsely adorned philosophy, while the other is the origin of knowledge, belief and wisdom.

Again, thanks to God, that He makes it possible to solve a tremendous matter pertaining to Divine Lordship by means of a rule of logic, namely the difference between a universal having particulars or individuals and a whole formed of parts.[38] The manifestation[39] of His Grace and Unity—the concentration of the manifestations of His Names on a single thing—may be compared to the universal having particulars or individuals. The manifestation of His Majesty and Oneness—the manifestation of one of His Names on a group or a whole—may be compared to the whole formed of parts. The manifestations of Perfection and Grandeur encompass both. That is, Perfection in the view of the Majesty is like the universal in the view of the whole and the particular in the view of the part.

Know O friend! The world is the "contents" of the Hereafter and has a bearing upon the most important matters connected with the Hereafter. For example, consider the pleasure you take in eating and drinking. The One Who, in this fleeting, despicable abode giving no true pleasure, has included in your body

---

37. That is, a letter has no meaning of itself and therefore points to other than itself, such as the word of which it is a part and its writer, etc. But the word has a complete meaning of itself and therefore primarily points to itself. (Tr.)

38. For example, the human species has universality and an individual human being is a particular one from amongst that universal entity, while a human being is a whole entity formed of parts. A particular or individual carries all the attributes the species has, while a part does not have all the attribute the whole has. (Tr.)

39. God has two general kinds of manifestation: one is the manifestation of His Grace, which is the origin of mercy, forgiveness, provision and the like, the other the manifestation of His Majesty, the origin of glory, awe, wrath, chastisement, and so on. (Tr.)

senses, feelings, systems, organs, parts and instruments to taste all the material bounties and to sense the varieties of the manifestations of His Names on things pertaining to your physical existence—the Wise One Who has so has provided you with different senses—has certainly prepared for His guests everlasting feasts in the palaces *underneath which rivers flow and where they will remain for ever.*[40]

Know, O fearful, helpless Said! When you fear or love the created, fear becomes a painful trouble and love a distressing affliction. For you fear one who has no mercy for you or gives no ear to your requests, and you love one who does not recognize you or despises you because of your love or does not keep company with you, one who rather abandons you in spite of your desire. So, you should fear and love your All-Munificent and Compassionate Creator so that your love may become an innocent, eternal happiness without pain or humiliation, and your fear an agreeable humbling by taking refuge in the bosom of Mercy, just as an infant's fear of his mother which compels him to throw himself into her warm arms, becomes a pleasure for him.

Know, O friend! You are the fruit or seed of the tree of creation. Although with respect to your physical existence, you are a weak, impotent, despicable, small-sized individual being, the All-Wise Maker has favored you with a universal disposition. By giving life to your body, He has freed you from the confines of an insignificant, individual existence and enabled you to travel through all parts of this visible world with your very developed, inquiring senses so that each may obtain its particular nourishment. Also, by making you a human being, He has endowed you with a potential to flourish, like a tree growing from a seed, through all corners of the physical dimension of existence. Further, He has bestowed on you belief and the religion of Islam and thereby equipped you with a potential to acquire a universal existence. Furthermore, by favoring you with knowledge and love of Him, He has made you like a comprehensive

---

40. *al-Ma'ida*, 5.119.

light. Now, it is up to you to choose one of the two alternatives: if you attach yourself to the world and bodily desires, you will become a weak, humiliated individual. If you use all the instruments of your life, your senses and faculties, on behalf of the greatest humanity, which is Islam, then you will acquire a universal existence and become a central, illuminating lamp.

Know, O one who loves the worldly things with which he is connected only to the extent that his restricted physical existence allows him! Since you spend your love away from its proper place, you are distressed. If, however, you love the One of Unity and love other things on behalf of Him and by His leave, you will be saved from the distresses and pains of separation (from the worldly things you love). You will be like him who, by virtue of faithfully serving a king who has relations with everyone in his kingdom, hears with the ears of his lord and sees with his eyes whatever takes place throughout the kingdom as if present in all places and beside everyone at the same time. By using all the communicative systems the king uses, he hears all the pleasant music and sees all the beautiful scenes throughout the vast lands of the king.

Know, O one who shows great curiosity to learn about the moon and other planets! If you were told that someone has come from the moon to tell you about it, you would sacrifice half of your life to hear him. You would also sacrifice it for the sake of knowing about your future. However, there has come a man who tells you about Him in the realm of Whose rule the moon is less than a moth flying around a light: it flies around the light among innumerable candles hanging from the ceiling of the house which He has prepared for His guests. That man also tells about eternity and eternal life together with fundamental truths and awesome matters the least of which is more important than the explosion (destruction) of the earth and the moon. If you would like to hear him, give ear to the chapters of the Book he has brought which begin with *When the sun is folded up*,[41] and *When the heaven is rent asunder*,[42] and others like them.

---

41. *al-Takwir*, 81.1.   42. *al-Infitar*, 82.1.

Further, he shows you a straight, levelled path leading to unity and saves you from confusion in twisted, crooked ways of misguidance. He extends to your hand the "firm handle", a chain of ascension, which keeps whoever holds fast to it from drowning in the levels of darkness of the bewildering multiplicity of things. He also offers you the water of life, eternal life, from the pure source of belief, so that you may be saved from the fire of separation from all that you love in the world. Furthermore, he informs you of what pleases your Creator to Whose command the sun, the moon and all other stars are subjected and by Whose leave the earth was settled and stabilized, and of what He commands you to do. He also translates to you the communication and conversation of the King of eternity to Whose Power there is no limit with one infinitely weak and poor like you.

Such being the truth, should you not renounce your self in order to perceive the guidance of the Qur'an? Should you not forget your desires to give ear to the Messenger of the All-Merciful One? Should you not welcome His Messenger with belief and submission? Should you not sincerely love him who has come with peace and salvation, upon him be peace and blessings? Should you not feel the need of learning from him what our All-Affectionate Master, the All-Bounteous Owner, asks of us, may His Glory be exalted?

Know O friend! We see the All-Wise Maker with the perfection of His Wisdom and clearly witness that His acts are absolutely free from waste and futility. He weaves extensive, enduring and precious "textiles" from despicable and very small things. Again, by virtue of His acts being absolutely free from waste and pointlessness, He charges a single thing, each of the organs or apparatuses of man's body, for example, and especially those in his head, with a variety of very important duties. If a different organ the size of a mustard-seed were required to do each of the duties with which the organs in your head are charged, then your head would be as big as Mount Sinai. Do you not see the tongue—how, besides its other very important tasks, it functions as an inspector of the bounties stored in the treasury of the All-Merciful One, all edible things and beverages prepared in the kitchen of His Power? It has tasks to the number of the tastes of all kinds of food. Does this purposeful activity not point to the fact that the Maker is certainly weaving from the things moving in the flux of time, from (the contents) of past days, years and centuries, "textiles" for the world of the Unseen and the Hereafter by moving the "shuttle" of day for the alternation of day and night and the change of seasons? He also does the same weaving in man, who is the index of the universe. He records and permanently preserves the minutes of his life in the "textiles" or on the "sheets" of his memory, and employs death as a means of transportation from this visible, narrow world to the unseen worlds of purity and permanence. We hear from the sources of Revelation that the minutes of man's life return to him either darkened with heedlessness and sins or illuminated with the lamps of good deeds hanging from the links of those minutes.

Know O friend! The All-Beautiful, All-Wise Maker makes in greatly different sizes the members of each species of animals, especially including those flying on pairs of wings and fish, and angels and all other creatures from atoms to galaxies. He makes the small a specimen of the big. Some of His purposes for doing so are that man may be guided to truths and easily reflect on His creation and read and understand the missives of His Power, and that He may display the perfection of that Power and exhibit His two kinds of art, one originating in His Grace, the other in His Majesty. Things too small and discerned with difficulty usually remain unknown, so when they are "written" in "capital letters", they are saved from remaining unknown. Similarly, things too big for the eye to encompass and for the mind to comprehend also remain unknown. When they are "written" in relatively "small letters", they can easily be seen and understood. Despite this fact, the carnal, evil-commanding self taught by Satan thinks that the small size is the result of weakness or defect in artistry and therefore small things can be attributed to deaf and blind causes. It likewise claims that things being too big show the lack of any wisdom and purpose in them and are therefore attributable to chance.

Know O friend! It is said that the almost infinite multiplicity of things and the absolute abundance in provision mean futility and contradict wisdom. If there is only one purpose for the existence of things, especially of living beings, such multiplicity and abundance may be said to contradict wisdom in creation and life. However, there are innumerable purposes for each existent thing, which has also various tasks and a great variety of fruits. Do you not see that your tongue has as many tasks as the number of the hairs on your head? There are endless purposes for that abundance and with respect to tasks with which each thing is charged, there is never any contradiction with wisdom. Although an army is mainly charged with guarding the frontiers or defending the country (against possible foreign attacks), we feel compelled to have numerous troops, since an army has other functions and duties, such as representing the authority of a government and guarding the country also against internal conflicts.

Know O friend! A man can be seen together with his works of art, but there are seventy thousand veils between God and His works. If you could view the creatures of God all together at one time, the veils of darkness might be lifted, and then only the veils of light would remain. The most direct and shortest way to reach that level of vision is within you; it can be found in the outer world only by an intense love.

Know O friend! Each member of most of the reproducing species of plants and animals has a tendency or intention to invade the whole of the earth and capture it to use it as a place of worship by manifesting the Names of its Creator. Each of them has a particular type of worship of its Creator, Who alone infinitely deserves worship. If you like, look at a melon and its seeds, and fruit-bearing trees and the seeds in their fruits, and also at the fish and birds and their eggs. However, since the world is too small for all of them to fully realize their "intention", the all-encompassing Knowledge of the Knower of the seen and the Unseen, Who knows what has happened, what is happening and what is yet to happen, is expected to accept their intended worship.

Know O friend! Out of the purposes for the existence of things, the Qur'an sometimes mentions those related to man. This does not mean that those things were created only for the purposes mentioned. It is for drawing man's attention to their benefits for him and to the order and harmony they display and thereby to the Names of their Maker they point to. For man pays attention only to what is related to him and prefers a thing related to him even if so small as the tiniest particle in preference to a "sun" with which he has no relations. For example, *And the moon: We have determined stations (phases) for it,*[43] *that you might know the number of years and the reckoning.*[44] This is only one of thousands of purposes for the existence of the moon. It does not mean that the moon was created only for this purpose, which is mentioned because it is the most evident for man.

Know O friend! One of the inimitable stamps and the seals particular to Him, and also one of the most evident signs of unity of the boundless Power and endless Knowledge observed in the absolute authority over existence and the absolute firmness and facility in its creation and maintenance, is that innumerable different things are created from a simple single thing. For example, earth is the main element for all kinds of plants to come into existence and be maintained, and all the organs of an animal, including its flesh, bones, blood and tissues, are made from simple food. Again, a thing of the same nature and composition, man's body, for example, is made from innumerable kinds of food.

Glory be to Him Who has absolute power to make all things from a single thing and a single thing from all things.

Know O friend! In the Qur'anic statement, *or are We the sowers?*[45] there is a profound meaning. As you keep some of the

---

43. *Ya Sin*, 36.39.
44. *Yunus*, 10.5.
45. *al-Waqia*, 56.64.

seeds and store them to sow later, so also the Heir to all things, the Quickener, the Preserver, Who revives the earth after its death, records the results of the "deeds" of all plants and preserves them to scatter in many areas according to certain measures. Then, He causes them to produce leaves and blossom, as if each recited *When the records are laid open*.[46] Consider how ardently you take care of preserving some seeds and try to understand how perfectly the Absolute Preserver preserves innumerable of those delicate cases which contain the indexes of their parents determined by Destiny, from numerous changing and corrupting factors, and distinguishes them without the least confusion. This preserving does not leave you to your own devices so that you can do whatever you wish and then die for eternal rest. *Does man think that he will be left to roam at will?*[47] No! You will certainly be called to account for whatever you do, even the least of what you do.

Know O friend! One of the tasks with which man's life is charged is that judging from the particular attributes and essential qualities he and his species have, he should perceive the essential Qualities and Attributes of his Creator. But in order to understand His most comprehensive acts in the destruction and re-building of the universe and resurrection of all the dead together with all other disposals of His in the other world, you should consider His acts in the revival of the earth in spring and its death in autumn and winter. In order to see the like of the Supreme Resurrection and the interpretation of the verses such as *When the sun is folded up*,[48] reflect upon spring and autumn.

Know O friend! Islam is so comprehensive that its essentials encompass everything, every matter, from the most universal ones such as the Greatest Names and Attributes of the Owner of the Supreme Throne and the creation of the Supreme Throne, the heavens and the earth together with the angels particular to them, down to the most particular such as occurrences to man's

---

46. *al-Takwir*, 81.10.
47. *al-Qiyama*, 75.36.
48. *al-Takwir*, 81.1.

heart. They also encompass with its most firm principles what is between the heavens and the earth!

In the Name of God, the Merciful, the Compassionate.

Let not the life of the world beguile you, nor let the deceiver beguile in regard to God.[49]

Know, O one who invites Muslims to the worldly life which is a plaything in the hands of sleep and sport, urging them to leave the sphere of what God has made lawful out of pure things sufficient for them to satisfy their licit desires, and to enter the sphere of what God has forbidden out of bad, foul things, which will compel them to abandon some of the public symbols of their religion or even the religion itself altogether: in regard to them, you resemble a drunken one who cannot distinguish a wild, ravenous lion from a docile horse, or a hangman's noose from a child's skipping rope, or a gaping wound from an opening rose. He supposes the lion to be the horse; the noose to be the skipping rope, and the open wound a red rose. Despite this, he thinks himself as a guide putting things right. He comes to a man who is in a dreadful condition—a strange lion behind him waiting to attack, a gallows in front of him, and two grievous wounds on either side of his body. He has two kinds of medicine in his hand; if he uses them, his wounds will change into two red roses by God's leave. He has also two talismans, one in his tongue, the other in his heart. If he uses them, the lion behind him will change by God's leave into a horse taking him to the presence of his munificent master who invites him to the abode of peace to feast him, and the hangman's noose dangling from the tree of decay and mortality will change by God's grace into a means of transport to carry him through scenes continuously changing to increase the pleasure taken in the renewal of their beauties and their forms and favors through the days, seasons, years and centuries.

---

49. *Luqman*, 31. 33.

The drunken one says to that man:

– Leave those talismen and medicine! Come and let us play and amuse ourselves!

The man replies:

– What is allowed me to do by preserving those talismen and medicine is enough for my pleasure. There is no pleasure and happiness save by them. If it is possible for you to kill the lion of death which will die only in Paradise[50] and remove this device implanted in earth by the decree of the Ruler of the earth, that is, remove the device of decay and mortality, by changing the earth into something other than the earth, and if it is also possible for you to heal this wound of mine (the wound of impotence) invading all my life by changing my fleeting, perishable life into a permanent, everlasting one and cure that other wound invading all my being by changing my poor, destitute being into a perpetual, rich one, then let us do what you propose. Otherwise, O drunken devil, if you have no power at all to do those four things I have just mentioned, then go away! You can deceive only those drunken like yourself, who cannot distinguish between laughing and crying, permanence and transience, remedy and ailment, and deviation and guidance. As for me, God is sufficient for me, how good a Guardian He is, and how good a Helper.

Know O friend! The students of the corrupt, misguided civilization and the pupils of harmful, misguiding philosophy are drunken with their abnormal greed and unusual passions. They attempt to invite Muslims to follow foreign traditions and customs and abandon their public symbols radiant with the light of Islam. The students of the Qur'an respond to them:

– O misguided, heedless ones! If you are able to remove decay and death from the world and impotence and poverty from man, then you may be indifferent to religion and its public sym-

---

50. A Tradition says that on the Day of Judgement death will be brought in the form of a ram and slaughtered between Paradise and Hell, meaning that there will no longer be dying in both Paradise and Hell. *Muslim*, Hadith no. 2849; also recorded in *Bukhari*. (Tr.)

bols. Otherwise, keep silent and stop your clamouring, which is no more than the buzzing of a fly compared to the thunder-like cry of the four things mentioned above and the laws of creation and life proclaiming with their loudest voice the necessity of religion and following its public symbols. *When the Qur'an is recited, give ear to it and pay heed, haply so you will find, and be treated with, mercy.*[51]

Indeed, there is behind me the lion of the appointed hour of death ever-threatening me. If you give the ear of belief to the voice of the Qur'an, then that lion will change into a horse and separations (from those we love) into a *Buraq* (mount of the world of the Unseen) taking you to the Mercy of the All-Merciful, the All-Compassionate, to the Presence of my Master, the All-Affectionate, the All-Munificent. Otherwise, death is a rapacious lion which will tear me into pieces despite my desire, and eternally separate me from all that I love. Again, before me are the devices of decay and transience placed in alternating day and night, and the devices of perishing and separation appearing through the waves of seasons and years. These devices are placed to hang me together with all my beloved ones. If you pay heed with conviction to the guidance of the Qur'an, then these devices will become a mount on which to make a pleasant journey on the stream of time and ocean of the world to observe the operations of Divine Power through seasons changing and following one another by the wheel of the sun and the rotation of the earth wrapping around its head the turban of days and nights and wearing the garments of summer and winter one over the other. During that journey, you can also observe the continuous renewal of the manifestations of Divine Names on moving objects, in changing mirrors and on altering tablets through the alternation of days and nights.

Moreover, on my right side there is the invading wound of infinite poverty. I am poorer than all other animate beings, that is, I have as many material and spiritual needs as all other animal beings have, while my power to need them is lesser than

---

51. *al-A'raf*, 7.204.

that of a sparrow. If I cure that wound of mine with the remedy of the Qur'an, then that painful, absolute poverty changes into a pleasure-giving zeal to sit at the feast of Mercy, and into a pleasant appetite for the fruits of the Mercy of the All-Merciful, the All-Compassionate. The pleasure of feeling one's poverty and impotence before the Almighty, becomes much greater than that of being apparently rich and powerful. Otherwise, I am certain to suffer the pains of being needy and the humiliation of begging from and bowing before whoever I expect to satisfy my needs.

On my left side there is the deep wound of infinite impotence despite unending hostilities and dangers. The pain of fear destroys the pleasure of the worldly life. But if I pay heed in submission to the call of the Qur'an, then my impotence leads me to have trust in the Absolutely Powerful One and find a point of reliance to be secure against all hostilities. Otherwise, I will continue to suffer hostilities and dangers in my boundless impotence.

Furthermore, I am on a long journey extending through the grave and the Resurrection to eternity. Neither the world nor human reason show me a light to illuminate the veils of darkness enveloping the way, nor do they provide us with any food necessary for that journeying. Only by the light to be obtained from the sun of the Qur'an of miraculous exposition and the food to be had from the treasury of the All-Merciful One can we illuminate our way and go on journeying. Now, if you have something to keep me from this journeying provided it should not be in the form of highway robbery through misguidance, which means throwing me from the mouth of the grave into the dark pits of eternal annihilation, a state much more terrible and dreadful than the journeying itself, if you have that something, then declare it. Otherwise, keep silent and let the Qur'an say what it says. While I am "reading" these five "verses" in the book of creation—that is, the decay and ephemerality of the world, the death of man and his impotence and poverty, and the long journey required of man—how can I follow you, O conceited, deceived one, especially after I hear the Qur'anic verse, *Let not the life of the world beguile you, nor let the deceiver beguile in regard to*

God?[52] No one follows you except those drunken with the wine of politics or passion for fame, or ambition for praise, or ethnic or tribal preferences or the atheistic philosophy or modern dissipation. However, the blows struck against man, the terrible slaps he gets in the face, will bring him to his senses. Unlike an animal, man does not suffer only the pains of the present time, but in addition to the pains of the present, anxieties for future and the griefs of and for the past also strike him on the head.

If you do not desire to remain the most wretched of all animals and the most foolish and misguided of them, keep silent and give the ear of belief to the good news of the Qur'an: *Assuredly, God's friends no fear shall come upon them, neither shall they grieve. They believe and refrain from sins in fear of God. For them is good tidings in the life of the world and in the Hereafter. No change can there be in the words of God; that is the supreme triumph.*[53]

> *In the Name of God, the Merciful, the Compassionate.*
>
> *By the fig and the olive, and Mount Sinai, and this inviolate city. We indeed created man in the fairest stature, then We reduced him to the lowest of the low except those who believe and do good deeds; for them is a wage unfailing. What then shall contradict you as to the Judgement? Is not God the wisest of judges?*[54]

Know O friend! The firmness of the artistry in everything and its perfection point to the fact that the Maker of all things is present and near all things, while He is not contained by space at the same time. Because of man's need for all things from the smallest to the biggest, it does not befit him to worship other than Him in Whose hand is the dominion of all things and with Whom are the treasuries of all things. With respect to existence, invention, and doing good, man has a being very impotent and defective, more powerless than an ant or bee and weaker than a spider and gnat, while in regard with destruction and evil-doing,

---

52. *Luqman*, 31.33.
53. *Yunus*, 10.62–4.
54. *al-Tin*, 97.1-8.

it is greater than the heavens, earth and mountains. For example, when he does good, he can do it within the reach of his hand, while the evil he does may have a far-reaching influence.

The evil of denying the Almighty means condemning the whole of the universe or all creatures by reducing them from being the missives of the Lord and the mirrors of Divinity to being things consisting only in certain amounts of matter subject to change and decay with which chance plays aimlessly. With this evil, man himself is reduced from being a well-composed, harmonious piece of poetry displaying the manifestations of the Divine Names, and the seed of a permanent, everlasting tree, and a vicegerent of God on the earth superior to the greatest of creatures by virtue of bearing the Supreme Trust, to the lowest degree of being the most debased of mortal animate beings and the most powerless and destitute of them. Also, with respect to his ego, man has free will as weak as a hair, with a very little capacity, faint and short-lived like a distant flash of light and a very restricted, feeble existence. Whereas, in regard to his impotence and poverty, he has so great a capacity that he can be a vast mirror for the manifestations of the infinitely Powerful and eternally Wealthy One.

Again, with respect to his worldly, animal life, despite being like a seed endowed with innumerable apparatuses to grow into a tree spreading high into all corners of space, he is reduced to being one striving, like a hen scratching the soil, to obtain some mean substances, and thereafter to dissolve in earth. But in regard with his immaterial life, he is like a perpetual tree with the branches of desire extending into eternity.

Again, with respect to his working and efforts, man is a weak, impotent animal, having a narrow sphere with a radius as short as the reach of his hand. However, with regard to praying and asking, he is a noble guest of the All-Merciful One Who has opened for him the treasuries of His Mercy and subjugated to him all the marvels of His art, and has a vast sphere with a radius extending where his eyes, even his imagination, go, even vaster than that.

Again, with respect to the pleasures of his animal life and its perfectibility, tranquillity and stability, he is lower than a sparrow, for his pleasures are clouded by his griefs for the past and anxieties for future. Whereas in regard to the apparatuses given to him and the variety of his senses and feelings, and the developing capacity of his potentials, his main task in life is that he must observe all creatures with reflectively and contemplatively, and witness their glorifications of God. He must also pray to God for his needs and worship Him in due perception and acknowledgement of his impotence, poverty and defectiveness.

With respect to his nature so comprehensive that he may worship his Creator in many ways, he is many times superior to all other creatures. A man with a bit of intellect must conclude that all those apparatuses have been given to him for an eternal life, not for this transient one. For instance, if we saw that a man had given one of his servants ten gold liras to buy himself a garment of a particular cloth, which the servant did, and then gave another servant a thousand gold liras also to buy himself a garment, we would conclude that the thousand gold liras were not given to the second servant to buy a garment of the same cloth as the first bought. The cloth which the second servant should choose must be a hundred times more valuable than the other. If, despite this, because of his stupidity, that servant bought a garment of the same cloth as the first one had bought, he would certainly be sentenced to a long, severe punishment.

Despite (or, rather, because of) his lack of power and strength, man is many times stronger and more powerful than other animate beings, for through his prayer and asking for help, he is subjected to what he cannot obtain the least part of which with his own power. Like an infant, he reaches through his crying what he cannot reach with a power thousands of times greater than his own. He gains superiority to all other animate beings by other creatures being subjected to him, not through his own unassisted power of grasp, overcoming and attraction. Therefore, he should pronounce his impotence, weakness, poverty and destitution and implore God for help and supplicate and worship.

By virtue of observing the beauties of the perfections of the splendor of Divine Lordship, heralding the marvels of the manifestations of His sacred Names, perceiving the contents of the treasuries of His Mercy, knowing the gems stored in the treasuries of the manifested Names, studying and reflecting on the missives of the Pen of the Power, and looking forward to seeing the subtleties of His creatures, man is the noblest of creation and ruler of the earth.

In the Name of God, the Merciful, the Compassionate.

O mankind! You are poor before God and in absolute need of Him.[55]

Flee unto God.[56]

Know, O failing, helpless, poor Said! With respect to your selfhood, you are constantly imperfect, with boundless helplessness, infinite poverty, limitless needs and innumerable desires. As you are given hunger and thirst in order to know the pleasure of the Almighty's bounties, so also you are loaded with failures, poverty, impotence and neediness so that through the telescope of your failures, you should view the lofty works of the All-Glorified's Perfection, and using your poverty as a measure, you should view the degrees of His Wealth and Mercy, your impotence, His Power and Grandeur, and the variety of your needs, the variety of His bounties and favours.

The purpose for your creation is servanthood, which means declaring before the door of His Mercy—your failures with "I ask God for forgiveness" and "All glory be to God"; your poverty with "God is sufficient for us" and "All praise be to God" and begging from Him; your impotence with "There is no power and strength save with Him" and "God is the Greatest", and by asking Him for help. Thus the Beauty and Grace of His Lordship are seen in the mirror of your servanthood.

---

55. *al-Fatir*, 35.15.
56. *adh-Dhariyat*, 51.50.

In the Name of God, the Merciful, the Compassionate

Surely the pious will be in bliss. While the wicked will surely be in blazing Fire.[57]

Know, O heedless Said! Everyone will follow either of the two ways in the journey through life to the grave. Those two ways are of equal length but one of them is harmless; indeed, as is unanimously attested by the people of insight and discernment, there is great benefit in it. Nine out of the ten who follow that way obtain that benefit. As for the other way, while there is no benefit in it, there is, as is agreed by the people of discernment and religious scholarship, great harm in it. It is ninety-nine percent harmful, although the one following it, unlike those following the other way, does not have to carry any weapon and food. In appearance, he has no burden, nothing to bear. However, there is, on the back of his heart, a burden a hundred times heavier, and on the shoulders of his spirit, the burden of frights and terrors. The following parable will make perceptible to you what is conceptual or abstract:

For example, you desire to go to Istanbul or someone sends you there. There are two ways leading there one on the right, the other on the left, both being of the same length but different from each other with respect to the harm or benefit in them and ease or difficulty in following them. The people of discernment, observation and sufficient experience are agreed that on the right way there is very great benefit, with no harm at all, but those who choose to follow it are required to carry weapon and food. However, they go relieved of any burden on their hearts and spirits of fear and being obliged to others (for the satisfaction of their needs), a burden as heavy as mountains. By contrast, as millions of people of experience and religious scholarship attest, there is no benefit in the left way, although, in appearance, those following it have no burden, with neither weapon nor food to carry. However, the burden on the shoulders of their spirits because of the fear they suffer and on the back of their hearts caused by being obliged to others for the

---

57. al-*Infitar*, 82.13–4.

satisfaction of their needs is a thousand times heavier than carrying a weapon and food. Those who have either all but completed their journeying or witnessed what the wayfarers face both during and after journeying, inform us that those following the right way travel in security and, on reaching their destination, nine out of ten are welcomed with great reward. While those following the left, dangerous way suffer much fear and hunger during journeying and, because of fear and neediness, they have to bow in humiliation before everything or everyone. When they reach their destination, they are either called to account for their journeying or killed, and only one or, at the most, two out of ten can be saved. One with a bit of intelligence does not choose what is harmful for the sake of not having to carry any burden. How can something ninety-nine percent harmful be preferred to what is ninety-nine percent of great benefit?

The traveler is you. Istanbul is the intermediate world of the grave and the Hereafter. The right way is the way of the Qur'an requiring five daily prayers to be done after belief. The left way is the way of the sinful and rebellious. People of discernment and experience are saints who experience in person the pleasure in Islamic truths. A saint experiences what an ordinary man believes. As for the weapon and food, they are the religious obligations including the five daily prayers that include confirmation of Divine Unity which, in turn, includes having the points of reliance on Go and ask Him for help, which means placing one's trust in the All-Powerful, Preserving and Knowing One, and on the All-Wealthy, Munificent and Compassionate. Those following the way of the Qur'an are saved from bowing in humiliation before whatever or whoever they expect may benefit or harm them. For the conviction that there is no deity but God means that no one but He or save by His leave is able to give harm or benefit.

In the Name of God, the Merciful, the Compassionate
This life of the world is but a diversion and a sport; while the home of the Hereafter, that is Life if they but knew.[58]

---

58. *al-Ankabut*, 29.64.

Know, O Said journeying toward old age and to the grave and to eternity! Your Owner gave you the life of this world to obtain the necessities of both lives each according to its length. But you have spent all of it in this transient life which is only like a drop of mirage compared to an ocean. If you have enough sense, you should spend half or a third of it for the everlasting life. And yet, how strange it is that those foolish ones like you are called intelligent and learned.

For example, can there be one more foolish than this servant? His master gives him twenty-four gold liras and sends him from Burdur to Antalya (provinces in southern Turkey) and therefrom to Damascus, Madina and the Yemen. He orders him to spend the gold liras to buy what is necessary during the journey. He lets him go to Antalya however he wishes, whether on foot or by a vehicle, but after Antalya he has to continue his way by vehicle. If he buys a ticket, he can travel by ship or train or air and arrive in each city within a day. Whereas, if he does not have a ticket, he will have to travel alone with great difficulties.

However, that foolish traveler spends twenty-three gold liras in two days. He is told: "Spend at least the rest to buy the necessities of your journey. If you do that, your master may have mercy on you." But he answers: "I will not spend it on something which will probably give no benefit." Then he is told:

– How foolish you are! Your reason allows you to set aside half of your wealth to spend in a lottery in which a thousand people participate and therefore to take a great risk for the sake of a chance of one in a thousand. Yet your reason does not allow you to set aside one of the twenty-four parts of your wealth for the sake of a chance of nine hundred and ninety-nine out of a thousand, as is attested by millions of people of certified knowledge. While you accept the news or information an ordinary man gives about some possible material benefit you may obtain, why should you not accept the tidings given by the suns and stars of mankind? Furthermore, two men confirming a thing are preferred to thousands who negate or deny it. For example, the testimony of two men as to having seen the crescent of the holy month of Ramadan is preferred to thousands of others who deny its appearance.

The traveler in the parable is you. Burdur is your world. Antalya is the grave. Damascus is the intermediate world between this and the next. As for the Yemen, it is the realms after the Resurrection. The twenty-four gold liras are the twenty-four hours of a day. You spend twenty-three of them on the affairs of the transient life but show laziness when it comes to spending only one out of the twenty-four in doing the five daily prayers which will serve as the most essential food during the long journeying.

This parable explains one of the profound meanings of the verses: *Paradise shall be brought forward for the God-fearing, and Hell advanced for the perverse.*[59]

Know, O heedless one who has renounced the religious life for the sake of worldly benefits! I will speak to you in a parable containing truths pertaining to both the world and the religious life.

There were once two brothers, one well-disciplined and well-mannered, the other badly-behaved. They set out on a journeying and after a while they come to a fork in their road. The right fork required obligatory observance of the law which governed that road, while the left fork promised a certain kind of freedom, without any obligation.

The well-disciplined brother took the right fork, accepting dependence on law and order. The badly-mannered one took the left fork without undertaking any obligation. He headed for the north and reached a desert. Suddenly he heard a terrible sound and saw a lion ready to attack him. He ran away and, happening to come across a waterless well sixty meters deep, jumped into it. Half-way down, his hands met a tree growing out of the walls of the well. The tree had two roots. Two rats, one white and the other black, were gnawing away at them. The man looked up and saw that the lion was waiting at the top of the well. He

---

59. *al-Shu'ara'*, 26.90–91.

looked down and there was a horrible dragon almost at his feet, with its mouth as large as the mouth of the well gaping to receive him. When he looked around him, he saw harmful vermin everywhere. Then he looked again at the tree. It was actually a fig tree but it had a great variety of fruits .

There, hanging in the well, he was very much afraid. Although he was inwardly distressed about this situation and his spirit and heart were complaining, under the influence of his evil-commanding self, he pretended to himself that he was in a garden and began to eat of the fruits. As is declared in a *hadith qudsi* (a saying from the Prophet, the wording of which belongs to the Prophet but the meaning to God): *I treat My servant in the way he thinks of Me,*[60] this wretched man remained in the well in this terrible condition. He did not die but he did not live well either. And, because of his lack of understanding, he did not perceive that there could not have been any coincidences in those affairs.

Leaving that wretched man in the torment he suffered, let us follow the prudent, fortunate brother. Being a well-mannered one who always thought of the good, see how he benefited from where his brother got no benefit. He happened to enter a garden and came across, besides lovely flowers and attractive fruits, ruined or ugly things in it. He concerned himself with what was good and beautiful and therefore found ease and was generally happy with everything.

Having continued his way, that man too reached a desert and heard the sound of the lion which was about to attack him. He too was afraid but not as much as his brother, because he thought that the lion might be in the service of the ruler of the desert. This disciplined man also fled and jumped down a well sixty meters deep that happened to be there and, half-way down, caught hold of a tree having two roots. He too noticed a pair of rats gnawing at the roots of the tree. Looking up, he saw the lion and on looking down, he saw a dragon almost at his feet with a mouth as wide as the mouth of the well. He too was

60. *Muslim*, Hadith no. 2675; *Tirmidhi*, Hadith no. 3538; also recorded in *Bukhari*.

afraid but much less than his brother because, being wise and self-disciplined, he inferred that all those strange happenings were arranged by someone and constituted a sign. He thought that the one who must have arranged all those things was testing him. His fear turned into curiosity about knowing the one who made himself known by all those things. Then his curiosity aroused in him a love for the owner of the signs. On seeing the fig tree bearing a variety of fruits, his fear completely disappeared, because he came to understand that all those things were for a purpose. If not, the fig tree could not have borne the fruits of other trees. They must have been the foods that the ruler of the desert had prepared for his guests. His love of him aroused in the man the desire to discover what the signs meant and the key to the meaning of the signs was inspired in him. He called: "I have abandoned all other things for your sake and relied on you." Following that call, the wall of the well unexpectedly parted, and a door opened onto a wonderful, pleasant garden. He saw the dragon and the beast change into two servants inviting him in.

Now, compare the positions of these two brothers: one is about to fall into the mouth of the dragon, while the other is invited to enter a brilliant garden full of flowers and fruits. The former is terribly anxious and suffers fear bursting from the depth of his heart. The latter studies what he witnesses and his fear gives rise to love, respect and knowledge. The former is in loneliness, despair and gloom, while the latter sees himself in a friendly situation and is in hope and expectation. The former is the target of the attacks of terrifying enemies, while the latter is welcomed and served as a guest. The former adds to his distress by eating apparently delicious but actually poisonous fruits which are only presented as samples, not intended to be consumed for their own sake but to persuade the consumers to seek out the originals and become customers of them, while the latter postpones eating and enjoys the anticipation.

Now we can interpret the parable:

One of the brothers is the spirit of a believer and the heart of a righteous one, while the other is the spirit of an unbeliever and the heart of a rebellious sinful. Of the two ways, the one on the right is the way of the Qur'an and faith, whereas the other is the way of unbelief and rebellion. The desert is the world, and the lion who turns up unexpectedly is death. The well is the life of man, and sixty metres in depth is our average life span corresponding to sixty years. The tree in the well is life itself, the two rats gnawing its roots are day and night. The dragon in the well is the grave opening, opening on to the Hereafter. The vermin on the walls of the well are the troubles people face on this earth. And the fruits on the tree are the bounties of this world presented as samples from the blessings of the Hereafter, inviting customers towards the fruits of Paradise. The poisonous among them are the forbidden ones. As for the sign, it is the wisdom in creation, and the key, *God, there is no deity but He, the All-Living, the Self-Subsistent.* That is, "O God! You are the Object of my worship and (to obtain) your good pleasure is my aim in life."

The changing of the mouth of the dragon into a door to the garden denotes that the grave is the door to the Mercy of the All-Merciful One through the Garden for the people of the Qur'an and belief. However, for the people of misguidance and rebellion, the grave is the door to the dark pits of loneliness and terror in the intermediate world which is like a dungeon, like the belly of the dragon.

The ravenous lion changes into a disciplined and trained horse. This means that, for the misguided, death is an eternal separation from loved ones and a deportation from their false, worldly paradise into the dungeon of the grave. For the rightly guided, by contrast, it is a means of reunion with the friends and companions and of return to their home. It is for them a departure from the dungeon of the world into eternal gardens to receive the wage for the services done while in the world which will be bestowed out of the grace of the All- Affectionate and Bounteous and the All-Requiter of good and evil and Merciful One, may His Majesty be exalted and there is no deity but He.

Know, O conceited Said, who desires to be praised for even what he has not done! You have no right to be conceited and proud. For you are only the origin of evils and imperfections. If there is good in your selfhood, it is only in proportion to your partial free will, while your free will causes very great evils. Since your imperfections cause the fruits destined for you to fall, you deserve great losses and shame.

Your like is that of a foolish, conceited one who has entered into a commercial partnership with a group on a vessel. While all the others do their duties, he neglects to do his own, which is to turn the steering-wheel. As a result, the vessel sinks and they lose a thousand gold liras. They tell him that he must compensate them for the whole of the loss, but he responds: "No! Rather, we should share it among us." Afterwards, they set out on another voyage and this time they earn a thousand gold liras. They tell him that they should share the profit according to the capital of each. But the man answers: "No! Rather, all of the profit belongs to me. Did you not previously attribute all the loss to me? Now, all the profit belongs to me." They tell him:

– O ignorant one! The existence of something depends on the existence of all its parts and the presence of all the conditions necessary for its existence. This is why the fruits of existence are shared among its constituents. Profit is something which has a positive, sensed existence. Whereas loss means "non-existence" and something existent can go to non-existence by the destruction of a single part of it or the non-presence of one of the conditions for its maintenance.

O one whose name means prosperous (Said) but who is in truth wretched. One who causes something to go into non-existence is responsible for its consequences. Therefore, you have no right to be conceited and proud:

First of all, evil is from you while good is from your Lord.

Secondly, your evil is great and pervasive while your good is little and restricted.

Thirdly, you receive the wages for your good deeds in advance before you do them. All of the good deeds you are able to do during your whole life-time do not suffice to pay for even one-billionth of the blessing of your being made a Muslim human being. That being so, you must understand that Paradise is purely out of His Grace, and Hell is purely justice. For even the least evil act of man can cause a global destruction.

Fourthly, something becomes good if it is done for God's sake and it is only He Who causes something intended done for His sake to be achieved. Therefore, everyone is indebted to Him for his good deeds. That is why you must thank Him, without the pride or show which change good into evil. Unaware of this truth, you are full of conceit. You attribute the good of human beings to themselves and thereby cause them to be each like a Pharaoh. You share what belongs to God among those in rebellion against Him.

Again, in order to avoid responsibility, you attribute your evils to Destiny, although they originate in you. While you ascribe to yourself the good your Creator causes to issue from you out of His Grace, and seek to be praised for what you did not do. Discipline yourself according to the instruction of the Qur'an, which declares: *Whatever of good visits you, it is from God, and whatever of evil visits you, it is from your self.*[61] Take what belongs to you and do not usurp what does not. Further, discipline yourself according to the instructions of the Qur'an that an evil is returned with its equal while a good deed with tenfold. Therefore, do not go to excess in your enmity toward one who has done you an evil by also feeling enmity toward his relatives and the good attributes he has. By the same token, include in your love for a good, righteous man his kin and overlook his defects.

Know, O heedless Said! You abandon your duty and preoccupy yourself with the work of your Lord. This is due to your being an unfair, ignorant one. You abandon your duty of worship although it is easy for you to do, but load on your back, head

---

61. *al-Nisa'*, 4.79.

and weak heart the work of Lordship which can only be done by Him Who created you, fashioning and proportioning you, and composed you in whatever form He wished.[62] Mind your own business and commit His business to Him so that you may be at rest and ease. Otherwise you will become a wretched, rebellious and treacherous person.

Your situation is like that of a private whose essential duty is doing drills and fighting when necessary. The ruler of the country helps him with that duty by providing him with the necessary equipment. The duty of the ruler is to provide whatever that private needs, including his food, clothes, weaponry and medicine.

They see that private cooking food and ask him what he is doing. He answers: "I am working for the state"; he does not say: "I am working to prepare my food", as he knows that cooking food is not included in his duties. It is the duty of the state to prepare his food, including even putting it in his mouth if he is not able to do that due to some reasons such as illness. That being the case, a private doing trade to earn his living is ignorant, rebellious and treacherous, and therefore deserves chastisement. A private who neglects to do his drills and deserts the field is a traitor and deserving of a severe punishment.

O wretched Said! You are that private and the five daily prayers are the drill you are obliged to do. Your piety, avoiding major sins and struggling with the carnal self and Satan, is your fighting. This is the purpose for your creation and God is the Helper Who makes you successful in your struggle. As for providing your food and other necessities of your life and maintaining your life and the lives of your family, your Creator has undertaken them. However, He employs you in carrying out the means of knocking on the door of the treasuries of His Mercy to ask Him by speech and deeds. He employs you to follow the ways to the kitchens where His bounties are cooked so that you should ask Him in the tongue of either potential or needi-

---

62. *al-Infitar*, 82, 7-8.

ness or working or pronouncement for what He has assigned for you. How ignorant you are that you accuse Him concerning your livelihood while He provided you with the best of food while you were a little infant with no power and will at all. He provides for all creatures; no one undertakes their provision except the All-Hearing, the All-Knowing, the All-Powerful, the All-Wealthy Who makes the earth in summer a kitchen for His guests to pour His blessings in floods out of the envelopes of gardens and fill the pans of trees with the most delicious of foods. Besides performing your essential task, work for His sake and in His Name and by His leave to do the duties in which He employs you. Place your trust in Him and say: "God is sufficient for me and how good a Guardian He is! How good a Protecting Friend and how good a Helper!"

In the Name of God, the Merciful, the Compassionate.

When My servants question you about Me, (tell them) I am surely near. I answer the call of the caller when he calls to Me.[63]

Call upon Me and I will answer you.[64]

My Lord esteems you not at all were it not for your prayer.[65]

Know O one who claims that he prays but is not answered! Prayer (calling to God, supplication) is a type of worship. The fruit of worship is given in the Hereafter. The worldly results expected from worship are the occasions for it.

Sunset is the occasion for the prayer-service (*salat*) of evening and the eclipse of the sun is the reason for the prayer of eclipse, the purpose for which is not the ending of the eclipse. Again, drought is the occasion for the prayer of asking God for rain, which was not ordered so that rain would come. It is, again, another kind of worship done purely to obtain the good pleasure of God, although it is necessary to continue it until rain comes. When rain comes, the time appointed for it ends.

63. *al-Baqara*, 2.186.
64. *al-Ghafir* (*Fussilat*), 40.60.
65. *al-Furqan*, 25.77.

Also, the assaults of wrongdoers upon Muslims and their being struck by misfortunes are occasions for another, particular, kind of prayer which should be continued so long as those conditions prevail. If relief from them becomes possible as a result of prayer, it is light upon light. If they continue, it is not proper to say that prayer has not been accepted, rather, we should say that the time of prayer has not ended yet. As for God's promise to answer prayer in *Call upon Me and I will answer you*, answering prayer does not mean accepting it and giving what is asked. Every prayer is answered but giving what is prayed for depends on Divine Wisdom.

For example, you call your doctor, saying "O doctor!" He answers: "I am at your service." You say: "Give me that food or medicine." He gives either what you want or what is better than it, or he does not give it as it is harmful to your health. Since we suppose that prayer is said in order to achieve a worldly aim, we think that it has not been accepted when we have not been able to achieve it. For instance, we think that the prayer for rain is ordered so that rain may come and therefore do it for that purpose, not purely for God's sake, and, consequently, it is not accepted.

Know O friend! Revolutions cause a deep rift to open between the two sides (in conflict), and in order to pass from one side to the other, there must be a bridge between them. Nevertheless, bridges may be of different kinds and shapes according to the nature of revolutions and the rifts opened. Sleep is a kind of bridge between this world and the world of symbols or immaterial forms. The intermediate world is also a bridge between the world and the Hereafter. Again, spring is a bridge between winter and summer. After the Resurrection, since there will take place numerous mighty revolutions, its bridges will be extremely strange, curved and amazing.

Know O friend! In the phrases frequently mentioned in the Qur'an such as *Unto Him is your return;*[66] *Unto Him you are re-*

---

66. *al-An'am*, 6.60.

turning;[67] *to Him is the homecoming,*[68] and *unto Him is return,*[69] in addition to a threat for the rebellious, there is mighty good news and a great consolation. For these verses tell mankind:

– Death, decay, transience and separation from the world are not the doors opening on eternal extinction in dark pits of non-existence and annihilation. Rather, they are the doors opening on going to the Presence of the King of eternity. This good news saves the heart from the terrible pain of thinking of eternal separation from all that is beloved. Consider the appalling hellish state which unbelief causes: According to what the Almighty says, *I treat My servant in the way he thinks of Me,* since an unbeliever supposes death to be an eternal extinction and separation, his supposition becomes a painful torment for him.

Then consider how the pleasure arising from conviction of meeting with God is superior even to the pleasures of Paradise, and then think about the greater pleasures to be given by reaching the rank of being eternally approved by God and vision of Him. They are such that the physically hellish state a sinful believer suffers is like a pleasure of Paradise compared to the spiritually hellish state of an unbeliever who does not recognize his Creator. Even if there were no proofs for the eternal life and no means to obtain it, the supplications of the beloved of the Eternal, Beloved One, behind whom all the Prophets, saints and other believers stand in lines in that supreme prayer, would suffice as a proof and means. Is it at all possible that the greatest, most extraordinary and perfect beauty should be marred by the greatest ugliness and most bizarre defect —that the One Who hears the most secret entreaty of His most secret creatures for the satisfaction of their needs and meets them, does not hear and accept the loudest of voices rising from the earth to God's Supreme Throne, the most pleasant of supplications, and the most comprehensive of prayers for the satisfaction of the greatest and most urgent of needs? No! For He is the All-Hearing, the All-Knowing.

---

67. *al-Baqara,* 2.28.
68. *al-Ma'ida,* 5.18.
69. *al-Ra'd,* 13.36.

The Almighty's acceptance of that entreaty of His Messenger, upon him be peace and blessings, is the widest, most inclusive dimension of the Messenger's intercession and his being a mercy for the whole of creation.

Know O friend! Heedless people usually discuss the matter of Destiny and are occupied with man's free will and the creation of his deeds. However, they heedlessly deny Destiny and attribute things and events to chance, supposing themselves to be independent agents and sharing what belongs to God and His works among their fellow men and material causes. An unbelieving or heedless self denies God the creation and administration of things and events, even if they evidently confirm Him. Whereas a believing self which knows God attributes all things and events to God in belief and conviction. These two issues of theology (namely, denial or conviction and confirmation of God as the real Creator and Administrator of all things and events, including all of man's deeds) mark, according to those having sufficient knowledge of God and living consciously of the fact that God supervises all men all the time, the final point of belief in and reliance on God and the highest degree of believing in God's Unity and being a good Muslim. They serve also for a veil or border between men of awareness and heedlessness. O heedless, haughty ones! How distant you are from the truth and seeking it! If a believer advances in humility and servanthood and rises to the rank of denying human free will and attributing to God everything including man's deeds, this is harmless, as it is the result of being lost in or intoxicated with Divine love and Unity. In this case, the issues of denial (of man's free will) or its negation and confirmation no longer concern theology as a branch of (religious) sciences; rather, they become issues pertaining to the state of a believer arising from his love and belief.

Know O friend! Humility sometimes contradicts one's proclaiming God's blessings upon oneself. For proclaiming God's blessings sometimes give rise to pride and arrogance. Therefore one must be very careful and avoid exaggeration and excessive descriptions.

The middle way in one's proclaiming God's blessings on him is as follows:

Every blessing has two aspects: one pertains to the one on whom God has bestowed a blessing. This blessing becomes a sign to distinguish that one in the community. It leads him to take pride in himself and forget the One Who has given it. He goes so far as to arrogate it to himself, attributing it to his abilities or merits, and becomes haughty.

The other aspect pertains to the Bestower of blessings. The blessing displays His Munificence and Mercy and testifies to His Names. By bestowing blessings on His creatures, He pronounces some of the "verses" of His manifestations. Humility should be shown concerning the former aspect, while it becomes ingratitude concerning this second one. Provided they are wholly attributed to God and His Munificence, without feeling any pride in being honored with them, a man's proclaiming God's blessings on him becomes a praiseworthy gratitude.

O Yusuf Kishri![70] When you wear splendid clothes, Said says to you: "How beautiful you are!" You say: "Beauty belongs to the clothes, not to me." This is humility and a proclamation of the blessing.

Know O friend! When it is the time of receiving wages and sharing of rewards, the feelings of rivalry and jealousy start to stir. They are inactive at the time of working and rendering service. Rather, since the burden of the service on them is lightened and the difficulty of working lessened, the weak appreciate the strong and the lazy love the hard-working. However, since the world is the place of working for the Hereafter, of fulfilling the religious responsibilities to get the reward in the Hereafter, there must not be rivalry and jealousy in them. Rivalry and jealousy in religious services mean a lack of sincerity and purity of intention and signify that a jealous man is considering worldly rewards such as being appreciated and praised by people. Such a wretched one does not know that he thereby invali-

---

70. Yusuf Kishri was one of the pupils of Said Nursi. (Tr.)

dates his good deeds, makes people partners with God in giving reward and, let alone being praised by people, he is condemned by them.

Know O friend! God's creating a wonder or extraordinary
event by the hands of a beloved servant of His, which is called
karama, is different from His gradually leading another servant
to perdition by enabling him to do extraordinary achievements,
called *istidraj*. Karama, like a miracle worked by a Prophet, is an
act of God, and the servant who is honored with it knows that it
originates from the All-Glorified One, not from himself. He is
convinced that the Almighty oversees and protects him and
wishes him good. This strengthens his certainty about and reliance on Him. Sometimes he is conscious of the *karama* with
which he is honored and how it takes place and sometimes not.
It is safer and preferable for his belief and religious life that he
is not conscious of the fact that God creates *karama* through him.

For example, God may cause him to utter unconsciously what
occurs to another person's heart or mind or to show him scenes
from the Unseen so that the other may be guided to the Straight
Path. That beloved servant is in fact unaware of what God does
for His servants through him.

As for *istidraj*, for example, some things from the Unseen may
appear to a heedless, even, misguided, servant. Or he may work
some wonders. He attributes all of these to himself and his own
power or abilities and increases in conceit, vanity and being distant from God. He says, *"I have been given it only on account of
knowledge I possess,*[71] and it has manifested or taken place because of the purity of my self and enlightenment of my heart."

Those who are half-way yet in their spiritual journeying confuse *karama* and *istidraj* with each other. Whereas those who
have attained the highest ranks and realized self-annihilation
can clearly be aware of the things belonging to the Unseen with
their external senses which have developed so as to function as
if means for God to execute His decrees [as is declared in a *ha-*

---

71. *al-Qasas*, 28.78.

dith qudsi recorded in *Bukhari*: *When I love a servant of Mine, I become his ears with which he hears, his eyes with which he sees, his hands with which he holds, and his legs on which he walks*). Since their inner world is perfectly illumined and illuminates their outer world, they can clearly distinguish between *karama* and *istidraj*.

There is nothing that does not glorify Him with His praise.[72]

Know O friend! Every creature's glorification and worship have innumerable aspects. It is not necessary for the creature to be conscious of all of them.

For it is not incumbent upon a creature to be always conscious of its glorification. For example, an ignorant wage-earner works on a ship. He has to touch some of the pegs and nails on the vessel without knowing why and for what important uses the owner has required him to do this. What he knows is only the wages he receives and the pleasure of earning. He even thinks that the work he does was decreed only for his pleasure. Again, an animal is completely unconscious of why it mates and the consequences of mating; it does that only to satisfy its sexual desire. But an animal's ignorance of the purposes for its mating does not prevent reproduction and maintenance of its progeny and species. For instance, while satisfying their greed, ants unconsciously clean the face of the earth of the corpses of micro-organisms. Or a clock tells you how much time more of your life has passed but "knows" only the pain of the wear of its mechanism. Or a honeybee does what is does by the sweetness of Divine inspiration included in the particular pleasure it takes. Or vegetable, animal and even human mothers work due to the pleasure of affection, unconscious of the lofty purposes realized through them which embellish the home of the universe. It is as if their affection serves as a seed or measure for those purposes.

It is sufficient for those to glorify and worship God that they

---

72. *al-Isra'*, 17.44.

know how to do their work. The Almighty declares: *Do you not see that all that is in the heavens and the earth glorifies God, and the birds spreading their wings. Each knows (how to do) its prayer and glorification; and God knows what they do.*[73] It is not necessary that they know that what they do is a glorification and are conscious of the nature of the prayer particular to each. It is enough that the thinking ones among creatures know that all creatures worship and glorify God. Indeed, it is enough that the Absolutely Worshipped One knows that. Since creatures other than men are not obliged to consciously worship God, they do not have to specially intend to pray or glorify and be conscious of the nature of what they do. Actually, those creatures themselves are embodied words of glorification and by their lives they do another kind of glorification. They glorify (their Creator and Sustainer) in as many ways as willed by the All-Glorified, the All-Pure One, may His Majesty be exalted, and there is no god but He.

Know O friend! Bounties and blessings sent to you in great variety and decorating you from head to foot, reach you after passing through different veils according to certain measures and being filtered through diverse "nets" in a fixed order.

Know O friend! There is a very subtle point in selfhood. I think it is to serve for a window through which to look into eternity. For whatever it encounters or contacts, it tends to eternalize it. If worldly desires and fancies use it, it becomes an instrument to attract the building-blocks of the Hereafter to the world and attempts to build a worldly palace with them, and it eats up the fruits of the Hereafter in this transient world before they ripen.

Know O friend! Selfhood is a very strange thing. If it is purified and developed, it becomes a treasury of innumerable instruments and endless metres to perceive the manifestations of the treasuries of the Divine All-Beautiful Names; whereas, if it is seduced and stunted, it becomes a cave of snakes, scorpions and other kinds of vermin. What is preferable in respect of selfhood is its maintenance, not its annihilation. Maintaining it pur-

---

73. *al-Nur*, 24.41.

ified, as the Companions of the Prophet, upon him be peace and blessings, did, is more conformable to wisdom than its death or annihilation, which is the way followed by great saints.

Selfhood is in great hunger and immense needs and has strange tastes. When it is trained and purified, its qualities change: its blameworthy greed changes into a zeal difficult to satisfy; its vicious conceit becomes a means to be saved from all types of associating partners with God, and its intense love of itself changes into love of its Lord, and so on. Its evils turn into virtues.

Know O friend! A believing man derives his value from the artistry, the distinguished colouring and the embroideries of the manifestations of the Divine Names in his being. An unbelieving or heedless one is valuable only in proportion to his physical aspect. Also, when considered on behalf of the All-Glorified One and from the viewpoint of its being the place where all of the Divine Names are manifested, as the Qur'an teaches, this world becomes infinitely valuable. Whereas, if considered on behalf of itself and from the viewpoint of natural causes, as taught by corrupt philosophy, its value is reduced to its changing and lifeless material substance.

The knowledge about the universe derived from the Qur'an is infinitely superior to the knowledge taught by modern science and philosophy.

For example, the Qur'an says: *He has made the sun as a lamp.*[74] Look, O man, what a broad, profound view the Qur'an gives you with this expression to look at the chains of the manifestations of Divine Names! Despite its huge size, the sun is subjugated to you to serve as a light to illuminate your home and a fire to ripen or cook your food by the command of Him Who nurtures you. You have such a powerful and compassionate Owner that that sun and innumerable others like it are lamps in the mansion built for His guests amongst the everlasting ones.

Now consider what science or philosophy says: The sun is a

---

74. *Nuh*, 71.16.

huge mass of fire moving by itself. Our earth and other planets were detached from it and move in their orbits attracted to the sun by a gravitational force. This information gives you no more than a fright or a sense of wonder.

Know O friend! You have no right to demand a right from the Truth, Glory be to Him. Rather, what you must do is continually to thank Him. For His is all kingdom, the whole of creation, and His is all praise.

O God, O All-Merciful, All-Compassionate, All-Munificent! Make this book a substitute for me to bear witness to You after my death as follows: '

O God, O Lord of the chosen Muhammad! O Lord of Paradise and Hell! O Lord of the Prophets and the good! O Lord of the truthful and pious! O Lord of the young and old! O Lord of seeds and fruits! O Lord of lights and flowers! O Lord of rivers and trees! O Lord of what is manifest and what is secret! O Lord of day and night! We have You as a Witness, we have those bearing Your Supreme Throne as witnesses, we have all of Your angels as witnesses, we have all of Your creatures as witnesses, all of your Prophets, all of Your saints, all of Your signs of creation and speech, and all of the particles of the universe and its compounds are also witnesses as is also attested by Your beloved, upon him the best of blessings, the testimony containing all other witnesses, and by Your Qur'an, that we all bear witness that You are God, the Necessarily-Existent, the One, Single, the Besought-of-All, the Manifest Truth, the All-Living, the Self-Subsisting, the All-Knowing, the All-Wise, the All-Powerful, the All-Willing, the All-Hearing, the All-Seeing, the All-Speaking. Yours are the All-Beautiful Names. We also bear witness that there is no god but You, the One, without any partners at all. Yours is the dominion and ownership of all things and Yours is all praise. We ask You for forgiveness and turn in repentance to You. Again, we bear witness that Muhammad is Your servant, Your Prophet, Your Beloved, and Your Messenger, whom You sent as a mercy for all the worlds. Bestow peace and blessings on him, his family and His Companions until eternity. Amen. Amen. Amen.

This is to explain one of the jewels in the treasure of the verse:

I have not created jinn and mankind except to worship Me.[75]

Know, O Said who has forgotten his self and his vital duty, and is unaware of the wisdom in the creation of man and ignorant of what the All-Wise Maker has placed in those adorned creatures! The building of this universe and inclusion in it of the human world can be explained through the following parable:

There is a king who disposes treasuries full of a great variety of jewels and buried treasures. He is also extremely skilful in making very novel and magnificent things and is specialized in almost all of the sciences and crafts. That king wills to display the magnificence of his kingdom, the splendor of his wealth, the wonders of his artistry and the marvels of his skills. In short, he wills to see his magnificence, perfections and graciousness in both his own sight and the sight of others.

The king builds a huge palace with many floors. He divides every floor into different rooms according to the purposes of each and the requirements of the relevant sciences he knows. He decorates the palace with the jewels in his treasuries and the embellishments of his subtle artistry, and puts a mark or seal on each thing in it in a way to display his miraculous skills, knowledge and power. He lays in the rooms tables on which there are innumerable kinds of delicious foods to exhibit his munificence. He does many other things to show his hidden perfections. Then he invites his subjects to have a good time and gives an incomparable feast. It is as if each morsel is a product of hundreds of delicate skills and arts. Afterwards, he appoints a teacher to make known whatever is in that palace and the meaning of all the embellishments and decorations it has. The teacher is also to describe in what ways the furniture, the jewels and embellishments point to the perfections of the owner of the palace, and to teach people the manner of going into the palace and behaving toward its builder. He tells them:

---

75. *adh-Dhariyat*, 51.56.

– O people! My master wills to make himself known to you through whatever is in this palace, so know him. He also wills to make himself loved by you through these embellishments and bounties, so love him and display your love by appreciating them. He exhibits his mercy on you, so thank him. He manifests himself to you, so show zeal to go to his presence.

The teacher also says many other similar things. The people enter the palace and divide into two groups. One group look at whatever is in the palace and think that all that is seen and takes place must signify something very important. They turn to the teacher and say to him:

– Peace be upon you! Everything must be as you tell us. So, teach us what your master taught you.

The teacher speaks to them and they listen. They act in a way to please the king and the king, in return, calls them to his private, indescribably beautiful palace and, in a way befitting him, bestows on them all kinds of food and drink which, in appearance, resemble those in the other palace but which are infinitely more delicious.

The other group pay no attention to anything other than the food and act as if blind and deaf to all other beauties and distinctions of the palace. They eat as if they were animals and then sleep. They drink the beverages forbidden to them and, getting drunk, make loathsome utterances and do others much harm. As a result, the soldiers of the king seize them and put them in a dungeon.

You know that the king has built the palace for the purposes mentioned and made the realization of those purposes dependent on the existence of the teacher and the obedience of the people to him. So, it is worth saying: But for the teacher, the king would not have built the palace, and if the people do not pay heed to the instructions of the teacher, the palace will be destroyed and a new one built in place of it for different other purposes.

If you understand the meaning of the parable, you can see

into the truth. The palace is the world, the ceiling of which is adorned with glittering lamps and the floor with smiling flowers. The king is the monarch of eternity: *The seven heavens and the earth, and all that is in them glorify Him. There is nothing that does not glorify Him with praise.*[76] *God has created the heavens and the earth in six days, then seated Himself on the Supreme Throne, covering the day with the night it pursues urgently, and the sun, the moon, and the stars subservient by His command.*[77] The floors are the worlds within the world, and the jewels and embellishments are the miracles of His Power. The kinds of food are wonderful fruits of His Mercy. The treasuries full of jewels and the hidden treasuries are the Sacred Divine Names and their manifestations. All the beauties, designs and decorations point to those Names. As for the teacher, he is our master Muhammad, upon him be peace and blessings. Other Prophets, upon them be peace, are his friends and all saints, may God be pleased with them, his students. There are many obedient servants in the palace, who are the angels, upon them be peace. The people invited to the palace are human beings and other animate beings. The two groups are the people of belief and the Qur'an, which explains the meaning of all the "verses" of the book of the creation, and the people of unbelief and rebellion following their carnal selves and Satan. Those belonging to the second group are *deaf, blind and mute, more unable to find the straight path than animals.*[78] They are unaware of anything other than the worldly life.

The prosperous, pious ones paid heed to the servant who made his Lord known with his supplication such as *Jawshan al-Kabir* and communicated the holy Qur'an. They listened to the Qur'an and became observers of the beauties of the sovereignty of Divine Lordship. They exalted God and glorified Him, then proclaimed the marvels of the manifestations of the Sacred Names. They glorified God and praised Him, recognizing with their senses the contents of the treasuries of His Mercy and

---

76. *al-Isra'*, 17.44.
77. *al-A'raf*, 7.54.
78. *al-Furqan*, 25.44.

thanking Him. They also knew the jewels in the treasuries of the Names manifested in certain measures according to their capacity of receiving them and declared God All-Holy and extolled Him. They studied the missives of the Pen of Power, appreciating and reflecting on them. They took great spiritual pleasure in observing the beauties of creation and filled with love for the Creator, looked forward to going to His Presence.

They responded to the Maker's will to make Himself known through the miracles of His art, by trying to obtain knowledge of Him, and said in amazement: "Glory be to You! We are unable to know You as required by knowing You, O Known One, through all Your miraculous creatures." Also, they responded to His will to be loved by loving Him through the adornments of the fruits of Mercy. They responded to His turning or inclination to them with the pleasures of His bounties, by praising and thankfulness, and said: "Glory be to You! We are unable to thank You as required by thanking You, O Thanked One, through the praises of Your favors on the whole of creation, the exhibitions of all Your bounties and their tastes in the market of the universe, and the testimonies of the melodies of all the fruits of Your Mercy and Favoring."

They responded with prostration in love, amazement and utmost humility to His displaying of His Grandeur, Perfection, Beauty, Grace and Majesty in whatever is in the universe, in the mirrors of creatures coming to the world and then departing one after the other. To His showing His all-inclusive Mercy and infinite Wealth, they responded with acknowledgement of their own destitution and beseeching Him. They also responded to His exhibiting the subtleties of His Art with appreciation and observation and by bearing witness to them. To His proclamation of the sovereignty of His Lordship throughout the universe, they responded with belief in His Unity, obedience and worship in acknowledgement of their helplessness, weakness and poverty.

In short, they fulfilled their vital duties in this abode and were perfected, more sublime than all other creatures, observ-

ing the Supreme Trust they had borne as trustworthy vicegerents on the earth. Then their Lord invited them to the Abode of
Peace for eternal happiness and bestowed on them such bounties and blessings that neither eyes have ever seen them nor
ears heard, nor minds ever conceived of.

As to the other group of the vicious and evil-doers, they unbe-
lieved in the Maker and despised in their unbelief all of the creatures by reducing their value to their material substance only.
They denied all the manifestations of the Names and committed
an infinitely great crime to deserve an infinite punishment.

Know O wretched Said! Do you think that your duty in life is
maintaining it by considering only the needs of your carnal self
and serving your belly and desires? Or do you suppose that the
purpose for the inclusion of all those senses, feelings, systems,
organs, limbs, and faculties in the mechanism of your life is using them for the satisfaction of the fancies of your carnal self in
this fleeting life? No! They were included in your creation so
that you should use them to perceive all the varieties of the
bounties of the Almighty and the kinds of the manifestations of
His Names. By using all of your senses and faculties as measures, you must appreciate the contents of the treasuries of His
Mercy and find out and open the hidden treasuries of the manifestations of His Names, may His Majesty be exalted. Your vital
duty is to display among all your fellow-creatures the marvels
of the manifestations of His Names and then proclaim your servanthood both verbally and actively at the door of His Lordship. And then you must adorn yourself with the jewels of the
manifestations of His Names and exhibit them to the view of
the Eternal Witness. Also, you must understand the reverences
of glorification of living beings for the Bestower of Life and testify to them and call others also to the same testimony. Again,
using your attributes, qualities and acts as means of comparison, you must also perceive the Attributes of your Creator and
His sacred Essential Qualities. Also, considering your poverty
and impotence, you must understand the extent of the manifestations of His Power and Wealth.

The nature of life is that it must serve as a treasury of senses and faculties, a map, a sample, an index, and a measure, to know the marvellous works of the manifestations of the Names of the Creator of death and life. Your life may be pictured as an inscribed, heard and perceived word composed by the Divine Beautiful Names. Its reality is that it is a mirror for the reflection of Divine Unity. Its perfection and happiness lie in its being conscious of what it embodies and feeling love and yearning for Whom it serves as a mirror. As for other living beings, they have a share in some of these purposes but not as much as yours. For you are a comprehensive mirror, as the Creator Himself is narrated to have declared: *Neither the heavens nor the earth can "contain" Me, but the heart of My believing servant can "contain" Me.*[79]

In the Name of God, the Merciful, the Compassionate.

O God! O All-Merciful! O All-Compassionate! O Unique! O All-Living! O Self-Subsistent! O All-Judging! O All-Just! O All-Pure! For the sake of Your Greatest Name and for the sake of Your most wise Criterion (Qur'an), bestow blessings on our master Muhammad, your noblest Messenger, to the numbers of the particles of our bodies and the seconds of our lives. And send down on us and on the publishers of this book and on all other true believers peace of reassurance, tranquillity and conviction, as You sent it down on the Companions and family of Your chosen Prophet, upon him be peace and blessings. And send down on us and on other believing servants of Your religion peace of reassurance, sincere faith, perfect certainty, pure intention, and perfect firmness in the service of the Qur'an and belief. Secure us against our fears by removing the anti-religious novelties included in the principles and public symbols of Islam and give us relief by the declaration of the essen-

---

79. In *al-Fatawa al-Hadithiya*, Ibn Hajar Haythami comments on this narration: "It is narrated by the Sufis. However, it must not be taken literally in a way to associate union (with God) and incarnation" (as asserted in Christianity and some other religions). What this narration means is that the heart of a believer is of such quality that it can know God with all His Attributes, Names and acts and feel an overflowing love for Him. (Tr.)

tials of Islam throughout the world as soon as possible. And employ us in this sacred service. Secure us, secure our religion and its sincere servants, and secure all true believers against the attacks of heretics. Provide us and provide all sincere servants of Your religion with security and safety in religion and in both this and the other world. Cure us of our diseases and make the Qur'an as a cure for all our and their diseases. Include us and them among those who always praise and thank You. Amen. And all praise be to God. May God bestow blessings on our master Muhammad and on all his family and Companions. Amen.

INDEX OR BRIEF SUMMARIES OF THE TOPICS
DISCUSSED IN THE TREATISE

*No one has the right to complain about and object to the Maker of the universe (317)

*Who operates in a cell of the body is surely operating in the whole of the body. (318)

*How can it befit the Wisdom and Attribute of Preserving of the One Who preserves the eggs of vermin and fish and the seeds of plants for wise, merciful purposes, that He neglects to record and preserve your deeds? Those deeds are the seeds of the trees that will yield their fruit in the Hereafter, especially considering that you are a bearer of His trust and His vicegerent on earth. (318)

*The material existence of the meaning—letters and words—may change and be effaced but the meaning continues to exist. A covering may be rent apart but the essence or kernel remains. Clothes are worn out but the body survives and the body ruins but the spirit survives. The body gets old but ego remains young... Despite its putting on different "bodies", undergoing many changes and experiencing lots of different conditions, the "meaning" endures from the beginning of its life to its end and maintains its unity, that is, remains without changing. This shows that it will pass over the "ditch" of death and, freed from its hooks and stripped of its body, continue its journeying to eternity safe and sound. The strong tendency of material things—essentially subject to decay—to remain and survive clearly points out that simple things such as the meaning, light and spirit—essentially inclined to permanence—will remain eternally. (318-9)

*As material, solid things get larger, they lose their sensitivity to delicate, subtle things. Whereas, as light expands and spreads, it pervades more and penetrates more deeply into hidden and subtle things. (319)

*The grandeur of God's Divinity and Its dignity and absolute independence require that whether big or small, all things should be under His disposal. (319)

*The Qur'an considers and regards the level of understanding of the common people who constitute the absolute majority. In a matter possible to describe in different ways and degrees, it chooses the way most comprehensible by them. Otherwise, the argument would have been more abstruse than the conclusion. (320)

*It is one of the widest causes of misguidance that man supposes as known what he has familiarity with because of its being common and usual. Whereas in most cases such sort of familiarity may cause compound ignorance. Nevertheless, because of that kind of familiarity, man does not need to reflect on what is usual and common, although those he sees as common are miracles of Divine Power. He only pays attention to what he sees as extraordinary because of rarity. (322)

*The One Who prepares melons and apples for you to eat knows better than you what you need to eat and is aware of what your conscience takes pleasure in. Is it possible for the branches and stems of plants and trees to know that? Such means or causes of Divine bounties are only the channels of Mercy and canals of bounties. (324)

*The key of creation is in the hands of man, in his ego. Although the doors of creation seem to be open, they are actually closed. The Truth, glory be to Him, has entrusted man with a key with which all the doors of creation are opened and the treasury of the Creator is unveiled. The key entrusted to you is ego, which is itself an enigma. When you solve that enigma by knowing its nature, creation is opened to you. (327)

*Good deeds acquire vitality through sincere intention and are corrupted through show, ostentation and hypocrisy. Whereas the feelings for and (natural) tendencies toward good ingrained in conscience lose their purity through conscious intentions. (330)

*The universe is a tree, the basic elements like earth, water, air and fire being its branches, plants its leaves, animals its flowers and mankind its fruits. (330)

*The meaning of the verse *We have made them (shooting stars) missiles for devils*: (332–4)

*Things are recorded before and during their physical existence. Among the evidences showing that all things are recorded before their coming into existence are seeds, measures and forms, while fruits, which are the results of the lives of trees, explicitly show that things are recorded during their existence. (335)

*God destines and decrees, executes His decrees and spares (that is, He forgives and withdraws the execution of His decrees). (339–40)

*The reason for many Qur'anic verses ending with Divine Names: (340)

*Like love, helplessness is also a way leading to God, a way even more direct and safer than the way of love. This way (which is based on acknowledgement of one's helplessness before God), it is a more direct, safer and levelled way with four steps.(341–3)

*Worship is the result and price of the bounties already accorded to man. It is not the means of future, expected reward. (344)

*The infinite abundance of the members of species, especially those of little creatures, without the least defect in their structure and with perfect orderliness, points to, even explicitly shows, that there are no limits to the manifestations of the Maker and that He is absolutely different from all of them and all things are the same in relation to His Power and Necessary Existence. (344)

*The One with the All-Beautiful Names manifests Himself in the departments of His Sovereignty with His Names with one Name being dominant in a department and the others subordinate. (345)

*It is a peculiarity of the comprehensiveness of man's primordial nature that the All-Wise Creator has included in that small object innumerable meters to measure what is endlessly stored in His Mercy, and equipped him with countless faculties to understand what is contained in infinite number in the treasuries of His All-Beautiful Names. (347)

*Differences among creatures show purpose and rejects chance. (The facial differences among men are a clear evidence for this.) (349)

*The wisdom in God's giving respite to the unbelievers who only aim to live the worldly life is that, albeit unconsciously, they serve to manifest various blessings of God by their labor and artifices, and make arrangements, albeit without knowing, to display the beauties and excellencies of the works of Divine Art, offering them to the views of people. Unbelievers do that unknowingly as a clock tells you the time without knowing what it does. (350)

*Concerning the most evident and important matters, the Qur'an and the one on whom the Qur'an was sent down do not view the universe as modern science and philosophy do. (352, 392)

* O one long suffering for some particular misfortunes! Do not divide your "forces" of patience to confront both past and present misfortunes. Nor do you use up them against those like to come in the future. (353)

*The Traditions that some persons of defective understanding dismiss as being exaggerated in fact contain some valuable truths. (354)

*O soul enamoured of itself and relying on its physical existence! You became content with a drop from a mirage of the ocean of the water of life and a weak radiance at night from the sun of a clear day. (355–6)

*O man! There are awesome issues before you which compel every conscious being to pay attention to them. (357)

*Explanation of the meaning related to the letter and the meaning related to the name and the difference between a universal having particulars or individuals and a whole formed of parts: (358)

*When you fear or love the created, fear becomes a painful trouble and love a distressing affliction. (359)

*O friend! You are the fruit or seed of the tree of creation. Although with respect to your physical existence, you are a weak, impotent, despicable, small-sized individual being, the All-Wise Maker has favored you with a universal disposition. (359)

*Love of God and love of all else save Him: (360)

*Man who shows great curiousity to learn about, say, the moor and other planets at the cots of sacrificing half of his life must give heed to the awesome tidings given by the Prophet concerning his future. (360)

*We see the All-Wise Maker with the perfection of His Wisdom and clearly witness that His acts are absolutely free from waste and futility. He weaves extensive, enduring and precious "textiles" from despicable and very small things. Again, by virtue of His acts being absolutely free from waste and pointlessness, He charges a single thing, each of the organs or apparatuses of man's body, for example, and especially those in his head, with a variety of very important duties. If a different organ the size of a mustard-seed were required to do each of the duties with which the organs in your head are charged, then your head would be as big as Mount Sinai. (361)

and therefore to take a great risk for the sake of a chance of one in a thousand. Yet his reason does not allow him to set aside one of the twenty-four parts of his wealth for the sake of a chance of nine hundred and ninety-nine out of a thousand, as is attested by millions of people of certified knowledge. (376)

*A parable containing truths pertaining to both the world and the religious life. (377)

*The like of one conceited and proud, who desires to be praised for even what he has not done! (381)

*The existence of something depends on the existence of all its parts and the presence of all the conditions necessary for its existence, while something existent can go to non-existence by the destruction of a single part of it or the non-presence of one of the conditions for its maintenance. (381)

*Paradise is purely out of His Grace, and Hell is purely justice. (382)

*An answer to those who claim that their prayers are not answered and the meaning of answering. (384–5)

*In the verses such as *To Him is the homecoming* (5.18) and *unto Him is return* (13.36), in addition to a threat for the rebellious, there is mighty good news and a great consolation. (386)

*Divine Destiny and man's free will. (387)

*Humility sometimes contradicts one's proclaiming God's blessings upon oneself. The middle way in one's proclaiming God's blessings on him. (387–8)

*Rivalry and jealousy in religious services mean a lack of sincerity and purity of intention and signify that a jealous man is considering worldly rewards such as being appreciated and praised by people. (388)

*God's creating a wonder or extraordinary event by the hands of a beloved servant of His, which is called *karama*, is different from His gradually leading another servant to perdition by enabling him to do extraordinary achievements, called *istidraj*. (389)

*Every creature's glorification and worship have innumerable aspects. It is not necessary for the creature to be conscious of all of them. (390)

A Radiance from the Sun of the Qur'an

Know: The All-Wise Creator has installed in your body all those senses, feelings, and systems to perceive the variety of His bounties, and experience the diversity of the manifestations of His Names.

The purpose for your life is that you must display the works of the manifestations of His Names and exhibit their marvels before the eyes of creatures.

Your humanity lies in being conscious of this duty.

Your being a Muslim depends on your conviction of this honor conferred on you.

In the Name of God, the Merciful, the Compassionate.

Praise is from God and for God as it is deserved by God. Praise be to God for "praise is for God".

O God! We present to You before all the bounties and works of mercy, before all the instances of favoring and wisdom, before all the instances of life and death, before all animals and plants, before all flowers and fruits, before all the works of (Your) art and fashioning, before the universal order and harmony, before all the instances of coming to a halt and movement in all the particles of the world and in their compounds, the testimony that we testify that there is no god but God. He is One with no partners at all. His is the kingdom of all existence and His is all praise. He gives life and causes to die. All good is in His hand and He is powerful over all things. We also testify that Muhammad is His servant, Prophet, beloved, and Messenger whom He sent as a mercy for all worlds.

O God! Bestow blessings on Muhammad, the ocean of Your lights, the mine of Your mysteries, the sun of Your guidance, the spring of Your Favoring, the tongue of Your proof. He is the one representing the work of Your Power and Your love, the embodiment of Your Mercy, and the most beloved of the creation to You. Bestow blessings on all the other Messengers and Prophets, and on all the families and Companions of them all, and on the angels made near to You. Also bless Your righteous servants among the inhabitants of the heavens and earth, for the sake of Your Mercy, O Most Merciful of the Merciful.

Glory be to You, O One Whom the universe glorifies with Your praise with the tongue of Muhammad, upon him be Your best blessings and peace.

Glory be to You, O One Whom the world glorifies with the works of Muhammad, upon him be the most abundant of Your blessings.

Glory be to You, O One before Whom the earth prostrates under the Throne of Your Grandeur and glorifies with Your praise with the tongue of its Muhammad, upon him be the purest of Your benedictions.

Glory be to You, O One Whom all the believing men and women glorify with the tongue of their Muhammad, upon him be Your blessings for ever.

Glory be to You: I glorify You with the tongue of Muhammad, Your beloved, upon him be Your perfect blessings and radiant peace. Accept from me for (the sake of) Your Mercy, as You accepted from him.

Know O friend! The extremely comprehensive meaning of the verse, *The seven heavens and the earth and whoever is in them glorify Him. There is nothing that does not glorify Him with His praise,*[1] requires explanation. I tried to look into it and some words of explanation dropped into my heart from it to serve as a ladder to rise towards it. If you would like to absorb those words of explanation dripping from the ocean of this verse or descending from its very high heavens, give a keen, attentive ear to what follows:

---

1. *al-Isra'*, 17.44.

Glory be to You! We—the communities of mankind—are unable to know You as Your knowledge requires, O One known through the miracles of all Your works, the descriptions of all Your creatures, and the definitions of all existence.

Glory be to You, how immense is Your authority and how clear Your proof!

Glory be to You! We are unable to mention You as mentioning You requires, O One mentioned with the tongues of all Your creatures and works and with the breaths of all the words of the book of Your creation.

Glory be to You, how majestic is Your mentioning!

Glory be to You! We are unable to praise You as Your praise requires. You are praised through all the instances of Your Kindness displayed before the eyes of all those having sight, and through the exhibition of all Your bounties in the market of the universe before all those who witness them. You are praised through the joyful testimonies of all the fruits of Your Mercy Which gives shape to those fruits in the moulds of the universal order and balance.

Glory be to You, how vast is Your Mercy!

Glory be to You! We are unable to pay our duty of worship to You as Your worship requires, O One worshipped by all of the angels and other creatures of Yours in infinitely various ways of worshipping and praising.

Glory be to You! We are unable to glorify You as Your glorification requires, O One Whom *the seven heavens and the earth and whoever is in them glorify. There is nothing that does not glorify Him with His praise.* We believe. It is true.

Glory be to You, O One Whom all kinds of angels glorify in different tongues in various ways.

Glory be to You, O One Whom the universe glorifies with the mouths of its worlds, the limbs of its main parts, the cells of its limbs, and the particles of its cells, through the tongues of its purposeful order, magnificent balance, well-ordered working, and well-proportioned construction.

Glory be to You, O One Whom Paradise glorifies with the mouths of its gardens through the songs of its *houris*, the eulogies of its palaces, the odes of its trees, and the hymns of its fruits resembling one another, as their resemblances in this world glorify Him.

Glory be to You, O One Who alternates day and night and subjugates the sun and the moon. You are the One Whom the heavens glorify with their systems, and the mouths of their suns or stars through the tongue of their order and harmony and well-designed adornment, and through the tongue of their majestic radiance, their absolute obedience, their tranquillity and their purposeful movements.

Glory be to You, O One Whom the atmosphere glorifies with the mouths of its thunderbolts, lightning, winds, clouds, shooting stars and rain, through the words of its well-balanced order with many lofty purposes.

Glory be to You, O One Whom the earth glorifies, prostrated before the immensity of His Power with its Muhammad and Qur'an, with the mouths of its seas, mountains, rivers, trees, and its sounds and vibrations—that is, with the sounds of its plants and the movements of its animals. It glorifies You with its light-diffusing words and luminous letters—that is, its Prophets and saints—and through the tongue of its order, balance, life and death, and its poverty and dryness and its rich adornment by His generous leave and wise art.

Glory be to You, O One Whom the seas glorify with their words of strange animals, and through their songs and the tongue of their order, balance and the many purposes they serve.

Glory be to You, O One Who has made the earth as a cradle and mountains as pegs. The mountains glorify You with their mouths of springs, rivers and trees, and through the tongue of their balance, order, the purposes they serve and their treasuries.

Glory be to You, O One Who has made every living thing from "water", and Whom animate beings glorify with their mouths of senses, feelings, systems, organs, artistic structures and intellects and hearts. They glorify through the tongue of their well-proportioned designs, and they ask through their potential, and through the tongue of their needs, prayers, and their being provided, and the changes they undergo and their lives and deaths.

Glory be to You, O One Whom flying insects glorify with Your praise with their chants of thanksgiving. Birds glorify together with their chicks in their nests with their songs of gratitude, through the tongue of the order and balance in their creation and movements, and the tongue of their designs and adornment. They proclaim Your favors on them and thereby manifest their gratitude at the time of their tasting the fruits of Your Kindness and being fed with the works of Your Mercy. Vermin and wild animals also glorify You through the tongue of the excellent proportion and balance in their structures, and their forms, and being munificently fed.

Glory be to You! How fine and subtle is Your art and how penetrating Your rule and authority!

Glory be to You, O One Whom trees manifestly glorify at the time of their blossoming and coming to leaf and producing fruits, and at the time of the dancing of the fruits on their branches, with the mouths of their green leaves, smiling blossoms and laughing fruits. They glorify You through the tongue of their well-proportioned forms and designs, their taste, beautiful flowers, fine smells, and rich adornment. They also magnify You and proclaim the perfection of Your Caring, describe the manifestations of Your Attributes and Names, and interpret Your making Yourself loved by Your creatures. They do so with what comes out of the limbs of their fruits pertaining to the radiance of Your making Yourself loved by Your creatures and undertaking their provision.

Glory be to You! How subtle is the proof of You originating in Your Kindness, and how rich is Your Graciousness in making Yourself loved!

Glory be to You, O One Whom plants glorify with perfect clarity at the time of their blossoming and producing spikes and grain, with the mouths of their flowers and spikes and with the words of their seeds and grain, through the tongue of their subtly-proportioned forms and structures. Again, they magnify You, make You known and show Your "face" which makes Yourself loved, and they also describe Your Attributes, mention Your Names, interpret Your making Yourself loved and making Yourself known to Your servants.

Glory be to You! How subtle and varied is the evidence of You, and how radiant and enriched it is!

Glory be to You, O One Who sent down iron wherein is mighty power and uses for mankind, Whom minerals glorify with all their varieties, shapes, properties, uses, and embellishments, through the tongue of their well-established order and special balance.

Glory be to You, O One Whom elements glorify through their coming together to make compounds by Your command and Power.

Glory be to You, O One Whom particles glorify through the duties they do and through the tongue of the order and balance they display. They also glorify You in that, despite their absolute impotence in themselves, they perform mighty duties by Your Power. Each of them testifies to the necessity of Your existence through the tongue of their essential impotence to carry out the lofty duties in the subtle order of creation. For example, a very tiny seed bears on itself a huge tree. Again, every particle indicates Your Oneness with respect to its duties and that its movements are to contribute to the universal order. In short, a particle testifies to both Your necessary existence and Oneness, and every incident indicates that You are One and the Eternally-Besought-of-All. Rather, each and every thing indicates and bears witness that You are necessarily existent, One and Single, and Eternally-Besought-of-All. May Your Majesty be exalted, and there is no god but You, One, with no partners at all.

Know O friend! With all its limbs, organs and senses, your body essentially belongs to its Maker Who rears it and governs it, and what falls to your share in it is only your duty [to maintain and use it according to God's commandments].

If, by virtue of your using it properly, you can obtain a ray of awareness of how your body really is, it manifests that its Originator has absolute knowledge of it with its essence and all its aspects, and that His Names and Attributes are manifested on it.

If your body serves you in some way only in this moment, it is so precisely because it is under the service of its Maker at all times. It displays many marvelous works of its All-Wise Creator and, by fulfilling its "natural" tasks with a perfect order and through a wonderful mutual assistance, it exhibits the subtleties of the Almighty's Mercy and the "fibers" of His Wisdom.

You have a share in your body and the right to dispose it proportionately to your knowledge of it and to your share in maintaining it. With all its particles and compounds and with all its life and properties, it manifests that it belongs to its Maker and is under His absolute disposal. That being the truth, know your place and do not overstep your limits.

With all its aspects, your existence has a relation to the Almighty Truth and the creation. With respect to its relation to the Truth, you are a subtle work of art, a pure, clean work of the Creator of the heavens and the earth. As your share in your existence and its worth and perfection, it is enough for you that you know that you are a work of the art of the Maker Who has adorned the heavens with stars. It is enough to know that you have become a beloved, honorable brother of the universe which serves you.

As for your relation to the creation, you are composed of some elements which have come together and will soon part company with one another.

Do not wrong your body by appropriating it unjustly and breaking its relation from the Truth, which will make it worthless. Even if it were to last millions of years, a fruitless existence cannot be equal in value to one moment of a fruitful one, [which receives the manifestations of an absolute, eternal Existence]. Do you not see that your Originator took material elements and kneaded them with a perfect, most valuable part of creation, giving you a particular, definite existence out of the ocean of existence? How did they come together to form you? Do you see in the market of becoming and dissolution a shop wherein to buy eyes or a store wherein to find brains and tongues, or a machine to manufacture hearts and weave skins? No! Rather, your Originator has built you, created you in an exquisite, comprehensive form from a thing resembling nothing or from everything, so that nothing, even if it be the greatest of things, can hope to be the creator of another thing, even if it be the smallest. Something unable to create the heavens cannot claim that it can create, say, a gnat.

Know O friend! The All-Skillful Maker disposes matter and creates from it wonderful works of art. The value of matter itself cannot be equal to even a hundredth of the art. An antique work of art may fetch as much as a million dollars while its material is not even worth a few cents. If this antique is taken to the antiques market, it may be sold for its true value because of the art it contains and the name of the brilliant artist who fashioned it. Whereas, this work of art may only be sold for the price of the iron in the blacksmiths' market.

Most, even all, creatures are each an embodiment of art. Especially living creatures, most particularly the small ones among them, display perfect art despite the density of matter. So, whatever is in the universe has two aspects. For example, with respect to its material aspect and the worldly life, its provision serves for the maintenance of life and gives a particular, fleeting pleasure. Whereas, with respect to its being an art displaying the works of the manifestations of the Maker, it is a wonderful treasure, a pure, marvelous treasury. It serves for all the bounties of the Maker to be tasted and known, and for the manifestations of the Names of the All-Munificent Provider to be experienced, and it causes conscious beings to be enlightened by recognizing those Names. If you like, consider your tongue, which is only one of thousands of devices receiving and recognizing provision. Despite its small size, it contains as many instruments as the number of edibles and drinks. If the owner of a tongue is awakened to and becomes conscious of its significance, he will give thanks with each of those subtle instruments for all the varieties of bounties which the All-Providing offers him to taste out of His mercy.

It means being thankful for the bounties, and it is more pleasant than the bounties themselves, that one is conscious of being provided with them and perceives the favor or kindness of the Giver of bounties.

Know O friend! There is not anything made or created by Almighty God which is not orderly and balanced. The Originator has made it sound and well-ordered. Whatever is seen in this world, this transient home, is ordered according to accurate calculations, delicate balance, and extremely careful equilibrium. This balance and order imply, even explicitly indicate, the coming of the Resurrection and the awesomeness of the reckoning and Supreme Balance [by which men's deeds will be weighed] in the Hereafter. For whatever we witness here as seeds or foundations serves as indications, testimonies and signs of what will flourish in the Hereafter.

Whatever we observe in this realm of existence is but made or created. The sign of its being made is so clear as it would nearly announce it. Nothing contingent can be its own maker for it is too weak and impotent to be the real Maker of anything. For making or building, say, a plant or an animal requires different instruments, various tools and delicate balances like the balances used in the preparation of medicine. Nothing contingent has any of these, nor does it know how to use them, and therefore it cannot have created anything. Whatever is necessary for the existence and maintenance of a thing that can be found near or above or beneath or before or after it, it is but one of the radiances or manifestations of the Power of Him Whose treasures are between *KAF* and *NUN*.[2]

---

2. *KAF* and *NUN* are the letters forming *KUN* which means "be" and implies God's command to anything He wills to do or create: "*His command, when He wills a thing, is but to say to it 'Be!' and it is*" (36.82).

Among the Divine Names are some like the All-Speaking, the All-Providing, the All-Granting and so on, that admit apparent means to manifest themselves through veils and from behind walls. While some of them such as the Creator, the Inventor, the Giver of Life, and so on, do not admit means. However, the reason why the Names that admit means do so is not that they need means because of incompetence, but they admit them because their dignity and grandeur require them to be manifested behind veils and means.

Know O friend! I have seen on a tree growing in the desert two kinds of fruits and have been amazed at it. One kind of them resembled green grains, while the other a sort of peas or beans the size of fingers or a little less or bigger. They were curved and hollow as if waiting to receive "guests" into them. I took one of them and I had just opened it when numerous flying insects flew out into the air. Like birds or ants, they were in lines. It was nearly at sunset and they began to dance in ecstatic movements of the mentioning of God Almighty—do not think that they were playing; rather, they were rapturously mentioning the All-Merciful One Who keeps them in the air. The pods of broad beans served them as nests like a mother's womb, warm and fortified, in which they found delicious food.

This explicitly shows that it was neither those unconscious pods nor the insects themselves which had made the pods a home for the formation or origination and growing of the insects. For they are obviously unable to make that extremely wise arrangement. So it must be referred to someone else who must have absolute knowledge of both the beans and the insects all over the world. He must also be the one who knows all their needs and relations. Such a one can be only the One Who has absolute knowledge of and power over all things.

I ask you, O one who attributes disposal to others apart from God in the kingdom of God, who accepts the role of chance in the existence of the subtle works of God. How can that little tree hear or understand or know the tongue of those insects which lay their eggs on their branches, entrusting them to their preservation? Yet that tree provides for them a warm home in utmost caring like the womb of a mother and a swinging cradle in the air. The tree receives from the treasury of Divine Mercy delicious, sufficient food and stores it up in the nests on its branches for nothing in return for the creatures not belonging to its species, for the guests entrusted to its safekeeping by God. Such sort of mutual assistance among creatures is a clear sign that whatever is in the universe works at the service and under the direction and instruction of a single Lord, a singie Instructor, Who is the Besought-of-All.

Know O friend! When you look at those insects carefully, you see them mentioning their Creator in the air in the tongue of their manners, dispositions, well-arranged decorations and well-proportioned structures, even if you cannot understand their mentioning of the Creator in their particular languages. It is as if each insect were an articulate word. Like those insects, all the vermin in the soil also glorify their Creator in the tongue of their designs and decorations made by the Pen of Power, as they glorify Him also in their particular languages. This reality will provide you with four benefits:

First of all, it will give you a feeling of confidence that you see yourself in a stronghold formed by new births and infants brought up and adorned by the Caring of an All-Knowing, the Instruction of an All-Wise, the Favoring of an All-Munificent and the Compassion of an All-Compassionate One. You are always under the protection and consideration of that All-Knowing, All-Wise, All-Munificent and All-Compassionate One.

Secondly, you will be convinced that you are not one left to your devices with your head over your shoulder to do whatever you wish. Nor have you been left to the compassion of your selfhood unable to meet even the least of your limitless needs so that you sit rebuked and denuded, frightened of your absolute impotence and unlimited needs. For the perfect order and delicate balance you see in the life of those little creatures prevail likewise in the whole system.

O heedless one! Do those delicate "inscriptions", fine "books" inserted in big "letters" not tell you that you are also dependent on the same order? So come, awaken and observe the order or balance strictly. Whereas you play and amuse yourself like one of the insane in such a way as to destroy the balance.

Thirdly, this will suggest to you the conviction that the One to Whom you appeal for the satisfaction of all your needs and Whom you always fear is infinitely near to you although you are infinitely distant from Him. He disposes [all that is] in you and in your environment through His Power. In relation to that Power the smallest and the greatest, the least and the most, and the nearest and the furthest are the same. Nothing is difficult for Him at all, and He does not need to be in direct relation with creatures in His acts. Does this tell you that there is no reason for you to fear and be frightened? For wherever you are, His rules are prevailing there, wherever you turn, there is His "Face". You are at home, even if inside the earth. He always sees you even if you are in the belly of "non-existence". The hands of compassion, munificence and wisdom take you by His leave and command from one state and stage to the other. Before a hand leaves you, another is stretched to receive you in an orderly sequence. Chance can in no way intervene during your journeying. You are not wronged by non-existence, nor does mortality wrong you by eternal extinction. In whatever place you may be during your journey of existence there is an instance of non-existence; certainly, behind or beneath or within it you see one of the treasuries of Mercy full of what will remain forever of the same kind as what has perished.

Fourthly, what you observe in the realm of those little creatures will provide you with the evidence that everything is created or made by One Maker. This evidence is strengthened proportionately to their smallness and becomes clearer proportionally to their invisibility. For it is impossible for what is encompassed to be excluded from the disposal of the Creator of what is encompassing. The sign of being created is more evident in small beings than in big ones.

Know O friend! Your heedlessness of the Creator comes from four things:

The first is that you are so oblivious of your own self that your hair-like ego grows as a "thick rope". For when you forget God because of fancies and desires, He causes you to forget your own self, and, consequently, your ego grows thicker and thicker to swallow you up completely.

Secondly, you compare all other living creatures to yourself. For example, when you see an animal, although the animal is innocent, secured and happy in its life, you think of it as if it were a sorrowful man lost in thoughts and confused memories. You suppose its joyful dances as groaning with distresses.

Thirdly, since you restrict yourself to the manifestations of the Divine Name the Outward, to the extent that whatever you suppose as excluded from the sphere of [the authority and disposal of] this Name, does not belong to the One called by It. This is not the case at all. For the One called by this Name has many other beautiful Names. As He is above all that is above, He is also the Most Inward of the inward. He is the First, the Last, the Outward and the Inward.

Fourthly, Divine Manifestation of Oneness [that is, the concentration of almost all or many Names on a single thing] is the highest of the manifestations, besides being also the most distant and the most hidden. However, you desire to see it on all things manifestly. When you see an animal, by comparing it to yourself, under the influence of many of your feelings, you think of it as grieved on account of separation from its beloved ones or home and anxious about its future and provision. You are affected by it. However, if you considered it realistically, you would never see it as you suppose it.

As you make a mistake because of that comparison, you make another, greater, mistake due to another comparison. That is, you see, say, a honeybee. You unconsciously compare its Maker, the One, the All-Wise and Necessarily-Existent Who does not need to be in direct touch with His creatures and has no difficulty at all to create and govern, to contingent beings who are wretched, material and restricted. They have to be near to and in touch with their works and suffer difficulty in their working. Because of this comparison, you think that you and that creature—the honeybee—on which the Pen of the Maker is now operating as It always does, are near to the All-Holy, All-Transcendent Maker. It is true that He, may His essential Qualities be exalted, is near. He is nearer to you and every other thing than the nearest to you, nearer than your jugular veins. Whereas you and that creature are infinitely distant to Him. Consider a piece of glass. It shines with the reflection of the sun's light in it and becomes beautiful and adorned with the seven, refracting colors in the light of the sun. Because of its transparency, the "purity of its heart", a window or way is opened from that piece of glass to the sun and the sun is seen in it. However, if you stretch out your hand (to touch the sun), even if you were to stretch it out seventy, nay, seven hundred times as long as the radius of the earth, you will not be able to touch it. Only one who cherishes love for the sun in one's heart and lacks enough good sense, wishes to reach the sun through any of its rays. Such a one also wants to see in whatever thing the sun is reflected all that he hears or knows of the properties and functions of the sun manifested in the whole of that thing's system. If he cannot see all those properties and functions in the thing, he goes on to deny the existence of the sun in it or even the existence of the sun itself.

The heart of man is the mirror of the One, Eternally-Besought-of-All. However, unlike other mirrors, as Imam Rabbani explains, it is conscious of and has deeply-felt relation with what is manifested in it. Because of this, the heart has a capacity to feel countless instances of happiness.

If you ask how the wonderful activity in a living creature can be reconciled with the silence around it as if nothing happens and the invisibility of anything to show the activity, my answer is as follows:

If the activity belonged to material or natural causes or the living creature itself, then it would require that in every animal would exist an independent agent with an all-encompassing knowledge. It would require in every fruit a powerful maker for whose power the creation of the earth with all that is in it was not difficult. Then it would become possible to hear and observe the activity from outside. Nevertheless, consider the utmost security and safety observed in the space, the silence and tranquillity observed everywhere except the human realm, and the obedience, peace and restfulness ever-prevailing in the universe. All that is the work and law of the One Who when He wills a thing, *His command is but to say to it "Be!" and it is.*[3] He says: *There is not a thing but its treasures are with Us, and We send it not down but in a known measure.*[4] [If it is permissible to make a comparison to understand God's activity,] the relation between actions done by your hand and actions done with the speed of your imagination may be likened to the relation between your imagined actions and the actions of the Power of the Originator.

Know, O wretched, arrogant Said! Of your thousands of needs, only a few or even less than that are left to you to meet. The rest are committed to the care of your Creator Who created you first like a lump of dough and then shaped you in a fluid by His miraculous art so that you might be a mirror reflecting His Names. He opened your organs of hearing and seeing through His Mercy so that you might hear the truth and, by seeing the created, know the Creator. In the cavity of your mouth, He hung through His Favoring a tongue so that you might mention Him. He included in your head intellect to know Him and entrusted in your chest a heart to love Him. He treated you kindly in the darkness of desolation—the darkness of the womb—and disposed in you through His Lordship however He wished. He formed in your body through His Wisdom all those senses of many kinds and those organs of a great variety so that you might perceive all sorts of His bounties and recognize diverse manifestations of His Names.

---

3. *Ya Sin*, 36.82.
4. *al-Hijr*, 15.21.

O heedless, conceited one! While He has favored you with all such blessings, how much longer will you continue to accuse Him and rely on your own extremely insignificant, partial power? How much longer will you continue to commit your affairs to your own selfhood and wrong yourself by loading yourself with the burden you are unable to carry? What is the matter with you that you do not rely on Him Who holds you by the forelock and has undertaken to meet your needs? Rely on Him and embark on His ship floating in the flood of events and say, *In the Name of God is its course and its mooring*[5] so that you could rest upon the Judi of Islam[6] and repose yourself on the shore of salvation. Do you not see that the sun of life is about to set, the moon of body is eclipsed because of old age, and your head is shining with hoariness? There is no benefit from anyone except the Almighty; rather, there is great harm in whatever is outside His permission. Without Him, everything is harmful and hostile, while with Him you need nobody else. So, you must renounce whatever or whoever else other than Him.

Without Him, pains lying in every pleasure are more acute than the pleasures themselves, nay, pleasures are pure pains without Him. Therefore, *flee to God*[7], for with Him is everything; whatever perishable is with you, it exists permanently with Him. It perishes here; it does not last without Him, whereas it lasts with Him there. Besides, time is very limited. Do you not see that you suffer intoxication of death, for all of your life passes in intoxication. So, raise your head to free yourself from the world so that you may see that there are perpetual bounties, everlasting mercy and eternal love with Your Originator.

Know O bewildered thinker searching for truth! When your knowledge ends in something or when you see a sign of eternality in something, glorify the Almighty with His praise for you have approached the Truth. For being unknowable and eter-

---

5. *Hud*, 11.41.
6. Referring to the Ark of Prophet Noah, upon him be peace, which floated through mountain-like waves and settled on *al-Judi*, which is pbobably one of the hills of the mountain Ararat. (Tr.)
7. *adh-Dhariyat*, 51.50.

nality are titles or signs for the disposal of His absolute Lordship, may His Majesty be exalted.

Know, O one in doubts! When doubts attack you, look right. You will see the spheres of the disposals of His Creativity one within the other from the sphere of the solar system and planets to the sphere of atoms and particles, from the creation of the heavens to the creation of fruits, from the building of the earth to the invention of worms eating trees. All this points to the fact that the Pen "drawing" them is one and the stamp on them is also one. You are in the middle of the conical universe, bearing the Supreme Trust and having undertaken vicegerency—the responsibility to rule and improve the earth according to God's laws.

Then, look left. You will see the universal order judging and ruling with justice in every thing. You will also see the perfect balance preventing deviation in every thing.

The reality of creation will blow away your doubts and the universal order and balance will remove your confusions and bewilderment.

Afterwards, look at yourself so that you will see your self and body made or created from head to foot, from the smallest of cells to the whole of your body, which is in fact like a huge cell.

Then, look at your heart and then upwards. You will see the lights of the Light of Lights, Who has created the light, illuminated the light, and formed the light. The lights of His manifestation penetrate every thing, may His Majesty be exalted.

Know O friend! The use of comparative or superlative form in some of the Divine Names like the Most Merciful of the merciful, the Best of the creators, and God is the Greatest, etc., does not contradict the Divine Unity. For what is meant by them is to express the absolute, incomparable superiority of the Almighty over whatever or whomever else people may imagine to have Divine Attributes. Nor does this usage contradict the dignity of the One, the All-Overwhelming. For the purpose of it is not to compare the Attributes or acts of the Almighty and those of the created. For in relation to the Perfection of the Glorified One, whatever exists in the created in the name of perfection is only a reflected shadow. All the perfection shared by the created has no right to be compared with that of the Almighty. The purpose of this usage is to compare the particular effect of the manifestations of Divine Names on the things and the extent of the things being affected by them, and the effect of apparent means on the same things and the degree of the things being affected. It is like this:

A private sees his corporal as the greatest to pay respect and be thankful to. He is told that the king is greater and more merciful than the corporal. This does not mean comparing the king with the corporal, which would be satirical. Rather, it means warning the private that the king is worthier to be respected and thanked, and that it is only by the permission of the king and to the extent of the corporal's loyalty to the king that the corporal deserves respect and thanks.

We say of the Almighty, for example, the Most Affectionate of the affectionate or the Most Munificent of the munificent or the Most Dignified of the dignified, etc. By this we mean that the whole of the affection a man receives from all the affectionate ones in the universe cannot be equal to the care he receives from the infinite ocean of God's Mercy.

The One declared to be superior is Real, One and absolutely and incomparably superior, and He has the Name or the Attribute in question as essential to Him. Whereas the inferior ones are only nominal or imagined and represent the whole of the created. They have the attribute or name in question only as accidental and a dim shadow or manifestation of its original possessed by the Almighty. Combined together, all the created cannot have a real radiance of its original by themselves, as God declares: *Surely, those whom they invoke, apart from God, will never create a fly even if they combine together for the purpose.*[8]

Know O friend! The Name God contains the meaning of all

---

8. *al-Hajj*, 22.73.

the other Divine Beautiful Names and all the Attributes of perfection. Whereas, the proper names of all other beings point only to the persons of the beings who are called by them, without including their attributes. For the attributes of other beings are not indispensable to them, so their proper names do not point to their attributes or qualities. However, the Names and Attributes of the All-Holy One are indispensable to describe Him and Divinity particularly requires them. So the Name (the One) God, the "Proper" Name of the Divine Being, necessarily contains the meaning of all the other Divine Names and Attributes and points to them. Also, It rejects all others to which divinity is attributed, as in *There is no god but (the One) God*.

If you understood this, you can also understand that *There is no god but God* declares absolute Divine Unity and contains all the requirements or conclusions of Unity to the number of the Divine Beautiful Names.

This phrase contains thousands of phrases, for phrases such as this signify both confirmation and negation or rejection. Since the word (the One) God necessarily contains all the other Divine Names, *There is no god but (the One) God* also means *There is no creator, no provider, no self-subsistent, no owner, no originator, no overwhelming... but God*. Therefore, one who has progressed in his spiritual journeying means all these phrases while uttering *There is no god but God* and this phrase implies his spiritual ranks and states. Its repetition helps to increase and improve conviction.

Know O friend! If you know that whatever exists and whatever happens to you is from God, if you have conviction of this, then you should consent to both what is pleasing and what is harmful. If you do not consent, you will have to fall into heedlessness. This is so because God Almighty decreed apparent causes which make eyes blind to the truth. Things and events displeasing to man in the world are more than those that are pleasing, and the universe was not built according to the plans and desires of the wishful. Winds may blow against the desires of sailors. So, if a wishful one did not see the role of apparent causes in heedlessness of the Creator of causes, he would direct his improper, unjust objection, opposition, hatred, wrath, and grudge to the All-Wise Creator, the All-Munificent Master. When a heedless one throws his arrow of objection, he throws it to either Destiny or Satan but usually hits his own head or soul.

Know O friend! When you give due, careful consideration (to existence), you will surely understand that any contingent thing or being is as distant from creating as the infinitude of the Power necessary for the creation of anything.

Know O friend! Prayer is of three kinds.

The first kind is the prayer man does verbally. The cries of animals which each utters in its own tongue for the needs of which it is conscious are also of this kind.

The second kind of prayer is that which is done in the tongue of neediness. The prayers of all plants or trees, especially those that they do in spring, and the prayers animals do for their needs of which they are not conscious are of this second kind.

The third kind is the prayer done in the tongue of potential. The prayers done by all the creatures having the potential to grow, change and be perfected, are of this kind. As *there is nothing that does not glorify Him with His praise*, neither is there anything that does not pray to Him and thank Him either verbally or in person or in the tongue of disposition or state.[9]

Know O friend! A fruit-stone before growing into a tree, a sperm into a man, an egg into a bird, and a seed into a plant, is certainly under the direction, command and control of a perfect, penetrating knowledge. This is in order that it could be directed

---

9. While discussing prayer in *The Letters*, the respectable writer divides the first kind of prayer into two categories and says:

The first category consists of the supplications made in desperation or in connection with natural needs. Most of such supplications are accepted.

The second category consists of those prayers that we say every day. These are also of two types: one is active and by disposition, and the other verbal and from the heart. To plough the earth, for example, is an active prayer and means to knock at the door of the treasury of God's Mercy and Munificence, not to beg provision from the earth.

What reaches the Court of God from the whole universe is a kind of prayer. Causes are petitions to God to create the desired result. (*The Letters* 2, pp.108–9.) (Tr.)

or dispatched to the right path out of countless crooked and blind, dead-end ones. This knowledge pertains only to the Knower of the Unseen, Who fashions in the wombs as He wills, Who knows the past, the present and the future. A stone, sperm, egg, or a seed is like a prototype or an outline copied from the Manifest Book, which is one of the books of Destiny. Or it is like a table of contents extracted from the Manifest Record, one of the records of the Eternal Knowledge. Or it is like a set or embodiment of principles deduced from the Mother Book, one of the books of eternal Destiny, particularly from the "chapters" of balance and order of that Book. Or it is like a summary or synopsis or something representative formed by the All-Powerful, All-Knowing Lord of all things, may His Majesty be exalted.

Know O friend! A believer views a creature like a letter, which means almost nothing by itself but serves as a complementary part of the word to which it belongs. Whereas an unbeliever considers it on behalf of itself, restricting his view of it to the creature itself.

Every creature has two aspects, one concerning itself and its own attributes, and the other pointing to its Creator and His Names manifested on it.

The second aspect is more comprehensive and capacious. For every letter in a book points to itself only as a letter, while it means much more and serves a great deal more in the book where it is. It points to its author and describes him or her in many ways. In the same way, every creature, which is a letter from the book of Divine Power, points to itself and its apparent existence to the extent of its size, while pointing to its Eternal Designer in many respects and eulogizes His Names manifested on it.

It is an established rule that no judgement can be given on the basis of a letter, neither can a letter serve to draw a conclusion about something in the name of affirmation or denial. For this reason, mind does not go into details about it. Whereas, if mind concerns itself with a letter intentionally, then that letter becomes as if a word.

It is because of this that you see the scientific or philosophical books written about the universe as if very sound and full of meaning, whereas they are of little significance concerning the Creator. By contrast, theologians deal with philosophical and scientific matters not on behalf of themselves but as offering arguments for the existence and Unity of the Creator. It is enough for them that, for example, the sun is a lamp, the earth a cradle, night a covering, day a time to work for livelihood, and the moon a luminous thing. It is enough for them that the mountains are as pegs for the stability of the earth and to freshen air, store up water and minerals, protect soil and calm the wrath of the quaking earth by enabling it to breathe out. However, science deals with the sun as the center of its system, a huge fire so intense that all its planets including the earth fly around it like scattered moths. The view of theologians about the universe may sometimes be contrary to reality, however, since they are usually in conformity with what is apparent and the general viewpoint, they should not be contradicted. For this reason, even if their views of philosophical or scientific issues may be considered as weak and of no significance, their views of the essentials of theology are stronger than iron.

It is because of this that in the world the heedless and misguided may seem to have the upper hand in the beginning. It appears so as they are utterly inclined to the world with all their faculties and abilities in a way to declare: *(The life) is only our life of the world.*[10] Whereas, the end is for the righteous and God-fearing, for whom and for whose leader the Qur'an proclaims: *What is to succeed will be better for you than what is foregoing, as will the Hereafter than the world.*[11] *The life of the world is nothing but a pastime and a play. But best is the home of the Hereafter for those who keep their duty in fear of God. Still, will you not understand?;*[12] *The home of the Hereafter, that is life if they but knew.*[13] God is suffi-

10. *al-An'am*, 6.29.
11. *al-Duha*, 93.4.
12. *al-An'am*, 6.32.
13. *al-Ankabut*, 29.64.

cient for us, what a good trustee He is. How good as the Protecting Friend and how good as the Helper.

Know O friend! God's forgiving is an act of extra grace, while His punishment is pure justice. If a man takes poison, he deserves to be ill according to God's established law. If he does not become ill, it is because of God's extra grace and extraordinary favoring.

The relation between a sin and torment is so strong that it led the *Mu'tazilite*s to err in judging about it by attributing evil to other than the Almighty and concluding that every evil will certainly be punished. Whereas [even if it can never be said that it is incumbent on the Almighty to punish every evil or sin], its deserving punishment is not contradictory to the perfection of Divine Mercy. It is because the harm of evil, even though it be partial and little, affects all the threads forming the universal order which is of absolute, great good to all. Forsaking that great, absolute good for the sake of shunning a little evil or harm causes great evil or harm. This is contrary to the wisdom in the Justice of the All-Just, the All-Wise, the All-Munificent.

O wrong-doing, ignorant man! Avoid evil as much as possible. You will otherwise deserve the punishment for abandoning good and fulfilling the necessary conditions to obtain a result. Evil means and results in non-existence; the non-existence of some necessary part of the existence of something causes its complete non-existence, which means the nullifying of also all other parts. For the existence of something depends on not a single part but the presence of all the conditions for its existence. So, God's forgiving of an evil is purely an act of grace and points to His perfect graciousness. Furthermore, He punishes an evil with its like but rewards good with ten times of it, while their true deserts are otherwise. This also shows the extent of the injustices of mankind who judge the other way.

Know O friend! Man is subject to forgetting and the worst kind of forgetting is forgetting one's own self. Man's forgetting himself in transactions, serving, working and reflection is misguidance. But self-forgetting at the time of getting wages and rewards is a sign of perfection. People of misguidance and those of true guidance differ from each other in forge12tting and remembering. The misguided forget themselves at the time of working and practicing the principles of duty, while they recognize no limits to their unyielding self-conceit and arrogance. However, they remember themselves whenever the time of obtaining fruits, however despicable they are, arises.

But, a man who purifies his soul remembers himself at the time of working and starting a movement or giving service or thinking, as if he knew that he was responsible for setting a good example for others and had the foremost responsibility in fulfilling a work or duty. Yet he forgets himself in obtaining the results, getting the rewards and collecting the fruits. He does so to the extent that one gets the impression that he has worked not for his own, mortal self but, as if a slave, for his lord with the pleasure of sincerity and the results of his work mostly belong to his lord.

Know O friend! The solidarity and togetherness of the believers in their congregational worship and supplications has a very deep, important meaning. Each believer becomes like a brick in a firm building, benefiting from his brothers in belief thousands of thousands of times more than his own worship and supplication. When belief brings them together, each works for the whole and becomes an intercessor and supplicator for them, and one pleading mercy for them declaring their innocence. All of them together extol their leader, upon him be peace and blessings, especially. Also, every believer takes pleasure in the happiness of others like a mother, although herself hungry, taking pleasure in the satisfaction of her children, or like a compassionate brother who takes pleasure in the happiness of his brother. As a result, that wretched, mortal individual—man—has the capacity of worshipping the Creator of the universe in a comprehensive way and earning eternal happiness.

Look at the Prophet, upon him be peace and blessings: when you see him invoking "O Most Merciful of the merciful," you see the whole of his community responding to him saying, "O God! Bestow blessings and peace upon Your servant and beloved, Muhammad, the ocean of Your lights, the mine of Your mysteries, one diffusing remembrance of and gratitude to You, and openly proclaiming the beauties of the sovereignty of Your Lordship." They declare his innocence before their Lord, make him loved by Him Who sent him as a mercy for them and confirm his right and authority to intercede [for them with the Almighty]. Again, they proclaim, in the tongue of their absolute impotence and poverty, the absolute wealth of the absolutely Glorified One in His absolute, perfect independence. They also proclaim His absolute Liberality in His majestic Dignity and, in the tongue of their absolute servanthood, His absolute Lordship. Through such exalted solidarity and mutual helping, a believer rises from the lowest state of insignificance and helplessness to the highest position of being vicegerent of God on the earth, bearing the Supreme Trust and being an honored, respected one to whom the heavens and earth were subjugated.

Know O friend! A man who is far from something cannot know that thing as much and as well as another near to it, even if he is much more intelligent than the other. When they disagree on that thing, the one near is preferred. European philosophers and scientists who are engrossed in materialistic subjects are extremely distant to the high station of Islam, faith and the Qur'an. Even the greatest of them cannot be on a par with an ordinary Muslim who understands the Qur'an superficially.

This is my observation in exact conformity with the reality. Do not say: "How do those who discovered scientific realities such as the properties of lightning and steam and so on not understand the mysteries of truth and the lights of the Qur'an?" They cannot understand them because their minds are restricted to their eyes, and the eyes cannot see what the heart and spirit see, especially at a time when the hearts have died because of heedless absorption in naturalism. *God has sealed their hearts, ears and eyes.*[14]

---

14. *al-Nahl*, 16.108.

Know O friend! The greatest of ingratitude for bounties is
giving the Almighty no thanks for the bounties common to all
like hearing and sight and for the constant ones like light and
fire and those abundant and encompassing ones like air and
water. A man can thank God Almighty for the bounties particular to him or for those renewed for him or given to him at the
time of particular need. Whereas the bounties given uninterruptedly and abundantly are much more important and greater.
Their being abundant and encompassing point to their utmost
importance and their being constant indicate the greatness of
their value.

Know O friend! The verse *He keeps count of all things*[15] implies
the order, harmony, equality and proportionateness among the
numbers of the things neighboring or corresponding to or resembling one another, such as the fingers of the hand, the
grains in spikes or ears, seeds in fruits, and petals in flowers...
Glory be to Him Who keeps count of all things and Whose
Knowledge encompasses all things.

Know O friend! Fertilization and birth, together with compassionate raising or rearing, are two tasks common to all things
down to the least. An immediate reward or wage is given in return for them, which is the pleasure they provide. The comprehensiveness of the liberality of the All-Beneficent, the All-Munificent and the intense zeal of all reproducing things to carry
out these two tasks show that they take pleasure particular to
each in fulfilling that task. That degree of rewarding, mercy and
justice together with the Divine declaration, *My Mercy encompasses all things*[16] and many Prophetic Traditions confirm rewarding and retaliation among animals on Judgement Day.
They point to the fact that the souls of animals are preserved to
receive their last reward for their perfect obedience to Divine
rules.[17] After the settlement of mutual rights, the bodies of ani-

15. *al-Jinn*, 72.28.

16. *al-A'raf*, 7.156.

17. Abu Hurayra relates that God's Messenger, upon him be peace and blessings,
declared: Mutual rights will be settled on Judgement Day, to the extent that a horn-
less sheep will restore its right from another with horns. (*Muslim*, Hadith no. 2582).

mals will be made dust. However, it is possible that the whole of a species will be embodied in and represented by a blessed member such as the camel, ram, dog, hoopoe, and ant mentioned in the Qur'an...

Know, O wretched Said greedy for the maintenance of his material existence in this fleeting world, despite the fact that the world is subject to decay and only the All-Permanent One can maintain it. You can gain permanence only by turning toward the All-Glorified One and spending your life in His way.

Such being the case, why continue to insist on seeking permanence in this world? Rather, say: For permanence, it is enough for me that God, the Master, is the All-Permanent, and for the pleasure of permanence it suffices that I know Him as the All-Permanent, Worshipped One. As for the aim in seeking permanence, it is sufficient that I know Him as my All-Permanent Lord. With respect to the perfection expected from permanence, my belief in His being the All-Permanent Inventor is enough. Regarding existence, it suffices that I am a work of the Necessarily-Existent Being. As regards the worth of existence, it is sufficient that I am a work of the art of the Creator of the heavens and earth. In regard to the aim of existence, it suffices that I know that I am the painting of Him Who has adorned the heavens with stars and the earth with flowers. With respect to the pleasure of existence, it is enough for me to know that I am His creature and He is my Lord and Inventor. In respect of life, it suffices that I am an object of the manifestations of the Names of the Creator of death and life. As for life and its rights and aims, it is enough that, by virtue of my comprehensive existence, I exhibit amongst my perceptive brothers in the universe and announce in the market of the world the marvels of the works of the Names of the Creator of the heavens and earth. It is enough for the aim of life that I am a sample and embodiment of the works of the manifestations of His Beautiful Names. It suffices for life and its perfection that in the tongue of my disposition and manners I reflect the manifestations of the Names of Him by Whose command the heavens rose high and by Whose leave the earth has gained stability. It suffices for the pleasure of life that I know that I am His slave, creature and servant needy of Him, and He is my Creator, God, Lord, Originator, Owner, Merciful to me and sustaining me. And with respect to perfection, belief in God is enough, and God is sufficient for me against everything.

Know O friend! In belief in Divine Unity and attributing things to the One God there is infinite facility to the extent that existence would almost become necessary. Whereas in associating partners with God and attributing creatures to multiple "creators", there is infinite difficulty, to the extent that existence would become impossible. While existence gains infinite worth by being attributed to the One God, it loses all its value by being ascribed to multiple "pseudo-creators"—to themselves or nature or matter or chance and the like. Do you not see how a thing in the hand of a soldier is regarded as great and valuable by being attributed to the king, and the soldier's speech about the king attracts attention and is given much importance. Also, how easy it is to procure all the necessities of life from the treasuries of the king. Whereas, whatever the soldier has or speaks will lose all its value and importance if his connection with the king is cut by his rebellion to the king.

Know O friend! Whatever comes from the Almighty is the same, whether it brings harm or benefit, good or evil, or life or death by His Power and Destiny. For death is the beginning of another life, and evil and harm end in good and benefit respectively.

Know O friend! Owing to its comprehensive nature and numerous faculties, the spirit of man has the capacity for both limitless pleasures and unrestricted pains. He takes pleasure in the pleasures of his children, human brothers and sisters and other creatures, and suffers on account of their distresses.

Know O friend! If one looks at things in oblivion of one's self, realities change, like things seen in water the other way. Your ignorance leads you to regard yourself as knowledgeable.

Know O friend! What requires the repetition of some parts of the Qur'an also requires the repetition of (religious) recitations and prayers. For the Qur'an, besides being a book of truths and law and a book of Divine knowledge and wisdom, is also a book of recitation, prayer and call. Recitation requires reiteration, prayer repetition, and call re-affirmation.

Know O friend! It is one of the elevated virtues of the Qur'an that it arrives at Divine Unity after mentioning the realm of multiplicity, thus making a summary after exposition. After mentioning particular things, it concludes with the principles of the absolute Lordship and the rules of the encompassing Divine Attributes of perfection. Such conclusions serve as the results of the main parts of verses or as the effects of the causes dealt with in them. By doing so, the Qur'an aims to prevent the mind of the listener or reciter from being lost in particulars of existence and forgetting the grandeur of the rank of the absolute Divinity. It also shows the manner of the "intellectual" servanthood to the One of Grandeur, Awe and Greatness. Again, it broadens your mind from those particulars to their resemblances and teaches you that in every thing, even if it be the smallest, there is a clear, straight way to the knowledge of the Eternal King and observation of the manifestations of the Names of the One, the Eternally-Besought-of-All.

Through this style, the Qur'an shows the "sun" in a "drop of water" or the "manifestations of the colors in the light of the sun" on a "flower". It shows the sun shining with all its splendor at midday and thereby lifts your head to the sun so that you are not bewildered amidst the multiplicity of things and despise the sun.

For example, in *sura Yusuf*, after mentioning a particular, minor event—namely, the Prophet Joseph's plan to retain his brother with him—the Qur'an concludes: *Over every man of knowledge there is one who knows (better)*.[18] In *sura al-Hajj*, *They do not esteem God His rightful measure;*[19] in *sura al-Nur*, *When the children among*

---

18. *Yusuf*, 12.76.
19. *al-Hajj*, 22.74.

you come of age to *God is All-Knowing, All-Wise*;[20] and in *sura al-Ankabut, surely the frailest of houses* to *if they but knew*[21] are examples of this style of the Qur'an.

Know O friend! The blessing and help coming from saints and the enlightenment they diffuse are a sort of prayer done either through disposition or actively. The One Who guides and really helps is God. With respect to this, something appeared to me but I could not specify it distinctly. It is this: Man has an innermost sense or faculty. If he, even if he be a sinful transgressor, prays through it, he is certainly answered. It is such a faculty that if man swears by God through it that [something will happen], God does not disprove him.

Know O friend! O one convinced of (the occurrence of) past events but doubtful about the future! Go back to a few centuries before and suppose yourself as one of your forefathers. Then, look at your ancestors who have already been the creatures of the past and your future descendants who will possibly come one after the other. Is there anything different between these two wings? You will not be able to see the hand of anything— chance or something else—in them. As the preceding generations are doubtlessly the creatures of God, the future ones will also be so. Both are included in the Maker's Knowledge and are seen by Him. Returning your ancestors to life will not be more strange that the creation of your descendants. Rather, it will be easier, as the All-Glorified One declares: *It is easier for Him.*[22] If you compare the whole of creation and events with this particular, minor incident, you will see that all past events are miracles testifying that their Creator has absolute power to bring about all possible events and creatures. He has also absolute knowledge of all their minutest details and encompasses them with His Sight.

All those creatures and heavenly objects in the garden of the universe are miracles bearing witness and clarifying that their

---

20. *al-Nur*, 24.59.
21. *al-Ankabut*, 29.41.
22. *al-Rum*, 30.27.

Creator is powerful over all things and knows them. Similarly, all those flowering plants and species of adorned animals found in the garden of the earth are marvels of His Art and manifestly testify that their Maker is powerful over all things and knows them. In relation with His Power, creating (minute) particles and stars and causing trees to yield fruits and resurrecting the dead are the same. Re-building the children of Adam on their rotted bones is not more difficult for Him than causing the flowers of trees to re-open on their thin branches every year.

Know O friend! like the fruits of trees, drops of water whose form shows perfect, delicate order and balance are among the countless bounties of God. The One Who attaches infinite aims to a drop of water is He Who holds the whole of the creation in His Grasp and Whose treasuries are between *Kaf* and *Nun*. A drop of water is the bounty of Him Who has made the order "*Kun*" (be!) the infinitive (origin) of "*Kawn*" (the creation). All thanks and gratitude are to Him, the All-Glorified.

Know O friend! The frequent mentioning of the revival of the earth in the Qur'an, and the Qur'an's drawing the attention of mankind to soil, inspired to me that the earth is the heart of the universe and soil is the heart of the earth. The nearest of ways to the target goes through "soil" through the gate of humility and self-annihilation. Soil is nearer to the Creator of the heavens even than the highest of the heavens themselves. Because there is nothing else in the universe equal to soil in receiving the manifestations of Divine Lordship and the Names the All-Living and Self-Subsistent, displaying Divine Creativity and being the object of the activities of Divine Power.

As the "Throne of Mercy" is on water, the "Throne of Life and Reviving" is on soil. Soil is the most comprehensive of the mirrors (reflecting the manifestations of life). However transparent the mirror of a dense thing is, it shows that thing more clearly. Whereas, however dense the mirror of a luminous thing is, the reflection of the Names in it is more complete. Do you not see that air receives only a dim light from the radiance of the sun and water cannot reflect the colors of the sun, although it shows it to you with its light. As for soil, it shows through its flowers whatever there is in the light of the sun. Compared with the Light of the Eternal Sun, the sun is only a dense, shining drop. The adornment of soil and displaying in spring its finery— its countless flowers of infinitely various forms and colors and its beautiful, innumerable animals testifying to the perfection of Divine Lordship—is a witness to the Creator. If you like, look at that violet: how the hand of the All-Wise Maker disposes in it, coloring and adorning it.

Glory be to Him Who makes Himself known to us through His subtle Art, makes His Power known to His creatures through the marvels of His disposal in soil. This explains the meaning of the *hadith, A servant is the nearest to his Lord while he is prostrate before Him.*[23]

Such being the truth, do not be frightened of soil and entering in it, nor fear the grave and lying in it.

Know O friend! My intellect accompanies my heart in its journeying and the heart gives its findings to the hand of the intellect, which displays them, as it always does, in the form of parabolical evidences. For example, the All-Wise Creator is infinitely near (to His creatures) as He is endlessly distant from them. Also, as He is the most Inward of the inward, He is the most Outward of the outward. Again, He is neither within nor outside anything.

If you like, look at the works of His Mercy scattered on the face of the earth and the imprints or activities of His Power in the spheres of existence on the earth, so that you can see that manifest reality. Consider the two particles or flowers or fruits or bees of exactly the same sort or identity one in the farthest west, the other in the farthest east. With respect to apparent physical conditions, the Maker Who creates these two things in just the same moment must be distant from them. While from the viewpoint of the facility and speed of creation and the infinite abundance of creatures together with their absolute firm-

---

23. *Muslim*, Hadith no. 482; *Abu Dawud*, Hadith no. 875.

ness, the Maker is infinitely near to each. This is not like the nearness of the center of concentric circles to the points on them which differ in nearness to the center. For all things are equally near to the Maker Who makes everything infinitely firm and beautiful.

This arises from the qualities of the Sphere of Necessity—Divinity—the abstraction and immateriality of the inner dimension of existence and the unconditioned character of Divine Attributes and acts. This is also because of the character of the manifestations of Divine Names on creatures one by one as well as on the whole of existence at the same time, and the complete difference from the identity of the Original Agent and the object.

For example—and God's is the highest comparison—through its images in the mirrors of transparent objects and reflections on flowers, the sun is nearer to them than even themselves, while they are extremely distant from the sun. It is almost impossible to traverse the distance between the image (of the sun) in your mirror and its original.

Glory be to Him Who is absolutely free from having likes of His Essence, and absolutely exempt from having likes of His Attributes. He is the First, the Last, the Outward and the Inward, and He has absolute, perfect knowledge of all things.

O God, O All-Just, O All-Wise, O All-Knowing! There is not a single breath of wind, a single drop in clouds, a single sound in thunderbolts, a single flash of lightning, a single flower in gardens, a single fruit in orchards, a single bee in air, a single color in plants, a single work of art in animals, a single decoration in existents, a single particle in creation, a single instance of order and balance in creation, a single thing in the Divine Supreme Throne, a single act in the Divine Supreme Seat, a single star in the heavens, a single thing on the earth, that it does not testify that You are Necessarily-Existent, One, Single, Besought-of-All. There is not a single creature that does not explicitly testify that You are (the One) God, the Knower of the Unseen, the One Who brings forth grains and subjugates hearts. All of the creatures are under Your Power, with their hearts in Your grasp, forelocks in Your hand, and keys with You. There is not a single particle but it moves by Your leave.

O God of those who have already gone and those to come! O Lord of Muhammad, upon him be peace and blessings, and Abraham, Gabriel and Michael, upon them be peace! I ask You, for the sake of Your Greatest Name, the Light of Your Noble Face, Your right religion, Your Straight Path, the Seven of the Twice-Repeated (sura al-Fatiha), and the grand Qur'an, and for the sake of thousands of thousands of "Say: 'He is God, the One'", and thousands of thousands of the Opening Chapter of the Book, and for the sake of Your All-Beautiful Names, Your Greatest Name, the Sacred Black Stone, and Your Honored House—Ka'ba—and for the sake of the Night of Power and esteemed Ramadan, and for the sake of Your honored Prophets and Your noblest, beloved one, upon him be peace and blessings—I ask You for the sake of all those mentioned to have mercy on the community of Muhammad. Open their breasts for belief and Islam, keep us safe against heretics, protect our religion, brighten the evidences of the Qur'an, and exalt the Shari'a of Islam. Amen, O Most Merciful of the Merciful.

Addendum

In the Name of God, the Merciful, the Compassionate
Praise be to God, and blessings be upon His Prophet.

Know O friend! Nothing can be veiled from the pure, all-encompassing Light, nor can anything be outside the sphere of the limitless Power, otherwise what is limitless requires to be limited, which is inconceivable.

Also, the eternal, Divine Wisdom bestows blessing on everything according to the capacity of each—every thing takes from the ocean according to the volume of its pitcher. Nothing small can prevent the All-Wise, All-Powerful One Who creates everything with a certain measure from being concerned with large entities, nor can the large entities or species hinder the All-Encompassing, Immaterial, Outward and Inward One from being interested in the small ones or individuals. Something small is great in the art it contains, and a species of small creatures exists in more abundance than others of big ones. Absolute Grandeur never admits partners. An infinitely abundant creation with absolute facility and speed and absolute firmness shows that an All-Beautiful One wants to be known and see that His absolute Beauty and Perfection is observed. Together with this creation, the absolute Mercy and Wealth testified by whatever exists and takes place in the universe, and the existence of almost infinite number of reflective observers—all require without doubt the existence of species of micro-organisms and small, flying creatures in infinite abundance.

Know O friend! If your selfhood is more lovable to you than anything else because it is nearer to you than all other things, then your Lord must be more lovable to you than your own selfhood because He is nearer to you than your selfhood. Do you not see that the invaluable things—senses, faculties, etc.—

stored in you which are beyond your power and imagination, work under the guidance of your Lord?

Know O friend! There is no room for chance in the universe. Look at a garden to see infinite orderliness in infinite mixture and perfect distinguishing amidst perfect mixture of things. This points to the Wisdom of the Maker Whose Knowledge is all-encompassing.

Know O friend! If you do not attribute all things to the One Being, you will have to accept the existence of divinities to the number of God's manifestations on all individual existents in the universe. It is as if, after closing your eyes to the sun and remaining heedless of it, you see the images of the sun shining in the drops on the surface of the ocean. You see them as existing by themselves independently of the sun, and you will then have to accept the existence of as many suns as those drops. Whereas a drop cannot contain the smallest of stars, let alone containing the lamp of the world.

Know O friend! If you observe with attentive eyes, you will see that all species or kinds of creatures compete enthusiastically to present their adornments and subtleties of beauty to the view of the Majestic Observer Who constantly watches them. For all creatures observably bear subtleties of the firm, amazing art attracting all beholders. They compete to present their beauties and adornments to the view of the Eternal Witness because that Eternal Witness has created every creature to see in their mirrors the manifestations of the lights of His Beauty, Grace, Majesty, and Perfection. Then He calls all other conscious witnesses to see them in order to know Him, to discern that Secret Treasure.

The highest of the purposes for the existence of a thing, the loftiest of the rights of life, is its presenting itself to the view of its Creator and being watched by Him because it is a work of His Names. And the greatest of the pleasures of life is that a living being is conscious of being watched by Him.

A thing's being seen by other fellow-creatures is also another purpose for its existence. However, compared with the first purpose, the difference is as much as that between what is finite and the Infinite.

As for what people call the right of life, it is preserving and maintaining life. It is only one of the innumerable rights of life, the smallest and the least significant one, because life is among the highest, most elevated, most amazing and noblest miracles of the Power of the All-Living, Self-Subsistent, the One, Eternally-Besought-All. Maintenance of life is the means of this miracle being recognized and fulfilling its functions and is valuable only as a means. So, it cannot be elevated to the rank of an end or aim.

Do you think, O heedless one, that, a pomegranate, which is an amazing work of Divine art, is only for your eating in a minute? It is a word displaying the All-Glorified One Who forms it.

Know that the One Who has the most superior Beauty takes true pleasure in observing His Beauty and showing It to His creatures. Whereas it is impossible to feel the pleasure of relative superiority with the same strength. The One with essential Perfection and eternal, true, pure Beauty is loved because of Himself, Whose is the highest comparison, and Who informed us with the tongue of His Messenger, upon him be peace and blessings, who declared: *He has created the creation to be known*. That is, He has fashioned mirrors so that the manifestations of His Beauty, Who is loved because of Himself, may be observed in them.

Know, O mortal one! With respect to permanence, it suffices for you that after your death you will continue to exist in His Knowledge and before His eyes. Give all things to their true Owner and attribute them to Him to acquire satisfaction. Otherwise you will have to accept as many deities as the manifestations of God or the particles of the universe or the particles of soil, as has been mentioned many times in this book. For soil serves for innumerable living things of great variety to come into existence.

Glory be to Him Who is absolutely free from having likes both to His Essence and Attributes, and to Whose Oneness His creatures bear witness and to Whose Lordship His signs testify, and Whose Knowledge and Power encompass all things. May His Majesty be exalted, and there is no god but He.

INDEX OR BRIEF SUMMARIES OF THE TOPICS
DISCUSSED IN THE TREATISE

*An explanation of the verse, *The seven heavens and the earth and whoever is in them glorify Him. There is nothing that does not glorify Him with His praise* (17.44). (402–6)

*Man's body with respect to him and to its Creator. (407)

*Whatever we witness here as seeds or foundations serves as indications, testimonies and signs of what will flourish in the Hereafter. (409)

*Four things which cause one to be heedless of the Creator. (413)

*Without Him, pains lying in every pleasure are more acute than the pleasures themselves, nay, pleasures are pure pains without Him. Therefore, *flee to God*, for with Him is everything; whatever perishable is with you, it exists permanently with Him. (416)

*What is meant by the use of comparative or superlative form in some of the Divine Names like the Most Merciful of the merciful, the Best of the creators, and God is the Greatest, etc. (417)

*The Name God contains the meaning of all the other Divine Beautiful Names and all the Attributes of perfection. (418–9)

*If you know that whatever exists and whatever happens to you is from God, if you have conviction of this, then you should consent to both what is pleasing and what is harmful. (419)

*Kinds of prayer: (420)

*A believer views a creature like a letter, which means almost nothing by itself but serves as a complementary part of the word to which it belongs. Whereas an unbeliever considers it on behalf of itself, restricting his view of it to the creature itself. (421)

*God's forgiving is an act of extra grace, while His punishment is pure justice. (423)

*People of misguidance and those of true guidance differ from each other in forgetting and remembering. The misguided forget themselves at the time of working and practicing the principles of duty, while they recognize no limits to their unyielding self-conceit and arrogance. However, they remember themselves whenever the time of obtaining fruits, however despicable they are, arises. (424)

*Virtue of doing prescribed prayers in congregation: (424)

*European philosophers and scientists engrossed in materialistic subjects cannot be on a par with an ordinary Muslim who understands the Qur'an superficially in understanding the truths of Islam and the Qur'an. (425)

*Why insist on seeking permanence in this world? (427)

*Elevated virtues in the ways the Qur'an concludes its verses. (429)

*All those creatures and heavenly objects in the garden of the universe are miracles bearing witness and clarifying that their Creator is powerful over all things and knows them. (431)

*The earth is the heart of the universe and soil is the heart of the earth. The nearest of ways to the target goes through "soil" through the gate of humility and self-annihilation. Soil is nearer to the Creator of the heavens even than the highest of the heavens themselves. As the "Throne of Mercy" is on water, the "Throne of Life and Reviving" is on soil. (431)

*The All-Wise Creator is infinitely near (to His creatures) as He is endlessly distant from them. Also, as He is the most Inward of the inward, He is the most Outward of the outward. Again, He is neither within nor outside anything. (432)

*Nothing small can prevent the All-Wise, All-Powerful One Who creates everything with a certain measure from being concerned with large entities, nor can the large entities or species hinder the All-En-compassing, Immaterial, Outward and Inward One from being interested in the small ones or individuals. (435)

*O friend! If you do not attribute all things to the One Being, you will have to accept the existence of divinities to the number of God's manifestations on all individual existents in the universe. (436)

*The highest of the purposes for the existence of a thing, the loftiest of the rights of life, is its presenting itself to the view of its Creator and being watched by Him because it is a work of His Names. And the greatest of the pleasures of life is that a living being is conscious of being watched by Him. (436)

A Point from the Light of Knowledge of God, exalted be His Majesty

When I enter a garden, I choose the most beautiful flower or fruit in it. If it is difficult for me to pick it, I take pleasure in looking at it. If I come across a rotten one, I pretend not to notice it, according to the rule, *Take what pleases and leave what does not*. This is my style, and I request my readers also to behave in the same way.

They say that what I write cannot be clearly understood.

I agree. I write whatever occurs to my heart in the way it occurs. I feel as if I sometimes speak from the top of a minaret and sometimes from the bottom of a well.

Dear reader! As you read this treatise, I ask you to consider the following:

The one that speaks is my wretched heart.

The one I address is my rebellious selfhood.

The one who truly gives ear is one in search of the truth.

I believe in God, His angels, His Books, His Messengers, and the Last Day, and in Destiny, good and evil, being from Almighty God. Revival after death is true, and I bear witness that there is no god but God, and I also bear witness that Muhammad is His Messenger, upon him be peace and blessings.

In the Name of God, the Merciful, the Compassionate.

Praise be to God, the Lord of the worlds, and peace and blessings be upon Muhammad, the Seal of the Prophets, and on all his family and Companions.

Our aim and goal is God, *there is no got but He, the All-Living, the*

Self-Subsistent.[1] Among countless proofs of Him, we here adduce only four.

The first proof is Muhammad, upon him be peace and blessings. We explained this proof in the treatise *Gleams from Knowledge of the Prophet* [and also in the second treatise of this book titled *Droplets from the Ocean of Knowledge of the Prophet*].

The second proof is the universe, the macro-cosmos or macro-human. It is the observed, great book (of 1 creation).

The third proof is the holy Qur'an. It is the book in which there is no doubt, and which is the Sacred Word.

The fourth proof is the human conscience or consciousness, which is the juncture of the world of the Unseen and the material, visible world. Man's consciousness or conscience influences the intellect from which the ray of belief in the Divine Unity issues.

The first proof: It is the Muhammadan Truth, upon him be peace and blessings.[2]

This proof is furnished with Messengership and Islam. Messengership contains the testimony of the greatest concensus and most comprehensive agreement of all the Prophets, upon them be peace, and Islam bears the spirit of the Divinely-revealed religions and their confirmation based on Revelation.

The noble Messenger, upon him be peace and blessings, explains to mankind the existence of God and His Unity with all his truthful words affirmed by his manifest miracles, the testimony of the Prophets, upon them be peace, and the confirmation of all the Divine-revealed religions. He manifests, upon him be peace and blessings, that light (of Divine Unity) in the name of those purified, excellent ones among humankind, who all agree on this call.

---

1. *al-Baqara*, 2.255.
2. Muhammadan Truth is the truth represented by the Prophet Muhammad, upon him be peace and blessings, as a servant and Messenger of God Almighty, or it is the truth of which the Prophet Muhammad is the unique embodiment. (Tr.)

Is it at all possible that falsehood can have a hand in that pure, clear, evident truth which enjoys such strong confirmation and is discerned by the eyes penetrating all truths? No! It is utterly impossible.

The second proof: It is the book of creation.

All the letters and points of this book, individually and collectively, voice each in its particular tongue, *There is nothing that does not glorify Him with His praise,*[3] and proclaim the existence of the All-Great Creator and His Unity. Every particle of creation testifies with a true testimony to the necessary existence of the All-Wise Creator, exalted be His Majesty. While being hesitant among endless possibilities and probabilities where they will go, whether they will constitute building-blocks of a being, in what and what kind of being they will be put, each particle takes a particular route and puts on particular attributes. It is directed to a specific goal in accordance with certain established laws and ends in many amazing, purposeful consequences. It strengthens the belief in God, which is implanted in man's inner faculty by God so that he may find Him, and which is a sample in man of the unseen worlds.

Does a particle proclaim in its particular tongue the purpose of its All-Majestic Maker and His manifest Wisdom? Through its individual existence, particular attributes, and definite nature, every particle points and testifies to the All-Wise Creator. It acts as a building-block in the formation of compounds one within the other; taking a route among countless possibilities and probabilities, it sequentially takes up a position in a compound. The position it takes up has relations with all other positions and the particle fulfils many tasks issuing from those relations. As there is a strict balance and perfect harmony among the positions, each task the particle fulfils yields numerous, wise fruits. As all this corroborates the testimony of the particle to the Creator, in the tongue of its every act and the task it ful-

---

3. *al-Isra'*, 17.44.

fils, the particle proclaims the proofs of the necessary existence of its All-Majestic Maker and displays the purpose of its All-Wise Creator. It is as if it recites the noble verses declaring the Divine Unity. Its like is the like of a soldier who is charged with particular duties and has relations with all the divisions within an army in respect of those duties.

Then, are the proofs of (the existence and Unity of) Almighty God not more than all of the particles of creation? The saying, *The roads leading to God are to the number of the breaths of His creatures*, expresses a pure truth without exaggeration.

Question

Why can't all men find the All-Great Creator with their intellects?

Answer: Because of the perfection of His manifestation and His having no opposites at all.[4]

> Reflect on the lines of the universe, for
> they are missives to you from the High Abode.

This great book of creation displays orderliness as clearly as the midday sun and exhibits the miracle of Power in every word or letter in it. This book is composed so miraculously that, supposing the inconceivable, if each of the natural causes were a free agent, they would all prostrate themselves in utmost humility before this miraculousness, acknowledging: "Glory be to You. We have no power. Surely, You are the All-Mighty, the All-Wise."

As you can observe, there is so subtle, so delicate an order in this book that placing a new point in its exact place in it requires an absolute power able to invent the whole of creation. For each of its letters—especially those living ones among them—has inner relations with all its sentences, and each of its letters has a very strong connection with all the other words. Therefore, whoever has created the eyes of a gnat has also creat-

---

4. Everything in existence is known through its opposite. The Almighty alone has neither equals nor opposites. (Tr.)

ed the sun, and whoever has ordered the stomach of a flea has also ordered the solar system. If you like, refer to the verse *Your creation and resurrection are but as a single soul*[5] and see how truthful a witness comes out from the tongue of a bee, which is only one of the miracles of the Power or represents a small word in this book. Or, if you like, ponder over a micro-organism which, although so small that it cannot be seen with the naked eye, is a sample of creation. The One Who has "written" it in that miraculous fashion, has also "written" the whole of the universe. If you study it and discern the subtle mechanisms and wonderful systems installed in it, you will be convinced that it is impossible to attribute its existence and life to lifeless, simple, natural causes that are unable to distinguish between possibilities. Otherwise you will have to admit that in each particle of existence there is the consciousness of sages, the knowledge of scientists and the genius of statesmen or administrators and that they can communicate with one another without any media. That is a superstition of which even the superstitious are ashamed. There is no explanation of that mechanism of life other than to regard it as a miracle of Divine Power. It is the invention of the One Who has invented the whole of the universe and arranged its operation. Otherwise it would be impossible for the two main and most important of natural causes or laws, namely the force of gravitation and the force of repulsion, to come together in an atom.

The force of gravitation, the force of repulsion, motion and similar phenomena are the names of Divine principles or ways of operating represented as laws. They may be accepted as laws provided they are not promoted to being the foundation of an agent nature. Being only names or titles or having nominal existence, they should not be accorded real, external existence.

Question

Despite this manifest fact, why do some believe in the eternity of matter and attribute the formation of all species in exis-

---

5. *Luqman*, 31.28.

tence to the ramdom motions of particles or other similar things?

Answer: Approaching a matter only to be rationally convinced does not mean believing in God. They cannot perceive the corruption of the notion as their reasoning is based on a superficial view and imitation. Whereas if a man inquires into the matter closely in pursuit of the truth, he will conclude how illogical and irrational such a belief is. If still, despite this, he reaches such a belief, it is because of his heedlessness of the Creator, glory be to Him. How strange a deviation! How can one who finds it difficult to accept the eternity of God the Glorified and attribute the invention of things to Him—although eternity and creativity are among the indispensable Attributes of the Divine Essence—attribute that eternity and invention to countless particles and helpless things?

Recall this well-known incident: They were scanning the sky to see whether the new crescent had appeared to mark the beginning of the holy month of Ramadan. An old man claimed that he had seen it. Whereas what he had seen was only a white hair from his eyebrow which curved downward. So it is that hair-like things which make people blind to the truth.

Man is of noble character by creation. While in pursuit of truth, he sometimes encounters falsehood and keeps it in his breast; or while digging out the truth, misguidance falls on his head and, supposing it to be the truth, he puts it on.

Question

What are those things called nature, laws and forces by which they deceive themselves?

Answer: Nature is the comprehensive Divine *Shari'a* established for the order and harmony among the acts, elements and parts of the body of creation which is called the visible, material world. This *Shari'a* or law of creation is that which is also called the "way of God", and nature is the result of the whole of the nominal laws prevailing in creation.

What they call forces are the principles of this *Shari'a*.

Laws are elements of the same *Shari'a*.

However, the regularity of the principles and elements of this *Shari'a* leads to its being seen as "nature" with a real, external existence. Those who see nature as having real, external existence also regard it as an agent. Although it is impossible that the heart or mind is convinced of its being a true agent, yet because of fancying the denial of the All-Majestic Creator and the inability to understand the mircaluous works of the Divine Power which so amaze our minds, this blind, ignorant 'nature' may come to be considered as the origin of things.

Nature is something printed, it is not a printer. It is a design, not a designer; an object acted on, not an agent; a rule or measure, not an origin; an order, not an orderer; it is a principle with no power at all, a set of laws issuing from the Divine Attributes of Will and Power with no real, external existence.

Supposing a man in the prime of his youth comes to this exquisite world from another one and enters a beautiful, richly adorned palace. He sees no one in the palace to whom he can attribute its building and decoration. He catches sight of a comprehensive book containing a plan of the palace and the information about how the palace was built and furnished. Because of his ignorance and being obsessed with the builder, he fancies that book to be the builder of the palace. In the same way, because of their heedlessness of the All-Majestic Creator, some people deceive themselves into accepting the natural world as the originator of itself.

God has two kinds of *Shari'a*:

One is that which issued from the Divine Attribute of Speech and regulates or orders the acts of the servants issuing from their free will.

The other is that which has issued from the Divine Attribute of Will and Power and in fact comprises the Divine commands of creation and is the result of the Divine Way of acting.

The first *Shari'a* comprises comprehensible laws, while the second consists of the nominal laws, which are wrongly called the "laws of nature". They have no creative or inventive part in existence. Creation and invention are qualities of the Divine Power.

As we have frequently mentioned so far while discussing Divine Unity, each thing in existence is connected to all other things; nothing can exist or survive without the whole of existence. The one who has created a single thing has also created all things, and that one—the creator of all things—cannot be but the One, Eternally-Besought-of-All. By contrast, natural causes, to which the misguided ascribe creativity, are great in number and do not know one another. They are also blind. Attributing creativity to them means accepting that innumerable blind, lifeless things have come together by chance and formed that vast, orderly universe, [the existence, order and harmony of which manifestly require absolute knowledge, will, power, and wisdom]. *Then leave them to plunge and play.*[6]

To sum up: The observed order and regularity in the great book of the universe and the manifest miraculousness in its composition are two proofs of Divine Unity which show as clearly as the shining sun that the whole of the universe and whatever is in it are but the works of the absolute Power, infinite Knowledge, and eternal Will of God.

Question

How can the order, harmony and regularity be established?

Answer: Sciences function as if mankind's senses and "spies" that have discovered the order through deduction and induction. For each branch of sciences is based upon or studies one of the species or divisions of existence. It is in this order, harmony and regulartiy that the universal principles of sciences originate. Each branch of science comprises the universal principles and rules prevalent in the whole of the species it studies. The universality and uniformity of those principles point to the mag-

---

6. *al-An'am*, 6.91.

nificence of the order, because where there is no order it is impossible to infer universal rules. Man can discover that order by means of his spies of sciences and he sees again by means of those sciences that the macro-human being—the universe—is as orderly as himself. There is wisdom in everything; nothing is purposeless or left to its own devices.

This proof of ours, that is, the book of creation—with all its systems, with all its worlds of living creatures, with all its particles, proclaims Divine Unity: all together they declare: *There is no god but God.*

The third proof: It is the wise Qur'an.

When you listen to this articulate proof, you will hear it repeat: *There is no god but He.* This proof of ours is like an enormous tree whose boughs and branches hang down with innumerable, splendid fruits of truth. Since a tree with many lively fruits cannot have been grown from a rotten seed or stone, no one can doubt that the seed—which is Divine Unity—of this tree is sound and lively.

The branch of this tree stretching into the visible, material world bears fruits of the most sound and realistic commandments and rules, while its other, great branch extending into the world of the Unseen is laden with ripe fruits yielded by Divine Unity and belief in the Unseen.

If this comprehensive proof is closely studied with all its aspects, it will certainly be admitted that the one who communicated it was absolutely certain of its result—which is the Divine Unity—and felt no hesitation about its truth. He based all of his other claims on this firm result and made it a criterion to judge whatever exists in the universe. Such a basis, established so firmly and bearing a manifest seal of miraculousness, has no need to make show and pretensions and is absolutely independent of being pronounced true by others. Whatever it says and declares and whatever tidings it gives are all true.

All six sides of this luminous proof are transparent and clear:

there is the seal of manifest miraculousness on it, beneath it are logic and evidence; to its right side is the assent of intellect and to its left side is the testimony of conscience. Before it is good and happiness in both worlds, and it is founded on pure Revelation. Can doubt dare to enter this most formidable citadel?

There are four paths leading to the "throne" of perfections, which is knowledge of God, exalted be His Majesty:

The first is the path of the Sufis which is based on purification of the carnal self and spiritual illumination.

The second is the path of theologians who, to prove the existence of the Necessarily-Existent-Being, depend on the argument that everything comes into existence contingently, in time and space, its being existent or not are equally possible, which means that there is an Eternal One Who prefers their existence and brings them into existence by His Will.

Both of these two paths were deduced from the Qur'an. However, their followers have complicated them over time and therefore caused some doubts to infiltrate into them.

The third is the path of philosophers contaminated with doubts, hesitations and fancies.

The fourth and the best is the path of the holy Qur'an which clearly shows the "throne" of perfections with its miraculous eloquence, utmost beauty of style, directness and incomparable comprehensiveness. It is the most direct and shortest of the paths leading to God and the most inclusive for human beings.

There are four means to reach that "throne": inspiration, learning or study, purification and reflection.

The Qur'an follows two ways to lead to knowledge of God, glory be to Him, and prove God's Unity.

The first is the argument of favoring and purposiveness.

All of the Qur'anic verses which mention benefits or uses of things and the wisdom in or purposes for their existence "weave" this argument and serve as mirrors in which it is reflected.

This argument can be summarized as follows:

All things in the universe are made firmly and artistically and there is a perfect orderliness in creation. This is for certain purposes and uses. The orderliness in creation and the purposes and uses evident in the existence of all things indicate that the All-Wise Creator has certain wise purposes for creating them, and decisively reject chance and coincidence. For the firmness and orderliness clearly show the existence of will and intention. All of the sciences studying the creation testify to that orderliness and point to the uses and fruits hanging from the branches of existence like clusters and reveal the instances of wisdom and beneficial results behind daily, monthly and seasonal changes.

If you like, look at zoology and botany. There are hundreds of thousands of species of plants and animals in the world. Like mankind having a first, original ancestor—Adam, upon him be peace—each species has an original of its own kind. Each member of these species is like an exquisite, amazing mechanism bewildering minds. It is impossible, inconceivable, that fancied laws of nominal existence and ignorant, blind natural causes are the originators of those innumerable chains of beings. Each species and each member of the species proclaim that they issued forth from the hand of the wise, Divine Power.

The holy Qur'an teaches us this argument in the Divine saying, *Return your gaze; do you see any fissure?*[7] It explains this argument in a perfect and most beautiful way. By commanding us to reflect on creatures and mentioning their uses or benefits as Divine bounties, the Qur'an seeks to establish this argument in the mind, and then calls reason to ponder over them in the conclusions and divisions of verses. It illuminates the role of reason and stirs up conscience in the conclusions such as *Do they not know? Will they not reflect and learn the lesson? So, learn a lesson!*

The second argument of the Qur'an: It is the argument of invention, which can be summarized as follows:

---

7. *al-Mulk*, 67.3.

God Almighty has given each species and each member of every species existence particular to the tasks it will fulfil and the perfections it will achieve. There is not a species coming from eternity because every thing, every species, has a beginning and there is no thing, no species, whose existence is absolutely necessary. Every thing comes into existence by the will and preference of a Necessarily-Existent One, and it is equally possible for it to come into existence or not. This is an undeniable truth which cannot be changed. Evolution is also impossible, for mutations can occur only within a species and there are no intermediary species. If there were once species transformed into others by God for punishment, they did not survive. What they call matter is changeable and not independent of time and space, and therefore it has a beginning. Forces and forms are accidental and cannot be the origin of the diversity of the essences or substances of species. Something accidental cannot be essence or substance. All this leads to the conclusion that the substances of all species with all their diverse, distingushing attributes were created from non-existence. Generation or reproduction is only a later condition for continuance.

How strange it is that the minds of the misguided who cannot admit the eternity of the All-Majestic Creator—although eternity is one of His indispensable Attributes—can attribute eternity to matter, which is clearly and observable contained in time and space. Again, where can the tiniest particles that are blind, ignorant and helpless, find the power, stability and firmness before which the whole of the universe bow in submission and veneration? Also, how can inventing and originating—which are among the attributes of the Divine Power—be attributed to the most impotent and weakest of things, which are natural causes?

The holy Qur'an establishes this argument in its verses mentioning creation and invention and confirms that no one and no thing, including causes, other than God, the One, has creative power. Causes function only as veils before the Divine Power and Its grandeur in order to prevent the mind from drawing wrong conclusions about the All-Holy Divine Being by seeing with a superficial view the hand of His Power involved in mean affairs.

Every thing has two aspects:

One is its apparent aspect. It is like the dense, black face of a mirror. In this aspect of things opposites—small and great, good and evil, beatiful and ugly and so on—exist side by side. The role of causes concerning this aspect is displaying the Grandeur and Dignity of the Almighty.

The other is the inner, spiritual aspect. It is like the polished or transparent face of a mirror. This aspect is pure and absolutely beautiful and, as required by Divine Unity, causes do not have any role in it. Since things like life, spirit, light and existence have all directly been origininated by the hand of Power without the medium of causes, they are beautiful with respect to both their outer and inner aspects.

The fourth proof: It is man's conscience called conscious nature.

First, the natural or inborn qualities of things do not lie. A seed has an inclination to grow as if to say: "If I am planted, I will grow and yield fruit." It says truth. An egg has an inclination toward life as if to say: "I will become a chick" and it becomes so by leave of God. When a handful of water with the inclination of expansion on freezing says, "I will cover broader space", despite its hardness and firmness, even iron cannot resist it. All such inclinations as these are manifestations of the commands of creation issuing from Divine Will.

Second, man's senses are not restricted to the five known senses. He has many "windows" opening on the world of the Unseen. He also has many other senses the nature of which he is aware or unaware. For example, drive and energy are only two of his other senses which do not lie.

Thirdly, it is impossible for something fancied and of merely nominal existence to be the origin of external, visible existence. The point of reliance or support and the point of seeking help the necessity of which man feels in him are two essential aspects of his conscience or conscious nature. Man is noble in creation with an essentially pure spirit. Without these two points, he is reduced to the lowest of the low. Man's being without them is also irreconcilable with the wisdom, order and perfection in creation.

Fourthly, even if reason neglects to work properly and see the truth accordingly, conscience does not forget the Creator. Even if man's selfhood denies Him, conscience sees Him, reflects on Him and turns toward Him. Intuitive perception always stirs it up and inspiration illuminates it. Love of God always urges conscience to knowledge of the Almighty. This love which is compound yearning for Him, which, in turn, issues from compound desire coming from compound inclination is innate in conscience. The attraction (towards Him) ingrained in man's conscience is because of the existence of One Who really attracts.

After these preliminary notes, look into conscience to see how it is a proof, entrusted to the soul of every person, proclaiming Divine Unity. You will also see that as the heart pumps life into all the parts of the body, the source of (spiritual) life in it, which is knowledge of God, energizes and vitalizes the ambitions of man and his inclinations included in all his abilities and limitless potentialities. It pours into them pleasure and joy and increases their value. It also expands or develops and sharpens them. This is the point of seeking help.

Knowledge of God is a point of support and reliance for man in the face of the convulsions of life and flux of misfortunes. For man, if he does not believe in the All-Wise Creator in every act of Whose there is orderliness and wisdom, and instead attributes things and events to blind coincidences, relying on what has no power to resist misfortunes, he will tremble with fear of disasters and live in a hellish state. Man is not a being to fall into such a miserable state, for he is noble in creation with a potential to achieve all kinds of perfections. This cannot also be conconant with the prevailing, firm order in the universe. For the two points mentioned, the point of seeking help and the point of support and reliance, are necessary for man's spirit. The All-Munificent Creator diffuses the light of His knowledge into the conscience of every man through these two windows. Even if the eyes of the reason may become blind, the eyes of conscience are always open.

The testimony of all these four comprehensive arguments point to the fact that as the All-Majestic Creator is the Necessarily-Existent-Being, Eternal, One, Single, Unique, Eternally-Besought-of-All, All-Knowing, All-Powerful, All-Willing, All-Hearing, All-Seeing, All-Speaking, All-Living, Self-Subsistent, He is also qualified with all the Attributes of Majesty and Grace. For whatever all creatures have in the name of perfection, it comes from the shadow of the manifestation of the Majestic Creator's Perfection. Surely, the Beauty, Grace and Perfection are infinitely greater than the sum of the beauty, grace and perfection shared by the whole of the creation. Also, the All-Glorified Creator is free from all defects for defects originate from the insufficiency of the inborn capacities of material beings. The All-Glorified One is absolutely free from materiality and exempt from the qualities essential to the nature of the created.

There is nothing like Him; He is the All-Hearing, the All-Seeing.[8]

Glory be to Him Who keeps concealed because of the intensity of His manifestation.

Glory be to Him Who is hidden because of the lack of His opposite.

Glory be to Him Who is veiled by natural causes because of His Dignity.

Question

What is your opinion about the view of Unity of Being?

Answer: It comes from absorption in Divine Unity. Divine Unity is inwardly and deeply experienced and is not restricted to theory and thought. The profundity of absorption in Divine

---

8. *al-Shu'ra'*, 42.11.

Unity—following belief in God's Unity as the Lord and Deity—results in belief in the unity of the Power—that is, believing that there is none other than God Who has creative effect. Belief in the unity of the Power results in belief in the unity of dominion and ruling, which, in turn, ends in seeing what is witnessed as united—Unity of the Witnessed—and finally in the Unity of Being. This leads to seeing existence as one or united and then seeing what exists as united.

The sayings of some Sufi scholars uttered in ecstasies of spiritual delight and which go beyond what is really intended must not be taken as proofs for the truth of this way. If one who has not been able to save himself from the sphere of cause and effect, who organizes his life considering the law of causality, speaks about the Unity of Being inclusive of created entitites, he goes beyond his limits and to excess. Those who really sense and speak about the Unity of Being restrict themselves to the Necessarily-Existent-Being in isolation from the created and see God as the only existent being.

Seeing the result together with or contained in the evidence leading to it, that is, seeing the All-Majestic Maker as the only existent being in utter oblivion of the creation, comes from the absorption of the view and experience of the existence of the Divine Being. It is the result of seeing or perceiving Divine manifestations in the channels of existence and the flux of Divine effulgences in the inner dimension of things and the manifestation of Divine Names and Attributes in the mirrors of creatures.

My personal view of the Unity of Being is as follows:

Such a perception pertains to inner experience and sensing. However, due to the lack of more proper words to express their belief or inner experience, those who follow this way—the way of believing in the Unity of Being—interpret it as pervading Divinity and permeating Life in creatures. Whereas philosophers or those who try to find the truth with their intellects or sense-impressions have made this way of inner experience a philosophical or merely intellectual subject of discussion and therefore a source of false notions.

Besides the Sufis and Muslim philosophers and thinkers who speak of the Unity of Being, there are materialist, pantheistic philosophers who believe in the Unity of Being. However, what the Sufis and pantheistic philosophers mean by Unity of Being are absolutely cortradictory with each other. There are five significant differences between them:

The first is that the Sufi scholars restrict their view solely to the Necessarily-Existent-Being and are lost in reflection on Him with all their strength to the extent that they do not accept the existence of the universe. According to them, it is only the Necessarily-Existent-Being Who can be regarded as really existent. The existence of all others is illusory. Whereas, materialist philosophers and those with weak belief concentrate wholly on matter and fall distant from perceiving Divinity. They give priority to matter in existence and do not see anything else existent except matter or material things. Or since they continue to remain in misguidance, they see Divinity as contained in or embodied by matter or prefer to remain indifferent to Divinity because of their restricting their view to the universe.

The second difference is that the Sufis who believe in the Unity of Being see the universe as something witnessed or only sensed. However, the others regard the universe as really existent and believe in the unity of what exists materially.

The third difference: The way of the Sufi saints is a way pertaining to inner experience, while the others follow a purely rationalistic one.

The fourth difference: The Sufi saints are lost in the Truth the Almighty, and consider the universe from the viewpoint of Divinity. Whereas, the others are absorbed in creatures and reflect on them for their sake and from within that absorption.

The fifth difference: The Sufi saints worship God and love Him deeply, while the others adore their selves and follow their fancies. The way of the Sufis is as far from that of materialist philosophers as earth is from the highest heaven and as different from it as bright light is from thick darkness.

A note for further enlightenment:

Supposing the earth made up of small pieces of glass of different colors, each of those pieces would receive light from the sun and reflect it according to its size, shape and color. Although what each piece would receive and reflect is neither the sun nor its light itself, if each piece were to speak, it would say: "I am a sun."

Similarly, if the colors of those smiling, brilliant flowers were to speak, although they are manifestations of the seven colors in the light of the sun, each would say: "The sun resembles me" or "The sun belongs to me exclusively."

> Those illusions are traps for saints, whereas in reality
> they are the reflections of the radiant-faced in the garden of God.[9]

The way of those who believe in the unity of the witnessed or sensed in the name of existence is the way of sobriety, wakefulness and discernment, while the way of the Unity of Being is a way followed in the state of spiritual intoxication. What is safer is the way of sobriety and discernment.

> *Think about the bounties and blessings of God. Do no think about the Essence of God, because you are unable do that.*[10]

The reality of man: while man is unable to perceive it,
how can he perceive how the Eternal All-Compelling is?
He is the One Who originated things and built them.
Then, how can one who is a breath created, perceive Him?

---

9. Mawlana Jalal al-Din al-Rumi, *Mathnawi*, vol.1, p. 3.
10. A Prophetic saying. Tabarani, *al-Mu'jam al-Awsat*, 6456.

INDEX OR BRIEF SUMMARIES OF THE TOPICS
DISCUSSED IN THE TREATISE

*Among countless proofs of God Almghty, the following four are of great importance and prominence: The Prophet Muhammad, upon him be peace and blessings, the macro-cosmos or macro-human which is the observed, great book (of the universe), the holy Qur'an and the human conscience or consciousness, which is the juncture of the world of the Unseen and the material, visible world. Brief explanations of these proofs. (439-452)

*Despite all the proofs so manifest, why can't all men find the All-Great Creator with their intellects? (441)

*There is so subtle, so delicate an order in the book of creation that placing any point in its exact place in it requires an absolute power able to invent the whole of creation. (441)

*The force of gravitation, the force of repulsion, motion and similar phenomena are the names of Divine principles or ways of operating represented as laws. They may be accepted as laws provided they are not promoted to being the foundation of an agent nature. Being only names or titles or having nominal existence, they should not be accorded real, external existence. (442)

*Why do some believe in the eternity of matter and attribute the formation of all species in existence to the ramdom motions of particles or other similar things? (442-3)

*Man is of noble character by creation. While in pursuit of truth, he sometimes encounters falsehood and keeps it in his breast; or while digging out the truth, misguidance falls on his head and, supposing it to be the truth, he puts it on. (443)

*God has two kinds of *Shari'a*:

One is that which issued from the Divine Attribute of Speech and regulates or orders the acts of the servants issuing from their free will.

The other is that which has issued from the Divine Attribute of Will and Power and in fact comprises the Divine commands of creation and is the result of the Divine Way of acting. (444)

*How can the order, harmony and regularity in creation be established? (445)

*The Qur'an, as the proof of Divine existence and Unity, is like an enormous tree whose boughs and branches hang down with innumerable, splendid fruits of truth. The branch of this tree stretching into the visible, material world bears fruits of the most sound and realistic commandments and rules, while its other, great branch extending into the world of the Unseen is laden with ripe fruits yielded by Divine Unity and belief in the Unseen. (446)

*There are four paths leading to the "throne" of perfections, which is knowledge of God, exalted be His Majesty. The first is the way of the Sufis, the second the way of the theologians, the third the way of the philosophers and the fourth the way of the Qur'an.

The path of the holy Qur'an is the most direct and shortest of the paths leading to God and the most inclusive for human beings.

There are also four means to reach that "throne": Inspiration, learning or study, purification and reflection. (447)

*The Qur'anic arguments of favoring and purposiveness and invention. (447–9)

*Every thing has two aspects:

One is its apparent aspect. It is like the dense, black face of a mirror. *The other* is the inner, spiritual aspect. It is like the polished or transparent face of a mirror. (450)

*The natural or inborn qualities of things do not lie. A seed has an inclination to grow as if to say: "If I am planted, I will grow and yield fruit." It says truth. (450)

*The point of reliance or support and the point of seeking help the necessity of which man feels in him are two essential aspects of his conscience or conscious nature. (450)

*Man also has many other senses the nature of which he is aware or unaware. For example, drive and energy are only two of his other senses which do not lie. (450)

*Knowledge of God is a point of support and reliance for man in the face of the convulsions of life and flux of misfortunes. (451)

*The truth of the Unity of Being (*Wahdat al-Wujud*), and its difference from pantheism. (452–4)

Twelfth treatise

A Light from the Lights of the Verses of the Qur'an

In the Name of God, the Merciful, the Compassionate
. . . and from Him we seek help.

Praise be to God Who has guided us to this. We could not have found guidance if God had not guided us. Assuredly the Messengers of our Lord brought the truth.[1]

Peace and blessings be upon the Argument of the Truth to the creation, the king of the Prophets, proof of the purified scholars, and the beloved of the Lord of the worlds, and on his family and all of His Companions.

Know O friend! Whether it is a plain or a mountain or a valley or a desert or a sea or a piece of land on the earth, it bears various stamps of the One, the Eternally-Besought-of-All. A mountain, for example, shows that it is a property of the All-Glorified One with all the creatures that inhabit it such as animals of many species and trees of many kinds, which are all the All-Glorified's properties also. Again, it shows that it is also a creature of the Almighty as testified by the brilliant stamps on it such as various kinds of plants and species of birds. It also shows that it is one of His missives, exalted be His Majesty, as testified by the seals of the All-Glorified placed on all its corners such as adorned flowers and beautiful fruits. When you know that, for example, a single palm-tree and bee are the All-Glorified's property and creatures, you will understand that all palm-trees and bees are also His property.

What shows that the stamps and seals throughout the earth

---

1. *al-A'raf*, 7.43.

belong to the One Monarch and the Owner Eternally-Besought-of-All, is that all kinds of things are found almost throughout the world at the same moment. The identity in existence, invention, form, making and time evidently show that the Maker of all those things is the One and Single Whom doing or saying one thing cannot prevent from doing or saying another, nor hearing and meeting a need can confuse Him and hinder Him from hearing and meeting another, exalted be His Majesty.

Know O friend! If you would hear from me about the miraculousness of the Qur'an as it is flowing into me from the ocean of the Qur'an, listen to the following which in fact I address to myself:

O Said, heedless of himself and even his heedlessness!

Heedlessness, ingratitude and unbelief arise from groundless conceptions or notions. For when you look at something, especially a living one, and fall into heedlessness because of not attributing it to the Almighty—that is, the One God—you will have to concieve of impossibilities by attributing divinity to all particles and compounds of earth, air and water; you will have to admit as many deities as the manifestations of God. For you know that each particle of earth serves for the growth of all kinds of plants, trees, flowers and fruits. If you would like to attain greater certainty, put sufficient amount of earth in a pot. If you plant in it the seed of a fig tree, you will have a tree yielding figs; if you plant a seed of a pomegranate or apple tree, you will have a tree yielding pomegranates or apples, and so on. You know what great differences there are among those fruit-bearing trees. If the mechanism of Destiny operating in the seed of the fig tree is like, say, a sugar factory, the machine of Power working in the seed of the pomegranate tree may be like a textile factory. . .

Afterwards, in places of fruit-bearing trees, plant in your pot seeds of all kinds of flowers one after the other. You will have flowers in place of fruit-trees.

If, O owner of the pot, your heedlessness leads you to follow the way of materialists, then you will have to admit the existence in your pot of as many factories as the number of fruit-bearing trees in the world to make all the parts of infinitely various trees from roots to fruits, and as many mechanisms as the number of the flowers. The particles of earth must also have as much knowledge and power as to grow each tree and flower and the necessary capacity to distinguish them. If you attribute the existence of trees and flowers to nature, this time, you will have to admit that nature has numberless printing machines in each particle of earth. Seeds or fruit-stones are material things of almost the same structure and contents and resembling one another in formation and shape. So, seeds or stones growing each into a different tree or flower is like cotton of a few grams being woven into rolls of silk, satin, broadcloth, wool and so on. Verses such as *He created you from a single soul*[2] and *God has created every moving creature of water*[3] point to the fact that the substance from which you were created while it was something simple, not compound or composite like you, cannot be the origin of you. Whereas the invention of seeds or fruit-stones—each of which is, despite its simplicity, like a plan made by Destiny and, despite its small size, like an origin or nucleus containing all the principles of the existence of the tree or flower to grow from it—its invention with a composition that includes all the details of the tree or flower to grow from it as far as the tips of its twigs or petals, is a most evident testimony that its Creator cannot be other than the One Who has created the heavens and the earth and in relation to Whose Power minute particles and massive suns are the same.

If your heedlessness arises from materialism, then you will have to admit that in your pot there is a wonderful, intelligent power able to make and form all kinds of fruit-bearing trees and flowers, and a knowledge encompassing all of their features and properties down to the finest details. There has also to be a will with knowledge of all the principles and necessities of their existence. Again, the pot has to have the capacity to per-

2. *al-Nisa'*, 4.1.
3. *al-Nur*, 24.45.

form the functions of other Names of the One Who *shall roll up the heavens like a scroll rolled up for books,*[4] Who holds the earth in His hand disposing it however He wills, and man's heart between two fingers of His turning it however He wishes, and Whom something big or significant cannot hinder from being concerned with what is small or insignificant. He manifests the light of His Power on the Supreme Throne, on the sun and particles with the same facility, as the sun is reflected in both the surface of an ocean and a mirror and in drops or bubbles of water with the same ease all at the same time and with the same extent of radiance except for the capacity of things to receive it.

This is observed especially in spring when innumerable kinds of flowers, plants, trees and animals burst forth almost all at the same time in utmost abundance and with absolute facility and firmness.

You can make the same experiment a few times more, emptying your pot and then re-filling it from different places. It is certain that you will always obtain the same result.

Each flower, each fruit, each animal, each micro-organism is like a drop formed of constituents taken from all parts of existence with exact and subtle measures and according to absolutely precise calculations. Nothing or no one other than Him Who holds the whole of existence in His grasp disposing it however He wills and extracts this drop from existence with such measures and according to such calculations—nothing and no one other than Him Who makes each flower or each fruit or each animal a miniature of the whole of existence when He wills to create from non-existence, can create that drop.

Just as it will be necessary to admit the existence of as many suns as the transparent objects such as pieces of glass, drops of water, bubbles of oceans and the like, when the images of the sun is not attributed to the one sun in the sky, so too, an ungrateful unbeliever has to accept as many deities as all the particles of existence—as mentioned in *The Bubble* and *The Drop*—or

---

4. *al-Anbiya'*, 21.104.

as the manifestations of God—as discussed in the *Addendum to The Radiance.*

If you have understood what I told myself, you will have perceived only one ray of the lights of the Qur'an's miraculous explanations from the viewpoint of its meaning, for the issue we have just discussed is only one drop among the drops of the ocean of the Qur'an's meaning.

Know O friend! Among the artefacts of mankind there may be some worth thousands of dollars because of the art they contain while their material costs only five. Similarly, belief is an elixir changing decaying, coal-like substance of man into an enduring, jewelled diamond by connecting him to the All-Permanent Maker. By contrast, unbelief reduces him to the degree of coal subject to decomposition in earth.

Man is the most amazing one among the artefacts of the Eternal Maker Who *has created the heavens and the earth in six days*[5] and adorned the sky with stars and the earth with flowers. Created of clay like the potter's, subject to rapid disintegration, he is worth very little in respect of his material constituents. But, when considered with respect to the art he contains, his worth increases to the greatest extent. For he is a piece of poetry composed with the subtleties of the manifestations of the Divine Beautiful Names. He is a polished mirror to reflect the rays of the Eternal Sun.

Belief is a tie connecting man to its Owner and revealing the Divine art in man. It attracts sight and understanding to the fact that man is an artefact of God. Through this connection, man's value increases to the extent that Paradise will become its price. Again, through belief man rises to the rank of being God's vicegerent on the earth and bearing the Supreme Trust. As to unbelief, it cuts this connection and causes the Divine art in man to be concealed. As a result, man is reduced to his material substance only and loses all his value to the extent that an unbeliever wishes he had never existed or that he would become dust.

---

5. *al-A'raf*, 7.54.

In short: Man is like a machine furnished with millions of tools of measurement to weigh and experience the contents of the treasury of Divine Mercy, and the jewels of the Hidden Treasure.[6] It is such that as many devices for tasting as the number of the edibles were set in man's tongue so that he might taste all the varieties of the bounties of the Truth. When this machine is used in the light of the blessing of belief, it yields fruits preserved by the One Who never errs or forgets.

However, if this machine falls into the hand of unbelief, then it is as if that invaluable, matchless machine had fallen into the hand of a savage who does not recognize it and uses it merely to light a fire or make it burn more brightly.

O One in Whose hand is the dominion and keys of all things, Who grasps all things by the forelock, and with Whom are the treasuries of all things! Do not leave us to ourselves. Have mercy on us and illuminate our hearts with the light of belief and the Qur'an.

God's promise is true, so let not the life of the world deceive you, nor let the deceiver deceive you in regard to God.[7]

Know, O intoxicated, dissolute, heedless and misguided one! You have drowned in the marsh of the world and desire to cause people to stray by presenting that marsh as the source of happiness in order to console yourself. If you are able to change the nature of the following four realities, do whatever you wish:

The first reality is death. You cannot change it or remove it from life. Whereas it is a changing of residences in the view of a believer, in your view it is an eternal extinction.

The second reality is man's innate helplessness along with limitless needs and hostilities. Whereas, in truth, this condition invites man to rely on the absolutely Powerful One, as does helplessness, you make it an absolute helplessness [through unbelief] with no support of reliance and support.

---

6. Alluding to the *hadith qudsi*: *I was a hidden treasure. I willed to be known and created the universe.* (Tr.)

7. *Luqman*, 31.33.

The third reality is man's innate poverty. While it is a means of appealing to the treasure of the absolutely Wealthy One and an invitation to it, you make it a painful destitution increasing with the disgraceful habits of modern civilization.

The fourth reality is decay or disappearance. For the disappearance of pleasures is permanent pain, so there is no good in inconstant pleasure. While, in truth, disappearance or decay is a means of reaching everlasting pleasures, you make it painful decay leaving behind only sins and remorse.

One to whom it is possible for death to come at any time, who is enveloped by helplessness and surrounded by poverty on all sides, and who is on a continuous journeying, can be deceived in your sophistries only in the state of drunkenness, and drunkenness does not last for a long time. What they call the happines of life consists in wretchedness, and what they mean by happiness may be possible only by killing death or in utter oblivion of it, and removing helplessness or in extreme vanity, and eliminating poverty or complete madness, and by eternity of life or stopping the wheel of existence.

May God awaken me and you from the sleep of heedlessness which you accept as wakefulness, although it is the deepest part of sleep, and bring us to our senses by curing us of the insanity which you fancy to be intellectual enlightenment.

Know O friend! See how the All-Powerful Maker has spread millions of worlds of plants and animals on the face of the earth. Every world is like a sea whose drops are charged with cleaning. For example, ants are charged with cleaning the face of the earth of the corpses of some animals.

Similarly, water, air, light and earth, especially snow, are like oceans each drop of which is a duty embodied. These worlds are one within the other, while the All-Wise Maker also distinguishes each from them with its particular properties and duties. He displays infinite distinguishing amidst infinite mixture, to the extent that, for example, He places the world of ants or flies amongst the worlds of other living creatures by creating and causing them to die in a way particular to them. It is as if the face of the earth is only their home. No confusion is observed in their coming into existence and death. As each world of living creatures subsists amongst other worlds, each individual member of each species is also brought up amongst other individuals. Maintaining one world does not prevent the Maker from maintaining others, nor bringing up one individual hinders Him from rearing others.

O one whose eyes are blind because of naturalism and whose heart has been sealed! If you suppose nature as a printer and maker—while, in fact, it is something printed and made—then you will have to admit that in each piece of earth there are perfect printing machines much more in number than the whole of the printing machines in the world.

Know, O animal! Do not be proud of your being an animal as something greater than plants, for the art in plants is not lower in degree than that you contain. Do you not see that while the fleshy parts of all species of animals are almost of the same constitution and quality, the pulpy parts of the kinds of fruits are different from one another. This shows that the Pen of Divine Power works more deeply and delicately in them. Also, while animals and human beings reproduce by seven on average, plants usually reproduce by seventy or seven hundred or seven thousand. However, because of the weakness of their animal senses, fish are an exception to this. Abundant reproduction signifies the degree of importance attached to plants.

Again, plants and trees are in absolute reliance on God and therefore their food comes to them, as well as does the food of their offspring. It is as if the roots of every plant and tree were directly connected to the treasury of Mercy, there is an outlet from Mercy to it. Mercy shares the food of each tree among its parts according to the need of each—while giving to the "parents" pure "milk", it gives to the daughters—fruits—pure sherbet and to the sons—olives, for example—blessed oil.

O animal proud of itself! The reason why plants are preferred over you in the three respects mentioned—although they

are inferior to you—is your vanity and that you have some degree of will-power. So, submit to God and be saved.

Man was created a weakling.[8]

O man! Do not take pride over animals! The reason why you
have been given superiority over animals is your weakness and
impotence, just as an infant commands its parents and its elder
brothers or sisters with the power of its impotence and the
strength of its weakness. Can you see an animal more impotent
than you in procuring the necessities of its life? An animal can
acquire in twenty days or in twenty hours or in twenty minutes
what you can achieve in twenty years through studying and experience to maintain its life. You can procure by mutual assistance in a community what an individual animal achieves by itself. However, with respect to human perfection attainable only
by Islam and servanthood to God, an individual human being
can be equal to a species of animals.

You and I have two alternatives: we will be either lower than
the lowest of animals and weaker and more wretched than
them or more honored and perfect than all their species. Choose
whichever you wish. Anyway, be aware of your impotence and
weakness and know that your power and strength lie in prayer
and weeping before your Owner.

As for your accomplishments in which you take pride, they
are the works of His inspiration and favoring. He has made you
a specimen of all species or kinds of creatures so that He may
manifest His marvellous Beauty and Creativity through you and
cause you to taste all His bounties.

Know, O one who has doubts about the authenticity of the
Prophetic Traditions about the *Mahdi*,[9] the approaching of the
Last Hour and the great tumults predicted to take place after
the Prophet, upon him be peace and blessings! Do you seek conviction in all issues including even the secondary ones which

---

8. *al-Nisa'*, 4.28.

9. The *Mehdi*, literalling meaning one who guides, is the Muslim Messiah expected
by Muslims to come toward the end of time to deliver the oppressed. (Tr.)

are not concerned with fundamentals of belief? Whereas in some issues acceptance and non-rejection are enough; they do not demand certified belief so that you need evident proof.

Don't you know that, just as the profound, allegorical statements in the Qur'an need interpretation, so too the seemingly ambiguous, parabolic Traditions require interpretation and commentary? When you come across a narration attributed to the Prophet, upon him be peace and blessings, which seems to you contrary to reality, consider the following explanation:

It may be one among those borrowed from the commentaries on the Torah or related by Jewish converts whose narrations were mistakenly thought to belong to the Prophet, upon him be peace and blessings. Or it could be an explanatory addition by the narrator of a Tradition which was later taken as belonging to the Tradition itself. Or it may be a deduction from the Tradition by the narrators or a saying of one of the inspired traditionists mistakenly attributed to the Prophet, upon him be peace and blessings. Or again it may be one of the proverbial statements in circulation among the people which the Prophet, upon him be peace and blessings, uttered on an occasion for a certain purpose. So, one who encounters such a narration should not restrict himself to its apparent meaning. Rather, he should ponder over it and either take it as a saying uttered for guiding people to a truth or interpret it as a person asleep interprets in his sleep what a waking person sees. O awake one, you can interpret what a sleeping person sees [in his sleep]. So too, asleep in the heedlessness of this life, you may, if you are able to, interpret what he saw who was always awake, whose heart never slept and about whom God says, *The eye did not swerve nor waver*.[10]

Also, there is wisdom in the appointed hour of an individual being unknown so that he may always be alert for its coming and strive for his afterlife. It is the same wisdom that keeps hidden the Last Hour, which is the appointed hour of the world in

---

10. *al-Najm*, 51.17.

its entirety, so that the children of the world may always be alert for it. This is why the people in every century from the Age of Happiness to the present have looked out for it. That the Last Hour is kept hidden is not to do with the role of the Prophet; it has to do with the wisdom in this alert anticipation which removes heedlessness.

As for the differences in the narrations about the *Mahdi*, [the one promised to come near the end of time and eradicate wrong-doing and establish Islamic justice all over the world,] the reason is the same. The narrations about the *Mahdi* have come down in ambiguous form and therefore the people in every age have expected him. This has helped to reinforce the power of resistance of the believers, to strengthen their morale and remove their despair in every epoch when misguidance spreads and gains strength. It has also encouraged the Muslim scholars who strive to revive the Islamic principles and guide people to truth in a way expected from the *Mahdi*, their illustrious leader.[11]

Know, O Muslim in name and appearance only! In your imitation of the unbelievers (despite their dissipation) and in your opposition to the injunctions of Islam, you resemble a member of a clan who begins to blame that clan, to despise its chief and scorn its customs. He does so because he sees someone from a different and hostile clan who is proud of its virtues. The wretch thinks that by blaming his clan and scorning its customs, he will somehow become like the other one from the hostile clan. He does not realize that by such rejection and apostasy, he becomes foolish and disgraced and loses all support altogether.

Do you not see that a Westerner who rejects the Prophet Muhammad, upon him be peace and blessings, yet consoles himself with his Christianity and his Western civilization which contains elements of his nation's customs. It is possible for him to preserve in his spirit some laudable virtues and make praiseworthy efforts to improve his worldly life. This consolation

---

11. These issues are discussed by the writer more elaborately in *The Words*. See, Said Nursi, *The Words 1*, Kaynak AŞ. Izmir, 1997, pp. 448–64. (Tr.)

keeps him from seeing the veils of darkness in his spirit and the loneliness he must otherwise feel.

As for you, O apostate! If you deny the Prophet Muhammad, upon him be peace and blessings, and his accomplishments, you cannot accept another Prophet, nor your Lord, nor any real perfection. Look at the terrible ruin in your spirit and see the intensity of the darkness in your conscience and the gloom and despair in your heart! The ugliness of your inner world will soon become manifest and it will become clear that the superficial attractiveness of apostasy is uglier than the ugliness of an unbeliever. You will be like a carrier of poison, harmful to both yourself and the community.

Know, O one who suffers difficulty in understanding some of the awesome truths of the Qur'an such as are stated in the verses *He has created the heavens and the earth in six days*[12] and *The affair of the Hour is but like the twinkling of the eye*[13] and *Your creation and resurrection are as (the creation and resurrection of) a single soul*[14] and *Then it will be breathed into it a second time and lo! they have all stood up, staring*[15] and *That day We shall roll up the heavens like rolling up the scroll for books*[16] and so on.

The book of creation clearly observable interprets these Quranic verses and offers them to your understanding by showing you many physical realities comparable to them which you observe regularly [as, for example,] in the alternation of day and night and the changes of seasons and centuries.

If you seek conviction, open the treasure of the verse *Look at the imprints of God's Mercy, how He revives the earth after its death. Surely He is the Reviver of the dead (in the same way)*[17] so that you can clearly see the innumerable examples of the awesome realities which you deem unlikely.

---

12. *Yunus*, 10.3
13. *al-Nahl*, 16.77.
14. *Luqman*, 31.28.
15. *al-Zumar*, 39.68.
16. *al-Anbiya'*, 21.104.
17. *al-Rum*, 30.50.

For example, you witness in the revival of spring the resurrection of thousands of the worlds of plants and animals which
died in the doom of winter. They are all brought back to life in a
few days in definite order and appointed measures particular to
each. Most of those worlds are found in and adorn almost all regions of the earth. There are innumerable other examples of this.

Among those countless worlds, consider the world of trees,
within which are the many kinds of apple trees and each individual member of each kind. You will see three incidents of resurrection one after and within the other. First the tree bursts
into beautiful blossoms. Then follows its coming to leaf, producing well-proportioned, thrilling leaves. Lastly, it yields beautiful, delicious fruits. The One Creator does all these things on
the face of the earth and, by turning over the sheet of winter,
fills thousands of sheets each the size of the sheet of earth with
marvelous "words". He introduces Himself as the One Who *has
created the heavens and the earth in six days*, and Who does all the
things mentioned in the verses above.

Know O friend! Everyone has relations of love and affection
with his relatives, then with the members of his clan, then with
the members of his nation, then with the members of his race,
then with the members of his species—humankind—and then
with all parts and particles of existence. Even if unconsciously,
he is grieved because of their misfortunes and becomes happy
with their happiness. In particular, he feels himself together with
the community of the Prophets, saints and the pious because of
their perfection. A mother, for example, sacrifices herself and
disturbs her rest and peace for the sake of a single relative or
loved one. Because of what the world around him presents to
him, an individual immersed in heedlessness is not thereby able
to rid himself of distress. Rather, in addition to that inevitable
distress, he is crushed under the burdens of spiritual pains and
inward unrest. Even if placed in a paradise, he would be no better off than a firefly which gives out a brief, dim flash of light
and is then enveloped by darkness from all sides. Even this
fleeting light is a cause of harm to him in that it shows him the

distressing scenes around him. By contrast, assume he is able to get rid of heedlessness and consider all things and events in the light of belief in the Owner of existence Whose every act is good either by itself or by its consequences. Then a window will be opened from his heart to the lights of the Everlasting Sun illuminating all the past and future into eternity. He will be able to discern that all the love he shares out among all his loved ones is in fact for that One Who suffices and substitutes for all things and causes him to forget all others. Nothing can substitute for Him, for even one of the manifestations of His love. Even if a believer convinced of the truth of this were to be placed in Hell, he would enjoy some feeling of Paradise knowing that all his loved ones were saved from eternal extinction and separation and blessed with perpetual happiness.

O heedless Said! Give up supposing yourself as your owner and, submitting all your loved ones to their All-Munificent and All-Compassionate Owner, secure the salvation and happiness of them all.

Know O friend! Everything, including man's actions, is brought into existence by God. However, evils, defects, faults, and vices are the results of the nature and imperfect capacities of the created. The absolutely All-Liberal Creator responds with creation to whatever the created ask of Him in the tongue of their potential and disposition. Good and beauty are absolutely from Him. For it is He Who brings them into existence and requires them. As to ugliness and defects, it is again He Who creates them but without requiring them. All praise is always due to Him, for asking Him for beauty and good is like answer from Him and His Names. All glorification is also due to Him and He is absolutely free from all defects and ugliness, for it is creatures that seek and do vices and ugliness and the Almighty brings them into existence. However, He attaches many beautiful consequences to what seems as ugly. *Whatever good comes to you is from God, and whatever evil comes to you is from your selfhood.*[18]

---

18. *al-Nisa'*, 4.79.

Know O friend! All the species of creatures in the world, especially the species of plants and animals on the earth, are like the threads of an embroidery spread on the face of the earth one over the other, or like garments worn by the earth one under or over the other. Some of them are thinner, some shorter, some more loosely knitted, while some others are torn in winter and renewed in spring. However, all of them are woven in a perfect order and with perfect proportions. All species embrace one another and help one another in utmost zeal. Their members come together and separate on good terms.

Whatever exists is the textile of a Single Weaver and the servant of a Single Master. Everything is woven peculiarly to itself with different fibers characteristic to itself without any confusion or flaw. This testifies with a certainty based on observation that it is a work of the Art of the One to Whose Power and Wisdom there is no limit.

Observe the purposeful, peculiar adornment and furnishing of all creatures different from one another. This bears witness that the One Who has adorned and furnished the palace of the world with all those different species of creatures with different characteristics and features is He Who has created whatever is necessary for the maintenance of that palace. One of the most important purposes for its rich adornment is making its Maker known and that adornment is one of the most polished mirrors which reflect the truth that the Maker wills to make Himself known and loved.

If you like, look, among innumerable examples, at that yellow sunflower which closes at night and opens in daytime. Its Maker makes it a pleasant home for some tiny organisms or animals glorifying their Creator. A group of them inhabit a sunflower and that flower becomes like a garden or a palace or a village for them.

Glory be to Him Who manifests in all things His Grace, makes His Power known by His creatures and makes Himself loved by His servants through the rich adornment of His works of art, His Majesty be exalted and there is no god but He. *His word is true and for Him is the whole creation and His is the dominion over them.*[19] *He is not questioned concerning whatever He does.*[20]

Know O friend! He is not questioned concerning whatever He does, nor has anyone a right or any pretext to question Him. He disposes in His kingdom however He wishes and He is the All-Knowing, the All-Wise. He knows what we do not. Our ignorance of the wisdom in an event or in the existence of a thing does not mean that there is no wisdom in it. For the wisdom clearly observed in the absolute majority of things testifies to the existence of wisdom in all things and events.

For example, we grieve over the death of living beings. We may not discern any beauty or good in the shortness of the lives of some fine beings. We may not also perceive any instances of mercy in the decay of some living creatures in autumn or winter. However, all such objections or grief arise from our ignorance of the reality that a living being is like a soldier or servant charged with many tasks in life which are glorifying and praising the Creator of life and death. The purposes for their lives pertain to Him, be He glorified. So, their appearance in the arena of existence for a single moment or even their innate intention to fulfil their functions—like the intentions of seeds and fruit-stones to grow into plants or trees—may be sufficient to perform what is expected of their lives. And death is only a changing of abodes or a discharge from duties or a call to the presence of their Creator, as the Creator Himself decrees: *Then, they are resurrected and gathered in the presence of their Lord.*[21] It is only one of the signs of His Mercy's perfection that He does not usually postpone His creatures to the unbearable period of old age and allow them to remain long in the most severe, troublesome hardships of life. He discharges the lovers of flowers and those taking pleasure in vegetation from their duties. The Maker of those creatures, their Master, employs them during their lives according to the conditions in which they can fulfil their

19. *al-An'am*, 6.73.
20. *al-Anbiya'*, 21.23.
21. *al-An'am*, 6.38.

tasks easily. When the frown of the unbearable conditions of life because of old age or winter and extinction of their enthusiasm appears on their faces, the Mercy of the All-Merciful One comes to their assistance by granting them their discharge. In their place, He dispatches the likes of them, weaves them after their example, so that they too should glorify their Master. Those new-comers start off their tasks where their predecessors completed theirs.

O heedless, conceited one, supposing yourself to be the owner of your self and your life and fancying that your happiness lies in a continuous, easy life. You are wrong and deceive yourself. You compare your self-forgetting selfhood to an animal contented with its life and which, in fact, fulfils its tasks. The shouts of joy caused by the manifestations of the universal Mercy sound to you like lamentations. So, do not grieve about them because grief arises from compassion and pity. Rather, pity that self of yours which you compare to them and grieve over that.

As for allowing some animals to attack others, it is because that the weak ones attacked can develop their agility and potential or capacity to defend themselves and learn to know their faculties. When you compare the domesticated animals with wild ones of the same kinds, you can see this manifest wisdom.

Know O friend! Why do saints differ in the conclusions they draw through inspiration and spiritual unveiling while agreeing on the fundamentals of religion; why did saints and the Prophets preceding the Last One, upon him be peace and blessings, not elaborate the pillars of belief except Divine Unity, while the Qur'an and the one upon whom it was sent down explained all of them so clearly that they do not require further clarification? The reason is the intervention of certain veils between those pillars and saints and previous Prophets. Another reason is that the capacities differ in receiving the manifestations of the Divine Names that occur in different colors and intensity.

For example—and God's is the highest comparison—the sun has, by God's leave, a universal manifestation on all flowers and particular manifestation upon each species and upon every individual flower. According to a well-known theory, every flower receives its color from the refraction of the sun's light.

Also, the sun has, by the leave of its Originator, a universal manifestation of light on the planets and the moon, which reflects the sun's light on the sea and its bubbles and drops, and on land and the transparent things on it, and on air and its particles.

Again, the sun has, by the command of its Creator, a pure, universal reflection in the "mirrors" of the atmosphere and the surfaces of the sea. It has also particular reflections or images in the bubbles on the surface of the sea, the drops of water, molecules of air and flakes of snow.

The sun's manifestation on every flower, drop of water and air molecule, or every water-drop on a window or dewdrop on a flower, for example, is in two ways:

The first way is direct, without any ways, media or obstacles. (This way is represented by Prophethood.)

The second way is indirect, with the intervention of veils and media. In this way, the sun's manifestations are received according to the capacity and nature of "mirrors". (This way is represented by sainthood.)

With respect to the first way, the flower, drop of water and the dewdrop can say: "I am a mirror of the sun of the world", while with respect to the second, they can only say: "I am a mirror of my particular sun or the sun of my species." The particular sun of each or the sun of the species of each manifests itself behind veils or is obstructed by veils. Thus it cannot possess the properties of the sun of the world which causes the planets to revolve around itself, and heats and illuminates the earth and moves the wheels of the lives of plants and other things.

O friend! Let us suppose ourselves in their places. O dense carnal self, you will become the flower which takes on a color as an effect produced by a ray of the sun's light of a particular wavelength. Let this philosopher drowned in natural causes be the drop which receives from the moon a shadow of the sun's light. The poor dewdrop, destitute of any color, holds the image of the sun in the "pupil of its eyes".

The love of Him Who, out of His Grace, illuminates and adorns us, has moved us to approach Him and see Him. You, the flower, have risen to the rank of representing all flowers. But a flower is a dense mirror, where light is refracted and the seven colors in it dissolve. Therefore it veils the reflection of the sun. For this reason, you cannot be saved from separation and are confused between the qualities of the colors. You cannot be freed from separation caused by the barriers interposing. You can be freed on condition that you raise your head that is sunk in the love of your selfhood, and withdraw your gaze fixed on the merits and beauties you ascribe to your selfhood, and direct it to the face of the sun in the heavens. You should also turn your face, looking down to the earth to attract your sustenance which is in fact hastened to you, up to the sun. For you are a mirror of it, as it is a drop-like mirror shining in the heaven to a gleam from the lights of the Light, the Truth, glory be to Him. Nevertheless, you cannot see it in its real identity. You can only see it painted with the colors of your own attributes and telescope and restricted by your limited capacity.

You have advanced, O drop, as far as the moon by the ladder of science and philosophy and found it dense and dark, with neither light nor life. Your endeavor has all been in vain, and your knowledge has proven to be fruitless. You can only be saved from the darkness of hopelessness, the desolation of loneliness and the terror of that frightening solitude on condition that you abandon the night of naturalism and turn toward the sun of truth. Believe with certainty that the lights of that night are but shadowy reflections of the lights of the sun of daytime. However, you will not be able to see the sun clearly. You can see it only from beyond the veils woven by your knowledge and philosophy, and in a color produced by your capacity.

As for you, O weak and poor dewdrop, you advance by evaporating and rising into the air. The dense matter in your structure burns and then changes into light. Then you hold on to a ray from the rays of the manifestations of light. In whatever station you reach during your journeying upward, a window is opened to you to the sun. You see with certainty that it deserves the attributes it has and no veil or barrier, nor the limitedness of capacities and smallness of mirrors can restrain you from attributing to it all the works of its essential sovereignty. You have understood that what appears in the objects and is observed in the mirrors is not the sun itself but manifestations or colored reflections of it of some sort.

The three groups represented by the flower, drop of water and dewdrop in our comparison differ in the merits of the perfection they have obtained and in the details of the rank of certainty they have reached. But they are all agreed on affirming the truth.

Know, O man! You serve as a unit of comparison in five ways. You are a comprehensive index of the marvelous works of the manifestations of the Divine Beautiful Names. With your attributes and supposed lordship in your own sphere, you are a measuring instrument to know the all-comprehensive Attributes of God.

Second, you are a measure to reject all kinds and degrees of associating partners with Him in the universe. For when you are convinced that you belong to Him exclusively, being a property of Him, you believe that He has no partners at all in the universe. Whereas, if you give a third of your existence to Him, a second third to natural causes, and the last third to your own selfhood, then this sharing occurs throughout the universe. When you attribute to your ego even the smallest thing from His property, you will have to admit that every being and every natural cause has also a thing of the same size and thereby share God's property among others than Him.

Also, when your ego becomes unveiled to you, then the true map of the "natural" sciences and the knowledge of the outer world are opened to you. Whereas, when you forget your self, this knowledge becomes closed to you or changes into compound ignorance and useless sophistries.

Again, the keys of the hidden treasuries in Divine Names are in your hand. If you can perceive your limitless impotence, you will discover that your Creator has a limitless power, and if you find out your infinite poverty, you will see that your Provider has an infinite wealth. By such ways, the manifestations of His Names become luminous letters inscribed in the darkness of your existence. The more intense that darkness is, the more luminous they are.

With respect to these four ways mentioned, you are a being capable of receiving only, you have nothing (good) by yourself. You are a eulogy written in the language of "Be!" and it is.

As for the fifth way, you are an agent, an effective cause, one asking in the tongue of potential, neediness, actions and words. You are the origin of all vices, defects and sins, while your Creator is the source of all good, beauties, perfection and lights.

While the first four ways manifest the essence of everything with respect to your Creator and your relation with Him, the fifth one shows the degrees of the manifestations of His Names.

Surely, God has bought from the believers their selves in return for Paradise.[22]

Know O friend! *What deceives you with respect to your All-Munificent Lord*[23] Who buys from you His property[24] entrusted to you to benefit from it? He gives for it an extremely great price. He buys it while you continue to hold it in your hand and benefit from it. He buys it only to preserve it from being lost and that it may increase in value thousands of times. Profit upon profit upon profit...

But you, O heedless one, refrain from the transaction and breach His trust in you. You decrease its value from the highest

22. *al-Tawba*, 9.111.
23. *al-Infitar*, 82.6.
24. That is, your selfhood, body and existence or life, which are in fact His property. (Tr.)

of the high to the lowest of the low, and then it goes in vain. You come to be deprived of the great price He offers and endure sufferings, difficulties, pains and hardships to maintain it for a very short time and you endure also the sins you commit thereby. Loss upon loss upon loss...

Concerning this transaction, you resemble a wretched man standing at the top of a mountain. An earthquake takes place and, together with all others like that man, he falls into the depths of a valley and loses whatever is in his hand. In that state, he is like one "just about to fall into a pit of fire or an abode of ruin from the brink of a crumbling precipice". However, he still holds the marvelous device entrusted to him which contains countless measuring instruments and innumerable apparatuses able to produce limitless fruits and benefits. While he is in that state, the true owner of the machine, purely out of his compassion for the man, offers to buy it. He says to him: "In order to preserve it and return it after you are saved from this valley, I want to buy from you this property of mine as if it belonged to you. That is, you should use it, including all its instruments, in my infinitely spacious gardens to recognize and measure the contents of my overflowing treasures so that their value may increase and in return you can receive very high wages. Otherwise, it will become a lowly, ordinary device of the sort used in the narrow cavities of your abdomen. Compared with my gardens and treasures, how worthless and narrow your abdominal cavities are. How can those cavities contain the device entrusted to you which cannot be contained by even the whole world? Besides, I will give you a very high price in return for it. I will not take it over as long as you continue to stand on this mountain, rather, I will assume its preservation and management so that it will not cause you any difficulty to maintain it. If you accept the bargain, use it in my name and on my behalf. Use it in the manner of a soldier disposing what he holds in his hand in the name of the king and on his behalf, and without any fear of what will occur and grief for what has taken place. If you do not consent to the bargain, you will suffer loss upon loss and be treated as a breacher of trust responsible for its perishing."

The Qur'an describes this transaction to mankind and warns them: Buy it and gain an extremely high profit: *The home-coming of the Hereafter, that is Life if they but knew*[25]. While modern civilization and materialistic philosophy say: Appropriate it. It is but our life of the world.[26] Consider the difference between the illuminating Divine guidance and misleading human genius!

Know O friend! The All-Glorified One is near, but you are distant from Him. As He is near to you, He is also near to all members of mankind. As He is near to all members of mankind, He is also near to all other living beings and all creatures from the tiniest particles to ether and spirit beings and to those beyond your imagination.

If you want to be near to Him, you will have to develop and expand so as to be able to represent the whole of humankind and then acquire an absolutely universal existence representing the whole of creation. This means you will have to go beyond seventy thousand veils. If He is near to you and also near to every thing at the same time, you will also have to be near to every thing. Thereafter you encounter an infinite space between the contingency—the sphere of the creation—and the Necessity —the sphere of Divinity.

How is it possible to reach to the One infinitely distant in His nearness beyond thousands of worlds. If you desire to be near to Him, renounce your selfhood and annihilate it so as to remove the intervening distances and gain permanence with Him and acquire nearness to Him.

Know O friend! God is nearer to us than ourselves while we are infinitely distant from Him. Among the evidences of His nearness is His disposal of us. However, if we look for Him near what He disposes, we will find Him near all things. If we are able to reach Him by acquiring universality so as to repre-

---

25. *al-Ankabut*, 29.64.
26. *al-An'am*, 6.29.

sent the whole of the creation, then we will find Him beyond veils of light in the sphere of Necessity formed of the worlds of the Names, Attributes and Essential Qualities in His Dignity, Grandeur and Magnificence. Whereas if we look for Him through His nearness by renouncing our selfhood and annihilating it, then it will be easy to find Him, if He wills: there is no strength and power save with Him.

Know, O one who desires to know the difference between the wisdom of the Qur'an and the viewpoint of philosophy. Imagine that there is a copy of the Qur'an written in letters of different precious jewels-gold, silver, diamond, emerald, agate and others. Two persons have read and admired it. Then each has decided to write a book on the merits of that richly adorned copy.

One of those persons is a foreigner who cannot understand Arabic and is therefore unable to understand the meaning of the Qur'an. However, since he is an expert jeweler as well as a specialist in engineering, geometry, and painting, he has written a book on that copy discussing the visible beauties of its jeweled letters.

As for the other, on seeing the book, he understands that it is a very valuable, wise book—it is the wise Qur'an. He concerns himself not with the jewels used in writing it but with what is millions of times loftier, more beautiful, more adorned and valuable than the letters. So he has written a book discussing the jewels of its meaning, the lights of its mysteries, and the truths of its verses.

O you with a little sense and intellect! Which of those two books deserves to be recognized as one containing some of the wisdom of the Qur'an? If you understood this analogy, you can work out the truth of it. The copy of the Qur'an in the analogy is the universe and the two persons are the philosophers and scientists on the one hand, and the students of the Qur'an on the other.

Whoever places his trust in God, He is sufficient for him. [27]

Know, O Said! Happiness lies in trusting in God, so put your

---

27. *al-Talaq*, 65.3.

trust in God in order that you may find peace and rest in this world and find a great reward in the next.

The like of the one who puts his trust in God and another who does not is the like of two men who board a ship bearing heavy loads on their backs and head. One of them puts his load down and sits on it in peace of mind. While the other, out of stupidity and arrogance, does not do so. When he is told to lay his load down on the ship, he responds: "I am strong enough to carry it." They explain to him: "The ship carrying you is stronger and better able to carry it. As the journey proceeds, your load will grow heavier for your back and head. So, put it down and be relieved of your burden. If the owner of the ship sees you in this state, he will either think that you are mad and order your expulsion or, thinking that you are a traitor mocking his ship and ridiculing him, he will order your imprisonment. You will also be a laughing-stock before the other travelers. When you are no longer able to carry your load, you will have to either pretend to be strong, which means ostentation or a false show, or display arrogance or conceit, which means weakness and impotence." At last, the man perceives his mistake and, no longer obstinate, puts his load down and sits on it. Relieved, he says: "May God reward you; you have guided me to that upon which my ease, salvation and honor rest."

Know O friend! The verses of the Qur'an frequently conclude either with the Divine Beautiful Names themselves or with phrases implying them or with phrases ordering reflection and contemplation or calling to reasoning. The verses sometimes conclude with a general expression containing one of the purposes of the Qur'an—as if rays from the light of the elevated wisdom or sprinkles from the pure water of Divine guidance. That is, with its miraculous expressions, the Qur'an expounds the works and acts of the Maker and then concludes either with the relevant Divine Names or with affirmation of the Resurrection or Divine Unity or another pillar of faith.

For example:

He created for you all that there is on the earth; then He turned to the sky, fashioning it into seven heavens. He is the Knower of all things.[28]

Have We not made the earth a cradle, and the mountains as pegs. And We have created you in pairs. We have made your sleep for repose. We have made night a cloak, and We have made the day (a means or time of earning) livelihood. We have made above you seven strong (firmaments), and We have made a lamp therein blazing with splendor. We have sent down from the condensed clouds pouring water, so that We may bring forth grain and plants, and gardens thick with foliage. Surely the Day of Judgement is a fixed time.[29]

The Qur'an spreads before people's eyes the textiles of His Art and then concludes them with the Divine Names or with a reference to reasoning:

Say: "Who is it that provides for you from the sky and the earth, or who possesses hearing and sight; and who brings forth the living from the dead and the dead from the living, and who directs all affairs?" They will surely say: "God". Then say: "Will you not then improve your ways in fear of Him? Such then is God, your True Lord".[30]

In the creation of the heavens and the earth, and in the alternation of night and day, and in the ships sailing through the ocean for the benefit of mankind, and in the water which God sends down from the sky and with which He revives the earth after its death, and dispersing over it all kinds of beasts, and in the ordinance of the winds and clouds subjugated between the earth and sky: are signs for people who reason.[31]

Also, the Qur'an explains God's acts and then concludes with His Names or Attributes:

Thus Your Lord will choose you and teach you the interpretation

---

28. *al-Baqara*, 2.29.
29. *al-Naba'*, 78.6-17.
30. *Yunus*, 10.31-2.
31. *al-Baqara* 2.164.

of things and events, including dreams. And He will perfect His grace upon you and upon the family of Jacob as He perfected it to your forefathers Abraham and Isaac before you. Assuredly, your Lord is All-Knowing, All-Wise.[32]

Say: "O God, Owner of sovereignty! You bestow sovereignty on whom You will, and take it from whom You will; You exalt whom You will and abase whom You will. In Your hand lies all good. Surely, You are Powerful over all things."[33]

Again, the Qur'an mentions creatures and then employs the order, harmony, proportions and the fruits of their existence as mirrors to reflect the Names manifested on them, as if those creatures were words and the Names their meanings or water of life, seeds or essences:

Surely We created man from an extract of wet earth; then We placed him as a drop (of seed) in a safe lodging. Then We created the drop into a suspended clot, then We created the clot into a shapeless lump, then We created the lump into bones, then We clothed the bones with flesh, and then built it as another creation. So blessed be God, the Best of creators![34]

Assuredly Your Lord is God, Who has created the heavens and earth in six days, then was established on the Throne, covering the night with the day, which is in haste to follow it, and has made the sun and the moon and the stars subservient by His command. Beware, His is creation and commandment. Blessed be God, the Lord of the Worlds.[35]

Again, the Qur'an mentions some particular, changeable events and things and then concludes with universal, luminous, established Names or with phrases urging reflection or taking lessons:

He taught Adam the names, and then presented them to the angels: "Tell Me the names of these, if you are truthful." "Glory be

---

32. *Yusuf*, 12.6.
33. *Al 'Imran*, 3.26.
34. *al-Mu'minun*, 23.12–4.
35. *al-A'raf*, 7.54.

to You" they replied; "We have no knowledge save what You have taught us. Surely You are the All-Knowing, the All-Wise."[36]

And for you there is a lesson in the cattle (too). We give you to drink of that which is in their bellies, between bowels and blood, pure milk, palatable for those who drink. And of the fruits of the date-palm and grapes from which you derive strong drink and (also) good nourishment. Surely in this there is a sign for a people who use their intelligence. And Your Lord inspired the bee: "Build your homes in the mountains and in the trees, and in what they build. Then feed on every kind of fruit, and follow the paths of your Lord made smooth (for you)." There comes forth out of their bellies a fluid of many hues, wherein is healing for mankind. Indeed in this there is a sign for a people who reflect.[37]

Again, the Qur'an mentions vast things or things found in multiplicity and then places on them the signs of Divine Unity and concludes them with a general rule:

His Supreme Seat embraces the heavens and the earth, and it tires Him not to uphold them both. He is the High, the Tremendous.[38]

It is God, Who has created the heavens and the earth, and sends down from the sky rain and with it He brings forth fruits to be your sustenance. And He makes the ships to be of service unto you, that they may run upon the sea at His command, and has made of service unto you the rivers. And makes the sun and the moon, both constant in their courses, to be of service unto you; and has made of service unto you the night and the day. And He gives you of all that you ask Him; and if you were to reckon the favors of God, you would never be able to count them. Surely man is a wrong-doer, ungrateful.[39]

Again, He mentions apparent causes for things coming into existence and then draws attention to the real Agent Who creates them and their fruits, thus pointing out that it is impos-

---

36. *al-Baqara*, 2.31–2.
37. *al-Nahl*, 16.66–9.
38. *al-Baqara*, 2.255.
39. *Ibrahim*, 14.32–4.

sible for lifeless causes to know those fruits and purposeful results. Even if the causes seem to be near to the effects, there is a
very great distance between them, and it is there that the Divine
Names show forth in their splendor. It is not possible for the
vastest of causes to bring forth of themselves even the smallest
of effects. It is in the same way that the horizon seems to be
touching the mountains, although between it and them there is
a vast distance—the distance in which the stars reside:

> Let man reflect on the food he eats: How We pour water in show-
> ers, then split the earth in clefts, and cause the grain to grow on
> it, and grapes and fresh herbage, and olive trees and palm trees,
> and enclosed gardens dense with lofty trees, and fruits and pas-
> ture, as provision (from God) for you and your cattle.[40]

The phrase *provision (from God)* and mentioning the plants
and trees, each of which is an exquisite work of art with many
uses, show that apparent causes have no creative effect in their
coming into existence.

> Have you not seen how God drives clouds lightly forward, then
> gathers them together, then piles them in masses? And then you
> see the rain coming forth from their midst; and He causes clouds
> like mountains charged with hail to descend from the heaven, and
> He makes it to fall on whom He wills, and from whom He wills He
> turns it aside. The brightness of His lightning all but takes away
> the sight! God alternates the night and the day. Truly, in this is a
> teaching for men of insight. And God has created every creature of
> water; some of them go upon their bellies; and some of them go
> upon two feet, and some of them go on four feet. God creates what
> He pleases. Surely God is All-Powerful over all things.[41]

Again, the Qur'an mentions the extraordinary feats of God
so as to prepare minds to accept His wonderful acts in the Hereafter, or it mentions His future acts in the Hereafter in a way
that points to their likes which we witness here in this world:

> Has man not seen that We created him from a drop of seed? Yet,

---

40. *Abasa*, 80.24-32.
41. *al-Nur*, 24.43–5.

lo! he is an open opponent. And he has coined for Us a similitude, and has forgotten the fact of his creation, saying: "Who will revive these bones when they have rotted away?" Say: "He will revive them Who built them at the first, for He is All-Knowing of all creation, Who has made for you fire from the green tree, and behold! you kindle from it." Is not He Who created the heavens and the earth able to create the like of them? Most certainly He is, for He is the All-Knowing Creator .[42]

When the sun is folded up . . . .[43]

When the heaven is cleft asunder . . . .[44]

When the heaven is split asunder . . . .[45]

We see in the resurrection of spring numerous analogies for the Resurrection. For example, you see the like, nay the likes, of *When the pages (records of men's deeds) are laid open*[46] in the germination and growth of seeds and in fruit-stones the records of the deeds of their "mothers" and their life-histories.

Again, the Qur'an mentions particular purposes or events and then confirms and corroborates them with the Names as if they were universal rules:

God has heard the words of her who disputed with you concerning her husband and made her plaint to God. God has heard the arguments of both of you. Surely God is All-Hearing, All-Seeing.[47]

Glory be to Him Who carried His servant by night from the Sacred Mosque (Masjid al-Haram) to the Farthest Mosque (Masjid al-Aqsa') whose surroundings We have blessed, that We might show him some of Our signs. Surely He is the All-Hearing, the All-Seeing.[48]

Praise be to God, the Creator of the heavens and the earth, Who appoints the angels messengers having wings two, three or four. He multiplies in creation however He pleases. Surely God is All-Powerful over all things.[49]

---

42. *Ya Sin*, 36.77-81.
43. *al-Takwir*, 81.1.
44. *al-Infitar*, 82.1.
45. *al-Inshiqaq*, 84.1.

46. *al-Takwir*, 81.10.
47. *al-Mujadila*, 58.1.
48. *al-Isra'*, 17.1.
49. *al-Fatir*, 35.1.

Again, the Qur'an mentions the acts of ungrateful people with the doom threatened for those acts. Afterwards, it consoles them with the Names pointing to mercy:

> Say: "If there were other gods besides Him, as they say, they would certainly have sought out a way to the Owner of the Supreme Throne." Glorified is He, and High Exalted above all that they say. The seven heavens and the earth, and all who dwell in them glorify Him. There is not a thing that does not glorify Him with praise, yet you cannot understand their glorification. Surely He is All-Clement, All-Forgiving.[50]

An important topic

The Qur'an says: Say: "If the ocean were ink for the words of my Lord, assuredly the ocean would be used up before the words of my Lord were finished, even if We brought another (ocean) like it, for its aid.".[51]

If you ask in what ways the Qur'an is superior in value to all other kinds of speech, uttered or written down, the answer will be:

The Qur'an is the Word of God on account of His being the Lord of the worlds having the title the Deity of the worlds, and the Name the Lord of the heavens and the earth, and in respect of the absolute Lordship and the universal Sovereignty. It is so as part of the all-embracing Mercy and by reason of the magnificence and grandeur of Divinity, and it is a Book issuing from the all-encompassing field of the Greatest Name and addressing the circle encompassed by the Supreme Throne.

As for other words of God:

They are words of God on account of the particular manifestations of His Lordship and Divinity with particular Names and titles and as part of particular Sovereignty and Mercy. They are like most Divine inspirations. For this reason, a saint can say, "My heart informs me from my Lord"; he cannot say: "My heart informs me from the Lord of the worlds."

---

50. al-Isra', 17.42–4.
51. al-al-Kahf, 18.109.

A Prophet receives radiance and enlightenment from the manifestation of the Lord of the worlds with His Greatest Name in the mirror of the Supreme Throne, which is the "mother" of all thrones. Compared to this, how particular is the enlightenment and radiance you, O saint, receive from the manifestation of your Lord in the mirror of your heart according to the capacity of your heart! In order to understand the difference, you can consider the difference between the light of the sun reflected in your little, dim mirror and the light the sun provides to the whole solar system. The difference is also like the difference between a king's address to one of his subjects concerning a particular matter on the particular line of communication with that subject and the decree the king has issued to all of his subjects. He has issued the decree by means of his envoys on account of his being the supreme authority over the whole kingdom and the full majesty of that authority.

This significant reality also explains why most of the Divine Revelations came by means of the greatest of the angels, while inspirations come without his mediation and why even the greatest of saints cannot reach the rank of any of the Prophets. It also explains the reason for the supremacy of the Qur'an together with its incomparable dignity and sacredness and the sublimity and beauty of its miraculous conciseness. Again, it explains, in addition to many other mysteries, why it was necessary for the Seal of the Prophets, upon him be peace and blessings, to ascend to the heavens as far as the Farthest Lote Tree. It explains why he ascended to the *nearness of two bows' length* to supplicate to Him Who is nearer to him than his jugular vein, and then return to the world in the twinkling of an eye.

Like Knowledge and Will, God's Speaking to Himself (resembling endophasy) is one of His eternal Attributes. Its existence is known and its nature is unknown. And His words are without end.

Glory be to You! We have no knowledge save what You have taught us. Surely, You are the All-Knowing, the All-Wise.

In the Name of God, the Merciful, the Compassionate.
From Him we seek help.

In the Name of God. *Know* O friend! Either verbally or through the tongue of disposition or potential, everything says *In and with the Name of God.* For you see that, despite its essential impotence, every thing from tiniest particles to massive suns performs astonishing tasks one-billionth of which it is unable to do by its own power. This evidently shows that it does them by the Strength of an All-Strong, All-Mighty One; it undertakes those tasks in and with the Name of the All-Powerful, the All-Wise One.

Also, despite its utter ignorance, it does those tasks so wisely and orderly and in a way beneficial to all and so fruitfully that it is impossible for it to do one-billionth of it by itself. This is the clearest sign that it assumes those purposeful tasks in and with the Name of an All-Tremendous, All-Wise One. Every object works for the use of living creatures in and with the Name of an All-Merciful, All-Compassionate One and on behalf of an All-Knowing, All-Munificent One.

If you like, look at seeds and fruit-stones and see how each bears a tree or a plant. Look at trees and their fruits, at micro-organisms and other animals and the tasks they do. One sees a private gather together all the people of a town in a certain place, and then dispatch them to different places to do certain tasks. One will certainly conclude that that private gives orders by the power of the government or the sovereign and works in his name and employs the people on his behalf. Similarly, one with a bit of sense and intelligence will evidently understand that all those impotent, ignorant creatures do all their mighty tasks so wisely and orderly and so fruitfully in the Name of an All-Powerful, All-Knowing One. They act on behalf of an All-Mighty, All-Wise One, offering the fruits of their tasks in the Name of an All-Merciful, All-Compassionate One. Whatever task a creature does and produces fruits thereby is such that the universal Divine Mercy gives particular pleasure in return for it. It is like the pleasure a mother takes in her compassion for her children, or the delight a bee has in obeying the Divine inspiration in it to do what it does, or the pleasure a male takes in insemination. It is like the pleasure every living organism takes in eating, drinking and resting, or the pleasure a creature takes in putting its potential into effect, as in the germination and growth of plants, and so on.

The All-Wise Creator, the All-Munificent Owner assigns such pleasures as wages for the services creatures render and as appetites urging their actions.

Now, O man bearing the Supreme Trust!

How is it that you do not obey a law encompassing all things from the Supreme Throne to the tiniest creatures on the earth? And how can you dare to rebel against a principle put by the One Who has subjugated the sun and moon and employs stars and particles in His service?

Know O friend! The difference between the path of belief in the Divine Unity and atheism and heresy is like the difference between Paradise and Hell, and between what is absolutely necessary and what is [or should be] inconceivable. If you like, consider the following comparison:

Belief in the Divine Unity attributes all things to One Being and thereby decreases the difficulty and expenditure for their existence to the extent that in relation to the Power of that Being, suns and tiniest particles and few and innumerably many are the same.

Also, belief in the Divine Unity unveils the many purposes for the existence of things pertaining to their Maker. One of these purposes is that a thing manifests the Names of the Creator as if it were a comprehensive word bearing the meanings of the Names and pointing to them.

By contrast, the heedless and misguided people attribute the existence of a thing to numerous other things, to impotent, lifeless elements and deaf and blind forces and laws. They make the existence of things so difficult that it is as difficult for one thing to come into existence as for all things to do so. Again, they consider things only with respect to their benefits for mankind such as their being sustenance to maintain human lives, which is only one of many purposes for their existence.

The like of an atheist and a believer is two men who see the stone of a date-palm and start to describe it:

One of them says:

– It is an index of innumerable other indexes called stones or seeds. It makes known the meaning and essence of the tree destined to grow from it and describes the life-history of the tree which has produced it. It is a map showing the nature of the potentials of its tree and functions as a sort of machine weaving a date-palm.

The other says:

– No! With all its parts and leaves, the date-palm has gathered together to invent this stone, and equipped it with many instruments. But, it is of no use! The only purpose for the existence of this tree is to produce this stone, and yet this stone will be eaten by an animal or rot away in earth.

All things take place with an extreme facility despite their abundance, and despite their being intermingled with one another, every thing can be distinguished easily and an all-embracing order prevails in the universe. Is it possible for one with a bit of sense and consciousness to attribute even a single thing, a pomegranate, for example, to lifeless causes? Most of the things in existence co-operate for that single thing to come into existence, which is a sample of all things. Is it possible that such a thing—a pomegranate—has been created only for eating?

The universal wisdom has charged man's head with all the senses it contains with numerous tasks. If for each of these tasks a different instrument the size of a mustard seed were assigned, then the head of man would be as big as Mount Sinai.

Consider your tongue and the tasks it does. Tasting and

measuring all the contents of the treasures of Divine Mercy is only one of those tasks.

Is it possible that this universal wisdom (which charges a thing, however small it is, with numerous duties) has assigned for that pomegranate, a miraculous work of art, a single purpose, namely your eating it in a moment of heedlessness? As it is inconceivable that something the size of your head yields a fruit the size of a mountain, it is also and equally inconceivable that a thing the size of a mountain yields a single fruit like your head. Supposing such sort of inconceivability means seeing no difference between wisdom and futility and absurdity, seeing infinite wisdom identical with infinite futility and absurdity. Whereas like all other kinds of fruit, that pomegranate contains a long eulogy on the Divine Beautiful Names, explaining their meanings.

Glorified be Him in Whose work minds are amazed.

The following is a blossom of the tree of the verse *The seven heavens and the earth and all that is in them glorify Him. There is not any thing that does not glorify Him with praise.*[52]

The meaning of this verse was unveiled to me at a time when trees blossomed in spring. I went into ecstasies and reflected on their glorification. The following lines occurred to me:

In the Name of God, the Merciful, the Compassionate.

Praise be to God Whom all things glorify with the words particular to each, visible and perceptible. For example, lights, rivers, and rain clouds are the words of the source of light and water and air respectively.

Glory be to Him Whom praise:

the source of light with lights; water and air with rivers and clouds...

earth and plants with rocks and flowers...

---

52. *al-Isra'*, 17.44.

the atmosphere and trees with birds and fruits...

clouds and sky with rain and moons...

Light shines by His illuminating and displaying it.

Air produces waves by His disposing and charging it (with tasks).

Water bursts forth and flows by His subjugating and depositing it, which is evident praise for the One Who determines all things and appoints for each thing a particular nature.

Stones are adorned by His shaping and arranging them.

Flowers smile by His making them adorned and beautiful.

Fruits appear richly adorned by His favoring and graciousness, which is a manifest, comely praise for the One Who creates every thing with a particular nature.

Birds sing by His enabling them to speak and making them lovely.

Rain trills by His sending it down and making it vital for beings.

Moons move by His determining and directing, which is an eloquent glorification for the All-Determining, a luminous sign for the All-Overwhelming.

Glory be to Him Whom praise:

the heavens with constellations and light-giving objects...

the planetary systems with suns, stars and moons...

the atmosphere with thunderbolts, lightning and rain...

the earth with animals, plants and trees...

Trees praise Him with leaves and flowers, then with well-proportioned fruits.

When flowers stop praising, fruits begin to speak with an eloquent, light-diffusing praise.

A seed hymns silently by heart, full of mysteries;

a book is inscribed in it—the record of the life-history of its tree.

It voices the praise of the Splitter of grains, the Originator.

All plants praise, worship and glorify and are prostrate before the All-Determining.

The smiles of plants through their flowers are praise manifest for one able to discern.

Their sprouts and spikes are their mouths, seeds and grains the words of the poetry they recite...

Their proportions and orderliness are another tongue and their design is by the designing of the All-Illuminating.

Each is a work of art adorned by the All-Radiating.

With their being sustenance, their colors and smells, they describe and praise the Originator.

They describe His Attributes, make His Names known and interpret His will to make Himself known and loved.

The grains in the ears and flowers like eyes are "drops" of the manifestations of the Originator...

So that He may be loved by His servants and known by His creatures.

A tree in blossom

is an expression of praise in verse

with many "eyes" that have opened.

It has adorned its green parts for its festive day,

in order that its Lord may watch His illustrious works.

It exhibits the gems attached to it

to those having eyes to see;

and proclaims to mankind the wisdom in its creation,

with the treasury deposited in it by the Munificence of the Lord of fruits.

Glory be to Him Who does good whatever He does: how illustrious His proof, how clear His explanations!

Who is the All-Shaping Originator, the All-Able Creator, the

All-Illuminating Fashioner Who creates each thing with a
nature particular to it.

Look at His Mercy in the season of spring to see His art:

the season of spring is a festive day for His servants...

the day when His creation—trees and plants—adorn themselves...

Each plant manifests to the degree of its rank

the sovereignty of its King and the gifts of its Owner...

It is ready to receive and fulfil His orders;

renders much service in His Name...

It blossoms and yields fruits by His leave,

resembling a clean table for His guests...

Light, air, earth and water

are conveyors of His commands and bearers of His Throne,

publicizing His Art, illustrating His Wisdom.

Knowledge and Wisdom: light is their throne.[53]

Grace and Mercy: water is their throne.

Preserving and reviving: earth is their throne.

Command and Will: air is their throne.

Know O friend! All those elements are objects where His
Names are manifested; they are media, not sources or origins;
they are acted on, not agents. They are conveyors by His
Strength and carry what they carry by His leave, by His
Names... they do what they do by His Power.

If what falls to the part of things did not consist in this
only—that is, being objects where His Names are manifested,
being only passive media—then it would have been necessary
for earth, air, light and water to have in each of their particles or

---

53. That is, they pervade all existence or manifest themselves through light; in other words, light conveys them. The thrones to follow should be taken in the light of
this explanation. (Tr.)

atoms or molecules an infinite knowledge, power and creative ability.

For example, air passes through the atmosphere and visits the particles of all plants destined to grow.

Its passing causes to appear countless marvels—miracles of the Art of Him Who has created the heavens.

If it were possible for a particle, simple, lifeless, ignorant, to build those trees, to attach those fruits to trees and to shape those flowers, in short, to invent all those things;

and if it were able to bear this earth, this world, then you would have the right to have doubts about the Oneness of Him Who has no partners.

Or else, it is beyond doubt that none other than Him Who holds all creation in the grasp of His Power, in the grasp of His Wisdom, can claim any ownership and dominion of things.

For every grain or drop or particle works in the service of vegetation, fruits and flowers. If they were not employed by the Lord of the heavens, then each particle, grain and drop would have as great art and power as, and be wise enough, to invent and direct all those creatures.

Glory be to Him Whom trees praise with their leaves, flowers and fruits...

Bursting of flowers amidst multiplicity of leaves to lead the way to the growth of fruits,

and the growth of fruits in the lap of the flowers—which are daughters of trees—dancing in the hands of green branches, moved by enlivening breezes—

all is an eloquent speech extolling Him Who has built them, Who is the One, the Overwhelming.

Their mouths, letters, and words...are leaves, flowers and fruits.

Leaves dance in delight at mentioning the Creator...

Flowers smile in gratitude to the All-Able One for their adornment...

Fruits joy in what Mercy provides for them, singing sweet melodies,

well-ordered, well-proportioned, in shining colors...

artistically designed and embroidered, with wonderful shape;

richly adorned and marvelously painted, delicious in the eating.

The marvelous art they display, their being in great variety and with diverse skins—all this is in praise of the Originator and describes the All-Able.

They describe His Attributes and make His Names known, interpreting that He wills to be loved and manifests His Affection.

The drops of the manifestations of the Creator come out of the mouths of fruits that He wills to be known and loved by His servants and manifests His Compassion for His creatures in poverty.

Glory be to Him: how clear His proof is! how vast His Power! how manifest His Mercy! The All-Building, the All-Shaping, the All-Composing, the All-Arranging, the All-Spreading, the All-Promising.

Glory be to Him: how gracious His Majesty!

How majestic His Grace!

How great His Sovereignty!

(Look at the earth on which you live and say: God is the Greatest. Look at the universe and say: God is the Greatest, He is the All-Creating, the All-Acting. He is the All-Opening, the All-Knowing. He is the All-Giving, the All-Diffusing. He is the All-Mighty, the All-Wise. He is the All-Munificent, the All-Compassionate.)

If you would like to know the meaning of *God is the Greatest*, look at the universe. It consists in the shadows of His Lights, the results of His acts, the lines of the Pen of His Decree and Destiny, the embroideries of His Names, the mirrors of His Attributes.

Know and say: *God is the Greatest*. Look at the worlds. They are all held in the grasp of His Knowledge, in the grasp of His Power, in the grasp of His Justice, in the grasp of His Wisdom, well-ordered, measured, harmonious.

The order observed in the universe is by His ordering; the measure by His making measured, both of which—the order and measure—are two handfuls of the All-Merciful and the titles of two chapters from the Manifest Record, the Manifest Book. This book together with that Record are the evident titles of the Knowledge and Power of the All-Able, the All-Knowing, of the All-Just, the All-Wise. There is nothing outside the order of this system and the measure of this balance. This shows to one fair and sensible, one who has eyes in his head with which to see, that there is nothing in space and time excluded from the grasp of the disposal of the All-Merciful.

Look and say: *God is the Greatest*. He is the All-Just, the All-Ruling. He is the All-Wise, the All-Independent, Single One. He is One dispensing justice and acting wisely. For He is He Who constructed the building of the universe measuring with the rule of Will, and the ordering Wisdom. The principles of His Wisdom are the linkages among existents. He distinguished all things and beings as individuals by the principle of His Decree and the law of Destiny, His Determining. The laws of Destiny appoint the distinguishing lines of the forms of beings. He arranged the universe all orderly by the principle of His way of acting and the law of His practicing. The principles of His way of acting, the laws of His practicing, put creatures in order. For He does whatever He wishes and decrees whatever He wills in the heavens and the earth with the grace of Mercy and kindness of Favoring. He adorned the universe by the laws of Mercy and principles of Favoring, in which all the beauties observed in creatures have their source. He illuminated the universe by the manifestations of His Names and Attributes, which form the lamps of creatures in the heavens and earth.

Understand this and say: *God is the Greatest.* He is the All-Knowing Creator. He is the All-Wise Maker. The world and this normo-world—man—are works of His Power, inscriptions of His Determining. He originated the former and made it a place of worship; He invented the latter and made him a worshipper. He constructed the former, which is His property, and built the latter, who is His servant. His art in the former was manifested as a book, and His painting in the latter appeared as speech. His Power manifested on the former displays His Might and Honor, and His Mercy in the latter arranges His bounties on him. His stamp in the former is visible on wholes and parts, and His seal on the latter on the body as a whole and on its parts.

Look and say: *God is the Greatest.* He is the All-Able, the Enduring. He is the Originator, the All-Knowing. He is the All-Subtle, the All-Munificent. He is the All-Loving, the All-Compassionate. He is the All-Beautiful, the Tremendous. He is the Designer of the universe. If you know about the universe, it consists of parts each of which is a sample of the whole. It consists of worlds which, both as wholes and parts representing wholes, are lines and inscriptions of His Decree and pictures of His Determining whether with respect to arrangement of particles or ordaining of purposes or determination of forms.

Then comes appointment of limits according to dimensions and the Power works to individualize forms with the ruler and compasses of Destiny according to purposes appointed for each. Considering benefits with respect to each testifies to the fact that all the particular, distinguishing lines of each are drawn by the Pen of an All-Knowing, All-Wise One.

After individualization comes Favoring to adorn the forms with Its shining hand. Forms are adorned in the best way conceivable, which shows for a certainty to one having eyes to see that adornment and beauty are the works of His Grace, the signs of His Munificence.

After adornment comes His Munificence to embellish and make beautiful in a way to show that the All-Munificent wills to be loved by His creatures. He displays His desire to be known by men and jinn. All the beauties witnessed and all instances of kindness originate from His will to be loved and known. The Creator displays His will to be loved by making all His works beautiful. The All-Able shows His desire to be known by embellishing His works.

After the will to be loved comes His Mercy to send bounties and maintain His creation. He spreads His tables for the pleasure of living beings. The Mercy of the Creator is apparent on His works. The Pitying of the All-Providing shows Itself by fruits.

To sum up:

This world consists, observably, in the lines and inscriptions of His Determining—Destiny, embroideries of His Pen, embellishments of His Munificence, flowers of His Kindness.

When looked at with the view of belief and truth, it consists in the fruits of His Mercy, gleams of His Beauty, manifestations of His Majesty, mirrors of His Perfection.

What is observed in the name of beauty, what is displayed in the name of perfection—they are all moving and changeable mirrors, the shadows of His Light and signs of His Perfection. They point to the perfection of His works.

A perfect work testifies, as will be admitted by one having reason, to a perfect act. A perfect act points, as will be accepted by one having understanding, to a perfect title. A perfect title evidently indicates a perfect attribute. A perfect attribute necessarily shows a perfect essential quality or potential. A perfect essential quality or potential points, for a certainty, to the perfection of the Being Who is the Manifest Truth, establishing the degrees and raising by them, the Creator of the universe. This shows to one having eyes to see that the beauty apparent on things does not belong to them.

The disappearance of mirrors and decay of creatures while Divine Names and Attributes continue to manifest themselves and bring new creatures into existence is one of the clearest, most articulate proofs of the absolute Beauty and ever-renewed gifts of the Necessarily-Existent, the All-Permanent, All-Loved One.

Know and say: *God is the Greatest.* He is the All-Creating, the Great. He is the All-Acting, the All-Powerful. Worldly objects, earthly adornments, heavenly bodies, pearl-like stars... in the garden of the universe are miracles of His Power, witnesses of His Wisdom, and proofs of the One, the Unique, the All-Able, the Eternally-Besought-of-All.

Glory be to Him Who has made the garden of the earth the display-hall of His art. Plants in blossom, fruit-bearing trees, adorned animals, beautiful, lovely birds... are marvels of His Art, witnesses of His Knowledge, evidences of His Kindness.

The smile of flowers which are the ornaments of fruits in these orchards displays the will of the All-Merciful to be loved, and the desire of the All-Benevolent to be known by jinn and mankind and the spirits and animals, and also the compassion of the All-Pitying towards them.

Flowers and fruits, grains and seeds are miracles of Wisdom, gifts of Mercy, evidences of Unity. They are also presents offered in this world to give the good tidings that their likes will be given in the next. Again, they are truthful witnesses that their Maker has full knowledge of all things, is powerful over all things, and that He embraces all things with mercy and knowledge and with kindness and pre-arrangement (of all the necessities of their lives).

The sun or a tiny particle, a star or a flower, the earth or an egg—nothing is difficult for Him to create and maintain, to preserve and shape and to make and equip.

Understand this and say: *God is the Greatest.* He is the eternal Sovereign. He is the Ruler of eternity. He is the everlasting Lord.

Look at the face of the sky: you will see a silent peace, a purposeful movement, a splendid radiation, a smile in ornaments, a perfect, inviolable order.

The glittering of its stars proclaims the eternal Sovereignty to the intelligent.

These luminous objects, those revolving planets are radiant evidences and light-diffusing witnesses proclaiming the might and dignity of the Divine Grandeur, displaying the majesty of the Lord's Sovereignty, revealing the magnificence and vastness of His Power, and pointing to His all-comprehensive Wisdom.

Believe and say: *God is the Greatest.* His is the grandeur in the heavens and the earth, and He is the All-Mighty, the All-Wise.

Glory be to You, O One for Whose Necessary existence and Unity there are two witnesses in every thing.

Glory be to You O One for Whose Oneness and being Eternally-Besought-of-All there are two signs in every thing.

Glory be to You O One Whose stamp is placed on the forehead of creatures as a truthful witness and an articulate evidence.

Look at His works: you will see as brightly as morning an absolute abundance in absolute order. In creation and administration of all things, you will see an absolute order and balance despite absolute facility; an absolutely beautiful art despite absolute speed; an absolute firmness despite absolute abundance; an absolute facility despite absolute value; an absolute mingledness despite absolute distinguishment; an absolute agreement despite absolute distance; an absolute perfection despite absolute multiplicity.

This openly and decisively shows to one having reason, and compels the foolish hypocrite to admit, that the Truth is One, having an absolute Power, absolute Knowing.

Think about this and say:

There is no creator but He...

There is none other than He, Who originates each thing with a nature particular to it.

In the Name of God, the Merciful, the Compassionate.

Do you not see that to God prostrate all who are in the heavens and who are on the earth, and the sun and the moon, and the stars, and the mountains, and the trees, and the beasts and many among mankind? And many have been destined to punishment. Whoever God makes lowly, there is none to give him honor. Assuredly, God does what He wills.[54]

Know O friend! The holy Qur'an declares openly: All things from the Supreme Throne to the earth, from stars to insects, from angels to fish, and from planets to particles of matter worship God, prostrating to Him, and praising and glorifying Him in different ways particular to each. We will point to only a few of these ways:

For example—and God's the highest comparison—when a great king wants to have a vast city and a magnificent palace built, he employs four kinds of workers:

The first are his slaves. They are paid no wages or salaries. They take pleasure in whatever they do by his command, always speak in praise of him and are content with the honor of being attached to him and working on his behalf.

The second are some ordinary people whom the king employs in return for a small wage particular to them. They do not know what great purposes are intended for their work. Some of them even think that there is no purpose for their being employed except the small wage paid to them.

The third are animals belonging to the king himself. They have no wages other than fodder and pleasure they take in working in jobs fitted to their potential. There is a pleasure in putting potential into effect.

The fourth are the workers who know what they and other workers are doing and why they are working. They also know the purposes of the king. Workers of this class also have the du-

---

54. *al-Hajj*, 22.18.

ties of supervision over the other workers. They get wages in accordance with their ranks.

In the same way, the Owner of the heavens and the earth and their Builder employs and causes to worship the angels, animals, inanimate objects, plants and human beings. But He does not do so out of need for He is their Creator and the Creator of what they do. But it is required by His Dignity, Grandeur, and the essential qualities of His Lordship and so on. The angels do not gain promotion by endeavoring. Each of them has a fixed, determined rank, but receives a particular pleasure from the work itself and a radiance in proportion to his degree in the act of worship he does. The reward for their services is contained in the services themselves. Just as man is nourished with air, water, light and food, and derives pleasure from them, so are the angels nourished with the lights of remembrance, glorification, praise, worship, knowledge, and love of God, and receive pleasure from them. For, since they are created of light, light and the things close to light such as fragrant scents, are sufficient for their sustenance. They feel great happiness in the tasks they perform at the command of the One Whom they worship, in the actions they do for His sake, in the service they render in His Name, in the supervision they exercise through His view. They find great bliss in the honor they gain through connection with Him, in the "refreshment" they find in studying both the material and immaterial dimensions of His Kingdom, and in the satisfaction they have in observing the manifestations of His Grace and Majesty.

As for animals, since they have an appetitive soul and faculty of partial will, their work is not purely for the sake of God. Therefore, their Munificent Owner grants a wage to them in their work. For example, its All-Wise Creator employs the nightingale, renowned for its love of the rose,[55] to proclaim the intense relationship between the species of plants and animals.

---

55. In oriental literature the rose symbolizes a beloved woman, and the nightingale, the young man who loves her. The singing of the nightingale symbolizes the pathetic songs sung for the beloved and especially laments of separation from her. Said Nursi treats the nightingale as the representative of the animals that offers to

The nightingale is an orator of the Lord among the animals, which are guests of the All-Merciful One, and is charged with acclaiming the gifts of their Provider and announcing their joy therein. It has also the duty to announce the welcome offered to the plants in return for the help the plants offer to animals, and to declare on beautiful plants the intense need of animal species for plants, which is a need in the degree of love and passion. Again, it offers a most beautiful gratitude to the All-Majestic and Gracious and Munificent Lord of all kingdoms, with a most pleasing yearning and in a most delicate form.

The nightingale acts to achieve these aims for the sake of the All-Glorified One. It speaks in its own tongue; we understand these meanings from it, even if itself does not know the meaning of its melodies. The ignorance of the nightingale of all those aims with all their details does not mean that it is not employed for them. It is like a clock telling you the time although it is unaware of what it does. As for the nightingale's wage, it is the delight it derives from looking on the smiling flowers, and the pleasure it receives from conversing with them. Its touching songs are not complaints arising from animal grief, they are rather thanks for the gifts of the All-Merciful One.

You can compare with the nightingale the bee, the spider, the ant and the "nightingales" among insects and so on. For each of them, a particular pleasure as wages has been included in their duties. Like a private employed on an imperial vessel, they serve certain important aims and the art of the Lord.

They observe God's commands of creation and operation of the universe in perfect obedience and thereby display the purposes for their creation in His Name in the best way and spend their lives in fulfilling their tasks by His Power in the most wonderful fashion. In this manner they present the gifts of their wor-

God, on their behalf, their thanks for the flowers and other plants on which they live. So, according to him, the Prophet Muhammad, upon him be peace and blessings, is the nightingale of humankind who sings the praises of God on their behalf and conveys to God their worship and thanks. See, "The Fourth Branch of the Twenty-Fourth Word", *The Words 1*, Izmir 1997, pp.467–70. (Tr.)

ship and virtues of their submission to their Creator. Their worship and submission mean their actual manifestation of the purposes required of their lives by the Giver of Life.

As for plants and inanimate objects, since they have no free will, they are not paid certain wages. They do by God's Power and in His Name and purely for God's sake whatever they do and what is required of them by Divine Will. However, as can be concluded from observing them, the plants have some sort of pleasure in fulfilling their tasks but, unlike animate beings having free will, suffer no pains. The results of the works of plants and inanimate objects are more perfect than those of animals because no free choice has part in them. Among animal creatures which have some sort of choice, the work of those like the bees and others similar to them that are equipped with a kind of inspiration is more perfect than that of the others which rely on their own will.

As far as human beings are concerned, they resemble the angels in the universality of their worship, extent of their supervision, comprehensiveness of their knowledge and their being heralds of Divine Lordship. Indeed, man is more comprehensive in nature than angels. Since he has an appetitive soul disposed toward evil, he has a capacity for almost boundless advance or decline. With respect to seeking pleasure for himself in his work and a share for himself, he resembles animals and has two kinds of wages, one animal, insignificant and immediate, the other angelic, universal and postponed.

Since we have discussed in many parts of the *Risale-i Nur* the meaning, contents and results of man's worship and duty and the worship and glorification of plants and inanimate objects, we will not go into further elaboration here.

A complementary note for the discussion on the nightingale

Do not think that singing and announcing the praise and glorification of God Almighty to those with the power of hearing is particular to the nightingale only. Rather, every species has a "nightingale" of its own representing the finest feelings of that species with the finest glorification in the finest verse. The "nightingales" of vermin and insects, in particular, are both numerous and various. They sing their glorification in fine poetry to the other members of their species and give pleasure to whoever hears them.

Some of those nightingales are nocturnal. As if each were the leader of a circle reciting God's Names by heart, the poetry-reciting friends of all small animals sing their praises and glorification of God in the peaceful silence of night. The song is like a language common to all which everyone with the power of hearing and feeling can understand.

Another group of those animals is diurnal. During daytime in spring and summer, as if each were the leader of a circle reciting God's Names aloud, they proclaim the glorification in fine verse to all living beings from the "pulpits" of trees and arouse those hearing them to ecstasies.

The Prophet Muhammad, upon him be peace and blessings, is the most virtuous of all beings and the most excellent, the noblest, the most illustrious, the most profound, the greatest and the most honorable of nightingales. His voice is the loudest and most lyrical, his attributes are the most brilliant, his recitation of God's Names is the most perfect and comprehensive, and his thanks are the most universal. The Prophet Muhammad, upon him be peace and blessings, is the nightingale of mankind—singing in the garden of the universe, who, through his most pleasant tunes, has become the nightingale of all creatures in the heavens and the earth. Upon him, his family, and his peers—the other prophets—be the best of blessings and peace.

Know O friend! The fact that an animal is born into the world with the skills and practical knowledge it will need during its life, shows that it is sent to the world only to work (or to serve the purposes of its life), not to be perfected through learning.

However, man is born with utter ignorance and impotence and needs to learn throughout his life to meet the necessities of his life. This shows that he is sent to the world to be perfected through learning and worship, not to work only for his life. What he is required to do for his life is to arrange the "actions" of plants and animals which God has subjugated to him and to benefit from the laws of Mercy. His real duty is to worship and pray and supplicate to and beg from the One Who has subjugated to him the creation because of his infinite weakness and impotence and limitless poverty and neediness. He must acquire knowledge of Him Who has made him the most honored of the creation and equipped him with what he will need to worship. He must find happiness by studying creation and the wisdom in it in a way to lead him to knowledge of its Creator with His Names, Attributes, Majesty, Grace and Perfection. Any study which does not gain for him this knowledge is of no essential use and causes deviation.

O God! Make us Your servants sincerely worshipping You wherever and in whichever rank we are, and supplicating to You as our God and occupied with acquiring knowledge of You.

Know O friend! Since the All-Munificent Creator is absolutely free from any impotence and is perfectly munificent, He creates a particle as He creates the sun; He gives a particle the same sort of existence as He gives the sun.

Likewise, as He creates the smallest of plant-forms, He creates the biggest of trees. As He creates the angel superintending and managing the movement of the sun, He also creates the angel superintending and managing a single drop of rain. As He creates the biggest of animals, He also creates the smallest among them. From the smallest of creatures to the biggest, all worship Him and obey Him.

Whether small or big and existing in abundance or in few, limited numbers, all creatures have tasks proper to each and suitable to the purpose for the existence of each. They are appointed by the One: *When He wills a thing, His command (or what He does) is only saying to it "Be!" and it is. Glory be to Him in Whose hand the dominion of everything is and unto Him you are returning.*[56]

---

56. *Ya Sin*, 36.82–3.

Know O Muslim! The Islamic Shari'a gives you the possibility to make all of your everyday acts and deeds into a treasury for your afterlife and a great elixir. Your most ordinary actions can become an act of worship and your heedlessness can be changed into a peaceful occupation.

For example, consider and remember the relevant ordinance of Shari'a when you do shopping or business and utter the words decreed by it to conclude buying or selling. In addition to feeling a sort of exhilaration because of doing an act of worship, you will also get a (spiritual) reward in return for it.

Prosperous is he who changes his acts into acts of worship and thereby enlightens them by observing even the secondary ordinances of Shari'a. Happy is he whom God enables to follow the Prophet, upon him be peace and blessings, in all his acts and deeds and thereby make his transient life to yield innumerable fruits to last for ever. How unfortunate he is whom God has debased because of his following his animal desires and fancies and taking his carnal desires and whims for his god so that his life passes all in vain.

Know O friend! Among human beings some are shepherds who superintend the lives and functions of some species of animals. Among them, there are farmers occupied with growing certain plants. Similarly, among the angels some superintend animals scattered over the face of the earth and may therefore be called "shepherds". However, their superintendence is different from that of human beings and they do it purely in the Name of God, for His sake and by His command and Power. They observe the manifestations of Divine Lordship on the animal species and study the acts of the Power and Mercy on them. They inspire the Divine commands into them to conduct their lives.

Some of the angels superintend the spreading of plants in the fields of the earth by God's leave, Power and command and in His Name. Their superintendence consists in representing and proclaiming the plants' glorification of their Creator and their obedience to Him, in addition to arranging and protecting their use of the systems granted to them.

The angels have no true disposal of the animal and vegetable species with a creative effect—for on everything there is a special stamp showing that it is the Creator of all things Who has created and disposed it; the angels' superintendence is their worship of God. The Archangel Gabriel, upon him be peace, who is among those carrying the Throne of Divine Providence—those who convey Divine bounties to creatures by His Will, Power and leave and in His Name—does his duty of worship by superintending the plants on the face of the earth. There are many other angels each of whom superintends a particular species under his command. Also, there are angels superintending animal species.

If you like to understand this reality, look at the earth, how the All-Wise Creator has made it a vast field and a wide pasture for plants and animals. Then, look at the species of plants astonishingly distributed over the earth in an amazing order by scattering around their seeds according to the Wisdom of the All-Wise, All-Knowing Creator. Also, look at the animals distributed in a wonderful, astonishing way. They maintain their lives on land or in sea in an orderly fashion by the Favoring of their All-Wise, All-Munificent Creator, His Majesty be exalted, there is no god but He.

In the Name of God, the Merciful, the Compassionate.

O God! O All-Merciful! O All-Compassionate! O All-Independent! O All-Living! O Self-Subsistent! O All-Wise! O All-Just! O All-Pure, All-Holy! For the sake of Your Greatest Name, place the students of the "Risale-i Nur" who publish this "Mathnawi Nuriya" in "Janna al-Firdaws"—the Highest Floor of Paradise—and grant to them eternal happiness there. Make them always successful in the service of faith and the Qur'an. Record in their registers of deeds many (spiritual) rewards for each of the letters of this book. Amen. Amen. Amen, for the sake of Your Mercy, O Most Merciful of the Merciful.

Said Nursi

INDEX OR BRIEF SUMMARIES OF THE TOPICS
DISCUSSED IN THE TREATISE

*Whether it is a plain or a mountain or a valley or a desert or a sea or a piece of land on the earth, it bears various stamps of the One, the Eternally-Besought-of-All. (456)

*Heedlessness, ingratitude and unbelief arise from groundless conceptions or notions. (457)

*Among the artefacts of mankind there may be some worth thousands of dollars because of the art they contain while their material costs only five. Similarly, belief is an elixir changing decaying, coal-like substance of man into an enduring, jewelled diamond by connecting him to the All-Perma-nent Maker. By contrast, unbelief reduces him to the degree of coal subject to decomposition in earth. (460)

*Four realities the nature of which man is unable to change: (461)

*One to whom it is possible for death to come at any time, who is enveloped by helplessness and surrounded by poverty on all sides, and who is on a continuous journeying, can be deceived in sophistries of modern, misgudided ones only in the state of drunkenness, and drunkenness does not last for a long time. What they call the happines of life consists in wretchedness, and what they mean by happiness may be possible only by killing death or in utter oblivion of it, and removing helplessness or in extreme vanity, and eliminating poverty or complete madness, and by eternity of life or stopping the wheel of existence. (462)

*The All-Powerful Maker has spread millions of worlds of plants and animals on the face of the earth. Every world is like a sea whose drops are charged with cleaning. For example, ants are charged with cleaning the face of the earth of the corpses of some animals.

Similarly, water, air, light and earth, especially snow, are like oceans each drop of which is a duty embodied. (462)

*To remove the doubts about the authenticity of the Prophetic

Traditions about the *Mahdi*, the approaching of the Last Hour and the great tumults predicted to take place after the Prophet, upon him be peace and blessings. (464–6)

*Everything, including man's actions, is brought into existence by God. However, evils, defects, faults, and vices are the results of the nature and imperfect capacities of the created. (469)

*All species embrace one another and help one another in utmost zeal. Their members come together and separate on good terms. (470)

*God is not questioned concerning whatever He does, nor has anyone a right or any pretext to question Him. (471)

*The reason why saints differ in the conclusions they draw through inspiration and spiritual unveiling while agreeing on the fundamentals of religion; why saints and the Prophets preceding the Last One, upon him be peace and blessings, did not elaborate the pillars of belief except Divine Unity, while the Qur'an and the one upon whom it was sent down explained all of them so clearly that they do not require further clarification. (472)

*Man serves as a unit of comparison in five ways. (475)

*What deceives you with respect to your All-Munificent Lord Who buys from you His property—your selfhood and life— entrusted to you to benefit from it? He gives for it an extremely great price. He buys it only to preserve it from being lost and that it may increase in value thousands of times. (476)

*The like of him who does not sell God's property entrusted to him to God Himself. (477)

*If you want to be near to Him, you will have to develop and expand so as to be able to represent the whole of humankind and then acquire an absolutely universal existence representing the whole of creation. (478)

*An analogy to understand the difference between the wisdom of the Qur'an and the viewpoint of philosophy. (479)

*The like of the one who puts his trust in God and another who does not. (480)

*The verses of the Qur'an frequently conclude either with the Divine Beautiful Names themselves or with phrases implying them or with phrases ordering reflection and contemplation or calling to reasoning. The verses sometimes conclude with a general expression containing one of the purposes of the Qur'an—as if rays from the light of the elevated wisdom or sprinkles from the pure water of Divine guidance. That is, with its miraculous expressions, the Qur'an expounds the works and acts of the Maker and then concludes either with the relevant Divine Names or with affirmation of the Resurrection or Divine Unity or another pillar of faith. Examples: (481–6)

*In what ways is the Qur'an superior in value to all other kinds of speech, uttered or written down? (486)

*Whether it is a plain or a mountain or a valley or a desert or a sea or a piece of land on the earth, it bears various stamps of the One, the Eternally-Besought-of-All. (456)

*Heedlessness, ingratitude and unbelief arise from groundless conceptions or notions. (457)

*Among the artefacts of mankind there may be some worth thousands of dollars because of the art they contain while their material costs only five. Similarly, belief is an elixir changing decaying, coal-like substance of man into an enduring, jewelled diamond by connecting him to the All-Perma-nent Maker. By contrast, unbelief reduces him to the degree of coal subject to decomposition in earth. (460)

*Four realities the nature of which man is unable to change: (461)

*One to whom it is possible for death to come at any time, who is enveloped by helplessness and surrounded by poverty on all sides, and who is on a continuous journeying, can be deceived in sophistries of modern, misgudided ones only in the state of drunkenness, and drunkenness does not last for a long time. What they call the happines of life consists in wretchedness, and what they mean by happiness may be possible only by killing death or in utter oblivion of it, and removing helplessness or in extreme vanity, and eliminating poverty or complete madness, and by eternity of life or stopping the wheel of existence. (462)

*The All-Powerful Maker has spread millions of worlds of plants and animals on the face of the earth. Every world is like a sea whose drops are charged with cleaning. For example, ants are charged with cleaning the face of the earth of the corpses of some animals.

Similarly, water, air, light and earth, especially snow, are like oceans each drop of which is a duty embodied. (462)

*To remove the doubts about the authenticity of the Prophetic Traditions about the *Mahdi*, the approaching of the Last Hour and the great tumults predicted to take place after the Prophet, upon him be peace and blessings. (464–6)

*Everything, including man's actions, is brought into existence by God. However, evils, defects, faults, and vices are the results of the nature and imperfect capacities of the created. (469)

*All species embrace one another and help one another in utmost zeal. Their members come together and separate on good terms. (470)

*God is not questioned concerning whatever He does, nor has anyone a right or any pretext to question Him. (471)

*The reason why saints differ in the conclusions they draw through inspiration and spiritual unveiling while agreeing on the fundamentals of religion; why saints and the Prophets preceding the Last One, upon him be peace and blessings, did not elaborate the pillars of belief except Divine Unity, while the Qur'an and the one upon whom it was sent down explained all of them so clearly that they do not require further clarification. (472)

*Man serves as a unit of comparison in five ways. (475)

**What deceives you with respect to your All-Munificent Lord* Who buys from you His property—your selfhood and life— entrusted to you to benefit from it? He gives for it an extremely great price. He buys it only to preserve it from being lost and that it may increase in value thousands of times. (476)

*The like of him who does not sell God's property entrusted to him to God Himself. (477)

*If you want to be near to Him, you will have to develop and expand so as to be able to represent the whole of humankind and then acquire an absolutely universal existence representing the whole of creation. (478)

*An analogy to understand the difference between the wisdom of the Qur'an and the viewpoint of philosophy. (479)

*The like of the one who puts his trust in God and another who does not. (480)

*The verses of the Qur'an frequently conclude either with the Divine Beautiful Names themselves or with phrases implying them or with phrases ordering reflection and contemplation or calling to reasoning. The verses sometimes conclude with a general expression containing one of the purposes of the Qur'an—as if rays from the light of the elevated wisdom or sprinkles from the pure water of Divine guidance. That is, with its miraculous expressions, the Qur'an expounds the works and acts of the Maker and then concludes either with the relevant Divine Names or with affirmation of the Resurrection or Divine Unity or another pillar of faith. Examples: (481–6)

*In what ways is the Qur'an superior in value to all other kinds of speech, uttered or written down? (486)*Either verbally or through the tongue of disposition or potential, everything says *In and with the Name of God*. (488)

*A comparison to understand the difference between the path of belief in the Divine Unity and atheism and heresy, which is like the difference between Paradise and Hell. (489)

*A blossom of the tree of the verse *The seven heavens and the earth and all that is in them glorify Him. There is not any thing that does not glorify Him with praise*. (491)

*Meaning of *Glory be to Him* and *God is the Greatest*. (491-501)

*All things from the Supreme Throne to the earth, from stars to insects, from angels to fish, and from planets to particles of matter worship God, prostrating to Him, and praising and glorifying Him in different ways particular to each. (502)

*The fact that an animal is born into the world with the skills and practical knowledge it will need during its life, shows that it is sent to the world only to work (or to serve the purposes of its life), not to be perfected through learning.

However, man is born with utter ignorance and impotence and needs to learn throughout his life to meet the necessities of his life.

This shows that he is sent to the world to be perfected through learning and worship, not to work only for his life. (506-7)

*Every species has a "nightingale" of its own representing the finest feelings of that species with the finest glorification in the finest verse. Some of those nightingales are nocturnal. Another group of those animals is diurnal. The Prophet Muhammad, upon him be peace and blessings, is the most virtuous of all beings and the most excellent, the noblest, the most illustrious, the most profound, the greatest and the most honorable of nightingales. (505-6)

*Since the All-Munificent Creator is absolutely free from any impotence and is perfectly munificent, He creates a particle as He creates the sun; He gives a particle the same sort of existence as He gives the sun. (507)

*The Islamic Shari'a gives you the possibility to make all of your everyday acts and deeds into a treasury for your afterlife and a great elixir. Your most ordinary actions can become an act of worship and your heedlessness can be changed into a peaceful occupation. (508)

*Among the angels some superintend animals scattered over the face of the earth and may therefore be called "shepherds". However, their superintendence is different from that of human beings and they do it purely in the Name of God, for His sake and by His command and Power. Some of the angels superintend the spreading of plants in the fields of the earth by God's leave, Power and command and in His Name. (508)

Indexes

Index of God's Names and Attributes

Index of the titles of the Prophet Muhammad

Index of names of persons, peoples, places and books

Highest Realm, 206

I

Ibn Sam'un, 314
(sura al-)Ikhlas, 234
Intermediate realm (world), 222; 375
Istanbul, 374–5;

J

Jawshan al-Kabir, 346
Jesus, (religion of) —, 253
jinn, 19, 27; 334
Joseph, 429
Junayd an-Baghdadi, 28
Jupiter, 24

K

Ka'ba, 138; 198; 272
Kawthar, 330

M

Madina, 16; 376
Magians, 263
Mahdi, 464; 466
Makka, 16; 272; 307
Manifest Book, 64; 250; 270; 421; 497
Manifest Record, 421; 497
mankind (men), 19; 27; 324; 347; 505
Mawlana Jalal al-Din al-Rumi, 315
Messengers, 329
moon, 24
Morocco, 248
Moses, 212; 276; 291; —' staff, 212
Mother Book, 421
Muhy al-Din ibn al-'Arabi, 29; 323;
Muslims, 263–4; 366–7; 382; 385;

N

Nile, 206
Nimrod, 329;

P

Pages, 127
Paradise, 27; 59; 61; 67; 170; 286; 367; 382; 404; 460; gardens of —, 63; pleasures of —, 282; 386
Pharaoh, 329
philosopher(s), 179; 300; 329; 454; 479; Illuminist —, 222
pious (ones), 168; 468
Place of Supreme Gathering, 65; 67; (Plain of Resurrection); 198

Prophets, 61; 65; 69; 179; 328–9; 335; 386; 404; 468; 487
Psalms, 17, 29

Q

Qur'an, 3; 30; 34; 69; 74; 127; 131; 142; 145–6; 158; 174; 202; 210; 222; 252; 257; 260; 273; 277; 282; 292; 306–7; 319–21; 338–41; 350–52; 361; 369; 385; 392; 429; 439; 446; 457; 465; 472; 476; 480–84; 486–7;   — of grandeur, 124; — of wisdom, 124; holy —, 16; 448; 479; 502; miraculous —, 335; wise —, 29; 68; 479; call of —, 369; commandments of —, 180; guidance of —, 368; good news of —, 370; instruction of —, 382; lights of —, 425; miraculousness of —, 166; 233; people of —, 380; people of belief and —, 396; (each) *sura* of —, 184; truths of —, 467; (also see, Criterion, Eternal Word)

R

Rabbani Imam, 29; 140; 213
righteous and God-fearing, 421

S

Said, 213; 225; 236; 246; 252–3; 286; 307; 359; 373–6; 381–3; 394; 398; 415; 427; 469
saints, 61; 69; 323; 329; 335; 386; 404; 454; 468; 472; 487
Satan, 66; 144; 255; 263; 294; 383; 396; suggestions of —, 167; whispering of—, 167
scholars: — of Islam, 466; purified, exacting (truth-seeking) —, 61; 65; 69; 222; 329; truth-seeking —, 24
Scientists, 354; 479
Scriptures, 74; 357
Scrolls, 127
Shadheli, Shayth, 29
Shafi'i, Imam, 28
Shah Naqshband, 29
Sha'rani Imam, 323
Siberia, 248
(Mount) Sinai, 361
Subhan, 206
Sufyan ibn 'Uyayna, 158
Supreme Tribunal, 59;

T

Theologians, 422; 447
thinkers, 454
Torah, 17, 29

Index of words